Professional SQL Server 2000 Database Design

Louis Davidson

Wrox Press Ltd. ®

Professional SQL Server 2000 Database Design

© 2001 Wrox Press

All rights reserved. No part of this book may be reproduced, stored in a retrieval system or transmitted in any form or by any means, without the prior written permission of the publisher, except in the case of brief quotations embodied in critical articles or reviews.

The author and publisher have made every effort in the preparation of this book to ensure the accuracy of the information. However, the information contained in this book is sold without warranty, either express or implied. Neither the authors, Wrox Press nor its dealers or distributors will be held liable for any damages caused or alleged to be caused either directly or indirectly by this book.

Published by Wrox Press Ltd,
Arden House, 1102 Warwick Road, Acocks Green,
Birmingham, B27 6BH, UK
Printed in Canada
ISBN 1-861004-7-61

Trademark Acknowledgements

Wrox has endeavored to provide trademark information about all the companies and products mentioned in this book by the appropriate use of capitals. However, Wrox cannot guarantee the accuracy of this information.

Credits

Author
Louis Davidson

Additional Material
Gary Evans
Charles Hawkins
Chris Ullman
Adrian Young

Technical Reviewers
Martin Beaulieu
Michael Benkovich
Maxime Bombardier
Robert Chang
James R. De Carli
Robin Dewson
Mike Erickson
Edward J. Ferron
Scott Hanselman
Mark Horner
Simon Robinson
Marc H. Simkin
Richard Ward
Helmut Watson
Sakhr Youness

Technical Architects
Catherine Alexander
Kate Hall

Proofreader
Fiona Berryman

Category Manager
Bruce Lawson

Technical Editors
Howard Davies
Paul Jeffcoat
Gareth Oakley
Douglas Paterson

Author Agent
Tony Berry

Project Administrators
Avril Corbin
Cilmara Lion

Production Coordinator
Pip Wonson

Index
Bill Johncocks

Figures
Shabnam Hussain

Additional Figures
Pip Wonson
Simon Hardware

Cover
Shelley Frazier

Production Manager
Simon Hardware

About the Author

Louis is an avowed database nut. Currently he is toiling as the database architect for Education Networks of America in Nashville, Tennessee, not to mention writing this book and hopefully one more.

He has been designing and implementing Microsoft SQL Server databases for around nine years, since his brilliant failure as a LAN Administrator for the Church of God International Headquarters in Cleveland, Tennessee (yes, there is a Cleveland in Tennessee). As SQL Server came packaged with Visual Basic 1.0 back then, he has also been developing with that product for around nine years, although his VB skills have been progressively getting worse since version 4.0, as he has been focusing primarily on SQL Server.

Louis has spoken at several conferences, such as CA-World in 1999 and 2000, concerning implementing solutions with ERwin; and at PASS 2000 Europe, he gave two presentations, one on normalization and the other on query optimization.

At home there is a wife Valerie and a daughter Chrissy, whom he dreams of one day spending a free moment with, since he hasn't had any since the day that SQL Server and Visual Basic landed on his desk nine years ago…

Acknowledgements

> **This book is dedicated to the memory of my dad.**

I would also like to acknowledge the following, who directly or indirectly affected the process of making this book a reality:

- The Lord Jesus Christ who created me with the ability to design and program computer software.
- My wife Valerie and daughter Chrissy, who did not see me for six months without a laptop, even on vacation; thanks for the love and patience.
- My mom, without whom...
- Chuck Hawkins for helping the book go past my limitations in Chapter 13.
- Chip Broecker, Donald Plaster, Michael Farmer, all for being great mentors over the past years
- All the great people I currently work with, who have put up with me for months on limited sleep.
- All of the professors, academics, authors, etc, who, through classes, books, and web pages I have read over the years, have either directly or indirectly planted seeds of knowledge in my brain
- The staff at WROX, who (other than the long nights!) treated me extremely well and made this all happen.
- The editors of this book, who have helped to shape and mold the ideas from a bunch of disorganized ramblings to the book you have in your hands.

Table of Contents

Introduction   1

    What's Covered in this Book   2
    Who Should Read this Book?   2
    What You Need To Use this Book   2
    Conventions Used   3
    Customer Support   3

Part I – Logical Design   7

Chapter 1: Introduction to Database Methodologies   11

    Introduction   11
        History of Database Structure   12
    OLTP and Data Warehousing   13
        The Four Modules of the Modern Database System 14
            OLTP   14
            Operational Data Store (ODS)   15
            Data Warehouse   16
            Data Marts   17
            Architecture   18
    Case Study   19
        Relational versus Procedural Programming   20
            Looping   20
            Network Access   21
    An Overview of SQL Server Database Design Process   21
    Summary   22

Chapter 2: Gathering Information for a Database Project   25

    The Database Design Team   26
    Documentation and Communication   26
        Client Approval   27

Table of Contents

Minimum Information Requirements	**27**
Database Prototypes	**28**
Client Interviews	**28**
What Kinds of Things to Ask	30
Who Will Use the Data?	30
How Will the Data be Used?	30
What Do You Want to See on Reports?	30
Where Is Your Data Now?	31
How Much is this Data Worth?	31
How Will the Data in the New Database Fit in with the Other Data?	32
Are there any Rules that Govern the Use of the Data?	32
Other Places to Look for Data Rules	**32**
Request for Quote or Request for Proposal	32
Contracts or Client Work Orders	32
Level of Service Agreement	33
Don't Forget about Audits	33
Old Systems	33
Reports, Forms, Spreadsheets	33
Outline of the Case Study	**33**
Client Interview	34
Preliminary Documentation	35
Summary	**38**

Chapter 3: Fundamental Database Concepts — 41

Introduction	**41**
The Relational Model	**42**
Database	42
Table	42
Rows and Columns	45
Limiting the Values in a Column to Only Legal Values	46
Row Identifiers	50
Optional Column Values	52
Rowcount	53
Additional Considerations for Tables	53
SQL Operations	56
Restrict	57
Project	57
Join	57
Product	58
Union	59
Intersect	59
Difference	60
Divide	60
Other Operators	60
Relationships	61
Binary Relationships	61
Non-Binary Relationships	63
A Last Note on Relational/SQL terminology	64

Definitions of Essential Concepts — 64
- Functional Dependency — 64
- Multi-Valued Dependency — 65

Summary — 65

Chapter 4: Entities, Attributes, Relationships, and Business Rules — 69

Introduction — 69
- Divorcing Yourself from the Final Structure — 70
  - A Simple Example — 70

Identifying Entities — 71
- People — 72
- Places — 72
- Objects — 72
- Ideas — 73
- Documents — 73
- Other Entities — 73
- A List of Entities — 74

Identifying Attributes and Domains — 75
- Identifiers — 75
- Descriptive Information — 76
- Locators — 77
- Related Information — 78
- A List of Entities, Attributes, and Domains — 78

Relationships between Tables — 80
- One-to-n Relationships — 80
  - The "Has-A" Relationship — 80
  - The "Is-A" Relationship — 81
- Many-to-Many Relationships — 81
- Listing Relationships — 82

Identifying Business Rules — 83

Identifying Fundamental Processes — 85

Are We There Yet? — 86
- Identification of Additional Data — 87
- Review with the Client — 88
- Repeat until You get Customer Acceptance — 88

The Book Case Study — 88
- Client Interview — 88
- Documents — 90
- Bank Account Object Listing — 94
- Business Rules and Processes — 98

The Waterfall Method — 100

Summary — 101

Table of Contents

Chapter 5: Data Modeling — 103

Introduction — 103

Modeling Methodologies — 104
- UML — 104
- IDEF1X — 105

Use Cases — 105

Data Models — 108
- Entities — 109
  - Entity Type — 109
  - Naming — 110
- Attributes — 111
  - Primary Key — 111
  - Alternate Keys — 112
  - Foreign Keys — 113
  - Domains — 113
  - Naming — 115
- Relationships — 116
  - One-to-Many — 117
  - Identifying Relationships — 117
  - Non-Identifying Relationships — 118
  - Mandatory — 119
  - Optional — 119
  - Cardinality — 120
  - Role names — 121
  - Other Types of Relationships — 122
  - Recursive — 122
  - Categorization Relationships — 124
  - Many-To-Many — 125
  - Verb Phrases (Naming) — 126
  - Alternate Methods of Relationship Display — 128
- Descriptive Information — 131

Case Study — 133
- Use Case — 133
- Data Model — 135

Summary — 142

Chapter 6: Normalization Techniques — 145

Why Normalize? — 146
- Reducing NULLs — 146
- Eliminating Redundant Data — 146
- Avoiding Unnecessary Coding — 146
- Maximizing Clustered Indexes — 146
- Lowering the Number of Indexes per Table — 147
- Keeping Tables Thin — 147

The Process of Normalization — 147
- First Normal Form — 148
  - All Attributes Must be Atomic — 148
  - All Instances in an Entity Must Contain the Same Number of Values — 150
  - All Occurrences of a Record Type in an Entity must be Different — 150
  - Programming Anomalies Avoided by First Normal Form — 150
  - Clues that Existing Data is not in First Normal Form — 152
- Second Normal Form — 153
  - The Entity must be in First Normal Form — 154
  - Each Non-Key Attribute Must Describe the Entire Key — 154
  - Programming Problems Avoided by Second Normal Form — 155
  - Clues that your Entities are Not in Second Normal Form — 156
  - Coding Around the Problem — 157
- Third Normal Form — 157
  - The Entity must be in Second Normal Form — 158
  - Non-Key Attributes Cannot Describe Non-Key Attributes — 158
  - Programming Problems Avoided by the Third Normal Form — 159
  - Clues that your Entities are not in Third Normal Form — 161
- Boyce-Codd Normal Form — 162
  - Clues and Programming Anomalies — 165

Case Study — 165
- First Normal Form — 165
  - All Attributes Must be Atomic — 165
  - All Occurrences of a Record Type Must Contain the Same Number of Values — 167
  - All Occurrences of a Record Type in an Entity Must be Different — 168
- Boyce-Codd Normal Form — 168
  - Summary Data — 168
  - Multiple Fields with the Same Prefix — 169
  - Every Determinant Must be a Key — 169
- Model — 172

Summary — 172

Chapter 7: Advanced Normalization Topics — 175

Introduction — 175
- Fourth Normal Form — 176
  - Ternary Relationships — 177
  - Lurking Multi-valued Attributes — 182
  - Attribute History — 185

Additional Normal Forms — 187

Denormalization — 188

Case Study — 188

Summary — 195

Table of Contents

Chapter 8: Ending the Logical Design Phase — 197

Introduction — 197

Data Usage — 198
- Reporting — 199
  - Report Discovery Strategy — 200
  - Prototype Reports — 201
- Determine Data Usage and Ownership — 202
  - Security — 202
  - Known Architecture Limitations — 204
- Interfacing with External Systems — 204
  - Example 1 – A Problematic Enterprise Resource Planning System — 205
  - Example 2 – Another "How Not To Do It" Example — 205
  - Example 3 – Systems Suffering from Denormalization — 206
  - Additional Issues when Interfacing with Third Party Systems — 207
- Data Conversion Plans — 208

Planning for Volumetrics — 208

Project Plan — 209

Final Documentation Review — 209
- Future Requirements — 210

Case Study — 210
- Data Usage — 210
  - Reports — 212
- Interfacing to External Systems — 214
  - Data Conversion Plan — 215
- Volumetrics — 215
- Project Plan — 217
- Security — 218
- Final Documentation Review — 219

Summary — 219

Part II – Physical Design and Implementation — 221

Chapter 9: Planning the Physical Architecture — 225

Introduction — 225

Reporting Issues — 227
- Size of Data — 227
  - Complexity — 228
  - Search Requirements — 229
  - User Access Contention — 229
  - Timeliness — 229
  - Frequency — 230

Performance Concerns — 230
- Connection Speed — 231
- Amount of Data — 232
- Budget — 233
- Number of users — 234

Table of Contents

SQL Server Facilities — 235
Replication — 235
Linked Servers — 235
Data Transformation Services (DTS) — 236
Distributed Transaction Controller (DTC) — 236
SQL Data Management Objects (SQL-DMO) — 237
COM Object Instantiation — 237
SQL Mail — 238
Full Text Search — 238
SQL Server Agent — 239

Basic Topology Examples — 239
Thin Client versus Thick Client — 239
    Thick Client — 239
    Thin Client — 240
    Somewhere in Between — 241
Client to Data Configurations — 242
    Classic Client Server — 242
    Three-Tier Configuration — 242
    Heavy Use Web Servers — 243
    WAN — 244

Case Study — 245

Summary — 245

Chapter 10: Planning and Implementing the Basic Physical Architecture — 249

Introduction — 249

Database Generation Tools — 250

Physically Designing the Schema — 250
Transforming our Logical Design — 251
    Subtypes — 251
    Other Reasons to Stray from the Logical Design — 255
Tables — 255
    Naming — 256
    Owner — 257
    Limits — 258
Columns — 258
    Naming — 258
Choosing Data Types — 260
    Precise Numeric Data — 260
    Approximate Numeric Data — 265
    Date and Time Data — 266
    Binary Data — 269
    Character Strings — 270
    Variant Data — 272
    Other Data Types — 273
    User-Defined Data Types — 277
    Optional Data — 280
    Calculated Columns — 282

Table of Contents

    Physical-Only Columns   283
        Concurrency Control   284
    Collation (Sort Order)   286
    Keys   289
        Indexes   289
        Primary Keys   295
        Alternate Keys   297
        Naming   298
        Other Indexes   299
    Relationships   299
        Foreign Keys   300
        Naming   300
        Cascading Deletes and Updates   302
        Cross Database Relationships   304
    Sharing the Details of your Database with Developers   304
        Information Schema and System Stored Procedures   305
        New Descriptive Properties   308

Case Study   **313**
    Cleaning Up the Model   313
        Subtypes   313
        Simplification of Complex Relationships   316
        Domain Tables   316
        Trimming Down Unneeded Entities   317
        Correcting Errors in the Model   318
    Preparing the Model for Implementation   319
        Physical-Only Columns   319
        Primary Keys   320
        Data Types   323
    Physical Model   330

Summary   **332**

Chapter 11: Ensuring Data Integrity   335

Introduction   **335**

Example Tables   **336**
    User Defined Functions   337
        Scalar Functions   338
        Inline Table-Valued Functions   341
        Schema Binding   342
        Multi-Statement Table-Valued Functions   345
        What User Defined Functions Cannot Do   345
    Constraints   346
        Default Constraints   347
        Functions   349
        Check Constraints   350
        Handling Errors Caused by Constraints   357
    Triggers   359
        Coding Triggers   360
        Error Handling   369
        AFTER Triggers   371
        INSTEAD OF Triggers   378
        Uses of INSTEAD OF Triggers   382
    Client Code and Stored Procedures   387
        Mutable Rules   389

Case Study — 391

- Default Constraints — 392
- Check Constraints — 392
- Triggers — 398
  - Remove the Time from Transaction Dates — 398
  - Validate City and Zip Codes Match — 399
  - Transaction Allocations Cannot Exceed the Amount Stored — 400
- Optional Rules — 402

Summary — 403

Chapter 12: Advanced Data Access and Modification Techniques — 405

Introduction — 405

Query Considerations — 406

- Transactions — 406
  - Locking — 411
  - Primary Recommendations — 418
- Major Coding Issues — 420
  - Temporary Tables — 421
  - Cursors — 425
  - NULL Handling — 433
- Views — 439
  - What's New in Views? — 443
- Stored Procedures — 445
  - Returning Values from Stored Procedures — 446
  - Error Handling — 449
  - Encapsulation — 455
  - Security — 457
  - Transaction Count — 458
- Common Practices with Stored Procedures — 462
  - Retrieve — 463
  - Create — 467
  - Modify — 469
  - Destroy — 472
- Batches of SQL Code — 474
  - Single-Statement Batches — 474
  - Multi-Statement Batches — 475
- Compiled SQL vs. Ad Hoc SQL for Building Apps — 478
  - Ad Hoc SQL — 478
  - Compiled SQL — 480
  - Tips to Consider — 482

Security Considerations — 482

- Row-Level Security — 485
- Column-Level Security — 487

Cross Database Considerations — 488

- Same Server — 488
  - Same Server Naming — 489
  - Same Server Security — 489
  - Same Server Data Modification — 489
- Different Server (Distributed Queries) — 490

Table of Contents

Case Study — 491
- Base Stored Procedures — 491
  - Transaction Insert Procedure — 492
  - Bank Update Procedure — 493
  - Payee Delete Procedure — 495
  - Account List Procedure — 496
  - Transaction Type Domain Fill Procedure — 497
- Custom Stored Procedures — 497
  - Balance Account Use Case — 497
  - Get Account Information Use Case — 498
- Security for the Case Study — 500

Summary — 500

Chapter 13: Determining Hardware Requirements — 503

Introduction — 503

Types of databases — 504
- OLTP — 504
- OLAP — 504

Growth of OLTP Tables — 505
- Rapid Growth — 505
- Slow Growth — 505
- No Growth — 505

Growth of OLAP Tables — 505
- Batch Growth — 506
- Growth Through Company Growth — 506
- "We Need More Reports!" — 506
- Don't Forget the Indexes — 507

Calculating Complete Table Size — 507

Data Size Calculation — 507
- Reviewing Index B-Tree Structures — 510

Index Size Calculation — 511

Transaction Log Size — 514

Archive Data When it Makes Sense — 515
- The Cost of Archiving — 516
- Archiving Details — 516
- Archiving by Time Period — 516
- Archiving by Fact Table Date-Partitioning — 517
- Archiving by Fact Table Characteristics — 517
- Accessing Archived Data — 518

Server Performance — 519
- Memory Subsystems — 519
  - Memory Subsystems on Windows NT Server — 519
  - Memory Subsystems on Windows 2000 Server — 520

Table of Contents

Memory Performance Monitoring — 520
- The Art Of Performance Monitoring — 521
  - SQL Performance Monitoring and Bottlenecks — 522
- Memory Tuning: The Operating System and SQL Server — 522
- SQL Server 2000 Dynamic Memory Tuning — 523
- Free Memory Target — 524
- Multiple Instance Memory Tuning — 525
- SQL Server Process Memory Tuning — 526

Adjusting Server Performance — 526

CPU Subsystems — 528
- CPU Performance Monitoring — 528
- *Textile Management* — 529

Disk Subsystems — 530
- The Basic Disk Subsystem — 530
  - Write-caching and SQL Server — 530
- The RAID Subsystem — 531
  - RAID 0 — 531
  - RAID 1 — 532
  - RAID 5 — 533
  - RAID 10 – where 0+1 does not equal 1 — 533
- Multiple Controller/Channel Solutions — 534
- Disk Tuning and Performance Monitoring — 534

User Connections — 535
- Locking and Blocking — 537
  - Blocking Demonstration — 537
- Monitoring Blocking — 537

Case Study — 540

Summary — 544

Chapter 14: Completing the Project — 547

Introduction — 547

Performance Tuning — 548

Read-Only Support Databases — 549
- Modeling the Transformation — 551
  - Table Oriented — 552
  - Solution Oriented — 555
  - Performance — 556
  - Latency — 558
  - Implementation — 558
- Uses — 561
  - Simple Reporting Needs — 562
  - Operational Data Store — 563

Enterprise Data Models — 565

Table of Contents

Moving From a Test Environment — 567
- Development — 568
  - Development Hardware — 568
- Quality Assurance — 569
  - QA Hardware — 569
- Production — 569
  - Maintenance and Disaster Recovery Plans — 570

Case Study — 571

Summary — 574

Appendix A: Codd's 12 Rules for an RDBMS — 577

Rule 1: The Information Rule — 577
Rule 2: Guaranteed Access Rule — 578
Rule 3: Systematic Treatment of NULL Values — 578
Rule 4: Dynamic Online Catalog Based on the Relational Model — 578
Rule 5: Comprehensive Data Sublanguage Rule — 579
Rule 6: View Updating Rule — 579
Rule 7: High-level Insert, Update and Delete — 579
Rule 8: Physical Data Independence — 580
Rule 9: Logical Data Independence — 580
Rule 10: Integrity Independence — 581
Rule 11: Distribution Independence — 582
Rule 12: Non-Subversion Rule — 582
Conclusions — 582

A Guide to the Index — 585

Introduction

If you are standing in your favorite booksellers, flipping thorough this book because it is a WROX book, I know you are probably thinking, "Hey, where is all of the code, and settings and such like?" Well, this is not exactly that kind of book. (Not that there is anything wrong with that kind of book; I alone have a gaggle of them around my desk.) What I wanted to put together in this case was a database design book that balances on the thin line between the very implementation-oriented SQL Server books, where all they are concerned with are DBCC settings, index options and all of the knobs and handles on SQL Server, and the truly academic tomes that exist which go deep into the theory of databases, but provide little or no practical information.

This book covers the process of implementing a database from the point where someone mentions to you that they want a database, all the way through to generating tables and implementing access to these tables. This includes taking normalization of tables all the way to beyond fifth normal form.

> *The mission of this book is simple; to implement the world's first chain book, where if you buy ten copies of my book and send it to ten of your best friends, and instruct them to do the same, I will be able to buy a real nice computer with a DVD player.*

The real mission is not so straightforward though. I have reviewed lots of people's code over the years, and no matter how well the object models, supporting code, or even documentation was put together, the database generally ranged from bad to horrible. My desire is to provide the information database architects need to make building proper databases possible. For anyone who has had the pleasure of having to read a college database textbook, you know that they can be a bit on the dry side; in fact as dry as the Mohave Desert in a drought. This is actually too bad, since much of the information contained between the covers is useful and relevant.

So my mission re-stated is to end the communication breakdown between the egghead geniuses and we working programmers, in order to provide the necessary knowledge in a way applicable to the real world.

What's Covered in this Book

This is a book of two halves. The first covers the logical design of databases, and the second looks at the physical design and implementation. Each of these sections begins with an introductory page, containing a general overview, then a summary of the areas covered chapter by chapter. We won't reproduce this material here, instead please refer directly to these pages.

Who Should Read this Book?

Not every chapter of this book is necessarily relevant for everyone and parts of it will not appeal to every programmer. I wish it did, because there is stuff in every chapter that will enrich their ability to design and implement databases. However, this is a breakdown of what will be valuable to whom.

Database Architect

If you are already a database architect, who is responsible for gathering requirements and designing databases, with involvement/responsibility for implementation, then please read the entire book, possibly skipping the third chapter on a first reading.

Database Implementer

If you are only involved in the implementation of databases, a good part of this book will interest you, so that you understand the reasons why the "insane" data architect wants to implement a database with fifty tables when you think it needs only three.

A first reading might include Chapter 5 on Data Modeling, Chapters 6 and 7 on Normalization, then the entire Part II of the book. This section describes all of the techniques for implementing database systems.

Database Programmer

If you primarily write SQL Server code then much less of this book will be interesting to you as a first read. A good reading plan will include Chapter 5 on Data Modeling, Chapters 6 and 7 on Normalization, then Chapters 9 and 10 on implementing a database, followed by Chapters 11 and 12 on accessing data.

What You Need To Use this Book

For the first half of the book, we will be discussing logical data modeling. There are no software requirements for working through this part of the book.

In the latter half dealing with physical design, the only requirement for working through the examples is an installed copy of SQL Server 2000 and the Query Analyzer tool that comes with it. This can be any edition of SQL Server (Personal Edition upwards), as long as you can connect with Query Analyzer. You will need a database which you can access with a user that is a member of the db_owner role, as we will be creating all objects as the database owner.

If you do not have a copy of SQL Server, an evaluation edition is available on Microsoft's SQL Server website at www.microsoft.com/sql.

Conventions Used

You are going to encounter different styles as you are reading through this book. This has been done to help you easily identify different types of information and to help you keep from missing any key points. These styles are:

> **Important information, key points, and additional explanations are displayed like this to make them stand out. Be sure to pay attention to these when you find them.**

General notes, background information, and brief asides look like this.

- Keys that you press on the keyboard, like *Ctrl* and *Delete*, are displayed in italics
- If you see something like, `BackupDB`, you'll know that it is a filename, object name or function name
- The first time you encounter an **important word**, it is displayed in bold text
- Words that appear on the screen, such as menu options, are in a similar font to the one used on screen, for example, the File menu

This is how code samples look the first time they are introduced:

```
Private Sub Command_Click
    MsgBox "Don't touch me"
End Sub
```

Whereas code that you've already seen, or that doesn't relate directly to the point being made, looks like this:

```
Private Sub Command_Click
    MsgBox "Don't touch me"
End Sub
```

Customer Support

We want to know what you think about this book: what you liked, what you didn't like, and what you think we can do better next time. You can send your comments, either by returning the reply card in the back of the book, or by e-mail (to `feedback@wrox.com`). Please be sure to mention the book title in your message.

Wrox has a dedicated team of support staff, so if you have any questions please also send them to the above e-mail address.

Source Code

Full source code for examples used in this book, can be downloaded from the Wrox web site at: http://www.wrox.com.

Introduction

Errata

We've made every effort to make sure that there are no errors in the text or the code. However, to err is human, and as such we recognize the need to keep you informed of any mistakes as they're spotted and corrected. Errata sheets are available for all our books at www.wrox.com. If you find an error that hasn't already been reported, please let us know.

p2p.wrox.com

For author and peer support join the SQL Server mailing lists. Our unique system provides **programmer to programmer™ support** on mailing lists, forums and newsgroups, all *in addition* to our one-to-one e-mail system. Be confident that your query is not just being examined by a support professional, but by the many Wrox authors and other industry experts present on our mailing lists. At p2p.wrox.com you'll find a list specifically aimed at SQL Server developers that will support you, not only while you read this book, but also as you start to develop your own applications.

To enroll for support just follow this four-step system:

1. Go to p2p.wrox.com.

2. Click on sql_server as the type of mailing list you wish to join, then click on Subscribe.

3. Fill in your details and click on Subscribe.

4. Reply to the confirmation e-mail.

Why this System Offers the Best Support

You can choose to join the mailing lists or you can receive them as a weekly digest. If you don't have the time, or facility, to receive the mailing list, then you can search our online archives. Junk and spam mails are deleted, and your own e-mail address is protected by the unique Lyris system. Any queries about joining or leaving lists, or any other queries about the list, should be sent to listsupport@wrox.com.

Introduction

transaction

- transactionId: int NOT NULL
- accountId: int NOT NULL (FK) (AK1.1)
- number: varchar(20) NOT NULL (AK1.2)
- date: smalldatetime NOT NULL
- description: varchar(1000) NOT NULL
- amount: money NOT NULL
- signature: varchar(20) NOT NULL
- payeeId: int NULL (FK)
- userId: int NULL (FK)
- statementItemId: int NULL (FK)
- transactionTypeId: int NOT NULL (FK)
- autoTimestamp: timestamp NOT NULL

accountReconcile

- accountReconcileId: int IDENTITY
- statementId: int NOT NULL (FK) (AK1.1)
- reconcileDate: smalldatetime NOT NULL (AK1.2)
- autoTimestamp: timestamp NOT NULL

Part I – Logical Design

Logical database design is one of the most important tasks in any database project, and yet is probably also the least well understood. This part of the book specifically hopes to change that by mixing a little database theory with some practical advice, as well as considering some common techniques that are often overlooked.

In this section we lay the foundations for the physical implementation of our design in the second half of the book and in doing so cover the following material:

- **Chapter 1 Introduction to Database Methodologies** – As its name implies, a brief introduction to the different database methodologies that are commonly used to implement a fully featured database system, such as OLTP databases, Data Warehouses, Operation Data Stores and Data Marts.

- **Chapter 2 Gathering Information for a Database Project** – In this chapter we give an overview of the process of determining the requirements that the users will have of the database system, by looking at some of the more obscure places where important data hides.

- **Chapter 3 Fundamental Database Concepts** – A basic understanding of the concepts of relational theory is fundamental to the process of database design and is considered here. This will provide a basis for the development of our design.

- **Chapter 4 Entities, Attributes, Relationships, and Business Rules** – In this chapter we will begin the process of turning the information gathered in Chapter 2 into a logical design of our relational database, in particular by devising the entities we will require.

- **Chapter 5 Data Modeling** – Once we have discovered objects, we need to have a way to display and share the information with programmers and users. The data model is the most effective tool for depicting database design information.

Part I – Logical Design

- **Chapter 6 Normalization Techniques** – Normalization is the process of taking the information we gathered in Chapter 2, and developed in Chapter 4 and Chapter 5, and turning it into a well structured draft of the data model. In this chapter we consider the normalization rules we must follow in designing a well-structured model for our system.

- **Chapter 7 Advanced Normalization Topics** – This chapter builds on the previous one by extending the basic normalization techniques beyond those familiar to most programmers. In this way we are able to fine-tune our logical design so as to avoid, as far as is possible, any data anomalies.

- **Chapter 8 Ending The Logical Design Phase** – Once we have designed the "perfect" database, we need to return to the original specifications to ensure that the data we expect to store will serve the data needs of the users. By this point many programmers are ready to code away, but it is important to finish off the logical design phase, by double checking our model and its documentation to try and minimize the level of changes required when we come to physically implementing it.

Part I – Logical Design

Introduction to Database Methodologies

Introduction

Database design can be thought of as an interesting blend of art and science. The science of database design is well established, with a number of mature methods for designing database structures (such as normalization) which have been around for a long time. In fact they are almost ancient in computing terms, and it's not too difficult to follow these rules when designing your database. As we will see, it is also relatively straightforward to translate such a design into SQL Server tables.

However, unless you are designing a very small database system, this isn't the end of the task. The art of database architecture is brought in when we need to incorporate distribution, clustering, redundancy, 24/7 support, stored procedures, triggers, constraints, integrity etc. into our database solutions. There isn't a set method for physically implementing a database, and that can make it tricky to decide what method is best.

This book will try to present good techniques that will hopefully help you to design better databases. I aim to present the information in a way which is clear enough for novices, but at the same time helpful to even the most seasoned professional.

One thing should be made clear before we go too much further. The design and architecture of a database is a very different role to those of database setup and administration. For example, as a data architect, I seldom create users, perform backups, or indeed set up replication or clustering, etc. This is the job of the DBA. When I worked for smaller shops, these types of tasks were in my domain, but I never felt I did a very good job of them.

Chapter 1

In this book we will be looking in depth at how to design, architect and implement the SQL Server database tables and their accompanying access methods; but we won't go into as much detail when we cover the physical hardware, system software, and other aspects of a database system.

History of Database Structure

The structure of databases has changed significantly in the last few decades. Originally, there wasn't any choice but to structure databases in ways optimized for the limited hardware on which they were stored. In the early 1970's E.F. Codd, a mathematician by training and at the time a researcher for IBM, introduced a new concept which was destined to change forever the way in which data would be stored. His principles of what would become the **relational model** were way ahead of their time. Many programmers liked his ideas, but couldn't implement them due to hardware limitations.

Codd's research is realized in his three rules of **Normalization**. These rules have been expanded on since Codd's original work, and we will explain all of the well accepted normalization rules later in Chapters 6 and 7. While I will make no direct reference to his works, nearly every bit of relational database theory is built upon his now classic paper *"A Relational Model of Data for Large Shared Data Banks"*. Whilst you could simply read this paper, or indeed C.J. Date's *An Introduction to Database Systems* (widely regarded as the industry "bible"), these tend to be very dry and academic. I am going to present the important ideas in a real-world way which is relevant to the database designer, and easy for him to digest.

> *"A Relational Model of Data for Large Shared Data Banks"* may be found at
> http://www1.acm.org/classics/nov95/toc.html.

Relational database theory has continued to evolve, and stricter and stricter rules regarding database structure have been formulated, by E.F. Codd and others. These rules are very valuable and are in general use today, but the relational model has not been in practical use for as long as the theory has existed. We will discuss the model and its advantages in detail later on, but for now, just take it that normalization requires an increase in the number of database tables, and any refinements to Codd's theory further increases the number of tables needed. Because of the extra hardware requirement this brings about, it has not been easy to sell the benefits of greater normalization to typical database programmers. Add to this the fact that a large number of tables with large numbers of joins bogged down the database server hardware and software of the 1980's and 1990's, and it's not hard to see why database developers failed to properly structure their databases, as much from technological limitations as from lack of understanding.

Fortunately, recent advances in technology mean that things are looking up. Hardware has improved by leaps and bounds in the past ten years, and database server software has been improved using algorithms that have actually been around for twenty years, but weren't used due to the previously discussed hardware limitations. Optimizations to database servers for specific uses such as OLTP and OLAP, plus the fact that Microsoft completely rewrote SQL Server to work optimally with both Windows and the Intel platforms in the past few years has given rise to incredible performance and reliability increases. These factors, along with operating system refinements and concepts such as **data warehousing** (discussed later in this chapter), have produced database servers that can handle structuring data in a proper manner, as defined thirty years ago.

Databases built today are being designed to use better structures, but we still have poorly designed databases from previous years. Even with a good basic design, programming databases can prove challenging to those with a conventional programming background in languages such as C, C++ or Visual Basic. This is because the relational programming language, SQL, requires the programmer to rethink the whole programming paradigm: sets and relations instead of ifs and loops. One SQL statement can expand to hundreds, if not thousands, of lines of procedural code, and in some cases, it does. This is not to say that Transact-SQL (T-SQL), the language of SQL Server, does not have support for loops, and all of the other basic programming language constructs, but even in T-SQL, the more work we offload onto the relational engine, the better. The other problem with SQL that is worth mentioning is that it is relatively easy to learn the basics, and as such it is typically not taken as seriously as other "real" programming languages. However, programming complex SQL is not easy, and so should not be taken lightly.

This chapter aims to introduce the reader to the basic concepts behind database paradigms, in particular the differences between OLTP and OLAP databases, as well as taking a look at the difference between both SQL and T-SQL and procedural programming languages, with the aim that in the future we will only have well designed databases.

OLTP and Data Warehousing

An **Online Transactional Processing (OLTP)** database is probably what most people are thinking of when they talk of a database, as it deals with the current data needed for the business operations. Data Warehousing is a wonderful, relatively new breed of database paradigm that allows for extremely complex reporting by building repositories for historical data separate from the transactional data. By allowing us to keep large quantities of historical data, it empowers the users to investigate long range trends in business history, whilst avoiding any performance hits for transactional activities.

There is a tremendous difference between these two paradigms, which can be summarized as follows:

- **Online Transaction Processing (OLTP)** systems deal with data that is used for transactions. The database is optimized to respond quickly to the insertion of new data, or the modification/deletion of existing data. It is designed to be responsive even when the amount of data is very large, and there are a large number of transactions.

- **Data Warehousing** solves issues which OLTP systems have in producing reports. OLTP systems have always been sluggish in reporting, since they are optimized to deal with constant modification of the stored data. When reporting, we may want to query and perform calculations on large amounts of data, and this can seriously reduce the responsiveness of our database. In addition, data updates in the middle of a report may lead to a different outcome. Data warehouses overcome this by storing the data in a manner which is efficient for complex queries – the data is optimized for a defined set of questions. Also, it is a recent history of the data that is stored – you don't query the actual, live, version of the data, but a copy which is read only to the user.

This is a little bit simplistic but should be effective in giving you the basic explanation of the differences between OLTP and Data Warehousing. In the following section, we will break down the different modules that make up each of these technologies.

Chapter 1

The Four Modules of the Modern Database System

Over the past ten years or so there has been a lot of discussion about how corporate data should be structured. We will look at one of the major designs that have been agreed upon by many database experts. The approach is to break down the entire system into functional modules that serve different needs, instead of just forcing a single technology to perform all the tasks. The different modules are:

- **OLTP** – The OLTP database stores current data – that's to say data which the database needs to run its business; it's only necessary to keep a small amount of history.
- **Operational Data Store (ODS)** – Consolidated data used for day to day reporting. Such data is frequently consolidated from several disparate sources, with some degree of pre-aggregation performed, in order to save query time.
- **Data Warehouse** – Grand data store for holding nearly all organization data and its history.
- **Data Mart** – Specialized data store optimized for aggregations, used for specific situations, and held as a subset of the data warehouse. Data marts are generally processed using a technology known as **Online Analytical Processing (OLAP)**.

Referring to these as *modules* may seem incorrect, but the term module is used here to indicate that they are each part of an integrated database system. Each module plays a very different role. For one reason or another not every database system will require every module. The two biggest factors in choosing which are necessary are the amount of data that needs to be stored, and concurrency (which defines how many users will be accessing the data at any given time). Smaller systems may be able to handle the reporting load without building costly additional modules to handle reporting needs. The only problem is to define what constitutes a smaller system? Chapter 9 will deal specifically with these issues in some detail.

Let's now look a little more closely at the four modules we introduced above.

OLTP

The OLTP database contains the data used in everyday transactions in the process of conducting business. It has transient qualities in that it reflects current processing, and serves as the source where data about the enterprise resides. It is characterized by having any number of concurrent users creating, modifying, and deleting data. All corporate data should be stored or have been stored (in the case of historical data) in an OLTP database.

The structure of the OLTP data store is built using normalization, the special structuring method mentioned earlier. Normalization reduces the amount of redundant data, helping to prevent modification anomalies – such as would occur if you had the customer address stored in two places in the database, and only altered it in one. Normalization is covered in detail in Chapters 6 and 7.

A primary goal of the OLTP database is integrity of current corporate data. This is achieved by following two important principles:

- Storing each current piece of data in a single place where it can be edited, so that any change is reflected everywhere else that it is used.
- Providing transactional support, so that multiple database alterations all have to take place together. If one of the alterations in the transaction fails, none of the others should be allowed to occur. The rest of the transactions up to that point should be *rolled back*.

A side effect of this, however, is that querying to find useful information can be laborious due to the strict structure of the data. As the OLTP database is designed with transactional performance and integrity in mind, data is stored in a manner that allows it to be written, but not necessarily read, efficiently. The user will often have to query numerous tables to get a meaningful set of information. This book focuses on the structure and implementation of an OLTP database. For smaller (there is that term again!) systems you may only need to implement this type of database.

As an example of the use of OLTP type databases, consider a bank that has customers with various amounts of money stored in their accounts. The bank will typically have a database that contains the names and contact information of all its customers. The bank is also likely to have many distributed databases to handle all of the different account types and monetary transactions its customers make. It might seem like all of this data could be located in the same database, but, since a bank has tremendous amounts of data about monetary transactions spanning different branches, different states and even different countries, as well as a large body of contact information about its customers, it is more likely that these details will be held on separate databases. The bank may also have databases (or the same database if it is so inclined) for prospective customer contact information, etc. Each of these databases would be an OLTP type database.

Banking systems are among the most complex OLTP databases in today's global economy. Whilst it is easy for you to use an ATM card anywhere in the world, without (in all probability) ever being able to withdraw more money than you actually have in your account, a massive distributed OLTP database system is required to accomplish this.

I ought to clarify what I mean by a **transaction** before I move on. OLTP databases do not only have to deal with monetary or numeric transactions. The term transaction refers to the mechanism by which you are able to ensure **referential integrity** (in other words, preserving the defined relationships between tables when records are entered or deleted) and **atomicity** (the concept that something should act as a single unit). For a database, this means that you have a known set of outcomes depending upon whether one operation (or a group of operations) fails or succeeds. We will cover transactions and how you will use them in your database code in Chapter 12. The most important thing to understand is that one of the main characteristics of OLTP databases is the employment of mechanisms to keep the data contained in them from being corrupted by anything the user does.

Operational Data Store (ODS)

The idea of the ODS is to have a database where all of the data you need to run your business on a day-to-day basis is located. A limited amount of historical data may be stored depending upon your requirements.

The ODS is designed to try and address some of the problems associated with the OLTP concept which can be summarized as follows:

- ❑ OLTP databases generally have a complicated structure with many tables. The data structures can be quite complex to understand, and querying information may require creative use of the SQL language. In my experience, novice query writers may bring an OLTP system to its knees by writing inefficient queries due to a lack of understanding of the inner workings of SQL Server.

- ❑ Many OLTP databases have a large number of detailed records. Day-to-day operations probably don't require access to every transaction created during the day, but will likely need to be able to obtain summations of the data. If you ran multiple queries on the OLTP system, all of the transactions would need to be re-calculated every time a query was made.

❏   Not all data is stored in a single source. A typical organization may have data important to the operation of the business stored in many data sources. Much as we would like to see it change, much of the world's data is still housed on mainframes in non-relational databases written in COBOL.

In the ODS, data is consolidated from all the disparate sources in an organization, and summarized as needed. It can be refreshed as frequently or infrequently as required. The data is characterized by having few, if any, allowable user-modifications, with a moderate amount of history maintained to handle the day-to-day questions and show short term trends.

In the bank scenario, the ODS would likely have all of the transactions for the past day, and possibly the past week or month, stored in a manner where a simple query would show you any answers you wanted. Some aggregated data may be stored if it is frequently needed. For example, an account list might be stored where a customer's current account balance for the previous day is viewable. This kind of data could then be queried by the customer to see their balance for the previous day, as well as any transactions that have been cleared. Hence the entire account need not be summarized every time the customer wants to see their account information. Additionally, notices could be sent based on the data from the summarized rolling account balances.

Storing summarized data is not a requirement for the ODS. It may just be necessary to make a set of tables that are simpler to query, so that the users can perform *ad hoc* enquiries. A great example of ODS is a database placed on notebook computers for sales staff who are on the road, or in PDAs for people who walk/work around the office, and don't have a permanent desk. Hence the goal of the ODS can be met by providing users with Operational Data and keeping them up-to-date on the short term trends that they need for making daily decisions.

Data Warehouse

The primary use of the data warehouse is to support decision making, by storing as much historical information from the organization as is necessary. **Decision support** is a pretty generic term that refers to being able to answer the difficult questions about how an enterprise is doing. Better decisions can be made when more data specific to the needs of the user is available to be looked through, summarized, and queried. A proper decision support system can form the "intelligence hub" for an organization. For example, if the sales group in your company was able to see sales trends over a ten year period, correlated with the current advertising models in use at any given time, it would certainly be better than having a single year of the same data. Or a month for that matter. Another goal of the data warehouse, as with the ODS, is to separate the active transactional processing from the reporting aspects of the database system, so that we can do more intensive querying that will not affect our users' ability to create and access the data in our OLTP systems.

An older copy of the data from the OLTP database is stored in the data warehouse. The frequency of updating the information is based on the amount of data, the needs of the users, and the time available to do the copying. This data is stored in a manner efficient for querying – this is a different structure to that which is efficient for modifications. No modification should ever be made to the data in the warehouse; any changes should be made to the operational database. The only time that the warehouse changes is when it gets the most up-to-date set of information from the operational database. You should also never use the data to ask questions that require an up-to-date exact answer. The data warehouse is used solely for historical analysis of data.

Introduction to Database Methodologies

A comprehensive data warehouse would take several years' worth of data from all heterogeneous sources within an organization – such as legacy mainframe systems, SQL Server and Oracle databases – and transform it into a single database using common structures. In this manner, the valuable data from legacy databases in an organization can be combined with all of the newer, well-structured databases (as well as third-party databases that are used for various tasks) into one common set of structures which can be used to mine the information needed to make decisions. For instance, human resources data could come from one third party system, general ledger from another, and router IP addresses from a third. All of these databases may supply a piece of the puzzle that will provide your users with the complete picture they need to make a decision.

As will be discussed later, one of the most important things you have to consider when you are designing the entire database system is the potential range of questions that may be asked. While many questions can be answered directly from the OLTP database ("What is customer X's current account balance?") many will have to be pushed out to a data warehouse ("Over the past year, what is the average amount of money customers have debited or credited to their accounts in ATM's in each region of the country"). The data warehouse is an ideal place to bring together difficult-to-associate data in a manner that your users can deal with.

A data warehouse is a tremendous undertaking – not to be taken lightly. It should not be considered just a quick item to build. You will likely want to bring in data from many disparate sources, some of which may change as time passes, especially when the data comes from third party sources (new vendor for the HR database, new version of another system, and, my favorite, systems from companies your own company has just acquired are but a few examples).

While the banking data warehouse is likely to be huge, it would probably be used heavily by the bank's sales and marketing teams. They would use the data to answer questions such as which of their programs has worked best when, and what kinds of programs to implement when. The actuarial staff would probably look at the data to see trends in interest rates vs. foreclosures. Having such a vast collection of information in a database makes the new technologies available in SQL Server 2000 so important to data warehousing.

Data Marts

A data mart is a distinctive segment of a data warehouse and usually pertains to either the specific needs of a division or department, or a specific business purpose within an organization. It is built using special database structures known as star or snowflake schemas. **Star schemas** are actually simple databases, with a single **fact table** (a table containing information that can be summarized to provide details regarding the history of the operation of the organization) connected to a set of **dimension tables** that categorize the facts in the fact tables. It should be noted that the data in the fact table is primarily numeric. **Snowflake schemas** are simply an extension of star schemas where the fact tables may also be dimension tables.

The other important term from data marts that we must introduce are **cubes**. A cube is another of those fairly strange terms, but it describes how the OLAP tools technology organizes the dimension tables of our star or snowflake schema. The dimensions of the fact table are described by the dimensions of the cube, whilst each cell of data in the cube represents a fact containing a level of detail for the different dimensions of the cube. Consider the following three questions:

- How many viewers in total were there of our website in 2000?
- How many viewers in total of our website were there in 2000 and what areas did they visit?
- What kinds of viewers of our website in 2000 did we have and what areas did they visit?

Each of these questions will use a different number of dimensions to solve the problem. Our fact table would be concerned with a numeric count of users at a low level, and the dimension tables would be used to group and slice the data according to a user's needs. The cubing mechanisms can be used to pre-aggregate the answers to parts or all of the questions that a user might ask, in order to make answering the question quicker for the users. An in depth explanation of these data structures is beyond the scope of this book. More details can be found in *"Professional SQL Server 2000" (Wrox Press, ISBN 1861004486)* and *"Professional Data Warehousing with SQL Server 7.0 and OLAP Services" (Wrox Press, ISBN 1861002815)*.

Data marts may use SQL Server (though they do not have to) to store their data, but the data is not necessarily accessed using classic SQL commands (though when SQL Server is used to store the dimensional data it is an option). Data marts usually use OLAP servers to do much of the aggregation prior to the user asking for the data. There exists an SQL-like language to access the data in a data mart (**Multidimensional Expressions** or **MDX**), though technically it does not work directly against the data mart data. However, data is usually accessed using a tool with no coding. Suitable tools include Microsoft Excel, Microsoft Access, Cognos Impromptu, and Lotus Approach to name but a few. The data in data marts is read-only by definition (save for the processes that periodically refresh it, of course).

The main purpose of the data mart is to show trends, regional or any grouping of data that the user may want, by separating the contents of a massive data warehouse into smaller segments that are reasonable to access and manage. Each data mart will be architected in such a manner as to solve a very specific set of problems.

Consider the example of an online bookseller. A data mart that their marketing department would no doubt want to have would deal with products sold. The main fact table would contain numeric sales figures, such as quantity of items sold, and their price. Then dimensions would be modeled for the date of sale; where on the site the user got the information (did they search directly for the item, did they do a general author search, or did we entice them to purchase by flashing their information on the screen); the customer information (where were they from, what kinds of personal information did they give); and finally the products that were purchased. From this information we can see what sales were made over a quarter to persons in Topeka, or any other combination of the dimensions, and so build vague, or very specific, queries to answer questions. In the case of our OLTP databases, this would take hundreds of lines of SQL code (and I can verify this from painful personal memories).

In the banking example, data architects (or indeed end users) may create specific data marts for different users of the data warehouse. For instance, a marketing user may have a data mart with banking customers segregated by income level, region of the country, payment amounts, interest amounts, and on-time information. From this, queries can be formulated showing the customers from each region, by each income level, who made their payments on time, for which interest level. This could be very powerful information when formulating new deals with special rates in different parts of the country.

Architecture

The overall architecture of the final database solution will vary depending on the size of the problem you are trying to solve. In the following diagram, we take a typical larger system, and break it down so we can see the flow of data through the full database solution.

Introduction to Database Methodologies

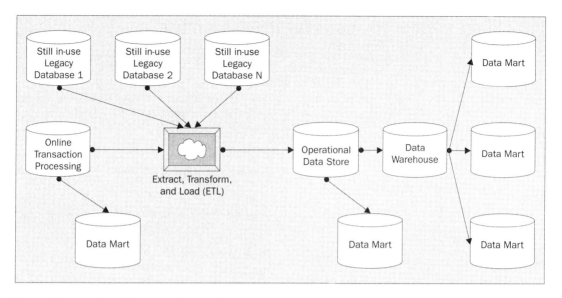

You will notice that there are a lot of data marts scattered about the diagram. Data marts are easiest to build from the data warehouse, since the data warehouse already has historical information, but they can be built at any step along the way.

Note that we take our source data in the legacy databases and OLTP databases and transform it for use in the ODS. In reality, we do somewhat the same thing in every step of the process, from the ODS to the data warehouse, and on to the data marts. Generally, once you have transformed it into an ODS-like format, you won't have to make too many changes to get the data into the data warehouse format. Actual scenarios may vary from situation to situation.

Case Study

Throughout the book, we will create a case study looking at the process of developing a database. This will incorporate all aspects of design, from the initial design ideas, through interviewing clients, modeling the database, creating it using SQL Server, choosing hardware, and building access to it.

The topic of the case study will be a personal checking account register. While the actual amounts of data that will be stored in the resulting databases (which are located on the Wrox website at www.wrox.com) will be much smaller than might normally require advanced data warehousing, it is merely a manageably sized example.

The choice of a checking register gives just enough leeway to show many of the different types of relationships, structural problems, etc. that will be encountered when creating a real database. Some level of multi-user functionality can be incorporated into the design by having an interface for multiple checking account users to enter debits and credits at the same time. This will allow us to consider the design and implementation of the ODS database, the use of SQL Server utilities to perform the tasks of extracting data from the OLTP databases, transforming the data into a different form, and loading that data into the data mart (generically known as **ETL** for **Extract**, **Transform**, and **Load**) .

Chapter 1

Relational versus Procedural Programming

The paradigm of relational programming is so different from procedural programming that it will cause plenty of grief if the differences are misunderstood. Relational programming is all about specifying what you want, then letting the relational engine do all of the work, and procedural programming is all about efficient looping. The primary relational language (and the only one we will be considering from now on) is SQL. It is assumed that you, the reader, have experience in using SQL, as we will be presenting all of our examples in T-SQL, the language of Microsoft SQL.

Whilst there are differing opinions as to the breadth of difference between the two paradigms, the different methodologies which each entails mean that careful thought must be given to which is most appropriate to the task in hand.

In Chapter 3 we will be looking at the basics of relational theory in more depth and how it relates to SQL.

Looping

In procedural programming, the primary way to access data is by looping through arrays of data. We can imagine a program written so that the programmer executes a SELECT statement to fill an array of data from one table (call it outerTable), and then executes a SELECT statement to get an array of data from another table (call it innerTable). He may then find the information he's after by using two nested loops as in the following:

```
For Each row In outer table
   For Each row In innerTable
       ` ...check for some equality then do some action
   Next row In innerTable
Next row In outerTable
```

This code is what SQL Server does behind the scenes when it queries two tables. But it is extremely bad programming practice to write a routine like this, as the following SQL code performs the same query.

```
SELECT *
FROM innerTable
   JOIN outerTable
       ON innerTable.key = outerTable.key
```

SQL Server is optimized to perform this operation, and the server has a higher performance than the client. Whilst this is a simple code example, the same principles are involved when performing complex queries – it's always best to offload as much work as is possible onto the server. This is called joining the tables. The resulting set of data returned by the query can be further filtered and refined by modifying the selection parameters.

It is important to learn to let SQL Server do as much as possible, since it is made for the purpose of manipulating data alone. This is especially important because some queries in a well structured database can include ten, twenty, or even more tables. The more tables involved, the harder it is to implement SQL without using joins (as joins are the representation of tables relationships). In Chapters 10, 11, and 12 we will use SQL is some depth, as we look at how to build and access our data in the databases we will create. This book is certainly not a SQL reference manual; it rather focuses on how to apply SQL statements within database design.

Introduction to Database Methodologies

A good understanding of the SQL language is essential in order to manipulate data in a relational database, and enable the development of software that accesses such data. Procedural programmers that ignore this reality will simply not develop well-performing applications. Just as you use a hammer to drive a nail and a saw to cut wood, you need to use all the tools at your disposal (including both procedural and relational languages) to get the job done right. For good reading on this subject try the following books:

- *Instant SQL Programming (Wrox Press ISBN 1874416508)*
- *Professional SQL Server 2000 Programming (Wrox Press ISBN 1861004486)*
- *The Essence of SQL : A Guide to Learning Most of SQL in the Least Amount of Time, (Peer to Peer Communications, ISBN 0964981211)*

Network Access

One of the primary reasons you need to implement proper SQL code is network access. SQL database applications are inherently distributed between two or more computers. Currently, it is pretty rare to have a single user SQL database where the user works on the same computer as the data is located on. While this may not always be true (with SQL Server 2000 having its Microsoft Data Engine and CE versions to enable single user systems) the focus of our book will be on multi-user systems that involve two or more computers. However, all examples in the book can be implemented and tested on any edition of SQL Server.

To implement the looping example in the previous section, every row in the `innerTable` and `outerTable` would have to be retrieved over a network connection to the client. If the table was large, this would likely be a very slow operation, even on a relatively fast network.

The efficiency gained by utilizing the processor resources of the server allows multiple users to access the data quicker than if the work was performed on the client machines, not to mention that the amount of data that must be shuffled across the network will be smaller, minimizing the effect of network access speed. Although well designed systems will centralize processing, you often find that poorly performing applications are attempting to do the work that the database engine was designed to do.

An Overview of SQL Server Database Design Process

The process of designing a proper database system has a few things in common with designing efficient computer systems of any kind.

- It is a relatively straightforward task
- It can be very time consuming
- It seldom is done with the kind of vigor that is required

As we will contend over and over throughout the book, the database is the central focus in a large percentage of the computer systems that are being created today. Even in systems that do not focus on the database there is usually a requirement for some form of data storage. In this book we concentrate primarily on larger systems that have a database as the focus of the system. Examples of such databases are all around us, on the Internet, in our banks, government, companies, grocery shops, pharmacies, etc.

The process of designing such databases can be broken down into a few steps, as we will in this book:

- **Defining the Objective** – Don't laugh this off as being too obvious: most projects are plagued by the developers having no real idea of what the user base actually wants or needs because they jump to conclusions or fail to listen to the right users, or in some cases, any users at all. During this phase we will be defining the functional, performance, and reporting requirements for the final system we will be creating.

- **Logical Design** – The process of designing a logical path to achieve the objectives, done in an implementation independent way. One of the main reasons you will not see SQL Server referenced much in the first half of this book is because logical database design is independent of physical database design and implementation.

- **Physical Design** – Taking the logical design and adapting it to a real implementation. This design phase is concerned with determining how the database system will be physically implemented, using whatever hardware and software is available to us.

- **Physical Implementation** – The implementation phase of the project is concerned with actually laying out the physical data onto database servers and developing code to access the data.

- **Review** – The process of assessing whether the objectives were achieved. Sadly, the most overlooked part of a project because it takes too doggone long, and is no fun at all: testing, documentation, and all of the other things we hate to do but must. This should include a mechanism to utilize user feedback, and a maintenance plan to consider how to rectify any problems identified.

In this book, the first two steps are covered in the Logical Design part of the book, and the rest is covered in the Physical part.

Summary

In this chapter we have introduced the basic foundations of the modern database systems, especially OLTP and data warehousing methodologies. We have established simply that there are four primary parts to the enterprise database system. These can be summarized as:

- **OLTP (Online Transaction Processing)** for storing our current data in, with only a limited amount of the historical data retained to enable up-to-the-minute decisions.

- **ODS (Operational Data Store)** for building a storage mechanism for data needed to make day-to-day business decisions without interrupting the users in the OLTP database.

- **DW (Data Warehouse)** – not to be confused with the general term of data warehousing, the DW is used to store massive amounts of history to allow us to maintain a consolidated database of as many of our corporate databases to enable us to see trends over long time periods.

- **Data Marts** – often confused with OLAP or Cubes (which are technologies used in querying the data in the data mart), the data mart is used to take a slice of a data warehouse or in its absence, the OLTP or ODS data, and allow the user to view aggregated data in a flexible manner.

Introduction to Database Methodologies

The central focus of our book will be on the data, particularly the data in the OLTP database. The data, and hence the OLTP database, is the single most important part of any project. Some might argue otherwise, that, for example, proper design is the most important, or indeed the logical nature of the information (since it models how the enterprise does business). However, very few users are interested in the nature of the data, or indeed the interface they are using to access it, as long as they can view and manipulate the data they require. So many systems are out there that are clumsy to use, poorly thought out, yet they keep using them on and on. Processes change, as do ideas, but the data that is stored will live much longer than any interface, or even the process. One of the main tasks of database administrators everywhere is data conversion from one system to another. No matter how messed up the database structure may be from version to version, the data will still be used over and over again.

If you have ever done any programming, you will undoubtedly disagree with some of the opinions/ideas in this book. I fully accept that this book is not the gospel of St. Louis of Databases. My ideas and opinions have grown from ten years of working with, and learning about, databases, and as such I have supplemented them with knowledge from many disparate persons, books, college classes, and seminars. The design methodology presented in this book is a conglomeration of these ideas, with as much credit given to those other folks as I can remember. I hope it proves a useful learning tool, and that through reading other people's works, and trying out your own ideas, that you will develop a methodology which will suit you, and make you a successful database designer.

Gathering Information for a Database Project

In this chapter, we will go back to first principles and discuss the very first steps that should be taken when starting a database design project. Getting preliminary information for a new database project – such as deciding what is going to be stored in it – is one of the most important tasks you will have to do, though there can be constraints on time and resources in the real world, which mean that this process is not carried out as thoroughly as it should be.

Building your database without adequate preliminary analysis can be likened to building a house on sand, where, after the first floor is built, the sands shift and you have to start all over again. Situations frequently arise where, after a database has been built and deployed, a previously overlooked feature has to be included in the database which requires redesigning it from scratch. Proper analysis is the solid foundation so that a smooth, successful project is built.

As you gather the information for your database project, you should avoid the temptation to start imposing any kind of structure at this time. Do not define your tables and fields, etc. at this point even if you are experienced at database design. You should try to approach the process naively, never starting down a single path until you have consulted all parties involved in the project to listen to their ideas and needs. Too often we begin to impose a structure and a solution to a problem before we have enough knowledge of the task at hand, and this helps neither our customers nor ourselves. This chapter is placed prior to the definition of data modeling to emphasize this point.

The process of database design involves the collection of a significant amount of information. This information will be useful to other team members now and in the future to understand and support the system. A formal documentation policy needs to be considered.

The Database Design Team

In order to start the information gathering process, a database design team will need to be organized. While the team may only consist of a single person (which would likely be the case in small organizations or projects), there are at least four roles that need to be filled because each serves a very different essential purpose:

- The **Business Analyst** fleshes out the business requirements from the users and provides the design team with a functional specification which they develop into a technical specification. This role also acts as the user's advocate, making sure that the final project solution suits the specified business needs of the client. The role also involves making sure that any contracts, agreements, etc., are fulfilled.

- The **Data Architect** takes the functional specification and develops a technical implementation specification. (The system architect also helps with this task.) The data architect designs all the data storage and access architectures, and also chooses proper storage technologies based on what's needed. *This book focuses only on the responsibilities of this role.* Note that the data architect is not the same as the database administrator (DBA) who is concerned with implementation and deals with hardware, software, and making things run smoothly. The data architect is concerned with the way the database systems, relational or otherwise, fit together and are structured.

- The **System Architect** is in charge of designing the entire user interface and middle-tier business objects that the project will require, and is responsible for choosing the front end and middle tier technologies. The specific difference between this role and the data architect is that the latter is solely responsible for the database side of the project, while the system architect deals with everything else, though there would likely be some overlap between the roles.

- The **Project Manager** is the "boss" who is primarily responsible for making sure that every other team member does their bit, and handles scheduling.

Each of these roles will exist throughout the design and implementation process. There are other important roles that will contribute as well – for example, the project sponsor or client representative, who needs the project completed and provides the finance for development, testing, documentation, etc. However, the four roles listed above are the core group and to define others or to go into more detail is beyond the scope of this book. The reason for defining these roles at all is to show that, if different people perform each of them, the data architect can focus almost exclusively on how the data is stored.

Documentation and Communication

During this process of analysis, there is one good habit that you should adopt early on – document all the information that you acquire. Let me remind you that you might get hit by a bus tomorrow. Less morbidly, keep thinking that, "If something happens to me, someone else will have to take over my work." Another example – in our industry, it is becoming more difficult to hold onto the best employees. If someone leaves the project because a competitor offers them an unreasonably huge salary, the replacement will be placed on a steep learning curve to get up to speed, and the only way to help this along is to document all information.

So you should document, document, document! It is imperative that you don't keep everything in your head. The following are helpful guidelines as you begin to take notes on users' needs:

- Maintain a set of documents that will share system design and specification information. Important documents to consider include: design meeting notes, documents describing verbal change requests, and sign-offs on all specifications, such as functional, technical, testing, etc.
- Beyond formal documentation, it is important to keep the members of your design team up-to-date and fully informed. Develop and maintain a common repository for all of the information.
- Take minutes of meetings and keep notes of every suggestion, request, or idea that your customer voices.
- Note anywhere you add information that the users haven't approved.
- Set the project's scope early on and keep it in mind at all times. This will prevent the project from getting too big or diverse to be useful.

One of the primary jobs of the design team is to specify a scope statement (mission statement or mission objectives) that describes the parameters of the project. This will be consulted and compared to during the design and implementation, and upon completion. If, however, the project's objectives and aims are not decided at the scope statement stage, or nothing is written down, then there is a strong chance that there will be conflicts between yourselves and your clients as your ideas diverge. Such vagueness or indecision might cause unnecessary discussions, fights, or even lawsuits later on in the process. So, make sure your clients understand what you are going to do for them, and use language that will be clearly understood, but is specific enough to describe what you learn in the information gathering process.

Client Approval

As you go through the entire database design process, the client will no doubt change his mind on field names, field definitions, business rules, user interface, colors – just about anything that he can – and you have to prepare yourself for this. Whatever the client wants or needs is what you will have to endeavor to accomplish. The client is in ultimate control of the project and you have to be flexible enough to run with any proposed changes, whether minor or major.

After every meeting, summarize your notes in language that all the participants can understand and send them copies. Keep a folder with all of the responses you receive and forward this to the project manager.

At any time the client can tell you, "I never said that". If there is no documentation to back up what you are saying, this could spell trouble. So I'll say this again – keep documentation, and if you have to take a decision that the client will not like, you'll have the documentation as backup for your decision.

The best way to avoid conflict – and, as clients change their minds, "scope creep" *will* occur – is to make sure that you get your client's approval at regular stages throughout the design process.

Minimum Information Requirements

Regardless of whether you are a one-person team or a cog in a fifty-person design force, there is a set of basic information that the design team needs to gather during the early stages if they are to continue the design process.

To start with, you need a pile of notes, printouts, screen shots, CD-ROMs loaded with spreadsheets, database backups, Word documents, e-mails, handwritten notes, etc. No structure is necessary for this initial information, and it would probably be best at this point if there was no structure at all, though, of course, this is a personal matter. Some people would argue that you shouldn't just gather and go, but rather that you need to keep yourself organized from the onset so that, as you go through your information quest, you are able to ask increasingly intelligent questions. The reason I don't believe in having too much structure is that I have found that I tend to add weight to what is in the information. The real ordering should come when you begin analyzing your gathered information, which we will discuss later on.

We'll now take a look at the initial stages of the design process, and the sources of this basic information.

Database Prototypes

Prototypes are useful when developing large-scale systems that warrant this initial step. Their role is to be a "proof of concept" tool – an opportunity to flesh out with the design team and the users the critical elements of the project on which success or failure will depend.

Sometimes, as the data architect, you will be directed to take a prototype database that has been hastily developed and "make it work" or, worse yet, "polish the database up". Indeed, you may inherit an unstructured, unorganized prototype and your task will be to turn it into a production database. Scary words indeed.

Bear in mind that prototypes should only be considered as interactive pictures to get the customer to sign a contract with your company. Time and time again consultants are hired to develop a prototype that looks so good that it is figured it must be ready for enterprise deployment. Many people will say to you, "It looks like it works, so why toss it out?" The main reason is that, when making a prototype, you piece, slap, and hack together code as you come up with ideas in an unorganized way. Proper structure and forethought are tossed to the wind. Once the whirlwind prototype development is done, you have a UI and a functional database, but little or no thought has been put into its architecture, though it looks pretty. It is better to start from scratch once the customer has signed; developing the final application using structured and supported coding standards. As a data architect, it is very important that you work as hard as possible to use prototype code *only* as a working model, a piece of documentation that you use to enhance your own design. They help you to be sure you are not going to miss out any critical pieces of information that the users need – such as a name field, a search operation, or even a button (which may imply a data element) – but they should not tell you anything about architectural issues. Deal with these yourself. When it comes to enterprise database design, there can be no short cuts.

Client Interviews

In the big business, corporate world, it is unlikely that the data architect will meet the user, let alone formally interview them. The Project Manager, Business Analyst, and System Architect would provide all the information that he/she requires. There may be times, however, when the data architect actually gets involved in the interview process, depending on the structure of the actual design team. In my consulting experience, I have been in the role of actually attending the client interview/design sessions. On occasion, I've had to interview the interviewer to clear up inconsistencies!

Gathering Information for a Database Project

The client interview is where the database project really gets started. However, many clients generally think visually; they think in terms of forms, web pages, and simple user interfaces in particular. In many cases your clients will have absolutely no understanding or care about how the system is created. As the data architect, your job when involved with interviewing clients is to balance the customer's perceived need with their real need – a properly structured database that sits behind the user interface. Changing a form around to include a new text box, label, or whatever, is a relatively simple task, giving the user the false impression that creating a database application is an easy process. If you want proof, show the user a near-finished prototype application with no database support. The clients may be impressed that you have put together something so quickly, but then run it and watch it fall over. Rarely will it be understood that what exists under the hood – namely the database and the middle-tier business objects – is where all main work takes place.

An exhaustive treatment of interview techniques is beyond the scope of this book, but there are a few key points that should be mentioned. Firstly, the word *interview* is used instead of the word *interrogation*. The first suggests a one-on-one exchange of ideas, while the second implies the imposing of your ideas upon the paying customer. If you come across as overbearing and try to tell the customer what he/she wants, you will damage your relationship right from the start. Be tactful and don't give the impression that you know more that the customer does.

Try to set a basic agenda for the interview, so that you can be sure you cover the important areas, but have an open mind. As a starter, one simple question will serve you well: "What do you want from this project?" This lets your interviewees tell you what they want from the project. Encourage them to explain their initial ideas of how they would achieve it. This will all give you a clear explanation of what they want and why, preventing your preconceived ideas from altering how you address the problems that you are solving for the client. Be prepared to listen, take notes, ask questions, get clarification – and take more notes.

Make sure you treat every person that you interview for a project as an individual. Each person will likely have different viewpoints from every other person. Don't assume that the first person you speak to can speak for the rest, even if they are all working on the same project or if this individual is the manager. One-on-one sessions allow clients to speak their mind, without untimely interruptions from colleagues. Be mindful of the fact that the loudest and boldest people might not have the best ideas and the quiet person who sits at the back and says nothing may have the key to the entire project. Make sure you get everybody's opinions.

One technique that is useful to convey to the client that you understand what they are telling you is to repeat their most important points as you go through a meeting. This is also useful for clarification of unclear points and aids in the note-taking process. Audio or videotaping of meetings is a technique that some use, but it can seem invasive and make the clients feel uncomfortable, so should only be used in situations where it is deemed necessary due to previous communication problems. Never record any conversation without the interviewee's consent. If at all possible, have a person at meetings who has no responsibilities other than note taking.

As the data architect, you will have to recall much of what was said during these initial meetings, and this is vital in enabling those around you do their jobs. Herein lies the importance of documentation. If everything is written down and filed away, rather than just committed to memory, the clients can regularly review it. This means that, not only can you improve relations with your clients, but you also enhance your chances of identifying the data that they will want to see again, as well as providing the design team with the information required to design the final product.

Chapter 2

This book is born out of eight years of making mistakes in the database design process, and the client interview is one of the most fouled parts of the process that I have encountered. It might not seem a suitable topic for experienced programmers, but even the best of us need to be reminded that jumping the gun, bullying the client, telling them what they want before they tell you, and even failing to manage the user's expectations can lead to the ruin of even a well developed system. Good client interviewing technique is necessary for us to get a solid foundation for the design process. If you have a shaky foundation, the final product will likely be shaky as well.

What Kinds of Things to Ask

It is very important to make sure that whoever does the interviewing finds out the answers to the following questions:

Who Will Use the Data?

The answer to this question may indicate other personnel that you might want to interview, and will likely be of importance when you come to define the security for the system.

How Will the Data be Used?

Imagine you are asked to create a database of contacts. You will need to know:

- ❏ Will the contact names be used just to make phone calls, like a quick phone book?
- ❏ Will we be sending mass e-mail or post to the members of the contact lists? Should the names be subdivided into groups for this purpose?
- ❏ Will we be using the names to solicit a response from the mail, like donations, overdue bills, or new investors?
- ❏ How important is it to have each contact's correct title (for example, Dr. not Mr.)? Do we need any phonetic information – would we lose a sale if a user mispronounces a customer's name?

Knowing what your client is planning to use the data in the system for is a very important piece of information indeed. Not only will you understand the process, but you can also begin to get a good picture of the type of data that needs to be stored.

What Do You Want to See on Reports?

Reports are often one of the most forgotten parts of the design process. Many novice developers leave implementing them until the very last minute. However, users are probably more interested in the reports that are generated by the data than anything else that you will do. Reports are used as the basis of vital decision making and can make or break a company.

Looking back at the contact example, what name does the client want to see on the reports?

- ❏ First name, last name
- ❏ First name, middle name, last name
- ❏ Last name, first name
- ❏ Nickname

It is very important to try to nail these issues down early, no matter how small or silly they seem to you at this point. We will be looking at building a reporting infrastructure later in our project and this kind of information may be necessary.

One note of warning: while it is very important to get some idea of what data is needed on reports, you should be careful to avoid any discussions about their actual appearance. It is not the role of the data architect to go beyond the reports' data requirements.

Where Is Your Data Now?

It would be nice once in a while to have a totally new database with absolutely no pre-existing data. This would make life so easy. Unfortunately, this is almost never the case, except possibly with startup companies, but even they will have some data that they have been storing while getting started. Every organization is different. Some have data in one single location, while others have it scattered in many locations. Rarely, if ever, is the data already in well-structured databases that you can easily access. If that were the case, where would the fun be? Indeed, why would the client come to you at all? Clients typically have data in the following sundry locations:

- **Mainframe or legacy data**
  Millions of lines of active COBOL still run many corporations.

- **Spreadsheets**
  Spreadsheets are wonderful tools to view, slice, and dice data, but are inappropriate places to maintain complex databases. Most users know how to use a spreadsheet as a database but, unfortunately, are not so well experienced in ensuring the integrity of their data.

- **Desktop databases such as Access**
  Desktop databases are great tools and are easy to deploy and use. However, this often means that these databases are constructed and maintained by non-technical personnel and are poorly designed, potentially causing large amounts of problems when the databases have to be enlarged or modified.

- **Filing cabinet**
  Yes, there are still many companies that have no computers at present and maintain vast stockpiles of paper documents. Your project might simply to be to replace a filing cabinet with a computer based system, or to supply a simple database that logs the physical locations of the existing paper documents.

Data that you need to include in the SQL Server database you are designing will come from these and other weird and wonderful sources that you discover from the client.

How Much is this Data Worth?

It is also important to place value judgments on data. Just because data is available, it doesn't necessarily mean that it should be included in the new database. The client needs to be informed of all the data that is available and be provided with a cost estimate of transferring it into the new database. The cost of transferring legacy data can be high. In this way, the client is offered the opportunity to make decisions that may conserve funds for more important purposes.

How Will the Data in the New Database Fit in with the Other Data?

Once you have a good idea of where all of the client's important data is located, you can begin to determine how the data in your new SQL Server solution will interact with the data that will stay in its original format. This may include building intricate gateway connections to mainframes, linked server connections to other SQL Servers or Oracle boxes, or even linking to spreadsheets. We cannot make too many assumptions about this topic at this point in our design. Just knowing the basic architecture you will need to deal with can be very helpful later in the process.

Are there any Rules that Govern the Use of the Data?

Taking our previous example of contacts, we might discover that:

- Every contact must have a valid e-mail address
- Every contact must have a valid street address
- The client checks every e-mail address using a mail routine and the contact isn't a valid contact until this routine has been successfully executed
- Contacts must be subdivided by type

Be careful not to infer any rules like this. Confirm them with the client. Your final product might be unacceptable because you have placed a rule on the data that the client does not want.

Other Places to Look for Data Rules

Apart from interviews, there are other sources in which you can look to find data rules and other pieces of information relevant to the design project. Often the project manager will obtain these documents.

Request for Quote or Request for Proposal

Two of the primary documents are:

- **The Request for Quote (RFQ)** – a document with a fairly mature specification, which an organization sends out to firms to determine how much something would cost
- **The Request for Proposal (RFP)** – for less mature ideas that an organization wishes to expand on using free consulting services

A copy of an RFP or an RFQ needs to be added to the pile of information that you will need later on in the process. While these documents generally consist of sketchy information about the problem and the desired solution, you can use them to confirm the original reason for wanting the database system, and for getting a firmer handle on what types of data are to be stored within it.

Contracts or Client Work Orders

Getting copies of the contract is a fairly radical approach to gathering design information. Frankly, in a corporate structure, you will likely have to fight through layers of management to make them understand why you need to see the contract at all. Contracts can be inherently difficult to read due to the language that they are written in. However, be diligent in filtering out the legalese, and you will uncover a basic set of requirements for the database system – requirements that you must fulfill exactly or you may not get paid.

Note that not only is the contract to build the system important, but any contracts that the system you are building has to fulfill must be taken into consideration.

Level of Service Agreement

One important section of contracts that is very important to the design process is the required level of service. This may specify the number of pages per minute, the number of records in the database, etc.

Don't Forget about Audits

When you build a system, you must consider if the system is likely to be audited in the future, and by whom. Government, ISO 9000 clients, and other clients that are monitored by standards organizations are likely to have strict audit requirements. Other clients will also have financial audit processes. These audit plans may contain valuable information that can be used in the design process.

Old Systems

If you are writing a new version of a currently operating database system, then access to the existing system can be both a blessing and a curse. Obviously, the more information you can gather about where the system was previously is very important. All of the screens, data models, object models, user documents, and so on, are extremely important to the design process.

However, unless you are simply making revisions to the existing system, it is very important to only use the old database system as a reference point. It is very easy to think in terms of tweaking existing code and utilizing all of the features and data of the existing system as the basis of updating the system. In a minority of cases, this might be a correct implementation, but generally speaking, this is not true. On most occasions, the existing system you will be replacing will have many problems that need to be fixed, not emulated.

Reports, Forms, Spreadsheets

Quite a large percentage of computer systems are built around the filling out of forms – government forms, company forms, all kinds of forms. You can guarantee that all this data is going to be scattered around the company, and it is imperative to find it *all*. It is virtually certain that these sources will contain data that you will need for your project, so make sure that the client gives you all such items.

Outline of the Case Study

The main goal of the case study in this chapter is not so much to illustrate the information gathering part of the process – it is unlikely that the data architect will do this in most teams – but rather just to set up a manageable example that we can follow throughout the book. For convenience, we will imagine that we are a one-person design team (with the exception of some input from the business analyst) and we will also totally ignore any kind of user interface.

You receive an e-mail from the programming manager stating that the accounting department is going to need a database to handle checking account maintenance. After you have met with your IT manager, you are referred to the accounting manager, Sam Smith. You set up a meeting (interview) with Sam to get an idea of what the need is.

Chapter 2

Client Interview

These are the type of notes that you would make for this meeting:

> Meeting with Sam Smith, Accounting,
> Nov 24, 2000, 10 AM, Large Conference Room
>
> Attendees: Louis Davidson, Data Architect;
> Sam Smith, Accounting Manager;
> Joe Jones, Business Analyst
>
> Initial Meeting
>
> Additional documentation attached: Bank register, sample check, sample statement, as well as electronic format of statement.
> Currently using paper check register, just like a basic home register. Have looked at the possibility of using canned product, but we have found none that offer all that they want. And most offer way too many features.
>
> Need to have multi-user capabilities (entry and viewing). Share over intranet.
>
> Process:
> Need to have very up to date information about account.
> Currently balancing account once a month. Using the statement from bank. Takes an entire day to get balanced at least. Would like to keep the account balanced weekly using internet data.
> Only interested in checking, not savings, stocks, bonds, etc. Already have a system for this.
>
> Will be audited yearly by a major auditor. Don't have an audit plan as of yet.
>
> Once Sam was finished, asked him about vendor tracking:
> It would be nice to be able to have payee information for most of the checks we write.
> Also about categorizing check, Sam said it would be nice, but not completely needed at this point.

Gathering Information for a Database Project

Looking back over the notes, there are several items we need to gather from the accounting department: check register, bank statement, audit plan, and a voided check, if available.

Preliminary Documentation

Sample Check Register

Number	Date	Description	Category	Amount	Balance
12390	12/15/00	Pizza Hut	Employee Appreciation		
12391	12/15/00	Allied Mortgage	Building payment		
12392	12/16/00	TN Electric	Utilities		
12393	12/16/00	Deposit	N/A		

Chapter 2

Sample Bank Statement

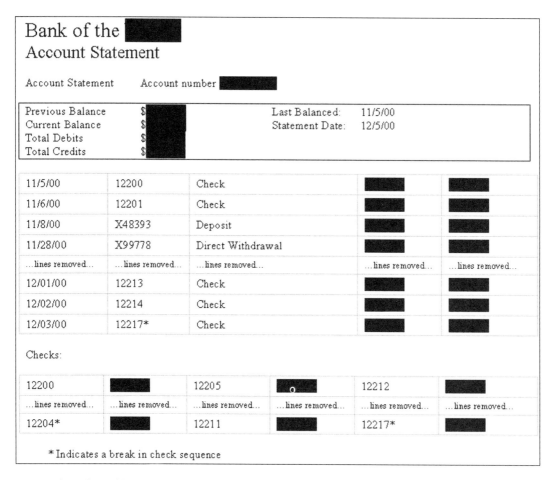

Notice that I have blacked out all figures in the above statements. Unless it is extremely important to have exact figures on documents, block out any sensitive information that might cause problems if it got into the wrong hands.

Gathering Information for a Database Project

Sample Bank Register Data Stream Format

Column	Data type	Required
Transaction Date	Date Only	Yes
Transaction Number	String(20)	Yes
Description	String(100)	Yes
Item Amount	Money	Yes

Note that this data stream is not from our analysis. Rather it is a paper document explaining what the bank will be providing to the client to support electronic balancing of accounts.

Sample Check

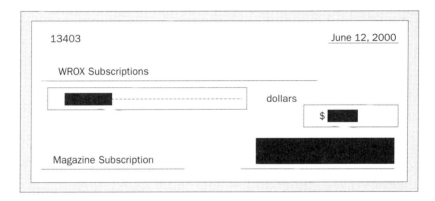

This is as far as we will take the case study in this chapter. We have now made a good start – the scope of our project is extremely small and we have gathered as much information as we can at this point – but there will come a time later on when we have to ask for more information. In later chapters, we will look back at these notes and documentation when we come to assemble the database itself.

Summary

In this chapter we have concentrated on a significant preliminary step in database design – the information gathering process. The real message behind all that we have seen is: get as much data as you can and document it. Look everywhere – leave no stone unturned as you procure as much information as the client is willing or able to give about the problem. Sometimes you will know exactly how to solve the problem even after the first e-mail. Other times, it will take a month of digging around to get enough information to tackle it. Designing well-structured systems and databases is hard work that takes a relatively long time to accomplish if done correctly. The first step is to understand the problem before you solve it.

Always keep in mind that it takes more time to redo a task than it does to do it right the first time. We will look at what "right" means during the physical data-modeling phase of database design. This comes *much* later in the process.

Gathering Information for a Database Project

3

Fundamental Database Concepts

Introduction

In this chapter, I aim to demystify the theory and terminology used by so many database academics. The group to which I belong is the hardcore of trench-level warriors who actually design good user databases to earn a living, and all this theory seems far removed from the world in which we live and work.

This may well leave you questioning whether reading about database design theory is at all worthwhile. Well, understanding the principles and theories that a technology is built upon is actually very important. For example, would you take your car to a mechanic who doesn't understand how spark plugs work, or fly in a plane with a pilot who doesn't understand the theory of flight? With this in mind, why should you expect your customers to come to you for database expertise if you don't understand the theory that supports database design?

That said, some of the terms and concepts used by academics could confuse and frustrate the best of us, partly due to their origins in mathematics. To compound this, there are some esoteric terms that would appear to most programmers to mean one thing, but in fact mean something altogether different. However, it remains important to gain some understanding of relational database theory, in order to be able to devise appropriate designs for such systems.

So, to figure out what the academic community are raving about, we are going to take a look at some of the simpler aspects of relational theory, comparing them to the SQL concepts and methods that we in the field should already know. As there are numerous other books on the subject, we are not going to delve too deeply into the academics' territory; rather we are going to try to provide a basic foundation in useful database concepts.

Chapter 3

This chapter will present the relational concepts from a largely SQL-oriented point of view. We will often touch on the implementation side of things which, though technically not what this part of the book is dealing with, cannot be avoided when giving our theoretical explanation in terms of concepts you'll be familiar with. However, we'll not get bogged down in implementation; it'll just be an overview. For further information, feel free to delve into the other sources suggested in Chapter 1.

During this chapter we will be looking at:

- The Relational Model – examining the terminology used for the essential blocks; we will then build upon this in later chapters
- Definitions of additional database concepts

The Relational Model

As mentioned in Chapter 1, E. F. Codd devised the relational model in the early 1970's. In this section, we will take a look at its more important parts from a Microsoft SQL Server standpoint.

As we will see, SQL Server implementation has much in common with this model, but is not nearly the same thing. Many relational purists cringe at how all of the variations of SQL (not just Microsoft's SQL Server) are implemented. This book is not the place to discuss their objections, and we intend to avoid any controversy with regard to this, as we look at the physical design and implementation parts of SQL Server.

Database

The first item that we need to define is a database.

> **Simply, a database is a collection of data arranged for ease and speed of search and retrieval.**

This could be a card catalogue at a library, a SQL Server database, or a text file. Technically, there is no corresponding concept in relational theory, but as we will make use of this term frequently, it is important that we introduce it.

> **In SQL Server, a database is a collection of objects and data that is grouped together logically.**

Table

One of the most common misconceptions about the relational model is that the term *relational* refers to the relationships between tables. In actual fact, it refers to the term **relation** (the mathematical name for a table), which is considered to be (almost) synonymous with the term table. As we will see, the relational model applies different names to not only what most programmers know primarily as a table, but also the elements contained within it.

The central most important element we deal with is the table itself. A table is the physical representation of some object, either real or imaginary. As you design tables, you will be looking for people, places, things (nouns) that you want to store information about. Understanding the concept of treating tables as nouns, and nouns as tables, is the first step to designing proper tables. Later, we will examine in more detail what we should store in tables, and the other structures covered in this section. Then, we start to look at how we identify tables and other objects in the next chapter.

The term *table* is a very implementation-oriented term and has the following meaning:

> **An orderly arrangement of data. Especially one in which the data is arranged in columns and rows in an essentially rectangular form.**

Two common versions of tables are: an Excel spreadsheet and the result of a simple SQL Query on the Northwind database. The latter is shown below:

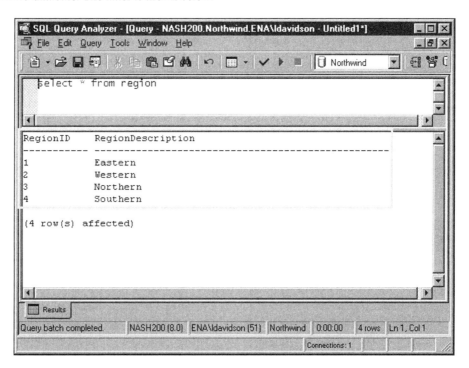

Even before computer spreadsheets, people were working on paper ones containing rows and columns (though they would not have called it a spreadsheet). We will take a more in-depth look at rows and columns later in this section.

As we mentioned earlier, a table is known as a relation, or more specifically, a named relation. As we will discuss later, tables and views are both considered named relations, and result sets are unnamed relations. Understanding this will help you to write better SQL.

The following table is just a very generic one of made up restaurants, with a few columns defined. Each of the terms in the table will be defined in full in this chapter.

Chapter 3

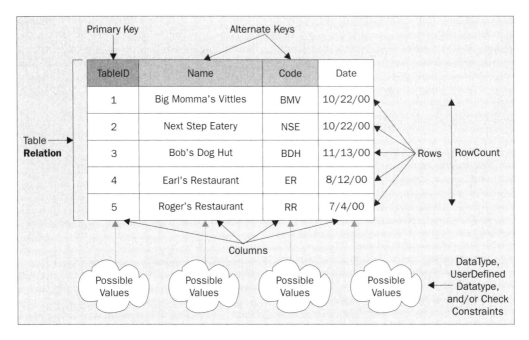

This is not to imply that a table and a relation are *precisely* the same thing. The following is the definition of a relation:

> **Relation**: A structure composed of attributes (individual characteristics, such as name or address, corresponding to the columns in a table) and tuples (sets of attribute values describing particular entities, such as customers, corresponding to the rows in a table). Within a relation, tuples cannot be repeated; each must be unique. Furthermore, tuples are unordered within a relation; interchanging two tuples does not change the relation.

This definition may seem a little confusing at the moment. Don't worry; everything will become clearer as we work our way through this chapter.

A relation is a very strict mathematical concept based on set theory, whilst a table is a physical implementation of a relation with special properties. That's to say, a relation can be used to define all tables, but not all relations can be manifested as a table. However, it is reasonable to suggest that the differences between the two are so subtle as to be nearly meaningless to the average database programmer.

Yet another term that we will use to mean a table is **entity**. The term entity is used frequently in logical modeling to mean the conceptual version of a table. I personally like this term, as it tends to really emphasize that a table is in fact a representation of something. "Table" is a very stark term that has a totally different meaning outside of computer science circles. The first time I told my wife I built a table she thought I might have been lying about my profession, "I thought you were in computers?" The term entity has fewer overheads and is less tied to implementation. In the next chapter, when we start to identify tables, we will first identify them conceptually as entities to avoid being forced into the structure that tables inherently have.

Rows and Columns

A row (or record) indicates an instance of whatever object is being physically represented by a table. The concept of an instance is related to object-oriented programming, but is treated differently in relational programming. In object-oriented (OO) programming (and even OO databases), a class is a general definition containing the attributes and methods that can operate on a specific instance of the class, commonly referred to as an object. In SQL Server, we deal with tables containing columns and rows. The table definition is much like the class in OO, and a specific instance of the table is a row, which is analogous to an object. While we have no methods for manipulating the data specifically implemented in the definition of a table, we do have specific SQL operations that we can use to interact with data in the tables.

The main reason for the distinction is really an implementation issue. Since SQL is heavily built around accessing data, it is very easy to see multiple instances of a SQL "object" at any one time, so many programmers fail to notice the parallels between an OO object and a SQL Server row. As we look further into data and object modeling in later chapters, we will highlight some of the parallels between OO methodologies and relational database programming.

As we can see in the figure below, the relational model has very different names for rows and columns. Rows are **tuples** (pronounced like couples) and columns are **attributes**. The term tuple is one of those funny technical terms that seems to either cause you to pause and think or make you giggle (which is what happened to me). According to legend, the word "tuple" has no other meaning, and you will not yet find it in any dictionary. Presumably it was coined during the formation of Codd's Relational Model specifically as a word with no preconceived notions attached to it. This avoids the confusion generated by terms such as table.

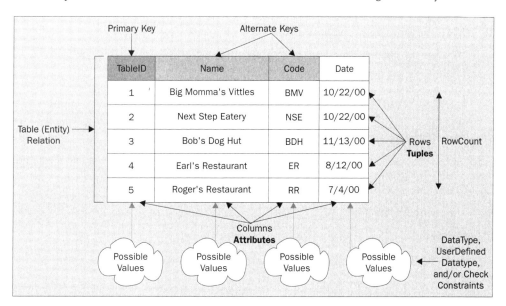

While the term tuple seems to be a pretty unobvious one to many programmers, attribute is a far better name for what a column represents. Each column should contain a characteristic or attribute of the instance of the row or tuple, or more simply put, each column contains an attribute that describes the row. When thought of in this manner, column usage makes way more sense. The analogy to OO properties should be reasonably obvious to anyone who has done any OO programming. A column is a property of an instance (or row) of a table (or relation/entity).

One of the tenets of relational theory is that attributes have no inherent ordering. You have probably realized from experience that columns in a table do have inherent ordering, as SQL users want a constant set of columns to be returned, not to mention that the columns have to be efficiently stored on some physical media.

The main point here is that you should never imply any meaning to the physical ordering of columns. There are a few common column-sorting basics that data architects generally follow when designing tables, such as primary keys at the left of the table, followed by more important columns near the left, and less readable columns near the right, but this is specifically for programmer or user convenience only. We will look at this further when we actually start to model tables in Chapter 5.

Each row in a table must contain the exact same set of columns. Each column must have a name which is unique amongst the columns in that particular table. This may seem kind of obvious, but is worth mentioning.

The last item we need to discuss is the **degree** of the relation, which corresponds to the number of columns in the table. This term is not used all that frequently, but I have seen it mentioned in some documents, and it is worth noting here for completeness.

The Attributes of an Attribute

I just had to give the above name to this section because it made me laugh. However, it is important to understand that each column in a table has columns of its own. The most important of these are (besides the column's name, which has been discussed):

- The legal values for the column
- Whether the column is part of the row identifier
- Whether or not the values are required or optional

The next few sections will deal with these in more detail.

Limiting the Values in a Column to Only Legal Values

SQL Server tables have several methods for restricting the values that can be entered into a column:

- (Base) data types
- User-defined data types
- Constraints
- Triggers and stored procedures

Each of these serves a distinctly different purpose and should generally be applied in the order listed. In relational terminology, as shown in the figure below, these are all considered under the heading **domains**. A domain is defined as the set of valid values for a given attribute. We will look briefly at the mechanisms in the upcoming sections.

Fundamental Database Concepts

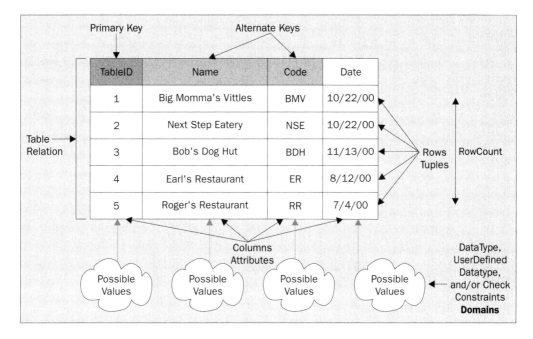

Base Data Types

A base data type is the simplest form of domain in SQL Server. The type of value is defined, as well as the intrinsic range of the input. One additional detail to mention is that every data type also supports a value of NULL, unless we specify otherwise. For example:

❑ An integer data type variable requires whole numeric input and may be between -2^{31} (-2,147,483,648) and $+2^{31}$ (2,147,483,647)

❑ A tinyint data type also requires whole numeric input, but has a range of non-negative integers between 0 and 255

❑ A varchar(20) requires ASCII character data between 0 and 20 characters

The base data type is the set of "primitive" data types that are defined by SQL Server. SQL Server defines the following base data types that can be used as column data types:

```
binary              numeric
big_int             real
bit                 smalldatetime
char                smallint
datetime            smallmoney
decimal             sql_variant
float               sysname
image               text
int                 timestamp
money               tinyint
nchar               uniqueidentifier
ntext               varbinary
nvarchar            varchar
```

47

There are two other data types: `cursor` and `table`, though neither can be used as the data type of a column.

Choosing the precise data type of a column is one of the most important choices you will make during the physical design process. During the logical phase of design, at a minimum, the general type of data that is to be stored will need to be determined. General classes of data types might include:

> binary
> blob
> character
> date
> logical
> numeric
> time

We will discuss data types in more detail in Chapter 10.

User-Defined Data Types (with Rules)

SQL Server allows the creation of customized data types based on existing ones. It is defined only in terms of a single base data type. A rule can then be created and associated with the new data type that restricts the stored values allowed in a column as desired. This enables you create many columns from the same template, and have it control the values that are entered.

If you are unfamiliar with user-defined data types, consult the SQL Server Books Online for more details.

As a simple example, you might want to define the following user-defined types:

- `IntegerFromOneToTen` – defined as an integer, with a rule that restricts values entered to between one and ten inclusive.
- `SocialSecurityNumber` – defined as a nine-character string, or an eleven-character string that is restricted to having dashes in the fourth and seventh places, and all other characters are numeric.

As you can see, many common data types can be created to help implement a domain of values that are legal for the column.

It should also be noted that user-defined data types need not be simple base data types as defined by relational theory. It is legal to have more complex data types as long as they do not have repeating groups in them. For example, you might have the following data type:

- `2DGraphPoint` – defined as X – integer, Y – integer

But you could not have a table data type with an unlimited number of attributes. This would only be legal in cases such as the graph point where the two values X and Y actually make up a single attribute, in this case location.

> *Note that Microsoft SQL Server does not currently support this.*

Constraints

A constraint is another mechanism that may be used to limit the values entered into a column.

- **NULL constraints** – The NULL constraint determines whether or not data has to be entered into a column. A NULL value in relational theory indicates that an attribute has an unknown value, generally thought of as a *maybe*. It is important to understand that when two NULL values are compared, they are never equal.
- **CHECK constraints** – Devices that allow us to define an allowable range of values for a column. For example, we can create a constraint on a column that stores the month of the year which only allows a value of 1 through 12.
- **Foreign Key constraint** – Devices that are used to make certain that a value in one table matches the key of a different table. They are used both to ensure data integrity and to maintain relationships between tables. While we will not cover these in any more depth in this chapter, it is important to simply mention their existence in the role of domain for a column.

Triggers and Stored Procedures

You can use triggers and stored procedures to implement a column domain, though they are generally used for much more powerful things. In this section we are focusing only on the domain aspect of using each device.

Triggers are devices that allow code to be fired whenever data in a table is entered or modified. Whilst they allow us to code complex domain rules that cannot be written into constraints, it is unusual for them to regulate the values being entered into a single column. The latter would only be the case if the rules were too complicated for a simple constraint, for example in automatically requesting clearance for the entry of a new value from a remote supervisor. We will examine triggers in more detail in later chapters.

The other SQL Server device available to implement a column domain is a stored procedure. Stored procedures are not the best way to do this, but again, there may be good reasons for doing so (for example, not allowing direct access to specific rows and/or columns of data). The primary problem is that for this to work we have to force all the modifications for a column to filter through a single stored procedure or duplicate lots of code for every case where a user needs to update data. The only time we need to resort to using stored procedures as domain enforcers is when the enforcement is optional or changing.

We should also briefly mention that while stored procedures can be used to implement domains; the same can be said for any code that is written to insert data into a column. In Chapter 11, we will cover triggers and stored procedures as a data integrity mechanism in great detail.

A Note About Terminology

In this book, we will generally use the term domain during logical design to indicate a data type description such as number, integer, string, etc. together with a general description of the legal values for the attribute. We will do our best to use the same domain for every column that has the same attributes.
For example, we might define the following domains in a typical database:

- **Amount** – a monetary value, with no domain, which always requires a value
- **String** – a generic string value which contains alphanumeric values, which always requires a value

- **Description** – a string value that is used to further describe an instance of a table, which always requires a value
- **FutureDate** – a date value that must be greater than the current date when entered, which always requires a value
- **SocialSecurityNumber** – an eleven character string of the format ###-##-####, which always requires a value

As we identify new attributes, we will see if the new attribute *fits* any existing domain, and if so, we assign it appropriately. If not, then we create a new domain. This will give us attributes that allow us to build databases in a quicker, easier, and more consistent manner.

We will use the term **business rules** to indicate the **predicate** for the table or database as a whole. A predicate is simply a rule that governs the values in the database. As an example of this let's consider the `SocialSecurityNumber` domain. This domain came with a predicate that the value stored in an attribute that used it would always be in the format "###-##-####". While I am not exactly enamored with the term business rules, it is a fairly common term in use today. We should note right here that we will continue to further define business rules throughout the book, as there are many different issues that surround this very broad term.

Very often we will not identify our business rules as part of the table definitions (or entities); rather, the business rules will be located throughout our documentation and implementation.

Row Identifiers

In relational theory, a relation may not have duplicate tuples. For those who have SQL Server experience, you would clearly want to jump and build an index to deal with this situation. However, in relational theory, there is also no concept of an index, since an index is a physical device and strictly speaking relational theory does not deal with implementation issues. In a physical table, there is no limitation that says that there must not be duplicate rows. However, in a practical sense, no two rows can be duplicates because there are hidden attributes in the implementation details that prevent this situation from occurring (such as a row number, or the exact location in the physical storage medium that you cannot actually see). However, it is always a bad situation when you can have duplicate rows for a number of reasons:

- It is impossible to determine which row is which, meaning that we have no logical method of changing or deleting a single row.
- If more than one object has the exact same attributes, it is likely to be describing the same object, so if we try to change one row, then the other row should change, this means we have a dependency.

To combat this, we have the concept of a **candidate key**. A key is used to require uniqueness over an attribute or set of attributes. An entity may have as many candidate keys as is required to maintain the uniqueness of its columns. Just as in SQL Server, we also have the concept of **primary keys** and **alternate keys**. A primary key is used as the primary identifier for a table, and alternate keys (implemented as unique constraints) are other fields over which uniqueness must be maintained, as we can see in the following table:

Fundamental Database Concepts

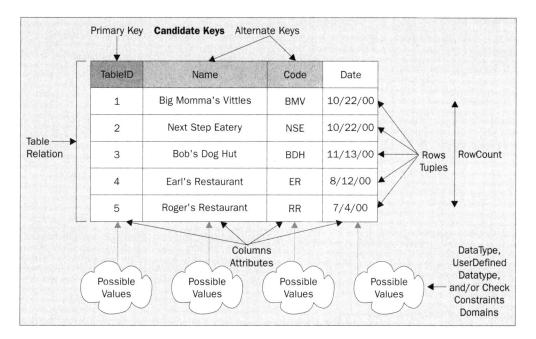

The choice of candidate keys is a very important one. A large percentage of databases errors come from not defining all the possible candidate keys. When we get to the normalization rules in Chapter 6, we will discuss specifics concerning the choices of candidate keys.

Composite Key

Keys, by definition, may be made up of any number of columns, though it is best to try and limit the number of columns utilized as much as is possible. Try to keep the number of columns as specific as possible, but if necessary, it may be as many columns as desired.

For example, you may have a Book table with the columns, Publisher_Name, Publisher_City, ISBN_Number, and Book_Name. For anyone who doesn't know, the ISBN number is the unique identification number assigned to a book when it is published.

From these attributes, we decide that we can define three keys:

- Publisher_Name, Book_Name – Obviously, a publisher will likely publish more than one book. Also, it is safe to assume that book names are not unique across all books. However, it is probably true that the same publisher will not publish two books by the same name (at least we will assume that it is true).
- ISBN_Number – We have already stated that ISBN_Number is unique.
- Publisher_City, ISBN_Number – Since ISBN_Number is unique, it follows that Publisher_City and ISBN_Number combined is also unique.

Both the first and third keys we have defined are composite keys. The third one needs a bit more discussion. The implication of this key is that in every city, you may reuse the ISBN_Number, a fact that is obviously not true. This is a very common problem with composite keys when not thought out properly.

51

Primary Key

The primary key is a key that is used to give a known interface to access a single row in a table. Usually, it is simply a pointer (to borrow a term from functional programming) to access the row, and should probably not be a mutable value, or at least it should be a value that changes very infrequently. The next section briefly introduces the key type (artificial key) that we will be using throughout this book, and is the one that will save you much trouble during implementation. We will discuss the precise logic surrounding this choice in the section on physical design, but for now it is enough to consider the meaning of the terms.

Artificial Keys

An artificial key is a contrived one, and the only reason for its existence is to identify the row. It is usually an automatically generated number (Identity column), or a GUID (Globally Unique IDentifier), which is a very large identifier that is unique on all machines in the world. The implementation of a GUID is beyond the scope of this book; however, full documentation is available from www.microsoft.com. The main reason for an artificial key is to provide a key that an end user never has to view, and never has to interact with. It serves simply as a pointer and nothing else. For anyone who does not understand pointers, they are a common construct from C, or any low-level programming language, used to point to a location in memory. The artificial key points to a position in a table. The table should have other keys defined as well, or it is not a proper table.

The concept of an artificial key is a kind of troubling one from the perspective of a purist. Since it does not describe the record at all, can it really be an attribute of the record? Artificial keys should probably not even have been mentioned in the logical design section, but it is important to know of their existence, since they will undoubtedly still crop up in some logical designs. In Chapter 6 we will discuss the pros and cons of such an approach.

Alternate Keys

Any candidate key that is not chosen as the primary key is referred to as an alternate key. Alternate keys are very important to a successful database. For one reason or another, most tables have more than one way of identifying themselves. This is particularly true when one uses artificial keys as primary keys.

Optional Column Values

This is a can of worms that I would rather not open, but I must. Tables may have columns for which the contents are not yet known or unnecessary in a given context. Unfortunately, there is only one mechanism to denote this fact built into SQL. This is the value NULL. It should be obvious from the list of different meanings of NULL that this is not the optimum way of handling such situations. Putting invalid data into the column (such as a date of Dec 31 9999) is even more troubling than NULL, for two reasons. Firstly, you may very well subsequently discover that you want to store data with the exact same value that you have just entered. Secondly, you may find that entering a value like this may not stand out to the user such that they understand what you are trying to do.

The Integrity Independence Law (Number 10 of Codd's 12 Laws, see Appendix A) requires that no column in the primary key can be an optional column. Boiled down to a single sentence: NULL is evil. Many theorists would prefer NULL to be done away with altogether. There are many reasons for this, as we will see in later chapters, but at this point we will stick to a very simple reason. NULL is defined as an unknown value, so no two values of NULL are equivalent. Also, in the way NULLs are implemented, seeing a value of NULL may have a couple of possibilities:

- ❏ I don't know the value yet
- ❏ I am never going to implement a value
- ❏ A value in this column does not make sense in this given situation

I would rather see a set of NULL-type values implemented to say why the column is NULL. There are set techniques for dealing with optional data without NULLs, but the implementation can require quite a few tables. We will discuss how to deal with NULL values in some depth in Chapter 12.

Rowcount

The number of rows in a table has a special name in relational theory. As shown in the figure below, it is called **cardinality**. This term is seldom used to indicate the number of rows in the table; however, the term is used to indicate the number of rows that can meet a certain condition. We will look at another form of cardinality when we discuss relationships later in this chapter.

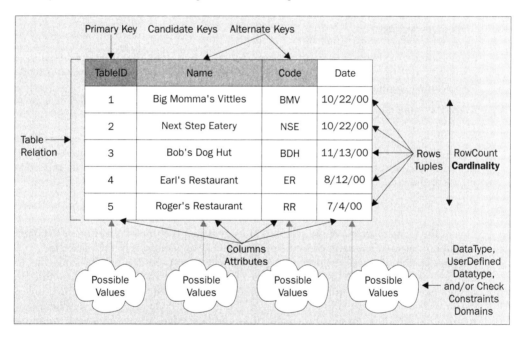

Additional Considerations for Tables

In this section we will look at some of the additional considerations that we have for tables in relational theory.

Foreign Keys

When is a key not a key? When it is a foreign key. Not a joke, but true. A foreign key is actually a column or combination of columns whose values match the primary key or unique key in the same, or another table. Existence of a foreign key in a table represents the implementation of a relationship between the tables. We will discuss relationships in more detail later in this chapter. A foreign key does not have to be a unique value.

The Integrity Independence Law (Number 10 of Codd's 12 Laws, see Appendix A) requires that for all non-optional foreign key values in the database, there must be a matching primary key value in the related table.

Views

Views are tables that do not exist as base (actual) tables – in fact, they are virtual tables. A view is the implementation of a named relation as we discussed back in the *Tables* section of this chapter.

Views appear as tables to the user and should cautiously be considered as tables. Based on Codd's laws (see Appendix A), views are supposed to be updateable, greatly enhancing their ability to perform these tasks. In fact, in SQL Server 2000, we can implement any view as being updateable by using several new features. This will be looked at in some detail in the *Physical Design* part of the book, as we look at what problems we can and cannot solve using views.

Views have many good uses and should be considered a part of logical design, as they can be used to solve some very important issues. Views can be used to:

- Implement security

    By including or excluding specific columns from the view definition, then specifically revoking rights from the base table and giving rights to the view, security can be provided for the excluded columns.

- Allow the same data to be viewed by different users in different ways

    By building different views of the data, users can be given a view that suits their needs. In this manner, data that is unimportant to the user can be hidden from them to improve readability. In addition to this, foreign key relationships can be resolved and data from the related table shown to the user.

- Provide logical data independence

    One of the primary tenets of the relational theory is that the implementation of the database should not make any difference to the users. If something changes in the database implementation, the user should not notice. Views can be used in much the same way to give the user insulation from base table changes. Obviously the view is dependent on the structure of the underlying table, but if you add a column, the view need not have it added, unless it is needed. If you remove a column or move it to a different table, the view could be modified to return a default value, or to get the value from the new table. Views are a very important part of any relational database implementation. However, they are considered a physical implementation issue, so this is the last time we will discuss views in this part of the book.

Relations

Codd's laws (see Appendix A) state that every database should be described in a logical level in the same way as user data, so that users with proper security can use the same relational language to view the user data.

Relational theory considers the makeup of a relation to have two parts:

- **Heading** – The set of *column name: data type name* pairs that define the columns of the table. This serves as a layer between the definitions that the SQL programmer sees and the actual implementation that the RDBMS programmer used to implement the database server architecture.

Fundamental Database Concepts

❑ **Body** – The rows that make up the table.

*In SQL Server, and most databases, we more frequently consider the catalog or, to use a SQL Server term, system tables as a collective description of the tables and other structures in the database. SQL Server exposes the heading or catalog in a set of tables known as the **Information Schema**. We will look further at the Information Schema in Chapter 10.*

Restricting the Values that Go into Tables

So far we have discussed restricting values that go into columns, which technically falls into this section. However, as we have already discussed the concept of a column domain, we now simply need to briefly discuss situations where you need to restrict data that is affected by other columns. We can break these down into three typical scenarios:

❑ Inter-column dependencies
❑ Inter-row dependencies
❑ Inter-table dependencies

Each of these poses quite a different type of problem to the implementation:

❑ Inter-column dependencies

Inter-column dependencies deal with the situation where the value stored in one column requires a certain domain of values in another column.

For example, say you have a field `hasDriversLicence` and `driversLicenseNumber`. If `hasDriversLicense` is `False`, then you do not want the user entering in a value for `driversLicenseNumber`.

Generally, you will solve this problem with a simple table `CHECK` constraint.

❑ Inter-row dependencies

Inter-row dependencies describe the situation where one row in the same table dictates the value in a different row.

An example of this might be a banking system. When a user goes to make a withdrawal from their account, all transactions they have previously made need to be summarized to see if they have enough money to make the withdrawal. Actually this might not be implemented in exactly this way, but logically speaking this is what occurs.

Generally this type of situation must be solved using a trigger, or less desirably, a stored procedure. One of the real problems with the inter-row dependencies in SQL Server is that it is easy enough to prevent overages (too many records of too high a value) but very difficult to prevent too few values from being entered. This topic will be returned to in Chapter 12, when we start to implement this sort of problem.

❑ Inter-table dependencies

Another situation might be where a value exists in one table, but you do not want this value to be filled in a related table.

An example of such a constraint might be personal information for a user. One table will keep a record of the person's name and age, and another table may intend to store their address and phone number. If the person is under a certain age, it may actually be illegal to store their address and phone number.

As with the inter-row dependencies, this must also be solved using a trigger, or less desirably, stored procedure. The same difficulties exist with inter-*table* dependencies as they do with inter-*row* dependencies.

Predicates

We have discussed predicates for attributes, but now we must look at predicates that govern the use of the table. As a reminder, the term *predicate* is a fancy way of saying a rule that governs the values in the database. The predicate of every table should be stated during logical design as fully as possible. By listing the predicates for the table in prose, they have meaning to the developer as well as the user who needs to ratify the rules. The predicate should contain any rule that governs the input of data.

This is a very hard habit to get into, but it will pay dividends. In the next chapter, we will look at developing predicates for the tables we discover.

SQL Operations

One thing that should be noted when discussing relational technology is the relational operators in T-SQL. We are not going to go too far into this discussion, but some mention of these operators needs to be included in any relational model discussion simply for completeness.

In this section we will take a brief look at the relation operators that make up the relational algebra that is the basis for all SQL implementations. As we hinted at earlier, all result sets that are returned from the SQL SELECT statements can be thought of as tables (although they are not physically stored as such). Note that a table must have a unique name for every column that is returned, but this is not always true for SQL result sets (even though it should be). It is important to remember this basic tenet as you write SELECT statements of your own, and is the reason that using SELECT * is particularly nasty, a point that will be reinforced in Chapter 12. The tables that are formed as a result of any SQL operation are referred to as unnamed tables, as opposed to tables and views, which are named.

Originally, Codd formulated eight relational operators. Most of these take the form previously mentioned with one or two relations into the operator, a single relation out. Only one of these did not fit this mold, and is not implemented in SQL. The following relational operators are the list of operators as first described by Codd in 1972 in *Relational Completeness of Data Base Sublanguages*. They are listed in the order that they are presented in the text, as each logically adds to the previous one.

- Restrict
- Project
- Join
- Product
- Union
- Intersect

Fundamental Database Concepts

- Difference
- Divide

There has been quite a bit of research in this area, and quite a few operators have been added over the years. The original eight will serve to give a brief introduction to the relational operators. We will take a brief look at each of the original operators, and leave it to the reader to do further reading on the subject if desired.

It is important not to confuse these operators with any keyword used in an actual SQL dialect. The actual set of SQL operators has been borne out of twenty years worth of attempts to create a relational language that end users could use easily, while also performing an incredible number of operations.

Restrict

The restrict operator is used to limit the rows of a table to those that match a given criteria. This is directly analogous to a simple `SELECT` statement's `WHERE` clause. For example:

```
SELECT    fieldname, fieldname2, … , fieldnameN
FROM      tablename
WHERE     fieldname > value
```

The `WHERE` clause is the implementation of the restrict operator, and it should also be noted that the output of this entire operation is an unnamed table that contains the single field `fieldname` and contains all of the rows where `fieldname` is greater than `value`. In the `WHERE` clause, we can use any of the common comparison operators (=, >, <, >=, <>, `LIKE`, etc.).

Project

The project operator is used to limit the number of columns in the resulting output table. In the next example, we will expect that there exists more than the single column in the table:

```
SELECT    DISTINCT fieldname1, fieldname2
FROM      tablename
```

In this manner you can vertically sub-divide the resulting table into a single column, or combination of columns. In relational theory, any duplicate values would be removed, so we have included the SQL keyword `DISTINCT` to remove the repeat values.

A common question that arises is "why is there no `DISTINCT` operator in relational theory?" Every operator in our discussion here takes in one or two relations, and returns a relation. By definition, a relation does not have any duplicate rows. Since the output of our query would be a relation, it will have no duplicates, and the `DISTINCT` operator is effectively redundant. In essence therefore, the `DISTINCT` operator is built in.

Again, this is one of the most important differences between the definition of a table and a relation.

Join

The join operator is used to associate one table with another, based upon the matching of column values, usually the primary key of one table with the foreign key of another.

```
SELECT    fieldname
FROM      tablename1
              JOIN tablename2
                  ON tablename1.key1 = tablename2.key1
```

I feel this operation also needs to be stated using a more relational algebraic style. The relational algebra style shows how limited in scope the relational operators are in comparison to the far more functional SQL language.

```
JOIN    tablename1
WITH    tablename2
OVER    key1
```

This notation actually is much clearer, but does exactly the same thing. This, of course, only works when the key names are the same. The reason that I show this notation is that I want to make clear that the JOIN in the first code snippet can be thought of as a single table. Next let's look at the effect of chaining together two join operations, as in the following query:

```
SELECT    fieldname
FROM      table1
              JOIN table2
                  ON table1.key1 = table2.key1
              JOIN table3
                  ON table2.key2 = table3.key2
```

The first join operation can be considered as:

```
(SELECT *
 FROM    Table1
     JOIN table2
         ON table1.key1 = table2.key1)
                          = derivedTable1
```

So we could rewrite our query as:

```
SELECT    fieldname
FROM      derivedTable1
              JOIN table3
                  ON derivedTable1.key2 = table3.key2
```

This is as far as we will delve into joins in this section. The point of this section has been a simple introduction to how the join operator works, and relating it to current join technology in SQL Server. In Chapters 11 and 12, we will look at this concept again.

Product

One of the least useful and most dangerous of the operations is the product operation. The product operator takes two tables and builds a table consisting of all possible combinations of rows, one from each table. In SQL this is denoted by the CROSS JOIN statement.

Fundamental Database Concepts

```
SELECT    fieldname
FROM      tablename1
          CROSS JOIN tablename2
```

To better explain this operation, consider the following:

Table1:	Fred	Table2:	Sam	→	Table1 product Table 2	Fred	Sam
	Wilbur		Bugs			Fred	Bugs
			Ed			Fred	Ed
						Wilbur	Sam
						Wilbur	Bugs
						Wilbur	Ed

You can see that the number of rows that will be returned by the product operator is the number of rows in Table 1 multiplied by the number of rows in Table 2. This number can get quite large, contain duplicate and useless rows, and choke your server quickly, so there are not too many practical uses of the product operator.

Union

The union operator takes as an input two tables of the same structure and builds another table with all of the rows in either of the tables, but removing duplicates in the process:

```
SELECT    fieldname
FROM      tablename1
UNION
SELECT    fieldname
FROM      tablename2
```

Table1:	Fred	Table2:	Fred	→	Table1 union Table 2	Fred
	Wilbur		Wilbur			Wilbur
			Babe			Babe

This is a good time to remind you that the two input tables to the union operator must be of the same type, but this does not mean that they have to be base tables. The table may also be a derived table formed from the project operator, as discussed earlier.

Intersect

The intersect operator is very close to the union and join operators. The intersect operator is pretty much the opposite of the union operator. It takes two tables of the same structure, removes the values that do not exist in both inputs, and returns the resulting table.

Table 1:	Jeb	Table 2:	Jeb	→	Table1 intersect Table 2	Jeb
	Silver		Howie			Carney
	Carney		Billy			
			Carney			
			Bob			

Intersect is not implemented properly in the SQL syntax. This code snippet shows the primary way to implement an intersect in SQL.

```
SELECT   fieldname
FROM     tablename1
            JOIN tablename2
               ON tablename1.fieldName = tablename2.fieldName
```

Difference

Difference is an operation that is used quite often when implementing a system. Just like union and intersect, difference again requires tables of the same structure. The gist of the difference operator is that we want every value in one table where there does not exist a corresponding value in the other. This is in contrast to the intersect operator which *removes* a value if it does not appear in both tables.

Difference again does not have a specific keyword in SQL. It can be implemented in its most simple form by using the NOT IN operator as shown here:

```
SELECT   fieldname
FROM     tablename1
WHERE    fieldname NOT IN (SELECT   fieldname
                           FROM     tablename2)
```

If you have done any SQL programming, you will probably note that this implementation is possibly not optimal, though in the logical sense, this is the best implementation. While we should not typically be formulating queries in the logical modeling phase of database design, if we need to, we should always use the most straightforward representation of the query we want.

Divide

The divide operator is one of the stranger operators, and one that you will probably never use. It takes two relations, one with a single column, one with two columns, and returns a table of values that match (in the column that is specified) all values in the single column relation.

There is no clear way to implement this in a way that will be clear in SQL, so we will omit it from our discussion here, as it is not terribly useful for most database architects and SQL programmers.

Other Operators

Additional operators can be separated into two classes, modification types (INSERT, UPDATE, DELETE) and additional retrieval types. We will not be discussing the modification type operators in this chapter, as they are very close to how SQL implements them, and also they have very little logical modeling relevance. We will be discussing them in some detail in Chapter 12.

As far as the retrieval operators go, there have been other relational operators defined in the (nearly) thirty years since the formulation of these eight base operators. In fact all of the **DML** (**Data Manipulation Language**) commands in SQL Server are either a result of, or an extension of, these basic operators. We should also note that the **DDL** (**Data Definition Language**) is basically for defining our objects, and while there would be no relational operator equivalent, any relational language would have to implement some form of DDL to build the objects for the DML.

I've stretched the limits of this book's scope by covering these eight original operators. The purpose of this section on the relational operators was not to replace or even supplement the various textbooks on the subject, but rather to give insight that will help us to know the basics of where the SQL operations came from. Understanding the fundamentals of SQL will help us when we are logically designing our databases and writing our code.

Relationships

We have already mentioned the concept of the primary key and the foreign key. Now let us put them together and look at the object that they form: the **relationship**. Relationships are what make the tables that you have created useful, taking the place of repeating groups by linking tables together. However, there is one point that we must make at this juncture. The relationship types we will be discussing in this section need not be of the form of one table's primary key being referenced by another table via a foreign key. While it is true that this is how all relationships will eventually be physically realized in the database implementation, logically it can take several primary key-foreign key relationships to convey a simple logical relationship. In this section, we will discuss the logical relationship types and will leave the discussion on physical implementation for later in the book.

Relationships can be divided at this point into two basic types that we need to understand:

- Binary relationships
- Non-binary relationships

The distinction between the two types lies in the number of tables involved in the relationship. A binary relationship involves two tables, while non-binary relationships involve more than two tables. This may seem like a small distinction, but it really is not. SQL and relations are limited to binary relationships, while there is no such restriction in the real world. When you design databases you must keep this in mind, and learn to document each of the possible situations. When we look at data modeling in Chapter 5, we will discuss how to represent each of these in a data model.

Binary Relationships

Binary relationships are relationships between two tables. Most of the relationships we deal with on a regular basis will fit into this category.

The number of child rows that may participate in the different side of the relationship is known as the cardinality. We will look at the different cardinalities of binary relationships in this section.

One-to-n Relationships

One-to-n relationships are the class of relationships where one table migrates its primary key to another table as a foreign key. The table that contains the primary key is known as the **parent** table and the table that receives the primary key, and uses it as the foreign key, is the **child** table.

Chapter 3

This parent-child terminology only considers itself with the relationship between the two tables. A child may have many parents, and a parent may have many children.

The one-to-n relationship is the most common relationship type you will deal with. However, there are several distinct possibilities for the cardinality of this relationship. There are:

- **One-to-one relationships** – A relationship of one-to-one cardinality indicates that for any given parent, there may only exist a single instance of the child. An example of this type of relationship might be House to Location, as illustrated in the figure below. A house is obviously in only one location. The discussion of why this would not be in the same table will be left for a later time.

House Id	House Type
1001	1
1002	2
1003	1
1004	3
1005	4

House Id	Location
1001	Database Drive
1002	Administration Avenue
1003	SQL Street
1004	Primary Key Place
1005	Business Rules Boulevard

- **One-to-many relationships** – The one-to-many relationship is the most important relation type. For each parent, there may exist unlimited child records. An example one-to-many relationship might be State to Address, as illustrated by the figure below. Obviously there are many addresses for a single state, though an address can only be in one state.

State Id Number	State
1	Amabala
2	Aksala
3	Sasnakra

State Id No.	Address	No. of bedrooms	No. of bathrooms
1	402 Database Drive	1	1
1	1222 Administrator Avenue	2	1
2	23 Login Lane	2	1
2	246 Cardinality Close	1	1
2	893 Server Street	3	2
3	107 Query Quay	2	1
3	293 Primary Key Place	4	2

❑ **One-to-exactly-n relationships** – Actually the one-to-one relationship is merely a specialized version of this relationship type. This is a rarely used relationship type, but it does actually get used on occasions. For example, a rule might be made that a user may only have two e-mail addresses. The following figure shows how one-to-two relationship cardinality might be used to enforce the User to E-mail relationship:

Employee Reference Number	Name
5001	Bob
5002	Fred
5003	Jean

Employee Reference Number	Email Address
5001	dbo@wrox.com
5001	dbo2@wrox.com
5002	serveradmin@wrox.com
5002	fred@wrox.com
5003	md@wrox.com
5003	jean@wrox.com

❑ **Recursive relationships** – Recursive relationships are where the parent and the child are the same table. This kind of relationship is how you implement a tree using SQL constructs. If you implement a recursive relationship of cardinality one-to-two, you can implement a tree-like data structure. The classic example of the recursive relationship is a bill of materials. Take an automobile. In and of itself, it can be considered a part for sale by a manufacturer, and each of its components, which also have part numbers, are a part that makes up the whole. Some of these components are also made up of parts. In this example, the automobile could be regarded as made up recursively of the automobile part and all of its constituent parts.

Many-to-Many Relationships

The other type of binary relationship (actually the second most common relationship type) is the many-to-many relationship. Instead of there being a single parent and one or more children, there would be more than one parent with children. This is impossible to implement using just two tables, but we will leave the implementation of many-to-many relationships until the physical modeling part of the book and Chapter 10.

An example of a many to many relationship is a car dealer. Take nearly any single model of car, and it is sold at many different car dealers. Then take one car dealer. It in turn sells many different car models.

Non-Binary Relationships

Non-binary relationships involve more than two tables in the relationship. This is far more common than one might expect. For example:

Wrox provides Books for Book Sellers to sell.

This is referred to as a ternary relationship because it involves three tables. We deal with such relationships by breaking them down into 3 tables with 2 or more relationships.

- Wrox provides Books
- BookSellers sell Books
- Book Sellers are supplied by Wrox

However, from these three relationships, you cannot exactly infer the original ternary relationship. All you can infer is that:

- Wrox supplies books to someone
- Book Sellers sell books supplied by some publisher
- Wrox provides something to Book Sellers

From these relationships, you cannot exactly infer the original statement that Wrox provides Books for Book Sellers. This is a common mistake made by many data architects. The original relationship will likely be identified during the design phase, then not quite put together properly when you begin to develop relationships.

The proper solution to this sort of problem would be to have a table for Publishers (Wrox), one for Product (Books), and one for Stores (Book Sellers). Then you would have a table with three binary relationships, one from each of these tables. This solves the problem (for now). In Chapter 7, on advanced normalization rules, we deal with the problems that arise when you have to store relationships with greater than two tables.

A Last Note on Relational/SQL terminology

In this book, we will stick to SQL style terminology except where it makes sense not to. It is important to understand the basic underpinnings of relational theory, but there is no need to confuse anyone who hasn't read this chapter or done any serious study of databases.

SQL terminology may not be perfect (and indeed it is not) but it is nevertheless how most programmers think, even those who care about relational theory.

Definitions of Essential Concepts

Before moving out of this chapter on fundamental database concepts, there are a couple of additional concepts that need to be introduced. They will become very important later in the process (and possibly clearer), but an introduction to them is important in this chapter.

Functional Dependency

The term **Functional Dependency** is one of those terms that sound more difficult than it is. It is actually a very simple concept. If we run a function on one value (call it Value1) and the output of this function is *always* the exact same value (call it Value2), then Value2 is functionally dependent on Value1.

This is a pretty simple, yet important, concept that needs to be understood. Correctly implemented functional dependencies are very useful things, whilst improper functional dependencies are at the very heart of many database problems.

There is an additional confusing term that is related to functional dependency. This term is **determinant**, which can be defined as, "Any attribute or combination of attributes on which any other attribute or combination of attributes is functionally dependent." So in our previous example, `Value1` would be considered the determinant. Two examples of this come to mind:

- Consider a mathematical function like 2 * X. For every value of X a particular value will be produced. For 2 we will get 4, for 4 we get eight. Any time we put the value of 2 in the function we will always return a 4, so in this case 2 functionally determines 4 for function 2 * X.

- In a more database-oriented example, consider the serial number of a product. From the serial number, additional information can be derived, such as the model number, and other specific fixed characteristics of the product. In this case, the serial number functionally determines the specific fixed characteristics.

If the situation seems familiar, it is because any key of a table will functionally determine the other attributes of the table, and if you have two keys, such as the primary key and alternate key of the table, the primary key will functionally determine the alternate key and vice versa. This concept will be central to our discussions of normalization in Chapter 6.

Multi-Valued Dependency

A less intuitive concept to understand is that of the multi-valued dependency. In our previous section, we discussed functional dependency in a single-valued case.

As an illustration of a multi-valued dependency, let's consider the fact that this book was written by a single author, so if we run the author function on this book, we would have a single value every time. However, if there existed a technical editor function, it would return many values, as there are several technical editors of this book. Hence, technical editor is multi-dependent on book.

We will come across the concept of functional dependency again later in Chapter 6.

Summary

In this chapter we have buzzed through thirty years of research in only a few pages. We have defined many of the terms and concepts that are so very pervasive both in our current corporate "just get it done" culture, and in "blue-sky research" circles. The world needs both of these groups to work together. We also looked at some of the building blocks of the relational programming language SQL.

In the following table we equate common SQL Server database terms, with their synonyms from relational theory and to a lesser degree, logical design terminology:

Common Term	Synonym
Table	Entity (specifically in logical design), Relation (more used in theory discussions)
Column	Attribute
Row	Tuple

Table continued on following page

Chapter 3

Common Term	Synonym
The legal values that may be stored in a column, including datatypes, constraints, etc.	Domain
Rowcount	Cardinality
Number of Columns	Degree

My true hope is that this chapter will be kind of a technical conference level overview of these topics that at the very least will give you enough theoretical understanding to make designing databases understandable, or at the best, will make you want to go out and read more on the subject so you can see all of the information I passed over too quickly, fully explained. Of course my real fear is that E. F. Codd himself will read my book and come to my house to berate me for taking years and years, and pages and pages, of well thought out writings and research and turning it into twenty pages or so. In that vein, I do hope that you will pursue this subject further, as it will make you a far better database architect/programmer.

Having taken a brief theoretical stop on our trip to Database Land, we will return to our case study in the next chapter as we begin to really get the process rolling.

Fundamental Database Concepts

4

Entities, Attributes, Relationships, and Business Rules

Introduction

Now that we have looked at the basic building blocks of databases, we need to begin to identify these building blocks within the preliminary information we gathered during Chapter 2. I will admit that we could be considered over-cautious in our approach here, but this is "best practice", and many accomplished programmers are likely to have their entire implementation in their heads by now. That's also true of me; however, the results I achieve are always far better when I take these preliminary steps in approaching a new database design project. The more we can follow the proper path of design, the better the outcome. The methods in this chapter could help you avoid the perils of increasing maintenance costs in your project, lessen the frequency with which you will have to go back later to change your structures and code, and generally decrease the risk of failure.

In Chapter 2, the information-gathering phase, we collected a mass of information which is cluttering up your desk at the moment. In this chapter, we will add structure to this information, and then gain an overview by summarizing it. We will go through everything – identifying and assigning initial names to tables, relationships, columns, and business rules – making sure that we consult our users for any additional information.

When we finish with this process, we will have our foundation documentation which is still in a format that we can share with the user without the baggage of the technical talk and diagrams (which we will start to develop later on).

Divorcing Yourself from the Final Structure

For those readers who are new to database design, or who haven't yet designed any tables, the principles outlined in this chapter should be followed to ensure the best result for your project. If you already know how to build a table you might question the simplistic nature of how we progress through this chapter. You may already have some idea of which tables need to be broken down into which constituent parts. However, while doing such operations at an early point in the design process might seem advantageous for shortening development time, you will pay the price in due course when you have to go back and modify the database, by inserting columns, for example, because you neglected to spend time reviewing your strategy with your client. Also, don't forget to continue to update your documentation, since the best documentation in the world is useless if it's out of date.

Once you have built a database or two (or two hundred for that matter) you will probably find divorcing yourself from the final structure very hard to do. When you listen to the client explaining what he wants, you will probably find yourself envisioning a table-like structure before you've even finished hearing what he had to say; it will be almost second nature to you. Unfortunately, this is not the best situation to be in when you are in this discovery/organizing phase of the database design process.

It is up to you to ignore these feelings of organizational desire until the time is right. Regardless of the tools used to actually consolidate the information (ER diagramming tool, OO diagramming tool, word processor, or even pencil and paper), the urge to try to build a database at this point in the process needs to be fought. Why is that? The answer is very simple. In your zeal to put together your database application, valuable information would likely be missed and some of the important steps that we will discuss in the coming chapters will also likely be overlooked. At this point you should restrict yourself to going through all of the documentation you have gathered to look for the following items:

- Entities and Relationships
- Attributes and Domains
- Business Rules

By doing this you are likely to end up with a much smaller pile of documentation, maybe ten percent of the size of the original pile, whilst still being sure that you have not overlooked any important data. At this point you can secure acceptance from the user before you begin applying a very rigid series of processes, outlined in the next three chapters, to the output of this discovery process.

We mentioned in Chapter 3 that, from that chapter onwards, we would use more implementation-oriented terms to describe an object unless it made sense not to. In this chapter, we will make use of the terms "Entities" and "Attributes" as we will be looking for objects that may never appear as physical structures. We will begin to use implementation-oriented terms as we start to move towards structures that will begin to resemble what we know as tables and columns.

A Simple Example

We will illustrate what we have just read using the following example, which could easily be a snippet of notes from a typical design session.

> *They have customers that they sell used products to, usually office supplies, but they have furniture as well. They identify customers by a number generated by their current system. They also sell new stuff, but used is where they make their money. Invoices are printed on a weekly basis, but they make deliveries as soon as a customer makes an order if they are trusted (no particular credit problems). Any changes to the invoice need to be documented. They ship all products from the warehouse downtown.*
>
> *They need to store contact information for each customer – phone numbers (fax and voice), address, and e-mail addresses. They would like to be able to fax or e-mail product order confirmations. They also want to have free notes for contacts so they can keep a journal of contacts.*

Through each of the following sections, we will scan the documentation for pieces of information that need to be stored. Sounds simple enough, eh? It really is much easier than it might seem.

Identifying Entities

Entities are really some of the more simple objects to locate while you are scanning through documentation. Entities generally represent people, places, objects, ideas, or things referred to grammatically as nouns. This is not to say that entities only store real things. Entities can also be abstract concepts, for example, "new products" is an abstract concept that is not physical but is a convenient way to group a range of products. Actually, a more reasonable definition of what an entity is used for is to store all of the descriptive information necessary to fully describe a single person, place, object, or idea. For example:

- ❏ Person: May represent a student, employee, driver, etc.
- ❏ Place: A city, a building, a road, etc.
- ❏ Object: A part, a tool, a piece of electronics, etc.
- ❏ Idea: A requirement document, a group (like a security group for an application), a journal of user activity, etc.

Note that there is overlap in several of the categories (for example, a building is a "place" or an "object"). You will seldom need to discretely identify that an entity is a person, place, object, or idea. However, if you can place it within a given group, it can help to assign some attributes, like a name for a person or an address for a building.

For those who have experience with relational databases, how an entity is implemented in an actual database table will probably be very different from the initial entities you specify. It is important not to worry about this at this stage in the design process – we should try hard not to get ourselves too wrapped up in the eventual database implementation.

The reason why we are interested in distinguishing between people, places, and objects is that this will help to define some basic information we will need later, as we begin the implementation further on in the book. Also, this will help us to ensure that we have all the documentation necessary to describe each entity.

People

Nearly every database will need to store information on people entities of some sort. Most databases will have at the very least some notion of a user. While not all users are people, a user is almost always thought of as a person, though a user might be a corporation or even a machine like a networked printer. As far as real people are concerned, a single database may need to store information on many people. For instance, a school's database may have a student entity, a teacher entity, and an administrator entity. It may also require only a single table to represent all three. This is a matter that we will look at closer in later examples.

In our example, two people entities can be found – contacts and customers:

> *need to store contact information for each **customer** ...*

> *... a journal of **contacts** ...*

The contact and customer information we will need to store has yet to be described, and we cannot know whether or not they will be considered as separate entities at this point in the documentation process. We will look at the specific attributes for the contacts and customers when we get to the attribute section of this chapter.

Places

There are many different types of places that users will want to store information on. There is one obvious place entity in our sample set of notes:

> *products from the **warehouse** downtown.*

Note though that contacts and customers obviously have postal addresses identifying their locations.

Objects

Objects refer primarily to physical items. In our example, we have three different objects:

> *... that they sell used **products** to, usually **office supplies**, but they have **furniture** as well.*

Products, office supplies, and furniture are objects, but notice that furniture and office supplies are also products. However, it won't come as a shock to you to realize that products, office supplies, and furniture will have *very* different attributes. Whether or not we can roll up the three objects into one abstract entity called products, or whether we will need to treat all three as separate entities, will totally depend on what the purpose of the particular database you are designing.

Ideas

There is no law requiring that entities should be real objects or even physically exist. At this stage of discovery, we will have to consider information on objects which the user wants to store that do not fit the already established "people", "places", and "objects" categories, and which may or may not be physical objects.

Documents

For many, the term "documents" normally refers to tangible pieces of paper containing information that the clients needs to keep track of. This may seem like splitting hairs, but this is not really the case. What if we make a copy of the piece of paper? Does that mean there are two documents, or are they both the same document? In our example, we really are simply referring to multiple pieces of paper:

Invoices are pieces of paper that are mailed to a customer after the delivery of their products. However, we only know that the invoices are printed on physical paper, but when they are mailed or even how they are delivered is unknown at this stage. At this point just identify the entities and move along; again, we will add our guesses as to how the data is used later in this process.

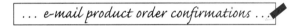

Here we have a type of document that is not written on paper – an e-mail message.

Other Entities

At this stage of discovery, we will have to consider information on entities that the users want to store which do not fit the already established "people", "places", "objects", and "documents" categories.

Audit Trails and Database Logs

A typical entity that you will need to define is the audit trail or a log of database activity. This is not a normal entity in that it stores no user data and, as such, should generally be deferred to the physical design stage. The only kinds of entities that we are concerned with at this point are those that users wish to store data about. As such, statements such as the following should not be dealt with at this stage but left until the implementation:

Events

Event entities generally represent verbs or actions.

Whether deliveries are recorded in some physical document is not clear at this point; the statement merely shows that an event has taken place. These events are important and users will want to schedule events or produce data resulting from an event's occurrence. In our example, it may be that we document events after they occur, so it may end up becoming a log of deliveries made.

Another type of event for you to consider might be things like meter readings, weather readings, equipment measurements, etc.

Records and Journals

The last of the entity types that we will examine at this stage is a record or journal of activities. Note that I mean records in a non-database sort of way. This could be any kind of activity that a user might previously have recorded on paper. In our example, the user wants to keep a record of each contact that is made.

... so they can keep a journal of contacts.

This is another entity type that is similar to an audit log but would potentially contain more information, such as notes about a contact, rather than just a record that a contact had taken place.

A List of Entities

So far we have identified the following list of preliminary entities.

Entity	Description
Contact	People who are points of contact for customers that we need to communicate with
Customer	Organization or individuals that products, office supplies, and/or furniture are sold to
Warehouse	Locations where objects are stored for sale
Deliveries	Events when sold items are delivered to customers
Products	Items that are sold
Office Supplies	A type of product
Furniture	A type of product
Invoice	A physical document that is issued to a customer to request payment for items sold
Product Order Confirmation	An electronic (possibly the only format) document that allows us to alert a customer that an order has been placed
Journal	A listing of all communication with a contact
Journal Entry	The actual record of the contact
Physical Modeling note:	
log any changes to invoices	

The descriptions are based on the facts we have carefully derived from the preliminary documentation.

Note that in the description for contact, we have avoided making any kind of assumptions about how the data is used while fully describing the basics of what is true, based on what has been previously agreed upon.

Now we have a list of all of the entities that have been specified in our previous documentation. At this point we are still iterating through what the client told us. When we begin to analyze what has been specified we can start to look for details that the client did not give us. Rather than filling in these holes with assumptions and guesswork, we should (ideally) prepare a list of questions and deliver them to the business analyst, who will revisit the client to extract more information.

- Do you have just one warehouse?
- Are your customers typically individuals or large conglomerates?
- Are there other types of products that you sell? Or are furniture and office supplies so important that you need to store special information about them?

Identifying Attributes and Domains

The primary reason for saying attributes instead of columns here is that we will be looking for items that identify, make up, and describe the entity you are trying to represent, or – to put this into computing terms – the properties of an entity. For example, if the entity is a person, attributes might include driver's license number, social security number, hair color, eye color, weight, spouse, children, mailing address, and e-mail address. Each of these things serves to represent the entity in part. However, from our definition of what a column must store, we know that it must be a single piece of information, though an attribute has no such requirement.

Identifying which attributes can be associated with an entity requires a different approach from identifying the entities themselves. Attributes will frequently be found by noting adjectives that are used to describe an entity you have previously found.

As data domain information is generally discovered at the same time as the attributes, we will look for this now as well.

Identifiers

The reason why we start with identifiers is that they are the most important. Every entity needs to have at least one identifying attribute or set of attributes. Without attributes, there is no way that different objects can be identified later on in the process. These identifiers are what we defined as keys in Chapter 3. In the above example, one such identifier is shown as follows:

> *They identify customers by a **number** generated by their current system.*

Almost every entity that you discover in this phase of design will have some easily found identifier. The reason for this is that, at this point, you are dealing with entities that are easy to pick out because they have natural identifiers.

It is also important to make certain that what you think of as a unique item is actually unique. Look at people's names. To us they are almost unique, but there are actually hundreds of Louis Davidsons in the United States, and that is not really a common name. There are thousands, if not millions, of John Smiths out there!

Some common examples of good identifiers are:

- For people – social security numbers (in the USA); full names (not always a perfect identifier); or other IDs (like customer numbers, employee numbers, etc.)
- For transactional documents (invoices, bills, computer generated notices) – these usually have some sort of number assigned when they are sent to other organizations
- For books – the ISBN numbers (titles are not unique)
- For products for sale – product numbers (product names are not unique)
- For companies that clients deal with – these are commonly assigned a customer/client number for tracking
- For buildings – the complete address including Zip/Postal code
- For mail – the addressee's name and address, and the date it was sent

There are many more examples, but by now you should understand what we mean when we talk of identifiers. Thinking back to the relational model we discussed in Chapter 3, each instance of a relation (or row if you will) must be unique. Identifying unique natural keys in the data is the very first step in implementing a design. Some of the identifiers listed above cannot be guaranteed to be unique; for example, in the case of company numbers and transactional documents, the identifiers could be sequential numbers, which are not natural keys.

However, in many cases these values are **smart** keys which means they have other information embedded within them. In most cases, the smart key can be disassembled into its parts. In some cases, however, the data will probably not jump out at you. Take the following example of a product serial number: XJV10229392.

- **X** – Type of product – tube television
- **JV** – Subtype of product – 32" console
- **102** – Lot that the product was produced in – the 102nd batch produced
- **293** – Day of year
- **9** – Last digit of year
- **2** – Color

Smart keys have their purpose, but for logical design we need to find all of the bits of information that make them up.

Descriptive Information

Descriptive information is one of the easiest types to find. Adjectives used to describe things that have been previously identified as entities are very common, and will usually point directly to an attribute. In our example, we have different types of products: new and used.

> *... they sell **used** products to ... They also sell **new** stuff ...*

One great thing here is that we have now identified the possible domain of an attribute. In this case, the attribute is "Type of Product", and the domain seems to be "New" and "Used". Of course, it is possible that this may subsequently be resolved into two attributes – an "Is New" attribute and an "Age of Product" attribute – or possibly a single attribute – "Year of Production".

In our next example, we see that we will need to have an attribute that identifies the customer's credit worthiness:

> ... as soon as a customer makes an order if they are **trusted** (*no particular credit problems*).

How they find out whether the customer has credit problems is something we will definitely want to question at some point, as we will want to know more about how the database can facilitate the process of managing credit worthiness. On the other hand, the following example:

> ... both phone numbers (**fax and voice**), address ...

gives the impression that we have a contact entity which has an attribute of phone number with a domain of fax and voice. This is a good place to insert a little reminder that one of the major difference between a column and an attribute is that a column is a physical representation of a single piece of information stored in the same physical entity or table, while an attribute may not be physically stored in the same table.

Locators

Locators are used as a way to locate something, from a physical resource to a categorization, and to differentiate and locate a value in a table. An example of a locator is shown here:

> They ship all products from the warehouse **downtown**.

Here we have a warehouse location. The warehouse can only have one address, so it is a specific locator. Note that it is not clear from this sentence fragment whether or not they have more than one warehouse. One thing for sure, we have at least one warehouse that is downtown.

In this next example we have four very typical locators:

> ... store **contact information** for each customer, both **phone numbers** (**fax and voice**), **address**, and **e-mail addresses**.

Most entities that are connected with organizations will have many phone number, address, and e-mail address attributes. In our example we have four attributes for the contact entity. A further review will do a better job of determining all the actual needs when it comes to this information, but this is a pretty good list of what is important to the user.

You may be wondering why we think of an address as a single attribute, when you well know that an "address" consists of apartment number, street, city, state, zip code – several attributes. The answer to that is that all of these make up the address, and that thinking of all of this as a single attribute is the level that we are at right now. This will make more sense later on when we start the structuring process but, for now, it should be enough to realize that when a user sees the word "address" in the context of our example, they think of a generic address used to locate a physical location. In this manner you can avoid any discussion of how the address is actually implemented, not to mention all of the different address formats we will likely need to deal with when we come to physically implement the address attribute later in the book.

The last attribute we will look at comes from the following sentence:

> *They would like to be able to **fax or e-mail** product order confirmations . . .*

The fax or e-mail attribute goes to the delivery mechanism that we will be using to pass on the product order confirmation. We will certainly want to keep a record of how and when we sent this to the customer. Hence we will need an attribute describing the delivery mechanism on the product order confirmation table.

Related Information

In some cases (though not in our example) we will have related information that we will need as attributes for our entities. Some examples of this might be:

- Additional materials – Anywhere that you have an entity which describes a book or some other type of media (think Amazon.com), you will likely want to list additional resources that the user can also look up.

- Contacts – We have already seen a contact table, but a contact is also technically an attribute of an entity. Whether or not you decide that the contact is a separate entity at this point or later on, the final database will end up looking exactly the same, because the process of normalization (Chapters 6 and 7) ensures that attributes which should really be entities are restructured accordingly.

- Web sites, FTP sites, or other assorted web resources – You will often need to identify the web site of an entity, or the URL of a resource that is identified by the entity; such information would be defined as attributes.

A List of Entities, Attributes, and Domains

The following table shows the entities, along with descriptions and column domains. The attributes of an entity are indented within the entity column.

Entities, Attributes, Relationships, and Business Rules

Entity	Description	Column Domain
Contact	People who are points of contact for customers that we need to communicate with	
Fax phone number	Phone number to send facsimile messages to the contact	Any valid phone number
Voice phone number	Phone number to reach contact over voice line	Any valid phone number
Address	Postal address of the contact	Any valid address
E-mail address	Electronic mail address of the contact	Any valid e-mail address
Customer	Organizations or individuals that products, office supplies, and/or furniture are sold to	
Customer Number	The key value that is used to identify a customer	Unknown
Credit Trustworthy?	Tells us if we can ship products to customer immediately	True, False
Warehouse	Locations where objects are stored for sale	
Location	Identifies which warehouse – there may only be one at this point, since single domain value identified	'downtown'
Deliveries	Events when sold items are delivered to customers	
Products	Items that are sold	
Product Type	Identifies different types of products that they sell	'Used', 'New'
Office Supplies	A special type of product that is sold	
Furniture	A special type of product that is sold	
Invoice	A physical document that is issued to a customer to request payment for items sold	
Product Order Confirmations	An electronic (possibly the only format) document that allows us to alert a customer that an order has been placed	

Table continued on following page

Entity	Description	Column Domain
Delivery Mechanism Type	**Identifies how the Product Order Confirmation is sent to the customer**	**'Fax', 'E-mail'**
Journal	A listing of all communication with a contact	
Journal Entry	The actual record of the contact	
Physical Modeling note:		
log any changes to invoices		

Note the use of the term "Any valid". The scope of these statements will need to be reduced to a reasonable form. Many databases that store phone numbers and addresses cannot cope with all of the different formats used in all regions of the world, mainly because it is no simple task.

At this point we have defined a list of entities and the attributes that we have identified thus far. Note that we still have not begun to add anything to the design at this process. It might also be interesting to note that we have a document that is almost a page long and we simply analyzed two small paragraphs of text. When you do this in a real project, the resulting document will be much larger, and there will likely be quite a bit of redundancy in much of the documentation. You will no doubt do a better job of discovering what data is needed than we have in the preceding few pages!

Relationships between Tables

The most important decisions you will make about the structure of your database will usually revolve around relationships.

One-to-n Relationships

In each of the one-to-n (that is one-to-one or one-to-many) relationships, the table that is the "one" table in the relationship is considered the parent, and the "n" is the child or children.

The one-to-n relationship is frequently used in implementation, but is uncommonly encountered during early database design. The reason for this is that most of the natural relationships that users will tell you about will turn out to be many-to-many relationships.

There are two prominent types of one-to-n relationships that we need to discuss. They are really quite simple and an experienced database designer will recognize them immediately.

The "Has-A" Relationship

The main special type of relationship is the "has-a" relationship. It is so named because the parent table in the relationship has one or more of the child entities employed as attributes of the parent. In fact, the "has-a" relationship is the way you implement an attribute that often occurs more than once. Some examples:

- Addresses
- Phone Numbers
- Children

In our example paragraph, we had:

> *... store **contact** information for each **customer** ...*

In this case, we have a customer entity that has one or more contacts. You will see this type of relationship many times, and also note that it forms the basis of the solution derived by using the fourth normal form, which we will look at in Chapter 6.

Another example of a "has-a" relationship is found in the following example:

> *... for **contacts** so they can keep a **journal** of contacts.*

In this case a contact has many journal entries. It is not likely that a journal entry will be associated with multiple contacts.

The "Is-A" Relationship

Another special case of the one-to-n relationship is the "is-a" relationship. The gist behind an "is-a" relationship is that the child entity in the relationship extends the parent. For example – cars, trucks, R/Vs, etc. are all types of vehicle, so a car **is a** vehicle. The cardinality of this relationship is always one-to-one, as the child entity simply contains more specific information that qualifies this extended relationship. The reason for having this sort of relationship is conceptual. There would be some information that is common to each of the child entities (stored as attributes of the parent entity), but other information that is specific to each individual child entity (stored as attributes of the child entity).

In our example, we have the following situation:

> *... they sell used **products** to, usually **office supplies**, but they have **furniture** as well.*

In this example we have an entity, products, which is very generic. The product entity is unlikely to have much information about what constitutes office supplies, or what a piece of furniture is made of. This approximates to the concept of inheritance in OO databases.

> Note: The "is-a" relationship is loosely analogous to a subclass in OO programming. In relational databases there is no such concept as a subclass, though this may change in the next SQL specification. We will discuss this topic further when we come to modeling the database.

Many-to-Many Relationships

The many-to-many relationship is used far more often than you might think. In fact, as we begin to refine our design, we will use them for a large proportion of our relationships. However, at this point in the process, only very few many-to-many relationships will be recognized. In our example, there is one that is obvious:

Chapter 4

> ...*customers* that they sell used ***products*** to ...

If we use a simple one-to-many relationship, we would be stuck with either one customer being able to buy many products or each product only able to be sold to a single customer. Alternatively, one product could be sold to many customers but each customer could only purchase a single product. Obviously neither of these is realistic. Many customers can purchase many products and many products can be sold to many customers.

Listing Relationships

Let's look at the document we are working on once again, this time having removed the attributes we added in the previous section to save space and make what we have done clearer.

Entity	Description
Contacts	People who are points of contact for customers that we need to communicate with
Have journal entries	**To identify when they contact people at the customer's address**
Customers	Organization or individuals that products, office supplies, and/or furniture are sold to
Purchase Products	**Customers purchase products from the client**
Have contacts	**To store names, addresses, phone numbers, etc. of people at the customer's address**
Warehouses	Locations where things are stored for sale
Store products to ship	**Products are stored at the warehouse for sale to customers**
Deliveries	Events where sold items are delivered to customer
Products	Items that are sold
Can be sold to customers	**Customers can purchase any of the products that are sold**
Office Supplies	A type of product
Is a Product	**Office Supplies are simply extensions of products, presumably to be able to show more information**
Furniture	A type of product

Entity	Description
Is a Product	**Furniture are simply extensions of products, presumably to be able to show more information**
Invoice	A physical document that is issued to a customer to request payment for items sold
Product Order Confirmation	An electronic (possibly the only format) document that allows us to alert a customer that an order has been placed
Journal	A listing of all communication with a contact
Journal Entry	The actual record of the contact
Physical Modeling note:	
log any changes to invoices	

Identifying Business Rules

Business rules can be defined as statements that govern and shape business behavior. Depending upon an organization's methodology, these rules can be in the form of bulleted lists, simple text diagrams, or other formats. For our concerns, we will primarily look at rules that are basically the same as the predicates we discussed in the previous chapter, and cover any criteria that do not fit precisely into our mold of table, column, and domain. Implementability is not implied by the existence of a business rule at this point in the process. All we want to do is gather business rules that are concerned with data for later review.

When defining business rules, you may end up with some duplication of rules and attribute domains, but this is not a real problem at this point. It is important to get as many rules as possible documented, as missing business rules will hurt you more than missing attributes, relationships, or even tables. New tables and attributes will frequently be found when you are implementing the system, usually out of necessity, but finding new business rules at a late stage can wreck the entire design, forcing an expensive rethink or an ill-advised "kludge" to shoehorn them in.

Recognizing business rules is not generally a difficult process, but it is time consuming and fairly tedious. Unlike entities, attributes, and relationships, there is no straightforward specific clue for identifying all of them. However, my general practice when I have to look for business rules is to read documents line by line, looking for sentences including language like "once…occurs", "…have to…", "…must…", "…will…", etc. But documents don't always include every business rule. You might look through a hundred or a thousand invoices and not see a single instance where a client is credited money, but this doesn't mean that it never happens. In many cases business rules have to be mined from two places:

- Old code
- Clients

Getting business rules from either of these sources is never overly pleasant. Not every programmer out there writes wonderfully readable code. If you are lucky, your business analyst will interview clients for their rules.

In our "snippet of notes from the meeting" example, there are a few business rules that we can define. For example, we have already discussed the need for a customer number attribute, but were unable to specify a domain for the customer number, so we take the following sentence:

> *They identify customers by a number generated by their current system.*

and derive a business rule like this:

> **Customer numbers are generated from an algorithm in their current system. (Check for meaning in their current numbers.)**

Another sentence in our example suggests a further possible business rule:

> *Invoices are printed on a weekly basis ...*

From the above statement we might derive this rule:

> **Invoices may only be printed on a given day each week.**

However, is this an actual business rule? It is unlikely that the client would want to tie the system down so that it only allows invoices to be printed on a certain day in the week. However, you might interpret that this is precisely what the client specified from the original documentation. This is likely to be one of the situations where the English language is not technically precise enough to specify important details in such a short form. The above extract from the example documentation might be implying that the client anticipates they would only have enough invoices to print weekly, or that it is just convenient to print them weekly. We will have to find out what was meant by this statement when the document we produce is reviewed with the client.

The last business rule we can identify comes from this part of the document:

> *... but they make deliveries as soon as a customer makes an order if they are trusted (no particular credit problems).*

We saw this before when we looked at attributes, but therein also lies a highly important business rule:

> **Deliveries should not be made immediately to customers if they are not credit trusted.**

Of course, we need to qualify:

- ❏ what does "immediately" mean here?
- ❏ how do we assess the credit-worthiness of the client?
- ❏ when we are finally able to ship products to the customers, how will payments be made and how will the deliveries be made?

These issues also need to be clarified in further consultation with the client.

This section on business rules is hardly complete. It was easy to give examples of tables, attributes, and relationships, but business rules are far more obscure in nature. To make our example such that a more complete set of business rules could be derived, we would have had to greatly increase the amount of information in the example documentation, which would have made the identification of entities and attributes unnecessarily complicated. It is simply very important to locate every conceivable place where a specific business rule can be derived that governs how data is used and which has not been specifically handled by column domains. Establishing business rules is a potentially long drawn out process that cannot be sidestepped or cut short in a real project. Missing or incomplete business rules will cause big problems later.

Identifying Fundamental Processes

A process is basically a coherent sequence of steps undertaken by a program that uses the data that we have been identifying to do something. As an example, consider the process of getting a driver's license (at least here in Tennessee):

- Fill in learner's permit forms
- Obtain learner's permit
- Practice
- Fill in license forms
- Pass driving exam
- Have picture taken
- Receive license

Each of these steps must be completed before the following steps can proceed. Processes may or may not have each step enumerated during the logical phase, and certainly will have business rules that govern them. In the Tennessee license process, you must be fifteen to get a learner's permit, you must be sixteen to get the license, you must pass the exam, practice must be with a licensed driver, etc. If you were the business analyst helping to design a driver's license project, you would have to document this process at some point.

Identifying processes is very relevant to the task of data modeling. Many procedures in database systems require manipulation of data, and processes are critical in these tasks. Each process will usually translate into one or more queries or stored procedures, which may require more data than we have specified.

In our example, we have a few examples of such processes:

> *They have customers that they sell used products to ...*

This note tells us that there is a means of creating and dealing with orders for products being bought by the client. On the surface, this may not seem like a ground-breaking revelation, but there will likely be records in several tables to facilitate the proper creation of an order. We have not yet specified an order table or order items, or even prices of items, though we would undoubtedly need to do so.

> *Invoices are printed ...*

We have made a note of invoices, but this "Print invoices" process may require additional attributes to identify that an invoice has been printed or reprinted, who the print was for, and whether it can be reprinted. Document control is a very important part of many processes when helping an organization that is trying to modernize a paper system. Note that printing an invoice may seem like a pretty inane event – press a button on a screen and paper pops out of the printer. All we have to do is select some data from a table, so what is the big deal? However, when we print a document we may have to record the fact that the document was printed, who printed it, and what the use of the document is. We might also need to indicate that the documents are printed during a process that includes closing out and totaling of the items on an invoice. The most important point here is that we cannot make any assumptions.

Other basic processes that have been listed are:

- **Make delivery** – from "... they make deliveries as soon as a customer makes an order if they are trusted ..."
- **Modify invoice** – from "Any changes to the invoice need to be documented."
- **Ship product** – from "They ship all products from the warehouse downtown."
- **Send product order confirmation** – from "... fax or e-mail product order confirmations."
- **Contact customer** – from "They also want to have free notes for contacts so they can keep a journal of contacts."

Each of these processes identifies a unit of work that must be dealt with during the implementation phase of the database design procedure.

Are We There Yet?

It should be very obvious that not all the entities, attributes, relationships, business rules, and processes from even our simple example have been identified at this point. In this section we will briefly cover the steps involved in completing the task of establishing a working set of documentation.

Each of the following steps may seem pretty obvious, but they can easily be overlooked or rushed through in a real life situation. The real problem is that, if you don't go all the way through the discovery process, you will miss a tremendous amount of information, some of which may be vital to the success of the project. Frequently, when an architect arrives at this particular point, he/she will try to move on and get down to implementing. However, there are at least three more steps that we must take before we can start the next stage in the project.

- Identify additional data needs
- Review the progress of the project with the client
- Repeat the process until we are happy, *and* the client is happy and signs off on what we have designed

Note that this sort of procedure needs to be going on throughout the whole design process, not just the data-oriented parts.

Identification of Additional Data

Up until this point, we have made certain not to broaden the information that was included from the information-gathering phase. The purpose has been to achieve a baseline to our documentation, so we can stay faithful to the piles of documentation we originally gathered. Mixing in our new thoughts prior to agreeing on what was in the previous documentation can be confusing to the client, as well as to us. However, at this point in the design, we need to change direction and begin to add the attributes that we naturally recognize the need for. Usually there is a fairly large set of obvious attributes and, to a lesser extent, business rules that have not been specified by any of the users or initial analysis.

For each of the ideas and items that we have identified so far, we need to go through and specify additional attributes that we expect will be needed. For example, take the contact entity we defined earlier:

Entity	Description	
Contact	People who are points of contact for customers that we need to communicate with	
Attributes		
Fax phone number	Phone number to send facsimile messages to the contact	Any valid phone number
Voice phone number	Phone number to reach contact over voice line	Any valid phone number
Address	Postal address of the contact	Any valid address
E-mail address	Electronic mail address of the contact	Any valid e-mail address
Relationships		
Have journal entries	To identify when they contact the customer's people	

We would likely want to note that a contact would need the following additional attributes:

- **Name** – The contact's full name is probably the most important attribute of all.
- **Spouse Name** – The name of the contact's husband or wife. This kind of information is priceless when making contacts if you want to personalize your message to the person, or ask about their family.
- **Children**
- **Birthdate** – If the person's birthday is known, a card may be sent on that date.

There are certainly more attributes that we could add for the contact entity, but this set should make the point clearly enough. There may also be additional tables, business rules, etc. to recommend to the client so, in this phase of the design, document them and add them to your lists. One of the main things to make sure of is that your new data items stand out from those already agreed from previous consultations with the client and the preliminary documentation.

Review with the Client

Once you have finished putting together this first draft document, it is time to meet with the client. It is important to show them everything that you have and not to miss anything out. It is absolutely essential to have the client review every bit of this document, so that they come to understand the solution that you are beginning to devise for them.

Of course, the client may have little or no database design experience and may require help and explanation from you in order to better understand your design. You might even find it worthwhile to make two documents, one for the client in layman's terms and an internal, more detailed one for your design team's use.

It's also worthwhile devising some form of sign off document, which the client signs before you move forward in the process. This could well be a legally binding document.

Repeat until You get Customer Acceptance

Of course, it is unlikely that the client will immediately agree with everything you say, even if you are the greatest data architect in the world. It usually takes several attempts to get it right, and each iteration should move you and the client closer to your goal. As you get through more and more iterations of the design, it becomes increasingly important to make sure that you have your client sign off at regular times; you can point to these documents when the client changes his/her mind later on.

> *This one hurts, especially when you do not do an adequate job of handling the review and documentation process. I have worked on consulting projects where the project was well designed, and agreed upon, but documentation of what was agreed upon was not made too well (a lot of handshaking at a higher level, to **save** money!). As time went by, and many thousands of dollars were spent, the client reviewed the agreement document and it became obvious that we did not agree on much at all. Needless to say it didn't work out too well.*

The Book Case Study

Now we come to our real database design example. Going back to our case study, started in Chapter 2, we need to begin the process of entity discovery following the guidelines already presented in this chapter.

Client Interview

It is always best to start with the client interview notes. First, we go through and mark all of the items that we expect to represent entities. In our example, we will **bold** these items.

> *Meeting with Sam Smith, Accounting, Nov 24, 2000, 10 AM, Large Conference Room*
> *Attendees: Louis Davidson, Data Architect; Sam Smith, Accounting Manager; Joe Jones, Business Analyst*
> *Initial Meeting*
> *Additional documentation attached: Bank register, sample check, sample statement, as well as electronic format of statement.*
> *Currently using paper **check register**, just like a basic home register. Have looked at the possibility of using canned product, but we have found none that offer all that they want. And most offer way too many features.*
> *Need to have multi-user capabilities (entry and viewing). Share over intranet.*
> *Process:*
> *Need to have very up to date information about **account**.*
> *Currently balancing account once a month. Using the **statement** from **bank**. Takes an entire day to get balanced at least. Would like to keep the account balanced weekly using internet data.*
> *Only interested in checking, not savings, stocks, bonds, etc. Already have a system for this.*
> *Will be audited yearly by a major auditor. Don't have an audit plan as of yet.*
> *Once Sam was finished, asked him about vendor tracking:*
> *It would be nice to be able to have **payee** information for most of the checks we write. Also about categorizing **check**, Sam said it would be nice, but not completely needed at this point.*

We have found the following initial set of entities to deal with:

Entity	Description
Check	A paper document that is used to transfer funds to someone else
Account	A banking relationship established to provide financial transactions
Check register	A place where account usage is recorded
Bank	The organization that has the checking account that the checks are written against
Statement	A document (paper or electronic) that comes from the bank, once per calendar month, that tells us everything that the bank thinks we have spent
Payee	A person or company that we send checks to

The next step is to go through the document and look for attributes (which we will **bold underline**) and relationships, which we will highlight in gray.

> Meeting with Sam Smith, Accounting, Nov 24, 2000, 10 AM, Large Conference Room
> Attendees: Louis Davidson, Data Architect; Sam Smith, Accounting Manager; Joe Jones, Business Analyst
> Initial Meeting
> Additional documentation attached: Bank register, sample check, sample statement, as well as electronic format of statement.
> Currently using **paper check register**, just like a basic home register. Have looked at the possibility of using canned product, but we have found none that offer all that they want. And most offer way too many features.
> Need to have multi-user capabilities (entry and viewing). Share over intranet.
> Process:
> Need to have very up to date information about **account**.
> Currently balancing account once a month. Using the **statement** from **bank**. Takes an entire day to get balanced at least. Would like to keep the account **balanced weekly** using **internet data**.
> Only interested in checking, not savings, stocks, bonds, etc. Already have a system for this.
> Will be audited yearly by a major auditor. Don't have an audit plan as of yet.
> Once Sam was finished, asked him about vendor tracking:
> It would be nice to be able to have **payee** information for most of the checks we write.
>
> Also about **categorizing** check, Sam said it would be nice, but not completely needed at this point.

At the moment, there really isn't a whole lot of information to be gleaned from these notes. You may find that the client interview uncovers very little information, in which case we may want to review why we didn't get the information that we sought. Were we talking to the wrong people in the organization, or were we asking the wrong questions? It is tough answering the question "How did I fail?" – but doing so will make you a much better Data Architect in the future.

Documents

Our case study documentation is fairly lame (to keep the example short and sweet) but, fortunately, we have several documents that will shed quite a bit of light on our solution. We will look at these documents now and mark the attributes (and possibly entities) that we find. The first document we will look at is the sample check. This sort of document is a designer's dream. Since we have identified the check entity, each of the fields in this document is likely to be an attribute.

Entities, Attributes, Relationships, and Business Rules

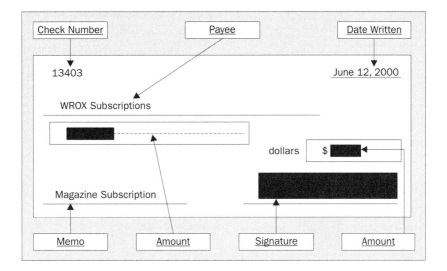

Two things to note from our check:

- The amount is specified twice on the check, providing a measure of redundancy and protection from fraud which is not necessary at this level of design.
- Payee has already been specified as a "has-a" type relationship, which is in essence an attribute of the table, so we will not need to specify it again as an attribute.

The next thing we will look at is the sample check register. It is simply a record of each check as it is entered.

Number	Date	Description	Category	Amount	Balance
12390	12/15/00	Pizza Hut	Employee Appreciation		
12391	12/15/00	Allied Mortgage	Building payment		
12392	12/16/00	TN Electric	Utilities		
12393	12/16/00	Deposit	N/A		

Account.Running Total

We note that the numbers, dates, descriptions (payee), categories, and amounts are derived from checks themselves, but the balances are new. The balance attribute does not fit so well with the check entity, but it does make sense for an account entity. Hence, we will add a balance attribute to the account entity.

Next, we need to look at the bank statement. We will mark all of the different attributes just as we did on the check. The bank statement will provide attributes for several entities.

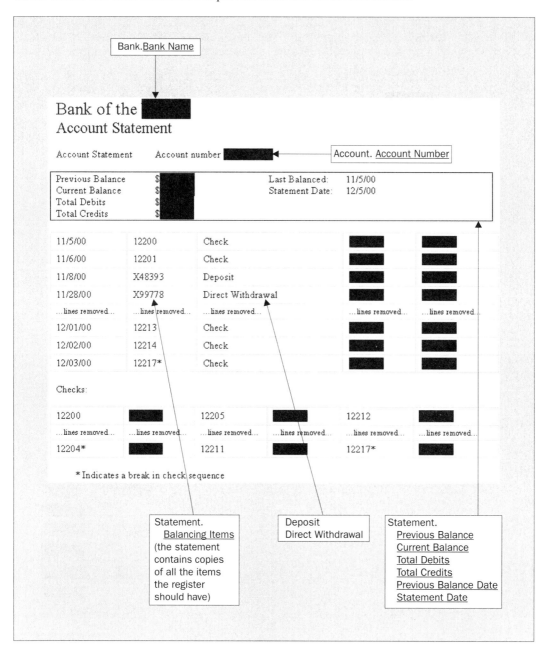

The bank statement has given us several attributes for the Bank, Account, and Statement entities. Here we define two new entities:

- **Deposit** – used to add money to the account
- **Direct Withdrawal** – money removed from the account without issuing a paper check

Entities, Attributes, Relationships, and Business Rules

Again we have the check date, check number, check amount, and running total (all blacked out for reasons of privacy and security, though it is always a good idea to get sight of some uncensored documents to get an idea of the scale of figures and their format – for example, do check numbers have leading zeros?). We also note that the Deposit and Direct Withdrawal entities have apparently the same attributes, and they are all in the same table with the running total. So the Deposit and Direct Withdrawal entities will have Date, Number, and Amount attributes. The running total again is the total for the account.

The final piece of documentation we have to look at is the electronic format of the bank register. The electronic version is notably sparser than the paper version. There may be more to the electronic feed, but this is all that we are currently given. This also may be the only thing that we are given because it is truly all we will need to balance the account.

Column	Data type	Required
Transaction Date	Date Only	Yes
Transaction Number	String(20)	Yes
Description	String(100)	Yes
Item Amount	Money	Yes

Transaction.
  Transaction Date
  Transaction Number
  Description
  Item Account

While there are no new attributes for existing entities, there is mention of a new entity, the Transaction. Interestingly, the bank uses this entity with these attributes to report the values of several other entities. This leads me to believe that there is likely to be a single object that also represents checks, deposits, and direct withdrawals. This indicates that we will have a Transaction entity, with "is-a" relationships to the Deposit, Direct Withdrawal, and the Check entities.

Once we have worked our way through all of our documents, we need to finish our entity document. We will mark any additional attributes that we add in the far left hand column.

Chapter 4

Bank Account Object Listing

So this is the draft document that we produce from our initial analysis:

Entity		Description	Domain
Transaction		A logical operation that puts in or takes out money from our account	
	Attributes		
	Transaction Date	The date that the check is presented and money is removed from the account	Valid Dates
	Transaction Number	A unique number that is used to identify a transaction	A string
	Description	A string description of what the transaction was for	A string
	Item Amount	The amount of money to be added to or withdrawn from the account	Real number to two decimal places
Check		A paper document that is used to transfer funds to someone else	
	Attributes		
	Check Usage Type	Used to categorize what check	*Unknown*
	Check Type	Used to categorize the check	*Unknown*
	Check Number	Number used to uniquely identify the check	Integer
	Date Written	The date that the check was written	Valid dates, possibly no future dates
	Amount	The amount of money to be withdrawn from the account and remitted to the payee	Real positive number to two decimal places
	Memo	Brief description of what the check was used for	Text
	Signature	The signature of the person who can sign the check – we likely will simply keep the text version of the name signed	Text
	Relationships		
	Has Payee	Used to identify the payee that the check was sent to	
	Is a transaction	Defines that a deposit is a subclass of the transaction	

Entities, Attributes, Relationships, and Business Rules

	Entity		Description	Domain
	Payee		A person or company that we send checks to	
		Attributes		
NEW		Name	Name of whoever money is being paid to	String
NEW		Address	Address of the payee	Any valid address
NEW		Phone Number	Phone number of payee	Any valid phone number
	Deposit		Used to add money to the account	
		Attributes		
		Date Written	The date that the check was written	Valid dates, possibly no future dates
		Deposit Number	Number used to uniquely identify the check	Integer
		Amount	The amount of money to be added to the account	Real positive number to two decimal places
		Description	Description from the electronic feed	String
		Relationships		
		Is a transaction	Defines that a deposit is a subclass of the transaction	
	Direct Withdrawal		Used to take money from account without any paper trail	
		Attributes		
		Date Withdrawn	The date that the check was written	Valid dates, possibly no future dates
		Number	Number used to uniquely identify the check	Integer
		Amount	The amount of money to be removed from the account	Real positive number to two decimal places
		Description	Description from the electronic feed	String
		Relationships		
		Is a transaction	Defines that a deposit is a subclass of the transaction	

Table continued on following page

Entity		Description	Domain
Account		A banking relationship established to provide financial transactions – we likely will need to be able to deal with multiple banks	
	Attributes		
	Account Number	Number that uniquely identifies the account	*Unknown, set by bank, likely a string*
	Balance Date	Date and time the checking account was balanced	Valid Dates
	Running Total	The current amount of money in the account	Real positive number to two decimal places
	Relationships		
	Balanced Using Statement	Identifies where the data came from to balance the account	
	Has Transactions	Transactions are made on an account to get money in or out of the account	
Check Register		A place where account usage is recorded	
	Attributes		
	Register Type	Describes the type of register we are using to hold the account records	'Paper'
Bank		The organization that has the checking account that the checks are written against – we likely will need to be able to deal with multiple banks	
	Attributes		
	Bank Name	The name of the bank we are dealing with	String
	Relationships		
	Sends Statement	The bank sends a statement so we can balance the account	
	Have Accounts	Identifies the bank of an account	

Entity	Description	Domain
Statement	A document (paper or electronic) that comes from the bank once a calendar month that tells us everything that the bank thinks we have spent	
Attributes		
Statement Type	Identifies the type of statement received from the bank	'Internet Data', 'Paper'
Previous Balance	Specifies what the balance was supposed to be after the last statement was balanced	Real number to two decimal places
Previous Balance Date	Specifies the date that the account was last balanced	Date
Current Balance	Specifies what the balance of the account is after all of the items in the statement have been reconciled	Real number to two decimal places
Statement Date	Specifies the date that the statement is produced – this will likely be the day that the statement was created by the bank	
Total Credits	Sum of all items that have added money to the account during the statement period	Real positive number to two decimal places
Total Debits	Sum of all items that have subtracted money from the account during the statement period	Real negative number to two decimal places
Balancing Items	All of the items that the bank has processed and is now reporting back to us	Array of transaction (checks, deposits, direct withdrawals) objects

You can probably see that we are getting to a point where, even for such a small example, this format of documentation is unwieldy. In the next chapter we will discuss data modeling, which provides a method of gathering and presenting this data that is much easier to work with. That is not to say that this manner of specification has no merit. At the very least, you need to be able to produce a document of this sort to share with the clients. This is the reason that we have gone through this exercise, and have not gone directly into data modeling. The document we have produced does a fair job of describing what we are trying to implement, in a way that can be read by the technical and non-technical alike.

Chapter 4

Business Rules and Processes

For business rules and processes, we go back and look at our client interview notes. Business rules are in gray highlight. Processes are in boxes.

> Meeting with Sam Smith, Accounting, Nov 24, 2000, 10 AM, Large Conference Room
> Attendees: Louis Davidson, Data Architect; Sam Smith, Accounting Manager; Joe Jones, Business Analyst
> Initial Meeting
> Additional documentation attached: Bank register, sample check, sample statement, as well as electronic format of statement.
> Currently using **paper check register**, just like a basic home register. Have looked at the possibility of using canned product, but we have found none that offer all that they want. And most offer way too many features.
> [Need to have multi-user capabilities] (entry and viewing). Share over intranet.
> Process:
> Need to have very up to date information about **account**.
> Currently balancing account once a month. Using the **statement** from **bank**. Takes an entire day to get balanced at least.
> [Would like to keep the account **balanced weekly** using **internet data**].
> Only interested in checking, not savings, stocks, bonds, etc. Already have a system for this.
> [Will be audited yearly by a major auditor]. Don't have an audit plan as of yet.
> Once Sam was finished, asked him about vendor tracking:
> It would be nice to be able to have **payee** information for most of the checks we write
>
> Also about **categorizing check**, Sam said it would be nice, but not completely needed at this point..

This documentation gives us the following:

Business Rule		Description
	Must have multi-user capabilities	It is likely that more than one person will need to enter transactions at the same time
	Account must be balanced weekly	We need to be able to balance the account more frequently than the typical once a month, presumably to reduce the time it takes to balance by finding missed transactions more often
	Will be audited yearly	Some outside firm will check our numbers yearly to make sure that everything is in good shape, likely we will produce some documentation to facilitate this process.
New	User should get a warning if they attempt to withdraw too much money	Just an idea that the user may want to help avoid an overdrawn account
New	Should not be able to enter transactions that are in the future	Possibly to avoid accidentally post-dating a check

Process		Description
	Balance Account	Reconcile all transactions that the bank thinks we have to make sure that we have all of them recorded
	Audit Account	Process to make sure that everything actually works as documented
New	Enter Transaction	Enter a new deposit, check, or direct withdrawal

There are probably more business rules and processes to be suggested, but what we have is a solid start. At this point you would take your draft document to your client for approval.

Chapter 4

The Waterfall Method

The final thing we should note is that you might need to carry out this whole process many times, depending on how well you perform the process as laid out in this chapter. For those who have project management experience, you may well think that the process outlined in this book is precisely the Waterfall Method, which describes the software design process like this:

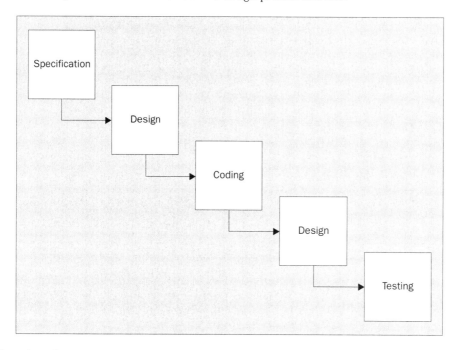

This does describe in some way what we are doing here in our database design project.

> However, in practice, this process would be more complex than depicted in the figure above. In fact, it would show a cycle rather than just linearly stepped boxes. As part of the testing phase, new criteria may need to be incorporated into the design and new specifications defined, which mean that the whole process has to restart. Each run of the cycle is called an iteration. Any software product or application will undergo many iterations before it gets to its final shape. The problem with adding the cycle information is that we may go from coding back to design, or from design back to specification. If everything goes perfectly according to plan, then the above diagram does illustrate the complete design process. Of course, the solution has to be built eventually and the key to this is trying to limit the number of iterations whenever possible. A few large changes are much more desirable than many smaller changes.

Summary

In this chapter we have looked at the process of discovering the entities that will eventually make up your database solution. We have weeded through all of the documentation that had been gathered during the information-gathering phase. We did our best not to add our own contributions to the solution until we had processed all of the initial documentation. It should be noted that this is no small task; in our initial example, we had just two paragraphs to work with, yet we ended up with about a page and a half of documentation from it. We also conducted interviews with the client and obtained a sign off.

It should be noted here that recording all of this information in a simple text document is not ideal. We have done it this way to keep it simple for the purposes of this book, but normally we would use a specialized tool to generate this kind of documentation for us. The data modeling process, which we will go on to in the next chapter, will generate skeleton documentation with blank spaces in it for you to enter your information.

Up until now, we have only been involved with the specification part of the process. This really cannot be helped. Any development process that requires data storage needs to be specified *completely* prior to moving onto the design phase. The implementation design phase will be covered in the second half of this book when we get to physical design. Once the process outlined in this chapter is complete, we have almost everything we need to gather from the client before we build a precise data specification.

5

Data Modeling

Introduction

The term data modeling is often used in a very broad sense to describe the entire process of database design. This is not really a bad thing, but it is not the way we will be using it. In this chapter, we will use it to mean the process of developing graphical representations of data structures.

The document that we started to develop in the previous chapter got very unwieldy in a short space of time, and identifying the relationships between the different entities was becoming very difficult. Hence, we need some way to represent the information that we created as tables in a document in a more easily understood format. To do this, we draw graphical models (pictures) to transform the document into a picture.

There are many types of models or diagrams: process models, data flow diagrams, data models, sequence diagrams, the list could go on for quite some time. We, however, will be focusing on two particular models:

- **Use Case** – a model that is a member of a larger specification known as UML, used to model the needs and requirements of the users. Use cases attempt to include all information known about the project, whilst being readable by both users and designers.
- **Data Models** – models which center wholly around representing the data structures in a relational database.

Before we look at the above models in more detail, let us briefly discuss the modeling methodologies we will be using in each case.

Chapter 5

Modeling Methodologies

Use cases actually come as a part of a larger specification called **UML**, or **Unified Modeling Language**. The UML specification does not have data modeling tools for relational databases (it is an object-oriented technology), so we will need to use a different data modeling methodology.

We make our choice of data modeling methodology by finding the one that is easiest to read, whilst displaying and storing everything that we require. In this book we will focus on one of the most popular modeling formats for relational databases, **IDEF1X** (**Integration Definition For Information Modeling**), and then briefly touch on another fomat, **Information Engineering**.

While the data modeling methodology may be a personal choice, economics, company standards, or features usually influence tool choice. In this chapter we will try to take a fairly non-partisan look at some of the tool features that are required or desirable if we want to extend basic graphical modeling. All of the information found in the document we created in the previous chapter needs to be represented and stored in the data model, and we need to be able to get the data out, to share with the client and programmers.

UML

UML is the *de facto* standard methodology for specifying and documenting the components of object-oriented software systems and is due largely to the work of three men: Grady Booch, Ivar Jacobson, and Jim Rumbaugh. Each of these men had their own (or parts of their own) methodologies, but these were fused together as the men began to work together at Rational Software on the Rational Rose product. It is not, however, a closed methodology, and is being employed and standardized in the tools offered by many large corporations today. Currently at version 1.3, full documentation can be found at http://www.rational.com/uml .

> *The corporations that are listed on the UML specification are: Rational Software, Microsoft, Hewlett-Packard, Oracle, Sterling Software, MCI Systemhouse, Unisys, ICON Computing, IntelliCorp, i-Logix, IBM, ObjecTime, Platinum Technology (CA), Ptech, Taskon, Reich Technologies, Softeam.*

It is probably important to mention here that UML is not just a modeling methodology, but is really a complete object-oriented design method. Whilst a modeling methodology is simply a method of graphically displaying the components of a computer system, a design method entails system design, from the cradle to the grave.

We have far less lofty requirements of UML; we want to model the processes that we discovered in the last chapter. The other purpose is to give a straightforward explanation of why the data modeler should care about UML, as we will not be using it to build or model our relational data, since, as we stated earlier, its primary focus is not on relational database technologies.

UML is made up of quite a few distinct models, each one of which is used to represent the components of a system, but we are only going to deal with one of them. For the pure data architect, doing nothing but building a relational database, most of the models are probably not all that interesting, except for the use case diagram. Later we will give a brief overview of use cases to a level that will get us through our task of designing a database system.

IDEF1X

To cover all of the existing modeling methodologies would be next to impossible. They all serve quite the same purpose, and all have nearly the same objects displayed in slightly different ways. In this chapter, we will be focusing on one of the most popular of them: IDEF1X, which is based on Federal Information Processing Standards Publication 184 from September 21, 1993. To be fair, there are several modeling methodologies that are pretty much equal for data modeling, such as Information Engineering, and Chen ERD models, and if you are a user of one of these methodologies then you are likely to be very attached to it, and will probably not wish to change technologies on the basis of this chapter. However, all examples throughout the book will be in the IDEF1X format.

IDEF1X was originally developed by the US Air Force in 1985 to meet the following requirements:

- Support the development of data models
- Be a language that is both easy to learn and robust
- Be teachable
- Be well tested and proven
- Be suitable for automation

For a full copy of the IDEF1X specification, go to http://www.qd.cl/webpages/idef/idef1/idef1x.html.

IDEF1X does a very good job of meeting the above requirements, and is implemented in many of the popular design tools, such as CA ERwin, Embarcedero ERStudio, and Microsoft Visio's Enterprise Edition. It is also supported by other public domain tools, which can be found on the Internet.

Now we've discussed the methodologies we'll be using, let's see how we apply them to our models.

Use Cases

As described in the UML Notation Guide, version 1.1, published September 1, 1997 (the full document is available at http://www.rational.com/uml), use case models represent the functionality of a system or a class as it manifests itself to external users within the system.

A use case model describes:

- Systems components modeled as use cases
- Users of the system modeled as **actors**
- Relationships between the actors and use cases

In a very simple manner, use cases represent abstractions of dialogs between the actors and the system. They describe potential interactions without going into the details. This type of information is essential to the database architect, as we always need to identify the users who will be accessing the database, and what they want to do. There are a few very important reasons for this:

- Security
- Ensuring the data required to support the process exists
- Building stored procedures and triggers to support the processes

As we will see in the next section, data models do not deal with processes or users whatsoever. While use cases are part of UML, they are frequently used not only by strict object-oriented designers, but also by system architects of all types to give a basic blueprint of the actions that must take place for success. Different designer/architect types will need to drill down on different parts of the use case diagram using different modeling technologies (as we will with data models).

There is no set manner for describing a use case, but there is a specific type of model. Use cases are very simple diagrams and there are only two symbols employed on a use case diagram.

The first symbol is the **actor**, which is a stick figure:

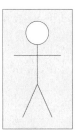

The actor represents a user, system, or piece of hardware that performs an action in the system.

The second symbol is the use case, represented by a simple ellipse with the name of the use case inside:

To model the fact that an actor uses the action in the use case, the two symbols are connected by a single line, also known as the **communicates relationship**:

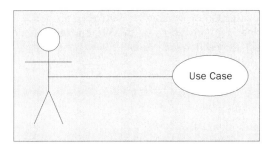

Use cases may also be related to one another in two ways:

- By using another use case to get its purpose completed – the **uses relationship**
- By extending another use case to specialize its behavior – the **extends relationship**

These are modeled in a very obvious manner:

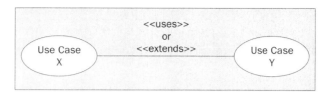

For example, let's say we want to model the process of getting a book published. We have at the very least the following actors: publisher, printer, editor, and (hopefully) writer. Then we would need the following use cases: suggest book, accept book, write book, edit book, print book, and (my favorite) pay for book. This probably doesn't include all of the actors or use cases required to model the book publishing process, but it's good enough for our example. From this we get the following model:

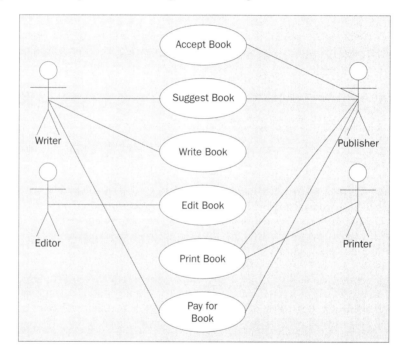

One thing that may seem confusing about this diagram is that accept book comes prior to suggest book. There is no ordering inherent in a use case diagram. Ordering comes later in the process. In fact in a very large use case diagram there could be hundreds of use cases employed with many actors.

Each use case will typically have data stored to explain what it stands for. The following table shows a possible description for one of our use cases:

Name	Write Book
Description	The process of taking an idea and expanding it into several hundred pages

Table continued on following page

Pre-Conditions	Book must have been suggested and approved Outline must have been completely fleshed out and ready to write
Post-Conditions	A written piece of prose will be completed and ready for editing
Steps to complete	Take outline Write introduction Write all chapters Write Summary

Between the model and the descriptions, we can see, at a glance, not only who the users are, but also what their interactions are with our system of writing a book. Note that both the publisher and printer are involved in the use case: Print Book. The publisher orders the printing to take place, and the printer actually does the printing.

Whichever tool is used to build the use case diagram, it is important that it can store detailed information about each use case or actor in the model. Good tools, available from the vendors listed earlier, will allow us to generate tremendously useful reports from the data we enter into the model. I leave it to you, the reader, to delve further into UML, at the very least so that you will be able to understand the models that your business analyst and system architects will produce. One of the better books on the subject is *"Instant UML"* (*Wrox Press, ISBN 1861000871*).

Data Models

There are two basic types of data model, the **logical** and the **physical**. During the process of designing a database system, we first build a logical model and then one or more physical models based on this. If the process goes well, the entire logical model should be functionally equivalent to the physical model(s) once the entire logical model is materialized. No data that the user needs to see should appear in the physical model without being in the logical model.

The logical model represents the basic unchanging nature of the information that the client needs to maintain. A logical model can be implemented in a number of different ways, depending upon the needs of the physical implementation. Regardless of whether we use SQL Server 2000, Oracle, Access, or even Excel to implement our data stores, the logical model should remain unchanged.

During logical modeling we are mostly concerned with making sure that every piece of information is documented, such that it can be stored somewhere. Therefore, as we progress through the process of normalization in the next two chapters, our model will grow, from the largely disorganized mass of entities that we started to deal with in the previous chapter, into a very organized set of entities. By the end of the process we should have identified every single piece of information we may possibly wish to physically store.

The major distinction between the logical and physical models is implementation. Since we use the same modeling language, the logical model will always pretty much resemble the physical model, but during the logical modeling phase of the process it is best to force yourself into ignoring the **HOW** and totally focus on the **WHAT** that will go into the database.

Data Modeling

The physical model, which we will look at in Chapter 10, provides the detailed plan of action for the implementation of the database. This model is where we will take the entities we discovered in the previous chapter and turn them into tables. Many different processes are possible, depending on the purpose and usage of the data in the database and these will be discussed in the second half of the book. While the logical model should be complete enough to describe the business, the physical data model we will implement later may make trade offs for performance versus efficiency.

If the two will differ so much, what is the purpose of logical modeling? This is a valid question. By documenting what should be the optimal storage of data from a consistency standpoint, we increase our ability to produce the best physical databases possible, even if we have to deviate a bit (or a lot) from the logical model. The logical model remains the driving document for later changes to the system and will not be overly perverted by storage details.

Entities

In the IDEF1X standard, **entities** (which are synonymous with tables) are modeled as rectangular boxes, which is actually true for most data model methodologies. There are two different types of entities that we model: **identifier-independent** and **identifier-dependent**, also frequently referred to as **independent** and **dependent** respectively.

Entity Type

The independent entity is so named because it has no primary key dependencies on any other entity, or to put it in other words, there are no foreign or **migrated** keys in the primary key.

In Chapter 3, we discussed foreign keys, but IDEF1X introduces an additional term, which is somewhat confusing, but more illustrative than foreign key, migrated. The term migrated is common and is included in the specification, but it can be misleading, as to migrate means to move. Rather than actually being moved, it refers to the primary key of one entity being "migrated" (copied) as an attribute in a different entity, thus establishing a relationship between the two entities. Hence, it is "independent" of any other entities. All attributes that are not migrated are owned, as they have their origins in the current entity.

The independent entity is drawn with square edges thus:

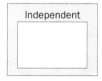

The dependent entity is the converse of the independent entity, as it will have the primary key of another entity migrated into its primary key. We will seldom end up using dependent entities in the physical modeling phase of design. This is because the primary key of an entity should not be editable in a database, and certainly not when it has dependent entities relying on it. Certainly, the concept of a cascading update does exist, so it is less of a problem, but we will see later in Chapter 10 the inherent difficulties in building entities in this manner. We will also look deeper at the idea of independent and dependent entities in the section of this chapter about identifying and non-identifying relationships.

The dependent entity is drawn with rounded off edges:

What we are beginning to see here is a bit of a chicken and egg situation. The dependent entity is dependent on a certain type of relationship. The later section on attributes has some information that relies on certain types of relationships that we have not yet covered. However, we clearly cannot wait until after we look at relationships to introduce the material we need to cover. If this is your first time ever looking at data models, this chapter may require a re-read to get the full picture, as the concept of independent and dependent objects are linked to relationships.

Naming

Though how we name entities is not a part of the IDEF1X specification, while we are building entities we must mention this subject. One of the most important aspects of designing or implementing any system is how you name your objects, variables, etc. Naming database objects is no different, and actually, it is possibly more important to name database objects clearly than it is for other programming objects. The names you give your entities (and attributes for that matter), will be translated into entity names that will be used by programmers and users alike. The logical model will be considered your primary schematic of how the database was conceived, and should be a living document that you change before changing any physical structures.

A few basic guidelines for naming entities:

- Entity names should never be plural. The primary reason for this is that the name should refer to an instance of the object being modeled rather than the collection. Besides, it sounds silly to say that you have "an automobiles record". No, you have an automobile record. If you had two, you would have two automobile records. (However, note that the system tables in SQL Server are all plural, which I personally mimicked during my formative years.)

- The name given should directly correspond to the essence of the entity. For instance, if you are modeling a record that represents a person, name it *person*. If you are modeling an automobile, call it *automobile*. Naming is not always this cut and dried, but it is wise to keep names simple and to the point.

Entity names frequently need to be made up of several words. It is totally allowable to have spaces in them when multiple words are necessary in the name, but it is not required. For example an entity that stores a person's addresses might be named: *Person Address*, *Person_Address*, or using the style I have recently become accustomed to, and the one that we will use in this book: *personAddress*. A common name for this type of naming is **camel notation**, or mixed case.

Note that we are in the logical modeling stage. We generally would want to avoid implementing spaces in the names of our physical structures. While it is allowable to have names with spaces, it is not a good idea for usablility. In SQL Server you would have to address these names surrounded by square brackets, [like this].

Data Modeling

No abbreviations are to be used in the logical naming of entities. Every word should be fully spelled out. Abbreviations tend to confuse the matter. However, abbreviations may be necessary in the physical model due to some naming standard that is forced upon you. If you use them, then you need a way to ensure an attribute uses the same abbreviation every time. This is one of the primary reasons to avoid abbreviations, so you don't get attributes named "description", "descry", "desc", "descrip", and "descriptn" all referring to a description attribute. More will be said in Chapter 10 concerning physical naming. One word of warning though, it is important not to go overboard with long descriptive sentence names for an entity, such as *leftHandedMittensLostByKittensOnSaturdayAfternoons* (unless the entity stored therein is unique from *leftHandedMittensLostByKittensOnSundayMornings*), on-screen truncation will make it difficult to read the name. A better name might be *mittens* or even *lostMittens*. Much of what is encoded in that name will likely be entities in their own right: *Mittens, Mitten Status, Mitten Hand, Mitten Used By, Kittens*, etc. However, this falls more readily under the heading of normalization, and will be discussed further in Chapters 6 and 7.

Attributes

All attributes in the entity must be uniquely named within it. They are represented by a list of names inside of the entity rectangle:

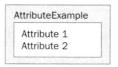

Note: This is technically an invalid entity, as there is no primary key defined (as required by IDEF1X). We will cover keys in the following section.

At this point, we would simply enter all of the attributes that we have defined in the discovery phase. In practice, we might well have combined the process of discovering entities and attributes with the initial modeling phase. It will all depend on how well the tools you use work. Most data modeling tools cater for building models fast and storing a wealth of information to document their entities and attributes.

In the early stages of logical modeling, there can be quite a large difference between an attribute and a column. As we will see in the next two chapters, the definition of what an attribute can store will change quite a bit. For example, the attributes of a person may start out as simply address and phone number. However, once we normalize, we will break these down into many columns (address into number, street name, city, state, zip code, etc.) and likely many different entities.

Primary Key

As we noted in the previous section, an IDEF1X entity must have a primary key. This is convenient for us, as in Chapter 3 we defined that for a tuple, or an entity, each record must be unique. The primary key may be a single attribute, or it may be a composite key (defined earlier as keys with multiple fields), and a value for all attributes in the key must be required (physically speaking, no nulls are allowed in the primary key). Note that no additional notation is required to indicate that the value is the primary key.

The primary key is denoted by placing attributes above a horizontal line through the entity rectangle:

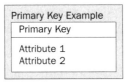

In the early logical modeling phase, I generally do not like to assign any meaningful primary key attributes. The main reason for this is to keep the model clean. I tend to add a meaningless primary key to migrate to other entities to help me see when there is any ownership.

As we will see later in this chapter, the meaningless primary key will contain the name of the entity, so when we create relationships that cause key migration, whatever primary keys we choose will migrate to the child entity in the relationship. As it is likely that we will not choose the primary key that will eventually be implemented, I generally model all candidate keys (or unique identifiers) as alternate keys (non-primary key unique keys). The result is that it is very clear in the logical model what entities are in an ownership role to other entities.

> *This is certainly not a requirement in logical modeling, but is a personal preference that I have found a useful documentation method to keep models clean and corresponds to my method of implementation later. Using a natural key as the primary key in the logical modeling phase is not only reasonable but to many architects preferable. I tend to try to equate even my logical objects to object oriented classes which are identified not by a primary key, but rather a pointer.*

Alternate Keys

Which brings us to our next topic, alternate keys. As previously defined in Chapter 3, alternate keys are a set of one or more fields whose uniqueness we wish to guarantee over the entire entity. Alternate keys do not have special symbols like primary keys, and are not migrated for any relationship. They are identified on the model in a very simple manner:

```
Alternate Key Example
Primary Key

Alternate Key (AK1)
Alternate Key 2 Att 1 (AK2)
Alternate Key 2 Att 2 (Ak2)
```

In this example, there are two alternate keys *groups*: group AK1, which has one attribute as a member, and group AK2, that has two. One extension that ERwin (a data modeling tool built by Computer Associates: http://ca.com/products/alm/erwin.htm) uses is shown here:

```
Alternate Key Example
Primary Key

Alternate Key (AK1.1)
Alternate Key 2 Att 1 (AK2.1)
Alternate Key 2 Att 2 (Ak2.2)
```

Data Modeling

Note that there is an added <*position number*> notation tacked onto the AK1 and AK2 to denote the position of the attribute in the key. In the logical model, technically this information should not be displayed, and certainly should be ignored. Logically, it does not matter which attribute comes first in the key. When a key is physically implemented, it will become interesting for performance reasons only.

Foreign Keys

Foreign keys are also referred to as migrated attributes. They are primary keys from an entity, which serve as a pointer to an instance in the other entity. They are again a result of relationships which we will look at in the next section. They are indicated much like alternate keys by adding the letters "FK" after the foreign key like this:

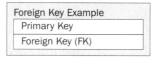

The diagram doesn't show what entity the key is migrated from, and confusion can arise, depending on how you choose your primary keys. This is a limitation of all modeling methodologies, as it would be unnecessarily confusing to the process if we displayed the name of where the key came from for a few reasons:

- ❏ There is no limit (nor should there be) on how far a key will migrate from its original owner
- ❏ It is also not unreasonable that the same attribute might migrate from two separate entities, especially early in the logical design process

This is one of the reasons for the primary key scheme we will employ in our logical model where we will simply build a key named <*entityName*>Id as the key for an entity. The name of the entity is easily identifiable, and is clearer in my opinion.

Domains

Domain is a term that we are regrettably going to use in two very similar contexts. In Chapter 3, we learned that a domain is the set of valid values for an attribute. In IDEF1X, domains have a subtly different definition, which encompasses this definition, but with a useful twist. In this case, domains are mechanisms that not only allow us to define the valid values that can be stored in an attribute, but also provide a form of inheritance in our data type definitions. As examples:

- ❏ **String** – a character string.
- ❏ **SocialSecurityNumber** – a character value with a format of ###-##-####.
- ❏ **PositiveInteger** – an integer value with an implied domain of 0 to max(integer value).

We can then build subtypes that inherit the settings from the base domain. We will build domains for any attributes that we use regularly, as well as domains that are base templates for infrequently used attributes. For example, we might have a basic character type domain, where we specify that all character data was not required. We might also define domains named *name* and *description* for use in many entities, and they will define that these values are required.

In logical modeling, there are just a few bits of information that we are likely to store, such as the general type of the attribute – character, numeric, logical, or even binary data. We must keep these domains as implementation independent data type descriptions. For example, we might specify a domain of:

113

Chapter 5

- **GloballyUniqueIdentifier** – a value that will be unique no matter where it is generated.

  In SQL Server we might use a uniqueidentifier (GUID value) to implement this domain. In Oracle, where there is not exactly the same mechanism, we would implement differently; the same would be true if we used text files to implement the data storage.

When we start physical modeling, we will use the very same domains to inherit physical properties as well. This is the real value in using domains. By creating reusable template attributes that will also be used when we start creating columns, we reduce the amount of effort it takes to build simple entities, which make up the bulk of our work. It also provides a way to enforce company-wide standards by reusing the same domains on all of our corporate models.

Later on, physical details such as data type, constraints, and nullability will be chosen, just to name a few of the more basic physical properties that may be inherited. Since we should have far fewer domains than implemented attributes, we get the double benefits of speedy and consistent implementation. However, we may not employ the inheritance mechanisms when we are building our tables by hand. Implementation of domains is strictly based on the tools used.

For example we might define the following hierarchy:

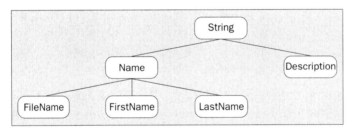

Where `String` is the base domain from which we then inherit `Name` and `Description`. `FileName`, `FirstName`, and `LastName` are inherited from `Name`. During logical modeling, this might seem like a lot of work for nothing, because most of these domains will share some basic details, such as not allowing NULLs, or blank data. However, you may not always require a `FileName`, whereas you may always require a `LastName`. It is important to implement domains for as many distinct attribute types as possible, in case you discover rules or data types that are common to any domains that you set up.

Domains are one of the most exciting features of IDEF1X. They provide an easy method of building standard attributes, reducing both the length of time required for such builds, and the number of errors that occur in doing so. Specific tools implement domains with the ability to define and inherit more properties throughout the domain chain to make creating databases easier. Obviously, if you are building your databases and models by hand, it is less likely that you will implement your tables using the inheritance of domains.

Domains or the datatype may be shown to the right of the attribute name in the entity, as such:

```
domainExample
attributeName: domainName
attributeName2: domainName
```

So if we had an entity that held domain values for describing a type of person, we might model:

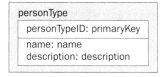

In this case we have three domains:

- **PrimaryKey** – which is a row pointer for a migrating foreign key. Implementation is not implied by building a domain, so we can implement this value in any manner we decide.
- **Name** – a generic domain for holding the name of an instance of an entity. By using this as our standard name domain everywhere we want a name, we maintain consistency. If a given entity name does not fit the same mold, we can create a new domain.
- **Description** – the same type of domain as the name domain, except to hold a description.

Naming

Attribute naming is a bit more interesting than entity naming. We stated that the entity name should never be plural. The same is technically true for attributes. However, at this point in the modeling process, we will still have attribute names that are plural. Leaving the name as a plural can be a good reminder that we expect multiple values. For example, we might have a *Person* entity with a *Children* attribute identified. The *Person* entity would identify a single person, and the *Children* attribute would be there to identify sons and daughters of that person.

Standards for naming attributes have always been quite a hot topic with several different naming schemes having been developed over the previous 30 years of databases. We will look at those in Chapter 10, when we begin to implement our database. The naming standard we will follow is very simple.

- Generally, it is not necessary to repeat the entity name in the attribute name, except for the primary key. The entity name is implied by the attribute's inclusion in the entity. Since the primary key will be migrated to other entities, this small concession makes dealing with migration simpler, as we don't have to rename every attribute after migration, not to mention making joins cleaner in SQL.
- The chosen attribute name should reflect precisely what is contained in the attribute and how it relates to the entity of the record.
- As with entities, no abbreviations are to be used in the logical naming of attributes. Every word should be spelt out in its entirety. If any abbreviation is to be used, due to some naming standard currently in place, then a method should be put into place to make sure that it is used consistently, as was discussed earlier in the chapter.

Consistency is the key to proper naming, so if you, or your organization, do not have a standard naming policy, it would be worthwhile developing one. My naming principle is to keep it simple and readable, and to avoid abbreviation. This standard will be followed from logical modeling into the physical phase. Whatever your standard is, establishing a pattern of naming will make your models easy to follow, both for yourself and for your programmers and users. Any standard is better than no standard.

Another step you should take is to inquire about your client's (or employer's) naming standards to promote future supportability, rather than create new standards.

Chapter 5

Relationships

Up to this point, the constructs we have looked at are pretty much constant across all data modeling methodologies. Entities are always signified by rectangles, and attributes are always words within the rectangles.

However, relationships are a very different matter. Every methodology does relationships different. IDEF1X is quite a bit different from all others, in a primarily good way. The reason I favor IDEF1X is its way of representing relationships. To make this clear, we need to take a look at the terms **parent** and **child,** and an example of a relationship between them.

From the glossary in the IDEF1X specification, we find the following definitions:

- **Entity, Child** – The entity in a specific connection relationship whose instances can be related to zero or one instance of the other entity (parent entity).
- **Entity, Parent** – An entity in a specific connection relationship whose instances can be related to a number of instances of another entity (child entity).
- **Relationship** – An association between two entities or between instances of the same entity.

These are remarkably lucid definitions to have been taken straight from a government specification. Every relationship is denoted by a line drawn between two entities, with a solid circle at one end of that line.

The primary key of the parent is migrated to the child. This is how we denote a foreign key on a model.

We will attempt to go through all of the different settings in the IDEF1X methodology, followed by a brief look at some of the other methodologies that it will be necessary for us to understand, as not everyone will use IDEF1X. There are several different types of relationships that we will look at:

- Identifying
- Non-Identifying
- Optional
- Recursive

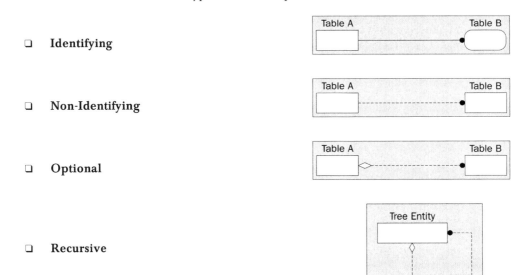

Data Modeling

- Categorization or Sub Types

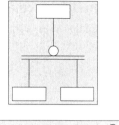

- Many To Many

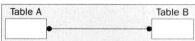

One-to-Many

The **one-to-many** relationship is really kind of a misnomer, and can be considered as a one-to-any relationship. It encompasses *one-to-zero, one, many,* or perhaps *exactly n* relationships. Technically we will see that it is more accurately one-to- (from m to n), as we are able to specify the many in very precise (or very loose) terms as the situation dictates. However, the more standard term is one-to-many and we will not try to make an already confusing term more so.

There are two main types of one-to-many relationships, the **identifying** and (unsurprisingly) the **non-identifying.** The difference, as we will see, is where the primary key is migrated. There are quite a few different permutations of one-to-many relationship settings, and we will look at all of the them and how to denote them in this section.

Identifying Relationships

The **identifying relationship** indicates that the migrated primary key attribute is migrated to the primary key of the child as follows:

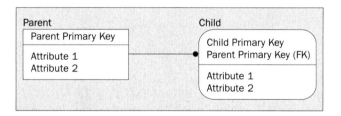

Note that the child entity in the relationship is drawn as a rounded-edged square, which means it is a dependent entity. The reason this is called the identifying relationship is that we will have to have a parent instance in order to be able to identify a child instance record. The essence (defined as "the intrinsic or indispensable properties that serve to characterize or identify something") of the child instance is defined by the existence of a parent.

In other words, the identification and definition of the child record is based on the existence of the parent record. An example is a purchase order and its line items. Without the purchase order, the line items would have no reason to exist.

117

Non-Identifying Relationships

The **non-identifying relationship** indicates that the primary key attribute is not migrated to the primary key of the child. They are used more frequently than the identifying relationship. Whereas identifying relationships were based on needing the existence of the parent to even have a reason to exist, the non-identifying relationship is (not surprisingly) just the opposite. Taking the example of the purchase order, consider the product vendor. They do not define the existence of a line item. Vendor in this case may be required or not required as the business rules might dictate, but generally business rules will not dictate whether a relationship is identifying or non-identifying; the data itself will by its fundamental properties.

Non-identifying relationships are modeled by a dashed line:

Why should you use an identifying instead of a non-identifying relationship? The reason is actually pretty simple. If the parent entity (as we stated in the previous section) defines the essence of the child, then we will use the identifying. If on the other hand, the relationship defines one of the child's attributes, then we use a non-identifying relationship.

As another contrasting example, consider the following:

- **Identifying** – Say you have an entity that stores contacts and an entity that stores the contact's telephone number. The *contact* defines the phone number, and without the contact, there would be no need for the *contactPhoneNumber*.

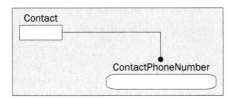

- **Non-Identifying** – Taking the enties that we defined for the identifying relationship, along with an additional entity called *contactPhoneNumberType*. This entity is related to the *contactPhoneNumber* entity, but in a non-identifying way, and defines a set of possible phone number types ("Voice", "Fax", etc.) that a *contactPhoneNumber* might be. The type of phone number does not identify the phone number; it simply classifies it.

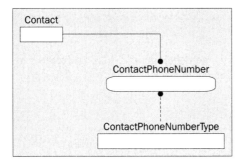

*The contactPhoneNumberType entity is commonly known as a **domain entity** or **domain table**. Rather than having a fixed domain for an attribute, we design entities that allow programmatic changes to the domain with no re-coding of constraints or client code. As an added bonus we can add columns to define, describe, and extend the domain values to implement business rules. It also allows the client user to build lists for users to choose values with very little programming.*

There are two different classes of non-identifying relationships, mandatory and optional. We will now take a closer look at these in the next two sections.

Mandatory

Mandatory non-identifying relationships are so called because the migrated field in the child instance is required. When this relationship is implemented, the migrated key should be marked as NOT NULL.

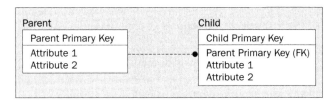

Note that the child entity does not have rounded off corners in this example. This is because both enties are independent, since none of the primary key attributes for the child are foreign keys.

Another example of such a relationship might come from a movie rental database:

The relationship might be `Genre <classifies> Movie`, where the `Genre` entity is the one entity, and `Movie` is the many. It would be mandatory that every movie being rented must have a genre so that it can be placed on the shelves.

Optional

We may not always want to force the child to have a value for the migrated key. In this case we will set the migrated child key to **optional,** which if implemented in this manner will dictate allowing null values. Since the non-identifying relationship denotes that the parent is an attribute of the child, this is the same as having an optional attribute (nullable attribute).

We signify this by an open diamond at the opposite end of the line from the black circle, as shown:

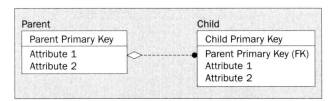

If you are wondering why there is not an optional identifying relationship, it is due to the fact that you may not have any optional attributes in a primary key; this is true for IDEF1X as well as SQL Server 2000.

For a one-to-many optional relationship, consider the following:

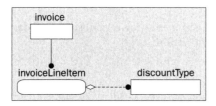

The *invoiceLineItem* entity is where items are placed onto an invoice to receive payment. Then consider that we sometimes will apply a standard discount amount to the line item. The relationship then from the *invoiceLineItem* to the *discountType* entity is an optional one.

Cardinality

The cardinality of the relationship denotes the number of child instances that can be inserted for each parent of that relationship. The following table shows the six possible cardinalities that relationships can take on.

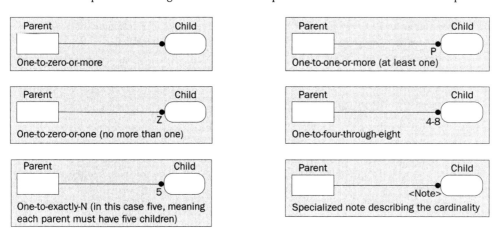

A possible use for the one-to-one-or-more might be to represent the relationship between a guardian and a student in a school database:

I like this example, because it expresses the need extremely well. It says that for a *guardian* record to exist, a student must exist, but a student record need not have a guardian for us to wish to store their data.

Another example that I really like to look at when discussing cardinality is the following. Consider the case of a club that has members and certain positions that they should or could fill:

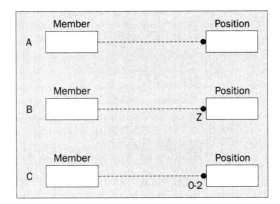

In example A, we are saying that a member can take as many positions as there are possible positions. In the second, we are stating that they can only serve in one position, and in the final 0, 1, or 2. They all look about the same, but the Z or 0-2 has great meaning.

I considered including examples of each of these cardinality types, but in most cases it was too difficult or too silly, so we have merely mentioned a few of the more typical ones. However, it is very nice to have them available in case they do become necessary.

Role names

A role name is an alternative name we give an attribute when we use it as a foreign key. The purpose of a role name is that we sometimes need to clarify the usage of a migrated key, because either the parent entity is very generic and we want to specify a very specific name, or we have multiple relationships from the same entity. As attribute names must be unique, we have to assign different names for the child records. In our example:

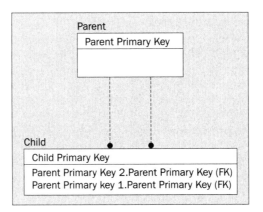

We have two relationships from the parent entity to the child entity, and the migrated attributes have been named as [Parent Primary Key 1] and [Parent Primary Key 2].

Chapter 5

As an example, say you have a *User* entity, and you want to store the name or ID of the user who created an *Object* entity. We would end up with a situation like this:

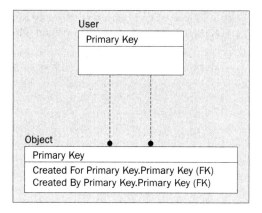

Note that we have two relationships to the *Object* entity from the *User* entity. One is named [Created For Primary Key] and the other is [Created By Primary Key].

This example also shows why you would put the name of the entity into the primary key attribute. When you migrate the primary key to another entity, it is important to know what the original parent entity is. Since we have a [Primary Key] attribute in the *Object* entity, we would have had to name the first attribute as well as the second.

Other Types of Relationships

There are a few other, less important relationship types that are not employed that much. However, they are extremely important to understand.

Recursive

One of the more difficult relationships to implement, but one of the most important, is the **recursive relationship**, also known as a **self-join**, **hierarchial**, **self-referencing** or **self-relationship**. This is modeled by drawing a non-identifying relationship not to a different entity, but to the same entity. The migrated key of the relationship is given a role name (and I generally use a naming convention of adding "parent" to the front of the attribute name, but this is not a necessity).

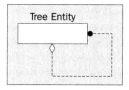

Data Modeling

The recursive relationship is useful for creating tree structures, as in the following organization chart.

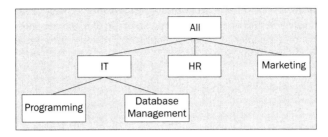

To explain this concept we will need to look at the data that would be stored to implement this hierarchy:

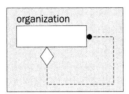

We will treat the *organizationName* as the primary key and *parentOrganizationName* as the migrated, rolenamed attribute that indicates the self-reference to the join:

```
organizationName                parentOrganizationName
-------------------------       -------------------------
All                             <null>
IT                              All
HR                              All
Marketing                       All
Programming                     IT
Database Management             IT
```

The org chart can now be rebuilt by starting at 'All', and getting it's first child, 'IT'. Then we get the first child of 'IT', 'Programming'. 'Programming' has no children, so we go back to 'IT' and get it's next child, 'Database Management', etc. The recursive relationship is so named because a popular algorithm for implementing such data structures in functional programming languages uses recursion to handle the process we simulated in our example.

As one final example, consider the case of a person entity, where we store the name, address, etc. of people that we deal with. If we wish to build this entity with the ability to point to a spouse, we might design the following:

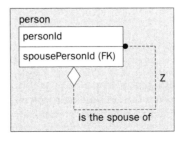

Notice that we also set this as a one-to-zero-or-one relationship, since (in most places) a person may only have a single spouse.

Categorization Relationships

Categorization relationships (also referred to as sub-types) are another special type of one-to-zero-or-one relationship used to indicate whether one entity is a specific type of a generic entity. Note also that there are no black dots on either end of the lines; the specific entities are drawn with rounded off corners, signifying that they are indeed dependent on the generic entity.

Using this type of relationship we have three distinct parts:

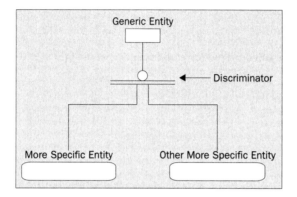

- **Generic Entity** – This is an entity that contains all of the attributes that are common to all of the sub-typed entities.

- **Discriminator** – This is an attribute that acts as a switch to determine the entity where the additional, more specific information is stored.

- **Specific Entity** – This is the place where the specific information is stored, based on the discriminator.

For example, let's look at a video library. If you wanted to store information about each of the videos that you owned, regardless of format, you might build a categorization relationship like:

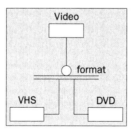

These types of relationships are typically known as "is-a" relationships – a VHS is a video, and a DVD is a video.

In this manner, you might store the title, actors, length and possibly description of the content in the *Video* entity, and then, based on format which is the discriminator, you might store the information that is specific to *VHS* tapes or *DVD* in their own separate entities, like special features and menus for DVDs, long or slow play for VHS tapes.

There are two distinct types of categories, **complete** and **incomplete**. The complete set of categories is modeled with a double line on the discriminator, and the incomplete with a single.

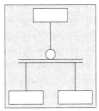 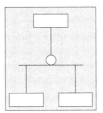

Complete set of categories   Incomplete set of categories

The primary difference between the complete and incomplete categories is that in the complete categorization relationship, each generic instance must have one specific instance; in the incomplete case this is not necessarily true. For example, we might have a complete set of categories like this:

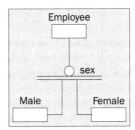

This relationship is read: "An employee *must* be either be male or female." This is certainly a complete category as there are no other recognized sexes. However, take the following incomplete set of categories:

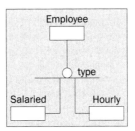

In this case we have an incomplete sub-type, because employees are either salaried or hourly, but there may be other categories, such as contract workers. We may not need to store any additional information about them, so we do not need the specific entity. This relationship is read as: "An employee can be either salaried or hourly or other."

Many-To-Many

The many-to-many relationship is also known as the non-specific relationship, which is actually a better name, but far less well known. It is very common to have many-to-many relationships in our logical models. In fact, the closer you get to a proper database model, the more you find that every relationship will be of the many-to-many type. In the early stages of modeling, it is helpful to define relationships as many-to-many even if you can see them changing during implementation.

They are modeled by a line with a solid black dot on either end:

Note that we cannot actually implement this relationship in the physical model, so we frequently go directly to a more implementation-specific representation:

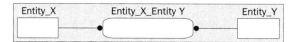

Here the intermediate *Entity_X_Entity_Y* entity is known as a **resolution entity**. In our modeling, we will stick with the former representation when we have not identified any extended attributes to describe the relationship, and the latter representation when we have.

To make that a bit clearer, let's look at the following example:

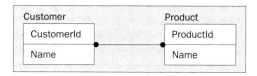

In this situation, we have set up a relationship where many customers are related to many products. This is a very common situation, as we seldom create specific products for specific customers; rather, any customer can purchase any of the products. At this point of modeling, we would use the many-to-many representation. However, if we discover that the customer can only be related to a product for a certain period of time, we might choose to represent this by the other representation:

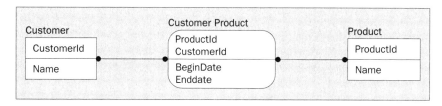

In fact in most cases, we will find that the many-to-many relationship will require some additional information to make it complete.

Verb Phrases (Naming)

Relationships are given names, which are called **verb phrases**, which make the relationship between a parent and child entity a readable sentence, which incorporates the entity names and the relationship cardinality. The name is usually expressed from parent to child, but can be expressed in the other direction, or even in both directions. The verb phrase is located on the model somewhere close to the line that forms the relationship:

The relationship should be named such that it fits into the following general structure for reading the entire relationship.

parent cardinality – parent entity name – relationship name – child cardinality – child entity name

For example, the following relationship:

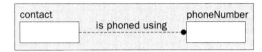

Would be read:

One contact is phoned using zero, one, or more phoneNumber(s).

Of course, the sentence may or may not make perfect grammatical sense, as this one brings up the question of how a contact is phoned using zero phone numbers. Obviously if we were trying to present this to a non-technical person, it would make more sense to read it as:

One contact can either have no phoneNumber or may have one or more phoneNumbers.

Obviously the modeling language does not take linguistics into consideration when building this specification, but from a technical standpoint, it does not matter that the contact is phoned using zero phone numbers, since it follows that they have no phone number.

Being able to read the relationship helps us to notice obvious problems. For instance, the following relationship:

looks fine at first glance, but when read like this:

One contactType classifies zero or one contact

it doesn't make logical sense. Likely we will want to correct this situation in our model to:

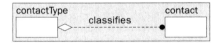

which now reads:

One contactType classifies zero or more contacts.

Note that the type of relationship, whether it is identifying, non-identifying, optional, or mandatory, makes no difference when reading the relationship.

We can also include a verb phrase that reads from child to parent. For a one-to-many relationship this would be of the following format:

one child record *(relationship)* exactly one parent record.

In the case of our first example, we could have added an additional verb phrase:

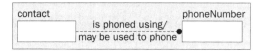

This would be read exactly opposite to the previous examples, as:

One phoneNumber may be used to phone exactly one contact

Since we are going from the many to the one, we will always know that the parent in the relationship will have one related value, and since we are reading in the context of the existence of the child, we can also assume that there is a single child record to consider in the sentence.

Alternate Methods of Relationship Display

In this section we will attempt to briefly describe two other modeling methodologies that you will likely run into frequently when designing databases for SQL Server 2000.

Information Engineering

The information engineering methodology is very well known and widely used. It is really quite popular, and does a very good job of displaying the necessary information. It is also known affectionately as the crow's foot method.

By varying the basic symbols on the end of the line, we can arrive at all of the various possibilities for relationships.

The following table shows the different symbols that we can employ to build relationship representations:

Symbol	Description
	Many – The entity on the end with the crow's foot denotes that there can be greater than one value related to the other entity
	Optional – Indicates that there does not have to be a related instance on this end of the relationship for one to exist on the other. What has been decribed as Zero-or-More as opposed to One-or-More.
	Identifying Relationship – The key of the entity on the other end of the relationship is migrated to this entity.
	Non-required Relationship – A set of dashed lines on one end of the relationship line indicates that the migrated key may be null.

Data Modeling

For example:

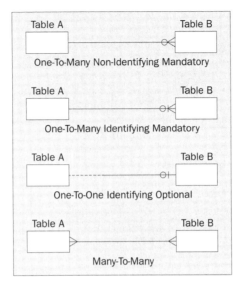

The attributes are shown in much the same method as IDEF1X uses, inside the rectangle. This notation is not as clean as IDEF1X, but it does a very good job and is likely to be used by some of the documents that we will come across in our work as a data architect. IE is also not always fully implemented in any tools. However, the circle and the crow's feet are generally implemented properly.

Further details regarding this methodology can be found in "*Information Engineering*" (*Prentice Hall, ISBN 013464462X (vol. 1), 0134648854 (vol. 2), and 013465501X (vol. 3)*).

Chen ERD

The Chen ERD methodology is quite a bit different, but is pretty self-explanatory. In the following graphic, we present a very simple diagram with the basics of the Chen diagram shown.

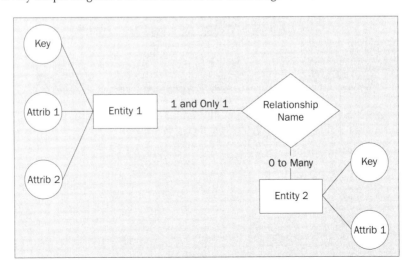

Each entity is again a rectangle; however, the attributes are not shown in the diagram, but are attached to the entity in circles. The primary key is denoted as double underlined. The cardinality for a relationship is denoted in text. In the example, it is *1 and Only 1 Entity1 <relationship name> 0 to Many Entity2.*

The primary reason for including the Chen ERD format is for contrast. At least one other methodology (Bachman) implements attributes in this style, where they are not displayed in the rectangle. While I understand the logic behind this (they are separate objects), I have found that models I have seen in this format seemed overly cluttered, even for very small diagrams. It does, however, do an admirable job with the logical model and does not over rely on an arcane symbology to describe cardinality. While I am not saying it does not exist, I personally have not seen this implemented in a database design tool other than Microsoft Visio, but many of the diagrams you will find on the Internet will be in this style, so it is interesting to understand. Further details can be found in *The Entity Relationship Model – Toward a Unified View of Data,* (*ACM Transactions on Database Systems, Volume 1, No. 1 (March 1976), pp 9-36*).

Microsoft SQL Server Diagram Tools

In the Enterprise Manager of SQL Server, a new tool was added to version 7.0 that was pretty neat; a database diagram tool. It also has a fairly interesting manner of displaying entities. The following is an example of a one-to-many relationship:

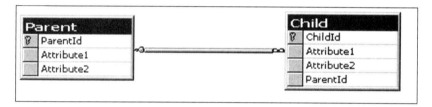

The primary keys are identified by the little key in an attribute. The relationship is denoted by the line between the entities with the one end having a key, and the many end having an infinity sign.

We can display the entities in several formats, such as just showing the names of the entities, or showing all of the attributes, with datatypes:

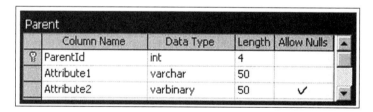

In the following graphic, I have made a model of the entire `Northwind` database using the diagramming tool to show that it does in fact do a good job of displaying the model:

Data Modeling

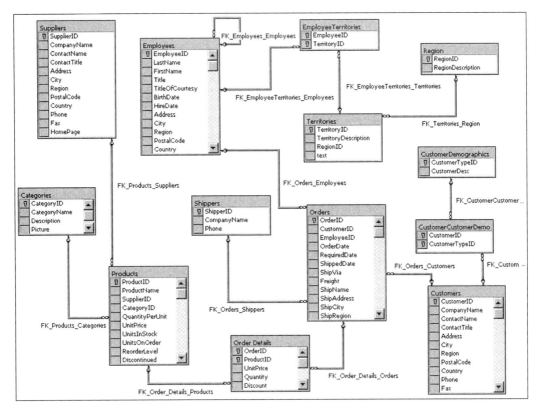

However, while it does have its place, it is not a full featured data modeling tool and should probably not be used as such if possible. We are including the SQL Server modeling methodology because it is included in SQL Server and it is understood that in some situations it is the best tool that you may have access to. It is only a physical modeling tool, and it does give access to all implementation specific features of SQL Server, including the ability to annotate our tables and columns with descriptive information. It is a great tool for sharing the current structure with database developers. Since it is implementation specific, if we decide to implement a relationship in a trigger it will not know that it exists.

In most cases these tools are not the optimal way to see actual relationship information that is designed into the database, but it does give a serviceable look at the database structure when needed.

Descriptive Information

We have drawn our entities, assigned attributes and domains to them, and and set up relationships between them, but we are not quite done. We have discussed naming our entities, attributes, and even our relationships, but even with well-formed names, there will still likely be confusion as to what exactly an attribute is used for.

We must add comments to the pictures in our model. Comments will let the eventual reader, and even yourself, know what you originally had in mind. Remember that not everyone who views the models that we create will be on the same technical level, in that some will be non-relational programmers, or indeed users or (non-technical) product managers who have no modeling experience.

131

We have already had a good start on this process in the previous chapter, where we added this information to our Word document. It should be noted that once we find a data modeling tool we are comfortable with, we will be able to enter all of the data we entered in the previous chapter and more. This will prove much faster than using a Word document to store all of the information we put into our document, and then transferring it to a data model.

Descriptive information need not be in any special format; it simply needs to be detailed, up to date, and capable of answering as many questions as we can anticipate will be asked. Each of these bits of information should be stored in a manner that makes it easy for users to quickly tie it back to the part of the model where it was used, and should be stored either in a document or as metadata in a modeling tool.

Questions such as:

- What is the object supposed to represent?
- How will be it used?
- Who might use it?
- What are the future plans for the object?

The scope of the descriptions should not extend past the object or entities that are affected. For example, the entity description should refer only to the entity, and not any related entities, relationships, or even attributes unless necessary. Attribute definitions should speak to only the single attribute, and where their values might come from.

Maintaining good descriptive information is eqivalent to putting decent comments in code. As the database is always the central part of any computer system, comments at this level are more important than any others. For example, say we have the following two entities:

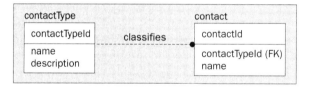

We might have the following very basic set of descriptive information stored to describe the attributes that we have created:

Entities:

Contact		Persons that can be contacted to do business with
	Attributes	Description
	Contacted	Primary key pointer to a contact
	contactTypeId	Primary key pointer to a contactType
	name	The full name of a contact

ContactType		Domain of different contact types
	Attributes	Description
	contactTypeId	Primary key pointer to a contactType
	name	The name that the contact type will be uniquely known as
	description	The description of exactly how the contact should be used

Relationships:

Parent Entity Name	Phrase	Child Entity Name	Definition
ContactType	**classifies**	contact	Contact type classification. Was required by specifications.

Case Study

In our previous chapter, we had built a document that has all of the different objects that we need to model. In this case study, we simply want to transfer all of the information that we put in the document and turn it into a set of graphical models where that makes sense.

Use Case

We start with the use case, because that is generally the first model that you need to create. In our case study, the interviewer has identified two actors, a general account user and the accounting clerk. Whilst an account user will want to be able to perform actions such as getting account information, withdrawing money, making deposits and so on, the accounting clerk needs to be able to do tasks such as accessing accounting information and entering tranasactions. We can summarize the actors and use cases we have identified as being of interest to us when we start to build security and write procedures, as follows:

Actors:

Name	Description
General Account User	Any user who can deposit or withdraw money from the account
Accounting Clerk	User who has the ability to enter and maintain accounts

Use Cases:

Name	Description
Get Account Information	Allows users to retrieve account information such as name of bank, balance, etc.
Enter Transaction	Allows user to record that a transaction has occurred
Enter Check	Allows user to specifically record a check type transaction

Balance	Allows user to reconcile items that have been reported by the bank
Download Statement	Allows user to download the items from the bank that the bank has committed
Withdraw Money	Users getting money from account to spend
Make Deposit	Users putting money into account
Write Check	Users writing a paper document and giving it to another person to transfer funds

In developing a real system, the use case is a very important part of design. However, since our example is actually tailored around keeping it simple, we will not be working too hard at getting a perfect use case model. The following use case is a possible outcome of the analysis we have performed:

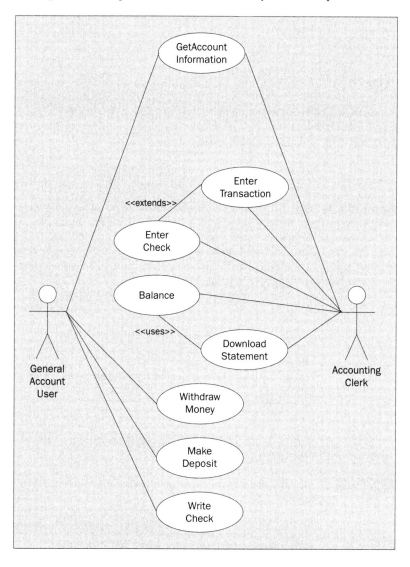

Though far from a complete process analysis, this model gives a good set of use cases and actors for our minor checking account system. Note that we have worked in an example of <<*uses*>> and <<*extends*>> to make our example more complete. Balance uses download transactions (if possible) to go out and get the transactions from the electronic source, and **enter check** <<*extends*>> **enter transaction** because a check has pretty much the same information as a general transaction, with a few additions. We have not included deposits or direct withdrawals as separate use cases, to save space.

This is as far as we are going to go with the use cases. What we have given here is simply a teaser, specifically to help us, as data architects, to build a model that explains what the processes in our system are. Further details can be found in the specification (the full document is available at http://www.rational.com/uml), or by reading Pierre-Alain Muller's *"Instant UML" (Wrox Press, ISBN 1861000871)*. Then you can get one of the several UML tools available and begin using use cases and UML. UML is likely to be around for quite a while and a thorough understanding of it will make it easier to communicate with the non-relational analysts that we have to deal with.

Data Model

Once we have finished identifying processes, we move to the main business of building a data model to establish our preliminary database architecture. The first step in data modeling is to model the entities and attributes that we have previously identified.

> *Note: For the rest of the case study, we are usually going to assume that any definitions that we have previously added are contained in the model. We cannot expand all of the fields to show definitions. We will, however, try to give definitions for all new objects that we create.*

So we simply create entities for each of our objects adding all of the attributes, choosing a base type domain as follows:

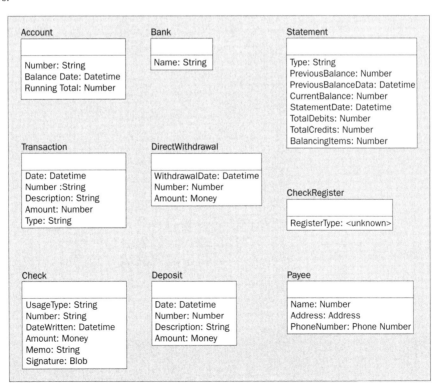

Now we have all of the entities from the previous chapter's case study in a far more compact and easy to follow format.

The next step is to identify any relationships where the two objects are basically the same thing, and implement them as sub-types. We have one such example in our case study in that the *check, deposit,* and *directWithdrawal* entities are all just types of transactions.

Note that we have added the type attribute as our discriminator for the subtypes, and have removed all of the attributes that that were duplicates of the ones that were already in the transaction entity.

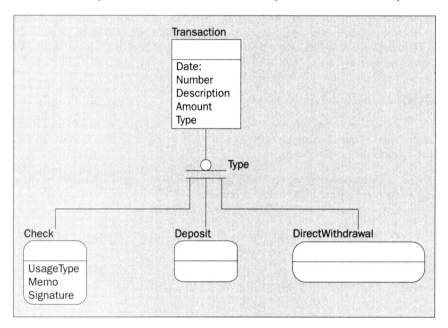

Data Modeling

The next step is to add and name all of the relationships on the model. We still have not added primary keys to the model, so we don't have any migration of keys at this point. It makes the implementation cleaner to start with. We will actually add them as our last step.

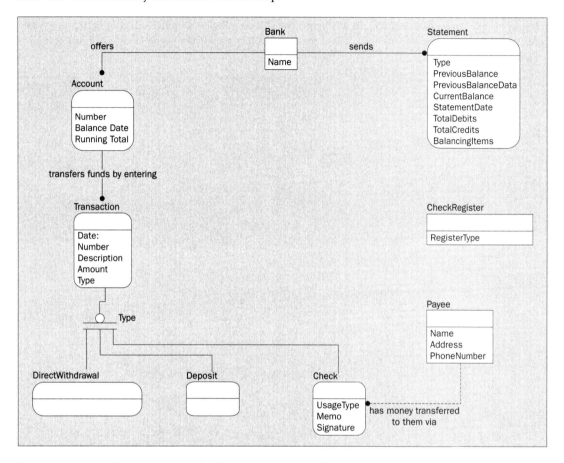

Notice that we see the payee-to-check relationship as a non-identifying relationship. This is because a check is not identified by its payee, since payee is merely an attribute of a check. It is, however, required.

The final step in building our initial model is to identify any natural unique keys in the data. For instance, in the *account* entity, the number is likely to be a unique value. In the *bank* entity, we have a name of the bank that should be unique. *Transactions* will probably have a unique number to identify them. Our guesses will sometimes be right and sometimes not quite so right, but they are logical guesses. As always, anytime you guess you must verify, and your model and supporting documentation should always give an indication when you do so.

For example, in the *transaction* entity we have set the *number* attribute as unique. This makes logical sense on first pass, but as we progress we will (hopefully) realize that a transaction's number is only unique for a given account. There are several wrong ways to deal with this situation such as appending the number of the account to the start of every transaction. (This is what is known as a **smart**, **intelligent** or **compound** key and it may be hard to readily decipher, as it does not stand out on the data model.). The right implementation will be to add the *account* entity's primary key to the alternate key we have devised. This will mean that our model now looks like this:

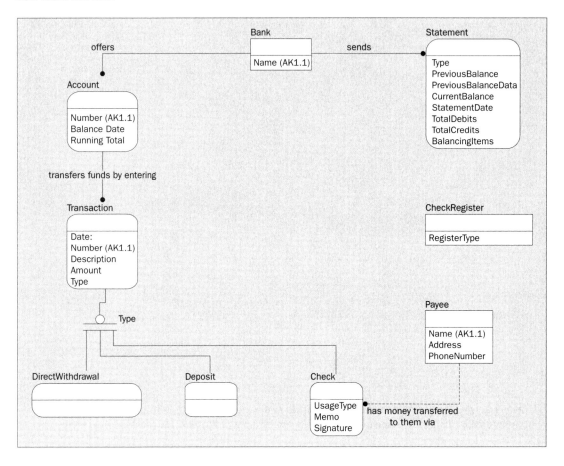

Data Modeling

In this model, typically we will use integers as the primary key, so they need not be editable. It also makes the choice easy at this point. The choice of primary key is largely a personal choice, but in this book we have made the point of generally sticking with using a more pointer-oriented primary key. We will expound on why to physically implement keys in this way in Chapter 10. However, as we have said earlier, by not choosing a proper primary key at this point, we do not end up with a messy model developed from keys migrating about.

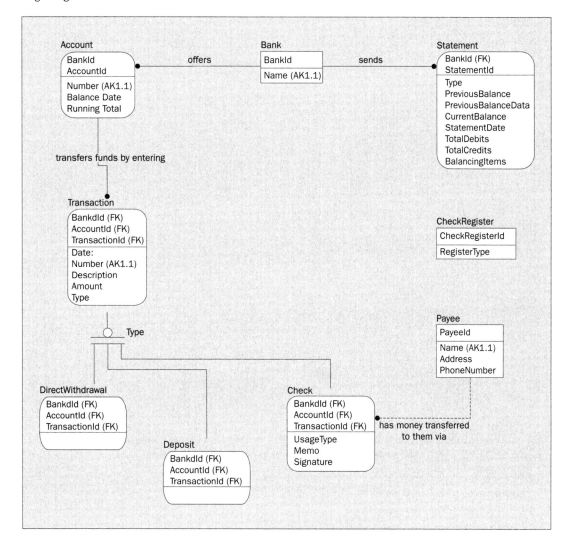

The final step we need to take is to choose logical domains for each of the attributes. The idea at this point is to try to group like attributes in the same domain, as, for example, in the case of the *date* attribute in *transaction*, the *previousBalanceDate* in *statement* and the *balanceDate* in the **account** entity. For the primary key attributes, we will give them a domain of primary key, and leave it at that for now. Our model now looks like this:

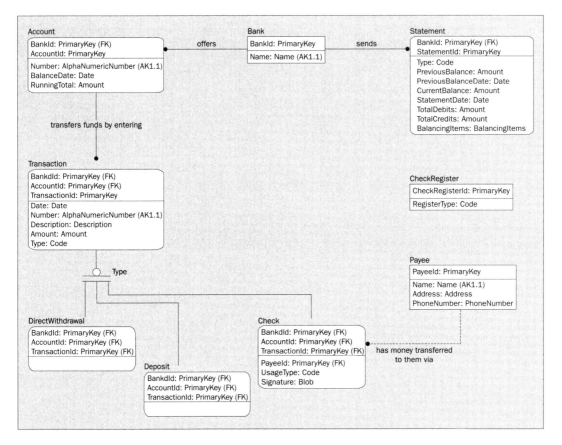

We will continue to assign domains to every one of the attributes that we create as we continue through the logical modeling phase. At this stage we have discovered and used the following domains:

Address	Includes an entire address
AlphaNumericNumber	A value which is generally referred to as a number but actually allows alpha and numeric data
Amount	A monetary value
BalancingItems	Group of items we need in order to balance account
Blob	Picture, document store in Binary Large Object format
Code	A value used as a kind of a text pointer

Data Modeling

Date	Date value
Name	The readable tag that is assigned to an instance of an entity for easy access
PhoneNumber	Entire phone number
PrimaryKey	Used as a pointer to an instance

We will not do too much more in terms of assigning predicates to them at this point, as we will be making quite a few changes to the model in the next few chapters, and we will no doubt discover more domains (and remove a few). We will however keep up with the process of adding domains, any time we create a new attribute, as our model becomes more mature.

As you can see, the model is beginning to get a bit larger, as well as showing signs of an implementable structure. We will be making a lot of changes to the structure in the upcoming chapters, but the final structure will still vaguely resemble what we have here.

At this point, we will take the definitions that we gathered previously, into our attributes. As an example, we will take the *statement* entity:

Statement	Represents a document (paper or electronic) that comes from the bank once a calendar month that tells us everything that the bank thinks we have spent
Attributes	**Description**
bankId	Primary key identifier for a bank
statementId	Primary key identifier for a statement instance
type	Identifies the type of statement gotten from the bank
previousBalance	Specifies what the balance was supposed to be after the last statement was balanced
previousBalanceDate	Specifies the date that the account was last balanced
currentBalance	Specifies what the balance of the account is after all of the items in the statement have been reconciled
statementDate	The date that the current statement was issued
totalCredits	Sum of all items that have added money to the account during the statement period
totalDebits	Sum of all items that have subtracted money from the account during the statement period
balancingItems	All of the items that the bank has processed and is now reporting back to us

Chapter 5

Summary

In this chapter we have looked at taking the textual design we arrived at in the previous chapter, and putting it into a more concise graphic format.

We have introduced two specific modeling types, namely the UML and IDEF1X data models. We took a brief look at UML, and specifically use cases, primarily to enable us to draw use case diagrams to model the processes that we will no doubt discover during the database design phase.

In data modeling, we focused heavily on the IDEF1X modeling methodology, taking a detailed look at the symbology we will need in our design work. The base set of symbols that we have outlined, will enable us to fully model our logical databases (and later physical databases) in great detail.

The last point to be made was that for every entity, and every attribute we discover during the process we should at the very least identify the following detailed properties:

Property	Purpose
Name	Name that will fully describe the purpose for the entity or attribute.
Description	Full explanation that when read within the context of the attribute and entity will explain what the purpose of the attribute is for programmer and user alike.
Predicates (Domain)	Generally, predicates indicate ANY rules that govern our data in or out of our database. It is generally acceptable to simply set a domain (single column predicate based on constraints and data types during physical modeling) and document other predicates at a table or database level.

We will use this descriptive information later in the process to build our check constraints, our triggers, etc. in order to protect and use the data to produce a bulletproof data store. In this way the user can have confidence that what they specified, and agreed to, will indeed be what is stored in the database.

Having considered the symbology we require to model our database, we now need to go on to consider normalizing our design, and will do so in the following chapters.

6

Normalization Techniques

No matter what database system you are designing, normalization is a vital process that needs to be performed to ensure that the database contained within your system is both accurate and doesn't contain duplicated information. Normalization can be summed up in a single sentence, "Every entity in your database needs to have a single theme". (http://www.gslis.utexas.edu/~l384k11w/normstep.html.)

The different levels of normalization of a database indicate how well the structure adheres to the recognized standards of database design, although after the third level there is some contention among database developers as to how useful the further levels are. We'll consider these arguments in the next chapter.

As you might have guessed, database structure is one of the most polarizing topics for the database architect. Disagreements often arise between database architects and client developers over how to store data. Why? Because no two database designs are the same and there are always several correct ways to structure a database. In this chapter and the next we will look at the guidelines which help avoid the many, many ways you can structure a database poorly.

An Online Transaction Processing (OLTP) database that hasn't been normalized is generally quicker to build for a client the first time as there are far fewer tables. This benefit soon disappears when minor user changes are required after the system is in production. Expert database designers realize that changes in data structure have large costs associated with them. When there are no rows in a table and no code to access the tables, structure changes may simply take minutes. When we have added a hundred rows to a table, with seven of its related tables having ten rows each, and programmers having written hundreds of lines of code, we can easily burn an hour of prime surfing time changing the table structure. If there are a million rows in the table, forget about it. Once we have changed the table structure, we then have to change all of the code that accesses the table. Normalization will also save a great deal of storage space as a major goal is to avoid repeating data.

The process of normalization also ensures consistent entity structures which will help us to avoid modifying our existing entities in the future. If we have done a decent job on the data-gathering portion of the project, when we are finished, the normalization process should have weeded out most of the trouble areas in the database. Obviously I am not saying that, once you have implemented your design, you can't change it, as expansions and changes in business practice could create much needed amendments. However, it is easier to add new information and new entities to a fully normalized database.

This chapter and the next will go through the recognized techniques of normalization, and you will see that the results of normalization will minimize the inclusion of duplicated information in your databases, and make them easier to manage and modify, and also more secure – although it will create a lot more entities.

Why Normalize?

There are many reasons to normalize data structures.

Reducing NULLs

NULLs can be very detrimental to data integrity and performance, and can make querying the database very confusing. However, NULLs are an entire subject in their own right; a lot of space can be devoted to how SQL Server 2000 handles them and how you can avoid them or minimize their impact in your databases. So, rather than digressing here, the rules of NULL handling will be covered in Chapter 12 in more depth. However, the process of normalization can lead to there being fewer NULL values contained in your database.

Eliminating Redundant Data

Any editable piece of data that isn't a primary key of a table (or part of one) but is a foreign key (or part of one) that occurs more than once in the database, is an error waiting to happen. No doubt we have all have seen it before – a person's name stored in two places, then one version gets modified and the other doesn't, and suddenly we have two names where before there was just one.

The problem with storing redundant data will be very obvious to anyone who has moved to a new address. Every government authority requires you to individually change your address information on tax forms, driver's licenses, auto registrations, etc., rather than one change being made centrally.

Avoiding Unnecessary Coding

Extra programming in triggers, stored procedures, or even in the business logic tier, can be required to handle the non-normalized data and this in turn can impair performance significantly. This is not to mention that extra coding increases the chance of introducing new bugs into the labyrinth of code that is required to maintain redundant data. Many database projects fail due to the enormous requirement of keeping redundant data in sync.

Maximizing Clustered Indexes

Clustered indexes are used to natively order a table in SQL Server. They are special indexes in which the physical storage of the data matches the order of the indexed fields, which allows for better performance of queries using that index. Typically, they are used to order a table in a convenient manner to enhance performance. Each table may have only a single clustered index. The more clustered indexes you have in your database the less sorting you may have to do, and the more likely it is that queries will be able to use the MERGE JOIN – a special type of very fast join technique that requires sorted data. Sorting is a very costly operation that should be avoided if possible. Clustered indexes and indexes in general will be covered in great detail in Chapters 10 and 14.

Lowering the Number of Indexes per Table

The fewer indexes per table, the fewer the number of **pages** that might be moved around on a modification or insertion into the table. By pages, we're not referring to web pages, but rather the SQL Server concept of pages. In SQL Server, data and indexes are broken up and stored on 8K pages. Of course SQL Server doesn't keep the whole database in memory at any one time. What it does do is keep a "snapshot" of what is currently being looked at. To keep the illusion of having the whole database in memory, SQL Server moves the pages in and out of a high speed fast access storage space when they are required, but this space can only contain a limited number of pages at any one time. The pages are therefore moved in and out of the space on the principle that the most frequently accessed remain in. The operation of moving pages in and out of memory is costly in terms of performance. Therefore, to keep performance as high as possible, you want to make as few page transfers as possible.

When a table has many columns, you may need quite a few indexes on a table to avoid retrieval performance problems. While these indexes may give great retrieval gains, maintaining indexes can be very costly. Indexes are a very tricky topic because they have both positive and negative effects on performance and require a fine balance for optimal utilization.

Keeping Tables Thin

When we refer to a thinner table, we mean that there is a relatively small number of columns in the table. Thinner tables mean more data fits on a given page in your database, therefore allowing the database server to retrieve more rows for a table in a single read than would be otherwise possible. This all means that there will be more tables in the system when we are finished normalizing. There is, however, a common sense cut-off point and I don't recommend having one column tables. Also bear in mind in a typical OLTP system, very few columns of data are touched on every data modification, and frequently queries are used to gather the summary of a single value, like an account balance. High performance is required for these sorts of queries.

The Process of Normalization

If we recall our single sentence description of normalization from the first paragraph of this chapter – "*Every table in your database needs to have a single theme*" – we can take this to mean that each table should endeavor to represent a single entity. This concept will become excruciatingly apparent over the next two chapters as we work through the process of normalization.

Normalization is a process. There are seven widely accepted types of normalization, as follows:

- First Normal Form
- Second Normal Form
- Third Normal Form
- Boyce-Codd Normal Form
- Fourth Normal Form
- Fifth Normal Form
- Domain-Key Normal Form

Chapter 6

In 1972, E. F. Codd presented the world with the First Normal Form, based on the shape of the data, and the Second and Third Normal Forms, based on functional dependencies in the data. These were further refined by Codd and Boyce in the Boyce-Codd Normal Form. This chapter will cover these four in some detail.

During the discussion of normalization in this chapter and the next, we will step through each of the different types, looking to eliminate all of the violations we find by following the rules specified in each type. We might decide to ignore some of the violations for expediency, and we will look at these as we go along. It is also critical not only to read through each form in the book, but to consider each form as you are performing logical modeling. It should be very clear, once we get to the end of the next chapter, that the Third Normal Form is not the magical form that some database architects would have you believe.

First Normal Form

The **First Normal Form** deals with the shape of attributes and records. It is the most important of all the normal forms.

This form is also used in the definition of the relational model of databases, and the definition of the First Normal Form is one of Codd's Twelve Rules, which are not actually about normalization, but rather a set of rules that define a relational database. These rules are listed and discussed in Appendix A.

Entities in First Normal Form will have the following characteristics:

- All attributes must be atomic, that is, only one single value represented in a single attribute in a single instance of an entity
- All instances in a table must contain the same number of values
- All instances in a table must be different

First Normal Form violations manifest themselves in the physical model with messy data handling situations, as we will see shortly.

All Attributes Must be Atomic

An attribute can only represent one single value, it may not be a group. This means there can be no arrays, no delimited data, and no multi-valued attributes stored in a field. To put it another way, the values stored in an attribute cannot be split into smaller parts. As examples, we will look at some common violations of this rule of the First Normal Form.

E-mail Address Fields

In an e-mail message, the e-mail address is typically stored in a format such as:

`name1@domain1.com;name2@domain2.com;name3@domain3.com`

This is a clear violation of First Normal Form as we are trying to store more than one e-mail address in a single `e-mail` field. Each e-mail address should form one separate field.

Normalization Techniques

Names

Consider the name "John Q Public". This is obviously a problem, as we have the first name, middle initial, and last name in a single field. Once we break the name into three parts, we get the fields `first_name`, `middle_initial` (or `middle_name`, which I prefer), and `last_name`. This is usually fine, since a person's name in the U.S.A. is generally considered to have three parts. In some situations, this may not be enough, and you may not know the number of parts until the user enters the data. Know your data requirements.

Telephone Numbers

Consider the case of the telephone number. American telephone numbers are of the form "1-423-555-1212" plus some possible extension number. From our previous examples, you can see that there are several fields embedded in that telephone number, not to mention possible extensions. Additionally, there is frequently the need to store more than just American telephone numbers in a database. The decision on how to handle this situation may be totally based on how often you store international phone numbers, as it might be impossible (might be, I haven't tried, so I cannot be one hundred percent sure) to build a table or set of entities to handle every situation.

So, for an American style telephone number, we would need five fields for each of the following parts: C-AAA-EEE-NNNN-XXXX

- (C) Country code – This is the one that we dial for numbers that are not within the area code, and signals to the phone that we are dialing a non-local number
- (AAA) Area code – Indicates a calling area that is located within a state
- (EEE) Exchange – Indicates a set of numbers within an area code
- (NNNN) Number – Number used to make individual phone numbers unique
- (XXXX) Extension – A number that must be dialed once you connected using the previous numbers

Addresses

You should know by now that all of an address should be broken up into fields for street address, city, state, and postal code (from here on we will ignore the internationalization factor, for brevity.) However, street address should also be broken down, in most cases, into number, street name, apartment number, and post office box. We will mention street addresses again shortly.

IP Addresses

IP addresses are a very interesting case because they appear to be four pieces of data, formed like BY1.BY2.BY3.BY4 where BY is short for Byte. This appears to be four different attributes, but is actually a representation of a single unsigned integer value based on the mathematical formula $(BY1 * 256^3) + (BY2 * 256^2) + (BY3 * 256^1) + (BY4 * 256^0)$. Hence, if you have IP address 24.32.1.128, it could be stored as $404750720 = (24 * 256^3) + (32 * 256^2) + (1 * 256^1) + (128)$. How you actually store this value will depend in great part to what you will be doing with the data. For example:

- If you deal with an IP address as four distinct values, you might store it in four different fields, possibly named `ipAddressPart1`, `ipAddressPart2`, `ipAddressPart3`, and `ipAddressPart4`. Note that, since there will always be exactly four parts, this type of storage does not violate the First Normal Form rules; all instances in an entity must contain the same number of values. This is covered in the next section.

- One valid reason to store the value as a single value is range checking. If you have one IP address and need to find out when an address falls between the two other IP addresses, storing the addresses as integers allows you to simply search for data with a where clause, such as:

"where `ipAddressCheck` is between `ipAddressLow` and `ipAddressHigh`".

We'll move on the second rule of the First Normal Form now.

All Instances in an Entity Must Contain the Same Number of Values

This is best illustrated with a quick example. If you have an entity that stores a person's name, then, if one row has one name, all rows must only have one name. If they might have two, all instances must be able to have two. If they may have a different number we have to deal with this a different way.

An example of a violation of this rule of the First Normal Form can be found in entities that have several fields with the same base name suffixed (or prefixed) with a number, such as `address_line_1`, `address_line_2`, etc. Usually this is an attempt to allow multiple values for a single field in an entity. In the rare cases where there is always precisely the same number of values, then there is technically no violation of First Normal Form. Even in such cases, it is still not generally a good design decision, as users can change their minds frequently. To overcome all of this, we would create a child entity to hold the values in the malformed entity. This will also allow us to have a virtually unlimited number of values where the previous solution had a finite (and small) number of possible values. One of the issues that you will have to deal with is that the child records you create will require sequencing information to get the actual rows properly organized for usage. Note that the actual implementation of addresses will certainly be based on requirements for the system that is being created.

We can use cardinality rules as described in the previous chapter to constrain the number of possible values. If we need to choke things back because our model states that we only need a maximum of two children, and a minimum of one child, cardinality provides the mechanism for this.

All Occurrences of a Record Type in an Entity must be Different

This one seems obvious, but needs to be stated. Basically, this indicates that every First Normal Form entity must have a primary (or unique) key. Take care, however, because just adding an artificial key to an entity might technically make the entity comply with the letter of the rule, but certainly not the purpose. In the next chapter we will expand upon this idea.

Programming Anomalies Avoided by First Normal Form

Violations of the First Normal Form are obvious and often very awkward if the columns affected are frequently accessed. The following examples will identify some of the situations that we can avoid by putting our entities in the First Normal Form.

Modifying Lists in a Single Field

The big problem with First Normal Form violations is that relational theory and SQL are not set up to handle non-atomic fields. Considering our previous example of the e-mail addresses attribute. Suppose that we have a table named `person` with the following schema:

```
CREATE TABLE person
(
    personId int NOT NULL IDENTITY,
    name varchar(100) NOT NULL,
    e-mailAddress varchar(1000) NOT NULL
)
```

Normalization Techniques

If we let our users have more than one e-mail address and store it in the e-mail address attribute, our `e-mail` field might look like: "Davidsons@d.com;ldavidson@e-mail.com". Also consider that many different users in the database might use the `Davidsons@d.com` e-mail address. If we need to change the e-mail address from `Davidsons@d.com` to `Davidsons@domain.com`, we would need to execute code like the following for every person that uses this e-mail address:

```
UPDATE person
SET e-mailAddress = replace(e-mailAddresses,'Davidsons@d.com',
      'Davidsons@domain.com')
WHERE e-mailAddress like '%Davidsons@d.com%'
```

This code doesn't seem like trouble, but what about the case where there is also the e-mail address `theDavidsons@d.com`? What if we don't want to change this value? Since the code that you write should work in *all* cases, this would be unacceptable, since the preceding UPDATE statement would have unwanted side effects in such cases.

Modifying Multi-Part Fields

The programming logic required to change part of the multi-part field can be very confusing. Take, for example, the case of telephone area codes. In the United States, we have more phones, pagers, cell phones, etc. than the creators of the area code system ever thought of, and so they frequently change or introduce new area codes.

If all values are stored in atomic containers, updating the area code would take a single, easy to follow, one-line SQL statement like this:

```
UPDATE phoneNumber
SET areaCode = '423'
WHERE areaCode = '615' AND exchange IN ('232','323',…,'989')
```

Instead, we get the following:

```
UPDATE phoneNumber
SET phoneNumber = REPLACE(phoneNumber,'-615-','-423-')
WHERE phoneNumber LIKE '_-615-___-____'
   AND substring(phoneNumber,7,3) IN ('232','323',…,'989')
```

Note that `substring()` *is a T-SQL Extension not in standard SQL.*

This example requires perfect formatting of the phone number data to work, and that seldom occurs without extreme amounts of code up front. All this when using a simple format would suffice to take care of all these issues.

Modifying Records with Variable Numbers of Facts

One of the main problems with allowing variable numbers of facts in a given record is dealing with the different situations that come up when you have to deal with one of the fields instead of the other. Say we have a very basic structured table such as:

```
CREATE TABLE payments
(
    paymentsId int NOT NULL IDENTITY,
```

```
    accountId int NOT NULL,
    payment1 money NOT NULL,
    payment2 money NULL
)
```

Where the user has to make two payments (for some reason), the following code snippet is indicative of what would be required to enter a payment:

```
UPDATE payments
SET payment1 = case WHEN payment1 IS NULL THEN 1000.00 ELSE payment1 END,
    payment2 = case WHEN payment1 IS NOT NULL AND payment2 IS NULL THEN
    1000.00 ELSE payment2 END
WHERE accountId = 1
```

Of course, this is not likely to be the exact manner for solving this problem, but even if this logic is done on the client side by giving multiple blocks for payments, or we pre-determine which of the payments needs to be made, it should still be clear that it is going to be problematic to deal with.

The alternative would be to have a table that is built like so:

```
CREATE TABLE payment
(
    paymentId int NOT NULL IDENTITY,
    accountId int NOT NULL, --foreign key to account table
    date datetime NOT NULL,
    amount money
)
```

Then, adding a payment would be as simple as adding a new record to the payment table:

```
INSERT payment (accountId, date, value)
VALUES (1, 'June 12 2000', $300.00)
```

This is certainly a better solution. One of the main problems with this example is that date is not an atomic data type (in other words, it is itself a multi-valued field). In fact, SQL Server simply has a datetime data type that is really several fields all rolled up into one; day, month, year, hour, minute, seconds, milliseconds, etc. The datetime data type is one of the annoying features of SQL Server that we frequently have to use for convenience reasons, but since it stores multiple values, it is not technically in First Normal Form. There is a host of functions in SQL Server designed to make up for the fact that datetime (and smalldatetime) are not proper relational database data types.

There are situations where it is prudent to implement our own date or time user-defined data types and deal with time variables in a reasonable manner.

Clues that Existing Data is not in First Normal Form

Next we're going to take a look at how you might go about recognizing whether the data in your database is already likely to be in First Normal Form or not.

Normalization Techniques

Data that Contains Non-Alphabetic Characters

By non-alphabetic characters we mean commas, brackets, parentheses, pipe characters, etc. These act as warning signs that we are dealing with a multi-valued field. However, be careful not to go to far. For instance, if we were designing a solution to hold a block of text, we have probably normalized too much if we have a word entity, a sentence entity, and a paragraph entity. This clue is more applicable to entities that have delimited lists.

Fieldnames with Numbers at the End

As we have noted, an obvious example would be finding entities with *child1*, *child2*, etc., attributes or, my favorite, *UserDefined1*, *UserDefined2*, etc. These are very blatantly wrong.

This is a very common holdover from the days of flat file databases. Multi-table data access was costly, so they put many fields in a single table. This is very detrimental for relational database systems.

Second Normal Form

The next three normal forms we will look at are all concerned with the relationships between attributes in an entity and the key in that entity, and all deal with minimizing improper functional dependencies. We will see that certain kinds of relationship between the key and other fields are undesirable and need to be eliminated. As you will recall from Chapter 3, being functionally dependent implies that, if we run a function on one value (call it Value1) and the output of this function is *always* the exact same value (call it Value2) then Value2 is functionally dependent on Value1.

For example, consider the following situation. We have three values: Owner Name, Product Type, and Serial Number. Serial Numbers imply a particular Product Type, so they are functionally dependent. If we change the Product Type but fail to change the Serial Number, then our Serial Number and Product Type will no longer match and the three values will no longer be of any value. The user will have no idea if the Owner owns the item denoted by the Serial Number or the Product Type.

The following saying will help you to understand what the Second Normal Form, Third Normal Form, and Boyce-Codd Normal Form are concerned with:

> *Non-key fields must provide a detail about the key, the whole key, and nothing but the key.*

This means that non-key fields have to further describe the key of the record, and not describe any other attributes.

Let's start with the **Second Normal Form** which is perhaps the simplest of these normal forms. An entity complying with Second Normal Form has to have the following characteristics:

- ❑ The entity must be in First Normal Form
- ❑ Each attribute must be a fact describing the entire key

> **Second Normal Form is only relevant when a composite key (a key composed of two or more columns) exists in the entity.**

153

The Entity must be in First Normal Form

This is very important; you need to go through each step of the normalization process to eliminate problems in your data. It may be hard to locate Second Normal Form problems if you still have First Normal Form problems.

Each Non-Key Attribute Must Describe the Entire Key

This indicates that each non-key attribute must depict the entity described by **all** attributes in the key, and not simply parts. If this is not true and any of the non-key attributes are functionally dependent on a subset of the attributes in the key, then you are going to have data modification anomalies. For example, consider the following structure:

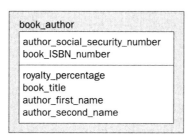

The `book_ISBN_number` attribute uniquely identifies the book, and `author_social_security_number` uniquely identifies the author. Hence, these two columns create one key which uniquely identifies an author for a book. The problem is with the other attributes. The `royalty_percentage` attribute defines the royalty that the author is receiving for the book, so this refers to the entire key. The `book_title` describes the book, but does not describe the author at all. The same goes for the `author_first_name` and `author_last_name` fields. They describe the author, but not the book at all.

This is a prime example of a functional dependency. For every value you have in the `book_ISBN_number` column, you must have the same book title and author. But for every `book_ISBN_number`, you do not have to have the same `royalty_percentage` – this is actually dependent on *both* the author and the book deal, and not one or the other.

Hence we have problems, so we need to create three separate entities to store this data:

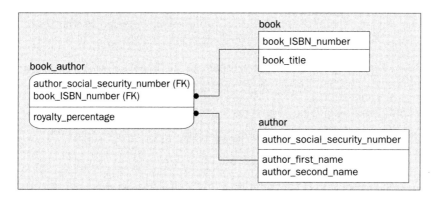

Normalization Techniques

After we split the entities, we see that the `royalty_percentage` attribute is still a fact describing the author writing the book, the `book_title` is now a fact describing the entity defined by the `book_ISBN_number`, and the author's name attributes are facts describing the `author` entity, identified by the `author_social_security_number`.

Note that the `book` to `book_author` relationship is an identifying type relationship. Second Normal Form violations are frequently modeled logically as identifying relationships where the primary key of the new entity is migrated to the entity where the original problem occurred.

Our previous illustration demonstrates this concept quite well. In the corrected example we have isolated the functional dependencies such that attributes that are functionally dependent on another attribute are functionally dependent on the key.

Since there are no columns which are not functionally dependent on a part of the key, these entities are in Second Normal Form.

Programming Problems Avoided by Second Normal Form

All of the programming issues that arise with the Second Normal Form, as well as the Third and Boyce-Codd Normal Forms, deal with functional dependencies. The programming issue is quite simple. If you can run a statement like this on our example table:

```
UPDATE book_author
SET book_title = 'Database Design'
WHERE book_ISBN_number = '923490328948039'
```

and modify more than one row, there is a problem with our structures.

The real crux of the problem is that many programmers do not have their database design thinking caps on when they are churning out applications, so we get tables created with client screens like this:

Consider what happens if we use this screen to change the title of a multi-author book in a database which has `book_author` tables like that shown in the first diagram in the previous section, *Each Non-Key Attribute Must Describe the Entire Key*. If the book has two authors, there will be two `book_author` tables for this book. Now a user opens the editing screen and changes the title, as shown here. When he saves the change, it will only alter the `book_author` table for **Fred Smith**, not the `book_author` table for his co-author. The two `book_author` tables, originally for the same book, now show different titles.

This problem is rectified by using the Second Normal Form, as shown in the second diagram in that section. In this form, the `book` table will connect to two `book_author` tables. Changing the title in this editor screen will change the `book_title` field in this single `book` table; the two `book_author` tables are only linked to the `book` table by the `book_ISBN_number` field, so the database will still show both authors as having co-authored the same book. Everything remains in synch.

Clues that your Entities are Not in Second Normal Form

The clues for detecting whether your entities are in Second Normal Form are not quite as straightforward as the clues for the First Normal Form. They take some careful thought, and some thorough examination of your structures.

Repeating Key Fieldname Prefixes

This situation is one of the dead giveaways. Revisiting our previous example:

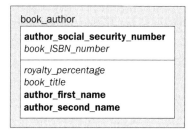

we had `author_first_name` and `author_second_name`, which are functionally dependent on `author_social_security_number`. We also have `book_title` and `book_ISBN_number` with the same situation.

Having such obvious prefixes is not always the case, but it is a good thing to look for as this is a rather common mistake made by novice designers.

Repeating Groups of Data

More difficult to recognize are the repeating groups of data. Imagine executing multiple SELECT statements on a table, each time retrieving all rows (if possible), ordered by each of the important columns. If there is a functionally dependent attribute on one of the attributes, anywhere one of the fields is equal to X, we will see the dependent field, Y.

Take a look at some example entries from the following table.

author_**social_security_number**	book_**ISBN_number**	royalty_ percentage
DELA-777-888	1-861-000-156-7	2
DELA-777-888	1-861-000-338-1	3
GIBB-423-4421	1-861-000-156-7	3

book_title	author_first_name	author_second_name
Instant Tiddlywinks	Vervain	Delaware
Beginning Ludo	Vervain	Delaware
Instant Tiddlywinks	Gordon	Gibbon

(This is a single table but I had to split it so that it could fit on the page.)

Book_title is, of course, dependent on book_ISBN_Number, so any time we see an ISBN number = 1-861-000-156-7, we can be sure that the book title is "Instant Tiddlywinks". If it isn't, then there's something wrong in the database.

Composite Keys with a Non-Foreign Key

If there is more than one attribute in the key that isn't a foreign key, any attributes that describe those attributes are likely to be violating the Second Normal Form.

Coding Around the Problem

Scouring the database code is one good way of discovering problems, based on the lifespan of the system we are analyzing. Many times a programmer will simply write code to make sure the Second Normal Form violation is not harmful to the data, rather than remodeling it into a proper structure. At one time in the history of the Relational Database Management System, this may have been the only way to handle this situation; however, now that technology has caught up with the relational theory, this is far less the case.

It is important to understand that I am not trying to make the case that theory has changed a bit due to technology. Actually, relational theory has been very stable throughout the years with little changing in the past decade. Ten years ago, we had quite a few problems making a normalized system operational in the hardware and operating system constraints we had to deal with, so corners were cut in our models for "performance" reasons.

Using current hardware, there is no need to even begin to cut normalization corners for performance. It is best to resolve these issues with SQL joins instead of spaghetti code to maintain denormalized data. Of course, at this point in the design process, it is best to not even consider the topic of implementation, performance, or any subject where we are not simply working towards proper logical storage of data.

Third Normal Form

An entity that is in **Third Normal Form** will have the following characteristics:

- ❑ The entity must be in Second Normal Form
- ❑ An entity is in violation of Third Normal Form if a non-key attribute is a fact about another non-key attribute

We can rephrase the second bullet like so:

All attributes must be a fact about the key, and nothing but the key.

Chapter 6

The Third Normal Form differs from the Second Normal Form in that it deals with the relationship of non-key data to non-key data. The problems are the same and many of the symptoms are the same, but it can be harder to locate the general kind of violations that this form tends to deal with. Basically, the main difference is that, data in one field, instead of being dependent on the key, is actually dependent on data in another non-key field. The requirements for the Third Normal Form are as follows.

The Entity must be in Second Normal Form

Once again, this is very important. It may be hard to locate Third Normal Form problems if you still have Second Normal Form problems.

Non-Key Attributes Cannot Describe Non-Key Attributes

If any of the attributes are functionally dependent on an attribute other than the key, then we are again going to have data modification anomalies. Since we are in Second Normal Form already, we have proven that all of our attributes are reliant on the whole key, but we have not looked at the relationship of the attributes to one another.

In the following example diagram, we take our book entity and extend it to include the publisher and the city where the publisher is located.

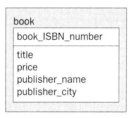

Title defines the title for the book defined by the book_ISBN_number, price indicates the price of the book, publisher_name describes the book's publisher, but publisher_city doesn't make sense in this context, as it does not directly describe the book.

To correct this situation, we need to create a different entity to identify the publisher information.

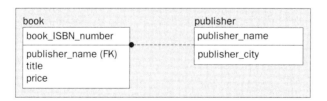

Now the publisher entity has only data concerning the publisher, and the book entity has book information. What makes this so valuable is that, now, if we want to add information to our schema concerning the publisher, for instance contact information, or an address, it is very obvious where we add that information. Now we have our publisher_city attribute identifying the publisher, not the book. Once we get into physical modeling, we will discuss the merits of having the publisher_name attribute as the primary key, but for now this is a reasonable primary key, and a reasonable set of attributes.

Note that the resolution of this problem was to create a **non-identifying** relationship publisher → book. Since the malevolent attributes were not in the key to begin with, they do not go there now.

All Attributes Must be a Fact Describing the Key, and Nothing but the Key

If it sounds familiar, it should. This little saying is the backbone for the whole group of normal forms concerned with the relationship between the key and non-key attributes. Remember it, as it may save your database project one day.

Programming Problems Avoided by the Third Normal Form

While the methods of violating the Third Normal Form are very close to the violations of the Second Normal Form, there are a few important differences. As we are not dealing with key values, every attribute's relationship to every non-key attribute needs to be considered, and so does every combination of attributes. In the book example, we had the following entity structure:

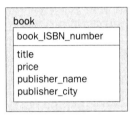

While, for the sake of brevity, I jumped right to the obvious violation, it is not always so easy to spot Third Normal Form violations. Every attribute should be considered against every other attribute. If entities are of reasonable size (I generally find that ten to twenty attributes in an entity is probably as many as you can have without violating some normalization rule, though this does not always hold), then the process of weeding out Third Normal Form problems will not be too lengthy a process. In our example, we need to check each attribute against the other three attributes. As there are four attributes, we need to consider the $N * (N - 1)$ or $(4 * 3) = 12$ (ignoring the fact that we will be checking some values more than once) different permutations of attribute relations to be safe. In our example entity we must check:

- `title` against: `price`, `publisher_name`, and `publisher_city`
- `price` against: `title`, `publisher_name`, and `publisher_city`
- `publisher_name` against: `price`, `title`, and `publisher_city`
- `publisher_city` against: `price`, `title`, and `publisher_name`

From this we notice that, when we check `publisher_name` against the other three attributes, it becomes clear that `publisher_city` is functionally dependent on it, hence a Third Normal Form violation.

Once you have designed a few thousand entities, you will begin to see common attributes that will jump out as problems, and only a few attributes will have to be considered in your normalization checks. We will look at many such examples during the case study section of this chapter.

Note too that our example has tailored names to make it seem simple, but in reality, names are often far more cryptic. Consider the following entity:

These names are probably less cryptic than those you might actually come across in some legacy database entities; however, they're already ambiguous enough to cause problems. City seems almost fine here, unless you consider that most books don't have a city attribute, but publishers might. The following example code shows what happens if we want to change the city attribute and keep it in synch.

Take, for example, the situation where we have the table as built previously:

```
CREATE TABLE book
(
    ISBN varchar(20) NOT NULL,
    pubname varchar(60) NOT NULL,
    city varchar(60) NOT NULL,
    title varchar(60) NOT NULL
    price money NOT NULL
)
```

This has the Third Normal Form violations that we have identified. Consider the situation where we want to update the city field for ISBN 23232380237 from a value of Virginia Beach to a value of Nashville. We first would update the single record:

```
UPDATE book
SET city = 'Nashville'
WHERE ISBN = '23232380237'
```

But since we had the functional dependency of the publisher to city relationship, we now have to update all of the books that have the same publisher name to the new value as well:

```
UPDATE book
SET city = 'Nashville'
WHERE city = 'Virginia Beach'
    AND pubname = 'Phantom Publishing' --previous publisher name
```

While this is the proper way to ensure that the batch code updates the city properly, as well as the book, in most cases this code will be buried in your application, not tied together with a transaction, much less one in a batch. Any errors in one UPDATE statement and your data can be compromised. For existing SQL Server applications that you are redesigning, you can employ the SQL Server Profiler to check what SQL is actually being sent to SQL Server from your application.

Normalization Techniques

Clues that your Entities are not in Third Normal Form

The clues for Third Normal Form are quite similar to those for Second Normal Form, as they are trying to solve the same sort of problem – making sure that all non-key attributes refer to the key of the entity.

Multiple Fields with the Same Prefix

Revisiting our previous example:

It is obvious that `publisher_name` and `publisher_city` are multiple fields with the same prefix. In some cases the prefix used may not be so obvious, such as `pub_name`, `pblish_city`, or even `location_pub`; all good reasons to establish a decent naming standard.

Repeating Groups of Data

Much the same as for the Second Normal Form, but you need to consider more permutations – as we have discussed.

Summary Data

One of the common violations of the Third Normal Form is **summary data**. This is where fields are added to the parent entity that refer to the children records and summarize them. Summary data has been one of the most frequently necessary evils that we have had to deal with throughout the history of the relational database. There are several new features in SQL Server 2000 that we will employ to help avoid summary data in our implementation, but in logical modeling there is *absolutely* no place for it. Not only is summary data not functionally dependent on non-key fields, it is dependent on non-entity fields. This causes all sorts of confusion as we shall demonstrate. Summary data should be reserved either for physical design or the Data Warehousing steps.

For clarification, take our following example of an auto dealer. They have an entity listing all of the automobiles they sell, and they have an entity recording each automobile sale:

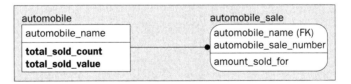

Instead of calculating the total number of vehicles sold and their value when needed, the designer has decided to add fields in the parent entity that refer to the child records and summarize them. This may seem fine, but the complexity of the implemented system has increased by at least an order of magnitude, as we will have to have triggers on the `automobile_sale` entity that calculate these values for any change in the `automobile_sale` entity. If this is a highly active database with frequent records added to the `automobile_sale` entity, this will tend to slow the database down considerably. On the other hand, if it is an often inactive database, then there will be very few records in the child entity, and so the performance gains made by being able to quickly find the numbers of vehicles sold and their value will be very small anyway.

161

Boyce-Codd Normal Form

During my discussions of the Second and Third Normal Forms, I was purposefully vague with the word **key**. As I have mentioned before, a key can be *any* candidate key, whether the primary key or an alternate key. However, the main concern of the Second Normal Form and the Third Normal Form is the primary key.

The **Boyce-Codd Normal Form** is actually a better constructed replacement for both the Second and Third Normal Forms. Note that, to be in Boyce-Codd Normal Form, there is no mention of Second Normal Form or Third Normal Form. The Boyce-Codd Normal Form actually encompasses them both, and is defined as follows:

- All attributes are fully dependent on a key
- An entity is in Boyce-Codd Normal Form if every determinant is a key

So let's look at each of these rules individually.

All Attributes are Fully Dependent on a Key

We can rephrase this like so:

All attributes must be a fact about a key, and nothing but a key.

This is a slight but important deviation from our previous rules for Second Normal Form and Third Normal Form. In this case, we don't specify *the entire* key or just *the* key – now it is *a* key. How does this differ? Well, it does and it doesn't. It basically expands the meaning of Second Normal Form and Third Normal Form to deal with the very typical situation where we have more than one key.

It is noted that the attribute must be fully dependent on a key, and this key is defined as the **unique identifier**. The unique identifier should be thought of as the address or pointer for the entity, regardless of whether we use a natural key or otherwise. The **entity**, as defined, is the logical representation of a single object, either real or imaginary. If you think of *every* key as the entity's ID badge, or Social Security Number, or whole name, you can begin to understand what each of the attributes should be like.

For example, let's take a person who works for a company and model them. First we choose our key, let's say Social Security Number.

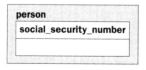

Normalization Techniques

Then we start adding the other attributes we know about our employees – their name, hair color, eye color, the badge number they are given, their driver's license number, etc. So we have the following entity:

Careful study of the entity shows that it is in Third Normal Form, since each of the attributes further describes the entity. The `first_name`, `height`, `badge_number`, and others all refer to the entity. The same may be said for the `social_security_number`. It has been chosen as the key, primarily because it was the first thing we came upon. In logical modeling, the choice of which field is a primary key isn't all that meaningful, although it is usually better to choose the right one. (A large discussion of proper primary keys will be dealt with in Chapter 10.) In most cases, even in the logical modeling phase, we will simply use an artificial key as discussed in Chapter 3.

The following sentence basically explains Second Normal Form and Third Normal Form:

> **All attributes must further describe the entity, the whole entity, and nothing but the entity.**

As long as you understand this concept, data modeling and normalization become much easier.

An Entity is in Boyce-Codd Normal Form if Every Determinant is a Key

The second part of the quest for Boyce-Codd Normal Form is to make sure that every determinant is a key, or a unique identifier for the entity. Our definition of a determinant in Chapter 3 was as follows:

> **Any attribute or combination of attributes on which any other attribute or combination of attributes is functionally dependent.**

Based on our study of the Second and Third Normal Forms, we can see that this is basically the definition of a key. Since all attributes that are not keys must be functionally dependent on a key, the definition of a determinant is the same as the definition of a key.

The Boyce-Codd Normal Form simply extends the previous normal forms by saying that an entity may have many keys, and all attributes must be dependent on one of these keys. We have simplified this a bit by noting that every key must uniquely identify the entity, and every non-key attribute must describe the entity.

What the Boyce-Codd Normal Form acknowledges is that there can be many keys in an entity. These are referred to as candidate or alternate keys. One interesting thing that should be noted is that each key is a determinant for all other keys. This is because, in every place where you see one key value, you could replace it with the other key value without losing meaning. This is not to say that an alternate key cannot change values – not at all. The driver's license number is a good key, but if the Department of Motor Vehicles issues all new numbers, it is still a key, and it will still describe the entity. If the value of any candidate key changes, this is perfectly acceptable.

With this definition in mind, let's take the example entity we are modeling for this section and look at it again.

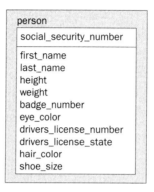

What we will be looking for now is attributes or groups of attributes that are dependent on the key, and also will be unique to each instance of this entity.

First_name will not be by itself, and it would not be a very good assumption to assume that first_name and last_name are. (It all depends on the size of the target set as to whether or not you are willing to accept this. You would likely want to include middle initial and title, but still this is not a good key.) Height describes the person, but is not unique. The same is true for weight. Badge_number certainly should be unique, so we will make it a key. (Note that we don't have badge_issued_date, as that would refer to the badge and doesn't help the Boyce-Codd Normal Form example.) drivers_license_number is probably unique, but you should definitely consider variations across state. hair_color and shoe_size describe the person, but neither could be considered unique. Even if you take the person's height, weight, eye_color, hair_color, and shoe_size together, you could not guarantee uniqueness between two random people. So now we model the entity as:

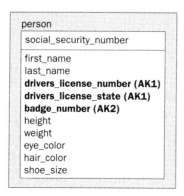

Normalization Techniques

We now have three keys for this object. When we do the physical modeling, we will choose the proper key from the keys we have defined, or use an artificial key. As discussed in Chapter 3, an artificial key is simply a value which is used as a pointer to an object, much like `badge_number` is a pointer that a company uses to identify an employee, or the government using Social Security Numbers to identify individuals in the United States.

It is also worth considering that an SSN is not always a very good key either. Even if you are dealing only with people in the USA, there are plenty of people that do not have a SSN. And certainly if you ever have to accommodate people from outside the USA, then SSN will never work – take it from someone who has had to fix systems with this assumption! It will certainly depend on the situation, as there are many situations where you are required to have a SSN, and some where you must either have a SSN or Green Card to identify the user as a valid resident of the US. The situation will always dictate the eventual solution, and it is simply up to the data architect to choose the appropriate path.

When choosing a key, we always try to make sure that keys do not overlap. For instance, `height` is not a unique key, but `height` and `badge_number` is! It is important to make certain that individual parts of unique keys cannot be guaranteed unique by themselves, otherwise mistakes can be made by accidentally putting non-unique data in the columns that need to be unique.

Clues and Programming Anomalies

The clues for determining that an entity is in Boyce-Codd Normal Form are the same as for Second Normal Form and Third Normal Form. The programming anomalies cured by the Boyce-Codd Normal Form are the same too.

The main point to mention here is that, if you get all your determinants modeled during this phase of the design, when you go to implement the database you will be far more likely to implement the determinants as unique keys. This will prevent users from entering non-unique values in the columns that need to have unique values in them.

This completes our overview of the first four normal forms. We will look at the Fourth and Fifth Normal Forms in the next chapter, but now we'll implement our newly learned concepts into our case study.

Case Study

For this chapter, we will go through each of the normal forms and correct our model according to the rules, then move on to a completed diagram.

First Normal Form

Our model has a few violations of the First Normal Form. We will break down each of the different violations that may occur.

All Attributes Must be Atomic

We have one example of this sort of violation. It occurs in the `statement` entity. We should recall that this entity represents the statement that the bank sends each month so that the client can reconcile all of the checks they have hand entered as they actually occurred. The `[balancingItems]` attribute contains all of the transactions that the bank has recorded and needs to be matched up to items in the register. However, this attribute will contain many rows and many fields, hardly atomic.

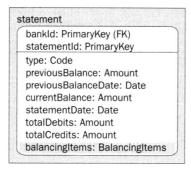

So, we need to add a new entity to contain these items. As we do not know exactly what will go into this entity, we will let the attributes migrate from the `statement` entity, then add another pointer to the primary key for uniqueness.

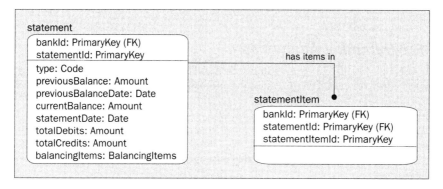

A different type of violation of this same kind must also be looked at. Consider the `payee` entity and the two fields `address` and `phoneNumber`.

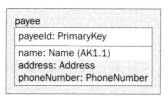

For our example, we will just look at the `address` attribute. The address is made up of several parts, the street address lines (usually we are happy with two lines to store street information), city, state, and zip code. We will also expand the `phoneNumber` field as we discussed earlier.

Once we have finished this process, we are left with the following result:

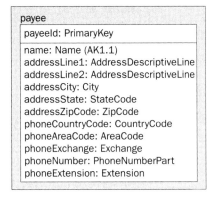

There are no fields now in this example which obviously violate the First Normal Form and therefore are not atomic. Actually, we could make the case that the `addressLine1` field is not atomic, since it will contain street number, street name, and other pieces of information. However, we are not going to model these attributes in our example diagram yet in an attempt to keep things simple.

Notice that we created domains for each new attribute. `addressLine1` and `addressLine2` are the same sort of item. Also of note is the `phoneNumber` attribute. It has the same name as before, but it has a different meaning, as a phone number is made up of country code, area code, exchange, and number. As it has a different meaning, we created a new domain with a new name, since in practice we may still have entities that use the domain.

All Occurrences of a Record Type Must Contain the Same Number of Values

In our new `payee` entity, we have put together a common set of attributes that violate this part of the rule, the `addressLine1` and `addressLine2` fields. While this is a common solution to the address problem, it is a violation nonetheless. Having a fixed number of address line fields has bitten me several times when addresses needed more, sometimes even four or five of them. Since not every address will have the same number of items, this is a problem. We solve this by adding another child entity for the address line information:

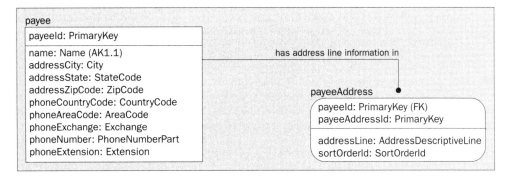

This may seem a bit odd, and it is, considering the way databases have been developed for long periods of time. However, this address design gives us the flexibility to store as many pieces of information as we may need, instead of having to add columns if the situation requires it. This is also a good example of normalization creating more entities.

Chapter 6

All Occurrences of a Record Type in an Entity Must be Different

We have begun to take care of this by adding primary keys and alternate keys to our entities. Note that simply adding an artificial key will not take care of this particular rule. One of our last physical modeling tasks will be to verify that all of our entities have at least one key defined that does not contain a non-migrated artificial key.

Boyce-Codd Normal Form

Since Boyce-Codd is actually an extension of the Second and Third Normal Forms, we can consider every one of the violations we have discussed all together.

Summary Data

Summary data fields are generally the easiest violations to take care of. This is because we can usually just prune the values from our entities. For example, in the `account` entity, we can remove the `[Running Total]` attribute, as it can be obtained by summing values that are stored in the `transaction` entity. This leaves us with:

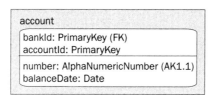

On the other hand, we have what appear to be summary fields in the `statement` entity:

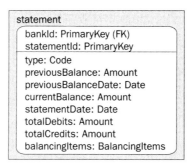

We have `previousBalance`, `currentBalance`, etc. – in fact, all of the fields other than `type` – referring to some other entity's values. However, in this case, we might want to accept this. As the `statement` entity is referring to a document, namely the statement from the bank, it could well come in handy to have these fields so we can store what the bank *thinks* is on the statement. We will likely want to keep these fields and use them to validate the data we will be storing in the `statementItem` entity.

Normalization Techniques

Multiple Fields with the Same Prefix

We have a very good example of this kind of problem in the `payee` entity we have created. `phoneCountryCode`, `phoneAreaCode`, etc., all have the same prefix (note that things won't always be so obvious, as we have discussed previously); likewise for `addressCity`, etc.

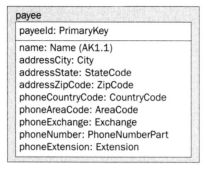

Phone numbers and addresses are technically things in and of themselves. Each of the phone fields doesn't really describe the `payee` further, but the existence of a phone number does. The same goes for the `address` fields. Hence we break them down further like so:

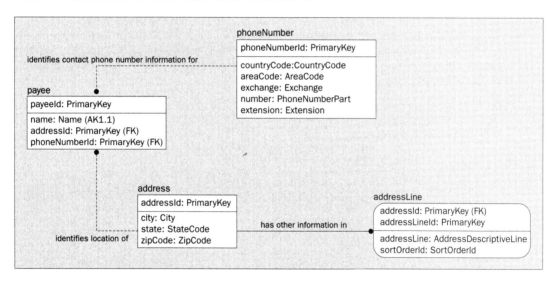

Now we have satisfied the idea that every field refers to a key, as the `address` and `phoneNumber` refer to the payee's address and phone number, the `address` is defined by its city, state, and zip, plus the street information in the `addressLine` entity. The `phoneNumber` is defined by its attributes as well.

Every Determinant Must be a Key

This is where things can get messy. Consider the `payee` entity in our previous example. The `payeeId`, a primary key, and `name` are the determinants for the entity. As we have discussed previously, we have the following set of dependencies:

- For every value of `payeeId` you must have the same `name` value

❑ For every value of `name`, you must have the same value for `addressId` and `phoneNumberId`

❑ It is not true that, for every value in `addressId` and `phoneNumberId`, you have to have the same value for `name`, as an address or phone number might be used for several payees

The real issue here is choosing a proper set of keys. Using an artificial key as a pointer, even in the logical modeling phase, tends to cover up a major issue. Every entity must contain unique values, and this unique value must not include just a single meaningless value, as an artificial key is meaningless except as an ownership pointer. In the case where there is more than one key, we need to identify a candidate key from the migrated key and another attribute in the entity.

First we take the phone number entity:

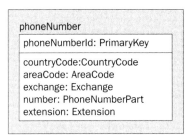

It has no key defined, so we must make one. In this case, the entire entity *without the primary key* will be a key. This illustrates one of the main reasons to maintain single themed entities. Now that we have the phone number isolated, we are able to make certain that if two payees have the same phone numbers, we don't duplicate this value. By doing this we keep things clear in our later usage of these values, as if we see duplicate phone numbers, things will get confusing.

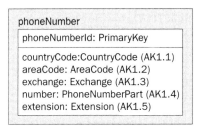

Next we look at the `address` entity:

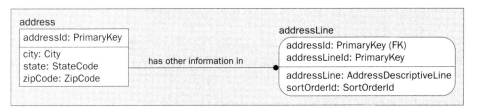

This is a very interesting case to deal with. There is no way that we can make the `city`, `state`, and `zipCode` unique, as we will almost certainly have more than one address of the same type. In this case, the uniqueness is determined by the `city`, `state`, `zipCode`, plus any `addressLine` items, which is a valid situation. We may not have any uniqueness on the values in the `addressLine` entity either, since as it is a logical part of the `address` entity, and `address` relies on it for uniqueness. We cannot very well model into the situation that only one address may contain the information "101 Main Street". This will not do.

We will not implement this situation in this precise manner, because it is too difficult. But, logically, this is a more appropriate way to model the data at this point.

Finally, consider the `transaction` entity:

```
transaction
bankId: PrimaryKey (FK)
accountId: PrimaryKey (FK)
transactionId: PrimaryKey
date: Date
number: AlphaNumericNumber (AK1.1)
description: Description
amount: Amount
type: Code
```

In this set of attributes, we have a key which is made up completely of migrated keys (`bankId`, `accountId`) and another artificial key. Basically, the meaning of this is that the migrated account key defines part of the transaction and it is up to us to look for the proper additional attribute. In this case it will be the `number`, as this is the number that the bank uses to identify a transaction, and we had previously chosen it as a key of its own:

```
transaction
bankId: PrimaryKey (FK) (AK1.1)
accountId: PrimaryKey (FK) (AK1.2)
transactionId: PrimaryKey
date: Date
number: AlphaNumericNumber (AK1.3)
description: Description
amount: Amount
type: Code
```

We must then go through each of the other entities, making sure a proper key is assigned, and more importantly, that there are no attributes that have functional dependencies on another attribute. Of course, this is if we have determined enough attributes at this point, as, in the case of `statementItem`, we have not determined any values.

Consider also that, now, `bankId`, `accountId`, and `transactionId` functionally determine the attribute `number`, and `bankId`, `accountId`, and `number` functionally determine the `transactionId`. This is a valid situation, which is pretty interesting!

One additional point should be made concerning the subtyped entities of `transaction`:

```
check
bankId: PrimaryKey (FK)
accountId: PrimaryKey (FK)
transactionId: PrimaryKey (FK)
payeeId: PrimaryKey (FK)
usageType: Code
signature: Blob
```

No additional keys are required for this entity as it is in a one-to-one relationship with the transaction entity, hence its primary key is a valid key.

Model

Here is our model after normalizing up to the Boyce-Codd Normal Form. Note that many of the common modification anomalies should be cleared up. It is far from complete, however. To keep the model simple, we still have not added any further information to it. We will present a final model with additional fields in the last section of the logical modeling part of the book.

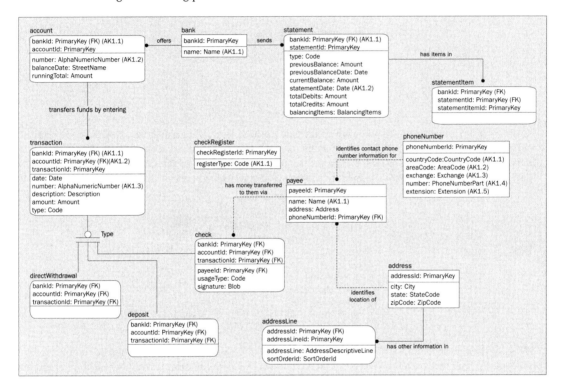

Summary

In this chapter, we have begun the process of turning our random table structures into structures that will make the storage of data much more reliable. By building these structures in a very specific manner, we will derive a set of entities that are resilient to change and that fewer modification anomalies.

This can all seem from the outside like one of the more baffling processes within computer science. This probably explains why a lot of developers don't normalize their databases. However, there's no reason why it should be so. Behind the sometimes esoteric jargon is a set of simple, well-formed rules that lay down how databases should be designed. As for the end result, the case study should demonstrate that the resulting entities we developed are cleaner, tidier, and safer for our data entry, even though the data that is stored will look less and less meaningful to the casual observer.

Now the obvious question: Can we normalize our data any further? Since I have alerted you to the fact that there are seven normal forms of interest, and we have only looked at four, you know the answer to this question is yes.

On the other hand, *should* we normalize further? Yes! The Third Normal Form has long been identified as the most important plateau of data modeling, and it may be that, when we come to physically implement our solution, we do not go beyond this level. However, we are currently in the logical modeling phase and we must not concern ourselves yet with performance issues; we should aim for an ideal model. Working through the next normal forms will uncover addition problems with our data that we may not see otherwise.

transaction

- transactionId: int NOT NULL
- accountId: int NOT NULL (FK) (AK1.1)
- number: varchar(20) NOT NULL (AK1.2)
- date: smalldatetime NOT NULL
- description: varchar(1000) NOT NULL
- amount: money NOT NULL
- signature: varchar(20) NOT NULL
- payeeId: int NULL (FK)
- userId: int NULL (FK)
- statementItemId: int NULL (FK)
- transactionTypeId: int NOT NULL (FK)
- autoTimestamp: timestamp NOT NULL

accountReconcile

- accountReconcileId: int IDENTITY
- statementId: int NOT NULL (FK) (AK1.1)
- reconcileDate: smalldatetime NOT NULL (AK1.2)
- autoTimestamp: timestamp NOT NULL

7

Advanced Normalization Topics

Introduction

If you have heard it once, you have probably heard it a million times: "This database is in Third Normal Form, so let's build tables!" In this chapter we will look at further methods for normalization that are just as important as the first three, though they are not commonly used because of perceived drawbacks in terms of both the time taken to implement them, and the cost in performance of the resulting database. We looked in the previous chapter at some of the different programming anomalies that the Third Normal Form remedies, but, as we shall discuss below, there may still be some problems remaining in our logical design, mostly caused by the presence of ternary relationships. In essence, while most people think they have completed the normalization process on reaching Third Normal Form, what they really should be concerned with is *at least* reaching Third Normal Form in their logical model. A degree of judgement is required in physically implementing a design, and determining what level of normalization is appropriate. However as a general guide, the designer should always attempt to normalize all entities to as high a form as possible. If, in testing the system, there are found to be performance issues, then these can be addressed by denormalizing the system, as will be touched on briefly later in this chapter and also in Chapter 14.

> *This chapter is, in my opinion, the most critical to understand. The methods in this chapter are exceedingly easy to do, and if I have done my job, easy to understand. There are some very important misconceptions about the normal forms past the third being meaningless and they are very wrong. I feel that once you actually normalize to the Fourth level, you will not even consider going back.*

Fourth Normal Form

Our rules of normalization so far resolved redundancies amongst columns in an entity, but did not resolve problems that arise from entities having composite primary keys whilst still possessing redundant data between rows. Normalizing entities to **Fourth Normal Form** addresses such problems. In a simple case, moving to Fourth Normal Form will take care of problems such as the modelling of an attribute that should store a single value but it ends up storing multiple values. The second type of problem is more elusive. Consider the case of an entity of students in a class (note that multiple classes present a very different problem). We need to store the teacher of each student, so we put those in the classAssignment entity as:

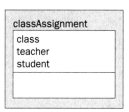

However this is unsatisfactory since we have the related attributes class, teacher and student in the same entity. To change this to Fourth Normal Form, we have to break up this ternary relationship. In order to do this we note that the relationship centers on the class attribute, since a class has one or more teachers, and indeed one or more students. Our modified design now looks like this:

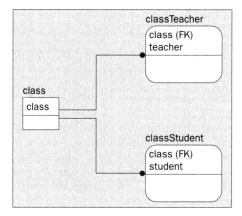

This example illustrates that the following conditions must be met for an entity to be in Fourth Normal Form:

- The entity must be in **Boyce-Codd Normal Form** (BCNF). This condition ensures that all keys will be appropriately defined, and all values in an entity will be properly dependent on its key.

- There must not be more than one **multi-valued dependency** (MVD) represented in the entity. No more than one attribute can store multiple values that relate to a key in any entity, otherwise there will be data duplication. In addition it should be ensured that we don't repeat single valued attributes for every multi-valued one.

We shall look at a few examples to help make these ideas clearer. Let's first look at the three main forms that Fourth Normal Form violations take:

- Ternary relationships
- Lurking multi-valued attributes
- Status and other attributes of which we need to know the previous values

Ternary Relationships

We briefly looked at ternary relationships back in Chapter 3. Not all real relationships will manifest themselves in a binary-type relationship, and the ternary relationship is really quite common. Any place where we see three (or more) identifying or mandatory non-identifying relationships in an entity, we are likely to have trouble.

Take as an example, a situation where we have designed a set of entities to support a conference planner, storing information concerning the `session`, `presenter`, and `room` where a session is to be given:

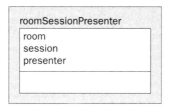

Let us also assume the following set of very open business rules are being enforced:

- More than one presenter may be listed to give a presentation
- A presentation may span more than one room

The figure below models the relationship: **presenter-*presents*-session-*in*-room**.

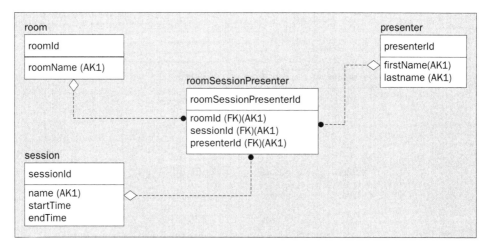

As a reminder, each of these values is nullable, as denoted by the diamond on the opposite end of the line.

Each of these entities is a Boyce-Codd Normal Form entity; however the relationship between the three is troubling. Let's look at a set of sample data:

Session	Presenter	Room
101	Davidson	River Room
202	Davidson	Stream Room
202	Hazel	Stream Room
404	Hawkins	Brook Room
404	Hawkins	Stream Room

In the first row, there is no problem, as we have one row for the `session` *101*, which has one `presenter` *Davidson* and one `room`, the *River Room*. A problem becomes apparent in the next two rows, as one `session` *202* has two different `presenters`, and yet a single `room`. This forces us to repeat data unnecessarily in the `room` attribute, since we have now stored in two places that `session` *202* is in the *Stream Room*. If the `session` moves, we have to change it in two places, and if we forget this property, and update the `room` based on a value that we are not currently displaying (for example through the use of an artificial key), then we end up with:

202	Davidson	Stream Room
202	Hazel	'Changed to Room'

In this example, we have duplicated data in the `session` and `room` attributes, and the *404* `session` duplicates `session` and `presenter` data. The real problem with our scenario comes when adding to or changing our data. If we need to update the `session` number that *Davidson* is giving with *Hazel* in the *Stream Room*, then two rows will require changes. Equally, if a `room` assignment changes, then several rows will have to be changed.

When entities are implemented in this fashion, we may not even see all of the rows filled in as fully as this. In the following entity we see a set of rows that are functionally equivalent to the set in the previous entity.

Session	Presenter	Room
101	Davidson	<null>
101	<null>	River Room
202	Davidson	<null>
202	<null>	Stream Room
202	Hazel	<null>
404	<null>	Brook Room
404	Hawkins	<null>
404	<null>	Stream Room

Advanced Normalization Topics

In this example, we have nulls for some rooms, and some presenters. We have eliminated the duplicated data, but now all we have is some pretty strange looking data with nulls everywhere. Furthermore we are not able to clearly use nulls to stand for the situation where we don't yet know the presenter for a session. We are in fact storing an equivalent set of data to that in the previous example but the data in this form is very difficult to work with.

To develop a solution to this problem let's first make the presenter the primary entity:

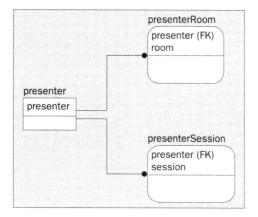

Note that our original implementation was as non-identifying relationships. To keep the diagrams as clear as possible, we will look at the relationships in terms of identifying relationships.

Then we take the data in the roomSessionPresenter entity and break it into these entities:

Presenter
Davidson
Hazel
Hawkins

Presenter	Room
Davidson	River Room
Davidson	Stream Room
Hazel	Stream Room
Hawkins	Stream Room
Hawkins	Brook Room

Presenter	Session
Davidson	101
Davidson	202
Hazel	404
Hawkins	404

This is obviously not a proper solution, because we would never be able to determine what room a session is located in, unless a presenter had been assigned. Also, *Davidson* is doing a session in the *River Room* as well as the *Stream Room,* and there is no link back to the session that is being given in the room. When we decompose any relationship and we lose meaning to the data, the decomposition is referred to as a **lossy decomposition**. This is one such case, and so is not a reasonable solution to our problem.

Next we try centering on the `room` where the sessions are held:

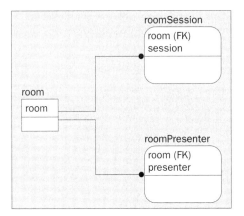

Taking the data and fitting into the entities once again:

Room
River Room
Brook Room
Stream Room

Room	Presenter
River Room	Davidson
Stream Room	Davidson
Stream Room	Hazel
Stream Room	Hawkins
Brook Room	Hawkins

Room	Session
River Room	101
Stream Room	202
Brook Room	202
Stream Room	404

Again, this is a lossy decomposition, and as such is an improper solution, because we are unable to determine, for example, exactly who is presenting the *202* presentation. It is in the *Stream Room*, and *Davidson*, *Hazel*, and *Hawkins* are all presenting in the *Stream Room*, but they're not all presenting the *202* `session`. So once again we need to consider another design. This time we center our design on the sessions to be held:

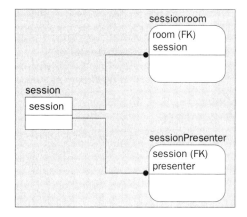

Looking at the data:

Session
101
202
404

Session	Room
101	River Room
202	Stream Room
404	Brook Room
404	Stream Room

Session	Presenter
101	Davidson
202	Davidson
202	Hazel
404	Hawkins

We have finally hit upon a solution to the problem. From this data we are able to determine precisely who is presenting what and where and we will have no problem adding or removing presenters, or even changing rooms. Take for example session *404*. We have the following data in the `sessionRoom` and `sessionPresenter` entities for this session:

Session	Room
404	Brook Room
404	Stream Room

Session	Presenter
404	Hawkins

To add a presenter named Evans to the slate, we simply add another row:

Session	Presenter
404	Hawkins
404	Evans

Thus this is a proper decomposition, and will not have the problems we outlined in our original entity. Our final model looks like this:

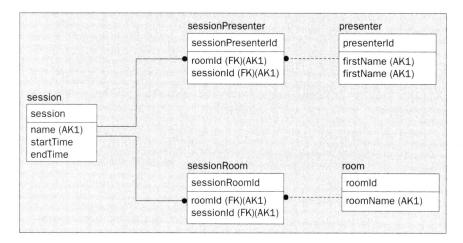

Now that we set the session separate from the presenter, and the nulls are no longer required in the foreign key values, since if we want to show that a room has not been chosen, we don't create a sessionRoom record. The same is true if we haven't yet chosen a presenter. More importantly, we can now set multiple rooms for a session without confusion, and we certainly cannot duplicate a value between the session and the room.

If we need to have additional data that extends the concept of sessionPresenter, for example to denote alternate presenter (or indeed primary and secondary presenter), we now have a logical place to store this information. Note that if we had tried to store that information in the original entity it would have violated Boyce-Codd Normal Form since the alternatePresenter attribute would only be referring to the session and presenter, and not the room.

Lurking Multi-valued Attributes

We consider some attributes to be **lurking** because they do not always stand out as problems at first glance. In an attempt to illustrate this idea, let's consider the following design model:

Advanced Normalization Topics

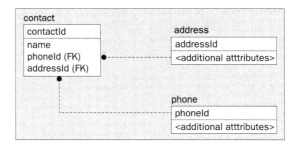

A problem arises here when we consider the `contact` entity, since we have three attributes: the contact's `name` (assume that this name is in First Normal Form), the `phone` number, and `address`. The `name` is fine, as every contact has a single name that we will refer to them by, but these days, many people have more than one address and phone number! We therefore have multi-valued attributes which require further normalization in order to resolve them. To allow for such multiple address or phone numbers we might modify our design as follows:

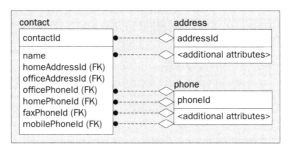

Whilst having multiple phone numbers is not a First Normal Form violation (since they are all different types of phone numbers, rather than multiples of the same type) we do have a further problem. Since we have simply added the type attribute to the name of the attribute (for example **home**AddressId, **fax**PhoneId) we will have further multi-value attribute problems if, for example, the user has two fax phones, or indeed two mobile phones. Furthermore, we are in the less than ideal situation of needing multiple nullable values for each of the attributes when they do not exist. This is a messy representation of the relationship. For example, if the client requires a spouse office phone number attribute for a contact, we will have to change the model, in all probability leading us to re-writing the application code.

Let's further modify the design, so as to have separate `contact` and `contactInformation` entities:

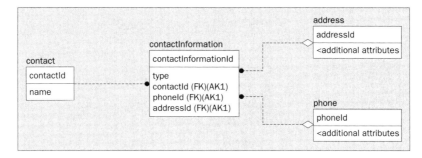

The `type` attribute denotes the type of contact information that we are storing in an instance, so we can now have a `contactInformation` instance with a `type` of Home, and attach an address and phone number to it. This will now allow us to add as many phone numbers and addresses, as a user requires. However, since address and phone are held in the same table, we'll end up with null values where a contact has different numbers of home addresses and phone numbers.

At this stage we have to make a decision as to how we want to proceed. We may want a phone number to be linked with an address (for example linking home address with home phone number). In our case what we will do is to split the `contactInformation` entity into `contactAddress` and `contactPhone` (though this should not be considered as the only possible solution to the problem):

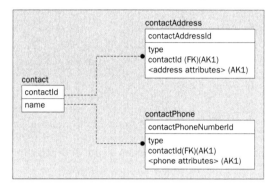

This modification has eliminated the remaining multi-valued dependencies, since we can now have many addresses and many phone numbers, independently of one another, and are able to define as many types as desired without the necessity of modifying our entity structures. However, we can take one further step, by modeling the phone number and address as different entities in the logical model, and adding domain entities for the type column. In this way we can prevent users from typing "Home", "Homer", "Hume", etc. when they mean 'home'. It will also give us a user configurable constraint so we can add additional types without having to change the model. We will add a description attribute to the domain entities allowing us to describe the actual purpose of the type. This allows for situations such as where we have an address type of "Away" that is pretty standard for a given organization, but confusing to first time users. A description such as: "Address for contact when travelling on extended sales trips" could then be assigned. Our final model now looks like this:

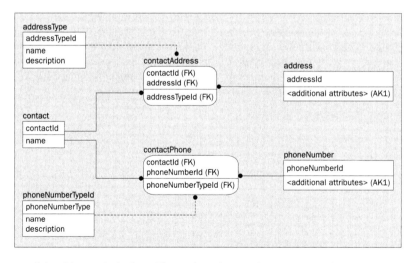

It should be noted that I have made the additional attributes of `address` and `phoneNumber` alternate keys, to avoid duplicating an address every time that it is used in the system. This way if we have five contacts that have the same address for their office, we only have to change one item. What looks like overkill can therefore actually have benefits, though when you began to physically model these entities it will be a judgement call as to whether or not to implement to this level, bearing in mind any performance tuning issues which may arise.

Advanced Normalization Topics

Attribute History

We may also encounter problems with our design model in a situation where we need to store status type information for an instance of some entity. For example, in the following diagram, we have built two entities that store the header of an order, as well as a domain entity for the order status:

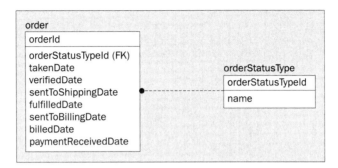

The problem here is that the order status changes (and hence the value of the `orderStatusTypeId` attribute) based both on the values of the other date fields, and other external factors. For example, when the order is taken from the customer, the `takenDate` attribute would be filled in with a date. The order then might be in 'Pending' status. After the customer's payment method has been verified, we would then modify the `verifiedDate` attribute with the date verified, and set the status to "InProcess". "InProcess" could actually mean more than one thing, such as "sent to shipping" or "bill sent".

What we are concerned with here is the `orderStatusTypeId` attribute on the order entity. It contains the current status for the order instance. How do you answer questions about when an order got sent to the shipping department, or when the order verification department verified the order? The modeller of the data has added several fields in the order entity to store these bits of information, but what if it failed verification once? Do we care? And is the `fulfilledDate` the date when the order was either fully shipped or canceled, or strictly when it was fully shipped so we need to add another attribute for `canceledDate`?

To solve this problem we will have to change our model to allow the storing of multiple values for each of the attributes we have created.

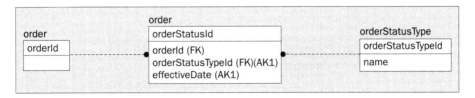

Now whenever the order status changes, all we have to do is add a record to the `orderStatus` entity. Whatever the record with the latest `effectiveDate` value is the current status. It would also allow us to have more than one status value at a time. For instance, not all statuses are fulfilled in a sequential fashion. In an `order` type entity, for instance, you may send the invoice to be verified, then once it is verified, send it to be processed by shipping and billing at the same time. With the new structure that we have created, when our order fails to be shipped, we can record this. We can also record that the client has paid. Note that, in this case, we only want to model the status of the overall order, and not the status of any items on the order.

Solving this type of Fourth Normal Form situation will sometimes require a state diagram to determine in what order a status is achieved. For example, the following diagram can be used to describe the process of an order being taken, from the time it was ordered to the time it was closed out. (Canceling or modifying an order, or indeed backorders, will not be considered in this example.)

185

Chapter 7

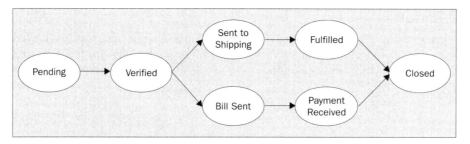

We can model this kind of simple state diagram fairly easily with one additional entity:

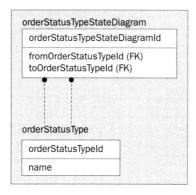

Consider that we had our four states in the `orderStatusType` entity

orderStatusTypeId	Name
1	Pending
2	Verified
3	Sent to Shipping
4	Bill Sent
5	Fulfilled
6	Payment Received
7	Closed

To define our state diagram we would need the following instances in the `orderStatusTypeStateDiagram` entity (leaving off the pointer this time, and including Name for clarity):

fromOrderStatusTypeId	Name	toOrderStatusTypeId	Name
1	Pending	2	Verified
2	Verified	3	Sent To shipping
2	Verified	4	Bill Sent
3	Sent to shipping	5	Fulfilled

fromOrderStatusTypeId	Name	toOrderStatusTypeId	Name
4	Bill Sent	6	Payment Received
5	Fulfilled	7	Closed
6	Payment Received	7	Closed

In this manner, we can see whether or not we are in a particular state, what state we were previously in, and what state we can be in next. It also allows us to define the flow of our business rules in data rather than hard coding a bunch of fixed values.

In this case our status may go through several values, and in fact may have multiple statuses at any given time. You would have to document business rules outlining exactly how the process works in a given situation, and in reality it is the exception processing that requires the most amount of time, with up to 80 per cent of coding time generally spent on the exceptions to the rule.

Additional Normal Forms

In this section we will make brief mention of a pair of additional Normal Forms that exist, though we will not be including any examples of them, as they are often considered too esoteric, and are generally only practiced during ordinary logical modeling. However, they are worth at least a mention for the sake of completeness.

Fifth Normal Form – Unlike the examples we have considered above, not every ternary relationship can be broken down into two entities related to a third. If this is the case then the entities are in Fourth Normal Form. The aim of the Fifth Normal Form is to ensure that any ternary relationships that still exist in a Fourth Normal Form entity can be decomposed into entities and then rejoined to one another to produce the original entity. If this cannot be done, then the relationship is implying information that is not true. Having said that, the cases that the Fifth Normal Form deals with are very esoteric and as such are usually ignored.

Domain Key Normal Form – An entity is in Domain Key Normal Form if every constraint on the entity is a logical consequence of the definition of keys and domains. Donald Fagin was the first person to devise a formal definition in 1981.

Let's review what each of these terms means.

- ❑ "Key" means any candidate key, which uniquely identifies each row in an entity.
- ❑ "Domain" means any limitation on the kind of data to be stored in the column. This can also be data enforced using foreign keys, if the resulting entity is defined properly and in at least Fourth Normal Form.
- ❑ "Constraint" indicates any rule dealing with attributes (this includes edit rules, interrelation constraints, functional dependency, and multivalued dependency, but NOT time-dependent constraints).

This is considered the "perfect" normal form since an entity with no insertion or deletion anomalies is, and must be, in Domain Key Normal Form.

Denormalization

Denormalization is used primarily to improve performance in cases where over-normalized structures are causing overhead to the query processor and in turn other processes in SQL Server, or to tone down some complexity to make things easier to implement. As we have tried to highlight in this chapter, while it can be argued that denormalizing to Third Normal Form may simplify queries by reducing the number of joins needed, this risks introducing data anomalies. Any additional code written to deal with these anomalies will need to be duplicated in every application that uses the database, thereby increasing the likelihood of human error. The judgement call that needs to be made in this situation is whether a slightly slower (but 100 per cent accurate) application is preferable to a faster application of lower accuracy.

It is this book's contention that during logical modeling, we should never step back from our normalized structures to proactively performance tune our applications. As our book is centered around OLTP database structures, the most important part of our design is to make certain that our logical model represents all of the entities and attributes that the resulting database will hold. During, and most importantly, *after* the process of *physical* modeling, there may well be valid reasons to denormalize the structures, either to improve performance or reduce implementation complexity, but neither of these pertain to the *logical* model. We will always have fewer problems if we implement physically what is true logically, and so I would always advocate waiting until the physical modeling phase, or at least until we find a compelling reason to do so (like some part of our system is failing), before we denormalize.

Case Study

Let's now reconsider our logical model that we left at the end of the last chapter. If we apply what we have learnt in this chapter to our case study examples, then we discover three examples of Fourth Normal Form violations. These violations are actually more frequent than one might think, and it is not until you think through each of the attributes and their possible values that you begin to realize that you may need to extend your model.

Example 1 – Account.BalanceDate

This first example arises when we look at the `balanceDate` attribute in the account entity we originally designed:

```
account
bankId: PrimaryKey (FK) (AK1.1)
accountId: PrimaryKey

number: AlphaNumericNumber (AK1.2)
balanceDate: Date
```

The account will be balanced frequently, otherwise any missed transactions or bank mess-ups may cause us to accidentally run out of funds in the account. (If it isn't, then it will be as bad as my checking account was after I got out of college!) Since we store data each time the account is balanced, the `balanceDate` attribute represents a multi-valued dependency to the account and needs to be relocated. Breaking down this dependency, we introduce the `accountReconcile` entity, along with the `reconcileDate` and `periodEndDate` attributes. These allow for the fact that there may be some latency between the time the statement is received and when it is actually reconciled. The `reconcileDate` is defined as the date when the account was physically balanced. As a final touch, we can add the `statementId` attribute to the

Advanced Normalization Topics

`accountReconcile` entity, to record any information that the bank sent the user to balance the account. It will also be better to use the `statementId` as part of the primary key, since it identifies the reconciliation. With these modifications in place our logical model now looks like this:

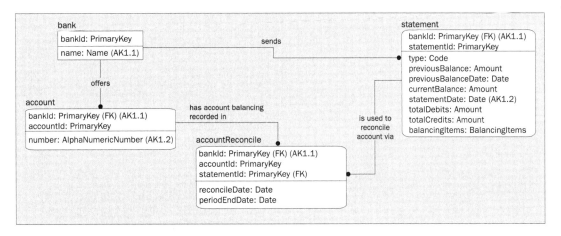

Example 2 – Payee.Address Id and Payee.Phone Number Id

The second example addresses a particularly common concern, that of needing to have multiple postal addresses and multiple phone numbers. We covered this earlier in the chapter, when we talked about lurking attributes, and we need to apply the same process to our case study. Our original model contained single entities for both `address` and `phoneNumber` as shown below:

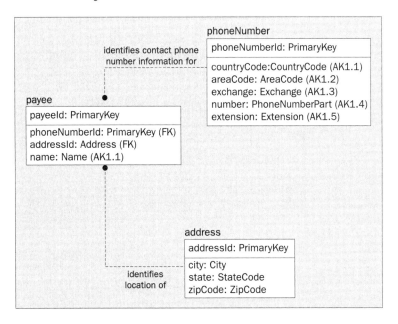

In order to be able to enter multiple phone numbers we create the `payeePhoneNumber` entity, and add a type domain entity to allow the classification of these numbers. In a similar fashion we create the attributes `payeeAddress` and `addressType`. Our corrected model design now looks like this:

189

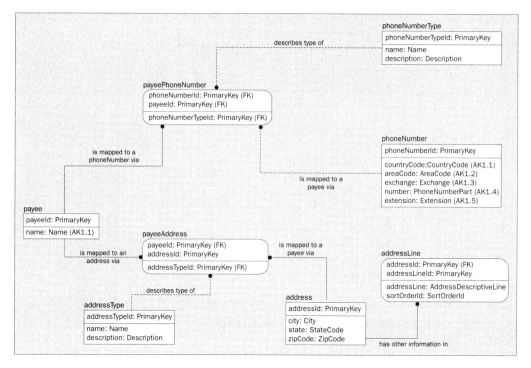

Note that now a payee is allowed to have many phone numbers and many addresses in a flexible manner that allows us to define new types of address without any additional coding; so the user will never be out of luck when he or she needs to store an address.

However if we take a closer look at the address entity there is still a problem, in that `city` and `state` are related (non key) attributes and therefore violate the third normal form by appearing in the same entity. Both of these are also related to the `zipCode` attribute, since if we know a zip code we can determine the city and state. Splitting the `address` entity leads us to the following modified diagram:

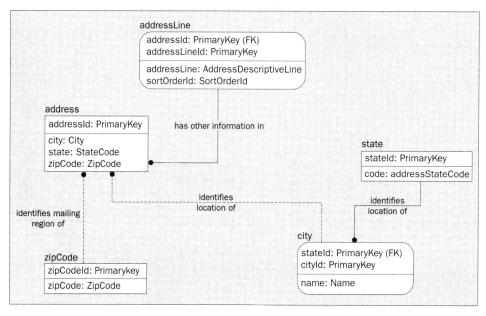

Advanced Normalization Topics

The next stage of the process is to determine the exact relationship between `city` and `zipCode`. Since one zip code may cover an entire small town, but a large city may contain many zip codes, the relationship is of the many-to-many variety. Having created city, state and address entities we now need to be able to combine their attributes to allow us to be able to search for addresses using full records. To do this we create a new entity, `zipCodeCityReference`, which brings together the attributes `CityID`, `StateID` and `zipCodeID`, and includes a new attribute `PrimaryFl`. The primary flag will allow us to set which city is the "primary" city in the `zipCode`, an attribute that the postal service will sell along with a database of zip codes and cities. In this way, our user can usually access full address details by entering only the `zipCode` attributes into an application. Building this into our model will give us:

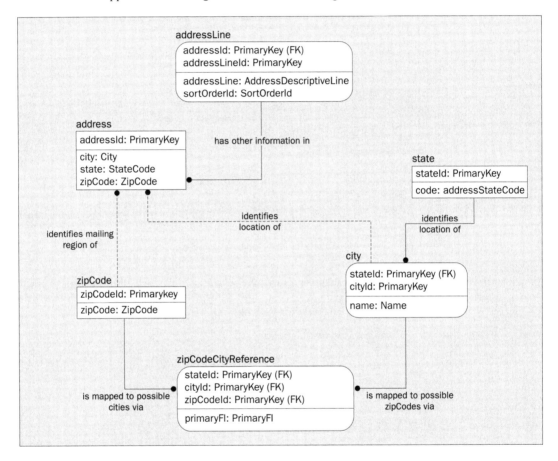

Example 3 – check.UsageType

The `usageType` attribute was first envisioned as a way to tag a check as being used for a certain purpose. In practice however, a single check can be written for many different purposes, and hence, we have a violation of Fourth Normal Form, since the user will not be able to put every usage of the check into a single value. To overcome this we create the `checkUsage` entity and associated type domain, in a similar fashion to that which we saw in the previous example. This gives us the following model:

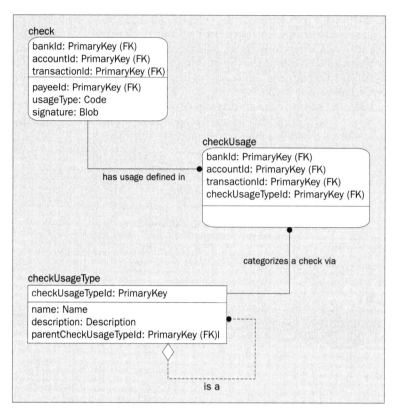

Note that the checkUsageType entity includes a recursive relationship that will allow the user to create a tree of usageTypes for check categorizations, since we now allow one instance of a checkUsageType to be owned by another. For example, we might define the following tree:

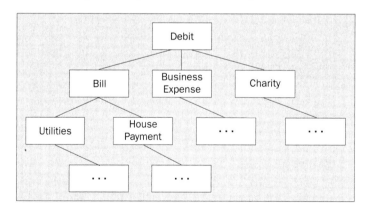

Now, (using an algorithm that we will touch on in the physical implementation part of the book in Chapter 12), we can summarize all of the bills, which in our tree includes utilities and house payments, or all debits, which includes business expenses, and charity.

Advanced Normalization Topics

I threw this example into the book to point out that recursive relationships are not terribly difficult to deal with. The base of the algorithm is pretty simple once you understand it. First you get all of the rows without parents, (Debit), and go down the tree one level at a time. First (Bill, Business Expense, and Charity) and in the next pass (Utilities and House Payment). On each pass through the tree, we simply summarize and add to the previous levels. As mentioned we will do a very simple example of this in Chapter 12.

Now we need to finish the `checkUsage` entity. We have allowed the user to determine multiple usages for a check, but we have not allowed them to allocate the amount of the check to go to each. There are two possible data solutions to the problem, either allocating check usage by percentage or amount. In our solution, we will choose to allocate by amount. Allocating by amount gives the user a way to discretely assign the allocation amounts to each usage type. If the amount of the check changes, the allocation will have to change. If you allocate by percentage, it is too easy to forget what values you were intending to set.

Hence, we end up with the following set of entities, with the new attribute `allocationAmount`:

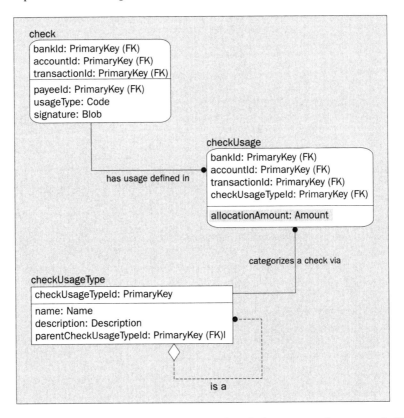

To our documentation, we will need to record our first identified inter-entity business rule. We will not allow the sum of the `checkUsage+allocationAmount` values to be greater than the transaction amount for the check. We should also have another rule that states that `checkUsage+allocationAmount` values never come to less than the transaction amount for the check. This is impossible to implement in SQL Server 2000, but needs to be noted for middle-tier or front-end implementation since this is a type of constraint that SQL Server does not have (a database or end-of-transaction constraint, where following a transaction we check to make sure that everything is in balance).

193

Chapter 7

We now have most of the attributes that we would need to actually implement our checking system. We will not be enhancing the attributes of the model by adding any further information in this normalization exercise. It is very important at this stage that we review the model that we have created over and over again. This is doubly important in a real world case!! It is also time to review the data model with the client to make certain that the model precisely models their business. In the upcoming chapters we will occasionally have to make changes to our structures as we do some further review and begin to consider how the users will be using the data.

The final logical data model of our system is as follows:

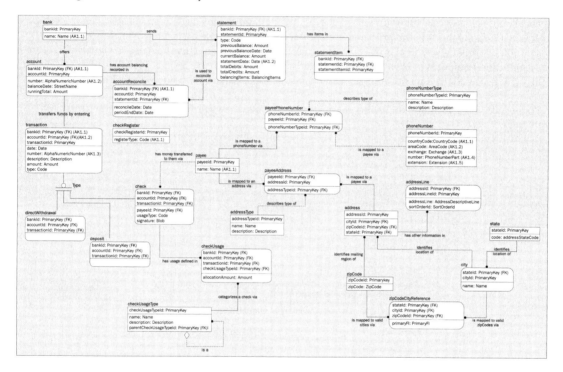

Summary

In this chapter we have presented additional criteria for normalizing our databases beyond the forms presented in the previous chapter. At this stage it is pertinent to quickly summarize the nature of the Normal Forms we have outlined in this, and the preceding Chapter:

First Normal Form	All attributes must be atomic, one single value per attribute
	All instances of an entity must contain the same number of values
	All occurrences of an entity in an entity must be different
Second Normal Form	The entity must be in First Normal Form
	All attributes must be a fact about the entire key and not a subset of the key
Third Normal Form	The entity must be in Second Normal Form
	An entity is in Third Normal Form if every non-key attribute is a fact about a key attribute
	All attributes must be a fact about the key, and nothing but the key
Boyce-Codd Normal Form	All attributes are fully dependent on a key; all attributes must be a fact about a key, and nothing but a key.
	An entity is in Boyce-Codd Normal Form if every determinant is a key
Fourth Normal Form	The entity must be in Boyce-Codd Normal Form
	There must not be more than one multi-valued dependency represented in the entity

All of the information we have learned in these two chapters can then be boiled down into a single statement:

> **All entities must be relations and must be single themed!**

By making them identify a SINGLE person, place, thing, or idea, we reduce all of the modification anomalies on the data we have stored. In this way, any time we change an attribute of an entity, we are simply changing the description of that single entity, and cannot effect an incidental change in the data.

The definition of a relation was presented in Chapter 3. This covers the first normal form requirements, and single-themed covers all of the others. The process of stepping through all of the normal forms will get us to a place where our databases require very little special coding to keep the data clean.

In the next chapter we will look at the issues that remain in wrapping up the logical design phase of our project.

SQL Server 2000 Database Design Professional

8

Ending the Logical Design Phase

Introduction

Let us review what we have achieved so far at this point of the book:

- ❑ We have gathered all the information
- ❑ We are well versed in relational theory
- ❑ We have learned a bit about UML
- ❑ We have built a use case diagram
- ❑ We have designed a logical model of our database using the IDEF1X modeling methodology
- ❑ We have normalized our data

Now we are almost ready to start our database implementation. But there are a few issues to clear up before we start creating tables and generating code.

While we are still in a phase of the project where we have quite a bit of contact with the users, this is the best time to get answers to the last few questions. What we will be doing is not exactly logical modeling, but it is not exactly physical modeling either, and some would say this is the bit that makes the difference between a brilliant project, and a merely adequate or even sub-standard one. At this point we may also consider having a review meeting with the project sponsor for a last check on whether the design covers all the requirements. Also, consider preparing a sign-off document for supporting documentation.

Chapter 8

From a database standpoint, we now have a very well structured data model; we have a good idea of who the users will be, and we have detailed the different processes that we will need to implement. In this chapter, we will take a brief look at the tasks that we have to finish prior to beginning the implementation, and we will examine the final technical issues that are critical to getting the database implemented properly:

- Data usage
- Volumetrics
- Project plan
- Final documentation review

Each of these is important to the process of implementing the database that we will begin in the next chapter. Taking care of these important technical issues now will allow you to make changes if you missed something, which may happen, as no one is perfect.

Another great practice when designing a database (or any other type of application for that matter) is to enlist the aid of other developers to validate your design, as well as to bounce ideas off them. Hold a meeting with them and explain the objectives of the application, the major obstacles, the known business process, and your proposed design. Having your data model represented in easy-to-view diagrams will make it easy for your associates to understand and criticize your work, even those who are not database architects. Let them look things over, evaluate what has been done, and provide you with feedback. This "peer review process" will almost always save you time and energy since any given applications will have similarities with other applications. By enlisting the help of others, you can learn a few things from how they approached their designs. Take the ideas and suggestions offered in the reviews and evaluations to refine your model and add more detail.

Lastly, no matter how good a job you do at the initial interview stage, you will rarely extract descriptions of every bit of data from your clients. Take the time to meet with clients and ask them a few more questions – this is the point where you must make clear what is not possible. Also, you must point out what assumptions you have made during the logical design and what the impacts may possibly be. This is not so much to cover your back as to leave the client with realistic expectations for the project. If the design does not match the desires of the client, it is critical to work out the details now, even if the outcome is to go back to the start of the process and discover what was misunderstood, or even cancel the project.

The truth will always set you free, and the time for the user to discover the gory details of how little you understand their business is not after the database is implemented and they find they cannot do their job.

Data Usage

So far, we have mapped out what data we need and what it is needed for. We have taken copies of the client's reports, screens, and documents to try to glean the data we will need to store, but we have not fully considered what that data will actually be used for. In this section we will look at:

- Reporting
- Data usage and ownership

❏ Interfaces to external systems
❏ Data conversion plans

Reporting

Reporting is one of the most important parts of the database system. Almost every bit of data that we have been modeling will need to be viewed by someone in the organization in some way, either directly or perhaps as part of a calculation.

In the course of many projects, reporting can be treated as an add-on and frequently the design and implementation of reports is put off until after the project is nearly complete. This is certainly not what we are advocating, but it can happen. This is more common with corporate/internal projects, but it does happen on consulting/external projects as well.

The following Gantt chart shows a typical project time line:

ID	Task Name	Start	End	Duration
1	Implement Module1	2/1/2001	02/03/2001	22d
2	Implement Module2	28/02/2001	26/03/2001	19d
3	Implement Module 3	13/03/2001	13/04/2001	24d
4	Design Reports	13/04/2001	13/04/2001	1d
5	Implement Reports	16/04/2001	18/04/2001	3d

Even when a reasonable amount of time is scheduled for reports, it is frequently tagged to the end of the design period, since we really must finish designing the database before we can start querying and actually implementing reports from it. Then, if the project time line slides – as they have a tendency to do for one reason or another – the time allocated for reports can be pinched even tighter.

Sometimes, when the clients begin to realize that it is getting late in the process and the reporting design still hasn't been done, they will mention it and force the issue, making sure that their reports are considered. However, even if clients don't jump up and down shouting about how important reports are to them, users *always* care tremendously about reports, as this is how they usually run their business. Reports are how they get the information out and look at it, slice it, dice it, plan for it, and – most important of all – get paid for it. In some cases, reports are the only bit of a project that the user will see.

So what are we saying? Before we end the logical design phase, it is very important to make sure that we understand what the user wants to get out of the database. Even if we cannot do a full design of the reports, at the very least we need to understand what the needs are going to be and get the general structure right.

Chapter 8

Report Discovery Strategy

There are two different types of report we need to be concerned with:

- **Standard Reports** – The reports that the user must have to get their jobs done. Frequently, these are very simple reports. They generally make up the core of a user's needs.

- **Specialized Reports** – Reports that allow users to go the extra mile, by giving them more than the average information that they would think of themselves.

These are two distinctly different things. Standard reports are reports that take no special skills to develop – for example, the displaying of the account balance. It is expected that your system will be able to produce these reports. Specialized reports are those that aren't quite so expected – they're the ones that take some specialist skill or understanding of the business process – for example, consolidating accounts on a multi-national corporation. In this phase of the project it is extremely important to plan for both.

Standard Reports

Most database systems have some fixed set of required reports that are necessary for the running of the business. These may be daily, weekly, or yearly reports, all fixed to show performance of the situation that is modeled by the database system you have created. High profile examples that we see all of the time might include:

- Neilson ratings – There is a database somewhere capturing every television show that test people watch, based on boxes they have in their houses. Daily, hourly, and weekly, it ranks the television shows based on the number of users who watch. These numbers are used to determine which shows stay and which go.

- Movie Ticket Sales – Every week in the papers there is always a list of the top ten grossing movies of the week. This comes from a typical database just like any other.

A less high profile example might be:

- Utility Bill – A report of a meter reading, amount being charged, previous charges, and possibly even last year's charges.

- Traffic Report – In an area where I recently lived (Virginia Beach, VA.), there were cameras and detectors set up all over the highways, which provided commuters with online reports of traffic flows.

Specialized Reports

Beyond the scope of the standard reports, the users that you talk with will have special desires for the data that you will be storing in the database. It is important to meet with the clients to identify how these special reporting requirements can be met. Users frequently have great ideas in their heads waiting to get out, and they won't always be listened to.

Keep in mind that the realities involved in implementing a report, or the storage for it, are not important during the interview – though be careful not to be the one to plant unrealistic ideas in the mind of the client (you will have created an unwritten specification).

Ending the Logical Design Phase

The simplest strategy to employ is to ask the users to list all of the questions that they might conceivably want to ask of the data that you will be storing. This serves two very important purposes. We get:

- An idea of what types of things they are thinking of for the future
- To see if we have overlooked anything in our original database design

Taking our report examples, the following types of question might be asked:

- Neilson ratings – The user would probably like to know about the person who was watching the TV program, whether they were watching or taping it, and if they watched the tape after they recorded it.
- Movie Ticket Sales – The age and gender of the people seeing the movie, when they saw it, how many were in the average party, and how many people walked out because they found it dull.
- Utility Bill – How the values were affected each day by the weather, holidays, or any other situation.
- Traffic Report – Trend analysis on how many vehicles are on the road, how the traffic flowed during the day, the effects of accidents, etc.

There are many challenges in developing reports for the user. In fact, at first it may even seem impossible. However, by breaking down the requirements and evaluating them, you will be in a better position to advise on what is possible and what is not. Reporting requirements should be prioritized and then, taking into account time and resources, broken down into required and future needs. Note that, as the designer, you must not be afraid to say no if a reporting requirement is actually impossible to fulfill.

Take the utility bill report we mentioned previously:

- **Required Needs: Reading of meter, amount being charged, previous charges**
- **Future Needs**: Last year's meter reading
- **Impossible Needs**: Daily values (cannot be made due to the limitations of the analog equipment)

Document, document, document! This information will be important to someone. If you are the data architect with a large organization, you may not get to ask these types of questions – it will be someone else. And never hide "the impossible" from the members of the design team. It may not be impossible – that is why we have teams.

Prototype Reports

Once we have defined what reports are necessary, we need to build prototypes of what the reports will need to look like and what data will be placed on them. Nearly every computer system design uses prototypes of the screens that make up an application, as a blueprint of what the client wants and what we will deliver. We must establish the same kind of thing for reports.

There are two schools of thought when it comes to what kinds of data to put on the prototype report. I present them both here for you:

❑ Using unreal data. This is not to say that we make the data bizarrely unrealistic to the client, but keep your sample data unreal enough to avoid drawn out discussions of how the exact situation in the report has never actually happened, though it might have, etc. Prototype reports merely reflect possible sets of data for a given reporting situation, not an exact situation. In many cases, the client's exact current data will not be fully understood until later in the development process.

❑ Using realistic data. By making the proto-type report as close as possible to the final report, it gives the user a feeling of how well the data is understood. Using current and familiar data draws the user closer to the design. In addition, it provides early feedback to the designers of the report as to whether they understand the requirements, and whether their design will produce the desired result.

I generally fall in the first camp, but it is totally dependent on the situation, the client, and – most important – how vital reports are to the process. In some cases they are very central, and in others they are ancillary. If we must understand the report before the rest of the system can be successfully built, then using realistic data will give the best results.

Determine Data Usage and Ownership

Understanding what the data will be used for and who owns it is a critical factor for the completion of the logical phase. First off, we need to check that our understanding of the following is still up-to-date:

❑ Who will be using the data and what will they be doing with it?

❑ Who will be allowed to do what, to what data?

❑ From where will they access it?

❑ What applications will be used to access the data?

❑ How many users will access the data?

❑ How many of these users will need to access the data concurrently?

These points should have been covered during the early analysis. However, it is incumbent on us to make certain that we totally understand the needs for the data, considering we may have discovered new data during the logical modeling phase. We will now move on and begin to deal with complex architecture issues like security and data access architecture.

Security

Unless the client has a predefined architecture for securing their data from unwanted modification/access, the matter of security frequently gets pushed even further back than reporting. While it may possibly be the least important part of the project to the data architect, it is certainly important to the database administrator, so it is not something that can be simply ignored.

When it comes to reports, security is an issue that is ultra-important. Its importance tends to depend on the information contained in the reports that the client may be using, but seldom will an organization want every user to have access to all data. A good approach is for the designer to establish a "reports classification table" and seek instructions from the project sponsor on the classification of each report and which users or user groups will have access to each report.

Ending the Logical Design Phase

Including security information in the use case descriptions of every actor in the system is a very useful technique. Security is implied by every process on the use case diagram, since, if the use cases include every possible report and every possible process, it will follow that if a use case is not linked to a user, then they cannot perform some function.

For example, take our example use case from the text of Chapter 5:

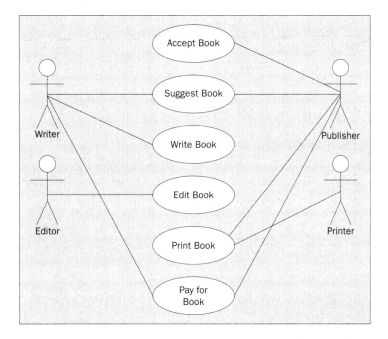

Each of the use cases will be a module in the system, so the writer will need to have access to whatever data it takes to map the "Write Book" module work. No one else will have access to this data unless it is used in a different module as well:

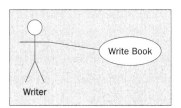

Now consider what happens if we add a report called the "Book Report". We create a use case for it and note that it gives quite a bit of information like name, description, picture, staff comments, and sales information:

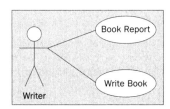

The writer may be able to view the report, but his view should be limited and will lack things like detailed sales information, for instance. In the actor definition structures, we might include:

Name	Author
Description	The actor who writes the text of the book
Security Notes	May only see the light version of the book report, as it contains sensitive information

Of course, you will probably use some form of tool that should either have space for such documentation or notes fields to use instead. In the "Book Report" use, we will document the versions and security constraints for the report, along with how it is used.

Known Architecture Limitations

We will look at determining final architecture later in the book, but I introduce it here, as this stage in the process is probably the last chance you will get to ask the client questions regarding the actual demands that will be placed on the database. We need to know about:

- Connection type – How will the clients actually access the data; from the web, from local applications?

- Programming issues – What languages are they married to? Or can we use whatever we want to?

- Likely system demand – Minimum and maximum number of users on the system, and the required hours of operation.

- Hardware limitations – This could be political or budgetary, but imagine if we figure that the user is going to purchase a million dollars worth of equipment, and they figured on five thousand.

- Physical limitations – Networking issues like lack of bandwidth, or even better, not enough room to fit certain equipment in the secured closet that was set aside for the server.

We need to get some handle on limitations to **performance** (how fast the database goes) and **scaleability** (how performance changes as the number of users increases) before we get down to physical implementation.

Interfacing with External Systems

When I speak of "External Systems", I refer to other databases that are not a proper part of our database, but with which we need to interface. Common examples include any off-the-shelf product (human resources system, payroll system, etc.) that an organization has which needs to communicate with our database.

The main problem with external systems is that, for whatever reason, some were poorly designed. Quite a few off-the-shelf systems still in use today were developed as mainframe systems and hastily ported over to a relational database system because it was the fashion, with little understanding of relational programming.

Ending the Logical Design Phase

The examples in this section are based on real world situations so, even if they seem unreal, they do mimic real problems in real products. They are included mostly for shock value, but also to give some idea of what may be ahead of us if we wait too late in the process before taking into account the external systems that we need to interface with.

Example 1 – A Problematic Enterprise Resource Planning System

A purchasing and requisitioning application I have worked with had nearly a thousand tables, but only one domain table to serve as the domain for all tables in the system. Instead of having a single table modeled like:

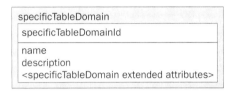

…for each place where they needed one – for example, payment type, resource type, purchase type, etc. – some programmer got the bright idea to implement a single table like this:

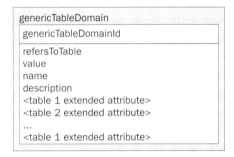

The programmer's idea must have been that, in getting a single table to do many things, he/she would only need a single editor to manage all domain values.

Unfortunately, there are quite a few major problems with using SQL on the data in this implementation. We will ignore the obvious implementation difficulties (like not being able to use declarative referential integrity since the specialized tables required a key value, which is not possible in any RDBMS), and stick to the data conversion issues. There were over eighty different distinct values in the domain table's `refersToTable` column. Since this method of building a domain table was non-standard, no data conversion tool supported this type of query, and the new system we were developing certainly did not mimic this design. Many, many queries had to be hand coded to extract the data.

Example 2 – Another "How Not To Do It" Example

The next example arose with a third-party product I have had the "pleasure" to interface with, and it makes the previous situation look easy. I was implementing a system that had to interface with one of our business units that we had been using for quite a while, and could not be replaced. The system stored its data in SQL Server, but was implemented in such a manner as to hinder interfacing with other systems. The database used structures that masked the column names in such a way that you had to go through their interfaces just to figure out what a table had in it.

For example, the following table shows the metadata that is used to define the fields in a table:

Actual Table Name	Actual Column Name	Logical Field Name (the field name that we want to know the field as)	Type	Nullable
TABLE1	COLUMN1	KeyId	Varchar(30)	No
TABLE1	COLUMN2	CreatedBy	Sysname	Yes
TABLE1	COLUMN3	CreateDate	Int	No
TABLE1	COLUMN5	ModifyDate	Datetime	No
TABLE1	COLUMN6	Field1	Varchar(10)	Yes
TABLE1	COLUMN7	Field2	Varchar(10)	Yes
TABLE1	COLUMN8	Field3	Varchar(15)	Yes
...	...	...	...	...
TABLE1	COLUMNn	FieldN	Varchar(30)	Yes

The designers of the product did this to encapsulate the implementation away from the users. As a mechanism to prevent competitors from gaining an understanding of their structures, it works fabulously. However, building an interface to retrieve data from these tables was a nightmare, requiring statements such as:

```
SELECT    COLUMN7 as field1,
          COLUMN8 as field2,
          COLUMN9 as field3,
          COLUMN10 as field4,
          COLUMN11 as field5,
          ...
          COLUMNnn as fieldN
FROM      TABLE1
WHERE     COLUMN9 = '<field1Value>'
```

Performing data conversions, by building statements to modify the data in the tables from our new system, was a very heinous and time-consuming task.

Example 3 – Systems Suffering from Denormalization

One of the more frequent problems you will face with other systems is denormalization. These systems may be denormalized for many reasons. Maybe the database designer wasn't very proficient or maybe it is a legacy system where the technology doesn't support full normalization. It is not at all uncommon to see a database with one, two, or maybe three tables where fifty are required to properly flesh out the solution. For example, we know that a table which models a person should only have attributes that specifically describe the person, but a poorly designed table may look like this:

Ending the Logical Design Phase

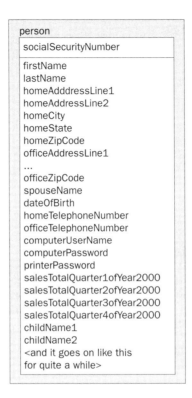

Hopefully you won't come across a table as ridiculously denormalized as this one, but even the least amount of denormalization in the source system will require complex queries to load the data into our tables.

Additional Issues when Interfacing with Third Party Systems

One of the primary issues when interfacing with external third party systems is coupling. The reason we have modeled our entire database without care for external interfaces so far is that, for the most part, it is important to keep our systems loosely coupled to systems that are out of our control. It is generally a good idea to import data from external tables into structures that we have designed – insert the data into a set of intermediate tables that will work as an import layer, and will always work regardless of the external system being used.

Another technique for integrating with external systems that share similar but different data structures is to build views on the data contained in the external systems. Imagine you have a Stock-Keeping Unit system with a core SKU table that stores the data in a particular structure, and a cash register system which stores it in a slightly different format, but from which we need to access the same information. The abstraction layer created by the views allows the core system to be modified without needing to change the external cash register system.

Another good reason for identifying all external systems to which we might need to interface is that we don't want to start a data store for information that already exists and is available to us. There's no point in creating a new `employee` table if an external system has an employee table that we can use.

Data Conversion Plans

We also need to take into consideration the fact that we are possibly replacing a system that is currently in use, even if it is a paper-based system. While data conversion is not so much a logical design issue, we still need to sketch out plans for conversion. Many projects fail due to the lack of plans for getting data from an existing system.

Granted, once your SQL Server 2000 database has been implemented properly, it will likely be so much better than the previous system, but people won't be very happy if it takes a huge effort to make the transition from old to new. Worse still, you will likely have changed data rules that will invalidate the previous system's data, especially when regarding unique data values. It is often true that much old data won't fit into a new database without some degree of massaging, due to the sloppy programming and/or design used in the old system.

Planning for Volumetrics

Volumetrics is defined as "of or relating to measurement by volume", and deals with determining how large your tables and database will grow. This type of information will be very useful when we get to physical modeling. Typically, you will get some idea of the size of the tables you are designing from conversations with the client and by looking at previous systems you are replacing.

Volumetrics is more of a physical modeling matter and we will cover it properly later in the book. However, it is best to begin to nail down some basic information that we will need to estimate database size and growth.

There are a few basic pieces of information that you can start to gather at this point in the process:

- Average length of attribute data (including text and BLOB data)
- Percentage of data that will be filled in for every attribute
- How much data will likely be in the table initially
- Number of rows in a table and by how much this number will grow
- How long the life of the project is expected to be

For example, in our customer database we might have the following table of values to help estimate database sizes:

Table Name	Initial Rows	Growth in Rows per Month	Max Rows
customerType	4	0	20
customer	0	30	3000
order	0	1000	Unlimited

In this case, we are saying that we will start out with 4 rows in the customerType table, that we don't expect much if any growth, and that we should plan on a maximum of 20 rows. In the customer table, we will start out with no data but we expect to add 30 rows a month, with an expected ceiling of 3000 rows. In the order table, we hope that we will keep adding 1000 rows a month forever.

Having this kind of information at the beginning of hardware planning will be extremely useful.

Project Plan

At this point I should mention the need for a project plan. Every step from here out will be relatively straightforward to plan for, once you have been through the process of creating databases ten or twenty times. The following bits of information should be included:

- What tasks need to be accomplished
- What tasks must be finished before others
- Milestones to reach for user review
- How long each task should take

The task of building the project plan will lie directly with the project managing team and, as such, is strictly beyond the scope of this book. Further information can be found in *Professional VB6 Project Management* by *Jake Sturm* (*Wrox Press, ISBN 1-861002-93-9*).

Final Documentation Review

Throughout the process of designing our system, we have amassed tons of documentation.

Final review means exactly what it sounds like. All documentation should be read through, corrected, and synchronized. This step is frequently missed or axed from project plans when time is short – which is exactly when good documentation can make a big difference. Throughout the design process, documentation frequently gets out of synch with itself, especially when a large team is involved.

As an example, I was the data architect on a project for a moderately sized manufacturing plant. The gist of the project was to store measurements on samples of the materials that they were producing, for quality control purposes. We gathered information about what they did, what they wanted, and how they would use the data. We determined their needs, mocked up screens, and designed a database for solving their problems. The problem was that, while we understood the fundamentals of their reporting needs, we did not understand everything that was required:

- The reporting was so complex – due to intricate calculations (one of the queries was over 250 lines of code) – that, when we had mocked up a test query and verified the results, we failed to check exactly how they would use the data. It took more than fifty old measurements to calculate a new value, and what happened if someone went back and changed one of those old readings…? They wanted graphs with the last hundred calculated values, so computing on the fly was not an option. We just failed to understand much of how these calculated values were used, or how to make them more valuable to their staff.
- Second, we failed to understand the organizational structure of the company we worked with. We dealt with the two people who were running the project and they seemed experienced enough, but looks were deceiving, unfortunately. During the design phase of this project, the primary user contact was still in training. Near the end of the six-month project, they finally understood the exact needs for the system we were developing, but it was too late in the process.
- The third problem was the worst. We failed to properly review our documentation and make sure that everything that was agreed upon was written down. We did this because it was a time and materials contract. Unfortunately, we had to give them an estimate of what the costs would be like. We got the figure wrong by at least 200%, and the project took three times as long to complete. Consequently, we lost the follow-up work to a different consulting firm.

The important moral in this story is that all three of these problems would have evaporated if we had fully reviewed the documentation and made the clients sign off on it. If our entire plan had been meticulously written down, the additional time required would not only have been accepted, it would have been foreseen. Instead, we got into trouble because we had other projects to move on to.

It is not always possible to document every last detail of a system you are endeavoring to build. However, it is extremely important at this stage to review the documentation, to make sure that what you have specified can actually be built in the amount of time you have suggested, and that the requirements on you are not too open ended. Regardless of what type of project it is – corporate, time and materials, or fixed bid – it will always make sense for you to protect yourself against poor documentation.

Future Requirements

As a final step, we should document any future requirements that the client may have for the system we are creating. As the designer, it is your job to try to discover what are the future plans for the project, and what requirements may arise from them. Wherever feasible, the design for the current project should be modified to take these into consideration, as long as it does not significantly increase costs. You will look pretty silly (and turn out to be a lot poorer) if, six months after a project completes, the client asks for what he considers to be a trivial change, and you have to tell him it will take six months to implement because you will have to change 50 tables – especially when you knew that this might have been a possible request from the outset.

A little advance planning might mean a two week turnaround, a happy customer, and possible future business. Obviously, you should not kill yourself trying to second-guess the client's every need or whim – you have to be sensible about this. Be upfront with the client. "If we spend an extra two days adding X, then it will make it much easier to add Y should you need it in the future." If the client says, "Nah! We'll never need that" then fair enough – but try to get that in writing! Be proactive. As a professional designer, you should be thinking beyond the simple limits set by the client. Suggesting possible future enhancements and planning for them shows you understand the client's business and rarely hurts the bank balance.

Case Study

When we last left our case study we had built our data model, we had made a use case model, and were ready to start building. But not quite – we still have a few more pieces of information to gather.

Data Usage

In our use cases, we identified two different users for the system, the general account user (the spender), and the accounting clerk (the recorder). We interview the client again to try to discover what kinds of uses might be made of the data. Through these discussions, we discover that we need to add a few additional use cases and an additional actor. The actor we failed to identify initially is the management user, a user who gets to look at summaries of accounts and the activities of the other account users. We defined three new use cases: summary reports, user reports, and account alerts. We will discuss exactly what the reports require in the next subsections, but the account alerts are defined as messages sent to the user to tell them that an account is in need of some attention, such as the general account being overdrawn.

Ending the Logical Design Phase

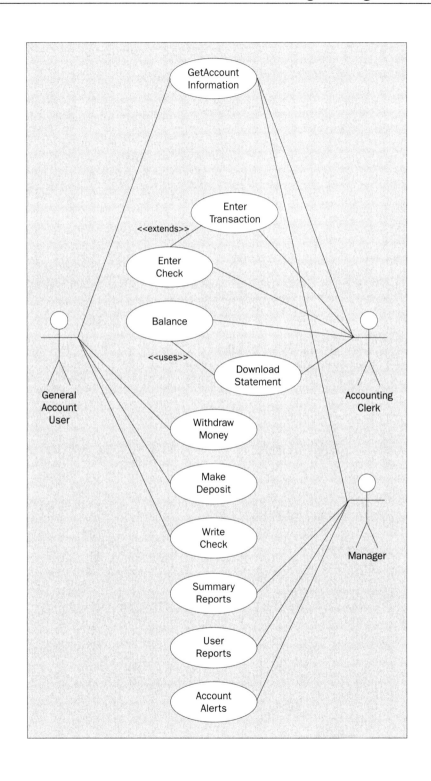

Chapter 8

Reports

When we ask the users what kind of reports they must have, we get the following list:

- **Account Summary** – Simply a categorized list of transactions, based on the `checkUsage` field. This report must let the user determine the level of subcategories to show. For instance, they could simply ask for all debits vs. credits, or another level down where they can see the basic categorization – all bills, business expenses, and charitable donations made (as we showed in the `checkUsageType` table example in the previous chapter).

- **User Activity** – A list of all transactions attributed to a given user, or simply grouped by user. Also needs to be able to show any transactions that have not been attributed to the user who actually spent the money.

- **Account Balance** – A list of all accounts and balances.

Further discussion leads the users to give us their specialized reports:

- **Spending Trends** – A very useful report that should be fairly easy to program, but is certainly not required, would be one that gives the trends of where the money goes in a more graphical easy-to-understand manner than the Account Summary Report.

- **Future Balance Estimator** – They would like to take spending for previous months and extrapolate to get an estimate of what they will probably spend in future months. This would be in lieu of a budget type tool. This report would also come in handy when building budgets.

- **Auto Check Writing** – Some time in the future they would like to have a facility to automatically pay bills, including the ability to have automatic payment with some intelligence built in, for situations where the required amount is not available in the account, etc.

They would also like to build data marts based on their data, in order to get multi-grouped reports based on payee, payee location, where the money goes, how much the amount was, etc. This is clearly above and beyond our current scope, but is very interesting to know.

Note that we have discovered at least one new data element and a new table for our database in the User Activity report. So we add a user table, and associate a user with a check and a deposit like so:

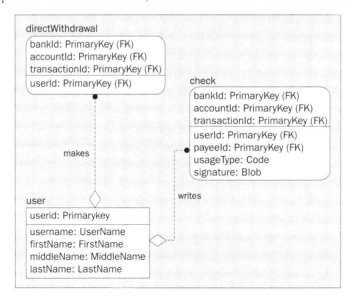

This will allow us to track the user who writes a check. This is another example of why we need to go through the entire design process, not leaving out any steps nor any stone unturned.

Prototype Report

We will now produce prototype reports of those listed in the previous section. To save space in this case study, I have I chosen just one – the Account Summary report – for illustration purposes.

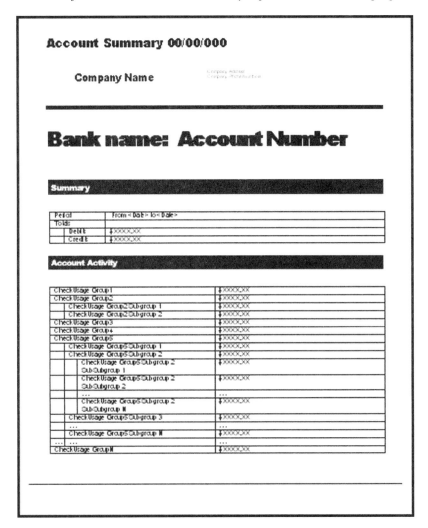

As you can see, we have added a simple summary to the basic requirements that we were given. We then have each of the check usage type groups summarized, and the amounts listed in the second column.

We will create prototypes for each of the three required reports. They are all that we will concern ourselves with here, because they should be well handled by our designed structures. The specialized reports that users have requested could be tackled in the next iteration of the system as follow on work.

Chapter 8

Interfacing to External Systems

The only external system that we will need to deal with belongs to the bank. As you will recall from the original interview documents, we have the format of the bank's automatic register, repeated here:

Column	Data type	Required
Transaction Date	Date Only	Yes
Transaction Number	String(20)	Yes
Description	String(100)	Yes
Item Amount	Money	Yes

Transaction.
   Transaction Date
   Transaction Number
   Description
   Item Account

In the paper version, they have extra summary type values that we apparently do not get from the electronic version. We will likely want to make our statement fields nullable, or possibly fill them in from a summary of items. We also need to add a few attributes to our data model for the `statementItems`, and we note that we had not even considered how an item would be considered reconciled. So we adjust our data model like so:

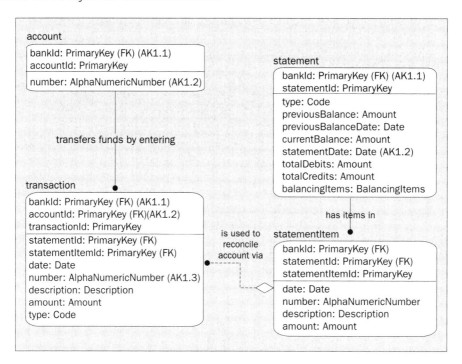

Note that we added the four attributes to the `statementItem` table for each of the fields in the bank's downloadable statement items. We also note that, in order to use these items for balancing, we need to link the item used for balancing to the item in the register.

> Just as would happen in real life, we are discovering new things about our solution as we go along. Note that we built a solid foundation in our opening chapters and all we are doing now is making important tweaks, closing important holes that we didn't find first time round.
>
> At this point we must attempt to avoid "analysis paralysis". By over analyzing, continually questioning the client, and making more and more changes to the design, we never actually get to the implementation phase. At some point a line must be drawn under the design, even it is not 100 per cent perfect. These shortfalls should be dealt with in the implementation phase.

Data Conversion Plan

In our system, the client has decided to start fresh in their check register; hence we will not have to do any data conversion. We will simply start the account out with a credit or debit for the initial balance.

This is the simplest type of data conversion plan – that is, none is necessary. As we are replacing a paper-based system, if the clients had wanted to do data conversion, they would have needed to enter all of the data by hand. Frequently this is not a possibility as it is too costly and problematic.

Volumetrics

For volumetrics, we build a simple table containing details of all of the other tables on our database, with the expected number of rows that the tables will initially contain. The best way to approach this is to take the system's important tables – as shown in our data model in Chapter 7 – and work from there. Say we decide that a good starting point for our estimates is the `transaction` table. We then simply inquire from the user about each table or group of tables, and extrapolate out to some of the other tables – especially the ones that we have added ourselves.

Note that we will also need to gather some statistics on columns. We will make quite a few decisions concerning how columns are implemented, and the users may be able to assist you in estimating their numbers. You can also refer to the existing system as a guide.

Let's take the transaction table first. In our case, the users have decided to start fresh with no actual transactions. They expect to have around 300 transactions per month, with 245 of those being checks, 5 deposits, and 50 direct withdrawals.

From there we get estimates on the number of different payees they want to start with, and how many they expect to add. We basically guess the rest of the numbers based on these values. For instance, from the estimate of 245 checks per month, we guess that they have 100 payees that they can set up, and they will likely add 30 new payees a month. Obviously, the more input you get from the clients, the better informed these estimates will be.

We end up with the following table of approximates that will need to be reviewed with the client.

Table Name	Initial Rows	Growth in Rows per Month	Max Rows
account	1	0	20
accountReconcile	0	1	36
address	50	30	600
addressLine	55	35	700
addressType	5	0	10
bank	1	0	5
check	0	245	10000
checkRegister	0	1	36
checkUsage	75	400	12000
checkUsageType	20	0	40
city	450	20	25000
deposit	0	5	4000
directWithdrawal	0	50	1000
payee	100	30	300
payeeAddress	100	30	600
payeePhoneNumber	100	30	600
phoneNumber	50	30	600
phoneNumberType	5	0	10
state	50	0	70
statement	0	1	36
statementItem	0	300	15000
transaction	0	300	15000
user	10	2	50
zipCode	1000	10	99999

Here is a description of the table's contents:

- Initial Rows – how many rows we expect to be added to the table when system goes live (zero indicates no rows yet).
- Growth in Rows per Month – the number of rows we expect the table to grow by (zero means little to no growth).
- Max Rows – a crude estimate of the maximum number of rows ever.

Project Plan

We make some estimates concerning how long the process will take in the project plan. For example, to finish the task of building this database, we might have a Gantt chart like this:

ID	Task Name	Start	End	Duration	May 2001					Jun 2001				Jul 2001			
					4/29	5/6	5/13	5/20	5/27	6/3	6/10	6/17	6/24	7/1	7/8	7/15	7/22
1	Physical Modeling	5/1/2001	5/7/2001	5d	■												
2	Design Data Protection	5/8/2001	6/1/2001	19d		■■■■											
3	Implement Access Code	6/4/2001	7/5/2001	24d							■■■■■						
4	Implement Reports	7/5/2001	8/15/2001	30d											■■■■■		

We would need to drill down into each task – perhaps:

Physical modeling:

Choose data types – 1 day
Designing optimistic locking mechanisms – 2 days

Or something like this. The amount of time things will take is really subjective, but should be based on previous experience and not on how much Dilbert we hope to read as we sit at our desk and look busy. As the project plan is beyond the scope of the book, we will not discuss it further.

Chapter 8

Security

Based on our use case from earlier in this chapter:

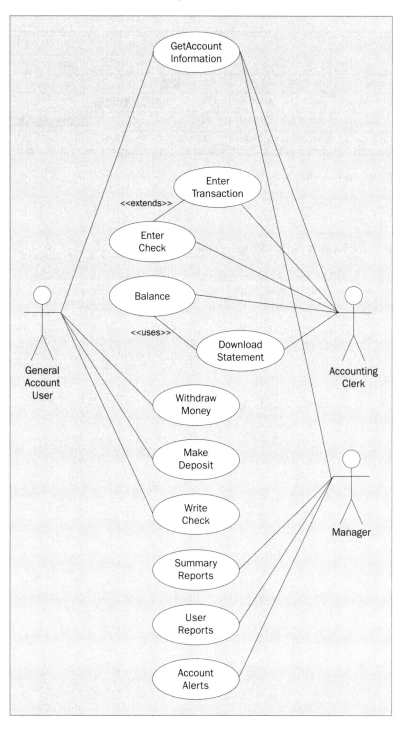

Since we have added new information as we discovered it, this should be a complete picture of how we will have to implement security. We can see that we have three user roles and several functional groups of items to consider. Each report has also been assigned a use case. This use case will be our template for implementing security later in the case study.

Final Documentation Review

Once we have finished, we stack up all of our papers, make copies, distribute them, and call a meeting a few days later. During this meeting, our goal is to get sign off; sign off that everything we have claimed in our documentation is precisely what the client wants. This is what I like to call the point of no return. Once the user signs off on the blueprints for the system, you are ready to start building. You should no longer spend very much time with the user, except for reporting progress.

This is not to say that our plans are fixed in stone, as we will likely find things that we did not do well enough. Hopefully, though, any changes will be in the form of an additional attribute, not an entire module of tables with screens.

Summary

The goal, however unreachable, of logical design is to discover everything that we need to implement a system. Once the implementation battle has begun, it can be very hard to change plans. However, I am assuming that, since you are reading this book, you at least have the common sense to not continue the *design-review-repeat* process forever until analysis paralysis sets in, but to find the best point when the design is ready to be implemented.

Throughout the entire logical design part of the book, we have been trying to design well enough to avoid having to change directions once we get rolling. We have gathered data, interviewed clients, pored over documentation, built models of our data, and finally normalized them, all so that they should be very close to being implementation-ready.

In this chapter we skirted very close to physical implementation in our attempts to finish off this part of the process. We have looked at planning our data needs, from security issues to reporting. We have also added our input to the project plan and have made some estimates concerning the size and growth of the data we will be storing in our tables.

Once this stage was complete, we reviewed the design – going back to make sure that we designed what we set out to design, and that any changes from the original requirements had been noted. If we are lucky, our documentation will now be in such a state that we do not need to actually go back and touch it again.

The output from the logical design phase is a blueprint, much like that which a building architect develops with a client, getting their hopes and dreams for the system, then tempering them with the reality and physics required to actually construct it. Once the client has approved the final blueprint, subcontractors are called in to add walls, lighting fixtures, plumbing, wires, and all the other various bits that go into putting together a physical structure.

Our blueprint is not unlike that of a building, with written descriptions, models, diagrams, etc. for physical implementation. The next phase of the project will now take us away from this very abstract world we have been living in, into the phase where we start hammering nails, erecting walls, and moving towards a database where our data can live and be safe.

Part II – Physical Design and Implementation

Physical database design and implementation is quite a different ball game to logical database design. Whereas in the logical phase, we went through our design concerning ourselves solely with getting "proper" structures, during the physical phase of the project, we tend to be more pragmatic. In this manner we turn our purely logical design into a practical design that we can implement.

While logical modeling is the hard part of the database design process, physical modeling shouldn't be viewed as a simple task. If you have not designed databases before, physical database implementation is very different from any other kind of computer software implementation that you may have been involved with, for one primary reason:

> The data structures in the database are normally the central part of the system being developed, hence the majority of the code in the project will rely on them. Any changes we implement therefore need to be carefully considered since they will have wide ranging implications for both the data structures themselves and the code we need to implement.

With this in mind, we move along into the following chapters:

- **Chapter 9 Planning the Physical Architecture** – In this chapter we will look at making the decisions concerning how we implement the architecture. Here we begin to take into consideration the number of users, system size, and how the data will be used.

- **Chapter 10 Planning and Implementing the Basic Physical Architecture** – In this chapter we will go through the mechanics of choosing data types, building tables, and creating indices.

Part II – Physical Design and Implementation

- **Chapter 11 Ensuring Data Integrity** – There are many different issues that govern the data integrity of our system. We will look at some of the different types of business rules we may wish to implement and how we can do so through the use of user defined functions and constraints.

- **Chapter 12 Advanced Data Access and Modification Techniques** – In this chapter we will look at some of the different methods of accessing the data in the databases we have created, in particular through the use of views and stored procedures.

- **Chapter 13 Determining Hardware Requirements** – One of the most difficult activities for many data architects is to translate the system requirements into actual hardware requirements. What disk format do I need? How much disk space do I need, and how will these requirements change in the future? How much RAM? How many processors? Too many questions. These are generally questions for the database administrator, but for many architects there may not be an administrator around to help make proper hardware decisions.

- **Chapter 14 Completing the Project** – In this chapter we will look at the end game. Once we have our data, our structures, and queries built, the project is over, isn't it? To wrap up our project we will consider the fine-tuning of our system, including considering performance issues concerning reporting needs, especially in high usage systems, and the system testing and deployment we must undertake. We will also look at drawing up disaster plans, in order to protect our data from all those mishaps that Murphy (in his famous law) predicted would occur.

Part II – Physical Design and Implementation

Planning the Physical Architecture

Introduction

In this chapter, we will be looking at how we should implement our database. In order to illustrate the type of judgements we may have to make, let's consider the following scenarios, and try to assess what each requires for successful implementation, such as separate read-only structures for reporting, a separate Operational Data Store, or simply additional hardware to improve query performance. Each is a realistic example of databases that are really quite commonplace today. Let's assume in each case that the logical design is an appropriate one.

Scenario 1

The database contains 100 tables. One of the tables will have a million rows and will grow at a rate of one hundred thousand rows a day. There are 2000 users entering data into the system, and only three people carry out reporting all day long.

Scenario 2

The database contains 20 tables. All of the tables have relations to at least one other table, and ten of the tables grow at a rate of 100 rows per day. Three people enter all of the rows twenty-four hours a day, whilst reports are run by an automatic process and sent via e-mail to the senior executives in the organization.

Scenario 3

The database has two million users, fifteen thousand of whom will be accessing the database at any given time. Every minute, each of the users will create two new records in a database.

The Solution

So which of these scenarios require special handling? Unfortunately, the answer is unclear since none of the scenarios contains sufficient information to allow us to make an informed decision.

In scenario one, for example, in order to determine whether there is a need to build a special database to support day-to-day reporting needs, we would need to know how long it takes for the two thousand users to enter the hundred thousand rows. This could take all day, or it could be rows from users who are actually machines that automatically enter data in an hour every day. Furthermore, whilst we would anticipate that data in this case has to be transformed, summarized, and stored in a data warehouse to do reporting against, the exact nature of any reporting needs is not outlined in this case.

Scenario two may seem simpler, since we might suppose that adding one thousand rows to a database a day is not that many, especially if a single user enters them. As an automatic process runs reports, we know that it can be scheduled to run at an opportune time. In this case we probably will not need any kind of special database for reporting, since the system should not be busy and so querying of the OLTP database can take place directly. However, we should take into consideration that we are going to add several hundred thousand rows per year to the database which, while certainly not a large number of rows, may be a problem depending on the type of data in the rows and the type of reporting required. Simple aggregations that are supported intrinsically by SQL Server will likely be no problem, while more complex statistical operations may require special handling. We will look deeper at the topic of complex reporting needs later in this chapter.

Scenario three is indicative of a website. It is also arguably the simplest of the scenarios to solve. The primary reason for this is that if you have a database with two million users, with fifteen thousand active connections, you will most probably have the money to throw as much hardware at the situation as is needed. However, aside from any hardware investment problems you may have, there are still important issues to resolve regarding the nature of the records that will be generated, and what reporting requirements there will be.

This chapter was actually the hardest of them all to write, since a good logical design is dictated by the problem being analyzed, without the tradeoffs required during implementation in allowing for performance and usability issues. Good logical modelers will generally come to similar conclusions for the same problems. We follow the same type of design methodology, regardless of whether we are working on a small database to store a television schedule, or a large database to store engineering quality control data. Once you have done it well once, you should be able to do it over and over again, with consistent, expected results.

Determining how the physical database solution should finally be laid out and implemented is a different story altogether. Here we must take a set of parameters and build the solution that represents the logical model in a manner that allows the business to meet all its expected requirements. Be certain that this is not always easy to get right every time. In implementation, you are not only considering your logical design model, but are also reliant on the work of your support colleagues (the DBA and database programmers) in making the best choices when selecting hardware, coding SQL procedures, and building transformations from the OLTP database to the ODS. It is not always possible for them to make the optimum choices and, since the database server is typically the central part of any system, it can often get the lion's share of the blame for system problems.

You may feel slightly daunted by the task at hand, but don't worry, as we will now start to look at all of the pre-implementation issues we need to deal with before creating tables. While we can't describe every situation you may encounter in physical implementation, we can at least consider the two main factors that we have influence over, namely:

- **Reporting** – A key issue in all our design work is balancing the need for frequent updating of our given database, with reading data in order to provide accurate reporting. Maintaining facilities to monitor the business is very important to the process of making informed decisions concerning tweaking that is required within the business to optimize its efficiency.

- **Performance** – Performance is a very different sort of issue. There are lots of situations where the well normalized database may provide less than adequate performance in relation to what is required. We will look at some of the basic things we can do to adjust performance, while still preserving our normalized database structures (in most cases).

It is our contention that the primary intent of building client-server systems is to allow changes to be made to our *current* data, and have it applied *immediately* – not to send off a query and wait for its completion. Hence we should do whatever we can to keep the OLTP system unencumbered by read only queries. Whilst we must consider performance, we should not in doing so compromise the integrity of the data that we store. It is the data architect's primary duty to store data that is needed, in a clean manner, protecting it from anomalies that occur in poorly structured databases.

Reporting Issues

Reporting seeks to arrange raw data into a meaningful format that will enable users to make timely and adequate decisions. As discussed in the previous chapter, reports are usually the most important part of the system to the end users, and in this section we will discuss some of the ways that reports can be optimized to fit into a range of database structures. Quite a few issues arise when we discuss accurate and timely reporting, not all of which are as obvious as one might think.

Size of Data

One of the most frequent problems in reporting is that the volume of data needed to answer a user's questions is too large to perform queries on in a reasonable manner. The nature of the problem is dependent upon what hardware you are running SQL Server on, be it a desktop computer with sixteen megabytes of RAM or a four-node cluster with 4 gigabytes of RAM each. Generally however, querying techniques need to be tailored to the volumes of data involved, though determining when "small" volumes become "large" ones can become somewhat problematic, as the following examples illustrate:

Imagine that the United States Government has a database somewhere that contains every social security number it has issued, along with every transaction that it has made to add money to, or to distribute money from, the social security accounts. It is clear that over the past 50 plus years, there would have been millions upon millions of records added each month.

While this may seem like a large quantity of data, it is dwarfed by databases being created by some Internet service providers and Internet sites in their desire to log every click, every purchase, and every search that their users perform. In this way, e-commerce web sites track as much information as they can about their visitors, in order to personalize their site to show goods that they predict the visitor will have an interest in. Such applications are likely to log immense amounts of information concerning the millions of daily visitors to such sites, all of which will be required for analysis by the sites' owners.

Another example of logging activities that are becoming commonplace is that of manufacturing quality assurance databases, where robots take hundreds and thousands of measurements a minute to ensure that the items being manufactured fall within a specified tolerance. This kind of application will obviously generate a tremendous number of records.

In these situations, there are a few basic approaches we can take to try to solve the problem:

- **Optimization** – If we are faced with a situation where we seem to be at an upper limit for the amount of data that our system can handle, there are many times when a simple change in our system set up (such as separating data out into different file groups) will correct the problem. Whilst features such as a large number of indexes (or indeed a lack of them), or poorly considered optimizer hints (overriding how the optimizer chooses to deal with queries), can kill performance, in many cases cries of "too much" anything may well have more to do with the less than optimal set up of the server or databases.

- **Data Access** – Consider a case where we were using a tool like Access, with linked tables. Performing a join in Access may well involve bringing each of the linked tables to the client before creating the join using its own query engine, which is not a great idea when we are dealing with thousands of rows, and is unfeasible in the case of millions of rows. However, the query might run admirably if performed using SQL Server. In many cases, problems with large amounts of data are linked more to the actual passing of data over a wire, rather than the SQL operation itself. More on data access times will follow later in this chapter.

- **Powerful hardware** – It is possible that we might be able to simply put together more efficient hardware that will handle the amount of data that we have to deal with. Using faster CPU, as much RAM as will fit in the machine, and fully optimized disk arrays may not be the only answer to the problem, but will certainly be a large part of it. We will discuss hardware in some depth in Chapter 13.

- **Reporting database** – As we have discussed in Chapter 1, and will implement in Chapter 14, we can build a copy of our data that contains the answers to many of the queries that the user will want to make, in order to support our day-to-day operations. In our e-commerce example above, it is a relatively fast process to build a cached copy of our data in order to answer queries on user activities. The alternative to this is to scan through all of the records that have logged all of the actions of not only the single user, but *all* the users that have been through the site: a *real* pain to carry out!

In all likelihood, we will end up using a mixture of these ideas, though the first two are a good place to start, since they don't require huge capital expenditures and are a great challenge (but don't let your manager hear you say that)!

Complexity

The complexity of the reporting required is directly dependent upon how we use basic SQL operations. Simple queries, using only intrinsic SQL operations, are generally no problem (though poorly designed queries can cause nasty situations, like forgetting a WHERE clause and duly locking up an entire table, preventing others from modifying it), but it is not always possible to restrict calculations to these operations alone. For example, I have implemented reports that utilize a single SQL statement containing over 300 lines of code. The length of code was due to the fact that it took around three lines of code to implement the standard deviation function used, and was needed 20 or so times within the SQL statement. Whilst the time required to execute the statement was not tremendous (in seconds) the operation proved costly in terms of resource utilization (disk and CPU usage) thereby limiting concurrency. What the users then wanted to be able to do was see the last 100 executes of this query on a graph, each aggregation using the previous 100 values in the table to make up the calculation. To execute the 300 line query 100 times, for the users to see 500 times a day, would have been unreasonable.

In this case, and in others which involve extremely complex reporting circumstances, it may become necessary to store some pre-aggregated data which violates the Third Normal Form, especially when additional data or business rules require the answers to the same queries to do their jobs. This is an illustration of the denormalization process that we touched on briefly in Chapter 7.

Note of course that the pre-aggregated data could come from calculations outside of SQL Server. When using pre-aggregated data you need to ensure that if the underlying data changes, the aggregation code is executed again and the stored values change. In our above example, a change of a single value could cost as much as 100 executes in order to repair the denormalized data. There is not much that can be done about this, as modification anomalies of this sort are at the core of the normalization argument. To ensure data integrity, all references to the same data must be changed simultaneously.

Search Requirements

If a report requires a large amount of search freedom (for example when users need to perform queries on many different fields from many different tables), this can increase complexity to the point that it is unmanageable. The tables in a normalized database are not optimized for querying, precisely because the process of normalization attempts to create single themed tables. One of the ways to work around this type of problem, is to use one of the new facilities contained in SQL Server 2000 – **Indexed Views**. This provides a means of pre-calculating a view based on its own definition, and so could be used to build a view that presents the users with the data in an understandable interface, which they can then query in a straightforward manner. This method suffers from the same performance issues that storing our own denormalized data does, since SQL Server has to maintain the indexed view in a similar manner whenever the underling data changes. Further details on indexed views can be found in "*Professional SQL Server 2000 Programming*" *(Wrox Press, ISBN 1861004486)*.

User Access Contention

For any given system, the more concurrent users there are, the more contention we are likely to have between them. In OLTP operations, transactions and queries should be designed to last for an extremely minimal amount of time. Reports are another matter. Many report queries can take quite a while to execute; it is not uncommon to have reports that take fifteen minutes, an hour, or even several hours to execute.

Problems may occur when, for example, you have a very patient and relatively knowledgeable user of your system, who writes *ad hoc* queries. If the user does not have any understanding of exactly how SQL Server works, then they may try and carry out queries that involve numerous joins between large tables of data, thereby taking many hours to complete their actions. In this way they are liable to eventually begin blocking other users' activities, despite the row-level locking facility implemented in SQL Server 7.0 in order to greatly decrease the likelihood of exactly this type of blocking scenario. However, the way that row-level locking was implemented allows the optimizer to choose between row-level, page-level, and table-level locks. When a user writes a particularly poorly constructed query that accesses many pages in a table, the optimizer will frequently escalate the locks to a page or even table lock. Frequently, when users perform such queries, the eventual locks will include pages and tables still being modified by the active users, causing a great deal of frustration!

Timeliness

Timeliness refers to how current the data needs to be in order to support the user's needs in making informed decisions. For example, suppose that we build an operational data store from our OLTP data, feed a data warehouse and data marts from it, and we refresh the data daily. This entire setup will be useless to the user if all decisions are to be made using up-to-the-second data.

How quickly we can provide data access depends not only on the amount of time it takes for the data to travel from one location to another (so called **latency**) but also on our design. Our different approaches may be summarized as:

- **Up-to-the-Second** – Up-to-the-second access is the most problematic as there is very little we can do about it. There are many ways to handle these needs and all of them cause us performance problems. We will frequently just have to build stored procedures that read data directly from our tables, accessing data in such a manner as to avoid locking data. If it is not possible to do this without a performance "hit", then we can include denormalized structures, or possibly even indexed views in our stored procedures. Sometimes the performance hit is unavoidable and actually represents an acceptable drawback in relation to our data presentation needs. Equally we may be able to devise a compromise situation, such as randomly sampling data, rather than including every value, to improve our speed of data retrieval.

- **Some allowable latency** – If you do not have instantaneous read need for data, we can use any of the other methodologies. We can build ODS structures that are refreshed as often as the data size (and business rules) allows. Care will need to be taken to ensure that the frequency of update is greater than the users needs.

- **Large latency** – When time is not a primary issue, and particularly when tremendously large amounts of historical data is involved (such as trend analysis over time), the data warehouse or companion data marts are the best approach, because we can have most of the possible (and all of the frequently used) aggregations and queries set up.

Frequency

Frequency in this context refers to the number of times a report will be run. One of the systems that I have previously worked on had a report that was considered central to their efforts. It was run every 24 hours at midnight and would take three hours to run. Since it was run during the slower hours of the day, the users could live with a small degree of performance degradation.

On the other hand, many other systems have users who need to keep tabs on how things are going throughout the day, such as a bank manager who needs to make sure that the bank has enough money on hand, or a broker who needs to have up-to-the-minute trend reports run on each of their clients or funds. Reporting of this type will probably require super-powered hardware and extremely optimized queries, as well as some denormalized structures.

Performance Concerns

If we take the example of a database built to monitor and store consumer activity at a website, which we discussed earlier, not only will this database be designed logically to log every activity, but we also might store every item, and every page that is displayed on the screen as well. This is a very large database (think terabytes), and with its data stored in a normalized fashion, a single database would possibly not be able to withstand both users modifying the data, and web users querying its pages. In the following section, we will look at some of the possible computer and networking configurations (commonly referred to as **topologies**) that we will use to combat a number of common performance issues.

Connection Speed

Of primary concern here are **Wide Area Networks** (WAN), as well as web applications (which one could technically regard as a WAN in different clothing). Let's take, as a very simple example, the classic two-tier client server system:

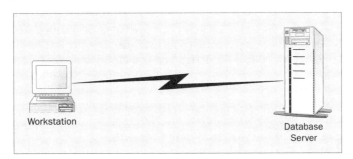

Varying the connection speed or distance between the client and the database server will considerably change the way we end up organizing our database system. In the following list, we will look at some of the common networking speeds and how they will affect our decision to vary from this simple topology:

- **Extremely fast connection, such as a 10Mbit, 100Mbit network or greater** – These types of connections are most commonly seen within a company's physical network. Unless we have database size issues, we should have little problem employing a simple two-tier client server system like we have in the diagram above. The user could connect directly to the SQL Server and require very few special optimizations.

- **Moderate connection, such as an ISDN, DSL, Cable** (2 Mbit down to 128Kbit) **connection** – In general basic client server applications are fairly workable over such connections, but we might need to ensure that we optimize all of our calls to the database, in order to reduce the number of bytes that go back and forth over the network and the number of separate communications involved. A possible enhancement would be to optimize our client software by caching frequent calls to the database that may be repeated, and to batch multiple operations together.

- **Slow connection, such as a Dial-up** (56Kbits in principle, often more like approximately 28.8Kbits) – Dial-up applications are more prevalent than one might realize. Many sales or support workers have dial-up connections that they use to run their database applications every night from their hotels. While users who access their applications via a dial-up connection are generally more understanding when it comes to access speed, the applications must work adequately. In these cases, we will certainly have to optimize the applications, or possibly even move to a use a replication scheme to present parts of the database to the client using some form of compression. We will discuss replication in some length later in this chapter.

No matter how fast the workstation or database server is, the speed at which you connect to the server is crucial to performance. If you are trying to push 1000 rows back to the client where the row has 3000 bytes, and you are doing this over a 128Kbit ISDN line, your client will be really unhappy with you, since it will take approximately 3 minutes (3000 * 1000 * 8 (bits per byte)) / (128 * 1000 = 187.5 seconds) to complete. This does not allow for either networking overhead, or indeed any other users. If ten users were trying to use the same bandwidth, then it would take 31 plus minutes for them to all receive their data!

Chapter 9

It should be noted that you could write your program so as to retrieve records and display them as needed, instead of retrieving all 1000 records at the same time. For instance, you could show 20 records in one page, and as the users scroll through the results, the remaining records would then be downloaded in chunks. However, for all of us who have used query analyzer and brought back 1000+ rows in a testing query in a half second (including both the query and fetching of the data), this would still prove frustrating.

The reality is that very few of the larger systems today are being built with a simple client-server architecture. Most of them have parts distributed all over the network, and even the world. The following example is a pretty wild looking design that includes web servers, data warehouses, and even a legacy mainframe system.

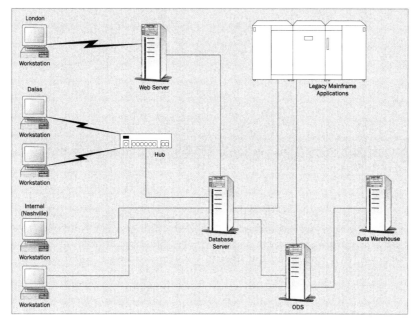

You can see from this diagram that the complexity of our solution is bounded only by the architect's imagination. Some organizations have tens or even hundreds of database servers, many of which are connected together via all sorts of connections with all sort of different reliability factors. In this case each one of the lines between items represents a network connection. At any of these connection points, we have speeds that may vary from blisteringly fast to doggedly slow, and each point should be considered as a liability (in design terms), since networks tend to be less than 100 per cent reliable.

Whilst it is important for the database designer to at least be aware of how connection speed affects the performance of applications, wider aspects of networking issues falls into the realm of the systems administrator.

Amount of Data

SQL Server 2000 is a very scalable database server. It scales from Windows Pocket PC handheld devices, through a single Pentium-200MHz laptop with thirty-two megabytes of RAM running Windows 95, or a dual Pentium III desktop with a half gigabyte of RAM, to a sixteen-server cluster of eight-processor servers with four gigs of RAM each, and everything in between. The amount of data you can support goes from a megabyte or two on your palmtop to multiple terabytes on the server cluster.

The size of data will make quite a bit of difference to our coding standards. We can get away with some programming conveniences (ignoring optimizations and such) with ease if our primary table in the database will have one thousand records as opposed to one billion. As an illustration, take this simple example:

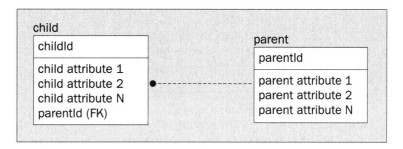

We will state as a matter of definition that if you have a record in the child table, the migrated key from the parent table must exist. Now consider the situation where we want to delete a record from the parent table. It then becomes apparent that the size of the child table will be extremely important. If there are ten rows in the child table, to delete a single row in the parent table you must scan through ten records: no big deal. If there are a million rows however, it is not quite so simple a task for SQL Server (even with indexes this could take an unreasonable amount of time). It follows that if you have a billion rows in the table, the row may not be able to be deleted in a fortnight. In this case, we would probably implement an additional column in the parent table to indicate that the record can no longer be used, but not actually delete the record. However setting this flag on the parent table only will leave records in the child table related to the flagged record, which require careful handling. Hence in either case we may not be able to handle the situation optimally.

Budget

Any solutions we devise must be based on what is appropriate for the organization, since increasing the size of the budget to pay for expensive hardware may not always be an option.

There are three main areas of concern:

- **Hardware** – Not enough can be said to emphasize how inappropriate hardware will cause you problems. In Chapter 13, we will look at sizing hardware for database growth, number of users, etc. Never skimp on production hardware is the simple message. In Chapter 14, we will discuss in some depth the concept of having at least three different environments, one each for development, testing, and production. In order to build, verify, and implement a proper database system, you will need at least two separate servers.
- **Software** – Budget sufficiently for the operating system, database software licenses, and any tools you will need for building the software. Read with care the licensing agreements on the software to avoid overpaying for your software.
- **Staffing** – Depending on the size of the project, you should be prepared to have staff capable of handling each part of the database system you develop. Very few database architects are also great networking specialists, great database administrators, and great documenters, great testers, great coders, and great...you get the point.

Number of users

One of the most difficult performance issues to deal with concerns the number of users (or connections) you will have to support. As each connection requires approximately 12 KB + (3 * (network packet size which varies but defaults to 4 KB)), or 24 KB, most system architects aren't exactly concerned with the number of users that a system will have. However, in this day of database supported websites, the user totals that could be accessing our database could be anything from 10 to 10 million or even more! In attempting to deal with such vast numbers of users there are a number of methods that we can use including:

- **Connection Pooling** – If a user connects and disconnects many times in their applications, it can be advantageous to use the connection pooling features in ODBC 2.5 and beyond, or OLE DB. They allow the drivers to let the user "think" that they disconnected but to actually hold the connection open waiting for a further command.

    As a brief word of caution, connection pooling does NOT do its own cleanup when you tell a connection to end. Most importantly any open transactions may not be closed out and could affect later connections, even in the case of multiple users sharing a connection, so suitable caution should be exercised.

- **COM+ (or any variation on the *n*-Tier applications)** – COM+ enables you to offload some of the processing that could have been done on the client end, and pool connections amongst many different users, so that you remove a good bit of the overhead of creating and destroying connections. By pooling connections, ten thousand concurrent connections can look like 1000, or even 100.

- **More Power, More Memory** – Just add more hardware doggone it! Unfortunately budget constraints may mean that this solution is not possible. As mentioned previously, each connection to the server requires ~24K of RAM. This may not seem like too big a deal, but if you have 10000 connections to the server, it could equal 240000K, which is a good part of the 256 MB that a standard SQL Server can use. If we add in the processor overhead of manipulating all that RAM over and over again, then we quickly see how problems can develop.

- **Clustering servers** – Microsoft SQL Server and Windows 2000 support clustering multiple database servers and treating them as a single server. Using clustering allows us to build very large, very powerful database server systems. The idea with these systems is to distribute the load of an application across a number of servers, such that as the number of requests increases so additional servers can be added in order to deal with the additional load. This process is known as **load balancing**. Since each server (ideally) is capable of handling a client's request individually then if one server breaks down, or there is a need for additional servers to be added to the cluster, there is no breakdown in performance. Further details regarding clustering can be found in *"Professional Windows DNA: Building Distributed Web Applications with VB, COM+, MSMQ, SOAP, and ASP" (Wrox Press, ISBN 1861004451)*.

- **Application specific read-only copies of data** – This is a technique that works well when building websites. Most of the data that we require when building data driven web pages is read only. For instance, consider a hypothetical product description database, in which we have all of our products stored in a very normalized set of structures, to avoid all of the pitfalls of redundancy. Then consider the web page that the user will see that has current price, color, sizes, shapes, specifications, etc. all listed on the same page. In this case we might build a table that has all of the values that the web page needs in one table, instead of fifty tables, and three hundred rows. We probably wouldn't want to pre-generate the entire user's page, since we certainly would want to be able to personalize it (add in discounts, etc.) and indeed change its look and feel on the fly. Additional storage will be required, but our processing needs will be greatly reduced thanks to the reduction in the number of joins performed.

Planning the Physical Architecture

SQL Server Facilities

Having considered many of the issues relating to the performance of our database systems, we should also consider the tools which SQL Server offers the designer. In this section we take a quick look at what they are and how they can be used primarily for those who have not had much use of SQL Server. For those who are regular SQL Server users: please skip this section and head for the topology examples in the next section.

Replication

Replication is a wonderful facility that assists in making copies of databases and maintaining them at some interval for us. This interval can vary from immediately to days or weeks. Replication can be carried out between SQL Servers, or even from SQL Server to Microsoft Access, Oracle, or almost any database that supports the Subscriber requirements for SQL Server (see SQL Server Books Online for more information).

A couple of terms that we need to introduce here are:

- **Publication** – The source of the data being replicated, though it may or may not be the original creator. Much like a physical printed publication (hence the name), a publication is a database that has been marked for other databases to **subscribe** to. The database is split up into tables marked for replication referred to as **articles.**

- **Subscription** – When a database uses a publication to get a replica of one or more articles of a publication, it is referred to as the **subscriber**. The subscription can be to a single article or all articles.

SQL Server provides four separate models for implementing replication:

- **Snapshot replication** – makes a copy of the data of the Publication database and replaces the entire set of data in the Subscription database on a periodic basis.

- **Transactional replication** – initially makes a snapshot of a Publication into the Subscription (just like snapshot replication), and then applies any transaction asynchronously to the Subscription as they occur on the Publication.

- **Merge replication** – allows you to have two databases (one of which is chosen as Publisher and the other as Subscriber) where you take all changes from the Publisher and add them to the Subscriber and *vice versa*. This allows you to edit data in either place and apply changes to the other automatically. Merge replication is very useful for mobile clients where maintaining a connection to the primary server is unfeasible. Merge replication also has default and custom choices to allow for conflict resolution in the case where multiple users edit the exact same pieces of data.

Linked Servers

Linked servers allow us to access heterogeneous SQL Server or OLEDB data sources directly from within SQL Server. Not only can we simply access it, but we are able to issue updates, commands and transactions on this data. For example, to access a SQL Server named LOUSERVER, we would execute the following:

```
sp_addlinkedserver @server = N'LinkServer',
    @provider = N'SQLOLEDB',
    @datasrc = N'LOUSERVER',
    @catalog = N'Pubs'
```

Then we can execute a query to retrieve rows from this datasource:

```
SELECT *
FROM LinkServer.pubs.dbo.authors
```

This is a simple example, but it illustrates our point succinctly. With linked servers you are able to access additional SQL Servers, Oracle Servers, Access Databases, Excel Spreadsheets, just to name a few. And the beauty of it is that you do not have to learn any additional syntax to access a myriad of different types of data. The ugly side of it is that to join the given set to another set, a great deal of data *may* have to be passed from one SQL Server into temporary storage on another, before the join is performed, which can have serious performance side effects.

Data Transformation Services (DTS)

When replication will not work due to changes (transformations, hence the name) that need to be made in the data, Microsoft has provided DTS. Using it, you can transform and transfer data between OLE DB sources. DTS also allows you to transfer indexes and stored procedures between SQL Servers.

Using DTS you can create packages that group together multiple transformation operations/objects that can be run either synchronously (one operation waiting for another to complete) or asynchronously using the full power of SQL Server. You can for example carry out data scrubbing (removal/cleaning of data) transformations from one table to another, with the ability to calculate new values using simple VB script.

DTS is a fully featured data scrubbing tool and as such has a plethora of settings and possibilities. Further details can be found in "*Professional SQL Server 2000 DTS*", (Wrox Press, ISBN 1861004419).

Distributed Transaction Controller (DTC)

DTC is the facility that implements a **two-phase commit** to allow you create a transaction that involves more than one server. The reason that the process is called a two-phase commit, is because each of the servers that are involved in the transaction is sent two special commands to start and end the process.

- ❑ **Prepare** – the transaction manager sends a command to each database server to its resource manager. The server then prepares to accept the commands that will be sent.
- ❑ **Commit or Rollback** – once the "user(s)" have completed whatever tasks and commands they want to execute, the commit or rollback phase begins, working much like you executed a commit transaction on each server.

In a strictly SQL Server coding manner, once DTC has been turned on, and you have created linked servers, you could use the following code to update the authors table both on the server where this code is executing, and the linked server.

```
USE pubs
GO
BEGIN DISTRIBUTED TRANSACTION
```

```
UPDATE authors
SET au_lname = 'Davidson'
WHERE au_id = '555-55-5555'

IF @@error <> 0
BEGIN
   ROLLBACK TRANSACTION
   GOTO exit
END

UPDATE linkserver.pubs.dbo.authors
SET au_lname = 'Davidson'
WHERE au_id = '555-55-5555'

IF @@error <> 0
BEGIN
   ROLLBACK TRANSACTION
   GOTO exit
END

COMMIT TRANSACTION

exit:
GO
```

Note that DTC controller works with data of any type where there exists an OLE DB driver that supports the distributed transaction interfaces. It should also be recognized that if DTC has not been installed the `BEGIN DISTRIBUTED TRANSACTION` statement will fail.

SQL Data Management Objects (SQL-DMO)

SQL-DMO is a set of COM objects that encapsulates almost every feature of SQL Server. From DMO you can carry out tasks such as creating tables and indexes, and automating object creation and administration tasks. The objects can be used from any tool that allows the instantiation of COM objects, such as Visual Basic, VB Script, VB for Applications, C++, and as you will see in the next section, SQL Server itself. There are many good examples in the SQL Server Books online that illustrate the power of SQL-DMO, and further details can also be found in *"Professional SQL Server 7.0 Development Using SQL-DMO, SQL-NS & DTS"*, (*Wrox Press, ISBN 1861002807*).

COM Object Instantiation

Another nifty feature that has existed since the 6.X versions of SQL Server is COM Object Instantiation. Using a pretty clunky T-SQL interface, you can make a call to most COM objects to have them do almost anything you require.

In the following example, we instantiate the SQLServer DMO object and then connect to it:

```
DECLARE @objectHandle int
@retVal int,

--instantiate the sqlserver object
EXECUTE @retVal = sp_OACreate 'SQLDMO.SQLServer', @objectHandle OUT
IF @retVal <> 0
```

```
    BEGIN
        EXECUTE sp_displayoaerrorinfo @objectHandle, @retVal
        RETURN
    END

    --connect to server
    EXECUTE @retVal = sp_OAMethod @objectHandle, 'Connect', NULL, 'LOUSERVER','louis',
    '<none of your business what my password is>'
    IF @retVal <> 0
    BEGIN
        EXECUTE sp_displayoaerrorinfo @objectHandle, @retVal
        RETURN
    END
```

While instantiating a COM object is very useful, it can also be a slow process. The object must be created (and memory allocated for it), executed, and finally destroyed, all in a manner that is specifically non-SQL like. Make use of this functionality only when a SQL based solution is not possible, or in procedures that you don't expect to be called that often.

SQL Mail

SQL Mail allows SQL Server to send and receive mail using a simple Outlook or Exchange interface and either an Exchange or POP3 server. The server can be made to answer e-mails that contain queries, returning the answering result set as an e-mail. It can also be added to stored procedures and triggers when required.

Examples of how useful this facility can be are tasks such as sending reminders for items on a calendar, or indeed sending warnings to tell the user that a certain condition has occurred, such as a negative balance on their bank account. In the following code snippet, we use SQL mail to send us a very happy e-mail:

```
    EXEC xp_sendmail @recipients = 'yourname@domain.com',
                    @query = 'select ''hi'' ',
                    @subject = 'SQL Server Report',
                    @message = 'Hello!',
                    @attach_results = 'TRUE'
```

Full Text Search

Full-text searching with SQL Server allows us to build very powerful searches that work much like any Internet search site would. Using full-text search lets us search through text columns as well as external system files. The query syntax for full-text search is simply an extension of regular SQL Server commands.

For example, consider the following query:

```
    SELECT title_id, title, price
    FROM pubs..titles
    WHERE CONTAINS (title, '"Database" near "Design"')
```

Using the CONTAINS keyword, we are searching not only for titles that have Database and Design in the title, but where they are close together.

Note that while full-text capabilities ship with SQL Server 2000, they do not come installed by default. If you try to execute that statement in `pubs` without configuring the `pubs` database, and also configuring the title column in the `titles` table for full-text support, the example above will fail with an error message. The full-text indexes are stored separately from the SQL Server, and as such may be slower than intrinsic SQL Server operations. Further details regarding setting up and implementing full-text search can be found in *"Professional SQL Server 2000 Programming" (Wrox Press, ISBN 1861004486)*.

SQL Server Agent

Last in our section on SQL Server Facilities, and far from least, is the job scheduling capability of SQL Server Agent, which is the glue that will make your systems operate. Replication uses the agent to process transactions, DTS packages can be scheduled to run at certain times, and you can also schedule your own stored procedures to execute and launch operating system programs.

Setting up the SQL Server Agent is beyond the scope of this book, and the reader should consult SQL Server Books Online for further details. Suffice to say that SQL Server has a built in facility that runs in its own security context that will execute almost anything your database will require.

Basic Topology Examples

In this section we will take a look at some of the more important topologies that we might choose to employ when we are building our applications.

Thin Client versus Thick Client

The "thickness" of a client relates directly to how much work the client program is responsible for. This should not be confused with the same term as it is used in describing the concept of a program written in a classic programming language like Visual Basic or C++ where all of the presentation logic is coded into the client program as opposed to delivered to the client.

Thick Client

The best example of a thick client would be an application written in Visual Basic that accesses a Text File database using ODBC. Since a text file is certainly not an RDBMS and as such cannot protect itself, you must include every bit of data validation code in the client.

A very thick client can be employed to reduce the bandwidth of an application, because, if every possible data issue has been handled by the front end, and there is no possibility of the server changing any values, we can trust that our data will be saved exactly as we entered it into the database. If an error does occur, it will be due to a SQL Server problem (such as a disk failure, or data corruption of some sort).

However, a thick client is not without its problems. Since you have already pre-validated the data, it seems like overkill to have SQL Server validate it. On the other hand, unless the client is the *only* method of getting data into the server, you leave your data open to errors whenever manipulation is done without the application. This may seem a small price to pay to have a user-friendly application, but rarely can all data edits be made strictly through a single piece of software.

Thin Client

On the other end of the spectrum is the thin client. In this scenario, the client code would not validate the data that is being entered at all, and would trust that the SQL Server mechanisms will take care of any errors and report them. A good example of a very thin client is the SQL Server Enterprise Manager query window:

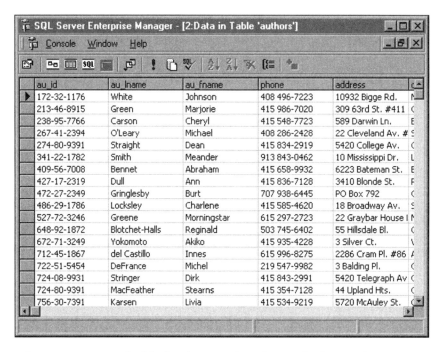

No matter what you enter into the blanks, the entry form here will take it and pass it to SQL Server. It in turn will take the data and save it unless it has been instructed not to do so. One of the great things about using thin SQL Server clients for all data editing is that you never have to worry about where the data comes from, since, if you have coded your server properly, all data in the database will be clean. Data is also validated once and only once. This will improve the performance of your applications, especially when the instances of errors are very low.

The downside is a decrease in application usability. Since the application has no idea of what the data should look like, it cannot assist the user in avoiding errors. This is very apparent in applications that have rules that affect more than a single column. Take the following example:

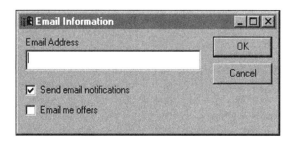

Planning the Physical Architecture

It is easy to see that we need to have a rule to prevent us from checking either of these checkboxes unless the user has an e-mail address. In the database this is simple to implement, but if we do not program any of this logic into the front end there is no way that we can avoid the following situation:

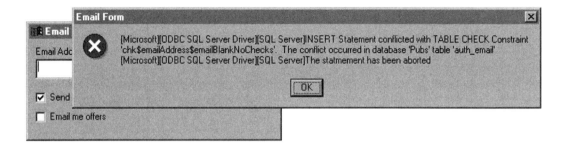

We could devise a fairly complex error-mapping scheme, in order to map the error in a more user-friendly format, but the underlying process will never be a very good way to handle the situation.

Somewhere in Between

Which brings us nicely to the "somewhere in between". The ideal client-server (or n-tier for that matter) applications would employ a domain-key normal form database, with a client that validates the least amount of data required to meet the user's needs, and be capable of handling any error messages that come back from the SQL Server. Certain types of rule are not suited for client-side enforcement, such as:

- Inter-table rules
- Uniqueness of data
- Foreign Key Relationships

For these rules you will certainly need to let the server handle the error and build a facility giving the user the error information in a reasonable manner. If we go back to our previous example VB form, we would need to do something like the following:

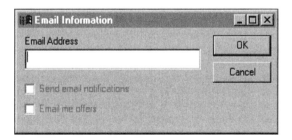

Here the two checkboxes have been disabled so that the user cannot interact with them until the e-mail address has been filled in. Just how far we go with the pre-validation of data is a cautious mix of usability with maintainability. (For example, changes to the data schema may also require changes to the VB program and, as a consequence, re-testing of both the schema and VB code). If we wanted to validate that the e-mail address typed in was valid, we might simply let the SQL Server perform the validation using a check constraint, mapping the check to a suitable message for the users.

Chapter 9

Client to Data Configurations

We will now look at some of the basic configurations that we can use when building database server systems. Whilst the group we will cover is not inclusive, it will certainly give us a basis for customized configurations that solve our own individual problems.

Classic Client Server

The old faithful, and yet still important after all these years. Ten years ago this was a very new concept. Nine years and three hundred and sixty four days ago we all began trying to come up with a better configuration, and whilst many applications are now of an *n*-tier type, client-server is still appropriate in a number of situations that SQL Server is employed in.

Basically, you have one or more workstations directly networked to a SQL Server database server. The connection needs to be a reasonably fast one, since primarily all that needs to be transmitted across the network are SQL commands sent to the server and a result set returned to the client.

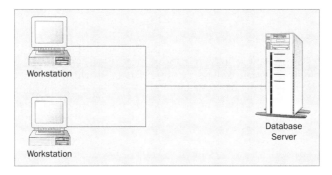

One of the primary merits of this configuration is simplicity. The client software sends commands directly to the database to retrieve or change what it needs. If these commands are well thought out and well encapsulated (a topic we will look at in some depth in Chapter 12), and the results we receive from the server are as narrow (as few columns as possible) and as short (as few rows as possible) as possible, attaining required performance will usually not be too difficult. If you have a relatively small number of users who access your data, this configuration is a suitable one. However what constitutes a "small" number will depend directly upon the type of hardware the database server is run on.

When the number of users grows very large, or you have to handle machine driven data entry, the overhead of the client server system configuration can get too much to bear. One of the primary reasons for this is that the most expensive operations are connecting/disconnecting to (and from) the server. Most applications require several connections to the server and, to reduce network overheads, are frequently written to hold onto their connections. As we have said previously, keeping around five to ten thousand open connections to the database server can be a heavy drain on processing resources.

Three-Tier Configuration

Three-tier configurations (and more generally *n*-tier configurations) are becoming very popular as a way to separate the presentation logic from the business logic and the business logic from the data logic. As depicted in the following diagram, the user's workstation never actually connects to the database server, it simply connects to a group of objects (usually written in a COM or CORBA compliant language):

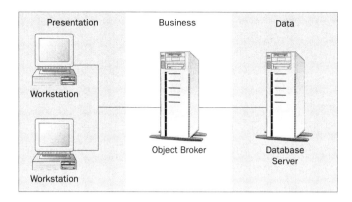

Ideally, the business objects that are in the business layer have two very important tasks:

Connection Pooling

To reduce the overhead of the client-server model, the object broker pools connections. Since clients tend to make the same requests over and over, whilst needing an open connection to the database server for a much smaller time than they usually have them, the object broker maintains a pool of connections that it uses to connect to the database server. You may also have many instances of objects cached for use on the object broker, as well having the ability to have multiple object brokers. Essentially, the philosophy behind this configuration is to take the job of connecting to the client out of the hands of the database server and put it on a more scalable device. Further details on this can be found in *"Professional Windows DNA: Building Distributed Web Applications with VB, COM+, MSMQ, SOAP, and ASP"* (Wrox Press, ISBN 1861004451).

Enforcing Business Rules

We may well encounter performance problems with certain business rules which appear somewhat arbitrary, and include a large number of AND, NOT and OR clauses that make them inefficient to code. An example of such a rule might be the following:

> *A user's subscription covers weekdays from Monday to Friday, but NOT Saturdays and Sundays, unless they take out the enhanced cover which includes weekends, though not bank holidays. If an engineer is requested outside the hours of 9 and 5 this will cost an additional fee, payable to the visiting engineer.*

Rules like this are generally not conducive to being dealt with in Transact-SQL code, since the handling will require feedback from the user after the first time they try to save the record, and the rules are liable to change frequently depending on management's changing needs. If we code in a functional language able to interact with the users, business rules are easier to implement, and indeed alter. As we will look at in the next two chapters, SQL Server rules should govern all non-changing rules that will be enforced on the data in the database.

Heavy Use Web Servers

Another scenario that is becoming somewhat more common is that of having thousands or even millions of read-only users connected to our database. In this situation, we can make one or more read-only copies of our data (in a heavily denormalized form). The load balancing switch (and a whole lot of setting up that is way beyond my core abilities) takes requests from the client, routes these requests to a webserver (each webserver being a copy of the same webserver), then the webserver calls one of the database servers (again routed by the load balancing switch). This is shown overleaf:

Chapter 9

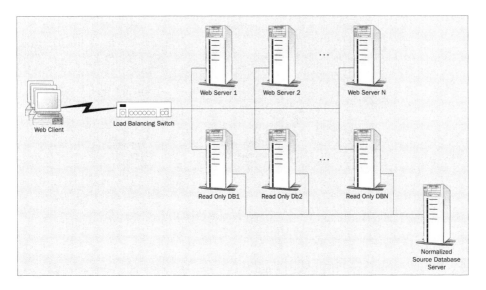

The normalized database is the source of all edits on the data, and if the user needs to modify data (such as make an order, or save some settings) then we can provide interfaces to the source database server or possibly to another server that we use only for editing data. Take for example a large media and books e-commerce site with tens of thousands of CDs, books, etc. All information regarding these items will exist in a normalized database configured so as to ensure data integrity. For performance reasons, we could take this data from its normalized form, and transform it into pre-built, pre-joined queries to build the web pages that the customers of the website will view. We might also partition the data across servers. Based on factors such as frequency of use, we might put classical music on one server, rock music on another, and so on.

WAN

In our global economy, many organizations are spread over an entire country, or indeed different continents. In some cases, we can build simple client-server, or even multi-tier applications that will be sufficient for our data editing needs. However, there are also many cases where it is impractical to edit and report on data over a WAN. Hence we can build a topology that is basically as follows:

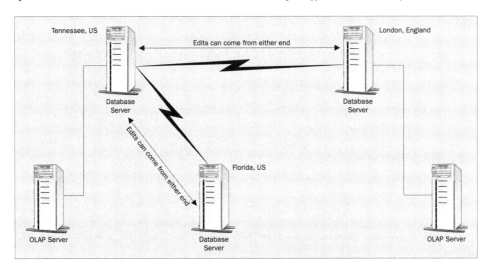

We can use merge replication to allow editing on either end of the pipe, then merge changes back into all of the servers. In this manner each of the offices in our diagram will feel as if they have their own database, where they could edit all rows in the database. We might partition the data to avoid having one user in Tennessee edit one row, at the same time as another in London, but we might simply let SQL Server's conflict resolution facilities handle the cases where this occurs.

Case Study

In our case study we are going to assume the simplest topology possible while still showcasing all of the ideas that we have looked at. We will use a simple client server setup with the addition of an Operational Data Store:

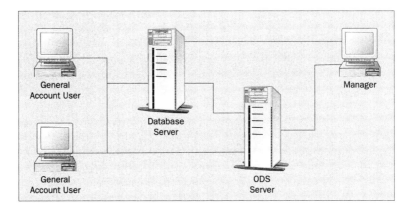

One of the main reasons to stick to a tried and true client-server topology is that we will be implementing business rules on the database server when at all possible. We will certainly discuss any situation where this client-server topology is a hindrance. One last thing that should be mentioned with regards to our decision to go in the client-server direction is that no matter which topology we need to implement, it is generally better to have as many of the rules implemented on the database server for reasons we have been over. We will implement them here as an example, and this is generally how I would implement the system.

Summary

As you probably have guessed from all the other chapters of this book, there are absolutely NO easy answers for dealing with the extremely wide range of possible situations/configurations/parameters that can affect the implementation. It is very important that, not only do you take what you have learned in this chapter, but depending on your role, you learn everything you can possibly learn about how SQL Server and its additional tools work, through referring both to other books (some of which we have mentioned in the text), and indeed SQL Server Books Online.

We have looked at merely a small subsection of the different possible ways to connect a database to a client, or to architect a solution. This chapter does not tell you everything you could possibly need to know about the physical architecture of a database design. That would require a whole book in itself. What we are aiming to do is give you the bulk of the information to allow you to get a feel for the subject, and work on 80 per cent of problems you will face, and decide where to find further information to tackle the remaining 20 per cent of problems.

The following chapter puts us back on track as we look in greater depth at the process of building tables, including a full look at the basic SQL Server objects, such as indexes and data types, that we will use to build our eventual databases.

Planning the Physical Architecture

Professional SQL Server 2000 Database Design

10

Planning and Implementing the Basic Physical Architecture

Introduction

Our goal in this chapter is to build the tables that will make up our database. We have talked about this process, planned it, even drawn pictures of it, but now it is time to physically begin. The process of generating OLTP tables can be laborious at times but, if you use any of the database design tools that are available, the task will be far easier. During this implementation phase, we have to reorganize our objects, add implementation details and finally turn it all into code.

In this chapter, we will build our code without the benefit of any tools or code generators, so you get to see exactly what is going on. Instead, we will be using Query Analyzer and hand editing the data definition language (DDL) for defining tables. We will look at the code to generate tables and relationships, but not code to define data domains, beyond that to choose data types. We will examine in some depth each of the intrinsic data types, discuss some of the extensions to these that we will possibly want to use, and define some basic columns and data types that we will likely want to reuse. The next chapter will deal with extending the definition of domains to further constrain data values beyond sizing or typing issues.

We will define the unique constraints and indexes on our tables, and will look at the physical on-disk structures of indexes and tables. A fundamental understanding of how indexes and data are stored will help to build the mental picture of what goes on inside SQL Server to store data and respond to queries. In turn, it will help us get a clear picture of what kind of index we need to use in different situations.

When we finish with the topics in this chapter, we will have a database schema comprising a group of tables with indexes and relationships. Our database will be far from complete, but we will have established a firm basis for the implementation of business rules which will be covered in the next chapter.

Database Generation Tools

What we are about to do should, in reality, never be done without a decent database generation tool. There are several excellent database generation tools that are also equally great for database modeling. Maintaining a database server is possible without them and there are plenty of database administrators out there that have dozens of text files representing their databases, but this is a monumental time waster.

During this phase of the implementation, many programmers will be eager to start writing code. If we have to build all of our tables and code by hand, it will take a huge amount of time to complete. The first system I wrote the database code for included over 800 stored procedures and triggers, developed by hand over eight months. That was eight years ago, and it was a fantastic learning exercise. Today, advanced database design tools let me build databases with comparable code in a matter of weeks.

> *There are tools that do much of the "detail" work for us, but if we do not have a full understanding of what they are doing it can make it very hard for us to be successful. Doing it by hand before using these great tools is worth all of the blood, sweat, and tears it will cost.*

However, in order to show you how the physical implementation process works, we are not going to use any of these tools for the next three chapters. We will build by hand the scripts that a tool would generate automatically. This will help us to understand what the tool is building for us. This is also a good exercise for any database architect or DBA to review the SQL Server syntax; just don't do this on a database with ninety tables unless you have eight months to spare.

We will be dealing primarily with a development database in these chapters. Development databases are characterized as containing data that has no actual business value. Developers should be able to modify or destroy any of the sample data (not structures) when developing code to access a database. Unfortunately, many programmers will beg for real data in the database straight away.

Physically Designing the Schema

In the logical design part of the book, we discussed in quite some detail how to design our objects. In this section we will begin to take this blueprint and develop actual database objects from it. Just as building engineers take an architect's blueprint and examine it to see what materials are needed and that everything is actually realistic, we will take our logical model and tweak out those parts that might be unfeasible or just too difficult to implement. Certain parts of an architect's original vision may have to be changed to fit what is realistic, based on factors that were not known when the blueprint was first conceived, such as ground type, hills, etc. We too are going to have to go through the process of translating things from raw concept to implementation. During logical design, we hardly looked at any real code examples and did our best to consider only features common to all relational database systems. The logical model we have designed could be implemented in Microsoft SQL Server, Microsoft Access, Oracle, Sybase, or any relational database management system.

From here on, I am going to assume that you have Microsoft SQL Server 2000 installed, and have created a development database to work with. We will look at many of the features that SQL Server gives us, though not all. For more information on Microsoft SQL Server 2000, read "*Professional SQL Server 2000 Programming*" by *Rob Vieira* (*Wrox Press, ISBN 1-861004-48-6*).

Throughout the chapter, our goal will be to map the logical design to the physical implementation in as faithful a representation as possible. We will look at the following:

- Transforming the logical design into our physical design
- Creating tables
- Creating columns
- Data types
- Physical-only columns
- Collation
- Keys
- Creating relationships
- Sharing your metadata with the developers

Each of these steps will be covered in detail, as a proper understanding of what is available is fundamental to getting the actual design and implementation correct.

Transforming our Logical Design

In days past, a section like this on physical design would have been much longer than just the few pages we have here. As we have already stated, hardware and software advances, coupled with data warehousing methodologies, potentially allow us to implement our database almost exactly as we logically designed it. However, care must still be taken when designing the physical database, as we should never try to implement something that is too difficult to use in practice.

Subtypes

We may have to stray away from our logical design when we deal with subtypes. You will recall that a subtype in database modeling terms indicates a specific type of one-to-one relationship, where we have one generic table – for example, `person` – and we then have one or more subtyped tables that further extend the meanings of this table – such as `employee`, `teacher`, `customer`, etc. They are particularly significant in logical design, but there are also good reasons to keep them in our physical design too.

> *Depending on how you end up doing your logical modeling, you may have to tweak more than just subtypes. Always bear in mind that there are as many ways of designing databases as there are data architects.*

I will now present examples of cases where we *will* and *will not* want to keep the subtyped tables.

Example 1

Say we have a `Movie` table that lists the names of movies (as well as other information, such as genre, description, etc.). We also have a `movieRentalInventory` table that defines videos or DVDs for rental. We specify a `number` to be used as the Alternate Key, and an `itemCount` that specifies the number of videos or discs that are in the rental package. There is also a `mediaFormat` column that shows whether the item is a video or a DVD.

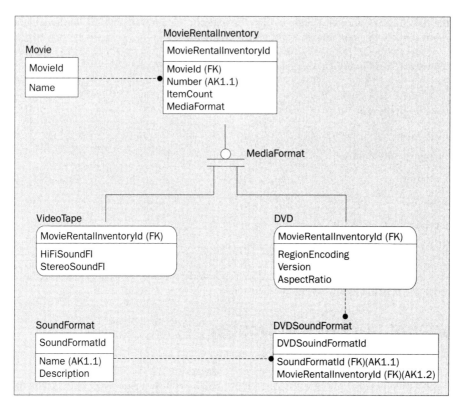

We define subtypes of the mediaFormat value for VideoTape and DVD. We need to know the format because DVDs have many more features than videos, the most important of which are region encoding and the sound format. We implement a special DVDSoundFormat for DVD as a many-to-many relationship – since DVDs support an ever changing set of sound formats – while, for the videoTape type, we just have fields for HiFi and stereo sound.

There are a few problems with this implementation:

- In order to create a new media rental, we have to create records in at least two tables (movieRentalInventory and videoTape or DVD, and another in DVDSoundFormat for a DVD). This is not a tremendous problem, but can require some special handling.

- If we want to see a list of all of the items we have for rental, including their sound properties, we will have to write a very complex query that joins movieRentalInventory with videoTape, and union this with another query between movieRentalInventory and DVD, which may be too slow or simply too cumbersome to deal with. (We will cover queries in some detail in Chapter 12.)

These are common issues with subtypes. What we have to decide is how valuable it is to keep a given set of tables implemented as a subtype. When considering what to do with a subtype relationship, one of the most important tasks is to determine how much each of the subtyped entities have in common, and how many of their attributes they have in common.

A simple survey of the attributes of the subtyped tables in this example shows that they have much in common. In most cases it is simply a matter of cardinality.

Planning and Implementing the Basic Physical Architecture

Take the DVD. Region encoding is specific to this medium, but some videos have different versions, and technically every video product has an aspect ratio (the ratio of the height and width of the picture) that will be of interest to any enthusiast. While it is true that we can specify the sound properties of a videotape using two simple checkboxes, we can use the same method of specifying the sound for a DVD. We will just have to limit the cardinality of `soundFormat` on a video to one, while DVD may have up to eight.

So we redraw the subtype relationship as:

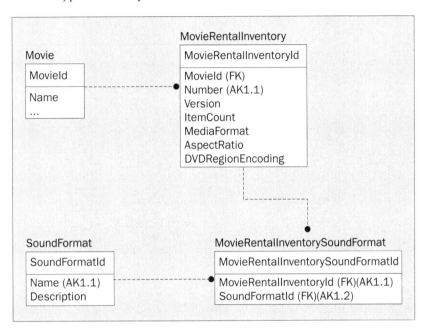

Note that this breaks the rules of normalization. However, it is really difficult to put together a way to deal with subtypes that does not compromise normalization if the two objects that the subtypes are approximating are basically the same thing.

The last point that has to be made is that, because we have changed our structure and are storing multiple types of information in the same entity, we now have to be careful not to allow improper data to be entered into the table. For example, when `mediaFormat` is video, the `DVDRegionEncoding` field does not apply and must be set to NULL. These business rules will have to be enforced using constraints and triggers, since the values in one table will be based on the values in another.

Rolling up (or combining) the subtype into a single table can seem to make implementation easier and more straightforward, while actually just offloading the work somewhere else. Knowing how the values are used will certainly help us decide if rolling up the subtype is merited.

Example 2

As a second example, let's look at a case where it does not make sense to roll up the subtype. You will generally have subtypes that should not be rolled up in the case where you have two (or more) objects that share a common ancestor, but, once subtyped, the subtypes of the items have absolutely no relationship to one another. Look at the following:

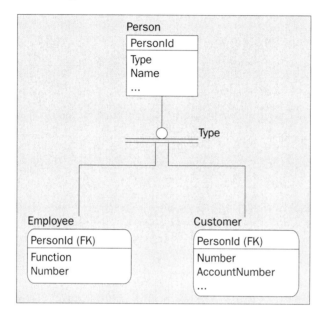

We have a person table which has a name and other attributes, including some that are implemented as additional tables with relationships to the person table (such as address, contact information, contact journal, etc.). In our example, employees and customers may both be people, but the similarities end there. So, in this case, it will be best to leave the subtype as it is.

The only problem here is that, when someone wants to look at the employee's name, you have to use a join. This is not a real problem from a programming standpoint, but it is from a technical standpoint. In many cases, the primary features that make subtypes more reasonable to use revolve around creating views that make the employee table look as if it contains the values for person as well.

Determining when to roll up a table is one of those things that comes with time and experience. As a guideline it is usually best to:

❑ Roll up when the subtyped tables are very similar in characteristics to the parent table, especially when we will frequently want to see them in a list together

❑ Leave as subtypes when the data in the subtypes share the common underpinnings, but are not logically related to one another in additional ways

Other Reasons to Stray from the Logical Design

The most frequent cause of straying from the logical model is denormalized structures – usually summary data to summarize a given set of rows, as in the following tables:

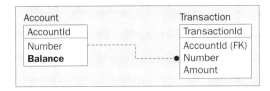

Here, the `balance` attribute will be equivalent to the summary of all of the transaction amount values for a given `accountId`. We will discuss how to implement this type of summary data using triggers, as sometimes introducing denormalized data may be required to solve a particular performance problem.

Introducing this at an early point of physical design may seem like a reasonable thing to do. However, It should be stressed that denormalization is not something that should be done unless there are compelling reasons. Usually, denormalization causes more problems than it solves. It can be hard for novice architects to understand why it is better to retrieve values through joins instead of propagating duplicate values all around a database to speed up a query or a set of queries. Joins in SQL Server are extremely efficient and very often will provide adequate performance.

Tables

Tables are the central objects in SQL Server. The basics of the table are very simple. If you look at the full syntax for the CREATE TABLE statement, you will see that there are many different optional parameters. Throughout this chapter, and part of the next, we will look at table creation statements and how best to choose what to do with each variation.

The first required clause is very straightforward:

```
CREATE TABLE [<database>.][<owner>.]<tablename>
```

We will expand upon the items between the angle brackets (< and >). Note that anything in square brackets ([and]) is optional and may be omitted.

- ❏ <database> – Usually you will not need to specify the database in your CREATE TABLE statements. If not specified, this will default to the current database where the statement is being executed.

- ❏ <owner> – This is the name of the owner of the table. This must be a current user in the database or dbo for the database owner. If the statement is executed by a member of the sysadmin server role, or the db_dbowner or db_ddladmin fixed roles, then an object can be created for any user by specifying a name.

> *Best practice is to minimize the number of owners. Having multiple owners causes "ownership chain" issues between dependent objects. It is most common to have all objects owned solely by a single user known as* dbo.

Naming

The entry for <tablename> gives the table a name. The name must fit into the system data type of sysname. In SQL Server, this is defined as a 128 character string using double-byte Unicode characters. The combination of owner and tablename must be unique in a database.

> *If the first character of the table name is a single # symbol, the table is a temporary table. If the first two characters of the table name are ##, it is a global temporary table. We will briefly mention temporary tables in Chapter 12, though they are not so much a part of database design as a mechanism to hold intermediate results in complex queries.*

SQL Server's rules for the names of objects consist of two distinct naming methods.

The first uses delimiters (either square brackets or double quotes) around the name (though double quotes are only allowed when the SET QUOTED_IDENTIFIER option is set to on). By placing delimiters around an object's name, you can use *any* string as the name. For example, [Table Name] or [3232 fjfa*&(&^(] would both be legal (but annoying) names. Delimited names are generally a bad idea when creating new tables, and should be avoided if possible as they make coding more difficult. However, they can be necessary for interacting with data tables in other environments.

The second and preferred naming method is to use non-delimited names, but they have to follow a few basic rules:

- The first character must be a letter as defined by Unicode Standard 3.1 (generally speaking, Roman letters A to Z, upper and lower case) or the underscore character (_). The Unicode standard can be found at **www.unicode.org**.
- Subsequent characters can be Unicode letters, decimal numbers, the ampersand (@), or the dollar sign ($).
- The name must not be a SQL Server reserved word. There is a pretty large list of reserved words in SQL Server 2000 Books Online (look in the *Reserved Keywords* section).
- The name cannot have spaces.

While the rules for creating an object name are pretty straightforward, the more important question is, "What kind of names should we choose?" The answer is predictable: "Whatever you feel is best as long as others can read it." This may sound like a cop-out, but there are as many different naming standards as there are data architects out there. The standard I generally go with is the standard we will use in this book, but it is certainly not the only way. Basically, we will stick with the same standard that we started with in logical naming. With space for 128 characters, there is little reason to do much abbreviating. It is most important to be clear when choosing names.

> *Since most companies have existing systems, it may be a good idea to know the shop standard for naming tables so that new developers on your project will be more likely to understand your database and come up to speed more quickly.*

As an example, let us name the object that we might use to store a television schedule item. The following list will show several different ways to build the name of this object:

- television_schedule_item – using underscores to separate values. Most programmers are not big friends of the underscore as they are cumbersome to program until you get used to them.

- [television schedule item] or "television schedule item" – delimited by brackets or quotes. Not favored by most programmers, as it is impossible to use this name when building variables in code, and it is easy to make mistakes with them.

- televisionScheduleItem – mixed case to delimit between words. This is the style that we will make use of in our case study, as it is the style that I like.

- tvSchedItem or tv_sched_item or [tv sched item] – abbreviated forms. These are problematic because you must be careful to always abbreviate the same word in the same way in all of your databases. A dictionary of abbreviations must be maintained or you will get multiple abbreviations for the same word, for example, description as desc, descr, descrip, and/or description.

Choosing names for objects is ultimately a personal choice, but should never be made arbitrarily, and should be based on existing corporate standards, existing software, and legibility.

Owner

The user who creates a database is called the database owner, or dbo. The dbo is a member of the system administrators or database creator system roles. Any user can be added to the database owners group in the database by being added to the db_owner role, which means that the user can create and delete *any* data, table, view, and stored procedure in the database.

When any non-dbo user creates an object, that object is owned by that user (and the dbo or db_owner roles). If a user called Bob tries to access a table without specifying an owner, like so:

```
SELECT * FROM tableName
```

SQL Server first checks to see if a table named tableName and owned by Bob actually exists. If not, it then checks to see if a table with this name owned by the dbo exists. If it does, and the dbo has not given Bob rights to access the table, the statement will give an error. To access a specific owner's table directly in code, we need to specify the owner of the table using a two part name, like so:

```
SELECT * FROM dbo.tableName
```

If we do specify a specific table and its owner, like we did in the previous line of code, and this table does not exist, then we raise an error.

The owner gets implicit rights to create, modify, and delete data from the table as well as the table itself. Any other user has to be given the rights to do so. At this point, it is simply important to understand that every table, view, and stored procedure in SQL Server has an owner.

We should also note that SQL Server uses a naming scheme with up to four parts:

[<server>.][<database>.][<owner>.]<objectName>

where:

- server – identifies the server where the object is located. For objects on the same server, the server name should be omitted. Objects on different servers can only be accessed if the system administrator has set up the server as a linked server.

- database – identifies the database where the object resides. If omitted, the object is looked for in the database from which the object is being accessed.

❑ `owner` – identifies the user who created/owns the object. If omitted, SQL Server uses the user who is connected as the default.

❑ `objectName` – identifies the name of the table, view, or stored procedure.

Limits

Before going any further, we need to look at a few of the limits that we will have to work with when building tables in SQL Server. Four limits are important to us when building a table:

❑ Number of columns – The maximum number of columns (that is, data fields) in a table is 1024. If the database is properly normalized, this is way beyond normal requirements.

❑ Number of bytes per row – The maximum number of bytes in a row is 8060. Unlike the number of columns, the maximum number of bytes is not quite as hard to reach. We will see why this is when we start to look at character and binary data.

❑ Number of bytes per index entry – The limit on this is 900 bytes and for good reason. A page is roughly 8000 bytes, so if an index was much larger than 900, it would become very ineffective.

❑ Number of indexes – The limit is 1 clustered and 249 non-clustered. We might get close to this limit in data warehousing systems. Having 250 indexes on a table in an OLTP system would reduce performance drastically because of the frequent modifications that are likely to be made to the data. We will discuss clustered and non-clustered indexes later in this chapter.

A more conclusive list of the basic requirements will be given in Chapter 13, when we look at hardware requirements.

Columns

The **bold** lines are the lines that we will use to define a column:

```
CREATE TABLE [<database>.][<owner>.]<tablename>
(
    <columnName> <data type> [<NULL specification>]
    -- or
    <columnName> AS <computed definition>
)
```

There are two types of columns that we will deal with, physical and computed (or virtual).

❑ **Physical columns** – This is an ordinary column where physical storage is allocated and data is actually stored for the value

❑ **Computed (or virtual) columns** – Columns that are made up by a calculation including any of the physical columns in the table

We primarily will deal with physical columns, but computed columns have some pretty cool uses.

Naming

The `<columnName>` placeholder is where you specify the name that the column will be known by.

Planning and Implementing the Basic Physical Architecture

The naming rules for columns are the same as for tables as far as SQL Server is concerned. As for how we choose a name for a column – again, it is one of those tasks for the individual architect, based on the same sorts of criteria as before (shop standards, best usage, etc.). The following set of guidelines will be followed in this book:

- Other than the primary key, the table name should rarely be included in the column name. For example, in an entity named `person`, we should not have columns called `personName` or `personSocialSecurityNumber`. No column should be prefixed with `person` other than the primary key of `personId`. This reduces the need for role naming (modifying names of attributes to adjust meaning, especially used in cases where we have multiple migrated foreign keys).

- The name should be as descriptive as possible. We will use very few abbreviations in our names. There are three notable exceptions:

    Complex names – Much like in table names, if you have a name that contains multiple parts, like "Conglomerated Television Rating Scale", you might want to implement a name like `ConTvRatScale`, even though it might take some training before your users become familiar with its meaning.

    Recognized abbreviations – As an example, if we were writing a purchasing system and we needed a column for a purchase order table, we could name the object PO because this is very widely understood.

    Data type indicators – We will sometimes add a short string (say, two characters) to the end of the column name. For example, a column that we use as a Boolean will end in the suffix "fl", short for flag, and a date column would end in "dt", obviously short for date. Note that we will not use these suffixes to indicate precise data types (for example, you might implement a Boolean with an int, tinyint, smallint, bit, or even a string containing "Yes" or "No").

Note that we left off any mention of a Hungarian style notation to denote the type of the column. I have never been a big fan of this style. If you are not familiar with Hungarian notation, it means that we prefix the names of columns and variables with an indicator of the data type and possible usage. For example, we might have a variable called `vc100_columnName`, to indicate a `varchar(100)` data type. Or we might have a Boolean or `bit` column named `bCar`, or `isCar`.

In my opinion, such prefixes are overkill since it is easy to tell the type from other documentation we can get from SQL Server or other methods. Our usage indicators typically go at the end of the name and are only needed when it would be difficult to understand what the value means without the indicator.

By keeping the exact type out of the names, we avoid clouding the implementation details with the entity identity. One of the beauties of using relational databases is that there is an abstraction layer which hides the implementation details. To expose them via column naming is to set in concrete what changing requirements may make obsolete (for example, extending the size of a variable to accommodate a future business need).

Domains

In logical modeling, the concept of domains involved building templates for data types and columns that we use over and over again. In physical modeling, domains are the same, but with additional properties added for physical needs.

For example, in the logical modeling phase, we defined domains for such columns as name and description, which occur regularly across a database. The reason for defining domains might not have been completely obvious at the time of logical design, but it becomes very clear during physical modeling. For example, for the *name* domain, we might specify the following:

259

Chapter 10

Property	Setting
Name	Name
Data type	varchar (100)
Nullability	Not NULL
Check Constraint	LEN(RTRIM(Name)) > 0 – may not be blank

Most tables will have a name column and we will use this very template to build them. This serves at least two purposes:

- ❑ Consistency – if we define every name column in precisely the same manner, there will never be any question about how to treat the column.
- ❑ Ease of implementation – if the tool you use to model/implement databases supports the creation of domain/template columns, you can simply use the template to build columns and not have to set the values over and over. If the tool supports property inheritance, when you change a property in the definition, the values change everywhere.

Domains are not a requirement of good database design, logical or physical, nor are they precisely used by SQL Server, but they enable easy and consistent design and are a great idea. Of course, consistent modeling is always a good idea regardless of whether or not you use a tool to do the work for you.

Choosing Data Types

```
<columnName> <data type> [<NULL specification>]
```

The `<data type>` placeholder is for choosing the data type for the column. Choosing proper data types to match the domain chosen during logical modeling is a very important task. One data type might be more efficient than another of a similar type. For example, storing integer data can be done in an integer data type, a numeric data type, or even a floating point data type, but they are certainly not alike in implementation or performance.

In this section, we will look at all of the intrinsic data types that are provided by Microsoft and discuss the situations where they are best used.

Precise Numeric Data

There are many base data types in which you can store numerical data. We will deal with two different types of numeric data: **precise** and **approximate**. The differences are very important and must be well understood by any architect who is building a system that stores readings, measurements, or other numeric data.

The precise numeric values include the `bit`, `int`, `bigint`, `smallint`, `tinyint`, `decimal`, and the `money` data types (`money` and `smallmoney`). Precise values have no error in the way they are stored, from integer to floating point values, because they have a fixed number of digits before and after the decimal point (or radix). However, when we must store decimal values in precise data types, we will pay a performance and storage cost in the way they are stored and dealt with.

bit

The bit has values of 0, 1, or NULL.

It is generally used as a Boolean. It is not the ideal Boolean because SQL Server does not have a distinct Boolean data type, but it is the best that we currently have. bit columns cannot be indexed – having only two values (technically three with NULL) makes for a poor index – so they should not be used in heavily searched combinations of fields. You should avoid having a bit field set to NULL if possible; including NULLs into a Boolean comparison increases the complexity of queries and will cause problems.

The bit column requires one byte of storage per eight instances in a table. Hence, having eight bit columns will cause your table to be no larger than if your table had only a single bit column.

int

Whole numbers from –2,147,483,648 to 2,147,483,647 (that is, -2^{31} to $2^{31} - 1$).

The integer data type is used to store signed (+ or –) whole number data. The integer data type is frequently employed as a primary key for tables, as it is very small (it requires four bytes of storage) and very efficient to store and retrieve.

The only real downfall of the int data type is that it does not include an unsigned version, which would store non-negative values from 0 to 4,294,967,296 (or 2^{32}). As most primary key values start out at 1, this would give us over two billion extra values for a primary key value. This may seem unnecessary, but systems that have billions of rows are becoming more and more common.

Another application where the typing of the int field plays an important part is the storage of IP addresses as integers. An IP address is simply a 32 bit integer broken down into four octets. For example, if you had an IP address of 234.23.45.123, you would take $(234 * 2^3) + (23 * 2^2) + (45 * 2^1) + (123 * 2^0)$. This value will fit nicely into an unsigned 32 bit integer, but not into a signed one. There is, however, a 64 bit integer in SQL Server that covers the current IP address standard nicely, but requires twice as much storage.

bigint

Whole numbers from –9,223,372,036,854,775,808 to 9,223,372,036,854,775,807 (that is, -2^{63} to $2^{63} - 1$).

The only reason to use the 64 bit data type is as a primary key for tables where you will have more than two billion rows, or if the situation directly dictates it like the IP address situation we previously discussed.

smallint

Whole numbers from –32,768 through to 32,767 (or -2^{15} through $2^{15} - 1$).

If we can be guaranteed of needing fewer than 32,767 items, the smallint can be a useful type. It requires 2 bytes of storage.

Using the smallint can be a tradeoff. On the one hand, it does save two bytes over the int data type, but frequently the smallint is not large enough to handle all needs. If the data can fit into the constraints of this domain, and your table will be very large, it may be worth using the smallint to save two bytes. For small to moderate databases, the possibility of running out of space and having to change all of the code to use a different data type can be too much to overcome. We will use the int data type for our database.

It is also generally a bad idea to use a `smallint` for a primary key (except in extreme situations, such as when we need trillions of rows or where a byte or two will make a performance difference). Uniformity makes our database code more consistent. This may seem like a small point but, in most average systems it is much easier to code when you automatically know what the data type is.

One use of a `smallint` that crops up from time to time is as a Boolean. I guess this is because, in Visual Basic, 0 equals `False` and −1 equals `True` (technically, VB will treat any non-zero value as `True`). Storing data in this manner is not only a tremendous waste of space (2 bytes versus potentially $1/8^{th}$ of a byte) but is confusing to all other SQL Server programmers. ODBC and OLE DB drivers do this translation for you, but even if they did not, it is worth the time to write a method or a function in VB to translate `True` to a value of 1.

tinyint

Whole numbers from 0 through 255.

The same comments for the `smallint` can be made for the `tinyint`. The `tinyint` types are very small, using a single byte for storage, but we rarely use them because there are very few situations where we can guarantee that a value will never exceed 255 or employ negative numbers.

The only use I have made of the `tinyint` over the years in previous versions of SQL Server is if I needed to group by a `bit` column. I could not do this directly so, if I ran a query like this:

```
SELECT bitColumn, count(*)
FROM testbit Group
GROUP BY bitColumn
```

I would get an error. However, I could write the following and it would work:

```
SELECT CAST(bitColumn AS tinyint) AS bitColumn, count(*)
FROM testbit Group
GROUP BY CAST(bitColumn AS tinyint)
```

SQL Server 2000 no longer makes this distinction, but this may still cause confusion if you have to write queries that need to port between versions of SQL Server.

decimal (or numeric)

All numeric data between $-10^{38} - 1$ through $10^{38} - 1$.

The `decimal` data type is a precise data type because it is stored in a manner that is like character data (as if the data only had 12 characters, 0 to 9 and the minus and decimal point symbols). The way it is stored prevents the kind of imprecision we will see with the `float` and `real` data types a bit later. It does however incur an additional cost in getting and manipulating values.

To specify a `decimal` number, we need to define the **precision** and the **scale**:

- ❑ Precision is the total number of significant digits in the number. For example, the number 10 would need a precision of 2, and 43.00000004 would need a precision of 10. The precision may be as small as 1 or as large as 38.

- ❑ Scale is the possible number of significant digits to the right of the decimal point. Reusing our previous example, 10 would have a scale of 0, and 43.00000004 would need 8.

Planning and Implementing the Basic Physical Architecture

Numeric data types are bound by this precision and scale to define how large the data is. For example, take the following declaration of a numeric variable:

```
DECLARE @testvar decimal(3,1)
```

This will allow us to enter any numeric values greater than −99.94 and less than 99.94. Entering 99.949999 works but entering 99.95 doesn't, because it will be rounded up to 100.0 which cannot be displayed by `decimal(3,1)`. The following, for example:

```
SELECT @testvar = -10.155555555
SELECT @testvar
```

returns −10.2.

When a computer programming language does this for you, it is considered an implicit conversion. This is both a blessing and a curse. The point here is that you must be really careful when butting up to the edge of the data type allowable values. Note that there is a setting – SET NUMERIC_ROUNDABORT ON – which will cause an error to be generated when a loss of precision would occur from an implicit data conversion. This can be quite dangerous to use and may throw off applications using SQL Server if set to ON. However, if you need to prevent implicit round-off due to system constraints, it is a very valuable tool.

Storage for the numeric types depends on how much precision is required:

Precision	Bytes Required
1 – 9	5
10 – 19	9
20 – 28	13
29 – 38	17

As far as usage is concerned, the `decimal` data type should generally be used sparingly. There is nothing wrong with the type at all, but it does take that little bit more processing than integers or real data and hence there is a performance hit. You should use it when you have specific values that you wish to store where you cannot accept any loss of precision. Again, the topic of loss of precision will be dealt with in more detail in the *Approximate Numeric Data* section.

Money Values

The money data types are basically integers with a decimal point inserted in the number. Since it always has the same precision and scale, the processor can deal with it exactly like a typical integer, and then the SQL Server engine can insert the decimal point back once the mathematical functions have been processed. There are two flavors of money variables:

- money – values from −922,337,203,685,477.5808 through 922,337,203,685,477.5807, with an accuracy of one ten-thousandth of a monetary unit. As would be expected, this is obviously a 64 bit integer and it requires eight bytes of storage.

- smallmoney – values from −214,748.3648 through +214,748.3647, with an accuracy of one ten-thousandth of a monetary unit. It requires four bytes of storage.

263

The money and smallmoney data types are excellent storage for most any requirement for storing monetary values, unless we have requirements to store our monetary values to greater than four decimal places, which is not usually the case in most situations.

Identity Columns

For any of the int or decimal (with a scale of 0) data types, we can create an automatically incrementing column whose value is guaranteed to be unique for the table it is in. The column which implements this identity column must also be defined as NOT NULL.

```
CREATE TABLE testIdentity
(
    identityColumn int NOT NULL IDENTITY (1, 2),
    value     varchar(10)   NOT NULL
)
```

In this CREATE TABLE statement, I have added the IDENTITY function for the identityColumn column. The additional values in parentheses are known as the seed and increment. The seed of 1 indicates that we will start the first value at 1, and the increment says that the second value will be 3, then 5, etc.

In the following script we insert three new rows into the testIdentity table:

```
INSERT INTO testIdentity (value)
VALUES ('one')
INSERT INTO testIdentity (value)
VALUES ('two')
INSERT INTO testIdentity (value)
VALUES ('three')

SELECT * FROM testIdentity
```

This produces the following results:

```
IdentityColumn  value
--------------  -----
1               one
3               two
5               three
```

The identity property is fantastic for creating a primary key type pointer that is small and fast. (Another reminder – it must not be the only key on the table or we technically have no uniqueness, except for a random value!) The int data type requires only four bytes and is very good, since most tables we create will have fewer than 2 billion rows.

One thing of note. Identity values are apt to have holes in the sequence. If an error occurs when creating a new row, the identity value that was going to be used will be lost. Also, if a row gets deleted, the deleted value will not be reused. Hence, you should not use identity columns if you cannot accept this constraint on the values in your table.

> *If you need to guarantee uniqueness across all tables, or even multiple databases, consider creating a column with the uniqueidentifier data type and with a default to automatically generate a value. We will discuss this implementation later in this section on data types.*

Approximate Numeric Data

Approximate numeric values contain a decimal point and are stored in a format that is fast to manipulate but they are only accurate to the 15th decimal place. Approximate numeric values have some very important advantages, as we will see later in the chapter.

Approximate is such a negative term, but it is technically the proper term. It refers to the `real` and `float` data types, which are IEEE 75454 standard single and double precision floating point values. The reason they are called floating point values is based on the way that they are stored. Basically, the number is stored as a 32 bit or 64 bit value, with four parts:

- **sign** – determines if this is a positive or negative value
- **exponent** – the exponent in base 2 of the mantissa
- **mantissa** – stores the actual number that is multiplied by the exponent
- **bias** – determines whether or not the exponent is positive or negative

A complete description of how these data types are actually formed is beyond the scope of this book, but may be obtained from the IEEE body at www.ieee.org for a nominal charge.

There are two different flavors of floating point data types available in SQL Server:

- `float [ (N) ]` – values in the range from $-1.79E+308$ through to $1.79E+308$. The `float` data type allows us to specify a certain number of bits to use in the mantissa, from 1 to 53. We specify this number of bits with the value in N.
- `real` – values in the range from $-3.40E+38$ through to $3.40E+38$. `real` is a synonym for a `float(24)` data type.

The storage and precision for the `float` data types are as follows:

N (number of mantissa bits for float)	Precision	Storage Size
1 – 24	7	4 bytes
25 – 53	15	8 bytes

Hence, we are able to represent most values from $-1.79E+308$ through to $1.79E+308$ with a precision of 15 significant digits. This is not as many significant digits as the numeric data types can deal with, but is certainly plenty for almost any scientific application.

Note that in the previous paragraph we said "represent most values". This is an issue that we must understand. There are some values that simply cannot be stored in floating point format. A classic example of this is the value 1/10. There is no way to store this value exactly. When we execute the following snippet of code:

```
SELECT CAST(1 AS float(53))/CAST( 10 AS float(53)) AS funny_result
```

We expect that the result will be exactly 0.1. However, executing the statement returns:

265

```
        funny_result
        -----------------------------
        0.10000000000000001
```

Even if we change the insert to:

```
        SELECT CAST(.1 AS float) AS funny_result
```

we get the same bad result. The difference is interesting, but insignificant for all but the most needy calculations. The `float` and `real` data types are intrinsic data types that can be dealt with using the floating point unit. In all processors today, this unit is part of the main CPU, so this is slightly more costly than integer math that can be done directly in the CPU registers, but tremendously better than the non-integer exact data types. The flaw is based on the way floating point data is stored. Any further discussion of floating point storage flaws is beyond the scope of this book.

The approximate numeric data types are very important for storing measurements where calculations are required. The round off that occurs is insignificant because there are still very few devices that are capable of taking measurements with 15 significant digits and, as you will likely be doing large quantities of mathematics on the measurements, the performance will be significantly better over using the decimal type.

When coding with floating point values, it is generally best to avoid trying to compare these values using the = operator for comparisons. As values are approximate, it is not always possible to type in the exact value as it will be stored. If you need to be able to find exact values, then it is best to use the numeric data types.

Date and Time Data

If you recall, this is not the first time we have discussed the `datetime` and `smalldatetime` data types. The first time we encountered them was when we were discussing violations of the First Normal Form. In this section we will present the facts about the `datetime` data types, then we will look at some of the alternatives.

smalldatetime

This represents date and time data from January 1, 1900, through to June 6, 2079.

The `smalldatetime` data type is accurate to one minute. It requires four bytes of storage. `smalldatetimes` are the best choice when you need to store the date and possibly time of some event where accuracy of a minute is not a problem. If more precision is required, then the `datetime` data type is probably a better choice.

datetime

This represents date and time data from January 1, 1753, to December 31, 9999.

Storage for the `smalldatetime` and `datetime` data types is interesting. The `datetime` is stored as two four byte integers. The first integer stores the number of days before *or* after January 1, 1990. The second stores the number of milliseconds after midnight of the day. `smalldatetime` values are really close to this, but use two byte integers instead of four. The first is an unsigned two byte integer and the second is used to store the number of minutes past midnight.

Planning and Implementing the Basic Physical Architecture

The datetime data type is accurate to 0.03 seconds. Using eight bytes, it does however require a sizable chunk of memory. Use datetime when you either need the extended range, or when you need the precision. There are few cases where you need this kind of precision. The only application that comes to mind is a timestamp column (not to be confused with the timestamp data type which we will discuss in a later section of this chapter), used to denote *exactly* when an operation takes place. This is not uncommon if we need to get timing information such as the time taken between two activities in seconds, or if we want to use the datetime value in a concurrency control mechanism. We will look deeper into the topic of concurrency control later in this chapter.

Using User-defined Data Types to Manipulate Dates and Times

A word about storing date and time values. Employing the datetime data types when you only need the date part, or just the time, is a pain. Take the following code sample. We want to find every record where the date is equal to July 12, 2001. If we code this in the very obvious manner:

```
SELECT *
FROM employee
WHERE birthDate = 'July 12,1967'
```

We will get a match for every employee where birthDate exactly matches "July 12, 1967 00:00:00.000". However, if the date is stored as "July 12, 1967 10:05:23.300" – as it might be by design (that is, she was born at that exact time), or by error (that is, a date control may send the current time by default if we forget to clear it) – we can get stuck with having to write queries like the following to answer the question of who was born on July 12. To do this we would need to rewrite our query like so:

```
SELECT *
FROM employee
WHERE birthDate >= 'July 12,1967 0:00:00.000'
AND birthDate < 'July 13,1967 0:00:00.000'
```

Note that we did not use between for this operation. If we had, the WHERE clause would have had to state:

```
WHERE birthDate BETWEEN 'July 12, 1967 0:00:00.00'
AND 'July 12, 1967 23:59:59.997'
```

...first to exclude any July 13 dates, then to avoid any round-off with the datetime data type. As it is accurate to 0.03 of a second, when it evaluates "July 12, 1967 23:59:59.997", it rounds it off to "July 13, 1967 0:00:00.00".

This is not only troublesome and cumbersome, but it can be inefficient. In the case where we do not need the date or the time parts of the datetime data types, it may best suit us to create our own. For example, let's take a very typical need for storing the time when something occurs, without the date. There are two possibilities for dealing with this situation. Both are much better than simply using the datetime data type, but each has its own set of inherent problems.

- ❑ Use multiple columns – one simply for hour, minute, second, and whatever fractions of a second you may need. The problem here is that it is not easy to query. You need at least three columns to query for a given time, and you will need to index all of the columns involved in the query to get good performance on large tables. Storage will be better, as we can fit all of the different parts into tinyint columns. If you want to look at what has happened during the tenth hour of the day over a week, then you could use this method.

267

- Use a single column that holds the number of seconds (or parts of seconds between midnight and the current time). This, however, suffers from an inability to do a reasonable query for all values that occur during, say, the tenth hour, and, if we specified the number of seconds, this would be every value between 36000 and 39600. However, this is ideal if we are using these dates in some sort of internal procedure that human users would not need to interact with.

Using these columns we could create user-defined functions to convert our data types to readable values.

As another example, we could create our own date type that is simply implemented as an integer. We could add a user-defined type named intDateType (more coverage will be allocated to this subject later in the chapter):

```
EXEC sp_addtype @typename = intDateType,
    @phystype = integer,
    @NULLtype = 'NULL',
    @owner = 'dbo'
GO
```

And then a user-defined function to convert our data values in the variable into a real datetime variable, to use in date calculations or simply to show to a client.

```
CREATE FUNCTION intDateType$convertToDatetime
(
    @dateTime   intDateType
)
RETURNS datetime
AS
BEGIN
    RETURN ( dateadd(day,@datetime,'jan 1, 2001'))
END
GO
```

From this basic example, it should be pretty obvious that the user-defined function will be an extremely important part of our coding of SQL Server applications. We will use them a few times in this chapter to illustrate a point, but we will cover them more fully in the next chapter, where we will make great use of them for protecting our data. We will see them again in Chapter 11 when we will be manipulating the data. At this point, it is merely important to note that these features exist.

To test our new function, we could start with looking at the second day of the year, by converting date one to a datetime variable:

```
SELECT dbo.intDateType$convertToDatetime(1) as convertedValue
```

which returns:

```
convertedValue
----------------------------------
2001-01-02 00:00:00.000
```

We would have to build several other data entry functions to take in a datetime variable and store it as a new data type. Though we have deliberately not gone into much detail with user-defined functions, I have suggested a range of possibilities to solve a date or time problem.

The datetime data type presents programmatic problems that you must deal with. Just be careful out there.

Binary Data

Binary data allows us to store a string of bits, with a range of one byte (eight bits) to around two gigabytes of bits (which is $2^{31}-1$ or 2,147,483,647 bytes).

A concept that we will begin to look at with binary data types is the use of **variable length** data. Basically this means that the size of the data store in each instance of the column or variable of the data type can change, based on how much data is stored. In all previous data types the storage was fixed, because what was stored was a fixed length representation of the value which was interpreted using some formula (for example, an integer is 32 bits, or a date is the number of time units since some point in time). Any data type that allows variable length values is generally a matter of stacking values together, like letters in a word. Variable-length data generally comprises two pieces – a value explaining how long the data is, and the actual data itself. There is some overhead with storing variable length data, but it is usually better than storing data in fixed length columns with considerable wasted space. Smaller data means more records per page, which reduces I/O, and I/O operations are far more expensive than locating fields in a record.

Binary data is stored in three different flavors:

- `binary` is fixed-length data with a maximum length of 8,000 bytes. Only use the `binary` type if you are certain how large your data will be. Storage will be equivalent to the number of bytes that we declare the variable for.
- `varbinary` is for variable-length binary data with a maximum length of 8,000 bytes.
- `image` is for really large variable-length image data with a maximum length of $2^{31}-1$ (2,147,483,647) bytes.

One of the restrictions of binary data types is that they do not support bitwise operators, which would allow us to do some very powerful bitmask storage by being able to compare two binary columns to see not only if they differ, but how they differ. The whole idea of the `binary` data types is that they store strings of bits. The bitwise operators can operate on integers, which are physically stored as bits. The reason for this inconsistency is actually fairly clear, from the point of view of the internal query processor. The bitwise operations are actually operations that are handled in the processor, while the binary data types are SQL Server specifics.

An additional concept we must discuss is how SQL Server stores huge data values such as image data commonly referred to as BLOBs or Binary Large Objects. When a data type needs to store data that is potentially greater in size than a SQL Server page, special handling is required. Instead of storing the actual data in the page with the record, only a pointer to another physical memory location is stored. The pointer is a 16 byte binary (the same data type as we have discussed) that points to a different page in the database. The page may have stored the value of one or more BLOB, and a BLOB may span many pages.

Uses of `binary` fields, especially the `image` field is fairly limited. Basically, they can be used to store any binary values which are not dealt with by SQL Server. We can store text, JPEG, and GIF images, even Word documents and Excel spreadsheet data. So why are the uses limited? The simple answer is performance. It is generally a bad idea to use the `image` data type to store very large files because it is slow to retrieve them from the database. When we need to store image data in the database, we will generally just store the name of a file on shared access. The accessing program will simply use the filename to go to external storage to fetch the file. File systems are built for nothing other than storing and serving up files, so we use them for their strengths.

Chapter 10

Character Strings

Most data that is stored in SQL Server uses character data types. In fact, usually far too much data is stored in character data types. Frequently, character fields are used to hold non-character data, such as numbers and dates. While this may not be technically wrong, it is not ideal. For starters, to store a number with eight digits in a character string requires at least eight bytes, but as an integer it requires four bytes. Searching on integers is far easier because 1 always precedes 2, whereas 11 precedes 2 in character strings. Additionally, integers are stored in a format that can be manipulated using intrinsic processor functions as opposed to having SQL Server-specific functions to deal with the data.

char

The `char` data type is used for fixed length character data. You must choose the size of the data that you wish to store. Every value will be stored with exactly the same number of characters, up to a maximum of 8060 bytes. Storage is exactly the number of a bytes as per the column definition, regardless of actual data stored; any remaining space to the right of the last character of the data is padded with spaces.

> *Note that versions of SQL Server earlier than 7.0 implement `char` columns differently. The setting `ANSI_PADDING` determines exactly how this is actually handled. If this setting is on, the table is as we have described; if not, data will be stored as we will discuss in the `varchar` section below. It is usually best to have the ANSI settings set to the most standard (or even the most restrictive) settings, as these settings will help you to avoid making use of SQL Server enhancements in your coding that are likely to not exist from version to version.*

The maximum limit for a `char` is 8060 bytes, but it is very unlikely that you would ever get within a mile of this limit. For character data where large numbers of characters are anticipated, you would use one of the other character types. The `char` data type should only be employed in cases where you are guaranteed to have *exactly* the same number of characters in every row and each row is not NULL. As such, we will employ this type very seldom, since most data does not fit the equal length stipulation.

There is one example where `char`s would be used that we will come across fairly frequently: identification numbers. These can contain mixed alphabetic and numeric characters, such as vehicle identification numbers (VINs). Note that this is actually a composite attribute, as you can determine many things about the automobile from its VIN.

Another example where a `char` field is usually found is social security numbers (SSNs).

varchar

For the `varchar` data type, you choose the maximum length of the data you wish to store, up to 8000 bytes. The `varchar` data type is far more useful than the `char`, as the data does not have to be of the same length and SQL Server does not pad out excess memory with spaces. There is some additional overhead in storing variable length data.

Use the `varchar` data type when your data is usually small, say, several hundred bytes or less. The good thing about `varchar` columns is that, no matter how long you set the maximum to, the data stored is the text in the column plus the few extra bytes that specify how long the data is.

We will generally want to choose a maximum limit for our data type that is a reasonable value, large enough to handle most situations but not too large as to be impractical to deal with in our applications and reports. For example, take people's first names. These obviously require the `varchar` type, but how long should we allow the data to be? First names tend to be a maximum of fifteen characters long, though you might want to specify twenty or thirty characters for the unlikely exception.

`varchar` data is the most prevalent storage type for non-key values that we will use.

text

The text data type is used to store larger amounts of character data. It can store a maximum of 2,147,483,647 ($2^{31} - 1$) characters, that is 2 GB. Storage for text is very much like that for the image data type. However, an additional feature allows us to dispense with the pointer and store text data directly on the page. This is allowed by SQL Server if the following conditions are met:

- The column value is smaller than 7000 bytes
- The data in the entire record will fit on one data page
- The Text In Row table option is set using the sp_tableoption procedure, like so:

```
EXECUTE sp_tableoption 'TableName', 'text in row', '1000'
```

In this case, any text columns in the table TableName will have their text stored with the row instead of split out into different pages, until the column reaches 1000 or the entire row is too big to fit on a page. If the row grows too large to fit on a page, one or more of the text columns will be removed from the row and put onto separate pages. This setting allows us to use text values in a reasonable manner, so that when the value stored is small, performance is basically the same as for a varchar column.

Hence, we can now use the text data type to hold character data where the length can vary from ten characters to 50 K of text. This is an especially important improvement for notes type columns, where users want to have space for unlimited text notes, but frequently only put ten or twenty characters of data in each row.

Another issue with text fields is that they cannot be indexed using conventional indexing methods. As discussed in the previous chapter, if you need to do heavy searching on text columns you can employ the full-text searching capabilities of SQL Server 2000. It should also be noted that, even if we could index text columns, it might not be that good an idea. Since text columns or even large varchar columns can be so large, making them fit in the 900 byte limit for an index is unfeasible anyway.

Unicode Character Strings

So far, the character data types we have been discussing have been for storing typical ASCII data. In SQL Server 7.0 (and NT 4.0), Microsoft implemented a new standard character format called Unicode. This specifies a sixteen bit character format which can store characters beyond just the Latin character set. In ASCII – a seven bit character system (with the eight bits for Latin extensions) – we were limited to 256 distinct characters, which was fine for most English speaking people, but was insufficient for other languages. Oriental languages have a character for each different syllable and are non-alphabetic; Middle Eastern languages use several different symbols for the same letter according to its position in the word. So a standard was created for a sixteen bit character system, allowing us to have 65536 distinct characters.

For these data types, we have the nchar, nvarchar, and ntext data types. They are exactly the same as the similarly named types (without the n) that we have already described, except for one thing: Unicode uses double the number of bytes to store the information so it takes twice the space, thus cutting by half the number of characters that can be stored.

> *One quick tip. If you want to specify a Unicode value in a string, you append an N to the front of the string, like so:*

```
SELECT N'Unicode Value'
```

Chapter 10

Variant Data

A variant data type allows you to store almost any data type that we have discussed. This allows us to create a column or variable where we do not know exactly what kind of data will be stored. This is a new feature of SQL Server 2000. The name of the new data type is `sql_variant` and it allows us to store values of various SQL Server-supported data types – except `text`, `ntext`, `timestamp`, and `sql_variant` (it may seem strange that you cannot store a variant in a variant, but all this is saying is that the `sql_variant` data type does not actually exist as such – SQL Server chooses the best type of storage to store the value you give to it).

The Advantages of Variant

The `sql_variant` data type will allow us to create user definable "property bag" type tables, that will help us avoid having very long tables with many columns that may or may not be filled in. Take the `entityProperty` table in the following example:

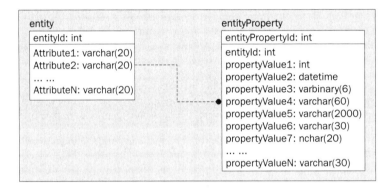

In this example, we have N columns with N data types that are all nullable to let the user store any one or more of the values. This type of table is generally known as a **sparse table**. The problem with this example is that, if the user comes up with a new property, we will be forced to modify the table, the UI, and any programs that refer to the columns in the table.

On the other hand, if we implement the table in the following manner:

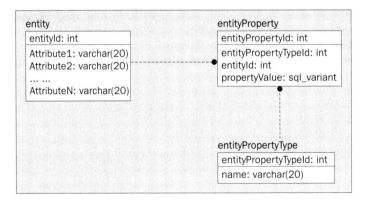

… then each of the properties that we implemented in the previous example, by adding a column to the `entityProperty` table, would now be added as an instance in the `entityPropertyType` table, and the value would be stored in the `propertyValue` column. Whatever type of data needed for the property could be stored as a `sql_variant`.

The `entityPropertyType` table could be extended to include many other properties without the user having to carry out major changes to the database. And if we implement our reporting solution in such a way that our new reports know about any changes, we will not have to recode for any new properties.

The Disadvantages of Variant

It is not easy to manipulate the data once it has been stored in a `sql_variant` column. I will leave it to the reader to fully read the information in SQL Server Books Online that deals with variant data. The issues range from:

- Assigning data from a `sql_variant` column to a stronger typed data type – we have to be very careful as the rules for casting a variable from one data type to another are difficult, and may cause errors if the data cannot be cast. For example, a `varchar(10)` value 'Not a Date' cannot be cast to a `datetime` data type. Such problems really become an issue when you start to retrieve the variant data out of the `sql_variant` data type and try to manipulate it.
- `NULL sql_variant` values are considered to have no data type – hence, you will have to deal with `sql_variant` nulls differently from other data types.
- Comparisons of variants to other data types could cause programmatic errors, because of the data type of the instance of the `sql_variant` value – the compiler will know if you try to run a statement that compares two incompatible data types, such as `@intVar = @varcharVar`. However, if the two variables in question were defined as `sql_variants`, and the data types don't match, then the values won't match due to the data type incompatibilities.

There is a function provided that discovers the data type of a value stored in a variant column:

```
DECLARE @varcharVariant sql_variant
SET @varcharVariant = '1234567890'
SELECT @varcharVariant AS varcharVariant,
   SQL_VARIANT_PROPERTY(@varcharVariant,'BaseType') as baseType,
   SQL_VARIANT_PROPERTY(@varcharVariant,'MaxLength') as maxLength
```

This returns:

VarcharVariant	baseType	maxLength
1234567890	varchar	10

Other Data Types

The following data types are somewhat less frequently employed but are still very useful.

timestamp (or rowversion)

The `timestamp` data type is a database-wide unique number. When you have a `timestamp` column in a table, the value of the `timestamp` column changes for each modification to each row. The value in the `timestamp` column is guaranteed to be unique across all tables in the data type. It also has a pretty strange name, as it does not have any time implications – it is merely a unique value to tell you that your row has changed.

The `timestamp` column of a table (you may only have one) is usually used as the data for an optimistic locking mechanism. We will discuss this further later in this chapter when we discuss physical-only columns.

The `timestamp` data type is a mixed blessing. It is stored as an eight byte `varbinary` value. Binary values are not always easy to deal with and depend on which mechanism you are using to access your data.

When using ODBC, or OLE DB and ADO, they can be tricky at first. This is due to the fact that they are binary values, and to retrieve them you have to use BLOB chunking mechanisms.

```
SET nocount on
CREATE TABLE testTimestamp
(
    value    varchar(20) NOT NULL,
    auto_rv  timestamp NOT NULL
)

INSERT INTO testTimestamp (value) values ('Insert')

SELECT value, auto_rv FROM testTimestamp
UPDATE testTimestamp
SET value = 'First Update'

SELECT value, auto_rv from testTimestamp
UPDATE testTimestamp
SET value = 'Last Update'

SELECT value, auto_rv FROM testTimestamp
```

which returns:

value	auto_rv
Insert	0x0000000000000089

Value	auto_rv
First Update	0x000000000000008A

Value	auto_rv
Last Update	0x000000000000008B

We did not touch the `auto_rv` variable and yet it incremented itself twice. However, you cannot bank on the order of the `timestamp` variable being sequential, as updates of other tables will change this. It is also in your best interest not to assume that the number is an incrementing value in your code. How timestamps are implemented is a detail that may change in the future (from SQL Server 2000 Books Online, "The definition of timestamp in a future release of SQL Server will be modified to align with the SQL-99 definition of timestamp."). If a better method of building database wide unique value comes along that is even a hair faster, they will likely use it.

You may create variables of the `timestamp` type for holding timestamp values, and you may retrieve the last used timestamp via the `@@dbts` global variable.

The topic of optimistic locks will be covered in greater detail in Chapter 12.

uniqueidentifier

A globally unique identifier (GUID) is fast becoming a mainstay of Microsoft computing. The name says it all – they are globally unique. According to the way that GUIDs are formed, there is a tremendously remote chance that there will ever be any duplication in their values. They are generated by a formula that includes the usage of the network card identification number (if one exists), the current date and time, a unique number from the CPU clock, and some other "magic numbers".

In SQL Server 2000, the `uniqueidentifier` has a very important purpose. When you need to have a unique key that is guaranteed to be unique across databases and servers, for example:

```
DECLARE @guidVar uniqueidentifier
SET @guidVar = newid()

SELECT @guidVar as guidVar
```

returns:

```
guidVar
------------------------------------------------------------
6C7119D5-D48F-475C-8B60-50D0C41B6EBF
```

They are actually stored as sixteen byte binary values. Note that it is not exactly a *straight* sixteen byte binary value. You may not put just any binary value into a `uniqueidentifier` column, as the value must meet the criteria for their generation which are not well documented for obvious reasons.

If you need to create a `uniqueidentifier` column that is auto-generating, there is a property you can set in the create table statement (or alter table for that matter). It is the `rowguidcol` property, and it is used like so:

```
CREATE TABLE guidPrimaryKey
(
    guidPrimaryKeyId uniqueidentifier NOT NULL
    rowguidcol DEFAULT newId(),
    value varchar(10)
)
```

We have introduced a couple of new things here – `rowguidcol` and default values – which we will examine properly in the next chapter. Suffice it to say that, if you do not provide a value for a column in an insert operation, the default operation will provide it. In our case, we use the `newId()` function to get a new `uniqueidentifier`. So when we execute the following insert statement:

```
INSERT INTO guidPrimaryKey(value)
VALUES ('Test')
```

and then run the following command to view the data entered:

```
SELECT *
FROM guidPrimaryKey
```

This returns:

guidPrimaryKeyId	value
8A57C8CD-7407-47C5-AC2F-E6A884C7B646	Test

The `rowguidcol` property of a column built with the `uniqueidentifier` notifies the system that this is just like an identity column value for the table – a unique pointer to a row in a table. Note that neither the identity nor the `rowguidcol` properties guarantee uniqueness. To provide such a guarantee, we have to implement this using unique constraints, which we will cover later in this chapter.

It would seem that the `uniqueidentifier` would be a better way of implementing primary keys, since, when they are created, they are unique across all databases, servers, and platforms. However, there are two main reasons why we will not use `uniqueidentifier` columns to implement all of our primary keys:

- ❑ **Storage requirements** – as they are sixteen bytes in size, they are considerably more bloated than a typical integer field.
- ❑ **Typeability** – As there are 36 characters in the textual version of the GUID, it is very hard to actually type the value of the GUID into a query, nor is it easy to enter.

cursor

A cursor is a mechanism which allows row-wise operations instead of the normal set-wise way. The `cursor` data type is used to hold a reference to a SQL Server T-SQL cursor. You may not use a `cursor` data type as a column in a table. Their only use is in T-SQL code to hold a reference to a cursor.

For more information on cursors, see "Professional SQL Server 2000 Programming" by Rob Vieira (Wrox Press, ISBN 1-861004-48-6).

table

The `table` data type has a few things in common with the `cursor` data type, but holds a reference to a result set. The name of the data type is really a pretty bad choice, as it will make the functional programmer think that they can store a pointer to a table. It is actually used to store a result set as a temporary table. In fact the `table` is exactly like a temporary table in implementation. The following is an example of the syntax needed to employ the `table` variable type.

```
DECLARE @tableVar TABLE
(
    id int IDENTITY,
    value varchar(100)
)
INSERT INTO @tableVar (value)
VALUES ('This is a cool test')

SELECT id, value
FROM @tableVar
```

Which returns:

Id	value
1	This is a cool test

Planning and Implementing the Basic Physical Architecture

As with the `cursor` data type, you may not use the `table` data type as a column in a table and it may only be used in T-SQL code to hold a result set. Its primary purpose is for returning a table from a user-defined function as in the following example:

```
CREATE FUNCTION table$testFunction
(
    @returnValue varchar(100)

)
RETURNS @tableVar table
(
     value varchar(100)
)
AS
BEGIN
    INSERT INTO @tableVar (value)
    VALUES (@returnValue)

    RETURN
END
```

Once created, we can invoke using the following syntax:

```
SELECT *
FROM dbo.table$testFunction('testValue')
```

Which returns the following:

```
value
-------------
testValue
```

User-Defined Data Types

We touched on these earlier when we were discussing how to manipulate the `datetime` data type.

The primary value of user-defined types is to allow the architect to build an alias for a frequently used data type. In the user-defined type declaration, we can specify:

- A name for the data type
- The system data type, including any length information
- Whether or not the data type will allow `NULL`s

To create a user-defined type for our corporate serial number, we might do the following:

```
EXEC sp_addtype @typename = serialNumber,
    @phystype = varchar(12),
    @NULLtype = 'not NULL',
    @owner = 'dbo'
GO
```

When the type is used, we can override the nullability by specifying it, but we cannot override the data type. We can then use this type much like we use all of SQL Server's data types – as a way to keep the implementation details of all usages of a type exactly the same. We can bind a rule (to limit values that are entered into it across all usages) and defaults (to give a default value if a value is not supplied) to the data type.

User-defined data types, as they are implemented in SQL Server, have some drawbacks that make them somewhat confusing to use:

- Error reporting using rules
- Inconsistent handling as variables
- Data types of columns defined with user-defined types will not change if the user-defined type changes

We will look into these problems now.

Error Reporting using Rules

It is possible to create a user-defined data type to encapsulate rules and error reporting. Create the user-defined type, create a rule for it, and bind it to a column. Now when a table is created with a column with the new data type, the rule is enforced, as expected. However, the error messages that are produced are worthless!

For example, let's create a very useful data type called `socialSecurityNumber`, add a rule, and bind it to a column.

```
--create a type, call it SSN, varchar(11), the size of a social security
--number including the dashes
EXEC sp_addtype @typename = 'SSN',
    @phystype = 'varchar(11)',
    @NULLtype = 'not NULL'
GO

--create a rule, call it SSNRule, with this pattern
CREATE RULE SSNRule AS
    @value LIKE '[0-9][0-9][0-9]-[0-9][0-9]-[0-9][0-9][0-9][0-9]'
GO

--bind the rule to the exampleType
EXEC sp_bindrule 'SSNRule', 'SSN'
GO

--create a test table with the new data type.
CREATE TABLE testRule
(
    id int IDENTITY,
    socialSecurityNumber   SSN
)
GO
```

This creates us a table with a column that should prevent an invalid SSN from being entered. So, in the following script, we will try to insert data into the table:

```
--insert values into the table
INSERT INTO testRule (socialSecurityNumber)
```

```
    VALUES ('438-44-3343')
    INSERT INTO testRule (socialSecurityNumber)
    VALUES ('43B-43-2343')    --note the B instead of the 8 to cause an error
    GO
```

The result we get back looks like the following:

Server: Msg 513, Level 16, State 1, Line 1
A column insert or update conflicts with a rule imposed by a previous CREATE RULE statement. The statement was terminated. The conflict occurred in database 'tempdb', table 'testRule', column 'socialSecurityNumber'.
The statement has been terminated.

You can see from this that the error message is not that helpful as it doesn't even tell us what rule was violated.

> *Note that, in our testing, we have the* NOCOUNT *option turned on for all connections. This setting will avoid the messages that tell us how many rows are modified by an action. In this case, this also makes for a better example. We can do this in code by specifying* SET NOCOUNT ON.

Inconsistent Handling of Variables

First, we will look at the handling of NULLs. When we created the type in the code in the previous *Error Reporting using Rules* section, we set its nullability to NOT NULL. Now run the following:

```
    DECLARE @SSNVar SSN
    SET @SSNVar = NULL
    SELECT @SSNVar
```

This code shows one of the inconsistencies of user-defined data types. When executed, we would expect an error to occur since the type did not allow NULLs. Rather, we get the following:

```
    SSNVar
    -----------
    NULL
```

This is fairly minor, but I would expect that the user-defined data type would not allow a NULL value.

Another problem associated with user-defined data types occurs when a variable is created according to the type – it does not employ the rule that was associated with it. It is possible to assign values to a variable defined using a user-defined data type with a rule, but these values cannot be inserted into a column defined with the same user-defined type. We show this effect here:

```
    DECLARE @SSNVar SSN
    SET @SSNVar = 'Bill'
    SELECT @SSNVar AS SSNVar

    INSERT INTO testRule (socialSecurityNumber)
    VALUES (@SSNVar)
```

This code results in this error:

```
SSNVar
-----------
Bill
```

Server: Msg 513, Level 16, State 1, Line 5

A column insert or update conflicts with a rule imposed by a previous CREATE RULE statement. The statement was terminated. The conflict occurred in database 'tempdb', table 'testRule', column 'socialSecurityNumber'.
The statement has been terminated.

In the next chapter we will look more closely at protecting our data from bad values, but at this point, we just need to understand why we are not employing what looks like such a useful encapsulation tool.

Note that rules are not the standard way of providing such protections – check constraints are. However, for a user-defined type to be of value to us, it should be an object in and of itself. For anyone that reads this book who really likes user-defined types, I think it was important to point out some of the biggest problems with them. Rules are in SQL Server 2000 as a backwards compatibility feature, and as such may not be around beyond the next version, depending on customer pressures to keep certain features. We will use check constraints, as they are bound directly to the column and not to the data type.

UDT Cannot be Modified When in Use

The data types of columns defined with user-defined types will not change if the user-defined type changes. This is the worst problem. Consider that we need to change a user-defined data type, say from `char(1)` to `varchar(10)`, for whatever reason. There is no facility to "change" the user-defined type, and we cannot drop it if it is already in use. Hence, we have to change the data type in every spot it has been used to the base type, change the type, and change the type back. Not pretty.

We will not employ user-defined data types in our case study for these reasons.

Optional Data

In Chapter 12, we will spend a good deal of time discussing the problems cause by use of NULLs as they apply to data retrieval. However, we need to look at why we would implement nullable columns. One of the goals of normalization was to remove as many of the NULLs from our tables as possible.

Before we get to how to implement NULLs, we need to briefly discuss what "NULL" means. While it can be inferred that NULL means that the data is optional, this is an incomplete definition. A NULL value should be read as "unknown value". In Chapter 12, we will present the truth tables for comparisons, but for now, we are saying that NULL means that the value of the column may be filled in the future.

In the column create phrase:

```
<columnName> <data type> [<NULL specification>]
```

we simply change the `<NULL specification>` to NULL to allow NULLs or NOT NULL to not allow NULLs. For example:

```
CREATE TABLE NULLTest
(
    NULLColumn varchar(10) NULL,
    notNULLColumn varchar(10) NOT NULL
)
```

Nothing particularly surprising there. If we leave off the NULL specification altogether, the SQL Server default is used. To determine what the current default property for a database is, we execute the following statement:

```
EXECUTE sp_dboption @dbname = 'tempdb', @optname = 'ANSI NULL default'
```

which gives:

OptionName	CurrentSetting
ANSI NULL default	off

To set the default for the database, you can use the sp_dboption procedure. (I would recommend that this setting is always off so, if you forget to set it explicitly, you won't be stuck will nullable columns that will quickly fill up with NULL data you will have to clean up.)

To set the default for a session use the following command:

```
set ansi_NULL_dflt_on off -- or on if you want the default to be NULL
```

Example:

```
--turn off default NULLs
SET ANSI_NULL_DFLT_ON OFF

--create test table
CREATE TABLE testNULL
(
    id    int
)

--check the values
EXEC sp_help testNULL
```

which returns:

Column_name	[...]	Nullable
id	...	no

Note that considerable stuff has been removed from the sp_help output here for space reasons. sp_help returns information about the table, columns, and constraints.

Alternatively, try:

```
--change the setting to default not NULL
SET ANSI_NULL_DFLT_ON ON

--get rid of the table and recreate it
DROP TABLE testNULL
GO
CREATE TABLE testNULL
(
    id    int
)

EXEC sp_help testNULL
```

which returns:

Column_name	[...]	Nullable
id	...	yes

Calculated Columns

Now we have introduced the data types, we will take a quick look at calculated columns. These are a really cool feature that was added in SQL Server 7.0. Strangely, they were not implemented in the Enterprise Manager, which simply destroyed them for you when you made any changes to the table, so you had to maintain them with script. In SQL Server 2000, this feature is properly supported.

```
<columnName> AS <computed definition>
```

Calculated columns can be used to take unreadable data and translate it into a readable format in the definition of the table. In SQL Server 2000, they can now be indexed – so they are even more useful.

An example where they came in handy in a database system I created was for building a grouping on the day, month, and year. In the following code, we have an example that is close to this. It groups on the second to make the example easier to test:

```
CREATE TABLE calcColumns
(
    dateColumn    datetime,
    dateSecond    AS datepart(second,dateColumn), -- calculated column
)

DECLARE @i int
SET @i = 1
WHILE (@i < 1000)
BEGIN
    INSERT INTO calcColumns (dateColumn) VALUES (getdate())
    SET @i = @i + 1
END

SELECT dateSecond, max(dateColumn) as dateColumn, count(*) AS countStar
FROM calcColumns
GROUP BY dateSecond
ORDER BY dateSecond
```

When this code is executed, it returns the following:

```
DateSecond        dateColumn                    countStar
----------------  ----------------------------  ----------------------------
20                2000-11-14 11:07:20.993       8
21                2000-11-14 11:07:21.993       900
22                2000-11-14 11:07:22.083       91
```

An almost dangerous feature with calculated columns is that they will be ignored when you are inserting data if you omit the insert field list. SQL Server will ignore any calculated columns and match the fields up as if they do not exist. For example, we create the following table:

```
CREATE TABLE testCalc
(
value varchar(10),
valueCalc AS UPPER(value),
value2 varchar(10)
)
```

Then we create some new values without the insert list:

```
INSERT INTO testCalc
-- We should have (value, value2) here
VALUES ('test','test2')
```

No error occurs. When we execute:

```
SELECT *
FROM   testCalc
```

we get back the following results:

```
Value         valueCalc               value2
-----------   ----------------------  -----------------
test          TEST                    test2
```

> **Regardless of calculated columns, it is poor practice to code INSERT statements with no insert list.**

Calculated columns are an extremely valuable feature, and should cause excitement to anyone who has ever had to type and retype column calculations over and over.

Physical-Only Columns

Not every column will be or should be denoted on the logical data model. In this section, we will discuss some of the reasons why we would have columns that do not fit the mold of a logical model column, but which are required in the physical implementation.

The primary reason for a physical-only column is that the column is not an attribute of the entity that the table is modeling. In other words, the column is required primarily for implementation purposes. Here are a few examples of situations when such columns are needed.

Chapter 10

Concurrency Control

When we have a database with more than one user, we need to implement some form of concurrency control mechanism. We want to make sure that, once a user gets a record that they want to change, no other user can make changes to the record, or we might lose information. There are two different methods for performing this task.

- **Pessimistic Locking** – this is implemented by having locks on any records that a user reads with intent to update. It is called pessimistic because it assumes that other users will likely be trying to edit the same record as the current user. This is a very high maintenance solution and is usually unnecessary, since in most cases no two users are likely to look at the same record at the same time. We would only use a pessimistic lock when it is completely necessary to make other clients wait until we are finished with the record before letting them get access to it. The problem is that we have to lock the record in such a way that *no one* else may look at it, or any other user may step on our changes after we have released our lock.

- **Optimistic Locking** – this is a far more popular solution. To implement an optimistic locking mechanism, we simply add a column to each table that changes every time a row changes in the database. For example, User 1 retrieves a row of values. Shortly afterwards, User 2 retrieves the same row. User 1 updates a record, and the value of the lock column changes. Now, if User 2 tries to modify the row, SQL Server checks the value of the lock column, sees that it has changed, and prevents User 2's update:

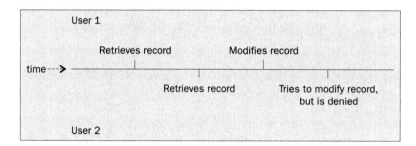

Implementing the optimistic lock is a fairly simple task, but note however that every process that uses the tables must adhere to the rules of the optimistic lock. If one process ignores it, the overall process fails.

There are a few ways to implement an optimistic lock:

- Using a timestamp column – As previously discussed, the timestamp column is a special column that changes every time a row is modified. Timestamp columns are the ideal manner for creating an optimistic lock.

- Using the last updated date and/or last updated user – Basically this is the same method, except that we add columns to store the user that last modified a record and the time of the modification. We do this through a trigger on the INSERT and UPDATE. This method is better in that it gives a human readable value for the optimistic lock, but worse in that it requires the overhead of coding triggers.

- Using all columns in the WHERE clause during modifications – This is the method provided by tools like Microsoft Access, when there is no timestamp column available. Basically, when doing a modification statement, we would include every column in the table in the WHERE clause. If the values have changed since we first retrieved the value, then someone else has likely fingered our data out from under us. Hence the optimistic lock will fail.

We will use the timestamp column, since it is quite easy to implement and requires absolutely no code whatsoever. So, we will build the following table:

```
CREATE TABLE testOptimisticLock
(
    id int NOT NULL,
    value varchar(10) NOT NULL,
    autoTimestamp timestamp NOT NULL, --optimistic lock
    primary key (id)                  --adds a primary key on id column
)
```

Then we execute the following script. The first step is to create a new row in the table and get the optimistic lock value for the row.

```
INSERT INTO testOptimisticLock (id, value)
VALUES (1, 'Test1')

DECLARE @timestampHold timestamp
SELECT @timestampHold = autoTimestamp
FROM testOptimisticLock
WHERE value = 'Test1'

--first time will work
UPDATE testOptimisticLock
SET value = 'New Value'
WHERE id = 1
    AND   autoTimestamp = @timestampHold
IF @@rowcount = 0
BEGIN
    raiserror 50000 'Row has been changed by another user'
END
SELECT  id, value FROM testOptimisticLock

--second time will fail
UPDATE testOptimisticLock
SET value = 'Second New Value'
WHERE id = 1
    AND   autoTimestamp = @timestampHold
IF @@rowcount = 0
BEGIN
    raiserror 50000 'Row has been changed another user'
END
SELECT  id, value from testOptimisticLock
```

This will return:

```
Id         value
---------- -----------------------
1          New Value
```

Server: Msg 50000, Level 16, State 1, Line 38
Row has been changed by another user

```
Id         value
---------- -----------------------
1          New Value
```

Record Disablers

A physical-only column that is of some importance in many applications that I have created is a record disabler. For example, take a domain table that defines the type of some record, say a `contactType` as in the following example diagram:

In the `contactType` table we have a `bit` column entitled `disableFl`. If this column has a value of 1, then we will not be able to use this value as a type of contact any longer. We will not have to delete or change any existing contact values to set this flag. (Note that this solution will require a trigger to enforce this rule – to check the value of `contactType.disableFl` – since this is an inter-table rule.)

Why would we want to do this? There are three very obvious problems we need to solve:

❑ If we only have 10 contacts, it would not be a problem to physically delete any rows in the contact table where the `contactType` instance is used. However, if we have 1,000,000 contacts, all of the contacts will have to be checked. This might be too much to deal with.

❑ While the user may not foresee any further use for a particular value, there may be no reason to remove the record totally from the database.

❑ There may be existing child records that we do not want to remove from the database.

Note that, where a list of `contactType` values is presented to the user, they would have to be filtered like so:

```
SELECT name
FROM contactType
WHERE disableFl = 0
```

This does imply some tradeoff in terms of query performance, so in cases we may need to balance the overhead of doing the delete versus the query costs. We might also implement both a delete and a disable flag – disabling during contentious times for our database and cleaning out the rows later in the night when everything is quiet.

It should be mentioned that `disableFl` is one of those attributes that requires Fourth Normal Form treatment, as we will probably want to know more than whether it is disabled – like *when* it was disabled, for instance. It would be possible of course to add a `contactTypeStatus` table, where we monitor the past and present status. In practice, this is rarely needed, but should certainly be considered on a case to case basis, as the first time you are asked when and why the `contactType` of "Active" was disabled and you cannot provide a simple answer, you are in trouble.

Collation (Sort Order)

The collation sequence for SQL Server determines how it will arrange character data when storing it, how data will be sorted when needed, and how data will be compared. SQL Server and Windows provide a tremendous number of collation types to choose from. To see the current collation type for the server and database, you can execute the following commands:

```sql
SELECT serverproperty('collation')
SELECT databasepropertyex('master','collation')
```

On most systems installed in English speaking countries, the default collation type is `SQL_Latin1_General_CP1_CI_AS`, where `Latin1_General` represents the normal Latin alphabet, `CP1` refers to code page 1252 (the SQL Server default Latin 1 ANSI character set), and the last parts represent case insensitive and accent sensitive, respectively. Full coverage of all collation types may be found in the SQL Server 2000 documentation.

To list all of the sort orders installed in a given SQL Server instance, you can execute the following statement:

```sql
SELECT *
FROM ::fn_helpcollations()
```

On the computer I do testing on, this query returned over 700 rows, but usually we will not need to change from the default that the database administrator initially chooses. There are a few important reasons to specify a different collation.

- ❏ **Case sensitivity** – depending on the application, there can be a need to have all of your code and data treated as case sensitive. This would certainly be on a case by case basis. Note that this makes your code and object names case sensitive too.

  Remember that case sensitivity causes searching difficulties. For example, when searching for all names starting with the letter "A", we have to search for all things starting with "A" or "a". We could use upper case functions for columns or variables, but this defeats indexing and is generally not a good idea.

- ❏ **Foreign character sorting** – the other reason is foreign characters. Using Unicode, you can use any character from any language in the world. However, very few languages use the same A-Z character set that English speaking countries use. In fact, nearly all other European languages use accented letters that are not part of the 7 bit ASCII character set. A possible use of a different collation type is in implementing columns for different languages. We will have an example of this later in this section.

In previous versions of SQL Server, the entire server had a single sort order. This meant that, in every database, in every table, in every field, in every query, you were forced to use exactly the same sort order. This leads to interesting difficulties, for example when trying to implement a case sensitive sort.

However, in SQL Server 2000, we can set the collation for our server and database as mentioned earlier, but also for a column, and even in the `ORDER` clause of a `SELECT` statement.

To set the collation sequence for a `char`, `varchar`, `text`, `nchar`, `nvarchar`, or `ntext` column when creating a table, you specify it using the `collate` clause of the column definition, like so:

```sql
CREATE TABLE otherCollate
(
    id integer IDENTITY,
    name nvarchar(30) NOT NULL,
    frenchName nvarchar(30) COLLATE French_CI_AS_WS NULL,
    spanishName nvarchar(30) COLLATE Modern_Spanish_CI_AS_WS NULL
)
```

Now, when we sort `frenchName` by columns, it will be case insensitive, but will arrange the rows according to the order of the French character set. The same applies with Spanish regarding the `spanishName` column.

In the next example, we look at another cool use of the COLLATE keyword. We can use it to affect the comparisons made in an expression. We do this by changing one or both of the values on either side of the expression to a binary collation. Let's create a table, called `collateTest`:

```
CREATE TABLE collateTest
(
    name    VARCHAR(20) COLLATE SQL_Latin1_General_CP1_CI_AS NOT NULL
)
insert into collateTest(name)
values ('BOB')
insert into collateTest(name)
values ('bob')
```

Note that for demonstration purposes, the COLLATE statement that I have included is the default for my server. This is likely to be your collation also if you have taken the default (we will assume this collation for the rest of the book).

We can then execute the following against the database:

```
SELECT name
FROM collateTest
WHERE name = 'BOB'
```

which returns both rows:

```
name
-------
bob
BOB
```

However, if we change the collation on the "BOB" literal, and execute it:

```
SELECT name
FROM collateTest
WHERE name = 'BOB' COLLATE Latin1_General_BIN
```

we only get back the single row that actually matches "BOB" character for character:

```
name
-------
BOB
```

You should have noticed that we only cast the scalar value "BOB" to a binary collation. Determining collation precedence can be a tricky matter and it is one that we will not cover here. In general, it is best to add the COLLATE function to both sides of the expression when performing such an operation.

In our case, instead of the collate on just the scalar, we would write it this way:

```
SELECT name
FROM collateTest
WHERE name COLLATE Latin1_General_BIN = 'BOB' COLLATE Latin1_General_BIN
```

We will not delve any deeper into the subject of collation. In the SQL Server documentation, there is a large amount of information about collations, including the rules for collation precedence.

Keys

As discussed in the logical modeling chapters, the defining of keys is one of the most important tasks in database design. In this section, we will not be looking at why we defined the keys we did, but rather how we implement them. There are several different types of keys that we have already discussed:

- **Primary** – contains the primary pointer to a row in the table
- **Alternate** – contains alternate pointers to a row in the table, basically any unique conditions that we wish to make certain exist amongst one or more columns in the table
- **Foreign** – foreign keys are pointers to primary keys in other tables

Primary and alternate keys are hybrid objects – part constraint, part index. Constraints declare that some factor must be true for an object. For keys, this is declaring that the values in the table must be unique.

Declarative key constraints are also implemented as indexes. If you do not understand how SQL Server stores data and implements indexes, please read the following section. It is vital to your understanding of physical modeling and your use of indexes and keys, not to mention your understanding of why we normalize our databases. Again, *"Professional SQL Server 2000 Programming"* by *Rob Vieira* (*Wrox Press, ISBN 1-861004-48-6*) contains more information.

Indexes

Any discussion on how to build constraints should begin with a discussion of the basics of index and table structures. Indexes are some of the most important objects involved in physical modeling. We use them to implement primary keys and alternate keys (unique constraints), and we can use them to improve performance. We will discuss performance-based indexes in Chapter 14.

Understanding how indexes work will give us a base level to determine what kinds of indexes to use. We will only give a brief treatment of how SQL Server implements indexes, as this is a complex topic outside the scope of this book.

Basic Index Structure

Indexes speed up retrieval of the rows in a table, and are generally, though not always, separate structures associated with the table. They are built by taking one or more of the table's columns and building a special structure on the table, based on those keys. There are two distinct classes of indexes:

- **Clustered** – orders the physical table in the order of the index
- **Non-Clustered** – completely separate structures that simply speed access

We can have unique type indexes of either class. Unique indexes are used not only to speed access, but to enforce uniqueness over a column or group of columns. The reason that they are used for this purpose is that, to determine if a value is unique we have to look it up in the table, and since the index is used to speed access to the data, we have the perfect match.

There are other settings but they are beyond the scope of this book (consult the *Create Index* topic in *SQL Server 2000 Books Online* for a full explanation of creating indexes). I will only present here the basic options that are germane to designing the physical structures. The additional settings affect performance as well as a few other features that are handy but beyond our scope.

Indexes are implemented using a balanced tree structure, also known as a **B-Tree**. In the following diagram, we give the basic structure of the type of B-Tree that SQL Server uses for indexes.

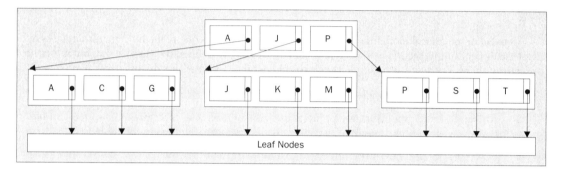

Each of the outer rectangles is an 8 K index page, which SQL Server uses for all data storage. The first page is shown at the top of the diagram:

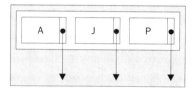

We have three values which are the index keys. To decide which path to follow to the lower level of the index, we have to decide if the value is between two of the keys. A to I, J to P, or greater than P. If the value is between A and I, we follow the first route down to the next level:

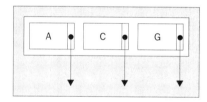

We continue this down to the leaf nodes of the index. We will look at leaf nodes when we come to discuss the details of clustered and non-clustered indexes. This structure is how all SQL Server indexes are implemented. However, one important detail should be noted. We have stated that each of these pages is 8 K in size. Depending on the size of your key (determined by summing the data lengths of the columns in the key, up to a maximum of 900 bytes), you can have anywhere from eight entries to over one thousand on a single page. Hence, these trees don't generally grow all that large, if designed properly. In our example, we used a simplistic set of index values to show how the index tree fans out.

In the next example, we build a basic table and basic indexes. We will use the same table in the rest of our examples in this section.

```
CREATE TABLE testIndex
(
    id int IDENTITY,
    firstName varchar(20),
    middleName varchar(20),
    lastName varchar(30)
)
CREATE INDEX XtestIndex ON testIndex(id)
CREATE INDEX XtestIndex1 ON testIndex(firstName)
CREATE INDEX XtestIndex2 ON testIndex(middleName)
CREATE INDEX XtestIndex3 ON testIndex(lastName)
CREATE INDEX XtestIndex4 ON testIndex(firstName,middleName,lastName)
```

If all is well, there will be no output from this statement. To drop an index you use the following statement:

```
DROP INDEX testIndex.Xtestindex
```

Clustered Indexes

The leaf nodes of the clustered index are the actual data pages. Hence, there can only be one clustered index per table. The exact implementation of the data pages is not a particularly important detail; rather, it is sufficient to understand that the data in the table is physically ordered in the order of the index.

When choosing what fields to use as the basis for the clustered index, it is best to consider it as the humanly readable index. In other words, if your table has an inherent ordering that will make sense for a human to scan, this is a good candidate for the clustered index. Take, for example, a dictionary. Each word in the dictionary can be thought of as a row in a database. It is then clustered on the word. The most important reason for this is that we frequently need to scan a group of words and their meanings to see if we can find the one we need. Since all of the data is sorted by word, we can scan the words on the pages without any trouble. We use much the same logic to decide whether or not to use a clustered index.

Clustered indexes should be used for:

- Key sets that contain a limited number of distinct values – since the data is sorted by the keys, when we do a lookup on the values in the index, all of the values we need to scan are visible straight away.

- Range queries – having all of the data in order usually makes sense when you have data where you need to get a range, like from "A" to "F".

- Data that is accessed sequentially – obviously, if you need to access your data in a given order, having the data already sorted in that order will significantly improve performance.

- Queries that return large result sets – this point will make more sense once we cover the non-clustered index, but having the data on the leaf index node saves overhead.

- Key sets that are frequently accessed by queries involving JOIN or GROUP BY clauses – frequently these may be foreign key columns, but not necessarily. GROUP BY clauses always require data to be sorted, so it follows that having data sorted anyway will improve performance.

Since the clustered index physically orders the table, inserting new values will usually force you to put new data into the middle of the table – the only exception to this is if you use a clustered index with auto incrementing (identity) type fields. If the new row will not fit on the page, SQL Server has to do a **page split** (which is when a page gets full, so the half of the data is split off to a new page – hence the name). Page splits are fairly costly operations and hurt performance since data will not be located on successive pages, eliminating the possibility of synchronous reads by the disk subsystem.

If you do not have a set of keys that meet one of the criteria for a clustered index, it is generally best to not build one. It is also important not to use a clustered index on columns that change frequently. Since the table is ordered by the values in the column, SQL Server may have to rearrange the rows on their pages, which is a costly operation. This is especially true if you have to do modification operations on the values in the key that subsequently change lots of different rows.

Another important point to note is that you should keep the clustering key as small as possible, as it will be used in every non-clustered index (as we will see). So, if you modify the cluster key, you add work for all non-clustered indexes as well.

For a clustered table, the row locator is always the clustered index key. If the clustered key is non-unique, SQL Server adds a random value to make it unique.

Non-Clustered Indexes

The non-clustered index is analogous to the index in a text book, with the book indexed on page number. Much like the index of a book, the non-clustered index is completely separate from the rows of data.

A leaf node of a non-clustered index contains only a pointer to the data row containing the key value. The pointer from the non-clustered index to the data row is known as a **row locator**. The structure of the row locator depends on whether the table has a clustered index or not. The upper levels of the index are the same as for the clustered index. We will look at diagrams showing the different row locators after a bit more discussion on the basics of non-clustered indexes.

We have discussed tables with clustered indexes – these are referred to as **clustered tables**. If we do not have a clustered index, the table is referred to as a **heap**. My dictionary's definition of a heap is, "A group of things placed or thrown one on top of the other." This is a great way to explain what happens in a table when you have no clustered index. SQL Server simply puts every new row on the end of the table. Note also that if you do a delete, SQL Server will simply pull out the row, not reusing the space. However, if you do an update, there are two possibilities:

- **Update in place** – the values are simply changed in the row
- **Delete and insert** – the entire row is deleted from the table, and then reinserted

There are several criteria that SQL Server uses to determine whether or not to perform an update on a row. Two of the more common ones include:

- Having an after update trigger on the table – when you have a trigger on the table that fires after the row is updated, the row is deleted first and then inserted.
- Trying to insert more data than the page will handle – if you have variable length data in your table, and you try to increase the size of the data stored, SQL Server will have to delete the row and reinsert it somewhere else, perhaps on a different page. This procedure differs from when there is a clustered index, because there is now no reason to do a page split in the middle of the structure; it is faster and easier to move the data to the end of the heap.

Planning and Implementing the Basic Physical Architecture

We now need to look at the two distinct types of tables and how their non-clustered row locators are implemented.

Heap

For the "heap" table, with no clustered index, the row locator is a pointer to the page that contains the row.

Suppose that we have a table called `ItemTable`, with a clustered index on the `description` column, and a non-clustered index on the `itemId` column.

In the following diagram we see that, to find `itemId` 3 in the table, we take the left branch of the tree because 3 is between 1 and 20, then follow that down the path between 1 and 10. Once we get to the page, we get a pointer to the page that has the value. We will assume this pointer consists of the page number and offset on the page (the pages are numbered from 0 and the offset is numbered from 1). The most important fact about this pointer is that it takes you directly to the row on the page that has the values that we are looking for. This is not how it will work for the clustered table, and it is an important distinction to understand.

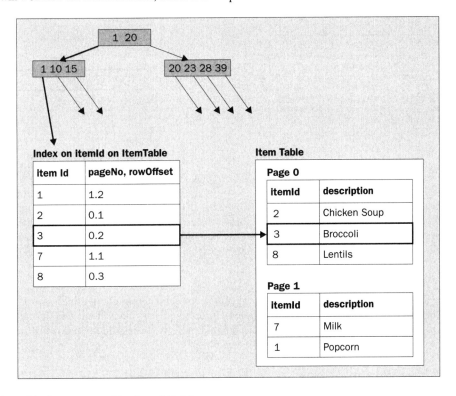

Non-Clustered Indexes on a Clustered Table

In this situation, when you have traversed the *non-clustered index* and arrived at its leaf node, instead of finding a pointer which takes you directly to the data, you are taken to the *clustered index*, which you must traverse to retrieve the data.

In the next graphic, the lower left box is the non-clustered index, as in our previous example, except that the pointer has changed from a specific location, to the value of the clustering key. We then use the clustering key to traverse the clustered index to reach the data.

Chapter 10

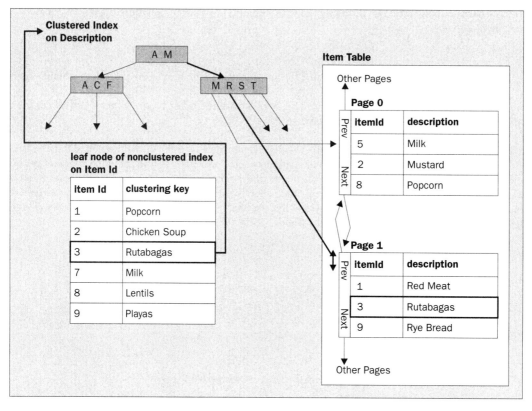

The overhead of this operation is minimal and it is "theoretically" better than having direct pointers to the table, because only minimal reorganization is required for any modification of the clustered index or the clustering key. When modifications are made, the pointers are not moved. Instead, a pointer is left in the table which points to the new page where the data now is. All existing indexes that have the old pointer simply go to the old page, then follow the new pointer on that page to the new location of the data.

Unique Indexes

The unique index is the second most important thing that you set when implementing your clustered index. You can create unique indexes for clustered and non-clustered indexes alike. It ensures that, among the index's keys, there cannot be any duplicate values. For example, if we created the following indexes on our test table:

```
CREATE UNIQUE INDEX XtestIndex1 ON testIndex(lastName)
CREATE UNIQUE INDEX XtestIndex2 ON testIndex(firstName,middleName,lastName)
```

we would not be able to insert duplicate values in the `lastName` column, nor would we be able to create entries that have the same `firstName`, `middleName`, and `lastName` values.

We typically do not use unique indexes to enforce uniqueness of alternate keys. SQL Server has a mechanism known as a UNIQUE constraint, as well as a PRIMARY KEY constraint that we will employ. Use unique indexes when you need to build an index to enhance performance.

It should also be noted that it is very important for the performance of your systems that you use unique indexes whenever possible, as it enhances the SQL Server optimizer's chances of predicting how many rows will be returned from a query that uses the index.

In our example, if we tried to run the following query:

```
INSERT  INTO testIndex (firstName, middleName, lastname)
VALUES ('Louis','Banks','Davidson')
INSERT INTO testIndex (firstName, middleName, lastname)
VALUES ('James','Banks','Davidson')
```

we get the following error:

```
Server: Msg 2601, Level 14, State 3, Line 1
Cannot insert duplicate key row in object 'testIndex' with unique index
'XtestIndex1'. The statement has been terminated.
```

While the error message could be much improved upon, it clearly prevents us from inserting the duplicate row with the same last name.

IGNORE_DUP_KEY

A frequently useful setting of unique indexes is IGNORE_DUP_KEY. By using this, we can tell SQL Server to ignore any rows with duplicate keys, if we so desire.

If we change our index in the previous example:

```
DROP INDEX testIndex.XtestIndex4
CREATE UNIQUE INDEX XtestIndex4
   ON testIndex(firstName,middleName,lastName)
   WITH ignore_dup_key
```

Then, when we execute the same code as before:

```
INSERT    INTO testIndex (firstName, middleName, lastname)
VALUES    ('Louis','Banks','Davidson')
INSERT    INTO testIndex (firstName, middleName, lastname)
VALUES    ('Louis','Banks','Davidson')
```

we get the following result:

```
Server: Msg 3604, Level 16, State 1, Line 3
Duplicate key was ignored.
```

This setting is probably not what you want most of the time, but it can come in handy when you are building a replica of some data. You can then insert the data without much worry as to whether it has been inserted before, as the index will toss out duplicate values. Note that this does not work on updates, only on inserts.

Primary Keys

Choosing a primary key is one of the most important choices we make concerning an individual table. It is the primary key that will be migrated to other tables as a pointer to a particular value.

In logical modeling, we chose to use a 4 byte integer pointer for entity primary keys, which migrate to dependent child tables in this manner:

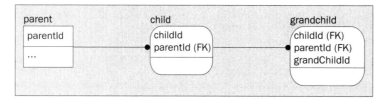

In physical modeling, this causes implemented keys to grow rather large, not so much in the sense of the size of the data but more in the number of values we have to deal with. Another problem with implementing the primary keys this way is that we tend to lose sight of the fact that the only key of a table must not be made up of meaningless columns. The migrated keys are fine, as they represent the values in the table that they came from but, by adding the unique value, we have essentially made this a meaningless key (since no matter what you add to a meaningless value you will always end up with a meaningless value). In logical modeling, this representation of the parent and child tables showed us that you could not have a `grandChild` without a `child` or a `parent`, and we always modeled an additional alternate key to make sure it was understood what the actual alternate key was. However, now that we are in the physical modeling stage, we will follow a slightly different strategy. Every table will have a single meaningless primary key and we will implement alternate keys in our tables, as shown in the following diagram:

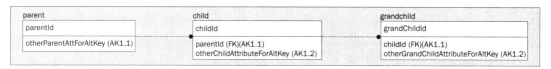

We will choose this method for the following important reasons:

- We never have to worry about what to do when the primary key value changes.

- Every table has a single column primary key pointer, and it is much easier to develop applications that access this pointer, because every table will have a single value as the primary key.

- Our primary key index will be very small, and thus operations that use it to access a row in the table will be faster. Most update and delete operations will likely modify the data by accessing the data based on primary keys which will use this index.

- Joins between tables will be cleaner to design, since all migrated keys will be a single field.

There are disadvantages to this method, such as always having to join to a table to find out what the value of the primary key actually means, not to mention other joins that will be needed to access data. Since the goals of our OLTP system are to keep keys small, speed up modifications, and data consistency, this strategy is not only acceptable, but favorable.

Implementing the primary key in this manner is very simple:

```
CREATE TABLE nameTable
(
    id integer NOT NULL IDENTITY PRIMARY KEY NONCLUSTERED
)
```

Note that you may not have any NULL columns in a primary key, even though you may have NULL columns in a unique index. The reason for this is actually pretty simple. The primary key is the record identifier, and a NULL provides no form of record identification.

Note also that we explicitly specified NONCLUSTERED. If we leave this specification off, the primary key constraints will be implemented using a clustered index, and frequently we forget this fact until it is too late.

The following will also work if you need to specify more than one column for the primary key.

```
CREATE TABLE nameTable
(
    id integer NOT NULL IDENTITY,
    pkeyColumn1 integer NOT NULL,
    pkeyColumn2 integer NOT NULL,
    PRIMARY KEY NONCLUSTERED (id)
)
```

Usually, when we implement the primary key as an integer pointer, we will not want to waste our clustered index on it. A primary key of this form should not be treated as any kind of ordering key. The reason for this is that you will seldom want to access rows in primary key order, or see a range of rows based on primary key. If ordering is required, it is best to add an additional column, because if you need to reorder for any reason, you cannot modify the value of an identity column, and should rarely modify the primary key for any reason.

As mentioned previously, if you have to provide for a key that is guaranteed to be unique across databases, or even servers, we can use the uniqueidentifier column with the ROWGUIDCOL property, like so:

```
CREATE TABLE nameTable
(
    id uniqueidentifier NOT NULL ROWGUIDCOL DEFAULT newid(),
    PRIMARY KEY NONCLUSTERED (id)
)
```

Note that the ROWGUIDCOL does not enforce uniqueness, nor does it provide its own default like the identity column. Only use the uniqueidentifier when necessary, as it uses sixteen bytes instead of four for the integer.

Alternate Keys

Alternate key enforcement is a very important task of physical modeling. When implementing alternate keys, we have two choices:

- Unique constraints
- Unique indexes

As an example, we take the nameTable and extend it to include a first and last name. We then want to implement a rule that we must have unique full names in the table. We could implement an index, like so:

```
CREATE TABLE nameTable
(
```

```
        id integer NOT NULL IDENTITY PRIMARY KEY NONCLUSTERED,
        firstName varchar(15) NOT NULL,
        lastName varchar(15) NOT NULL
    )
    CREATE UNIQUE INDEX XnameTable ON nameTable(firstName,lastName)
```

Or a unique constraint, like so:

```
    CREATE TABLE nameTable
    (
        id integer NOT NULL IDENTITY PRIMARY KEY,
        firstName varchar(15) NOT NULL,
        lastName varchar(15) NOT NULL,
        UNIQUE (firstName, lastName)
    )
```

While technically they are both based on unique indexes, unique constraints are the favored method of implementing an alternate key and enforcing uniqueness. This is because constraints are semantically intended to enforce constraints on data, and indexes are intended to speed access to data. In actuality, it does not matter how the uniqueness is implemented, but we certainly need to have either unique indexes or unique constraints in place.

One additional benefit of implementing them as constraints is the ability to view the constraints on the table by executing the following stored procedure:

```
    sp_helpconstraint 'nameTable'
```

This returns a result set of which the following is an abridged version:

constraint_type	constraint_name	[...]	constraint_keys
PRIMARY KEY (clustered)	PK__nameTable__1466F737	...	id
UNIQUE (non-clustered)	UQ__nameTable__155B1B70	...	firstName, lastName

This stored procedure will be used to view all constraints that we will add to our tables in the next chapters.

Naming

Naming of keys is relatively unimportant to the general structure of the table. However, it still pays to give the keys some recognizable name for use in error messages. SQL Server does not force us to give our indexes names. If we leave the name out of the constraint declaration as we have in the previous sections, SQL Server assigns a name for us. For instance, the following names were chosen when we ran the previous example code:

        PK__nameTable__1ED998B2
        UQ__nameTable__1FCDBCEB
        UQ__nameTable__20C1E124
        UQ__nameTable__21B6055D

These don't mean much to the human reader. While it is not hard to look them up with tools like Enterprise Manager, it is probably better to make them something more intelligible. The naming standard that we will use in this book is pretty simple:

```
<type><tableName>_<description>
```

For a primary key the type would be `PK`, and for an alternate key we would use `AK`. As for the `description`, we would omit that on the primary key because we can only have a single instance of a primary key. For the `description` of alternate keys, use either the column name for single columns or a brief description for an alternate key comprising more than one column. So, for our example, we would get the following:

```
CREATE TABLE nameTable
(
    id integer NOT NULL IDENTITY
        CONSTRAINT PKnameTable PRIMARY KEY,
    firstName varchar(15) NOT NULL CONSTRAINT AKnameTable_firstName UNIQUE,
    lastName varchar(15) NULL CONSTRAINT AKnameTable_lastName UNIQUE,
        CONSTRAINT AKnameTable_fullName UNIQUE (firstName, lastName)
)
```

This would leave us with these names, making it is easier to work out the role of the constraints:

PKnameTable
AKnameTable_fullName
AKnameTable_lastName
AKnameTable_firstName

Other Indexes

Any indexes that we add in addition to those used to enforce uniqueness should be taken care of when dealing with performance tuning. This is a very important point that I will make over and over. Indexes make accessing data in a certain way faster, but they also have overhead. Every time a change affects any of the columns that are indexed, the index must be modified. On a single change, this time is really small, but the more the active the system is, the more this will affect performance. In our OLTP system, only in extremely obvious cases would I advocate performance "guessing" – adding indexes before a need is shown – versus performance "tuning" where we respond to known performance problems. Only at this time will we be able to decide how a performance "tune" will affect the rest of the database.

Relationships

We have covered relationships in some length already, so we will not say too much more about why we would use them. In this section we will simply discuss how to implement relationships. The first thing we need to do is introduce a new statement. This is the `ALTER TABLE` statement:

```
ALTER TABLE <tablename>
```

The `ALTER TABLE` statement allows us to modify and add columns, check constraints, and enable and disable triggers. In this section, we will look at how to add constraints to tables. Note that you are also able to do this using the `CREATE TABLE` statement. However, since we frequently create all of our tables at once, it is better to use the `ALTER TABLE` command on pre-existing tables rather then having to create tables in order, such that parent tables are created before dependent child tables.

Chapter 10

Foreign Keys

The foreign key is actually just the primary key of another table migrated to the child table which represents the entity that it comes from. Implementing foreign keys is a fairly simple task in SQL Server 2000. There are several issues that we have to work through when creating relationships:

- Cascading deletes (if the parent row is deleted, then delete any related children values that refer to the key of the deleted row)
- Relationships that span different databases

The basic syntax of the ALTER TABLE statement for adding foreign key constraints is pretty simple (the ALTER TABLE command will be used many times throughout this chapter and the next to add constraints):

```
ALTER TABLE <tablename>
   ADD CONSTRAINT [<constraintName>]
   FOREIGN KEY REFERENCES <referenceTable> (<referenceColumns>)
```

Note that this code demonstrated the addition of a constraint. For other operations that you can carry out using ALTER TABLE, see the SQL Server 2000 documentation.

- `<tablename>` is the child table in the relationship
- `<referenceTable>` is the parent table in the relationship
- `<referenceColumns>` is a comma delimited list of columns in the child table in the same order as the columns in the primary key of the parent table

If you need to implement an optional relationship (where the migrated key is nullable) like the following:

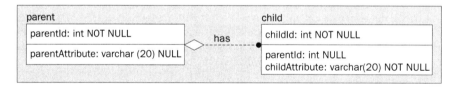

then this is implemented almost identically to the previous situation. The ALTER TABLE statement is the same, but you will notice that the `child.parentId` column is nullable. When the referencing key allows a NULL, SQL Server knows that you want it to be optional. You do not have to have a NULL primary key because, as we discussed, it is impossible to have a NULL attribute in a primary key.

It is as simple as this to protect the parent child relationships that we have set up in our design. We will present examples of relationships and cascading deletes, as well as a brief discussion of cross-database relationships, shortly.

Naming

When choosing names for our objects, we have usually created names that allowed the user to interact with the objects. For constraints and indexes, we need names that indicate the usage of the object. The same goes for the naming of relationships, though it is possible in certain circumstances to have chosen the same name for two relationships though we cannot implement this in SQL Server. Hence, we need to consider designing names for relationships.

Planning and Implementing the Basic Physical Architecture

The naming standard for relationships that we will adopt for this book takes the verb phrase from the logical model and includes the parent and child table names in the object name, to create a unique name as well as making any constraints easy to identify when listed by name.

We use the following template for our name:

    <parentTable>$<verbPhrase>$<childTable>

For example, let's look at our example pair of tables.

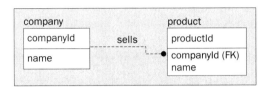

To implement this relationship, we would define the name as company$sells$product, and as with the naming of foreign keys, implement this using the following syntax:

```
ALTER TABLE product
    ADD CONSTRAINT company$sells$product FOREIGN KEY
    REFERENCES parent (companyId)
```

Note the use of the dollar sign in the name. Remembering back to our identifier standards we discussed earlier in the chapter, there are not any really good values to delimit or separate between parts of a name other than the dollar sign. Other than letters and numbers, we were allowed only three special characters: the dollar sign, the ampersand, and the underscore. The underscore is frequently used within the names of objects (instead of the camel case formatting that we are using). The ampersand is often used for variables, which these are not. Hence, for clarity, we will use the dollar sign between names.

> *My naming of objects is sure to raise some eyebrows but this is just my naming convention, and I use the dollar sign to break up parts of object names because it has no meaning in SQL Server, and I can use this convention regardless of the naming standard chosen. This is another area where personal taste comes into play.*

For instance, if we have the following tables on our model:

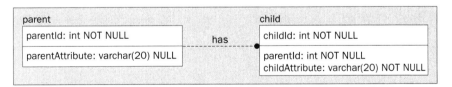

which could be implemented using the following create table script:

```
CREATE TABLE parent
(
    parentId      int IDENTITY NOT NULL CONSTRAINT PKparent PRIMARY KEY,
    parentAttribute   varchar(20) NULL
)
```

```
CREATE TABLE child
(
    childId       int IDENTITY NOT NULL CONSTRAINT PKchild PRIMARY KEY,
    parentId      int NOT NULL,
    childAttribute   varchar(20)NOT NULL
)
```

We would then implement the relationship using the following syntax:

```
ALTER TABLE child
    ADD CONSTRAINT child$has$parent
        FOREIGN KEY (parentId) REFERENCES parent
```

Once we have created this constraint, we can test it by trying to insert data into the parent and then the child tables:

```
INSERT INTO parent(parentAttribute)
VALUES ('parent')

--get last identity value inserted in the current scope
DECLARE @parentId int
SELECT @parentId = scope_identity()

INSERT into child (parentId, childAttribute)
VALUES (@parentId, 'child')

DELETE FROM parent
```

This causes the following error in the database when executed:

Server: Msg 547, Level 16, State 1, Line 1
DELETE statement conflicted with COLUMN REFERENCE constraint 'childhasparent'. The conflict occurred in database 'tempdb', table 'child', column 'parentId'.

Cascading Deletes and Updates

In our previous example, the database prevented us from deleting the parent table if a child table existed with a reference to the parent as an attribute. This is great in most cases, but there are cases where the data in the child table is so integrated with the data of the parent table that, when the parent table is changed or deleted, SQL Server would always seek to modify or delete the child record without any further interaction with the user.

Consider the case of a product and a table that stores descriptive specification information:

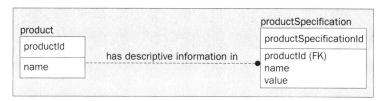

In this case, if we wanted to delete the product table, it's unlikely that we'd want to keep the productSpecification table either.

The ability to affect some implicit change automatically on a child table, as a result of an explicit action on a parent table, is known as **cascading** changes.

For a delete, you could set a constraint that would automatically delete the children of a relationship as a result of some action on the parent table. For an update, if you modify the value of the primary key of the parent table, then the change would cascade down to the child table's foreign key value. There is another lesser-used cascading action that SQL Server does not in fact implement – a type of cascading action where the child table is not deleted altogether but its key reference set to NULL. This can only be implemented on optional relationships as, if the foreign key value does not allow NULLs, it will fail. A discussion of how to implement such a situation will be left to the next chapter as it has to be built with triggers.

Two of the most exciting new features of SQL Server 2000 are the ability to have cascading deletes in declarative referential integrity, and cascading updates. In previous versions of SQL Server, a cascading operation required a trigger. This was troublesome because we could no longer employ foreign key relationships and tools that would use declarative relationships.

The syntax for implementing cascading operations is simple. We simply add ON DELETE CASCADE or ON UPDATE CASCADE to our constraint declaration:

```
ALTER TABLE <tablename>
    ADD CONSTRAINT <constraintName>
    FOREIGN KEY REFERENCES <referenceTable> (<referenceColumn>)
    [ON DELETE <CASCADE> | <NO ACTION>]
    [ON UPDATE <CASCADE> | <NO ACTION>]
```

Using the NO ACTION option for either of the declarations sets the relationship to the "normal" restrictive case – when a child record exists and a change to the key or a delete is affected on the parent, an error occurs.

> *No action may seem like a strange way to put it, but what is being said is that, if the delete fails, we take NO ACTION and end the operation.*

To continue our childhasparent constraint example, we just found out that, after creating the child record, we could not delete the original parent. So, we will adapt this example to allow cascading deletes.

```
--note that there is no alter constraint command
ALTER TABLE child
   DROP CONSTRAINT child$has$parent

ALTER TABLE child
   ADD CONSTRAINT child$has$parent FOREIGN KEY (parentId)
   REFERENCES parent
   ON DELETE CASCADE

SELECT * FROM parent
SELECT * FROM child
```

which returns:

parentId	parentAttribute
2	parent

childId	parentId	childAttribute
2	2	child

Then we run the delete and re-execute the selects:

```
DELETE FROM parent
SELECT * FROM parent
SELECT * FROM child
```

and this returns:

parentId	parentAttribute

childId	parentId	childAttribute

It would be trivial to implement an example of cascading an update in much the same way. Note, however, that the primary key cannot be implemented as an identity column to make use of the cascading update, since identity values cannot be updated.

Cross Database Relationships

The primary limitation on constraint-based foreign keys is that the tables participating in the relationship cannot span different databases. When this situation occurs, we must implement our relationships via triggers.

It is generally a bad idea to design databases with cross-database relationships. A database should be considered a unit of related tables that are always kept in synch. When we design databases that extend over different databases or even servers, we spread around references to data that is not within the scope of database, and we cannot guarantee its existence. However, there are times when cross database relationships are unavoidable.

Sharing the Details of your Database with Developers

In the logical modeling phase of design, we spent many hours entering definitions of our tables, columns, and other objects. In this section, we will look at some of the tools that we should give to our clients who will need to understand what we have created for them. These tools will provide reports of all the database objects and their properties, both implemented and informational.

However, building these reports, keeping them up to date, and distributing them can be quite a task. In keeping with the way we have built the rest of the book, we are going to only explore the tools that SQL Server 2000 provides for us. There are several methods that are built into SQL Server:

- ❑ The Information Schema and system stored procedures
- ❑ New descriptive properties
- ❑ Meta Data Services

We will be covering the first two in this list in some detail, but we will leave the Meta Data Services alone. They are very valuable but are not exactly practical from a simple usage standpoint. They are primarily used for exchanging metadata between modeling tools, DTS, and OLAP, and are not really relevant to the subject matter of this book. If you are interested, you can find out more about Meta Data Services in the SQL Server 2000 Books Online documentation.

Information Schema and System Stored Procedures

For simply letting your users look at the structures of your tables, SQL Server offers us the Information Schema and system stored procedures.

The Information Schema is a set of twenty views based on the ANSI SQL-92 standard definition of a mechanism to provide a standard set of meta-tables to foster cross-platform development. They define many of the objects in SQL Server – all those that are understood by the SQL-92 standard – and they provide a quick reference to the structures of our tables.

In these views, we tend to use a slightly different, but fairly easy to understand set of semantic representations for common objects:

SQL Server name	INFORMATION_SCHEMA (SQL-92) name
database	catalog
owner	schema
user-defined data type	domain

The following table gives a list of metadata procedures and the corresponding INFORMATION_SCHEMA views. The explanation in the third column of the table is simply a brief note of what the different procedures and views are used for. It is advisable for any database programmer to have a good understanding of how to use these objects to query the metadata of the model. The best way to do this is to look up the complete documentation on them in SQL Server 2000 Books Online.

So SQL Server offers two completely different ways of viewing the same system data. From a comparison of the two different methods, there are two things that stand out for me. The system stored procedures are very SQL Server implementation oriented. The INFORMATION_SCHEMA tables give the impression of being developed by a committee, where not everybody got their way. However, the definitions that they give tend to be generic but certainly very useful. In my opinion, it is best to use the INFORMATION_SCHEMA views whenever possible, because they are based on the SQL 92 standard and would likely be improved in the future. In addition, since every SQL 92 compliant database will eventually have an identical set of views implemented, using these views should facilitate understanding of other database systems.

System stored procedure	Corresponding INFORMATION_SCHEMA view	Explanation
sp_server_info	N/A	Gives a listing of settings and information concerning the server. Server information is not in the INFORMATION_SCHEMA.

Table continued on following page

System stored procedure	Corresponding `INFORMATION_SCHEMA` view	Explanation
`sp_databases`	SCHEMATA	Both give listings of the databases on a server. The SCHEMATA listing has more useful information about database creator while `sp_databases` gives the size of the database.
`sp_tables`	TABLES, VIEWS	Gives listings of the tables and views in the system. `sp_tables` lists system tables, user tables, and views. Strangely, the TABLES view lists tables and views, while the VIEWS view only lists views. It does have extended information about views, such as updatability, definition, check option, and a few other things.
`sp_columns`	COLUMNS	While the `sp_columns` procedure requires a parameter delineating the table it is used for and the COLUMNS view does not, both contain useful interesting information about columns.
`sp_stored_procedures`	ROUTINES	Both list stored procedures and functions, but where `sp_stored_procedures` has a few columns that have not yet been implemented, the ROUTINES view has lots. Both of these methods show hints of what is to come for SQL and SQL Server.
`sp_sproc_columns`	PARAMETERS	Both list the parameters of stored procedures and functions.
N/A	ROUTINE_COLUMNS	Lists the columns of the tables returned by functions, when they return tables, of course.
`sp_helptext`	VIEWS, ROUTINES	`sp_helptext` is one of those procedures that should be understood by any administrator. Using this procedure, you can get the text of any procedure, default, extended stored procedure (which returns the DLL it is in), and function in the system. The VIEWS and ROUTINES views are related because they too will return the definition of the view or routine, much like help text.

System stored procedure	Corresponding INFORMATION_SCHEMA view	Explanation
sp_column_privileges	COLUMN_PRIVILEGES	Both list the different rights available on the columns in the tables.
sp_special_columns	N/A	Returns the primary key of the table.
sp_statistics	N/A	sp_statistics displays information on a table's indexes. There is no information about indexes in the INFORMATION_SCHEMA.
sp_fkeys	TABLE_CONSTRAINTS, CONSTRAINT_TABLE_USAGE, REFERENTIAL_CONSTRAINTS, KEY_COLUMN_USAGE	sp_fkeys gives us a list of the foreign key constraints on a table. TABLE_CONSTRAINTS and CONSTRAINT_TABLE_USAGE list all constraints on the table, one from the tables perspective, and the other from the constraints. REFERENTIAL_CONSTRAINTS lists all of the foreign key constraints in the database. KEY_COLUMN_USAGE lists the columns in primary and foreign key constraints.
sp_pkeys	KEY_COLUMN_USAGE, TABLE_CONSTRAINTS	sp_pkeys gives a list of primary keys on a table. The TABLE_CONSTRAINTS has already been mentioned in the previous section on sp_fkeys.
sp_helpconstraint	REFERENTIAL_CONSTRAINTS, CHECK_CONSTRAINTS, TABLE_CONSTRAINTS, CONSTRAINT_COLUMN_USAGE, CONSTRAINT_TABLE_USAGE	sp_helpconstraint gives us an overview of a table's constraints. We have discussed all of the other INFORMATION_SCHEMA views already.
sp_table_privileges	TABLE_PRIVILEGES	sp_table_privileges displays a list of privileges available for a given table that may be granted. The TABLE_PRIVILEGES view lists one row for each privilege that has been granted to a user. They are related, but are actually opposite. sp_table_privileges is centered on what *can be* granted, while TABLE_PRIVILEGES is centered on what *has been* granted.

Table continued on following page

System stored procedure	Corresponding INFORMATION_SCHEMA view	Explanation
sp_datatype_info	DOMAINS	sp_datatype_info lists all data types that are available in the system and their properties, while the DOMAINS view lists only user-defined data types.
N/A	DOMAIN_CONSTRAINTS, COLUMN_DOMAIN_USAGE	Two additional views are added for domains that can really come in handy. DOMAIN_CONSTRAINTS lists all of the constraints (rules) that have been added to a domain. COLUMN_DOMAIN_USAGE lists every table where the domain has been used in a table.

There are some bits of information in this group of functions that we have not yet begun to discuss, most notably those functions that deal with privileges, which we will look at in Chapter 12.

It is left to the reader as an exercise to execute the procedures, look through the tables, and study SQL Server 2000 Books Online in the *System Stored Procedure* section (particularly the catalog procedures, but it is all good) as well as the section on the *Information Schema Views*. With a combination of catalog procedures, INFORMATION_SCHEMA objects, and T-SQL functions, we can get a look at almost every piece of metadata concerning the databases we have created.

New Descriptive Properties

In our modeling, we have created descriptions, notes, and various pieces of data that are extremely useful in helping the developer to understand the whys and wherefores of using the tables we have created. In previous versions of SQL Server, it was very difficult to actually make any use of this data. In SQL Server 2000, Microsoft introduced extended properties that allow us to store specific information about objects. This is really great because is allows us to extend the metadata of our tables in ways that can be used by our applications using simple SQL statements.

By creating these properties, we can build a repository of information that the application developers can use to:

- ❏ Understand what the data in the columns is used for
- ❏ Store information to use in applications, such as:
    - ❏ Captions to show on a form when a column is displayed
    - ❏ Error messages to display when a constraint is violated
    - ❏ Formatting rules for displaying or entering data

Extended properties are stored as `sql_variant` columns, so they may hold any data type other than `text` or `image` fields.

For the purposes of attaching extended properties, the objects in SQL Server have been classified into a three level naming scheme. The following tree illustrates this hierarchy:

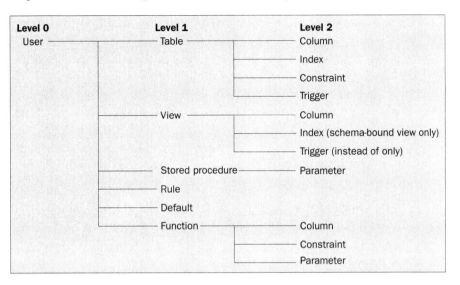

> Note: in this diagram we have mentioned a new term: schema-bound. Schema binding refers to a mechanism that is new to SQL Server 2000 where, when you create a schema-bound view or schema-bound user-defined function, you can instruct SQL Server not to allow any changes to the base tables it uses. We will cover this in greater detail in the next chapter.

These are the only objects on which we can define extended properties, as SQL Server will check the names that we use for these properties. The naming scheme is fairly simple. We can add a property to a user requiring no other information, but to add a property to a table, we first must have a reference to the user who owns the table. To attach one to a column, we must know the user who owns the table, as well as the table name and column name.

To maintain extended properties, we are given the following functions and stored procedures:

- `sp_addextendedproperty` – used to add a new extended property
- `sp_dropextendedproperty` – used to delete an existing extended property
- `sp_updateextendedproperty` – used to modify an existing extended property
- `fn_listextendedproperty` – a system defined function that can be used to list extended properties

In the following example, we will look at the specific syntax of each command as we use them, but it is important to understand the basic way they work. Each has the following parameters:

- `@name` – the name of the user-defined property.

- ❏ @value – what to set the value to when creating or modifying a property.
- ❏ @level0type – either user or user-defined data type.
- ❏ @level0name – the name of the object of the type that is identified in the @level0type parameter.
- ❏ @level1type – the name of the type of object that is on the level 1 branch of the tree under user, such as Table, View, etc.
- ❏ @level1name – the name of the object of the type that is identified in the @level1type parameter.
- ❏ @level2type – the name of the type of object that is on the level 2 branch of the tree under the value in the @level1Type value. For example, if @level1type is Table, then @level2type might be Column, Index, Constraint, or Trigger.
- ❏ @level2name – the name of the object of the type that is identified in the @level2type parameter.

For example, say we create a table named person with the following script:

```
CREATE TABLE person
(
    personId int NOT NULL IDENTITY,
    firstName varchar(40) NOT NULL,
    lastName varchar(40) NOT NULL,
    socialSecurityNumber varchar(10) NOT NULL
)
```

To do this, we are going to add a property to the table and columns named MS_Description. Why MS_Description? Because this is the name that Microsoft has chosen to use in the Enterprise Manager to store descriptions.

Note that this is subject to change. I found the name of the property by using the SQL Profiler to trace how SQL Server saved the property, and then fabricated my own version of the script. Profiling how Enterprise Manager does things is a quick way to discover how to script out tasks that are seemingly only possible using the GUI tools.

So we execute the following script after creating the table:

```
--dbo.person table gui description
EXEC sp_addextendedproperty @name = 'MS_Description',
    @value = 'Example of extended properties on the person table',
    @level0type = 'User', @level0name = 'dbo',
    @level1type = 'table', @level1name = 'person'

--dbo.person.personId gui description
EXEC sp_addextendedproperty @name = 'MS_Description',
    @value = 'primary key pointer to a person instance',
    @level0type = 'User', @level0name = 'dbo',
    @level1type = 'table', @level1name = 'person',
    @level2type = 'column', @level2name = 'personId'
```

```
--dbo.person.firstName gui description
EXEC sp_addextendedproperty @name = 'MS_Description',
    @value = 'The person''s first name',
    @level0type = 'User', @level0name = 'dbo',
    @level1type = 'table', @level1name = 'person',
    @level2type = 'column', @level2name = 'firstName'

--dbo.person.lastName gui description
EXEC sp_addextendedproperty @name = 'MS_Description',
    @value = 'The person''s last name',
    @level0type = 'User', @level0name = 'dbo',
    @level1type = 'table', @level1name = 'person',
    @level2type = 'column', @level2name = 'lastName'

--dbo.person.socialSecurityNumber gui description
EXEC sp_addextendedproperty @name = 'MS_Description',
    @value = 'descrip of sociSecNbr colmn',
    @level0type = 'User', @level0name = 'dbo',
    @level1type = 'table', @level1name = 'person',
    @level2type = 'column', @level2name = 'socialSecurityNumber'
```

Now when we go into Enterprise Manager, right-click on our table and select Design Table, we see our description like so:

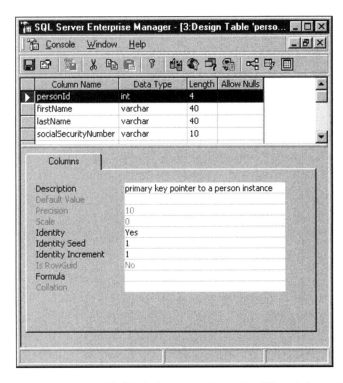

And looking at the properties of the table (click the icon to the right of **Save**) shows that we now have a description:

Chapter 10

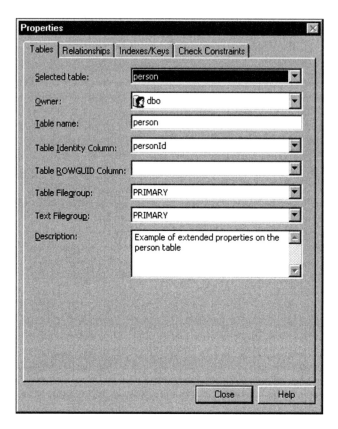

Obviously, this is not something that we would regularly do, but if we have advanced capabilities in our data modeling tools, we should be able to push out this data to make Enterprise Manager that much more useful as a tool for our programmers.

To change a property, we would use the following type of script:

```
--see if the property already exists
IF EXISTS ( SELECT *
    FROM ::FN_LISTEXTENDEDPROPERTY('MS_Description',
      'User', 'dbo',
      'table', 'person',
      'Column', 'socialSecurityNumber') )
BEGIN
    --if the property already exists
    EXEC sp_updateextendedproperty @name = 'MS_Description',
    @value = 'the person''s government id number',
    @level0type = 'User', @level0name = 'dbo',
    @level1type = 'table', @level1name = 'person',
    @level2type = 'column', @level2name = 'socialSecurityNumber'
END
ELSE
BEGIN
    --otherwise create it.
    EXEC sp_addextendedproperty @name = 'MS_Description',
```

```
        @value = 'the person''s government id number',
        @level0type = 'User', @level0name = 'dbo',
        @level1type = 'table', @level1name = 'person',
        @level2type = 'column', @level2name = 'socialSecurityNumber'
END
```

The `fn_listExtendedProperty` *object is a system defined function which we will discuss further in Chapter 12.*

Our final extension to this example is to add an extended property to the table that the user processes can use when executing the program. For this we will add an input mask property to the table, so that we can build a general method of data entry for the column.

```
exec sp_addextendedproperty   @name = 'Input Mask',
    @value = '###-##-####',
    @level0type = 'User', @level0name = 'dbo',
    @level1type = 'table', @level1name = 'person',
    @level2type = 'column', @level2name = 'socialSecurityNumber'
```

Note we can create *any* extended property we want. The names must fit into the `sysname` data type, and may include blank, non-alphanumeric, or even binary values.

This new documentation feature has some interesting possibilities for creating applications and making the most of the metadata we have stored in various locations, even beyond the tremendously valuable documentation uses. For more information, check the SQL Server 2000 Books Online section on *Using Extended Properties on Database Objects*.

Case Study

Returning to our case study, we now need to get down to building the physical structures to put the theory into practice. We will follow our prescribed path whereby we identify situations that are going to be too difficult to implement and drop them from the implementation, we then choose our primary keys and data types, and then present the physical model that we will implement. We will then use a T-SQL script to implement our database, including adding our description information from our initial analysis.

Cleaning Up the Model

The first step is to clean up any situations that exist in the model which are too difficult to implement. In some cases, we will have to leave out large areas of implementation that we would otherwise want, thereby ending up with a less than perfect solution. Depending on your situation, your tools, or even your corporate standards, we may have to change the way of implementing things, though we must still finish up with a solution that is functionally equivalent to the logical model. Each transformation we make in the model during the physical modeling phase should not change the set of data that is stored by our database, unless we discover further attributes that are required and which must be added to the logical model.

Subtypes

One of the most difficult situations to implement in SQL Server is the subtype. In our logical model (which we finished with last at the end of Chapter 8), we have an example of just such a case: the transaction subtype. We had modeled it as a complete subtype, that is, all possible cases were represented in the diagram.

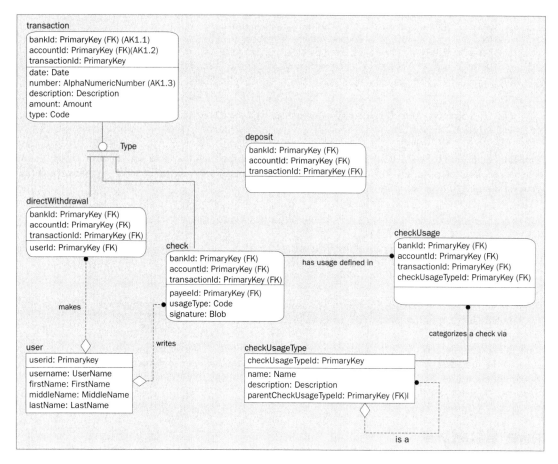

However, we did not identify any additional attributes for a "deposit" or "direct withdrawal" to add to the model. In this case, we could simply change our subtype to an incomplete version (where not every subtype value is actually materialized into a table) and remove the "deposit" and "direct withdrawal" entities. Depending on how large the subtype is (one or two attributes, or more, plus related tables) we may just want to assign these attributes to the parent of the relationship. This is what we will do in our example. The primary reason for this is practicality, since each of the subtypes is very close to the same object. Later, we will have to write some specialized code to protect the data from unreasonable data entry into the subtype tables.

In the subtype it is quite obvious which fields are valid, based on what value the discriminator is (in this case the discriminator is the type of transaction because it determines in which child table we should look for the subtype values), but once we take all of the attributes of all of the subtyped entities and reassign them to the parent, it can become less obvious. In our case, we have three attributes to deal with:

- `Payee` – checks always have payees. Direct withdrawals might do also, but deposits never have payees. We could enhance our tables to allow the documentation of where the money for the deposit comes from, but we won't do this because we want to keep a limit on the size of the project and because such a change would breach the implementation plans that were previously approved by the client.

Planning and Implementing the Basic Physical Architecture

- ❏ Signature – only checks have signatures. This attribute seems a little pointless, but we will leave it this way for the purpose of the example. If we were taking this system to full fruition, this attribute would probably extend to a large domain tree and would pertain to deposits, direct withdrawals, and checks. However, we will use the logic from the previous point and state that, as the client didn't ask for it, we don't put it in. We will also change this value to a string because we will only store the name of the person who signed the check, rather than a picture of the signature.

  Of course, if this were a real system, we would want to ask the client whether these modifications are acceptable and get another sign-off.

- ❏ checkUsageType – this one is pretty simple; we will change this to transactionAllocationType, where the user can set the usage/allocation for every type of transaction.

So we remodel the tables like this:

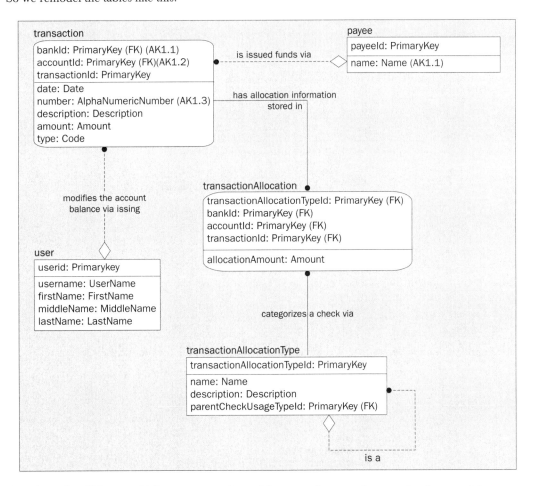

One thing should be noted. The transaction table cannot be named transaction because it is a reserved word and SQL Server will not allow us to use it in code. So we have several choices of ways to handle this.

❑ Rename the table to a different name, say `xaction`.

❑ Always refer to the table with bracketed notation: `[transaction]`.

Neither of these is overly pleasant, and transaction was the best name for the table and referencing tables. We will choose to keep the name transaction and use bracketed notation whenever using the table. This will keep the table name more recognizable to the client. We will only refer to the table as `[transaction]` when we are using it in code.

We will look at how to implement the specific data rules that we will have to handle in the next chapter.

Simplification of Complex Relationships

In some cases, we will model things during the logical design phase that are a little too complex to actually implement. In our logical model, we have one situation that we might find too difficult to implement as we designed it. In order to have a unique postal address, we have to look across two tables. In our model, the `address` and `addressLine` tables are like this:

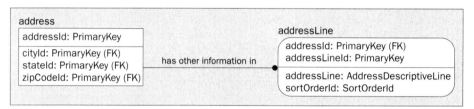

This allows for an address of unlimited size and structure, but this is probably not necessary for the physical implementation. So we will simply rebuild the address table as follows:

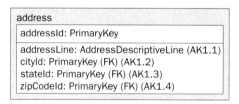

The `addressLine` field allows for all of the street, post office box, etc. information, the size of which we will decide upon when we choose data types.

Domain Tables

In the `transaction` table, we have a column named `type` to denote the type of transaction.

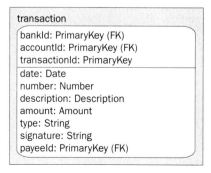

Planning and Implementing the Basic Physical Architecture

Usually, we will not want to have a freeform data entry field when we will need to be able to group on the field, or, in the case of the `transaction type` column, where we will likely need to use the domain value for special handling in our User Interface.

We might even want to add implementation-specific information to our address type table, such as icon file name locations, so that the UI could show a little check by the check type, an ATM card by the direct withdrawal, and so forth. In our `transactionType` table, we add name and description columns. This way we can include more information to explain what each value in the table means. Again, each of these attributes would have to be passed by the client and possibly added to the logical model. We see these changes, plus three other logical fields in the following diagram:

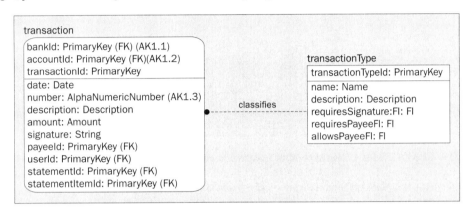

Now we can write code that forces the `signature` field to be filled in for a certain type of transaction, or we can specify that the payee is mandatory or optional. Building the UI would be easier, because we have data that will tell us when a value is required and changing the requirement will not require any extra code. Each of these flag fields would likely be considered logical fields because they support the implementation of information already in the current design.

We will also use this table as our transaction type for the `statementItem` table (though we will not use the flag fields). Since our transaction types will match the bank's, this keeps us from having duplicate data in the table, plus it will make matching the items during the balancing of the account much easier – but we will certainly not *require* that the transaction types match.

Trimming Down Unneeded Entities

After further review, we note that the `checkRegister` table will not really turn out to be an implemented table at all, since there will only be the electronic check register once the database is implemented. Hence, we remove it from our physical model, though it still has value in the logical model as it is an actual entity that we may have to deal with.

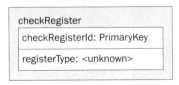

317

Correcting Errors in the Model

As we go through the process, we will find errors in the model even if we use the best modeling tools and work at an unhurried pace. For instance, in the original model we had the following relationship:

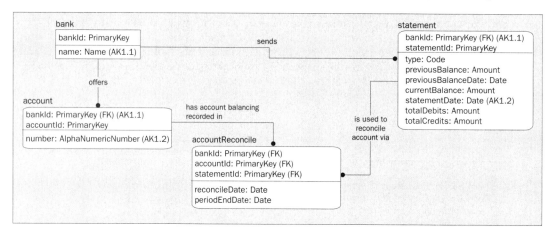

The error is the relationship between the `bank` and `statement` tables: "banks send statements". The relationship should be "banks send statements for accounts" and, to implement this, the relationship between `bank` and `statement` should be replaced by a relationship between `account` and `statement`. We move the `periodEndDate` column to the `statement`, as this will be a part of the statement rather than a value we store when we are marking the statement as reconciled. We will also drop the relationship between account and `accountReconcile`, since we will mark a statement as reconciled.

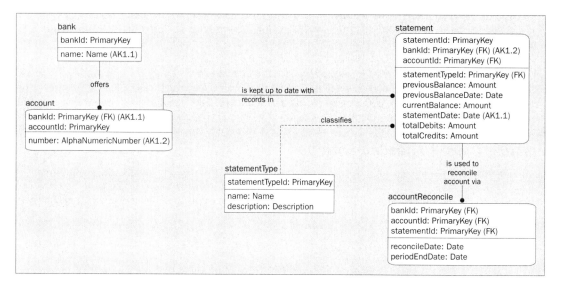

One of the interesting parts of this model is that, in order to find out when an account was last reconciled, we have to go through the `statement` table to the `accountReconcile` table. While this may seem odd to those uninitiated to normalized database programming, this is one of the tell-tale signs of a well designed database. In a larger system, you might have to go through five, ten, or twenty tables to find out information like this. The principle of having one piece of data stored in one place can make your databases more interesting to traverse, but on the other hand will eliminate redundant data and modification anomalies – if an account number is stored in more than one place and it needs to be changed, it has to be changed in every place otherwise your data would be inconsistent. As we will see in the next chapter, not having the ability to accidentally mess up our data is worth the extra initial coding pain.

You should not look at finding errors like this in your model as a failure. Very often we will miss stuff as we go through the design phase. Often our clients will make a change in their database requirements which we have to deal with. Errors cannot be eliminated as every database architect is human. Often, it isn't until you have completed the first draft of a design that you are able to spot the more complex problems and consider their solutions. Sometimes one design decision may determine or modify several others. Database design should always be an iterative process.

Preparing the Model for Implementation

Once we have cleared up the logical model in the way we have just outlined, we can move on to preparing our tables for generation. Here we should take steps to make the system easy to create, adding columns for optimistic locking and record disabling (and anything else that suits your particular needs). We will then add primary keys, unique keys, and finally choose data types.

Once we have completed these final tasks, we will be ready to script our database objects and implement the database in SQL Server.

Physical-Only Columns

As a brief reminder, physical-only columns do not relate to any of the database objects. They are simply included in the database to make coding easier. The two examples we have covered have already been added to the following table:

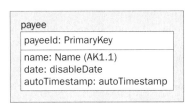

In this table we have a `disableDate` column as opposed to the `disableFl` we have previously discussed. `disableDate` sets the date and time after which the payee can no longer receive monies from transactions in our database. We could also add tables to store the reasons for and history of payee status, but we won't here to keep things simple. `disableDate` works the same way as `disableFl` except that, instead of a simple flag, we implement a date so we can see if we set it to some future date and time.

We have also added an `autoTimestamp` column to every table on the model, which, as we have previously discussed, will form the basis of an optimistic lock mechanism.

These are the only physical-only columns we will add to our current database.

Primary Keys

Primary key columns are technically physical-only columns, since we will never show them to the user and they exist primarily for our benefit in implementation, though we have represented them both on the logical and physical models.

Take this chunk of the model:

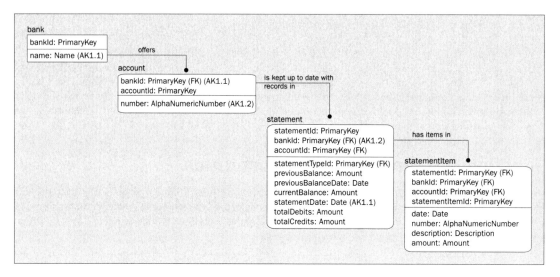

The `bankId` pointer migrates from the `bank` table all the way down to the `statementItem` table. This is fine for logical modeling but, for multi-part keys in physical tables, this cause more trouble than it is worth. The main reason for this is that we may need two, three, or even more columns to uniquely identify a table. If you have to join across ten tables to find related information, then you are in trouble. So, if our database was implemented as above and we asked the question – "For the First National Bank, in which cities did we spend the most money on textiles?" – this query would involve every table and, by the time that we had included all of the multi-part keys, the query would be unmanageable.

Another reason for making the primary key a physical-only column is that, if you change the composition of the *logical* primary key for the object, you do not affect the *implemented* primary key of the object. This will reduce the effect that the change will have on any dependent objects. In our example, take our "`bank` to `account` to `statement` to `statementItem`" set of relationships. If we decided that the `bank` table was no longer needed and we deleted the table from the model, the `account`, `statement`, and `statementItem` tables would have their primary keys changed:

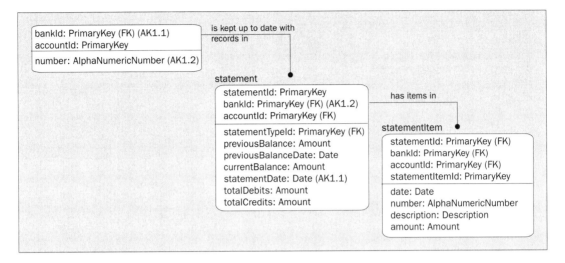

This is not an optimal solution to our coding problem because all of the code that used these entities would now be broken. However, if each table had a single column primary key, only the `account` table would be forced to change. The meaning of the objects would change since they would no longer be identified by the corresponding bank, but to the programmer, the actual values of the primary keys would still be the same. An account would still have statements and transactions.

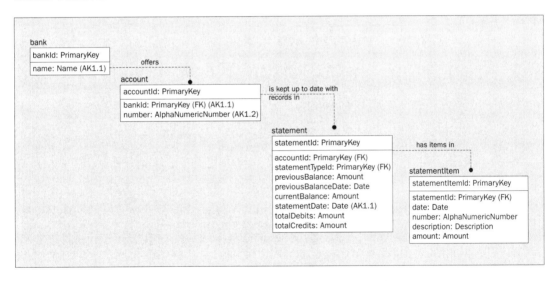

Now, note what happens when we remove the `bank` table from this model:

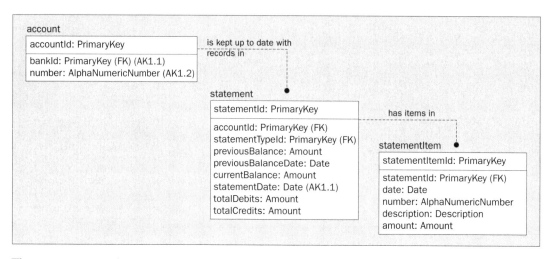

The `statement` and `statementItem` tables are unchanged. Hence, the programs that access them will not change. The `account` programs will only have to change to reflect there no longer being a `bankId` field in the table, a fairly minor change in comparison with what might have been required. Note that, once we have changed the keys, the implementation of the tables has changed, though what the tables represent has not.

One thing about the new tables – each one of them has a unique key which contains the migrated part of the previous primary key. For instance, before the changes were made the `statement` table looked like this:

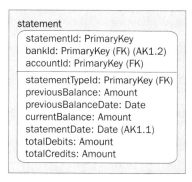

This table has no easily identifiable natural key, since we did not previously specify any alternate keys in our design. Upon further review, there is a possible key that we can use – the `date` value (likely with time stripped off). We have defined this program to allow online account balancing, which we might do daily but no more frequently than that (check with client before making such decisions). So, we could use the `date` as part of the alternate key, as modelled in the following diagram:

```
statement
------------------------------------
statementId: PrimaryKey
------------------------------------
accountId: PrimaryKey (FK)
statementTypeId: PrimaryKey (FK)
previousBalance: Amount
previousBalanceDate: Date
currentBalance: Amount
statementDate: Date (AK1.1)
totalDebits: Amount
totalCredits: Amount
```

Normally, we would not use dates in our keys, even alternate ones, if we can possibly help it – especially one that we implement as a full eight bit `datetime` value. There are two very important reasons to avoid this practice:

- Ease of accessing data – when we need to use the key to access a given row in the table, if our key is defined with the date value, it can be very hard to type in the actual value of the date by hand. For instance, a `datetime` value contains day, month, year, hour, minute, second, and parts of a second (and `smalldatetimes` include values up to the minute). This can be cumbersome to deal with, especially for the average user.

- Precision – in most cases, the precision of the date variables is more than is required for the average key. Usually, when you want to put the date in the key it is because you simply want the day and year.

In our case, we will use a `datetime` type, probably a `smalldatetime`, because we will want to be able to have a statement produced at multiple times during the day and it works best here. Plus, we will be stripping off some of the time values.

Data Types

During the modeling, we have chosen logical domains for our attributes. Now we will take our design and turn the attributes into real fields and assign real data types. To decide on data types, we will create a table of the domains that we have chosen, and then assign data types and definitions to them – choosing the data type, nullability options, and any additional information on a domain by domain basis. Once we have done this task, we will go through each of our tables setting the data type to the domain values we have chosen.

The domains that we have been applying to our logical model throughout this exercise have the form of:

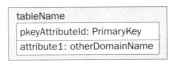

where `primaryKey` *and* `otherDomainName` *are considered the domain for the different attributes.*

The following list contains all of the domains that we have used by name. We will go through and make some guesses as to what the data type seems to call for, then, once finished with that, we will use these as first passes to our data type choices. We will find that there is a very good hit ratio and we will not have to change many. We will, however, have to go through all of the tables to verify they are right (of course we will only do a few tables here).

Name	Comment	Data type	Nullability
`addressDescriptiveLine`	Used to store the address information.	`varchar(800)` to keep unique index under 900 bytes	NOT NULL
`addressStateCode`	The two character state code that is recognized by the United States post office.	`char(2)`	NOT NULL

Table continued on following page

Name	Comment	Data type	Nullability
alphaNumericNumber	Alphanumeric "number" which is usually an alternate key value for a record in a table. An example is an account number.	varchar(20)	NOT NULL
amount	Generic domain for monetary amounts.	money	NOT NULL
areaCode	Code that identifies a dialing region of a state.	varchar(3)	NOT NULL
autoTimestamp	Automatically incrementing optimistic locking value.	timestamp	NOT NULL
countryCode	Dialing code that identifies the country being dialed.	char(1)	NOT NULL
date	Default datetime values. Defaults to smalldatetime values since we will seldom need the precision of the datetime data type.	smalldatetime	NOT NULL
description	Brief, unstructured comments describing an instance of a table to further extend another user's ability to tell them apart.	varchar(100)	NOT NULL
disableDate	Used to disable a record without deleting it, like for historical purposes.	smalldatetime	NULL
exchange	The area dialing code that comes before the telephone number.	char(5)	NOT NULL
extension	A string that allows a set of numbers that can be dialed after the connection has been made.	varchar(20)	NULL

Name	Comment	Data type	Nullability
firstName	Used to store a person's first name.	varchar(60)	NOT NULL
Fl	Generally a logical value. Implemented as a not null bit column where 0 is false and non-zero is true.	bit	NOT NULL
lastName	Used to store a person's last name.	varchar(60)	NOT NULL
middleName	Used to store a person's middle name.	varchar(60)	NOT NULL
name	The name that an instance of a record will be uniquely known as. This is not a person's name, rather, this is usually an alternate key value for an object.	varchar(60)	NOT NULL
number	General value that is a number. Defaults to integer.	int	NOT NULL
phoneNumberPart	The telephone number.	char(4)	NOT NULL
primaryFl	Bit flag that is used to point to the primary record of a group.	bit	NOT NULL
primaryKey	Auto generating identity column used as the pointer for an instance of an entity.	int	NOT NULL, IDENTITY
String	Generic string values. We used this as the default where we did not know what the string was going to be used for. NOT NULL by default.	varchar(20)	NOT NULL

Table continued on following page

Name	Comment	Data type	Nullability
Username	Used to store the name of a user in the system.	sysname (a SQL Server user-defined data type that they use to store usernames. We will store SQL Server names here to map to real names, as we will give rights to any user who has rights to enter a check to look at the transactions and/or accounts, based on the use cases.	NOT NULL
ZipCode	Five digit zip code that identifies a postal region that may span different cities, states, and may also simply identify a part of a city.	char(5) (Note that we have used the zipCode to link back to the city. This is done with the five character zipCode. We have ignored the +4 zip code again for simplicity.)	NOT NULL

It should be noted that all of my addresses and phone numbers are very US centred. This serves one purpose – simplicity.

Once our list has been completed, we step through each of the tables and look at each data type and NULL specification for every field, to see how the they work in the individual situation. If we find out that some do not match the specifications as outlined above, and assuming that we were going to repeat this process many times, we would likely want to create new domains for future use. We will not go along this route; rather, we will just make the necessary changes if there are any. One additional point – we will also want to finalize the definitions for our attributes, as we have added and changed many of them along the design path.

In each of the following sections, we will take one of our entities, match the domain name with those from the list, present what the default choices were for data types, and then follow that with a discussion and any overrides to data type from the default.

Planning and Implementing the Basic Physical Architecture

We start with the `bank` entity:

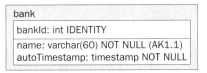

- **bankId**
  PrimaryKey, `int NOT NULL IDENTITY` – which is exactly what is needed.
  Define as: "Non-human readable pointer used to identify a bank instance."

- **name**
  Name, `varchar(60)` – which should be sufficient to handle any bank name.
  Define as: "The name that an instance of bank will be uniquely known as."

Note that we go for very technical definitions for the attributes, since these will be used by developers who have not been involved in the design phase and this will be the first time that they see the database specification. In logical modeling (from Chapter 4), we defined the "Bank Name" attribute as "the name of the bank we are dealing with", which means the same thing but is in a softer format that will be understood by all users. When developing systems using database modeling tools, you will need to be able to reconcile the definitions that we have chosen.

Finally, we end up with the following:

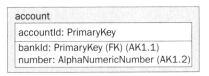

Note that we have also added the column `autoTimestamp`, defined as the "Automatically incrementing optimistic locking value". We will add this to all tables.

Next we look at the `account` table:

```
account
accountId: PrimaryKey
bankId: PrimaryKey (FK) (AK1.1)
number: AlphaNumericNumber (AK1.2)
```

- **accountId**
  primaryKey, `int NOT NULL IDENTITY` – which is exactly what is needed.
  Define as: "Non-human readable pointer used to identify an account instance."

- **bankId**
  primaryKey, `int NOT NULL` – which is exactly what is needed as it is a foreign key value with nulls not allowed.
  Define as: "Non-human readable pointer used to identify a bank instance."

- **number**
  AlphaNumericNumber, `varchar(20) NOT NULL` – which should be sufficient to handle almost any account number. Some additional research might be needed to determine if all of the client's values will fit.

327

Define as: "Account number that is provided by the bank to identify the account."
Note that while the value is referred to as a number, it is actually an alphanumeric string because it may contain leading zeros or letters.

This results in:

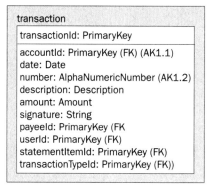

For our last illustration, let's look at the `transaction` table:

- **`transactionId`**
  PrimaryKey, int NOT NULL IDENTITY – which is exactly what is needed.

  Define as: "Non-human readable pointer used to identify a transaction instance."

- **`accountId`**
  PrimaryKey, int NOT NULL – which is exactly what is needed as it is foreign key with nulls not allowed.

  Define as: "Non-human readable pointer used to identify an account instance."

- **`number`**
  AlphaNumericNumber, varchar(20) NOT NULL – which should be sufficient to handle almost any check number, or number from the deposit or ATM (Automatic Telling Machine) slip. Some additional research might be needed to determine if all of the client's values will fit.

  Define as: "Account number provided by the bank to identify the account."

  Note that while the value is referred to as a number, it is actually an alphanumeric string because it may contain leading zeros or letters.

Planning and Implementing the Basic Physical Architecture

- **description**
  description, varchar(100) NOT NULL – in this case we should probably give them additional space to describe the use of a check, ATM, or deposit. However, we also have a checkAllocation table where usage is broken down. For this, we will change the description column type to varchar(1000), to give the freedom to describe the transaction in greater detail if required.

  Define as: "Unstructured comments, describing an instance of a transaction, to further extend another user's ability to tell them apart."

- **amount**
  amount, money, NOT NULL – these will be sufficient to describe the amount of a transaction.

  Define as: "The amount of money that is to change hands via the transaction."

- **signature**
  String, varchar(20) NOT NULL – this is where we would possibly want to extend the string to handle an entire name. We also might want to use some form of image data type to store an image of the signature. In our tables, we will simply choose to change it from a varchar(20) to a varchar(100), to allow the user to enter the name of the person to whom the signature belongs.

  Define as: "A textual representation of the signature that was entered on a transaction."

- **payeeId**
  primaryKey, int NOT NULL – which is *not* exactly what is needed as this is an optional relationship. So we make sure that this column is set to NULL.

  Define as: "Non-human readable pointer used to identify a payee instance which may only be filled in based upon the allowsPayeeFl value in the related transactionType table."

- **userId**
  primaryKey, int NOT NULL – which is not needed as this is an optional relationship. So we make sure that this column is set to NULL.

  Define as: "Non-human readable pointer used to identify the user who was responsible for the transaction."

- **statementItemId**
  primaryKey, int NOT NULL – which is not needed as this is an optional relationship. So we make sure that this column is set to NULL.

  Define as: "Non human readable pointer used to identify the statementItem that was used to reconcile this transaction item."

- **transactionTypeId**
  primaryKey, int NOT NULL – which is exactly what is needed as it is a required field.

  Define as: "Non-human readable pointer used to identify a transaction type record that identifies the type of transaction we are dealing with."

This results in the following table:

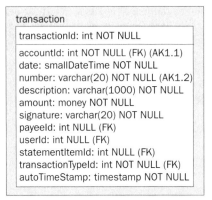

We continue through all of the tables in our model in this manner, until we have determined all of the data types and definitions. In the next two sections, we will display the final physical model that we will implement, followed by the script for the three tables we have created in this section. The entire schema script (and supporting code) will be located at www.wrox.com.

Before we continue, we need to make a note about collations (the character sets and ordering settings we looked at earlier) on data types. Setting individual column collations is quite an advanced topic, and useful for a very specific set of situations. In our case study we will not make use of collations, but I mention them again here to remind you that it is possible to set the collation of a single column if desired.

Physical Model

At this point, the model on paper should be given a "sanity check", preferably by a co-worker if possible, so that you can ensure your model is not only efficient and usable, but also understandable to someone else.

So we come to present the final physical model for our database system. As far as we are concerned, these are the models that we will implement and create on the database server:

Planning and Implementing the Basic Physical Architecture

Part One

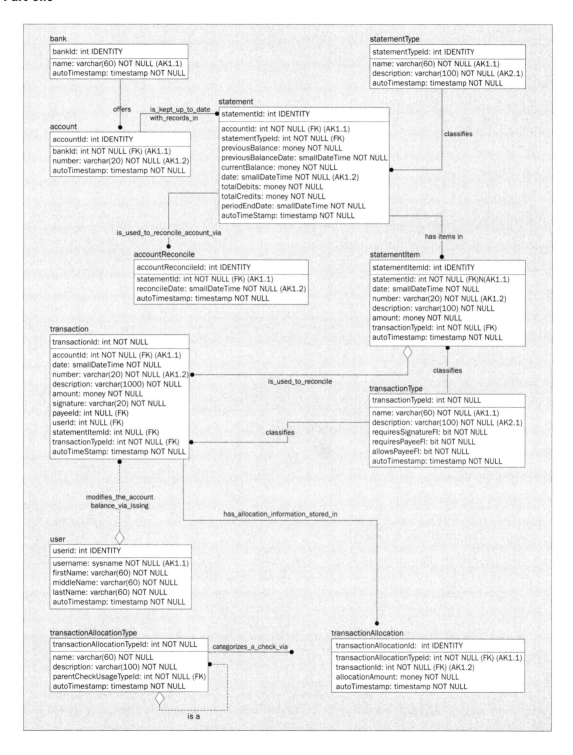

Chapter 10

Part Two

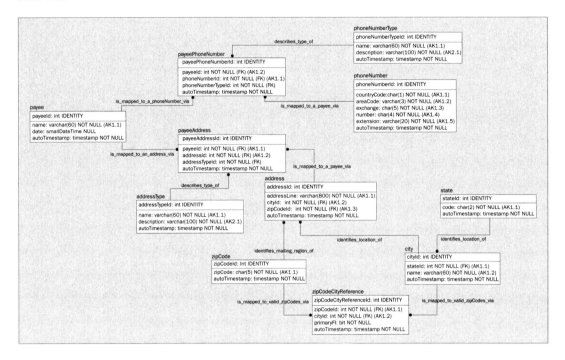

> The full version of the source code to create the database objects, along with PDF versions of the data models, will be available from www.wrox.com. The full script for even this small database is quite long, and is quite repetitive.

Summary

Well, this has been a long chapter covering a large amount of ground. It is chock full of information that is very important for every reader. Understanding how to build tables and how they are implemented is the backbone of every database designer's knowledge.

We have taken our logical model and examined each entity to determine how feasible it is to implement. We have dealt specifically with subtypes as they can be problematic. We have also considered possible deviations from our strict normalization rules in extreme cases (though we have fought this as much as possible), and cleaned our database structures by dealing with the errors that exist in the model.

After we were satisfied that we had a model we could implement, we took a deep look at SQL Server tables, walking through limits on tables and the CREATE TABLE and ALTER TABLE syntax. We noted the rules for naming objects, columns, indexes, and foreign key constraints.

The two most important sections of this chapter were on data types and indexes. When we are implementing our tables, it is very important to understand the conceptual way that our data will actually be stored in SQL Server.

We completed this process by defining the primary keys and at least one alternate key per table, and a `timestamp` column for the purpose of optimistic locking. The final model and a script to implement the system is available from the Wrox Press website.

In the next chapter, we will finish the task of implementing the OLTP system by implementing the business rules required to keep the data in our database as clean as possible.

11

Ensuring Data Integrity

Introduction

What we are concerned with in this chapter are the predicates and domains that have been specified during the design process. When we discuss data integrity, we are looking at applying a body of rules to a given table, or set of tables, to ensure that stored values are always valid. Maintaining our database in a state where data is always within our original design specifications is at the heart of a great implementation. No matter how good or bad the tables that have been designed, how the user perceives the database will be based on how well the data is safeguarded. When developing a data integrity strategy, we need to consider several different scenarios:

- ❏ Users using custom front end tools.
- ❏ Users using generic data tools such as Microsoft Access.
- ❏ Routines that import data from external sources.
- ❏ Raw queries executed by data administrators to fix problems caused by user error.

Each of these poses different issues for our integrity scheme, and what is more important, each of these scenarios (with the possible exception of the second) form part of every database system that we develop. To best handle each scenario, we must safeguard the data, using mechanisms that work independently of the user and which cannot accidentally be avoided. There are four possible ways we can use code to maintain consistent data:

- **Data types and constraints** are simple, straightforward resources that form an integral part of the table definition. They are very fast mechanisms that require little coding, and their use can give some important performance gains. Such constraints include actions such as defining data ranges in columns (for example, column must be greater than 10, or if column1 = 1 then column2 > 1).

  This is the best place to protect the data, as most of the work is handled by SQL Server, and the user cannot get around this by any error in an external program.

- **Triggers** differ from constraints in that they are pieces of code which you attach to a table (or tables). This code is automatically run whenever the event(s) you have specified occur in the table(s). They are extremely flexible and can access multiple columns, multiple rows, multiple tables, and even multiple databases. As a simple case, let's consider a situation where we want to ensure that an update of a value is performed on both the tables where it occurs. We can write a trigger which will disallow the update unless it occurs in both tables.

  This is the second best place to protect the data. We do have to code every trigger rule in T-SQL, but the user cannot get around this by any error in an external program.

- **Stored procedures** are pieces of code which are stored in the database, dealing with tables in a very flexible manner, such that different business rules can be applied to the same table under different circumstances. A simple example of a stored procedure is one which returns all the data held in a given table. In a more complex scenario, they can be used to grant different permissions to different users regarding manipulation of tables. This is not all that great a solution to protect the data, as we have to code the rules into any procedures that access the data. However, since it is in the central location, we can use this to implement rules that may be different based on various situations.

- **Client executable code** is useful to deal with situations where business rules are optional or are flexible in nature. A common example is asking the user "are you sure you wish to delete this record?" SQL Server is a server product, and if you ask it to delete data, it deletes data. Most server products work in this manner, leaving the client programs the responsibility of implementing flexible business rules and warnings. Bear in mind that applications come and go, but the data must always be protected.

In moving down this list the solutions become less desirable, yet each one has specific benefits that are appropriate in certain situations. All of these features will be considered in turn, however we will begin by introducing a new feature in SQL Server 2000 which is essential in building Constraints, Triggers, and Stored procedures. This feature is User Defined Functions.

Example Tables

In the examples provided to illustrate the various concepts under consideration throughout this chapter we will use the following tables:

```
CREATE TABLE artist
(
    artistId int NOT NULL IDENTITY,
    name varchar(60),
    --note that the primary key is clustered to make a
    --point later in the chapter
```

```
        CONSTRAINT XPKartist PRIMARY KEY CLUSTERED (artistId),
        CONSTRAINT XAKartist_name UNIQUE NONCLUSTERED (name)
    )

    INSERT INTO artist(name)
    VALUES ('the beatles')
    INSERT INTO artist(name)
    VALUES ('the who')
    GO

    CREATE TABLE album
    (
        albumId int NOT NULL IDENTITY,
        name varchar(60),
        artistId int NOT NULL,
        --note that the primary key is clustered to make a
        --point later in the chapter
        CONSTRAINT XPKalbum PRIMARY KEY CLUSTERED(albumId),
        CONSTRAINT XAKalbum_name UNIQUE NONCLUSTERED (name),
        CONSTRAINT artist$records$album FOREIGN KEY (artistId) REFERENCES artist
    )

    INSERT INTO album (name, artistId)
    VALUES ('the white album',1)
    INSERT INTO album (name, artistId)
    VALUES ('revolver',1)
    INSERT INTO album (name, artistId)
    VALUES ('quadrophenia',2)
```

User Defined Functions

User defined functions (UDFs) can be used to ensure data integrity, and are (in my opinion) one of the great new features of SQL Server 2000.

Basically, UDFs are closely related to stored procedures, but instead of being a resource primarily intended to modify data and return results, they are T-SQL routines that return a value. As we will see, the SQL Server compiler will not allow you to execute any data modification code from within the UDF, and as such UDFs can only be used for read-only operations. The value returned by a UDF can either be a simple scalar or a table or result set.

What makes them fantastic is that they can be embedded into queries, thereby reducing our need for huge queries with many lines of repeating code. A single function can hold routines that can be called from the query at will. In the remainder of the chapter and the next, we will make heavy use of UDFs to solve problems that in earlier versions of SQL Server were either impossible or very difficult to implement. UDFs have the following basic structure:

```
    CREATE FUNCTION [<ownerName>.]<functionName>
    (
        [<parameters>] --just like in stored procedures
    )
    RETURNS <data type>
    AS
    BEGIN
        [<statements>]
        RETURN <expression>
    END
```

In creating these functions, as opposed to stored procedures, there are a few very important differences in syntax that we need to remember:

- We use CREATE FUNCTION instead of CREATE PROCEDURE.
- Parentheses are always required regardless of whether there are parameters.
- RETURNS clauses are used to declare what data type will be returned. Note that the RETURNS statement is *mandatory* for a UDF, unlike in the case of a stored procedure.
- BEGIN and END are required for scalar and multi-statement table valued functions.

There are three distinct versions of UDFs which we will consider in turn.

Scalar Functions

Scalar functions return a single value. They can be used in a variety of places to implement simple or complex functionality not normally found in SQL Server.

Our first example of a scalar function is one of the simplest possible examples: incrementing an integer value. The function simply takes a single integer parameter, increments it by one and then returns this value:

```
CREATE FUNCTION integer$increment
(
    @integerVal int
)
RETURNS int AS
BEGIN
    SET @integerVal = @integerVal + 1
    RETURN @integerVal
END
GO
```

Note that I used the dollar sign naming again for functions. I name all functions, triggers and stored procedures in this manner, to separate the object (in this case integer) from the method (in this case increment). This is simply a personal preference.

We can execute this using the classic execute syntax from previous versions of SQL Server:

```
DECLARE @integer int
EXEC @integer = integer$increment @integerVal = 1
SELECT @integer AS value
```

Which will return:

```
value
-----------
2
```

Now that we have created a function and executed it, it is logical that we would want to call it from a SELECT statement. However, this is trickier than it might at first appear. If we try the following statement:

```
SELECT integer$increment (1) AS value
```

Then we get the following message:

Server: Msg 195, Level 15, State 10, Line 1
'integer$increment' is not a recognized function name.

UDFs require you to specify the owner of the function in order to successfully execute it.

```
SELECT dbo.integer$increment (1) AS value
```

We now get our desired result:

```
value
-----------
2
```

There is one other usage note that we have to mention. You may not pass user-named parameters to functions as you can with stored procedures. So the following two methods of calling the code will not work:

```
SELECT dbo.integer$increment @integerVal = 1 AS value
SELECT dbo.integer$increment (@integerVal = 1) AS value
```

Executing them will return:

Server: Msg 170, Level 15, State 1, Line 1
Line 1: Incorrect syntax near '@integerVal'.

Server: Msg 137, Level 15, State 1, Line 3
Must declare the variable '@integerVal'.

Unfortunately only the first error message makes any sense (the second one is trying to pass the Boolean value of (@integerValue = 1) to the function. Strangely, we can only use the @parmname = syntax with the EXEC statement, as we saw an example of above.

As a final example involving the incrementing function, we will increment a value three times, all in the same statement (note the nesting of calls):

```
SELECT dbo.integer$increment(dbo.integer$increment(dbo.integer$increment (1))) AS
value
```

which as expected will return:

```
value
-----------
4
```

Let's now look at a more complex example of a function that I'm sure many readers would have wanted to implement at one time: a function to take a string and capitalize the first letter of each word within it:

```
CREATE FUNCTION string$properCase
(
   @inputString varchar(2000)
```

339

```
    )
    RETURNS varchar(2000) AS
    BEGIN
        -- set the whole string to lower
        SET @inputString = LOWER(@inputstring)
        -- then use stuff to replace the first character
        SET @inputString =
        --STUFF in the uppercased character in to the next character,
        --replacing the lowercased letter
        STUFF(@inputString,1,1,UPPER(SUBSTRING(@inputString,1,1)))

        --@i is for the loop counter, initialized to 2
        DECLARE @i int
        SET @i = 1

        --loop from the second character to the end of the string
        WHILE @i < LEN(@inputString)
        BEGIN
            --if the character is a space
            IF SUBSTRING(@inputString,@i,1) = ' '
            BEGIN
                --STUFF in the uppercased character into the next character
                SET @inputString = STUFF(@inputString,@i +
                1,1,UPPER(SUBSTRING(@inputString,@i + 1,1)))
            END
            --increment the loop counter
            SET @i = @i + 1
        END
        RETURN @inputString
    END

    GO
```

So we can then execute the following statement:

```
SELECT name, dbo.string$properCase(name) AS artistProper
FROM artist
```

and get back the name as it was, and the name as it is now.

```
name                    artist
---------------------   ---------------------
the beatles             The Beatles
the who                 The Who
```

While this is certainly not the perfect function for changing a string into a title case, we could easily extend this to take care of all of the "special" cases that arise (like McCartney, or MacDougall).

The last example we will look at, accesses the album table, counts the number of records in the table and returns the number. What is nice about this function is that the caller won't be aware that the table is being accessed, since this is done from within the UDF. If we create the following function:

```
CREATE FUNCTION album$recordCount
(
    @artistId int
)
RETURNS int AS
```

```
    BEGIN
        DECLARE @count AS int -- variable to hold output

        --count the number of rows in the table
        SELECT @count = count(*)
        FROM album
        WHERE artistId = @artistId

        RETURN @count
    END
GO
```

Then we can execute it using a single `SELECT` statement:

```
SELECT dbo.album$recordCount(1) AS albumCount
```

and will return:

```
albumCount
-----------
2
```

However, if we were to execute it like this:

```
SELECT name,
    artistId,
    dbo.album$recordCount(artistId) AS albumCount
FROM album
```

It would return:

ArtistId	albumCount
1	2
2	1

The UDF will execute one time for each row. This is not a problem for such a small query, but performance will become an issue when we have bigger numbers of large tables.

Inline Table-Valued Functions

An inline table-valued function, also known as a single-statement table-valued function, is a more complex version of a scalar function, since it returns a table rather than a single value. In the following code example, we build a function that returns a table of album keys, filtered out by artist.

We should note in passing that we will refer to a function returning a table, while a result set comes from a procedure.

```
CREATE FUNCTION album$returnKeysByArtist
(
    @artistId int
)
```

```
    RETURNS TABLE
    WITH SCHEMABINDING
    AS
    RETURN (
        SELECT albumId
        FROM dbo.album
        WHERE artistId = @artistId )
```

Now, we can execute this function. But how? This is totally different from any resource we have had in SQL Server before now. We cannot execute it like a procedure:

```
    EXEC dbo.album$returnKeysbyArtist @artistId = 1
```

It returns an error:

Server: Msg 2809, Level 18, State 1, Line 1
The request for procedure 'album$returnKeysByArtist' failed because 'album$returnKeysByArtist' is a function object.

What we *can* do however, is substitute the call to the table-valued function in the place of a table in any query. We therefore execute the function like this:

```
    SELECT album.albumId, album.name
    FROM album
        JOIN dbo.album$returnKeysbyArtist(1) AS functionTest
        ON album.albumId = functionTest.albumId
```

which produces the following:

```
albumId     name
----------- -----------------------------
1           the white album
2           revolver
```

Is this better than a normal join? Not really. This is not a standard database programming operation and it would likely hinder the query optimizer from producing the most optimized code. However, it is a pretty cool way to build a custom piece of code that we can add to our toolbox if we have very small sets of data that we wish to use in our queries.

Schema Binding

In the declaration of our function, we flew past something that might be an unfamiliar term:

```
    WITH SCHEMABINDING
```

Schema binding is a new feature that SQL Server provides for functions and views, allowing you to take the items that your view is dependent upon (such as tables or views) and "bind" them to that view. In this way no-one can make alterations to those objects unless the schema bound view is dropped. This addresses a very common problem that has occurred since the first days of client-server programming. What if the server changes? How will the client deal with the change?

For example, in our existing function, we have used the album table. If we wanted to drop the album table:

```
DROP TABLE album
```

we would get the following error:

Server: Msg 3729, Level 16, State 1, Line 2
Could not DROP TABLE 'album'. It is being referenced by object ' album$returnKeysbyArtist'.

> Note that this is not a bad thing. Indeed, this demonstrates SQL Server's inbuilt mechanism for protecting its data.

So what if we wanted to simply alter the table? The UDF will disallow any attempt to alter a used column, although we *will* be allowed to either add a column or modify one that is unused. To illustrate this we will add a `description` column and then remove it to leave the table as it was:

```
ALTER TABLE album
ADD description varchar(100) NULL
ALTER TABLE album
DROP COLUMN description
```

which executes just fine. But if we try to drop a column that is accessed by a function, such as the `artistId`:

```
ALTER TABLE album
DROP COLUMN artistId
```

SQL Server knows that this column is being used by a function and tells us so:

Server: Msg 5074, Level 16, State 3, Line 1
The object 'album$returnKeysByArtist' is dependent on column 'artistId'.
ALTER TABLE DROP COLUMN artistId failed because one or more objects access this column.

You should always use schema binding on a production system that clients will be accessing. Obviously if you are going to be dropping and recreating a table frequently then schema binding might not be much of an advantage to you, but most tables in a deployed database will rarely, if ever change, and if they do, it is always wise to know the code that accesses them. There will be no performance issues, other than the speed with which the schema bound object can be modified.

If you do need to modify a table or column, you can either:

- turn off SCHEMABINDING, carry out the required modifications, and turn it back on again, or
- drop the function, modify the table or column(s) and then recreate the schema binding

An object may be schema-bound if the following conditions are true:

- All objects employed are schema bound.
- All objects are accessed using the two part name (`owner.objectName`).

Chapter 11

- All objects are in the same database.
- The user must have proper permissions to reference all the objects in the code.

For example, if we tried to alter our function in the following manner:

```
ALTER FUNCTION album$returnKeysByArtist
(
    @artistId int
)
RETURNS TABLE
WITH SCHEMABINDING
AS
RETURN (
    SELECT albumId
    FROM album ---- used to be dbo.album
    WHERE artistId = @artistId)
```

This will cause the following error:

Server: Msg 4512, Level 16, State 3, Procedure album$returnKeysByArtist, Line 9
Cannot schema bind function 'album$returnKeysByArtist' because name 'album' is invalid for schema binding. Names must be in two-part format and object cannot reference itself.

To remove schemabinding, simply execute the ALTER FUNCTION with no WITH SCHEMABINDING clause; for example, take the first function we built:

```
CREATE FUNCTION album$returnKeysByArtist
(
    @artistId int
)
RETURNS TABLE
WITH SCHEMABINDING
AS
RETURN (
    SELECT albumId
    FROM dbo.album
    WHERE artistId = @artistId )
```

To change this to run without schema binding, we should execute this code as:

```
CREATE FUNCTION album$returnKeysByArtist
(
    @artistId int
)
RETURNS TABLE
AS
RETURN (
    SELECT albumId
    FROM dbo.album
    WHERE artistId = @artistId )
```

Multi-Statement Table-Valued Functions

If single-statement table-valued functions were more complex scalar functions, multi-statement table-valued functions are even more complex! What makes them great is that you can define functions with relatively unlimited commands and build a single table, the nature of which we define in the function declaration. In our example, we will return all of the albums for a particular artist *and* set all of the names to upper case:

```
CREATE FUNCTION album$returnNamesInUpperCase
(
    @artistId int
)
RETURNS @outTable table (
    albumId int,
    name varchar(60) )
WITH SCHEMABINDING
AS
BEGIN
    --add all of the albums to the output table
    INSERT INTO @outTable
    SELECT albumId, name
    FROM dbo.album
    WHERE artistId = @artistId

    --second superfluous update to show that it
    --is a multi-statement function
    UPDATE @outTable
    SET name = UPPER(name)
    RETURN
END
GO
```

When we execute the following statement:

```
SELECT * FROM dbo.album$returnNamesInUpperCase(1)
```

it returns:

```
albumId     name
---------   ----------------------------------
1           THE WHITE ALBUM
2           REVOLVER
```

Their usage is much like the single-value table-valued functions, but they open up a number of new possibilities. Operations that were previously done using temporary tables with single use code can now be done in a function, where they can be reused, and without coding messy temporary tables.

What User Defined Functions Cannot Do

There are a few things that we cannot do using UDFs. The first thing to note is that there are a few important functions built-in to SQL Server that cannot be included in UDFs. The reasons for this are fairly simple: they are not deterministic. (Deterministic functions are those functions that when executed with a given set of parameters always return the same set of values.) The reasoning behind this is sensible. UDFs can be used to build calculated columns, or columns in views, and each of these can now be indexed. Indexing can only occur if the columns can be guaranteed to return the same values for each function call.

The following table lists the non-deterministic functions that cannot be used in UDFs:

@@CONNECTIONS	@@TOTAL_ERRORS	@@CPU_BUSY	@@TOTAL_READ
@@IDLE	@@TOTAL_WRITE	@@IO_BUSY	@@MAX_CONNECTIONS
@@PACK_RECEIVED	@@PACK_SENT	@@PACKET_ERRORS	@@TIMETICKS
TEXTPTR	NEWID	RAND	GETDATE
GETUTCDATE			

We will not list all of the functions in SQL Server and their deterministic status. This is fully covered in the SQL Server 2000 Books Online under the *Deterministic and Nondeterministic Functions* topic.

A second key point is that the state of the server and all data must be exactly the same as when you executed the statements. Hence, any changes that extend to objects that are not local to the function, such as sending back results, data, or data structures, cursors that are not local to the function, or any other modification to system state cannot be made. To illustrate this, let's create a function that will update all of the albums in our tables to "the Beatles", and then return the number of values we have updated.

```
CREATE FUNCTION album$setAllToTheBeatles
(
)
RETURNS int AS
BEGIN
    DECLARE @rowcount int

    UPDATE album
    SET artistId = 1
    WHERE artistId <> 1

    RETURN 1
END
```

This will fail upon compile because of the UPDATE:

Server: Msg 443, Level 16, State 2, Procedure album$setAllToTheBeatles, Line 9
Illegal use of 'UPDATE' within a FUNCTION.

Constraints

As we have seen before constraints are SQL Server resources that are used to automatically enforce data integrity. One of the greatest things about using constraints instead of triggers is that the query optimizer can use them to optimize queries. For instance, if you tell SQL Server that a certain variable can only have values between 5 and 10, and then perform a query for all rows that have the value of this variable greater than 100, the optimizer will know without even looking at the data that there will be no rows that meet the criteria.

There are five different kinds of constraints that we have in SQL Server:

Ensuring Data Integrity

- NULL – NULL constraints are not technically constraints, but are generally considered so.
- **Primary Keys** and **Unique Constraints** – to make sure that our keys contain only unique combinations of values.
- **Foreign Keys** – used to make sure that any migrated keys have only valid values that match the keys that they reference.
- **Default** – default constraints are used to set an acceptable default value for a column.
- **Check** – constraints that are used to limit the values that can be entered into a single column or an entire table.

Having previously considered the first three of these in Chapter 10, we will focus our attention on the latter two here:

Default Constraints

I consider default values to be a very important part of safeguarding data, in that if a user doesn't know what value to enter into a table, the value can be omitted and the default constraint will set it to a valid pre-determined value. Whilst we can prevent the user from entering invalid values, we cannot keep them from putting in illogical values. For example, consider that an experienced SQL Server user must enter a value into a column called boogleF1, which is a bit field (boogleF1 was chosen because it has just as much meaning to us as some of the fields that make sense to us have for other users). Not knowing what boogleF1 means, but forced to create a new record, the user may choose to enter a 0. Using default values gives the users an example of a likely value for the column. There is no question that setting default values for fields is very convenient for the user!

The command to add a default follows the following structure:

```
ALTER TABLE <tableName>
    ADD [ CONSTRAINT
    <DefaultName>
    DEFAULT <constantExpression>
    FOR <columnName>
```

We will use a similar naming structure to our previous naming, expanding the default name to use the following pattern:

```
dflt<tableName>$<columnName>$<genericDatatype>$<description>]
```

Resulting in the following alter syntax:

```
ALTER TABLE <tableName>
    ADD [ CONSTRAINT
    dflt<tableName>$<columnName>$<genericDatatype>$<description>]
    DEFAULT <constantExpression>
    FOR <columnName>
```

Of course we should know by now what the <tableName> and <columnName> placeholders are for, but what about the others?

❏ <genericDatatype> – We need to specify a generic data type. The reason for this is a matter of convenience. In our vault of generic objects, we will build up a group of default constraint definitions that we can use repeatedly. For example, if we were defining a constraint setting an integer column to a value of 1, we would not need a different default constraint in setting a `tinyint` (unlike the case of a `bigint` field).

❏ <description> – This is the general description of the purpose of the default, for example, if the constraint is used to keep all data in an integer column greater than zero, we might call it `greaterThanZero`. This description will make our default names more understandable. Not only that but, when considered as a "normalized", reusable package with the generic data type, we will have a default definition that will work for any situation where we need the same default values.

❏ <constantExpression> – A scalar expression which could either be a literal value, a `NULL`, or a function. We will look at several different scenarios for constant expressions in the following section.

Literal Defaults

A literal is a simple single value in the same data type that requires no translation by SQL Server. For example, the following table has sample defaults for a few data types:

Data type	Possible Default Value
`int`	1
`varchar(10)`	'Value'
`binary(2)`	0x0000
`datetime`	'12/31/2000'

So in our database, let's say we want to default all albums to "the Beatles" unless the user specifies otherwise, we might do a select from the artist table to see what the `artistId` of the Beatles entry is:

```
SELECT * FROM artist

artistId    name
----------- -----------------------
1           the beatles
2           the who
```

So we specify the following default value:

```
ALTER TABLE album
    ADD CONSTRAINT dfltAlbum$artistId$integer$one
    DEFAULT (1)
    FOR artistId
```

A word of warning about literal defaults. It is better not to supply a literal default value to a column that is part of a unique index. The reason is that since any column that has a default value set is unlikely to contain unique values. Also, in any index, having large numbers of repeating values is not going to be good for performance.

Ensuring Data Integrity

Functions

An alternative to hard coding a default value is to use a function to return the default value. Let's consider our earlier example when we wanted to set the default artist to "the Beatles". To do this we could add a field to the artist table, `defaultFl` with a default of 0. We would do this since we will only want to have a single value that was 1, plus we want to force the user to *choose* the default record.

```
ALTER TABLE artist
    ADD defaultFl bit NOT NULL
        CONSTRAINT dfltArtist$defaultFl$boolean$false
            DEFAULT (0)
```

We now set "the Beatles" row to 1:

```
UPDATE artist
SET defaultFl = 1
WHERE name = 'the beatles'
```

The table now includes a field where the user can choose which value is required as the default, so what do we do next? For each version of SQL Server, up to 2000, you could create a query that returns one row, like this one, which will return a single, scalar value. This will generate an error message however, so to be able to perform a query we write our own function:

```
CREATE FUNCTION artist$returnDefaultId
(
)
RETURNS int
WITH SCHEMABINDING
AS
BEGIN
    DECLARE @artistId int

    SELECT @artistId = artistId
    FROM dbo.artist
    WHERE defaultFl = 1

    RETURN @artistId
END
GO
```

and now if we execute the statement:

```
SELECT dbo.artist$returnDefaultId() AS defaultValue
```

we get this:

```
defaultValue
------------
1
```

So for our solution, we can code this:

```
ALTER TABLE album
   ADD CONSTRAINT dfltAlbum$artistId$function$useDefault
   DEFAULT dbo.artist$returnDefaultId()
   FOR artistId
```

Now we have the exact functionally that we were trying to get from the subquery, and in doing so we have created a function that any other process may employ. To test it out, we execute the following INSERT statement, leaving out the `artistId`:

```
INSERT INTO album(name)
VALUES ('rubber soul')

SELECT album.name AS albumName, artist.name AS artistName
FROM album
   JOIN artist
   ON album.artistId = artist.artistId
WHERE album.name = 'rubber soul'
```

Which we see contains the row that we created:

albumName	artistName
rubber soul	the beatles

Default constraints in SQL Server 2000 are a tremendously powerful resource with which to supply initial values to fields. Since you can set default values in one table from within another, there are few limits to their uses.

Check Constraints

Check constraints are used to disallow improper data being entered into our tables. Check constraints are executed after default constraints (so you cannot specify a default to supply an improper value) and INSTEAD OF triggers. They cannot affect the values that we are trying to put in the table and are used to verify the validity of the supplied values. There are two separate types of check constraint: column and table. Column constraints reference a single column, and are only used when the individual column is referenced in the modification. Table constraints are used regardless of which columns are referenced.

Fortunately for us, we do not have to worry about declaring a constraint as either a column constraint or table constraint. When SQL Server compiles the constraint, it verifies whether it needs to check more than one column and applies the appropriate constraint accordingly. In each of our examples of constraints, we will discuss whether it is a column or table constraint.

The basic syntax of the ALTER TABLE statement that concerns constraints is:

```
ALTER TABLE <tableName> [WITH CHECK | WITH NOCHECK]
   ADD [CONSTRAINT chk<tableName>$[<columnName>$<genericDatatype>$]<usage>]
   CHECK <searchConditions>
```

Some of the syntax will not be familiar, so here is an explanation of the new parts. When you create a check constraint, the WITH CHECK setting (as the default setting) gives you the opportunity to decide whether or not to check the existing data in the table. WITH NOCHECK allows existing data to be invalid, but will not allow future values to violate the constraint requirements. Sometimes the WITH NOCHECK setting may be necessary, if you are adding a constraint to an existing table where it is unrealistic to check all existing data, but you want to check all subsequent data entries. It is always good practice to avoid using NOCHECK unless absolutely necessary.

Ensuring Data Integrity

While it is obvious what `<columnName>` is referring to, why is it optional? It is simply a means to incorporate the column that you are trying to protect in the constraint's name. However, when we are dealing with a constraint that works with multiple columns, we should not include a column name in the name.

The `<genericDatatype>` value is simply a description of the data type class that the constraint could work on. When it comes to column check constraints, there is no reason why we should use different code for a `varchar(10)` or a `char(10)`, or even a `char(100)` if we simply want to ensure that the input value is greater than five characters long. Instead we can use the reference `string` in our code, to denote all of these data types. This is of course impossible in the case of a table check.

The `<usage>` value would basically be a small text string to explain what the constraint is used for. For example, if the check was to make sure that a value was between zero and ten, we would put `zeroThroughTen`.

The `<searchConditions>` value is analogous to the `WHERE` clause of a typical `SELECT` statement, with no subqueries allowed. It may access system and UDFs, and use the name or names of column in the table. However, it cannot access any other table, nor can it access any row other than the current row. If multiple rows are modified, the constraint deals with each row individually. The result of the `searchConditions` part must be a logical expression with only two possible values, `TRUE` or `FALSE`.

A common check constraint that we will add to most every string (`varchar`, `char`, etc.) serves to prevent blank data from being entered. For example, in our album table, we have a `name` column. This column does not allow `NULL`s, so the user has to enter something, but what about a single space character?

```
INSERT INTO album ( name, artistId)
VALUES ('',1)
```

If we allowed this in our database, we would certainly end up with a blank record because there would likely be one occasion where a user would enter a record prematurely having failed to input his or her name. The second time a space is entered instead of the name, an error would be returned:

Server: Msg 2627, Level 14, State 2, Line 1
Violation of UNIQUE KEY constraint 'XAKalbum_name'. Cannot insert duplicate key in object 'album'.
The statement has been terminated.

Alternatively, we may have a non-unique constraint bound column, like a description or notes field, where we might have many blank entries. So we might add the following constraint to prevent this from ever happening again:

```
ALTER TABLE album WITH CHECK
    ADD CONSTRAINT chkAlbum$name$string$noEmptyString
    --trim the value in name, adding in stars to handle
    --values safer than just checking length of the rtrim which
    --will be NULL if name is NULL, and a single char if not.  The coalesce
    --makes certain
    CHECK (( '*' + COALESCE(rtrim(name),'') + '*') <> '**' )
```

The final `CHECK` function here utilises the `COALESCE` operation to ensure that if there are no characters other than space then a zero length string is returned, and if a `NULL` is entered then it is returned. Of course, we know that we already entered a value that will clash with our constraint, so we get the following error message:

Server: Msg 547, Level 16, State 1, Line 1
ALTER TABLE statement conflicted with COLUMN CHECK constraint 'chkAlbum$name$string$noEmptyString'. The conflict occurred in database 'master', table 'album', column 'name'.

If we specify the constraint using WITH NOCHECK:

```
ALTER TABLE album WITH NOCHECK
    ADD CONSTRAINT chkAlbum$name$string$noEmptyString
    --trim the value in name, adding in stars to handle
    --values safer than just checking length of the rtrim
    CHECK (( '*' + COALESCE(rtrim(name),'') + '*') <> '**' )
```

The statement will be added to the table definition, though the NOCHECK means that the bad value is retained in the table. However, any time a modification statement references the field, the check constraint will be fired. The next time you try to set the value of the table to the same bad value, an error will occur.

```
UPDATE album
SET name = name
WHERE name = ''
```

This gives us the error message:

Server: Msg 547, Level 16, State 1, Line 1
UPDATE statement conflicted with COLUMN CHECK constraint 'chkAlbum$name$string$noEmptyString'. The conflict occurred in database 'master', table 'album', column 'name'.
The statement has been terminated.

In our next example we will look at ways to encapsulate into UDFs the code to perform both simple and complex checks. In the case of the function that checks for empty strings we can build our own UDF as follows:

```
CREATE FUNCTION string$checkForEmptyString
(
    @stringValue varchar(8000)
)
RETURNS bit
AS
BEGIN
    DECLARE @logicalValue bit
    IF ( '*' + COALESCE(RTRIM(@stringValue),'') + '*') = '**'
        SET @logicalValue = 1
    ELSE
        SET @logicalValue = 0

    RETURN @logicalValue
END
```

And then build constraints such as:

```
ALTER TABLE album WITH NOCHECK
    ADD CONSTRAINT chkAlbum$name$string$noEmptyString
    --trim the value in name, adding in stars to handle
    --values safer than just checking length of the rtrim
    CHECK (dbo.string$checkForEmptyString(name) = 0)
```

Ensuring Data Integrity

Now if the method ever changes, it is encapsulated within a function, and will only change in a single place.

Most check constraints will consist of the simple task of checking the format of a single field. In the next two examples, we will employ UDFs to provide generic range checking functionality and powerful rule checking which can implement complex rules which would prove difficult to code using straight SQL.

In the first example, we are going to add a catalog number column to the album table, and stipulate that the catalog numbers are alphanumeric values with the following format:

<number><number><number>-<number><number><alphaOrNumber><alphaOrNumber><alphaOrNumber>-<number><number>

An example of such a catalog number might be: '433-43ASD-33', with all characters in the string being required.

So we define a UDF called `album$catalogNumberValidate` that will encapsulate the validation of `catalogNumbers`. This function will have two purposes, namely validating the column in a check constraint, and validating any bulk row inserting and data cleaning. Our function will return a bit value of 1, 0, or NULL for a NULL value, that we can use to deal with the checking of the data.

The first step is to add our new column to the database.

```
ALTER TABLE album
    ADD catalogNumber char(12) NOT NULL
    --temporary default so we can make the column
    --not NULL in intial creation
    CONSTRAINT tempDefaultAlbumCatalogNumber DEFAULT ('111-11111-11')

 --drop it because this is not a proper default
ALTER TABLE album
    DROP tempDefaultAlbumCatalogNumber
```

Then we create our function that is used to check the values of the `album.catalogNumber` column:

```
CREATE FUNCTION album$catalogNumberValidate
(
    @catalogNumber char(12)
)
RETURNS bit
AS
BEGIN
    DECLARE @logicalValue bit
    --check to see if the value like the mask we have set up
    IF @catalogNumber LIKE
            '[0-9][0-9][0-9]-[0-9][0-9][0-9a-z][0-9a-z][0-9a-z]-[0-9][0-9]'
        SET @logicalValue = 1 --yes it is
    ELSE
        SET @logicalValue = 0 --no it is not
    --note that we cannot just simply say RETURN 1, or RETURN 0 as the
    --function must have only one exit point
    RETURN @logicalValue
END
```

We will check to see if the constraint works.

```
IF dbo.album$catalogNumberValidate('433-11qww-33') = 1
    SELECT 'Yes' AS result
ELSE
    SELECT 'No' AS result
```

which returns:

```
result
--------
Yes
```

All that is left is to build a function based check constraint:

```
ALTER TABLE album
    ADD CONSTRAINT
    chkAlbum$catalogNumber$function$artist$catalogNumberValidate
    --keep it simple here, encapsulating all we need to in the
    --function
    CHECK (dbo.album$catalogNumbervalidate(catalogNumber) = 1)
```

and testing the new constraint we see that the following incorrect catalog number makes the system generate an error:

```
UPDATE album
SET catalogNumber = '1'
WHERE name = 'the white album'
```

returning:

Server: Msg 547, Level 16, State 1, Line 1
UPDATE statement conflicted with COLUMN CHECK constraint 'chkAlbum$catalogNumber$function$artist$catalogNumberValidate'. The conflict occurred in database 'master', table 'album', column 'catalogNumber'.
The statement has been terminated.

Executing it with proper values will work just fine:

```
UPDATE album
SET catalogNumber = '433-43ASD-33'
WHERE name = 'the white album'
```

As a second example, let's add a column to the `artist` table that will hold the `LIKE` mask. Note that it needs to be considerably larger than the actual column, since some of the possible masks use multiple characters to indicate a single character. We should also note that it is a `varchar`, since using `char` variables as `LIKE` masks can be problematic due to the padding spaces.

```
ALTER TABLE artist
    ADD catalogNumberMask varchar(100) NOT NULL
    -- it is acceptable to have a mask of percent in this case
    CONSTRAINT dfltArtist$catalogNumberMask$string$percent
    DEFAULT (' per cent')
```

Ensuring Data Integrity

Then we build the function, and it will access this column to check that our value matches the mask:

```
ALTER FUNCTION album$catalogNumberValidate
(
   @catalogNumber char(12),
   @artistId int --now based on the artist id
)
RETURNS bit
AS
BEGIN
   DECLARE @logicalValue bit, @catalogNumberMask varchar(100)

   SELECT @catalogNumberMask = catalogNumberMask
   FROM artist
   WHERE artistId = @artistId

   IF @catalogNumber LIKE @catalogNumberMask
      SET @logicalValue = 1
   ELSE
      SET @logicalValue = 0

   RETURN @logicalValue
END
GO
```

Now we give the artist columns the correct masks:

```
UPDATE artist
SET catalogNumberMask =
         '[0-9][0-9]-[0-9][0-9][0-9a-z][0-9a-z][0-9a-z]-[0-9][0-9]'
WHERE artistId = 1 --the beatles

UPDATE artist
SET catalogNumberMask =
         '[a-z][a-z][0-9][0-9][0-9][0-9][0-9][0-9][0-9][0-9][0-9][0-9]'
WHERE artistId = 2 --the who
```

and we test that the function works like this:

```
IF dbo.album$catalogNumberValidate('433-43ASD-33',1) = 1
   SELECT 'Yes' AS result
ELSE
   SELECT 'No' AS result

IF dbo.album$catalogNumberValidate('aa1111111111',2) = 1
   SELECT 'Yes' AS result
ELSE
   SELECT 'No' AS result
GO
```

Now we can add the constraint to the table:

```
ALTER TABLE album
   ADD CONSTRAINT
   chkAlbum$catalogNumber$function$artist$catalogNumberValidate
   CHECK (dbo.album$catalogNumbervalidate(catalogNumber,artistId) = 1)
```

However our data does not match:

Server: Msg 547, Level 16, State 1, Line 1
ALTER TABLE statement conflicted with TABLE CHECK constraint 'chkAlbum$catalogNumber$function$artist$catalogNumberValidate'. The conflict occurred in database 'master', table 'album'.

We could use the NOCHECK option, since this will mean that any existing data will be improper when we save the constraint, whilst any new data will automatically be validated. There is an issue in this example however, in that the constraint will not prevent the user changing the mask. If this is a problem, we might need to implement a time based table, where we can state that the catalogue number mask will take a certain value for a publishing date in the period '1/1/1970' – '12/31/1995' and a different value for the period '1/1/1996' until the present.

For our example we will not use the NOCHECK option, just to show you how easy it is to find aberrations in the data. This query will find the problems in the table:

```
--to find where our data is not ready for the constraint,
--we run the following query
SELECT dbo.album$catalogNumbervalidate(catalogNumber,artistId)
   AS validCatalogNumber,
   artistId, name, catalogNumber
FROM album
WHERE dbo.album$catalogNumbervalidate(catalogNumber,artistId) <> 1
```

This gives us a list of rows with invalid data. Using similar code to our previous examples, we can correct the error and then add the constraint. Attempting to add an incorrect value:

```
UPDATE album
SET catalogNumber = '1'
WHERE name = 'the white album'
```

results in an error:

Server: Msg 547, Level 16, State 1, Line 1
UPDATE statement conflicted with COLUMN CHECK constraint 'chkAlbum$catalogNumber$function$artist$catalogNumberValidate'. The conflict occurred in database 'master', table 'album', column 'catalogNumber'.
The statement has been terminated.

Now we try a correct one:

```
UPDATE album
SET catalogNumber = '433-43ASD-33'
WHERE name = 'the white album'  --the artist is the beatles
```

Using these approaches, we can build any single row validation code for our tables.

However, there is a drawback to this coding method. As we described previously, each UDF will fire once for each row and each column that was modified in the update, and making checks over and over again may lead to a degradation in performance. The alternative method, as we shall present later on, would be to use a trigger to validate all table predicates in a single query.

Despite the drawback, this way of solving row validation issues is very clean, easy to understand and easy to maintain. However, if our check constraints are complex requiring access to many tables, performance may be affected and use of a trigger is more appropriate.

Handling Errors Caused by Constraints

Handling errors is one of the most important parts of writing any data-modifying statement in SQL server. Whenever a statement fails a constraint requirement, we have seen that an error message is generated. SQL Server provides us with very rudimentary error handling tools to determine what happened in a previous statement, and we will consider them here. Throughout this chapter, we have been executing statements to prove that constraints execute. When the constraints fail, we get error messages like this:

Server: Msg 547, Level 16, State 1, Line 1
UPDATE statement conflicted with COLUMN CHECK constraint 'chkAlbum$catalogNumber$function$artist$catalogNumberValidate'. The conflict occurred in database 'master', table 'album', column 'catalogNumber'.
The statement has been terminated.

This is the error message that the Query Analyzer tool sees, and is the error message that user applications will see. The error message is made up of a few basic parts:

- **Error number**, Msg 547 – the error number that is passed back to the calling program. In some cases this error number is significant; however in most cases it is simply enough to say that the error number is non-zero.

- **Level**, Level 16 – a severity level for the message. 0 – 18 are generally considered to be user messages, with 16 being the default. Levels 19-25 are really severe errors that cause the connection to be severed (with a message written to the log) and typically involve data corruption issues.

- **State**, State 1 – a value from 1 to 127 that represents the state of the process when the error was raised. Always 1 unless it is part of a RAISERROR statement.

- **Line**, Line 1 – the line in the batch or object where the error is occurring. Very useful for debugging purposes.

- **Error Text** – a text explanation of the error that has occurred.

However, in our SQL Statements we only have access to the error number. We do this simply using the @@error global variable.

```
SET @<errorVariableName> = @@error
```

This will capture the value of the error number of any message that has occurred as a response to the previous statement. This value will have a value of:

0	No error.
1-49999	System errors, either from constraints, or from real system errors that are not under our control. Examples of such system errors include syntax errors, disk corruptions, invalid SQL operation, etc.
50000	*Ad hoc* error messages with no number specified, or any general message that no user process will need to differentiate from any other message.

50001 and higher	User-defined. If the client system can make use of the error number, then it is not a bad idea to develop a corporate or personal standard for error numbers. We will look at error handling schemes in Chapter 12.

The maximum error number is the maximum value for the `bigint` *data type.*

When we execute an INSERT, UPDATE, or DELETE statement anywhere in our script, trigger, or stored procedure code, we must always check the error status of the command. Note that this value is changed for every command in our database, so any statement following *every* modification statement should get the value stored in @@error. (Also, you could get the value of @@rowcount after a SET statement, as this statement does not affect the @@rowcount value.)

What you do with the error value depends on the situation you face. It is generally better to execute every statement that modifies data inside its own transaction, unless you are executing a single statement. In the following example code, we will try to update an album with an invalid catalog number. This will raise an error that we will handle by issuing a RAISERROR which will inform the user what is happening. Each time we execute the UPDATE command again, we will check whether @@error variable is zero, and if not we will make sure that the command is not executed:

```
BEGIN TRANSACTION

    DECLARE @errorHold int

    UPDATE album
    SET catalogNumber = '1'
    WHERE name = 'the white album'

    SET @errorHold = @@error
    IF @errorHold <> 0
    BEGIN
        RAISERROR 50000 'Error modifying the first catalogNumber for album'
        ROLLBACK TRANSACTION
    END

    IF @errorHold = 0
    BEGIN
        UPDATE album
        SET catalogNumber = '1'
        WHERE name = 'the white album'

        SET @errorHold = @@error
        IF @errorHold <> 0
        BEGIN
            RAISERROR 50000 'Error modifying the second catalogNumber'
            ROLLBACK TRANSACTION
        END
    END

IF @errorHold = 0
    COMMIT TRANSACTION
ELSE
    RAISERROR 50000 'Update batch did not succeed'
```

Ensuring Data Integrity

Executing that batch we get back three errors:

Server: Msg 547, Level 16, State 1, Line 1
UPDATE statement conflicted with TABLE CHECK constraint
'chkAlbum$catalogNumber$function$artist$catalogNumberValidate'. The conflict occurred in database 'master', table 'album'.
The statement has been terminated.

Server: Msg 50000, Level 16, State 1, Line 12
Error modifying the first catalogNumber for album

Server: Msg 50000, Level 16, State 1, Line 33
Update batch did not succeed

By coding the extra error messages, we can build error reporting chains that tell us precisely where an error occurs in a batch, allowing for easy debugging.

Triggers

Triggers are a type of stored procedure attached to a table or view and are executed only when the contents of a table are changed. They can be used to enforce most any business rule, and are especially important for dealing with situations that are too complex for a check constraint to handle.

We will look at triggers as a means to do the following:

- Perform cross database referential integrity
- Check intra-table inter-row constraints
- Check inter-table constraints
- Introduce desired side effects to our queries

The main advantage that triggers have over constraints is the ability to directly access other tables, and to execute multiple rows at once. In a trigger we can run almost every T-SQL commands, except for the following:

```
ALTER DATABASE    CREATE DATABASE    DROP DATABASE
RESTORE LOG       RECONFIGURE        RESTORE DATABASE
```

We can have triggers that fire on INSERT, UPDATE, or DELETE, or any combination of these. We can also have multiple triggers, of different or the same types, on a table.

A word of warning: never include statements that return resultsets in a trigger unless this is allowable in *all* circumstances where the trigger might fire.

There are two different models of trigger:

- **Instead-of** – Meaning that the trigger operates instead of the command (INSERT, UPDATE or DELETE) affecting the table or view. In this way, we can do whatever we want with the data, either modifying it as sent, or putting is into another place. We can have only a single INSERT, UPDATE, and DELETE trigger of this type per table. You can however combine all three into one and have a single trigger that fires for all three operations.

❑ **After** – Meaning the trigger fires after the command has affected the table, though not on views. After triggers are used for building enhanced business rule handlers and you would generally put any kind of logging mechanisms into them. You may have an unlimited number of after triggers that fire on INSERT, UPDATE and DELETE or any combination of them. Even if we have an instead-of trigger, we may still have as many after triggers as wanted, since they can all be combined into a single trigger.

Coding Triggers

The following contains the basic trigger syntax:

```
CREATE TRIGGER <tableName$triggerType$usageType>
ON <tableName> | <viewName>
AFTER | INSTEAD OF
[DELETE][,][INSERT][,][UPDATE]
AS
<sqlStatements>
```

The following sections look at several parts of the CREATE TRIGGER statement that need further explanation:

❑ CREATE TRIGGER <tableName$triggerType$usageType>

The name of the trigger is not tremendously important, as you won't explicitly call it from code. I generally like to give them names that resemble all of the other objects we have seen previously, though as with every object we have built, the name is an extremely personal choice.

❑ INSTEAD OF | AFTER – tells the trigger when to fire, as we outlined above.

❑ [DELETE][,][INSERT][,][UPDATE] – We can specify one or more of these to tell our trigger when to fire, for example, specifying:

```
AFTER DELETE, INSERT
```

would give us a trigger that fired on DELETE and INSERT, but not UPDATE. Specifying:

```
INSTEAD OF INSERT, UPDATE
```

would give us a trigger that fired instead of INSERTs and UPDATEs, but DELETE would work as normal.

❑ <sqlStatements> – any SQL Statement.

The rest of this section will be devoted to which statements to put in the trigger. We will look at

❑ Accessing modified rows information

❑ Determining which columns have been modified

❑ Writing validations for many rows at a time

❑ Having multiple triggers for the same action (INSERT, UPDATE, DELETE)

❑ Error handling

Accessing Modified Rows

The best part about coding triggers is that no matter how many rows are being modified, we get access to them all. We access these values via two tables that let us see the state of our data before and after our modification. These tables are called the DELETED and INSERTED tables, and are tables in memory that only exist for the lifetime of the trigger, being inaccessible outside of its scope.

The INSERTED table will be filled in during an INSERT or UPDATE operation, and the DELETED table will be filled in during an UPDATE or DELETE operation. INSERT and DELETE operations are obvious, but the SQL Server's handling of an UPDATE is less so. All UPDATE operations in SQL Server are logically divided in to a DELETE and an INSERT operation, removing the rows that are going to be modified, then inserting them into the new format.

In the following example, we will build a trigger to show the contents of the INSERTED and DELETED tables after an UPDATE:

```
--build a trigger that returns as a result set as
--inserted and deleted tables for demonstration purposes
--only. For real triggers, this is a bad idea
CREATE TRIGGER artist$afterUpdate$showInsertedAndDeleted
ON artist
AFTER UPDATE -- fires after the update has occurred
AS

SELECT 'contents of inserted' -- informational output
SELECT *
FROM INSERTED

SELECT 'contents of deleted' -- informational output
SELECT *
FROM DELETED
GO
```

Then we run an UPDATE on the table that will set all names to upper case as an example of the differences between the INSERTED and DELETED table contents:

```
UPDATE artist
SET name = UPPER(name)
```

This returns the following four result sets:

```
--------------------
contents of inserted

artistId name ...
---------------------
1 THE BEATLES ...
2 THE WHO ...


--------------------
contents of deleted

artistId name ...
---------- ---------------------
1 the beatles ...
2 the who ...
```

Determining which Columns have been Modified

There are two functions that we can use in our triggers to determine which columns have been involved in either an INSERT or UPDATE operation, but note that there is no equivalent for a DELETE operation. We will use this so as to avoid checking data that has not been affected by the operation, and hence enhance the performance of our triggers.

Specifically, the functions get information from:

- The columns clause of an INSERT statement:

```
INSERT tablename (<column1>,<column2>,…,<columnN>)
```

- The SET clauses of the UPDATE statement:

```
UPDATE tablename
SET <column1> = value1,
<column2> = value2,
...
<columnN> = valueN
```

The first method of seeing that the column has been updated is the UPDATE(<columnName>) function. This will return a Boolean value that tells us whether or not the column has been referenced in the modification statement. For example, the following would check to see if the name or description columns had been modified:

```
IF update(name) OR update(description)
BEGIN
    <SQL statements>
END
```

As an example, we will create the following table:

```
CREATE TABLE columnUpdatedTest
(
    columnUpdatedTestId int IDENTITY,   --bitmask value 1
    column1 int,                        --bitmask value 2
    column2 int,                        --bitmask value 4
    column3 int                         --bitmask value 8
)
```

We can then define the following trigger and attach it to the table:

```
CREATE TRIGGER testIt
ON columnUpdatedTest
AFTER INSERT,UPDATE
AS
IF update(columnUpdatedTestId)
BEGIN
    SELECT 'columnUpdatedTestId modified'
END
IF update(column1)
BEGIN
```

```
    SELECT 'column1 modified'
END
IF update(column2)
BEGIN
    SELECT 'column2 modified'
END
IF update(column3)
BEGIN
    SELECT 'column3 modified'
END
GO
```

Now when we create a new record:

```
INSERT columnUpdatedTest(column1,column2, column3)
VALUES (1,1,1)
```

The following rows are returned:

```
----------------------------
columnUpdatedTestId modified

----------------
column1 modified

----------------
column2 modified

----------------
column3 modified
```

If we update a single column:

```
UPDATE columnUpdatedTest
SET column2 = 2
WHERE columnUpdatedTestId = 1
```

the same trigger now informs us:

```
----------------
column2 modified
```

The other method is worth a mention, but is not really all that practical. It is the columns_updated() function. By executing the columns_updated() function, we get back a hexadecimal integer with a bitmask of the columns in the table. For instance, in the table that we created, we have the following columns:

```
columnUpdatedTestId --bitmask value 1
column1             --bitmask value 2
column2             --bitmask value 4
column3             --bitmask value 8
```

The bitmask for every column in the table would be $1 + 2 + 4 + 8 = 15$.

So in the above trigger, we can use `columns_updated()` in place of `updated()` in order to get a bitmask of the columns that have been updated. For instance, if we insert all columns in an INSERT statement:

```
INSERT columnUpdatedTest (column1,column2, column3)
VALUES (1,1,1)
```

If we execute the `columns_updated()` function in an insert trigger, we get the following bitmask back:

0x0F

which is equal to 15, or the bitmask for the entire table as we displayed earlier. If we use the following code:

```
UPDATE columnUpdatedTest
SET column2 = 2
WHERE columnUpdatedTestId = 1
```

we then get the bitmask for this single column that we have changed, and not the one in the where clause.

0x04

So we can test to see which columns have been updated by using bitwise operations, by using code such as:

```
If columns_updated() & 4 = 4    -- the third column in the table has been
                                -- modified

If columns_updated() & 15 = 15  -- the first four columns have been changed.
```

So what is wrong with using the `columns_updated()` function? The code that is written using this function must change if our column order changes. This makes our code unpredictable as we have to check the trigger code if we add a column to any position in the table other than the end. The `update()` function is by far the most preferable way of checking modified columns. The `columns_updated()` function is shown here for completeness.

Writing Multi-row Validations

Since triggers fire once for a multi-row operation, statements within triggers have to be coded with multiple rows in mind. It is fairly easy to write triggers that only seek to correct a single row; however, every piece of code you write will typically need to look for rows that do not meet your criteria, instead of those that do. Unless you want to force users into entering one row at a time, you have to code your triggers in a way that recognizes that more than one row in the table is being modified. In the next example, we have built a trigger with two very similar validations, and whilst both work for single rows, only one will catch multi-row failures.

```
CREATE TRIGGER artist$afterUpdate$demoMultiRow
ON artist
AFTER INSERT, UPDATE --fires after the insert and update has occurred
AS
IF NOT EXISTS ( SELECT *
   FROM INSERTED
   WHERE name IN ('the who','the beatles','jethro tull')
   )
   BEGIN
      SELECT 'Invalid artist validation 1'
   END
```

Ensuring Data Integrity

```
    IF EXISTS ( SELECT *
        FROM INSERTED
        WHERE name NOT IN ('the who','the beatles','jethro tull')
        )
    BEGIN
        SELECT 'Invalid artist validation 2'
    END
GO
```

So we have written our trigger, and we want to test it. Since we are going to write a query that will work, we surround our INSERTs with BEGIN TRANSACTION and ROLLBACK TRANSACTION statements, in order to allow us to test the statement whilst preventing any of our data modifications from actually being saved to the table. The trigger we have written is for demonstration only, and in the sections written on the AFTER and INSTEAD OF triggers, we will look at possible ways to actually return errors from triggers.

```
BEGIN TRANSACTION
    INSERT INTO artist (name, defaultFl, catalogNumberMask)
    VALUES ('ROLLING STONES',0,' per cent')

    ROLLBACK TRANSACTION --undo our test rows
```

Here it returns the following:

```
--------------------------
Invalid artist validation 1

--------------------------
Invalid artist validation 2
```

because in both of our validations:

```
IF NOT EXISTS ( SELECT *
    FROM INSERTED
    WHERE name IN ('the who','the beatles','jethro tull'))
```

And:

```
IF EXISTS ( SELECT *
    FROM INSERTED
    WHERE name NOT IN ('the who','the beatles','jethro tull'))
```

'ROLLING STONES' does not fall within the boundaries. In the first, the name is not in the group, so no set of rows exists, which passes the NOT EXISTS test. In the second, the name is not in the group, so all rows are returned by the query, and a row does exist. Next we try a multi-row test.

The best way to do a multi-row test is to use a UNION:

```
SELECT 'ROLLING STONES',0,' per cent'
UNION
SELECT 'JETHRO TULL',0,' per cent'
```

365

which returns:

```
--------------  ---------- ---- ----
JETHRO TULL           0  per cent
ROLLING STONES        0  per cent
```

By carrying out such unions, in this case one valid and another invalid, we can test the multi-row capabilities of our triggers:

```
BEGIN TRANSACTION

INSERT INTO artist (name, defaultFl, catalogNumberMask)
SELECT 'ROLLING STONES',0,' per cent'
UNION
SELECT 'JETHRO TULL',0,' per cent'

ROLLBACK TRANSACTION --undo our test rows
```

This time only one of our validations fail:

```
-----------------------------
Invalid artist – validation 2
```

We have to look at why this has happened. In the following validation, the trigger will not send us a message:

```
IF NOT EXISTS ( select *
    FROM INSERTED
    WHERE name IN ('the who','the beatles','jethro tull'))
```

Since we have one row that meets the criteria (the one with the `jethro tull` entry) we have one row where `INSERTED.name` is in our test group. So a single row *is* returned, and a row does exist. This is a pretty common problem when writing triggers. Even after ten years of trigger writing, I must test my triggers to make sure I have not fallen into this trap. It is of course best to test each of your snippets of code like this to make sure that it can handle what ever data is thrown at it.

Note also that we will drop the `artist$afterUpdate$demoMultiRow` trigger from our database as it is no longer needed:

```
Drop trigger artist$afterUpdate$demoMultiRow
```

Having Multiple Triggers for the Same Action

One cool SQL Server 2000 feature is the ability to have multiple AFTER triggers to take care of different data validation operations. This allows us to build triggers that are very specific in nature, as in the following options:

- **Nested Trigger option** – a server global setting accessed via:

    ```
    sp_configure 'nested triggers', 1 | 0 - where 1 = ON, 0 = OFF
    ```

    If a cascading operation is carried out, then the triggers on all the participating tables are fired. There is a limit of 32 nested trigger operations. Note that we are able to build infinite loop triggers which will cascade the operation to one table, and if any modifies the initial table, then it will start the process over again. Nested triggers are set at the server level.

Ensuring Data Integrity

- **Recursive Trigger option** – a database-specific setting accessed via:

  ```
  sp_dboption '<dbName>','recursive triggers', 'TRUE' | 'FALSE'
  ```

  This causes triggers to be re-fired when the trigger executes modifications on the same table as it is attached to. This requires that the nested trigger option is set and is set at the database level.

In this example we will demonstrate how the nested and recursive trigger settings work. First, we create two very simple tables into which we can insert a single value:

```
CREATE TABLE tableA
(
    field varchar(40) NOT NULL
)
CREATE TABLE tableB
(
    field varchar(40) not NULL
)
GO
```

and then two very simple triggers each inserting the same values into the other table:

```
CREATE TRIGGER tableA$afterUpdate$demoNestRecurse
ON tableA
AFTER INSERT
AS

--tell the user that the trigger has fired
SELECT 'table a insert trigger'

--insert the values into tableB
INSERT INTO tableB (field)
SELECT field
FROM INSERTED
GO

CREATE TRIGGER tableB$afterUpdate$demoNestRecurse
ON tableB
AFTER INSERT
AS

--tell the user that the trigger has fired
SELECT 'table b insert trigger'

--insert the values into tableB
INSERT INTO tableA (field)
SELECT field
FROM INSERTED
GO
```

Now that we have our set up, we will turn off nested triggers for the server:

```
EXEC sp_configure 'nested triggers', 0 -- (1 = on, 0 = off)
RECONFIGURE       --required for immediate acting server configuration
```

367

Next we insert a row into `tableA`:

```
INSERT INTO tableA (field)
VALUES ('test value')
```

and the only trigger that fires is the `tableA` trigger:

```
---------------------
table a insert trigger
```

If we turn on nested triggers, and make certain that recursive triggers is turned off for our test database:

```
EXEC sp_configure 'nested triggers', 1 -- where 1 = ON, 0 = OFF
RECONFIGURE
EXEC sp_dboption 'bookTest','recursive triggers','FALSE'
```

then we can now execute the same code on `tableA`:

```
INSERT INTO tableA (field)
VALUES ('test value')
```

This time, we get something very different:

```
---------------------
table a insert trigger

---------------------
table b insert trigger

....................
---------------------
table a insert trigger

---------------------
table b insert trigger
```

Server: Msg 217, Level 16, State 1, Procedure tableB$afterUpdate$demoNestRecurse, Line 7
Maximum stored procedure, function or trigger nesting level exceeded (limit 32).

This is pretty much what we would have expected. A recursive trigger situation only occurs when the trigger acts upon the same table that it is set on. To illustrate this, just change the `tableA` trigger so that it inserts a row into `tableA` and not `tableB`:

```
ALTER TRIGGER tableA$afterUpdate$demoNestRecurse
ON tableA
AFTER INSERT
AS

--tell the user that the trigger has fired
SELECT 'table a insert trigger'

--insert the values into tableB
```

```
INSERT INTO tableA (field)
SELECT field
FROM INSERTED
GO
```

When we enter our single row:

```
INSERT INTO tableA (field)
VALUES ('test value')
```

the statement fails and rolls back the transaction. This illustrates that recursive triggers can only be used if you very carefully code the triggers so they cannot run more than 32 times:

----
table a insert trigger

----
table a insert trigger

....

Server: Msg 217, Level 16, State 1, Procedure tableA$afterUpdate$demoNestRecurse, Line 7 Maximum stored procedure, function or trigger nesting level exceeded (limit 32).

Error Handling

There are two ways to implement error handling using a trigger. Either the error handling code is placed in the trigger or it is contained within the client calling code.

Handling Errors within the Trigger

We saw in the section on constraints that we have to check for the error status after every SQL statement that modifies data. Sadly, handling errors in this manner does not help us that much when we get errors from triggers, for two reasons:

- **Executing a rollback transaction in a trigger rolls transaction and halts all execution of proceeding statements** – The crux of this problem is that there is absolutely no way to tell all triggers that the current operation failed and that only the single operation should be rolled back. Say you have several triggers working consecutively and you have nested transactions. If the final transaction fails, then the whole lot are rolled back regardless of the success of the previous transactions. You can't just roll back the failed transaction and continue with the successful ones.

- **If a severe error is detected, the entire transaction automatically rolls back** – The definition of a severe error is quite loose. It does however include constraint errors, so any data modifications we do in a trigger that violates another table's constraints not only fail, but once the trigger has finished, the transaction is rolled back and no further commands are executed.

There are three generic ways in which to handle errors in our triggers, which can be summarized as follows:

- Checking that the values in the table are proper
- Cascading an operation

❑ Calling a stored procedure

Checking that the Values in the Table are Proper

The basic method we will use to check the validity of a condition is as follows:

```
IF EXISTS ( SELECT *
FROM INSERTED
WHERE <condition is true for invalid values>)
BEGIN
--always raise another error to tell the caller where they are
RAISERROR 50000 'Invalid data exists in inserted table'
ROLLBACK TRANSACTION
RETURN   --note the trigger doesn't end until you stop it, as
         --the batch is canceled AFTER the trigger finishes
END
```

Cascading an Operation

In the next piece of code, we show the way to cascade an update of one value to another table:

```
DECLARE @errorHold int,     --used to hold the error after modification
   @msg varchar(8000)       --statement for formatting messages

UPDATE anotherTable
SET <column> = <value>
FROM anotherTable
JOIN INSERTED
ON table.tableId = INSERTED.tableId

SET @errorHold = @@error    --get error value after update

IF @errorHold <> 0          --something went awry
BEGIN
SET @msg = 'Error ' + CAST(@errorHold) + 'occurred cascading update to table'
--always raise another error to tell the caller where they are
RAISERROR 50000 @msg
ROLLBACK TRANSACTION
RETURN     --note the trigger doesn't end until you stop it, as
           --the batch is canceled AFTER the trigger finishes
END
```

Executing a Stored Procedure

The next piece of code demonstrates the method of calling a stored procedure from our trigger:

```
DECLARE @errorHold int,     --used to hold the error after modification
                            --statement holds return value from stored
   @returnValue int,        --procedure for formatting messages
   @msg varchar(8000)

EXEC @retval = <procedureName> <parameters>
SET @errorHold = @@error    --get error value after update

IF @errorHold <> 0 or @retval < 0    --something went awry
```

```
BEGIN
SET @msg = CASE WHEN @errorHold <> 0
THEN 'Error ' + CAST(@errorHold) + 'occurred cascading update to table'
ELSE 'Return value ' + CAST(@retval as varchar(10))
                + ' returned from procedure'
END
--always raise another error to tell the caller where they are
RAISERROR 50000 @msg
ROLLBACK TRANSACTION
RETURN --note the trigger doesn't end until you stop it, as
       --the batch is canceled AFTER the trigger
END
```

As we have seen, the error messages that we get back from constraints are neither very readable nor very meaningful. However, when we build triggers, we write our own error messages that can be made as readable and meaningful as we want. We could go further and put every database predicate into our triggers (including unique constraints) but this would require more coding and would not be that advantageous to us; triggers are inherently slower than constraints and are not the best method of protecting our data except in circumstances when constraints cannot be used.

Handling Errors in the Calling Code

The best part about error handling and triggers is that because the entire sequence of trigger commands is rolled back when an error occurs, there is no need to worry about external error handling other than monitoring the error status when protecting against constraint errors.

AFTER Triggers

As we have previously stated, **AFTER triggers** are so called because they fire after the data is actually in the table. This lets us verify that whatever the statement did to the data in the table doesn't violate our specifications.

> *In previous versions of SQL Server this was the only kind of trigger available, but instead of the keyword AFTER, you used the FOR keyword. In SQL Server 2000, the latter keyword should no longer be used as a trigger type, but it is retained for backward compatibility.*

Let's look at a simple example of an AFTER trigger by considering the status of the INSERTED table and the contents of the database table while the trigger is running:

```
CREATE TRIGGER artist$trInsertDemo ON artist
AFTER INSERT
AS

SELECT 'contents of inserted'
SELECT artistId, name --just PK and name so it fits on a line in the book
FROM INSERTED

SELECT 'contents of artist'
SELECT artistId, name
FROM artist
GO
```

THEN we execute an INSERT, setting the name value:

```
INSERT INTO artist (name)
VALUES ('jethro tull')
```

which returns the following result sets:

```
--------------------
contents of INSERTED

artistId  name
--------- -------------------------------------------------------
27        jethro tull


------------------
contents of artist

artistId  name
--------- -------------------------------------------------------
27        jethro tull
1         the beatles
2         the who
```

So we see that the row in the INSERTED table contains the data for the inserted row (naturally) and we see from the results of the second query that the table already contains the value that we passed in. (If we did this with an INSTEAD OF trigger, the second query wouldn't return us the new record.)

Implementing Multiple AFTER Triggers

Let's now extend our multiple trigger example from above, by altering the coding of the tableA$afterUpdate$demoNestRecurse trigger, so as to insert the name of the procedure into tableB.field enabling us to see the different triggers that are firing:

```
ALTER TRIGGER tableA$afterUpdate$demoNestRecurse
ON tableA
AFTER INSERT
AS
SELECT 'table a insert trigger'

INSERT INTO tableB (field)
VALUES (object_name(@@procid))    --@@procid gives the object_id of the
                                  --of the current executing procedure
GO
```

Then we create two more triggers which are identical to the first (though with different names):

```
CREATE TRIGGER tableA$afterUpdate$demoNestRecurse2
ON tableA
AFTER INSERT
AS
```

```
    SELECT 'table a insert trigger2'

    INSERT INTO tableB (field)
    VALUES (object_name(@@procid))
    GO

    CREATE TRIGGER tableA$afterUpdate$demoNestRecurse3
    ON tableA
    AFTER INSERT
    AS
    SELECT 'table a insert trigger3'

    INSERT INTO tableB (field)
    VALUES (object_name(@@procid))
    GO
```

Next, we clear out the tables:

```
    --truncate table deletes the rows in the table very fast with a single log
    --entry, plus it resets the identity values
    TRUNCATE TABLE tableA
    TRUNCATE TABLE tableB
```

and we insert a single row:

```
    INSERT INTO tableA
    VALUES ('Test Value')
```

which returns the following three rows:

```
----------------------
table a insert trigger

----------------------
table a insert trigger2

----------------------
table a insert trigger3
```

To show that the tables are as we expect, we execute select statements from the tables:

```
    SELECT * FROM tableA
    SELECT * FROM tableB
```

and we then see that `tableA` has the single row we expected and `tableB` has a row resulting from each of the three `tableA` triggers that were executed:

```
field
--------------------
Test Value
```

```
field
----------------------------------------
tableA$afterUpdate$demoNestRecurse
tableA$afterUpdate$demoNestRecurse2
tableA$afterUpdate$demoNestRecurse3
```

Finally, we want to show how you can reorder the execution order of the triggers:

```
EXEC sp_settriggerorder
            @triggerName = 'tableA$afterUpdate$demoNestRecurse3',
            @order = 'first',
            @stmttype = 'insert'
```

Note `@order` may be 'first', 'last', or 'none' to fire in an unspecific location. We can only set the first and last trigger to fire, whilst any other triggers fire in a random (as far as we are concerned) order. The `@stmttype` value may be 'insert', 'update' or 'delete'.

We can now execute the commands to truncate the table, insert a row, and finally select the rows from the table:

```
TRUNCATE TABLE tableA
TRUNCATE TABLE tableB

INSERT INTO tableA
VALUES ('Test Value')

SELECT * FROM tableA
SELECT * FROM tableB
```

and in this case we return a different order of triggers:

```
field
-------------------
Test Value

field
----------------------------------------
tableA$afterUpdate$demoNestRecurse3
tableA$afterUpdate$demoNestRecurse
tableA$afterUpdate$demoNestRecurse2
```

As a final note in this section I would urge caution in having multiple triggers for the same action on the same table. It is often simpler to build a single trigger that handles all of your trigger needs. We normally design our systems to use one INSTEAD OF trigger and one AFTER trigger for each operation when necessary. We will also seldom use a multi-purpose trigger that will fire on insert and update. Basically our principle is to keep it as simple as possible to avoid any ordering issues.

Using AFTER Triggers to Solve Common Problems

In this section we will look at how you use triggers to solve typical problems, such as:

- Cascading inserts
- Range checks

Ensuring Data Integrity

❑ Cascading deletes setting the values of child tables to NULL

It is important to consider that whatever we are doing with triggers depends on pre-existing data in our table passing all constraint requirements. For instance, it would not be proper to insert rows in a child table (thereby causing its entire trigger/constraint chain to fire) when the parent's data has not been validated. Equally we would not want to check the status of all the rows in our table until we have completed all of our changes to them; the same could be said for cascading delete operations. The three examples that follow are but a small subset of all the possible uses for triggers; they are just a sample to get things rolling. Each of the snippets we will present in the next three subsections will fit into a trigger (of any type) which will be of the following basic format:

```
CREATE TRIGGER <triggerName>
ON <tableName>
FOR <action> AS
------------------------------------------------------------------
-- Purpose : Trigger on the <action> that fires for any <action> DML
------------------------------------------------------------------
BEGIN
    DECLARE @rowsAffected int,      --stores the number of rows affected
        @errNumber int,             --used to hold the error number after DML
        @msg varchar(255),          --used to hold the error message
        @errSeverity varchar(20),
        @triggerName sysname,

    SET @rowsAffected = @@rowcount
    SET @triggerName = object_name(@@procid)        --used for messages

    --no need to continue on if no rows affected
    IF @rowsAffected = 0 return

    <insert snippets here >

END
```

We will generally write our triggers so that when an error occurs, we raise an error, and roll back the transaction to halt any further commands.

Cascading Inserts

By cascading inserts, we refer to the situation, where after a record is inserted into a table, then one or more other new records are automatically inserted into other tables. This is especially important when we are creating mandatory one-to-one or one-to-many relationships. For example, say we have the following set of tables:

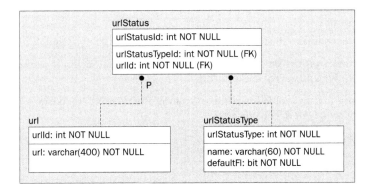

In this case the `url` table defines a set of URLs for our system, whilst the relationship between `url` and `urlStatus` is a one-to-many. We begin by building a trigger that inserts a row into the `urlStatus` table on an insert that creates a new record with the `urlId` and the default `urlStatusType` based on `defaultFl` having the value of 1. (We will assume for now that there is a maximum of one row with a `defaultFl` equal to 1, and will implement a check to make sure this is so.)

```
--add a record to the urlStatus table to tell it that the new record
--should start out as the default status
INSERT INTO urlType (urlId, urlTypeId)
SELECT INSERTED.urlId, urlType.urlTypeId
FROM INSERTED
    CROSS JOIN urlType      --use cross join with a where clause
                            --as this is not technically a join between
                            --INSERTED and urlType
WHERE urlType.defaultFl = 1

SET @errorNumber = @@error
IF @errorNumber <> 0
BEGIN
    SET @msg = 'Error: ' + CAST(@errorNumber as varchar(10)) +
                      ' occurred during the creation of urlStatus'
    RAISERROR 50000 @msg
    ROLLBACK TRANSACTION
    RETURN
END
```

A trigger might also be needed to disallow the deleting of the default urlType, since we would always want to have a default urlStatus value. However, creation of this trigger will leave a situation where we want to:

❑ Delete a `url`, but we cannot because of `urlTypes` that exist.

❑ Delete the `urlTypes`, but we cannot since it is the last one for a `url`.

This is a difficult situation to handle using conventional triggers and constraints, and may well be easier to solve by adding a field to the table informing the triggers (or constraints) that the record is available for deletion. This is a general problem in the case of tables where you want to implement a two-way relationship, but also want to enforce a one-way relationship under certain circumstances.

Range Checks

A range check means simply ensuring that a given range of data conforms to the data validation rules. Some examples are:

❑ Balancing accounts to make sure that there isn't a negative balance left by the transaction.

❑ Ensuring that a proper number of records exist for a relationship (cardinality), such as a "one-to-between-five-and-seven" relationship.

❑ Making sure that in a table (or group of rows in the table) there exists only a single record that is the primary or the default record.

Ensuring Data Integrity

In our example, we make sure that there is no more than a single default flag set to true or 1 in the table; the others must be 0 or false. We will also throw in, for good measure, code that will take any new value where the defaultFl field is 1 and set all of the others to 0. If the user manually sets more than one defaultFl field to 1, then a check is made afterwards to cause the operation to fail.

We will use as our example table the urlStatusType table we built earlier:

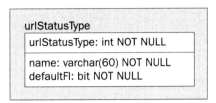

and we'll implement out range checking criteria as follows:

```
--if the defaultFl column was modified
IF UPDATE(defaultFl)
BEGIN
   --update any other rows in the status type table to not default if
   --a row was inserted that was set to default
   UPDATE urlStatusType
   SET defaultFl = 0
   FROM urlStatusType
         --only rows that were already default
   WHERE urlStatusType.defaultFl = 1
         --and not in the inserted rows
     AND urlStatusTypeid NOT IN
     ( SELECT urlStatusTypeId
       FROM inserted
       WHERE defaultFl = 1
     )

   SET @errorNumber = @@error
   IF @errorNumber <> 0
   BEGIN
      SET @msg = 'Error: ' + CAST(@errorNumber as varchar(10)) +
                 ' occurred during the modification of defaultFl'
      RAISERROR 50000 @msg
      ROLLBACK TRANSACTION
      RETURN
   END

   --see if there is more than 1 row set to default
   --like if the user updated more than one in a single operation
   IF ( SELECT count(*)
        FROM urlStatusType
        WHERE urlStatusType.defaultFl = 1 ) > 1
   BEGIN
      SET @msg = 'Too many rows with default flag = 1'
      RAISERROR 50000 @msg
      ROLLBACK TRANSACTION
      RETURN
   END
END
```

Cascading Deletes Setting the Values of Child Tables to NULL

When we have tables with optional alternate keys, instead of cascading on a parent delete, we may sometimes wish to remove the link and set any foreign key references to NULL. To do this in a DELETE trigger, we simply update every row in the child table that refers to the value in the row(s) we are deleting. Take the following relationship for example:

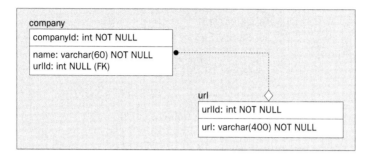

The url table contains all of the internet addresses for our system, and the company uses one of the values for a company URL. If we want to delete one or more of the url table's records, we do not want to delete all the companies that use the URL. So we might implement this by setting the child rows to NULL instead of deleting the rows themselves. Since SQL Server only implements a cascading delete where the child row is deleted, we will have to use a trigger. The trigger code that does this is:

```
UPDATE company
SET urlId = NULL
FROM DELETED
    JOIN company
    ON DELETED.urlId = company.urlId

SET @errorNumber = @@error
IF @errorNumber <> 0
BEGIN
    SET @msg = 'Error: ' + CAST(@errorNumber as varchar(10)) +
                        ' occurred during delete cascade set NULL'
    RAISERROR 50000 @msg
    ROLLBACK TRANSACTION
    RETURN
END
```

INSTEAD OF Triggers

INSTEAD OF triggers only fire in place of data manipulation operations, and before check constraints have been validated. You may only have a single INSTEAD OF trigger for each operation on each table. Note that while this trigger will be typically referred to as a "before trigger", it is more than that. When coding an INSTEAD OF trigger, we have to redo the operation in the trigger. For example, in the case of an INSTEAD OF DELETE trigger, the trigger contains a delete just like the operation which caused the trigger to fire in the first place.

The following example shows a trigger that will return the state of the INSERTED table and then the physical table.

Ensuring Data Integrity

```
CREATE TRIGGER artist$insteadOfInsert ON artist
INSTEAD OF INSERT
AS
--output the contents of the inserted table
SELECT 'contents of inserted'
SELECT * FROM inserted

--output the contents of the physical table
SELECT 'contents of artist'
SELECT * FROM artist
GO
```

Next, we execute an insert against the table:

```
INSERT INTO artist (name)
VALUES ('John Tesh')
```

and we get the following results:

```
--------------------
contents of inserted

artistId  name ...
--------- ----------------------------------------------------------- ----
0         John Tesh ...


------------------
contents of artist

artistId  name ...
--------- ----------------------------------------------------------- ----
1         THE BEATLES ...
2         THE WHO ...
```

This is exactly as we would expect; the trigger fired before the columns were in the table, which explains why John Tesh's record doesn't appeared in the second result set. However, if we look at the contents of the table now that the trigger has executed:

```
SELECT artistId, name
FROM artist
```

We get back:

```
artistId       name ...
---------      ----------------------------
1              THE BEATLES ...
2              THE WHO ...
```

This illustrates one difficulty with INSTEAD OF triggers, namely that any insertions are added to the INSERTED or DELETED table and not the database. This means that we have to manually insert the data into the table to make the trigger work properly. Therefore, INSTEAD OF triggers force us to completely reinvent the way we code data manipulation operations in order to make the most of them.

379

In the rest of this section we will look at some other problems with INSTEAD OF triggers, followed by a couple of very important uses that make them a very desirable addition to the SQL Server toolkit.

Caveats

The problems associated with INSTEAD OF triggers are as follows:

- You have to repeat the operation that the user has performed.
- It is not easy to do range checks on multiple rows.
- Cascading operations ignore instead-of triggers.

We will look at each of the difficulties in a bit more depth in the following sections:

You Have to Repeat the Operation that the User has Performed

In the following trigger, we show a simple demonstration of this:

```
CREATE TRIGGER artist$insteadOfInsert on artist
INSTEAD OF INSERT
AS

-- must mimic the operation we are doing "instead of".
-- note that must supply a column list for the insert
-- and we cannot simply do a SELECT * FROM INSERTED because of the
-- identity column, which complains when you try to pass it a value
INSERT INTO artist(name, defaultFl, catalogNumberMask)
SELECT name, defaultFl, catalogNumberMask
FROM INSERTED
GO

CREATE TRIGGER artist$insteadOfDelete on artist
INSTEAD OF DELETE
AS

-- must mimic the operation we are doing "instead of"
DELETE FROM artist
FROM DELETED
    -- we always join the inserted and deleted tables
    -- to the real table via the primary key,
    JOIN ARTIST
    ON DELETED.artistId = artist.artistId

go
```

Once we have created the triggers to operate instead of INSERT and DELETE, we test them:

```
INSERT INTO artist(name, defaultFl, catalogNumberMask)
VALUES ('raffi',0,' per cent')

SELECT * FROM artist WHERE name = 'raffi'
```

which returns:

Ensuring Data Integrity

```
artistId        name ...
----------      ----------------
14              raffi ...
```

Then we delete the row and execute a select to see if it exists:

```
DELETE FROM artist
WHERE name = 'raffi'

SELECT * FROM artist WHERE name = 'raffi'
```

which produces no output as the delete has done its job.

Not Easy to do Range Checks on Multiple Rows

In AFTER triggers, since the data has already been added to the table, it is easy to check to see if multi-row constraints were being met. However, INSTEAD OF trigger data has not yet made it to the database. In the next two samples of code, we will look at the two different methods required to validate that a table has only non-negative balances for an amount field, in an accountTransaction table, where balances are grouped by accountId.

AFTER Trigger for Comparison

```
IF EXISTS ( SELECT accountId
    FROM accountTransaction
    JOIN (SELECT distinct accounted FROM INSERTED) AS accounts
        ON accountTransaction.accountId = accounts.accountId
        GROUP BY accountId
        HAVING sum(amount) > 0)
BEGIN
    RAISERROR 50000 'Negative balances exist as due to operation'
END
```

INSTEAD OF Trigger

```
IF EXISTS( SELECT accountId
    FROM        --union inserted values with the transactions for
                --any accounts that are affected by the operation
      ( SELECT accountTransactionId, accountId, amount
        FROM INSERTED
    UNION
    SELECT accountTransactionId, accountId, amount
    FROM accountTransaction
    JOIN (SELECT distinct accounted FROM INSERTED) AS accounts
        ON accountTransaction.accountId = accounts.accountId
        --remove any accountTransactionRecords that we are
        --updating, by removing the rows that are now "deleted"
        WHERE accountTransactionId NOT IN (
            SELECT accountTransactionId FROM DELETED )
    ) as accountValues
        GROUP BY accountId
        HAVING sum(amount) > 0 )
BEGIN
    RAISERROR 50000 'Negative balances exist as due to operation'
END
```

In the AFTER trigger, all that was required was to check the current state of the table, while in the INSTEAD OF trigger, we had to add the values from the INSERTED table to the values in the actual table. One interesting thing to note is that is was not just a simple query of the INSERTED table. We always have to consider all of the rows in the current table that relate to the rows in the INSERTED table, which requires a complex JOIN.

Cascading Operations Ignore INSTEAD OF Triggers

One of the more troubling problems with INSTEAD OF triggers is that cascading operations ignore them, and so using INSTEAD OF triggers in enforcing business rules can prove problematic. For example, if in a given table the primary key changes to a value that would fail the checks in the INSTEAD OF trigger, the change will not be prevented, since the trigger will not fire. These limitations mean that INSTEAD OF triggers should not be used to enforce update business rules which involve the primary key, nor any business rules that involve deletes. This will not prevent us from using them for other purposes, which is what we shall turn to now.

Uses of INSTEAD OF Triggers

INSTEAD OF triggers can be used to automatically set or modify values in our statements. Knowing that INSTEAD OF triggers fire prior to both constraints and after triggers, they can be used to modify data *en route* to the table. We will consider three examples of how they can be used:

Automatically Maintaining Fields

As an example, we are going to build two triggers, an INSTEAD OF INSERT trigger and an INSTEAD OF UPDATE trigger, which will automatically set the first letter of the names of our artists to upper case, instead of the current all lower case format:

```
CREATE TRIGGER artist$insteadOfInsert ON artist
INSTEAD OF INSERT
AS
INSERT INTO artist(name, defaultFl, catalogNumberMask)
SELECT dbo.string$properCase(name), defaultfl, catalogNumberMask
FROM INSERTED
GO

CREATE TRIGGER artist$insteadOfUpdate on artist
INSTEAD OF UPDATE
AS
UPDATE artist
SET name = string$properCase(INSERTED.name),
    defaultFl = INSERTED.defaultFl,
    catalogNumberMask = INSERTED.catalogNumberMask
FROM artist
JOIN INSERTED ON artist.artistId = INSERTED.artistId
GO
```

To test our INSERT trigger, we execute the following:

```
-- insert fairly obviously improperly formatted name
INSERT INTO artist (name, defaultFl, catalogNumberMask)
VALUES ('eLvIs CoStElLo',0,'77_____')
```

```
-- then retrieve the last inserted value into this table
SELECT artistId, name
FROM artist
WHERE artistId = ident_current('artist')
```

which returns the required response:

artistId	name
19	Elvis Costello

Next we will test the UPDATE trigger. First, we check all of the values in the table as they stand right now:

```
SELECT artistId, name
FROM artist
```

This returns a list of untidily formatted rows:

artistId	name
19	Elvis Costello
1	THE BEATLES
15	The Monkees
2	THE WHO

Then we run the following query which looks as if it will set the names to all upper case:

```
UPDATE artist
SET name = UPPER(name)
```

However, we see that all of the rows are not in upper case, though they are now formatted in a tidier manner.

artistId	name
19	Elvis Costello
1	The Beatles
15	The Monkees
2	The Who

INSTEAD OF triggers are the best place to do this sort of data manipulation, since it saves us from inserting bad data, then having to take an additional step in an AFTER trigger to update it. Any time you need to extend the way that an INSERT, UPDATE, or DELETE operation is implemented in a generic way, INSTEAD OF triggers are great.

Conditional Insert

During our demonstration of error handling, a batch insert was created which added albums to a table based on the catalogNumber, while not matching the mask we had set up for an artist. Here, we will build a more streamlined example, where the table (or tables) in such a system will accept any data from the user, whilst placing any invalid data in an exception-handling table, so someone can later fix any problems. First we will have to drop the original constraint:

Chapter 11

```
ALTER TABLE album
DROP CONSTRAINT chkAlbum$catalogNumber$function$artist$catalogNumberValidate
```

At this point we are unprotected from any invalid values inserted into the `catalogNumber` field. However, we will build an `INSTEAD OF` trigger that will take all valid rows and insert (or update) them in the `album` table. If they are invalid, we will insert them in a new table that we will create called `albumException`, which will have the same structure as the `album` table, with a different primary key value and a new field called `operation` (for insert or update).

```
CREATE TABLE albumException
(
    albumExceptionId int NOT NULL IDENTITY,
    name varchar(60) NOT NULL,
    artistId int NOT NULL,
    catalogNumber char(12) NOT NULL,
    exceptionAction char(1),
    exceptionDate datetime
)
```

Now we create a simple `INSTEAD OF` trigger to intercept the user's data and attempt to validate the catalog number. If the data is valid, we update the table, otherwise it will be added to the exception table.

```
CREATE TRIGGER album$insteadOfUpdate
ON album
INSTEAD OF UPDATE
AS

DECLARE @errorValue int -- this is the variable for capturing error status

UPDATE album
SET name = INSERTED.name, artistId = INSERTED.artistId,
        catalogNumber = INSERTED.catalogNumber
FROM inserted
JOIN album
    ON INSERTED.albumId = album.albumId
    -- only update rows where the criteria is met
    WHERE = dbo.album$catalogNumbervalidate(INSERTED.catalogNumber,
        INSERTED.artistId) = 1

-- check to make certain that an error did not occur in this statement
SET @errorValue = @@error
IF @errorValue <> 0
BEGIN
    RAISERROR 50000 'Error inserting valid album records'
    ROLLBACK TRANSACTION
    RETURN
END

-- get all of the rows where the criteria is not met
INSERT INTO albumException (name, artistId, catalogNumber, exceptionAction,
                            exceptionDate)
SELECT name, artistId, catalogNumber, 'U',getdate()
FROM INSERTED
WHERE NOT(      -- generally the easiest way to do this is to copy
```

Ensuring Data Integrity

```
            -- the criteria and do a not(where ...)
            dbo.album$catalogNumbervalidate(INSERTED.catalogNumber,
            INSERTED.artistId) = 1 )

SET @errorValue = @@error
IF @errorValue <> 0
BEGIN
    RAISERROR 50000 'Error logging exception album records'
    ROLLBACK TRANSACTION
    RETURN
END
GO
```

Now, updating a row to a proper value can simply happen with the following statements:

```
-- update the album table with a known good match to the catalog number
UPDATE album
SET catalogNumber = '222-22222-22'
WHERE name = 'the white album'

-- then list the artistId and catalogNumber of the album in the "real" table
SELECT artistId, catalogNumber
FROM album
WHERE name = 'the white album'

-- as well as the exception table
SELECT artistId, catalogNumber, exceptionAction, exceptionDate
FROM albumException
WHERE name = 'the white album'
```

The catalog number matches what we have updated it to and there are no exceptions in the `albumException` table:

ArtistId	catalogNumber
1	222-22222-22

artistId	catalogNumber	exceptionAction	exceptionDate

Then we do an obviously invalid update:

```
UPDATE album
SET catalogNumber = '1'
WHERE name = 'the white album'

-- then list the artistId and catalogNumber of the album in the "real" table
SELECT artistId, catalogNumber
FROM album
WHERE name = 'the white album'

-- as well as the exception table
SELECT artistId, catalogNumber, exceptionAction, exceptionDate
FROM albumException
WHERE name = 'the white album'
```

385

We see that we have not updated the row – no error was returned, but we have now added a row to our exception table alerting us to the error:

artistId	catalogNumber
1	222-22222-22

artistId	catalogNumber	exceptionAction	exceptionDate
1	1	U	2001-01-07 01:02:59.363

It is left to the reader to create the INSTEAD OF INSERT trigger to accompany the UPDATE case. We would also probably want to extend the exception table to include some sort of reason for the failure if we had more than one possibility.

Views

In general, doing inserts, updates, and deletes on views has always had its drawbacks, because the following criteria must be met to execute a modification statement against a view:

- ❏ UPDATE and INSERT statements may only modify a view if they only reference the columns of one table at a time.
- ❏ DELETE statements can only be used if the view only references a single table.

However, by using INSTEAD OF triggers, we can implement the INSERT, UPDATE and DELETE mechanisms on views. In this example, we will create an extremely simple view and an insert trigger to allow inserts:

```
-- create view, excluding the defaultFl column, which we don't want to let
-- users see in this view, and we want to view the names in upper case.
CREATE VIEW vArtistExcludeDefault
AS
SELECT artistId, UPPER(name) AS name, catalogNumberMask
FROM artist
GO


-- then we create a very simple INSTEAD OF insert trigger

CREATE TRIGGER vArtistExcludeDefault$insteadOfInsert
ON vArtistExcludeDefault
INSTEAD OF INSERT
AS
BEGIN
   --note that we don't use the artistId from the INSERTED table
   INSERT INTO artist (name, catalogNumberMask, defaultFl)
   SELECT NAME, catalogNumberMask, 0 --only can set defaultFl to 0
                                    --using the view
   FROM INSERTED
END
GO
```

Then we simply insert using the view just as we would the table (excluding the identity column which we cannot set a value for):

Ensuring Data Integrity

```
INSERT INTO vArtistExcludeDefault (name, catalogNumberMask)
VALUES ('The Monkees','44_____')
```

However, the view has other ideas:

Server: Msg 233, Level 16, State 2, Line 1
The column 'artistId' in table 'vArtistExcludeDefault' cannot be NULL.

This is not what we expected or wanted. So we have to reformulate our insert to include the `artistId` and an invalid value. Now the insert works just fine:

```
INSERT INTO vArtistExcludeDefault (artistId, name, catalogNumberMask)
VALUES (-1, 'The Monkees','44_____')

SELECT * FROM vArtistExcludeDefault
WHERE artistId = ident_current('vArtistExcludeDefault')
```

which gives us back the value that we hoped it would:

artistId	name	defaultFl	catalogNumberMask
15	THE MONKEES	0	44_____

It should be noted that if we had two or more tables in the view, and we execute an insert on the view, we could insert data into *all* of the tables that make up the view. This neatly sidesteps the requirement that `INSERT` and `UPDATE` statements on views can touch only single tables at a time, which is very cumbersome. (Further details on views can be found in the next chapter.)

Client Code and Stored Procedures

For quite a while, there has been a programmatic drive to move much of the business rule implementation and data protection code out of SQL Server and into a middle-tier set of interface objects. In this way the database, client and business rules exist in three independently implementable units. Thus business rules that we may well have thought about implementing via constraints and triggers get moved out of this "data" layer, and into client-based code, such as a COM object and stored procedures.

Such a multi-tier design also attempts to make the life of the user easier, since users edit data using custom front-end tools, whilst the middle-tier services maintain and protect data that passes through them thereby insulating the users from all the required SQL code. Not only that, but these services can also directly handle any errors that occur and present the user with meaningful error messages. Since application users primarily edit rows one at a time, rather than a large number of rows, this actually works really great.

The other point is that, in most enterprise applications (for instance situations with hundreds of thousands of users on a web site), the database is usually considered as the "system bottleneck". Whilst it is possible to distribute the load on a single server, in many cases it can be much easier to spread the load across many application servers, as we touched on in Chapter 9.

However, almost any data protection mechanism that is enforced without the use of constraints or triggers may prove problematic. Let's consider our list of possible users that we introduced at the very beginning of the chapter, namely:

- **Users using custom front end tools**
  When users all use the custom front-end tools that are developed for the interface, there is no problem with employing the middle tier. In fact, it can have some great benefits, since as we have discussed, the object methods used to enforce the rules can be tuned for maximum performance.

- **Users using generic data tools such as Microsoft Access**
  Let's consider a case where a user needs to modify a set of "live" data, but only needs it for a week, or a weekend, and there is no time to write a full-blown application. We will not be able to let them directly access the data, as it is in a raw unprotected state. Hence, we will either have to code a relevant business rule into the Access database, or deny the user and make them wait until an application is created. This type of thing is relatively rare, and we can usually stop this kind of activity with strict policies against such access.

- **Data import routines that acquire data from external sources**
  Almost every system of any magnitude will include some import facilities to take data in a raw format from external systems, maybe from another part of your company or another company altogether, and place this data in a table on the database server. This can be in as simple a form as a user application to import a spreadsheet, or as complex as an interface between all of the schools in a state and the respective state department of education. The tools will range from user applications, DTS, or even BCP (Bulk copy program that comes with SQL Server). When the middle tier owns all of the business rules and data integrity checks, we will either have to go in through the middle tier (frequently one at a time) or extract all of the business rules and code them into our import routines.

- **Raw queries executed by data administrators to fix problems caused by user error**
  Almost anybody with administration experience has had to remove a few rows from a database that users have erroneously created but cannot remove, and in so doing have mistakenly deleted the wrong records, say active account records rather than inactive ones. In this situation, if we had business rules built into a trigger that allowed the deletion of inactive accounts only, an error message would have been returned to the user warning that active accounts could not be deleted. Obviously we cannot protect against a really bad action, such as systematically deleting every row in a table, but when a fully featured database is implemented and the data protected using constraints and triggers, it is next to impossible to make even small mistakes in data integrity.

As the data architect, I very much desire the possibilities offered by multi-tier development. However, the load of business rule and data integrity rule implementation should be "shared" between the middle tier and database server as appropriate. Two very specific types of such rules that are far better implemented in the database are as follows:

- **Any rule that can be placed in a NULL, foreign key or check constraint** – This is due to the fact that, when building additional external interfaces, this kind of check will generally make up quite a bit of the coding effort. Furthermore, base data integrity should be guaranteed at the lowest level possible, which will allow as many programs as possible to code to the database. As a final point, these constraints will be used by the optimizer to make queries run faster.

- **Rules that require inter-table validations** – This is the case where when we save a value, we must check to see if a value exists in a different table. The additional table will have to be accessed automatically to make certain that the state that was expected still exists. In some cases the middle-tier will try to cache the data on the database to use in validation, but there is no way to spread this cached data to multiple servers in a manner which ensures that the value we are entering has proper data integrity.

Having considered some of the possible drawbacks to middle-tier coding, let's now look at cases where a stored procedure or user code is the optimal place to locate the business rules.

Mutable Rules

These are rules that for a given set of criteria, on one occasion when they are met, the rule evaluates to true and an action is carried out, whereas on another occasion, the rule evaluates to false and a different action is carried out. The best litmus test for such a rule is to see whether the user is able to bypass it. For instance, in our chapter example, we could attempt to implement the rule: "The user should enter a valid artist for the album."

As a reminder, we have the album table that contains a not NULL foreign key relationship to the artist table. Hence, we are forced to put in a valid `artistId` when we modify the table. From here we have two courses of action.

- Make the `artistId` in the album table nullable and hence optional, allowing the user to select an album without supplying an `artistId`. To follow the rule "should", the front end would then likely pop up a dialog asking the user, "Are you sure you don't want to assign an artist to this album?"

- Alternatively, we could rephrase the business rule as "the user could enter an invalid artist". This would mean that the database could allow any value from the `artistId` and indeed let the client application handle the validation by checking the value to see if it is correct and then send a dialog stating: "Are you sure you don't want to assign an artist to this album?" or worse still: "You have entered an invalid `artistId`, you should enter a valid one". We would then have to drop the database validations in case the user says, "Nah, let me enter the invalid value."

The point I am trying to make here is that SQL Server cannot converse with the user in an interactive manner. The hard and fast trigger and constraint validations still depend largely on the process of submitting a request and waiting to see if it completes successfully, and we need a more interactive method of communication where we can influence events after the request has been submitted, and before the result comes back.

In the following examples, we will look at situations concerning rules that cannot be realistically implemented via triggers and constraints.

> *Admittedly where there's a will there's a way. It is possible, using temporary tables as messaging mechanisms, to "pass" values to a trigger or constraint. In this manner we can optionally override functionality. However, triggers and constraints are not generally considered suitable places to implement mutable business rules.*

Optionally Cascading Deletes

Cascading deletes are a great resource, but you should use them with care. As we have discussed, they automatically remove child records that are dependent on the content of the deleted parent record, and we would rarely want to warn the user of the existence of these child records before they are deleted. However this would not be ideal in the case of a bank account. Let's say that we have the following tables:

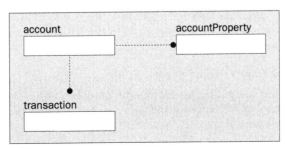

In this case, it will make sense to automatically cascade deletes of an accountProperty record if we want to delete a record from the account table. However, if an account has entries in the transaction table, we need to ensure that the user is aware of these, and so warn them if a cascading delete is requested. This will of course increase complexity, since we will not be able to delete an account, its properties and transactions in a single statement.

Instead of a single statement, we will have to execute the following steps:

- Run a SELECT statement for each child table that we will want to optionally cascade delete to, to show the user what exists.
- If the user accepts, execute a DELETE statement for each child table that had records related to our primary table, and in the same atomic operation, delete the row we are interested in.

This code could be built into a single stored procedure that checks for the children, and if they exist, returns a resultset of rows for the user to see what needs to be deleted. It will also include a parameter to allow the user to ignore the existence of rows and go ahead and delete them. The following is the basics of how we might handle this situation (note that for clarity of example, we have removed transactions and error handling, which will be covered in greater depth in the next chapter).

```
CREATE PROCEDURE account$delete
(
    @accountId int,
    @removeChildTransactionsFl bit = 0
) as

-- if they asked to delete them, just delete them
IF @removeChildTransactionsFl = 1
   DELETE [transaction] --table named with keyword
   WHERE  accountId = @accountId
ELSE --check for existance
  BEGIN
      IF EXISTS (SELECT *
                 FROM   [transaction]
                 WHERE  accountId = @accountId)
        BEGIN
            RAISERROR 50000 'Child transactions exist'
            RETURN -100
        END
  END

DELETE account
WHERE   accountID = @accountId
```

Now the user could try to execute the stored procedure with the flag equal to 0, and if any children existed, the user would get notification. If not, the account would be deleted, and presumably the properties would be removed as well via a cascading relationship.

Rules that are Based Upon How a Person Feels

Sadly for the system architect, this is a reality that must be faced. In a typical system, we will have many business rules that seem pretty obvious as hard and fast rules that cannot be broken. However a large number of mutable rules appear as hard and fast rules. As an example, let's consider the following statement:

It is the company's policy that we do not ship the product out to a customer until we have payment.

This doesn't seem at all problematic until we get a request for a shipment to take place as a goodwill gesture.

As a further example let's consider the following rule:

Products will be shipped out in the same sequence as the orders were received.

Consider the case of a quality control system that deals with Product Y. Let's say that a constraint is applied such that a given customer specification must be met otherwise the product cannot be shipped to the customer. So the user calls up and requests a large shipment, and the clerk who handles these orders calls up the user interface to choose some Product Y to ship. However there are not enough products to fulfil the order. When the clerk contacts the customer to inform him of this problem, the customer requests a closely related product rather than waiting for more Product Y to become available. What the clerk now discovers is that, as the business rules stand, he is unable to process this request, and so has to send it to the ordering manager to fulfill.

A stored procedure approach to this problem might allow users of a different security group to override the given settings where appropriate. In this way the clerk can get a list of Product Y to ship, choose materials, add them to an order, and press a button that starts shipping the product, calling a stored procedure `productOrder$ship`. This procedure will check that the product is within the customer specifications, and then set the order to be shipped. If it is out of specification, the procedure would deny the user. However, the ordering manager will have access to execute a different stored procedure, say `productOrder$shipOutOfSpec`, that would allow the user to ship an out-of-specification product.

Two things of note in this scenario are:

- The front-end would be responsible for knowing that the product was out of specification and not allowing the user to execute the `productOrder$shipOutOfSpec` procedure, but knowing this might be based on querying the rights on each stored procedure (using the `PERMISSIONS` function).

- `productOrder$ship` and `productOrder$shipOutOfSpec` would probably end up calling a different stored procedure that would be used to encapsulate the actual start of shipping the order. However, by presenting actual object and method names that are different, we can limit any situational coding in our procedures (if this type of user, do this, else do this) and present a secure interface based just on the stored procedures that are used for the enforcement.

The reality for a data architect is that there will always be those who work "outside the rules", for both proper and improper reasons, and we must take this into account whenever we build a truly user friendly system.

Case Study

In our case study, we will take the basic implementation that we produced in the previous chapter, implement the business rules that have been previously identified during the logical design phase, and add whatever data protection measures we deem necessary. We will follow the same path as we did during the chapter, building our constraints first, followed by triggers, then any optional rules that we have identified. We have already assigned data types, built `NULL` and foreign key constraints when we created our tables.

Default Constraints

When we build stored procedures to carry out inserts, we need to list all fields and supply values, even NULLs, to each one. If we use a default value for a missing column in an insert, this avoids problems that arise when deciding which values to default, and which the user planned on leaving NULL.

Note that we have built a `zipCode` to `city` reference table. It might seem a good idea to allow the user to simply choose the zip code or city and apply a default for the other one. However, it is impossible to do such a default as we have to enter the `city` and `zipCode` at the same time and defaults cannot access any other fields during the insert or update. We will use this table as a basis for a trigger validation later in the case study.

Bit Fields in transactionType

In the `transactionType` table, we have three fields where we can supply default constraints. We will set them to the most lenient settings.

- `requiresSignatureFl` – set to 0 to state that a signature is not required
- `requiresPayeeFl` – set to 0 to state that a payee is not required
- `allowPayeeFl` – set to 1 to state that they can put in a payee

which we script as follows:

```
ALTER TABLE transactionType
ADD CONSTRAINT dfltTransactionType$requiresSignatureFl$bit$false
DEFAULT 0 FOR requiresSignatureFl

ALTER TABLE transactionType
ADD CONSTRAINT dfltTransactionType$requiresPayeeFl$bit$false
DEFAULT 0 FOR requiresPayeeFl

ALTER TABLE transactionType
ADD CONSTRAINT dfltTransactionType$allowPayeeFl$bit$true
DEFAULT 1 FOR allowPayeeFl
```

Phone Number Fields

Another use for defaults is to set fields that users typically leave blank. Two fairly good examples are the phone number country code and area code. We would set the country code to '1', since this is the default for all United States phone numbers, and, say, '615' for the area code, or whatever the code is for the area where the users of the system are located.

```
ALTER TABLE phoneNumber
ADD CONSTRAINT dfltPhoneNumber$countryCode$string$charNumberOne
DEFAULT '1' FOR countryCode

ALTER TABLE phoneNumber
ADD CONSTRAINT dfltPhoneNumber$areaCode$string$localAreaCode
DEFAULT '615' FOR areaCode
```

Check Constraints

In almost any database we design, we will require far more check constraints than triggers or optional rules. Our database will be no different. As examples, we will be adding four different sets of check constraints, in order to disallow empty strings, prevent future financial transactions, force specification of the range of a financial transaction and to ensure that addresses may only have certain fields filled in a given condition. We will of course be building UDFs to support many of these constraints as needed.

Disallowing Empty Strings

In many string fields, we will wish to prevent our users from entering an empty string. As we discussed earlier in this chapter, we can prevent the entry of empty strings using this code:

```
CHECK (( '*' + COALESCE(RTRIM(<column>),'') + '*') <> '**' )
```

but in practice, we will want to encapsulate such algorithms into a function where possible. In this case, we will build the following function:

```
CREATE FUNCTION string$checkEntered
(
    @value varchar(8000)    --longest varchar value
)
RETURNS bit
AS
--used to check to see if a varchar value passed in is empty
--note: additional function required for unicode if desired
BEGIN
    DECLARE @returnVal bit --just returns yes or no

    --do an RTRIM, COALESCED to a '' if it is NULL, surround by *, and compare

    IF ( '*' + COALESCE(RTRIM(@value),'') + '*') <> '**'
        SET @returnVal = 1 --not empty
    ELSE
        SET @returnVal = 0 --empty

    RETURN @returnVal
END
GO
```

Now we test the code. When problems arise, it is always nice to be able to check the code quickly, so we test our constraint code by forcing it to fail and succeed as illustrated below:

```
-- empty condition
IF dbo.string$checkEntered('') = 0
    SELECT 'Empty'
ELSE
    SELECT 'Not Empty'

-- not empty condition
IF dbo.string$checkEntered('Any text will do') = 0
    SELECT 'Empty'
ELSE
    SELECT 'Not Empty'
```

As expected, the first code returns "Empty" and the second, "Not Empty".

Next we will want to create our check constraints. We could look at every field in the database we have designed and identify fields, but a better place to start is our domain list. In the following table we have all of the `varchar` and `char` domains we previously identified, and we determine which of them need to be validated with a check constraint.

393

Again keep in mind that our examples do not consider non-US address or phone numbers for simplicity of the example.

Name	Data type	Nullability	Check Non-Empty
addressDescriptiveLine	varchar(2000)	NOT NULL	Yes
addressStateCode	char(2)	NOT NULL	Yes
alphaNumericNumber	varchar(20)	NOT NULL	Yes
areaCode	varchar(3)	NOT NULL	Yes
countryCode	char(1)	NOT NULL	Yes
description	varchar(100)	NOT NULL	Yes
exchange	char(5)	NOT NULL	Yes
extension	varchar(20)	NULL	No, in this case if it is known that there is no extension, a blank would indicate that; if unknown, NULL fits
firstName	varchar(60)	NOT NULL	Yes
lastName	varchar(60)	NOT NULL	Yes
middleName	varchar(60)	NOT NULL	No, if the user did not give a middlename, a blank would signify
name	varchar(60)	NOT NULL	Yes
phoneNumberPart	char(4)	NOT NULL	Yes
string	varchar(20)	NOT NULL	No, as this is the generic case, these cases would need to be evaluated on a case by case basis
username	sysname (a SQL Server user-defined datatype that they use to store usernames. We will store SQL Server names here to map to real names, as any user who has rights to enter a check we will give rights to look at the transactions and/or accounts, based on the use cases.)	NOT NULL	Yes

Name	Data type	Nullability	Check Non-Empty
zipCode	char(5) (note that we have used the zipCode to link back to the city. This is done with the five character zipCode. We have ignored the +4 zip code again for simplicity.)	NOT NULL	Yes

To illustrate the way in which we format our constraints let's consider the example of the bank table. To build a constraint for its name column, we use the following:

```
ALTER TABLE bank
ADD CONSTRAINT chkBank$name$string$notEmpty
CHECK string$checkEmpty(name) = 1
```

The same would be true for the account table's number field:

```
ALTER TABLE account
ADD CONSTRAINT chkAccount$number$string$notEmpty
CHECK (dbo.string$checkEmpty(number) = 1)
```

Preventing Future Financial Transactions

Our specifications state that we shall prevent future transactions from being entered, so we will apply a constraint to prevent exactly this. In order to determine whether a transaction has yet occurred, we need to carry out some preliminary operations on our date-time data. For instance, we are not going to be storing the time in our transactions, so we need to strip off the time element of our date-time variables in our check constraint. We will implement our stripping of the time in our column in the trigger section of this chapter, but we will simply trust here that it has taken place.

The ability to check whether a date is in the future, or the past, is quite a useful facility, so we can build a UDF to do this for us:

```
CREATE FUNCTION date$rangeCheck
(
    @dateValue datetime,           -- first date value
    @dateToCompareAgainst datetime -- pass in date to compare to
)
RETURNS int
AS
BEGIN
    DECLARE @returnVal int
    IF @dateValue > @dateToCompareAgainst
    BEGIN
       SET @returnVal = 1           -- date is in the future
       END
    ELSE IF @dateValue < @dateToCompareAgainst
    BEGIN
       SET @returnVal = -1          -- date in is the past
    END
```

Chapter 11

```
    ELSE
        SET @returnVal = 0
    RETURN @returnVal            -- dates are the same
END
GO
```

Again we need to check out our function to make sure that it works:

```
--empty condition
SELECT dbo.date$rangeCheck('1/1/1989',getdate()) as [should be -1]
SELECT dbo.date$rangeCheck(getdate(),getdate()) as [should be 0]
SELECT dbo.date$rangeCheck('1/1/2020',getdate()) as [should be 1]
```

Of course I do apologize if the current year is greater than 2020 and you are still using this book. Please change this date as necessary!

We then create a function to strip off the time part of the date-time value:

```
CREATE FUNCTION date$removeTime
(
    @date datetime
)
RETURNS datetime AS
BEGIN
    SET @date = CAST(datePart(month,@date) as varchar(2)) + '/' +
                CAST(datePart(day,@date) as varchar(2)) + '/' +
                CAST(datePart(year,@date) as varchar(4))
    RETURN @date
END
GO
```

Now we can go to our transaction table and build a constraint against the date column as follows:

```
ALTER TABLE transaction
ADD CONSTRAINT chkTransaction$date$date$notFuture
--0 is equal, -1 means in the past, 1 means in the future
CHECK (dbo.date$rangeCheck(date,dbo.date$removeTime(getdate()) > 0)
```

Specifying the Range of a Financial Transaction

Going back to our `transaction` and `transactionType` tables:

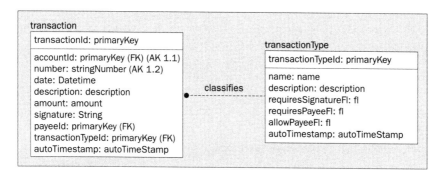

Ensuring Data Integrity

We need to make certain that all deposits are positive values, and that all checks and electronic withdrawals are negative values. Instead of building a check constraint based on the value of a foreign key, we could add a new column to the `transactionType` table called `positiveAmountFl`, but this is not flexible enough for our needs. Some items may allow negative values, zero or only positive numbers. We might also decide that a particular type of transaction has a maximum value imposed on it, such as an automatic "cash machine" withdrawal of 500 dollars. So a straightforward way to implement this would be to allow the user to create a range by adding the `minimumAmount` and `maximumAmount` attributes to our `transactionType` table:

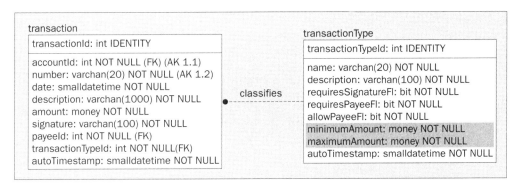

Here we add a simple constraint to make sure that the `minimumAmount` is not greater than the `maximumAmount` value we have entered:

```
ALTER TABLE transactionType
ADD minimumAmount money NOT NULL

ALTER TABLE transactionType
ADD maximumAmount money NOT NULL

--simple check constraint to make certain that min is less than max
ALTER TABLE transactionType
ADD CONSTRAINT chkTransactionType$minAndMaxRangeCheck
CHECK (minimumAmount <= maximumAmount)
```

Now we can create a UDF that will confirm that a value for a transaction of a given `transactionType` is within the range defined by the `minimumAmount` and `maximumAmount` columns:

```
CREATE FUNCTION transactionType$validateAmountInRange
(
    @transactionTypeId int,
    @amount money
)
RETURNS bit
AS
BEGIN
    --1 means within range, 0 out of range
    DECLARE @returnValue bit
    IF EXISTS ( select *
       FROM transactionType
       WHERE @amount NOT BETWEEN minimumAmount AND maximumAmount
          AND transactionTypeId = @transactionTypeId)
       BEGIN
```

397

```
            SET @returnValue = 0
        END
    ELSE
        SET @returnValue = 1
    END
```

Finally, we alter the transaction table and add a check constraint to validate the data as it is being entered into the table:

```
ALTER TABLE [transaction]
ADD CONSTRAINT chkTransaction$amountProperForTransactionType
AS
CHECK
   (dbo.transactionType$validateAmountInRange(transactionTypeId, amount) = 1 )
```

Note that the signature required constraint; payee required or payee allowed constraints based on the flags in the transactionType table would be built in much the same manner, so we will not include them here.

Triggers

Remove the Time from Transaction Dates

The first trigger we will create is an INSTEAD OF trigger to format the transaction date. There is no reason to store the time for the transaction date, and so we start out with our template trigger code, and add code to remove the time element from the dates using the function date$removeTime function used previously for a check constraint:

```
CREATE TRIGGER transaction$insteadOfInsert
ON [transaction]
INSTEAD OF INSERT
AS
-----------------------------------------------------------------
-- Purpose : Trigger on the insert that fires for any insert DML
--         : * formats the date column without time
-----------------------------------------------------------------
BEGIN
   DECLARE @rowsAffected int,    -- stores the number of rows affected
           @errNumber int,       -- used to hold the error number after DML
           @msg varchar(255),    -- used to hold the error message
           @errSeverity varchar(20),
           @triggerName sysname

   SET @rowsAffected = @@rowcount
   SET @triggerName = object_name(@@procid) --used for messages

   --no need to continue on if no rows affected
   IF @rowsAffected = 0 RETURN

   --perform the insert that we are building the trigger instead of
   INSERT INTO [transaction] (accountId, number, date, description,
                    amount, signature, payeeId,
                    transactionTypeId)
```

Ensuring Data Integrity

```
            SELECT accountId, number, dbo.date$removeTime(date) AS date,
                 description, amount, signature, payeeId, transactionTypeId
            FROM INSERTED

            SET @errorNumber = @@error
            IF @errorNumber <> 0
            begin
                SET @msg = 'Error: ' + CAST(@errorNumber AS varchar(10)) +
                                 ' occurred during the insert of the rows into ' +
                                 ' the transaction table.'
                RAISERROR 50000 @msg
                ROLLBACK TRANSACTION
                RETURN
            END
      END
```

The update trigger is 95 per cent the same code, so we will leave this to the reader.

Validate City and Zip Codes Match

In our `address` table, we have the `cityId` and `zipCodeId` fields which are foreign keys to the `zipCode` and `city` tables, respectively. We have also included a `zipCodeCityReference` table that is used to help the user select city and state from the zip code. We would fill this table from a zip code database which is commercially available (like from the US Postal Service). A final purpose of this table is to validate the `city` and `zipCodeId` values. As a reminder, here was the physical data model for these tables:

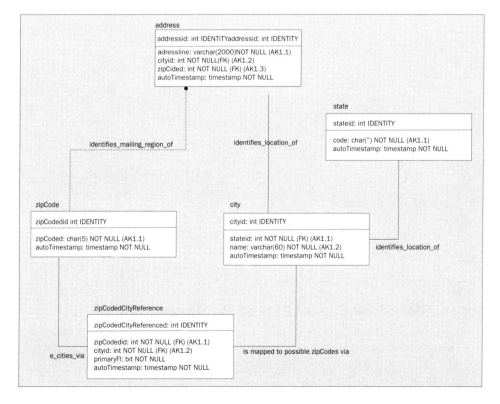

399

We can do this by making sure that the `cityId` and `zipCodeId` pair that has been entered is found in the reference table:

```
CREATE TRIGGER address$afterInsert
ON address
AFTER UPDATE
AS
--------------------------------------------------------------------------
-- Purpose : Trigger on the <action> that fires for any <action> DML
--------------------------------------------------------------------------
BEGIN
   DECLARE @rowsAffected int, -- stores the number of rows affected
   @errNumber int, -- used to hold the error number after DML
   @msg varchar(255), -- used to hold the error message
   @errSeverity varchar(20),
   @triggerName sysname,

   SET @rowsAffected = @@rowcount
   SET @triggerName = object_name(@@procid) --used for messages

   --no need to continue on if no rows affected
   IF @rowsAffected = 0 RETURN

   DECLARE @numberOfRows int
   SELECT @numberOfRows = (SELECT count(*)
                           FROM INSERTED
                              JOIN zipCodeCityReference AS zcr
                                 ON zcr.cityId = INSERTED.cityId and
                                    zcr.zipCodeId = INSERTED.zipCodeId)
   IF @numberOfRows <> @rowAffected
   BEGIN
      SET @msg = CASE WHEN @rowsAffected = 1
                     THEN 'The row you inserted has ' +
                          'an invalid cityId and zipCodeId pair.'
                     ELSE 'One of the rows you were trying to insert ' +
                          'has an invalid cityId and zipCodeId pair.'
   END
   RAISERROR 50000 @msg
   ROLLBACK TRANSACTION
   RETURN
END
```

The insert trigger is 99 per cent the same code, so we will leave this to the reader.

Transaction Allocations Cannot Exceed the Amount Stored

In this example, we consider the transaction allocation amounts for transactions. The field we are concerned with is the allocationAmount on the transactionAllocation table:

Ensuring Data Integrity

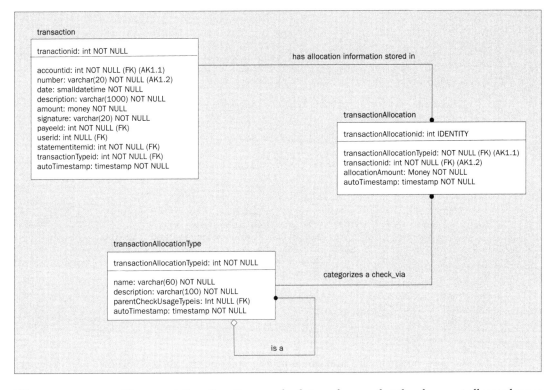

Whenever a user modifies an existing allocation, we check to make sure that they have not allocated more money to the transaction than actually exists. So we write the following trigger:

```
CREATE TRIGGER transactionAllocation$afterInsert
ON transactionAllocation
AFTER INSERT AS
-------------------------------------------------------------------
-- Purpose : Trigger on the insert that fires for any insert DML
--         : * protects against allocations that are greater than 100 per cent
-------------------------------------------------------------------
BEGIN
    DECLARE @rowsAffected int,      -- stores the number of rows affected
            @errNumber int,         -- used to hold the error number after DML
            @msg varchar(255),      -- used to hold the error message
            @errSeverity varchar(20),
            @triggerName sysname

    SET @rowsAffected = @@rowcount
    SET @triggerName = object_name(@@procid) --used for messages

    -- no need to continue on if no rows affected
    IF @rowsAffected = 0 RETURN

    -- get the total fo all transactionAllocations that are affected by our
    -- insert and get all transactions affected

    IF EXISTS (
        SELECT * FROM (
            SELECT transactionId, sum(amount) AS amountTotal
            FROM transactionAllocation
```

401

```
                                        --note this transactionId expands our
                                        --query to look at all allocations that
                                        --are for any transaction who's
                                        --allocation we have touched
           WHERE transactionId IN (SELECT transactionId fROM INSERTED)
           GROUP BY transactionId ) AS allocAmounts

        -- join to the transaction to get the amount of
        -- the transaction
        JOIN transaction
           ON allocAmounts.transactionId = transaction.transactionId

        -- check to make sure that the transaction amount is not greater
        -- than the allocation amount
        WHERE transaction.amount > allocAmounts.amountTotal )
        BEGIN
           SET @msg = CASE WHEN @rowsAffected = 1
                           THEN 'The row you inserted has' +
                                'made the transaction exceed its transaction. '
                           ELSE 'One of the rows you were trying to insert ' +
                                'has made the transaction exceed its ' +
                                'transaction.'
           END
        RAISERROR 50000 @msg
        ROLLBACK TRANSACTION
        RETURN
    END
```

Note that we solved a fairly complex problem using a complex query, and we have used neither cursors nor temporary tables. It is important to formulate our queries in triggers using as few operators as possible, so as to minimize the possibility of introducing logic errors into very hard-to-find places when building complex queries. There will always be trade-offs in usability versus readability/understandability. In most any system, slow triggers will be a problem, especially if we have to insert a large number of rows at a time.

Again, the update trigger for this and the `transaction` table is 95 per cent the same code, so we will not include it here.

Optional Rules

In our system, we have a few optional business rules that were specified that need implementing. Those that were identified in our original analysis were:

- **User should get a warning if they attempt to withdraw too much money** – We would likely create a stored procedure that checks the balance of the user account prior to saving a transaction amount. The client-side code would compare the balance with the amount of the transaction that was attempting to complete.

- **Account must be balanced weekly** – When starting up, the application would need to call a stored procedure that finds out when the account was last balanced, compares it to the current date, and issues a reminder or warning: a reminder might be sent to a manager to advise if balancing was severely overdue.

In the next chapter we will look at best practices when building stored procedures.

Summary

We have now finished with the task of developing the data storage for our databases. In the last chapter we built the physical storage for the data by creating the tables. In this chapter we took the next step and built a scheme to safeguard it. During this process, we looked at the following resources that SQL Server gives us to protect our data from having invalid values:

- **Defaults** – While it might not seem like defaults can be considered data protection resources, they can be used to automatically set fields where the purpose of the field might not be apparent to the user (and the database adds a suitable value for the field).

- **Check Constraints** – These are very important in ensuring that our data is within specifications. We can use almost any scalar functions (user-defined or system) as long as we end up with a single logical expression.

- **Triggers** – Triggers are very important resources that allow us to build pieces of code that fire automatically on any INSERT, UPDATE, and DELETE operation that is executed against a single table.

- **Stored Procedures/Front End Code** – We have simply made mention of these mechanisms of data protection because we want to ensure that they are used prudently in handling business rules.

Throughout this process we have made heavy use of user defined functions which are a new resource that SQL Server 2000 offers us. With them we can encapsulate many of the algorithms that we employ to enhance and extend our defaults, check constraints, triggers, and as we will find in the next chapter, stored procedures.

Once we have built and implemented a set of appropriate data safeguarding resources, then we can trust that the data in our database has been validated. We should never need to revalidate our data once it is stored in our database, but it is a good idea to do random sampling just to satisfy ourselves that there are no integrity gaps that have slipped passed us. Every relationship, every check constraint, every trigger that we devise will help to make sure this is true.

In the next chapter, we go on to look at some more advanced data accessing and modification methods, and in particular the use of views and stored procedures.

SQL Server 2000 Database Design Professional

12

Advanced Data Access and Modification Techniques

Introduction

In previous chapters, we have designed our databases, built our storage, and made protection schemes for our data. Throughout this book, we have assumed that the reader is relatively proficient in Transact-SQL, and has some experience of writing stored procedures and views, skills that we will further develop in the course of this chapter.

We will now meet more advanced concepts for accessing, creating, modifying, and deleting data in our OLTP database. We will discuss major query considerations, such as how transactions, temp tables, cursors, and NULLs make our coding both easier and more interesting. We will take an in depth look at the issues surrounding using views and stored procedures, and give a full discussion of the pros and cons of building applications using stored procedure access, *ad hoc* query access, and a mixture of both.

Once we have discussed querying matters, we will take a look at how we can use SQL Server security to limit access to the data in our systems. Finally, we will briefly examine how building applications that access data across different servers affects our architecture and coding.

One thing of note. For the data architect in some organizations, performing a few of the tasks described in this chapter will be beyond the call of duty. Perhaps creating stored procedures and views will come close to stepping on the DBA or database programmer's toes. Alternatively, it may well be that data architect is just one of many hats you must wear. Whatever the case, I feel that it is important for every data architect to endeavor not to lose those SQL coding skills, and a thorough understanding of these issues is very beneficial to the design role. If you're not skilled in SQL then you run the risk of designing a database that will cause the developers a lot of hassle to work with.

Query Considerations

In this section we will look at some of the important issues that need to be understood to implement efficient database access and modification features. Transactions, locking, NULLs, cursors, temporary tables, stored procedures, and views are all essential to the architecture of a database system.

We have discussed many of these earlier in the book. However, in this chapter, we are going to look at how these issues affect our coding of applications, rather than how they affect our creation of objects.

Transactions

Transactions play a very important role in how we access our data. A transaction is a sequence of operations performed as a single logical unit of work. There are four classic properties that transactions are required to support, commonly known as the ACID test. This is an acronym for the following:

- **Atomicity** – every action that participates in a transaction must be performed as a logical unit of work, such that every action either does or does not happen.

- **Consistency** – once the transaction is finished, the system must be left in a consistent condition, including physical resources like data, indexes, and the links between data pages.

- **Isolation** – all modifications within a transaction must be isolated from other transactions. When executing commands within a transaction, no other transaction may see data in an intermediate state.

- **Durability** – once the transaction has completed, all actions that have taken place in the transaction must be permanently persisted.

A transaction starts with a BEGIN TRANSACTION statement. Executing BEGIN TRANSACTION puts our connection to the database in a state where nothing that we do will be permanently saved to physical storage until we explicitly tell it to. We will examine this in the next set of examples.

In the first example, we will start a transaction, insert a row, and then roll the transaction back (in other words, the effects of the transaction are completely cancelled and the database returns to its original state). We will work with the artist table from the last chapter, and start by getting the base level list of artists in our table:

```
SELECT artistId, name
FROM artist
```

We see that we have three artists saved (keep in mind that the artistId column values will vary, depending on how many values you have entered, plus how many errors have occurred):

```
artistId    name
----------  -----------------------
27          jethro tull
1           the beatles
2           the who
```

Advanced Data Access and Modification Techniques

Next, we execute the following batch of commands:

```
BEGIN TRANSACTION --start a transaction

    -- insert two records
    INSERT INTO artist (name)
    VALUES ('mariah carey')
    INSERT INTO artist (name)
    VALUES ('britney spears')

    -- make sure that they are in the database
    SELECT artistId, name FROM artist
```

This returns the result:

```
ArtistId      name
----------    --------------------------
37            britney spears
27            jethro tull
36            mariah carey
1             the beatles
2             the who
```

Now we decide that we really don't want these records in our database, and so we roll back the transaction, followed by yet another check of the rows in the table:

As we will discuss later, having transactions span multiple executions is not the best way to deal with them, but I do this here to show you the values in the table.

```
ROLLBACK TRANSACTION
SELECT artistId, name FROM artist
```

Now the rows are gone, as if they never existed.

```
artistId      name
----------    --------------------------
27            jethro tull
1             the beatles
2             the who
```

Technically speaking, the rows did physically exist, but SQL Server has marked them so we can either commit them as a group or, in our case here, not commit them.

Transactions can be nested, such that, for every BEGIN TRANSACTION statement that we execute against the database, we have to execute one COMMIT TRANSACTION. On the other side of the coin, the ROLLBACK TRANSACTION statement undoes an unlimited number of transactions.

We can tell how many transactions have been started by examining the @@trancount global variable. In the following example we will show the effects of executing BEGIN TRANSACTION and COMMIT TRANSACTION statements, by looking at the @@trancount value before and after transaction commands:

407

```
SELECT @@trancount AS zero
BEGIN TRANSACTION
   SELECT @@trancount AS one
   BEGIN TRANSACTION
      SELECT @@trancount AS two
      BEGIN TRANSACTION
      SELECT @@trancount AS three
      COMMIT TRANSACTION
   SELECT @@trancount AS two
   COMMIT TRANSACTION
SELECT @@trancount AS one
COMMIT TRANSACTION
SELECT @@trancount AS zero
```

This returns the following output. Note that it increments from zero to three and then increments back down to zero.

```
zero
-----------
0

one
-----------
1

two
-----------
2

three
-----------
3

two
-----------
2

one
-----------
1

zero
-----------
0
```

We must commit every transaction or the resources will be locked from our other transactions, based on the isolation part of the ACID test. However, as we stated before, ROLLBACK rolls back all of the BEGIN TRANSACTION statements at once:

```
SELECT @@trancount AS one
BEGIN TRANSACTION
   SELECT @@trancount AS two
   BEGIN TRANSACTION
      SELECT @@trancount AS three
```

```
        BEGIN TRANSACTION
            SELECT @@trancount AS four
            ROLLBACK TRANSACTION
            SELECT @@trancount AS zero
```

This will return:

```
one
-----------
0

two
-----------
1

three
-----------
2

four
-----------
3

zero
-----------
0
```

This is a great thing and also a problem. For starters, you will likely have several COMMIT statements after the rollback, since you will usually use logic that states: if it works, commit it; if it doesn't, roll it back. After the rollback, we must then tell every following statement that we don't want to execute it. Hence, SQL Server gives us an additional resource for transactions that allows us to selectively roll back certain parts of a transaction.

Selective Rollback

The command is SAVE TRANSACTION. You can name a save point (based on the usual criteria for identifiers, though only the first 32 characters are significant) as:

```
SAVE TRANSACTION <savepoint name>
```

Then, if you decide that part of the transaction has failed, you can roll back part of the command but not the rest by executing a command like this:

```
ROLLBACK TRANSACTION <savepoint name>
```

> Note that this is different from BEGIN TRANSACTION <transaction name>.

So, in our final example on transactions, we will use the SAVE TRANSACTION command to selectively roll back one of the commands that we execute and not the other:

```
    BEGIN TRANSACTION --start a transaction

    --insert two records
    INSERT INTO artist (name)
```

```
        VALUES ('moody blues')

        SAVE TRANSACTION britney
        INSERT INTO artist (name)
        VALUES ('britney spears')

        --make sure that they are in the database
        SELECT artistId, name FROM artist
```

which gives this output:

```
        ArtistId    name
        ---------   ---------------------------
        45          britney spears
        27          jethro tull
        44          moody blues
        1           the beatles
        2           the who
```

Then we roll back to the `britney` save point we created, commit the major transaction, and select our rows to see the state of our `artist` table:

```
        ROLLBACK TRANSACTION britney

        COMMIT TRANSACTION

        SELECT artistId, name FROM artist
```

We see that it *has* rolled back the "`britney spears`" row but not the "`moody blues`" row.

```
        artistId    name
        ---------   ---------------------------
        27          jethro tull
        44          moody blues
        1           the beatles
        2           the who
```

We will make use of the SAVE TRANSACTION mechanism quite often when building transactions. It allows us to roll back only parts of a transaction and to decide what action to take. It will be especially important when we get to stored procedures, as a stored procedure is not allowed to change the value of @@trancount as a result of its operation.

The Scope of Transactions

A **batch** is a logical group of T-SQL statements that are parsed and then executed together. We use the GO statement to split code up into batches; GO is not a T-SQL command but just a keyword recognized by SQL Server command utilities like Query Analyzer.

A transaction is scoped to an entire connection to SQL Server, and may theoretically span many batches of statements sent between the client and the server. Note that a connection is not the same thing as a user. A user may have many connections to the server and, in fact, a user may be forced to wait for one of his/her own connections to complete a transaction before continuing with work. One transaction, or a set of nested transactions, has to be completed before the next one can start.

Advanced Data Access and Modification Techniques

How does SQL Server make sure that, if a connection is cut before a transaction has finished, everything is rolled back to its original state? How does SQL Server make sure that transactions do not overlap with each other, thereby violating the isolation requirement of the ACID test? In the next section we will take a look at the locking mechanisms that SQL Server employs to keep track of transactional activity on the database.

Locking

Locking in SQL Server is a bit like the occupied sign you find on a bathroom door. It tells the outside world that something is going on inside and everyone else will just have to wait.

Locking plays a vital role in ensuring transactions work correctly and obey the ACID rules. Rolling back one transaction would be dangerous if another transaction had already begun working with the same set of data. This situation – many users trying to access resources at the same time – is generally known as **concurrency**. In this section we will present a basic overview of how locking is internally implemented (as opposed to our treatment of an optimistic lock in Chapter 10) and how this prevents data corruption if multiple processes try to access the data simultaneously.

Lock Types

SQL Server internally implements a locking scheme that allows a transaction or operation to associate a token with a given resource or collection of resources. The token indicates to other processes that the resource is locked. SQL Server prevents the explicit setting or clearing of locks, so a resource with such a token is protected. Depending upon the level of usage, the following resources may be locked (the **lock types** are listed in order of decreasing granularity):

- **Row** – an individual row in a table
- **Key** or **Key-Range** – a key or range of keys in an index
- **Page** – the 8 KB page structure that has an index or data
- **Table** – an entire table, that is, all rows and index keys
- **Database** – an entire database (usually only used during database schema changes)

> Note that there is also an **extent** lock, which is normally used when allocating space in a database and which has a range of eight 8 KB pages.

The initial type of lock employed is determined by SQL Server's optimizer, which also decides when to change from one lock type to another in order to save memory and increase performance. Generally, the optimizer will choose the smallest lock – the row type – when possible but, if there is a likelihood of needing to lock all or a range of rows, the table type may be chosen. By using optimizer hints on our queries, we can adjust to some extent the types of locks used. This will be discussed shortly.

Lock Modes

To architect systems well, it is useful to understand how SQL Server selects the level granularity to employ. First we will describe the different **lock modes** that exist:

- **Shared locks** – these are for when you simply want to look at the data. Multiple connections may have shared locks on the same resource.

- **Update locks** – these allow us to state that we are planning to update the data but we are not ready to do so, for example if we are still processing a WHERE clause to determine which rows we need to update. We may still have shared locks on the table, and other connections may be issued during the period of time that we are still preparing to update.

- **Exclusive locks** – these give exclusive access to the resource. No other connection may have access at all. These are frequently employed after a physical resource has been modified within a transaction.

- **Intent locks** – these convey information to other processes that have or are about to create locks of some type. There are three types of intent locks: **Intent Shared**, **Intent Exclusive**, and **Shared with Intent Exclusive** (reading with intent to make changes). For anyone who has ever been around divers, intent locks are analogous to the buoys that divers place on the surface of the water to mark their position. Because we see the buoy, we know that there is activity going on under water. SQL Server sees these markers on objects and knows that, if, for example, an intent shared lock is located on a table, then it is not possible to get an exclusive lock on that table as other connections are using the resources already.

As with the previous list of resources that may be locked, there are a few additional modes that we will mention in passing but which are outside the scope of the chapter. **Schema** *locks are used when the database structure is changed, a stored procedure is recompiled, or anything else changes to the physical structure of the database.* **Bulk update** *locks are used when performing bulk updates. See SQL Server 2000 Books Online for more information.*

So, now we know that there are locks at various levels of the process, and any time we do anything in SQL Server, tokens are set that tell other processes what we are doing to the resource. This is to force them to wait until we have finished using the resource if they need to do a task that is incompatible with what we are currently doing – for instance, trying to look at a record that we are modifying or trying to delete a record that we are currently fetching to read.

Isolation Levels

Locks are held for the duration of atomic operations, depending on the operation we have asked SQL Server to perform. Consider, for example, that we start a transaction on a table called tableX:

```
SELECT * FROM dbo.tableX
```

Locks (in this case shared locks) are held on this resource for a period of time, based on what is known as the **isolation level**. SQL Server provides the following four isolation levels, ordered here from least to most restrictive:

- **Read Uncommitted** – ignores all locks and does not issue locks. In the read uncommitted isolation level, we are allowed to see data from atomic operations that have not been finished yet, and which might be rolled back. Note that no modification statement actually operates in this isolation level; if you modify a row within a transaction, you still leave locks that prevent others from corrupting changes.

    This is a very dangerous thing to do in general. Since we are allowed to see even uncommitted transactions, it is never clear if what we have read is of value. It can, however, be used during reporting if the reporting can accept the margin of error this may allow – the data is read in a way that may not meet all constraints laid down and it may vanish after reading.

- **Read Committed** – this is by far the most commonly used isolation level as it provides a reasonable balance between safety and concurrency. We cannot see uncommitted data, though we do allow unrepeatable reads (a condition where, if we read in a set of rows, we expect the rows to exist for the length of the transaction) and **phantom rows**, which are new records that are created by other users while we are in our transaction.

  Ordinarily, this is the best choice for the isolation level and is, in fact, the SQL Server default.

- **Repeatable Read** – a repeatable read guarantees that, if a user needs to carry out the same SELECT statement twice, and providing the user has not changed the data between these two SELECT operations, the user will get back exactly the same data twice. An unrepeatable read situation cannot guarantee this as another concurrent user might have changed the data.

  As you might guess, repeatable read takes the protection of the read committed isolation level and prevents unrepeatable reads by placing locks on all data that are being used in a query, preventing other connections from changing data that you have already read. When you execute a query the second time, it will return at least the same set of rows as it did the first time. However, it does not prevent phantom rows.

- **Serializable** – this isolation level places range locks on the indexes and data sets, thus preventing users from making any phantom rows.

To illustrate what I have been saying, let's look at an example of what can occur if we use the default read committed isolation level. First, we build a table that we will use for the test, and we add some records:

```
CREATE TABLE testIsolationLevel
(
    testIsolationLevelId INT IDENTITY,
    value varchar(10)
)

INSERT INTO dbo.testIsolationLevel(value)
VALUES ('Value1')
INSERT INTO dbo.testIsolationLevel(value)
VALUES ('Value2')
```

Now we can execute the following commands in one connection to SQL Server:

```
SET TRANSACTION ISOLATION LEVEL READ COMMITTED

--set for illustrative purposes only. If we do not set this on a connection
--it will be in read committed mode anyway because this is the default.

BEGIN TRANSACTION
SELECT * FROM dbo.testIsolationLevel
```

and we will see the following results:

```
testIsolationLevelId    value
----------------------  ----------
1                       Value1
2                       Value2
```

Using a different connection, we execute the following:

```
DELETE FROM dbo.testIsolationLevel
WHERE testIsolationLevelId = 1
```

Then, going back to our first connection – which is still open and within a transaction – we execute:

```
SELECT * FROM dbo.testIsolationLevel

COMMIT TRANSACTION
```

and we will have no problems deleting the row:

testIsolationLevelId	value
2	Value2

This was an *unrepeatable* read. Next, we drop the table, reinitialize, and rerun our little test – changing the isolation level to:

```
SET TRANSACTION ISOLATION LEVEL REPEATABLE READ
```

This time, when we try to execute the DELETE statement in the second connection, it will not complete until our first connection is completed. The second connection has been **blocked** (or locked out) by the first and cannot execute its commands. Hence, our second SELECT statement will return at least the same values – in other words, it is a repeatable read.

But we still have to consider the problem of phantoms (that is, phantom rows). We have prevented anyone from removing rows, but what about adding rows? From the name "repeatable read", we might tend to believe that we are protected against this situation. However, let's retry our situation again. We will drop the table and recreate it, inserting the same two rows. Then we execute the original transaction over connection one:

```
SET TRANSACTION ISOLATION LEVEL READ COMMITTED

BEGIN TRANSACTION
SELECT * FROM dbo.testIsolationLevel
```

and again we will see the following results:

testIsolationLevelId	value
1	Value1
2	Value2

In a second connection, we execute the following command:

```
INSERT INTO dbo.testIsolationLevel(value)
VALUES ('Value3')
```

Advanced Data Access and Modification Techniques

This is not blocked as the DELETE was, but is allowed. Now, if we execute the following command in the first conection as before:

```
SELECT * FROM dbo.testIsolationLevel

COMMIT TRANSACTION
```

We get an additional row:

```
testIsolationLevelId     value
------------------------ ----------------
1                        Value1
2                        Value2
3                        Value3
```

Now we have a *repeatable* read, but we have a phantom row too. Finally, if we go back and run this example one last time, but specify SERIALIZABLE as the isolation level, the INSERT in this example will have to wait for the connection to finish.

From our examples, the serializable isolation level seems like the best choice, because we might want to prevent other users from accessing our data at the same time as we are using it. If we are modifying data using a transaction, we will most likely want to ensure that a given situation exists until all the operations have completed.

Whenever we modify data, SQL Server places exclusive locks on the resources that we are modifying. If another user is trying to access that particular resource, it must wait. However, all of the other resources that are being used as part of the transaction are locked as well, and a concurrent user cannot access any of these resources while they are being used in the transaction. As the level of isolation increases, SQL Server must place and hold locks on resources for longer in the process:

- ❑ Read Uncommitted – no locks are issued and none are honored, even exclusive locks.
- ❑ Read Committed – shared locks are issued when looking at a resource, but once the process has finished with them, they are released.
- ❑ Repeatable Read – the same shared locks are issued as with read committed, however, they are not released until the end of the transaction.
- ❑ Serializable – all the ranges of data (including whole tables) that might meet the criteria in any reads we make are locked, and no outside user can make any changes to this data.

One thing of note. When using any isolation level other than serializable, we leave ourselves open to a very small hole in data integrity. Consider what happens in triggers and check constraints, which use functions to access other tables to see if conditions are being met prior to saving a record. Depending on our isolation level, we could check that a certain condition exists and, ten milliseconds later, another user could conceivably change data in our system to the point where the data is within specifications. Another ten milliseconds later we could commit the now invalid data to disk.

This is further evidence to support our earlier claim that the serializable level is the most suitable level for all of your transactions. However, we should state the reason why read committed is the default isolation level for SQL Server. It has everything to do with balancing the potentially conflicting issues of consistency and concurrency.

Using the serializable isolation level can prevent other users from getting to the data that they need, hence greatly reducing concurrency, especially when you have many users using the same resources. Using read committed leaves a hole in our defenses for an extremely small period of time (usually in the order of milliseconds), with minimal risk.

It is recommended that serializable or repeatable read only be used when they are absolutely necessary. An example of such a case might be a banking or financial system where even the smallest possible error in a user's account could cause real problems.

The other recommendation is to keep all transactions as small as possible, so as to keep locks as short as possible. This entails trying to keep transactions in a single batch. Whatever resources are locked during a transaction will stay locked while SQL Server waits for you to finish. Performance obviously gets worse the longer you wait and the greater the isolation level. SQL Server will always try to complete every batch it begins executing. If we are disconnected in the middle of an open-ended transaction, the connection will not die immediately, further compromising performance.

Optimizer Hints

At this point, we should make a brief mention of table level **optimizer hints**. When we do not want an entire connection or operation to use a particular isolation level, but we simply want a table in a statement to behave in a certain manner, we can specify the isolation level via an optimizer hint.

```
SELECT <fieldName1>, <fieldName2>, … , <fieldNameN>
from <tableName1> WITH (optimizerHint1, optimizerHint2,...,optimizerHintX)
WHERE <where conditions>
```

Imagine we have a `customer` table, for example, and an `invoice` table that has a foreign key to the customer table.

```
SELECT invoice.date AS invoiceDate
FROM dbo.customer WITH (READUNCOMMITTED)
JOIN dbo.invoice
    ON customer.customerId = invoice.customerId
```

In this instance, there would be no shared locks placed on the `customer` table but there would be on the `invoice` table as resources are accessed. There are optimizer hints for each of the isolation level values, as well as a few others to force certain kinds of locks:

- ❑ `READUNCOMMITTED` (also known as `NOLOCK`) – no locks are created or honored.

- ❑ `READCOMMITTED` – honors all locks, but does not hold onto the locks once it is finished with them (the default).

- ❑ `REPEATABLEREAD` – never releases locks once they have been acquired.

- ❑ `SERIALIZABLE` (also known as `HOLDLOCK`) – never releases locks until the transaction has ended, and locks all other statements from modifying rows that might ever match any `WHERE` clause that limits the selection of data in the hinted table.

- ❑ `READPAST` – only valid for `SELECT`s; this tells the query processor to skip over locked rows and moved to unlocked ones. Only ignores row locks.

- ❑ `ROWLOCK` – forces the initial locking mechanism chosen for an operation to be a row-level lock, even if the optimizer would have chosen a less granular lock.

Advanced Data Access and Modification Techniques

- ❏ TABLOCK – forces a table lock to be used even when a more granular lock would normally have been chosen.
- ❏ TABLOCKX – same as the TABLOCK, but uses exclusive locks instead of whatever lock type would have been chosen.
- ❏ UPDLOCK – forces the use of an update lock instead of a shared lock.

While each of these optimizer hints has its uses and can be helpful, they should be used with extreme care and, in most cases, it will be best to use isolation levels rather than trying to manipulate lock types and lock modes directly.

Deadlocks

A deadlock is a situation that occurs when two (or more) connections each have resources locked that the other connection needs. To illustrate, suppose we have two connections – A and B – which issue commands to update two tables – tableA and tableB. The problem occurs because connection A updates tableA first and then tableB, whereas connection B updates the same tables in the reverse order.

Connection A	Connection B
Connect to table A	Connect to table B
Table A locked	Table B locked
Update carried out	Update carried out
Attempt to connect to table B	Attempt to connect to table A
Locked out of table B	Locked out of table A

Since there is no WHERE clause, the entire table will have to be locked to perform the update, so a table lock is applied to tableA while connection A is using it. The same happens with connection B's command to update all of the rows in tableB. When the two connections try to execute their second UPDATE statements, they both get blocked – creating the deadlock. SQL Server then nominates one of the connections to become the deadlock victim and releases the other connection, rolling back the locks that were held on a resource.

To determine which connection ends the deadlock, SQL Server chooses the connection that is the least expensive to roll back. However, there are settings you can use to raise a connection's deadlock priority, to help SQL Server choose a less important connection to fail. The following SET command will set the connection deadlock priority to either LOW or NORMAL. NORMAL is the default; and a LOW setting for a connection means that it is most likely to be the victim of the deadlock and fail.

```
SET DEADLOCK_PRIORITY [LOW | NORMAL]
```

Deadlocks are annoying but fairly rare, and if you anticipate their occurrence and produce code to avoid them, they can be easily handled. You can simply code your application to look for a deadlock error message (1205) and have it resubmit the command; it is highly unlikely that you would get a deadlock the second time round.

Note that this is not to be confused with the blocking we discussed earlier. Deadlocks cause one of the connections to fail and raise an error; blocked connections wait until the connection times out – based on the LOCK_TIMEOUT *value – and then roll back the connection. You can set this* LOCK_TIMEOUT *property by executing:*

```
SET LOCK_TIMEOUT <timeoutTimeInMilliseconds>
```

The key to minimizing deadlocks is, once again, to keep transactions short. The shorter the transaction, the less chance it has of being blocked or deadlocked by other transactions. One suggestion that is continually mentioned is to always access objects in the same order in your transactions, perhaps alphabetically. Of course, such suggestions will only work if everybody abides by the rule.

Primary Recommendations

Here are two very important recommendations for any clients that will be using our data.

Avoid Long Running Transactions

We have seen this suggestion several times already. However, *how long* is a long transaction? A long running transaction may take half of a second, one minute, one hour, or even a day. What matters most is that we minimize the transactions that are affecting our users and their access to data.

Rather than loading values from an outside source directly into our users' table, it may be better to load the rows into a new intermediate table, then insert the rows into the users' table during off-peak hours. The overhead of doing this will be far less than bulk copying directly into a table.

In very exceptional circumstances when you can't realistically keep your transaction down to a short time, you will either have to redesign the procedure or live with it. When it comes to transactions lasting a couple of seconds or less, there is not much that can be done programmatically to reduce this stress. If this duration is not within acceptable levels, this is where performance tuning comes into play.

Transactions Should Not Span Batch Boundaries

If you are sending multiple batches of commands to the server, it is best not to start a transaction in one batch and finish it in another.

By following this *critical* recommendation, we can greatly reduce some of the more performance hindering situations that will occur.

Consider the following example. In the diagram we have two commands which update tableA and then tableB. It has been determined that we need to make these commands into a transaction, and we have built a tidy little set of methods for dealing with this situation. We call a begin_transaction() method that connects to the server and begins the transaction. Next, it sends a command to update tableA, followed by a command to update tableB, but somewhere during the last call, the LAN breaks down:

Advanced Data Access and Modification Techniques

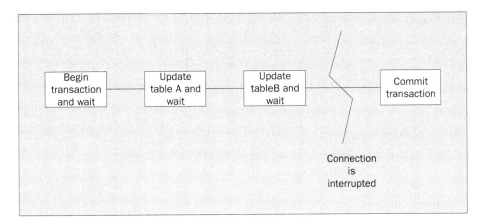

SQL Server will not see that your connection has been severed, so it keeps the connection open waiting for you to commit or roll the connection back. However, as you are now part way through the transaction, neither a commit nor a roll back will occur – until SQL Server realizes that the connection has been broken due to inactivity. Our data will be just fine as the transaction created update locks to protect it. The only problem is that – depending on the actual WHERE clause – the row, rows, or possibly the whole tableA table will be locked up tight. Hence, when another user comes by to simply look at a record in tableA, he/she is forced to wait or click the **Stop** button on the browser.

The answer to this problem is to roll these commands up into a single batch, which executes all at once. For instance:

```
Begin transaction

Update tableA
Update tableB

Commit transaction
GO
```

In this manner, if SQL Server gets the commands and begins to execute them, either *all* the operations will occur or none will. We will not end up with any locked resources.

So why on earth would a user consider sending transactions in multiple batches? A couple of reasons:

- ❑ Apparent speed – once each statement is finished, it is possible to update a progress bar and tell the user that tableA has indeed been updated, now I'm moving on to tableB, etc.

- ❑ It's easy to do without knowing it – especially using tools such as ADO. Consider the following ADO code sample, culled from SQL Server 2000 Books Online in the *Performing Transactions in ADO* section:

```
Dim cn As New ADODB.Connection
Dim rs As New ADODB.Recordset
. . .
' Open connection.
cn.Open
```

```
    ' Open titles table.
    rs.Open "SELECT * FROM titles", Cn, adOpenDynamic, adLockPessimistic
    ...
    ' Begin the transaction.
    rs.MoveFirst
    cn.BeginTrans

    ' User loops through the recordset making changes.
    ...
    ' Ask if the user wants to commit all the changes made.
    If MsgBox("Save all changes?", vbYesNo) = vbYes Then
       cn.CommitTrans
    Else
       cn.RollbackTrans
    End If
```

This code will do exactly what we were discussing above, but in a much nicer looking wrapper. By executing the BeginTrans method on the connection, a BEGIN TRANSACTION command is sent in one batch to the server. For each touch of a record in the loop (not coded, just mentioned), a data modification statement will be sent to the server. Finally, if all goes well in the code, the CommitTrans or RollbackTrans method will be called, sending a COMMIT TRANSACTION command. If there is any mistake inside here, or even a connection burp, then the users of the titles table will be waiting for quite a while. Note also that an adLockPessimistic lock is called for, which will likely implement an isolation level of read committed or possibly even serializable – so no other user can touch the rows while this user has them in this loop. A simple example of code for teaching how a few methods of the connection objects work, but it's not a good example to follow when building multi-user programs.

However, if we stored each statement in this situation, instead of actually sending them to SQL Server one at a time, we could execute the batch of statements once the user has finished. The user may have to wait a bit longer for the operation to finish than when each step was performed separately. Actually, less time will be taken overall but the user gets the impression that nothing is going on, and the time will *seem* longer. In this case, however, if the connection is interrupted after the server receives the batch of work, we can be sure that the user's changes will be applied and all locks used to maintain consistency will be immediately released.

By following the very simple rule of keeping transactions within the same batch, we will not leave transactions hanging as SQL Server will make sure that everything that is required for a transaction is ready before a single command is executed. If we get disconnected, we are guaranteed that either all or none of our command will be executed, and we will not affect any other user's performance any longer than necessary.

We will return to the topic of writing batch commands when we look at stored procedures later in this chapter.

Major Coding Issues

Any discussion of data access and modification techniques using queries would not be complete without covering three features that most affect SQL Server's performance:

❑   Temporary tables

Advanced Data Access and Modification Techniques

- Cursors
- NULLs

We will look at these topics in some depth, to make sure that you can deal with them effectively and avoid potential performance issues which can result from their misuse.

Temporary Tables

Temporary tables (usually called temp tables) were briefly mentioned earlier in the book when we were discussing table creation. They are like permanent tables, but are removed from the system when they go out of scope. There are two different kinds:

- Local temp tables (whose names are prefixed with #) are scoped to the connection to SQL Server.
- Global temp tables (names prefixed with ##) are allowed to be viewed by any connection and any user in the system. They do not fully go out of scope until the connection that creates them is destroyed *and* any other connections that are using the tables stop accessing them.

Temp tables allow us to create our own temporary storage and add some data into it, using the same INSERT, UPDATE, and DELETE statements as with permanent tables. They can also be indexed if necessary. In fact, a temp table is just an ordinary table that has a very short life span. Note too that any user can create them and use them as he/she sees fit.

> **In earlier versions of SQL Server, temp tables were frequently used as workarounds to overcome certain limitations. With SQL Server 2000, they should be far less frequently employed. Using a temp table in a query will always be slower than one executed in straight SQL.**

For example, imagine we want to try to determine the number of stored procedures and functions that have either two or three parameters. Using a temp table for this might seem the ideal solution:

```sql
--create the table to hold the names of the objects
CREATE TABLE #counting
(
    specific_name sysname
)

--insert all of the rows that have between 2 and 3 parameters
INSERT INTO #counting (specific_name)
SELECT specific_name
FROM information_schema.parameters as parameters
GROUP BY specific_name
HAVING COUNT(*) between 2 and 3

--count the number of values in the table
SELECT COUNT(*)
FROM #counting

DROP TABLE #counting
```

This code will return the right value (which of course will vary from SQL Server to SQL Server):

```
-----------
355
```

With a bit more thought, we can avoid using the temp table altogether and execute the query in SQL only – boosting the query's speed:

```
SELECT count(*)
FROM (SELECT specific_name
    FROM information_schema.parameters AS parameters
    GROUP BY specific_name
    HAVING count(*) between 2 and 3 ) AS TwoParms
```

We will explore this example of parameter counts again in the next section on cursors.

Temp tables could be avoided more easily if we all made better use of the following under-used T-SQL features:

- Derived tables – one of the most important additions to the T-SQL language has been the ability to include subqueries in joins. This is an extremely useful technique, and it allow us to do most of the things that we would previously have done with temp tables in our queries, like this:

    ```
    SELECT tableName.subqueryTableName,
           alias.subqueryTableNameId AS aliasKey
    FROM tableName
    JOIN ( select subqueryTableNameId, tableNameId
           from subqueryTableName ) AS alias
        ON tableName.tableNameId = alias.tableNameId
    ```

    The subquery acts exactly like a single-use view in the query and, as it allows you to use GROUP BY and HAVING clauses, you do not need a temp table to perform the query, which will be much faster because of this. Note that we can nest derived tables within other derived tables, if needed.

- UNION [ALL] – frequently, a temp table will be built to take two sets and put them together. In many cases, a UNION ALL could be used to put the sets together instead. There have been times when I have gained a 40 per cent speed improvement by using a UNION ALL where I might have used a temp table in the past. Also, if some final WHERE clause is applied to the entire set, we can put the unioned set in a derived table!

- Large numbers of tables in one query – in some cases, it may be prudent to divide long queries into smaller, more palatable chunks of code by breaking them up into calls to temporary tables. However, SQL Server 2000 will allow up to 256 permanent tables to be accessed in a single query, and it will often do a better job of choosing how to execute the query than you will.

This all sounds like the final nail in the coffin of temp tables. However, they can be useful when we need to manipulate the data in some manner that needs more than a single pass. I use temp tables quite frequently when implementing a recursive tree for display on the screen – adding the values for each level of the tree to the next level. A temp table is ideal in this specific situation because we have to iterate through the set to touch each level of the tree, and we need somewhere to store the intermediate values.

In this example, we will take a recursive table called `type`. Each of the types may have an unlimited number of subtypes. We need to order and display them as a tree, with sub-items directly following other subtypes. The tree of data has the following nodes that we will deal with:

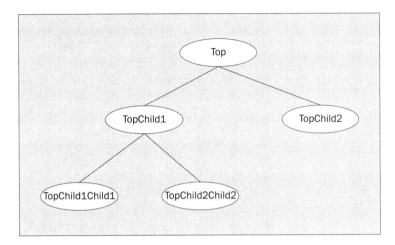

First, let's set up the scenario:

```
--first we create the type table
CREATE TABLE type
(
    typeId int,                 --not identity because we need to reference
                                --it in this test script
    parentTypeId int NULL,
    name varchar(60) NOT NULL,
)

--then we have to populate the type table
INSERT INTO type (typeId, parentTypeId, name)
VALUES (1, NULL, 'Top')
INSERT INTO type (typeId, parentTypeId, name)
VALUES (2,1, 'TopChild1')
INSERT INTO type (typeId, parentTypeId, name)
VALUES (3,1, 'TopChild2')
INSERT INTO type (typeId, parentTypeId, name)
VALUES (4,2, 'TopChild1Child1')
INSERT INTO type (typeId, parentTypeId, name)
VALUES (5,2, 'TopChild1Child2')
```

Now we build the query using a temp table that will display the tree. Note that we use the temp table here as an array to hold some values while we make extra passes – a SELECT statement will not suffice:

```
CREATE TABLE #holdItems
(
    typeId int NOT NULL,            --pkey of type table
    parentTypeID int NULL,          --recursive attribute
    name varchar(100),              --name of the type
    indentLevel int,                --level of the tree for indenting display
    sortOrder varchar(1000)         --sort order for final display
)
```

We now add the top of the tree items into the temp table:

```
--get the toplevel items
INSERT INTO #holdItems

-- First pass will start at indentLevel 1. We put the parent primary key into
-- the sortOrder, padded with zeroes to the right, then we will append each
-- level of child to each sublevel
SELECT typeId, parentTypeID, name, 1 AS indentLevel,
       LTRIM(replicate('0',10 - LEN(CAST(typeId AS char(10)))) +
       CAST(typeId AS char(10))) AS sortOrder
FROM dbo.type
WHERE parentTypeID IS NULL          --parent is NULL means top node
```

Then we have to code a loop to work down the table levels, one at a time, ordering the rows for output:

```
DECLARE @currLevel int
SET @currLevel = 2

WHILE 1=1                       -- since there is no repeat until in T-SQL
   BEGIN

      INSERT INTO #holdItems

      -- add the sort order of this item to current sort order
      -- of the parent's sort order
      SELECT type.TypeId, type.parentTypeID, type.name,
             @currLevel AS indentLevel,
             RTRIM(#holdItems.sortOrder) +
             LTRIM(replicate('0',10 - LEN(CAST(type.typeId AS char(10)))) +
             CAST(type.typeId as char(10)))
      FROM dbo.type AS type

      -- this join gets us the child records of the items in the
      -- #holdItemsTable
      JOIN #holdItems
         ON Type.parentTypeId = #holdItems.typeId

         -- currlevel tells us the level we are adding, so we need the parent
         -- in the @join
         WHERE #holdItems.indentLevel = @currLevel - 1

      -- if there are no children on the new level, we break
      IF @@rowcount = 0
         BREAK

      -- otherwise we simply increment the counter and move on.
      SET @currLevel = @currLevel + 1
   END
```

Now we have all of the data set up that we need to display the tree

```
SELECT typeId, parentTypeId, CAST(name AS varchar(15)) AS name, indentLevel
FROM #holdItems
ORDER BY sortorder, parentTypeID

-- drop table is not explicitly required if in a stored procedure or if
-- we disconnect between executions
DROP TABLE #holdItems
```

Advanced Data Access and Modification Techniques

This all yields the following set of rows:

```
typeId      parentTypeId name indent    Level
---------   ------------------------    --------------------
1           NULL                        Top 1
2           1                           TopChild1 2
4           2                           TopChild1Child1 3
5           2                           TopChild1Child2 3
3           1                           TopChild2 2
```

This forms the basis of a routine which deals with binary (recursive) trees coded in SQL tables. By extending this algorithm, we can do almost anything we need to do with binary trees, with remarkably good performance.

Don't forget though – if we could do this without the temp tables, it would be faster still. Basically, before using a temp table, make sure that it is not possible to code the solution without it.

Cursors

In SQL, the typical way to deal with data is a set at a time. We have seen this over and over again in our examples. However, it is not always possible to deal with data in a set-based manner. **Cursors** are a mechanism in T-SQL that allow us to get to an individual row and perform an action on it, rather than operating on a pre-selected group of rows.

There are two different types of cursors that are frequently used:

- **External, database API cursors** – these are specific cursors that are used to provide external interfaces to SQL Server. Common examples are ODBC, OLE DB, and ADO. Using cursors associated with these technologies, programmers can build streams of data for their applications.

    API cursors are primarily used by application programmers and, as such, are beyond the scope of this book.

- **Transact-SQL cursors** – these cursors are used in T-SQL code and we will look at them in detail in this section. We will use them to loop through SQL based steps to perform an action one row at a time.

People tend to have very opposite opinions of cursors in T-SQL code. The two main schools of thought are that:

- Cursors are evil
- Cursors are very useful tools that we must have available

The reasons why cursors have been described as "evil" are twofold:

- First, they tend to lead to poor implementations of solutions to problems that are better resolved using set-based SQL. In these cases, the performance of a query using cursors will frequently be an order of magnitude slower than when using set-based operations.

- Unless we use the proper cursor types, we will end up placing locks around our database for each row that we access. When using T-SQL cursors, this may be less of a problem since our T-SQL code will never have to wait for user interaction, but the problem certainly still exists.

The second school of thought on the use of cursors also rings true, as there are occasions where you do have to use them. With the advent of user-defined functions, however, there is really only one situation where the cursor provides the only possibility for implementation – when you need to perform some command on each row in a set. For instance, a cursor would allow you to perform a custom stored procedure, containing business logic, on every row in a table.

Let's now discuss the basic syntax of cursors. To employ a cursor, you need to use the `SET` command:

```
SET @<cursorName> = CURSOR
    [ FORWARD_ONLY | SCROLL ]
    [ STATIC | KEYSET | DYNAMIC | FAST_FORWARD ]
    [ READ_ONLY | SCROLL_LOCKS | OPTIMISTIC ]
    [ TYPE_WARNING ]
FOR <SELECT statement>
    [ FOR UPDATE [ OF <column1>, <column2>,...,<columnN> ] ]
```

> *If you have used cursors in the past, you are probably more familiar with the `DECLARE CURSOR` syntax. It is my opinion that using `SET` to set the cursor variable is a more coherent way of dealing with cursors. It leads to better code, since all cursors built this way are always local cursors and are dealt with in much the same manner as typical SQL Server variables. Because they are scoped to a particular batch, they do not have to be allocated and de-allocated.*

Name

```
SET @<cursorName> = CURSOR
```

This declares a variable as a cursor data type. This may then be passed around to different procedures as a parameter. It has the same scope as a typical SQL variable and this alleviates the need to explicitly close and de-allocate cursors.

Direction

```
    [ FORWARD_ONLY | SCROLL ]
```

It generally benefits you to use a `FORWARD_ONLY` cursor, unless you have some important reason to move back and forth in the table (`SCROLL`). Forward only cursors use less resources than scrolling ones as, once you have moved past the row, it can be discarded.

We usually will leave this setting blank as the `FAST_FORWARD` setting from the next set of optional parameters will not work with either `FORWARD_ONLY` or `SCROLL`, and `FAST_FORWARD` builds the most optimized cursor for typical use.

Cursor Type

```
    [ STATIC | KEYSET | DYNAMIC | FAST_FORWARD ]
```

With the `STATIC` option, SQL Server copies the data you need into its `tempdb` database and then you can move about in the set. No changes made to the underlying data will be seen in the cursor. This is the default.

`KEYSET` cursors simply make a copy of the keys in `tempdb` and then, as you request a row, SQL Server goes out to the physical table and fetches the data. You cannot see any new data, but you will see any changes to existing data, including deletes.

Advanced Data Access and Modification Techniques

DYNAMIC cursors are a bit more costly in terms of performance as the cursor values are not materialized into a working set until you actually fetch data from them. With KEYSET cursors, the members of the table are fixed at the time of the cursor's creation. DYNAMIC cursors have their members determined only as the cursor is moved.

The best choice is usually to specify a FAST_FORWARD cursor, but this setting precludes any of the direction settings and does not allow scrolling. This is not a static cursor because, if you make any modifications to the data, they will show up. In one of the examples shortly, we will show how this property can affect the cursors we use.

Updatability

```
[ READ_ONLY | SCROLL_LOCKS | OPTIMISTIC ]
```

The READ_ONLY option should be obvious, but the other two are less so. They both allow you to update the data in the cursor. However, it is generally not a great idea to make use of the positional updates in T-SQL code, as it can be really confusing to understand exactly where you are in the set.

If you really need to make updates, use an enhancement to the UPDATE statement with a non-static cursor type (KEYSET or DYNAMIC):

```
UPDATE <tableName>
SET <field> = value
FROM <tableName>
WHERE CURRENT OF @<cursorVariableName>
```

The CURRENT OF keyword tells the statement to modify the row that the cursor is currently positioned on. You can also do delete operations as well.

To carry out updates in the cursor, we can use the SCROLL_LOCKS and OPTIMISTIC settings. SCROLL_LOCKS will guarantee that our updates and deletes (made in the position specified by CURRENT OF) succeed by placing locks on the underlying tables. OPTIMISTIC uses the table's timestamp column or, if none is available, builds a checksum for each row. This checksum is used in just the same way as the optimistic lock we have discussed before, by recalculating prior to making a change to see if another user has modified the row.

However, unless you find a really good reason for updating data within a cursor, don't try it. It is much easier to do the same task using code like this:

```
UPDATE <tableName>
SET <field> = value
FROM <tableName>
WHERE <pkey> = @<variable 'fetched into' using cursor>
```

This does almost the same thing as the CURRENT OF cursor and is easier to read and debug, since we can print out the variable as we work through our examples.

Cursor Type Downgrading

```
[TYPE_WARNING]
```

If the SELECT statement that you have specified is unable to use a given cursor type, this setting requests an error message from SQL Server warning of this. Such a situation might arise if you try to use a KEYSET cursor on a set with no unique key with which to build the key set – SQL Server might choose to use a static cursor instead.

Cursor Performance

This example illustrates some of the performance issues with cursors. We seek to find out which stored procedures and functions in the master database have two or three parameters (as we did with the temp table example), based on the PARAMETERS view of the INFORMATION_SCHEMA. We will time the operation as it runs on my Dell 400MHz Pentium II laptop, with 256MB of RAM. First, we create a temp table using a cursor:

```sql
SELECT getdate()               -- get time before the code is run

--temporary table to hold the procedures as we loop through
CREATE TABLE #holdProcedures
(
    specific_name sysname
)

DECLARE @cursor CURSOR,        --cursor variable
        @c_routineName sysname    -- variable to hold the values as we loop

SET @cursor = CURSOR FAST_FORWARD FOR SELECT DISTINCT specific_name
FROM information_schema.parameters
OPEN @cursor                   --activate the cursor
FETCH NEXT FROM @cursor INTO @c_routineName   --get the first row

WHILE @@fetch_status = 0       --this means that the row was fetched cleanly
    BEGIN
        --check to see if the count of parameters for this specific name
        --is between 2 and 3
        IF ( SELECT count(*)
             FROM information_schema.parameters as parameters
             WHERE parameters.specific_name = @c_routineName )
                BETWEEN 2 AND 3
            BEGIN              --it was, so put into temp storage
                INSERT INTO #holdProcedures
                VALUES (@c_routineName)
            END

        FETCH NEXT FROM @cursor INTO @c_routineName   --get the next row
    END
```

and once we are done, we can count the number of records:

```sql
SELECT count(*)
FROM #holdProcedures

SELECT getdate()  --output the time after the code is complete
```

Advanced Data Access and Modification Techniques

Executing this statement, we get the following result:

```
-----------------------------
2001-01-10 23:46:59.477

-----------------------------
355

-----------------------------
2001-01-10 23:47:00.917
```

This indicates that the operation took around 1.5 seconds to execute. This is not too slow, but there is certainly a better way of doing this, as shown here:

```
SELECT GETDATE()     --again for demo purposes

SELECT COUNT(*)
--use a nested subquery to get all of the functions with
--the proper count of parameters
FROM (SELECT parameters.specific_name
      FROM information_schema.parameters AS parameters
      GROUP BY parameters.specific_name
      HAVING COUNT(*) BETWEEN 2 AND 3) AS counts

SELECT GETDATE()
```

This time we achieve a somewhat better result:

```
-----------------------------
2001-01-10 23:50:25.160

-----------------------------
355

-----------------------------
2001-01-10 23:50:25.823
```

It takes 0.7 seconds to run the query now, which is about half the time taken to do the same task using cursors. Additionally, the code is far less verbose and easier for SQL Server to optimize.

Hopefully, this goes some way to demonstrating that cursors are a large performance problem, taking up many more resources than set-based operations do.

Uses of Cursors

While I would warn against getting into the habit of using cursors, as I mentioned in the introduction to this section, they can be very useful in certain situations. Here are the circumstances under which I consider cursors to be very helpful:

- Executing system commands, such as DBCC, or system stored procedures
- Executing stored procedures for each row in a set
- Where we must access each row individually, rather than a set at a time

429

The first two of these should be fairly self-explanatory. A common example of a system stored procedure that we may need to execute using cursors is `sp_adduser`. If we are provisioning users, such as from a spreadsheet, we would likely import the data into a temp table in SQL Server, iterate through the values using a cursor, and add the new users to the database.

The second is different from the first, but not by much. If you have to execute a stored procedure once for each row in a set, you will usually have to employ a cursor. This is a relatively common activity (such as implementing business rules from a stored procedure) though it is not the optimal way to handle the situation, unless you are not the owner of the system you need to get the data into. For instance, if we do not own the system tables but we have to add data to them, we will probably accept that calling a stored procedure in a loop is the only way to carry out this task. If we were the owner of these tables, we could carry out this task using triggers instead.

The third situation is where we can get ourselves into trouble. There are an extremely limited number of reasons why we might have to go through each row in our set one after the other. The only common situation where I would use a cursor, and where I was not calling to some type of function, is demonstrated in the following example. Here we are going to implement an artificial sort order on a set. We will load the set with random values and finally, re-number the set in a uniform manner using a cursor. Consider that we have the following table:

```
-- table to demonstrate cursors
CREATE TABLE item
(
    itemId int IDENTITY
    CONSTRAINT XPKItem PRIMARY KEY,
    sortOrderId int
    CONSTRAINT xAKItem_sortOrder UNIQUE
)
```

The first step is to load the table by filling the sort order with random numbers:

```
DECLARE @holdSortOrderId int, @counter int
SET @counter = 1                           --initialize counter

WHILE @counter <= 5
   BEGIN
      --use random numbers between 0 and 1000
      SET @holdSortOrderId = CAST(RAND() * 1000 AS int)

      --make sure the random number doesn't already exist as
      --a sort order
      IF NOT EXISTS (SELECT *
                     FROM dbo.item
                     WHERE sortOrderId = @holdSortOrderId)
      BEGIN
         --insert it
         INSERT INTO dbo.item (sortOrderId)
         VALUES (@holdSortOrderId)

         --increment the counter
         SET @counter = @counter + 1
      END
   END
```

Advanced Data Access and Modification Techniques

Once we have loaded our table, we take a look at the results:

```
SELECT *
FROM dbo.item
ORDER BY sortOrderId
```

This gives us a fairly random set of numbers, which we will want to reorganize in the next step:

itemId	sortOrderId
4	29
2	35
1	71
3	72
5	81

Now we will build a cursor to move through all of the items in our table, ordered by the sort order, and we will update each row separately:

```
DECLARE @cursor CURSOR,                          --cursor variable
        @c_itemId int, @c_sortOrderId int, --cursor item variables
        @currentSortOrderId int              --used to increment the sort order
SET @currentSortOrderId = 1                  --initialize the counter

--use static cursor so we do not see changed values
SET @cursor = CURSOR FORWARD_ONLY STATIC FOR SELECT itemId, sortOrderId
        FROM dbo.item
        ORDER BY sortOrderId
OPEN @cursor                                 --activate the cursor

--get the first row
FETCH NEXT FROM @cursor INTO @c_itemId, @c_sortOrderId

--fetch_status = 0 says that the fetch went fine
WHILE @@fetch_status = 0      --this means that the row was fetched cleanly
   BEGIN
      --update the table to the new value of the sort order
      UPDATE dbo.item
      SET sortOrderId = @currentSortOrderId
      WHERE itemId = @c_itemId

      --increment the sort order counter to add 100 items of space
      SET @currentSortOrderId = @currentSortOrderId + 100

      --get the next row
      FETCH NEXT FROM @cursor INTO @c_itemId, @c_sortOrderId
   END
```

Because we added the line to output the keys of every row, we get the following output:

c_itemId	c_sortOrderId	current SortOrderId
4	29	1

c_itemId c_sort	OrderId current	SortOrderId
2	35	101

c_itemId c_sort	OrderId current	SortOrderId
1	71	201

c_itemId c_sort	OrderId current	SortOrderId
3	72	301

c_itemId c_sort	OrderId current	SortOrderId
5	81	401

Next we look at the values in the table:

```
SELECT *
FROM dbo.item
ORDER BY sortOrderId
```

If everything went well, the rows are output in the same order:

itemId sort	OrderId
4	1
2	101
1	201
3	301
5	401

But what if we change to a DYNAMIC cursor type, like the FAST_FORWARD cursor? If we change the FORWARD_ONLY STATIC part of the cursor declaration to FAST_FORWARD, we will get results like the following:

c_itemId c_sort	OrderId current	SortOrderId
4	29	1

c_itemId c_sort	OrderId current	SortOrderId
2	35	101

c_itemId c_sort	OrderId current	SortOrderId
1	71	201

c_itemId c_sort	OrderId current	SortOrderId
3	72	301

c_itemId c_sort	OrderId current	SortOrderId
5	81	401

c_itemId c_sort	OrderId current	SortOrderId
2	101	501

c_itemId c_sort	OrderId current	SortOrderId
1	201	601

c_itemId c_sort	OrderId current	SortOrderId
3	301	701

c_itemId c_sort	OrderId current	SortOrderId
5	401	801

c_itemId c_sort	OrderId current	SortOrderId
2	501	901

...and so on.

The reason for this is that the values in the cursor *change*, and end up reordered by the sort order. Since the sort order is changed to more than the next value of sort order, you can never get to the end of the chain.

> **Always specify the type of cursor you want, as you may get unpredictable results otherwise.**

NULL Handling

In Chapter 10, we discussed allowing fields to be nullable. In this section, we need to shed light on programming with NULLs and, especially, how NULL comparisons are handled in SQL Server and what this means to your code.

NULLs can be tricky to work with, and it's hard to avoid having them in your databases. This may seem a bold statement. Could we not set every field in the database to NOT NULL? Yes, but any time we use an outer join in a statement, the values that are not returned will all be filled with NULLs.

We will now examine a slightly different way of looking at what "NULL" refers to when used in a logical expression, and I am indebted to Dr David Rozenshtein for introducing me to this concept. We will see some of the more interesting problems that arise when dealing with NULL data, and which are commonly overlooked.

What does NULL mean? According to SQL Server 2000 Books Online, "A value of NULL indicates the value is unknown. A value of NULL is different from an empty or zero value. No two NULL values are equal. Comparisons between two NULL values, or between a NULL and any other value, return unknown because the value of each NULL is unknown."

So it is fairly clear that NULL means unknown. And this meaning serves us well in the case of a field being left NULL, and even in the case of a join, where the match of one set to another is unknown. However, when programming using three-value logic (true, false, and NULL) we have to be a bit craftier than that.

The problem is a fairly simple one to demonstrate. Consider the following statement:

```
SELECT CASE WHEN NOT(1=NULL) THEN 'True' ELSE 'False' END
```

It is obvious that (1=1) gives True and (1=0) gives False. What about (1=NULL)? I believe that False is the logical answer. And, obviously, NOT(False)=True. Yet executing this query returns a different value:

```
-------
False
```

Well – OK then – if NOT(1=NULL) is False, then NOT(NOT(1=NULL)) must be True, right? So we execute the following:

```
SELECT CASE WHEN NOT(NOT(1=NULL)) THEN 'True' ELSE 'False' END
```

This returns **False** again!

This fundamental property of three-valued logic is one of the least understood principles in SQL Server programming.

The problem lies with the definition of NULL as unknown. Logically speaking, what is the opposite of unknown? Known. So, consider that we replace (1=NULL) with Unknown because, logically, if NULL is Unknown then it is still Unknown if it is equivalent to 1. Therefore, NOT(1=NULL) must be NOT(Unknown). And this equals Known, right? Perhaps in an English lesson, but not in three-valued logic.

Maybe

What if we use Maybe instead of Unknown? So, (1=NULL) is Maybe. And the opposite of Maybe? Maybe.

Consider the following truth tables:

AND	True	False	OR	True	False
True	True	False	**True**	True	True
False	False	False	**False**	True	False

Taking a look at a few examples from this table, we see that `True AND True = True` and `True AND False = False`.

Next, we look at the standard truth tables including `NULL`. These tables come from SQL Server 2000 Books Online, but have `Unknown` replaced with my `Maybe`:

AND	True	False	Null	OR	True	False	Null
True	True	False	Maybe	**True**	True	True	True
False	False	False	Maybe	**False**	True	False	Maybe
Null	Maybe	Maybe	Maybe	**Null**	True	Maybe	Maybe

So we see that, while `True AND NULL = Maybe`, `True OR NULL = True`.

The other interesting comparison is `(NULL=NULL)`. It sure looks like `True`, but how can two unknown values be equal? They aren't – the result is `Maybe`.

Here are the `NOT AND` and `NOT OR` truth tables:

NOT AND	True	False	Null	NOT OR	True	False	Null
True	False	True	Maybe	**True**	False	False	False
False	True	True	Maybe	**False**	False	True	Maybe
Null	Maybe	Maybe	Maybe	**Null**	False	Maybe	Maybe

It is important to test these last two tables using `(1=1)` is `True`, `(1=0)` is `False`, and `(1=NULL)` is `Maybe`. For example:

```
SELECT CASE WHEN (NOT((1=1) OR (1=NULL)) AND (1=1))
            THEN 'True'
            ELSE 'False'
       END
```

We take each logical expression and evaluate it:

`(NOT(True OR Maybe) AND True) = NOT(True AND True) = NOT(True) = False`

which we see by executing the statement:

```
-------
False
```

An underlying issue in understanding some ugly logic errors in SQL Server programming is getting to grips with the fact that SQL Server evaluates the statement using the proper three-valued logic but, in the final analysis, treats the `NULL` value as `False`. However, since a great number of the most important queries you will write will include many search criteria, it is important to understand that the `NULL` value is kept as a `NULL` until the very end.

Chapter 12

Consider that we are looking at a WHERE clause for a given row, trying to figure out why it is not returning a value when we expect one:

```
WHERE NOT ((field1=@field1) OR (field2=@field2))
```

In the following line, we have replaced all of the field and variable values in the code with the data that is being compared:

```
WHERE NOT ((1=1) OR (NULL=NULL))
```

So we end up with NOT(True OR Maybe) = NOT(True) = False. This seems fairly reasonable. However, let's change the values just slightly:

```
WHERE NOT ((2=1) OR (NULL=NULL))
```

Now we have NOT(False OR Maybe) = NOT(Maybe) = Maybe.

> **Note though that, when SQL Server ends a comparison with the Maybe value, at that point it treats it as a False.**

Presumably it is safer to work in this pessimistic way, since a maybe could well be false.

> *While the ANSI standard for the comparison is that (NULL=NULL) evaluates to NULL, SQL Server 6.5 and earlier versions assumed that (NULL=NULL)=True. There is a setting in SQL Server 2000 (SET ANSI_NULLS) which allows this to be toggled so that we can make (NULL=NULL)=True. However, using this setting is not recommended unless you have backward compatibility issues. It tends to cause more trouble than it solves and the setting will likely not exist must longer.*

Problems with comparing data that includes NULLs are very common, and can only be combated by being extremely careful with NULL usage. We must be sure to understand that:

- (NULL = 3) has a value of Maybe
- (NULL > 3) also has a value of Maybe

And the example of where it will bite you: NOT(field1 = 3), where field1 is NULL, will evaluate to NOT(Maybe) = Maybe. SQL Server finally evaluates this to False.

IS NULL

The only comparison that works all of the time with NULLs is the IS NULL operator. We can discover which values are NULL by using:

```
WHERE field1 IS NULL
```

This will return True if the field is NULL, or False if it is not. There is also an IS NOT NULL operator which does the logical opposite of the IS NULL operator. Using these two operators, we can formulate proper comparisons with two values that are NULL. For example, if we want to determine whether two nullable values are "equal", meaning they have the same value or both are NULL, we would need the following three part comparison:

```
    WHERE field1 = @field1
      OR (field1 IS NULL
      AND field2 IS NULL)
```

This may seem pretty obvious but, of all the logical coding bugs I find and contribute to, by far the most pervasive are those involving transformations with a field that requires NULLs.

Suppose that we have a view from which I am building the transformation, and a child record of one of the tables – giving a person's address – is not available. However, not all people have an office address, so we have to use an outer join.

```
    CREATE VIEW v_person
    AS
    SELECT person.personId, person.lastName
           address.streetName
    FROM dbo.person AS person
    LEFT OUTER JOIN dbo.personAddress AS personAddress
        JOIN dbo.address as address
            ON address.addressId = personAddress.addressId
            AND personAddress.type = 1              --office address
        ON person.personId = personAddress.personId
```

Now a transformation query is built to insert any rows where the `personId` does not exist in the table. This is pretty easy to deal with. Next we code the following update statement to change the values for a person if any have altered:

```
    UPDATE person
    SET person.lastName = v_person.lastName,
        person.streetName = v_person.streetName,
        person.streetName = v_person.streetName
    FROM ODS..person AS person
    JOIN dbo.v_person AS v_person
        ON person.personId = v_person.personId
    WHERE person.lastName <> v_person.lastName
          OR person.firstName <> v_person.firstName
          OR person.streetName <> v_person.streetName
```

This looks pretty much correct, yet there is a gaping hole in there. Even assuming that all fields in our base tables do not allow NULLs, a left outer join exists in our view. streetName can be NULL. If the personAddress record does not exist, circumstances could arise where v_person.streetName is NULL but, if person.streetName is not NULL, this still evaluates to a False condition. Substituting real data into the following:

```
    WHERE person.lastName <> v_person.lastName
          OR person.streetName <> v_person.streetName
```

we get:

```
    WHERE 'Davidson' <> 'Davidson'
          OR 'Worthdale' <> NULL
```

Looking back at the truth tables, this evaluates to (False or Maybe) = Maybe. And SQL Server evaluates this to False! It is very easy to do this, so you must write queries such as:

```
WHERE person.lastName <> v_person.lastName
    OR   person.firstName <> v_person.firstName
    OR (person.streetName <> v_person.streetName
    OR (person.streetName IS NULL AND person.streetName IS NOT NULL )
    OR (person.streetName IS NOT NULL AND person.streetName IS NULL ) )
```

This code is painful to write, but it is the only way we can effectively deal with comparisons to NULL.

NULLs in other Operations

The last point to be made about NULLs concerns using them in other operations. When dealing with a NULL in a situation other than a logical comparison, it is best to consider it as Unknown. NULL does not mean, nor should it ever mean, "nothing". NULL is something, so it must be treated as such, though its identity is unknown. For example:

- Numerical calculations: NULL + 10 evaluates to Unknown since, if we don't know how many we start with, then adding 10 makes no difference.

- String concatenations: '*' + NULL + '*' also evaluates to Unknown, since there is no way of knowing what the string should actually be.

- NULL + NULL: obvious really, two Unknowns cannot possibly produce anything other than Unknown.

Hence, when dealing with an operation where one or more factors could well be NULL, you need to use one of several mechanisms that SQL Server provides – the keyword CASE, and the functions ISNULL and COALESCE.

For example, to perform the following concatenation:

```
SELECT '*' + @field + '*'
```

where @field may be NULL, and we wish to receive a non-NULL result if the @field is NULL, we can take the following three paths:

```
SELECT CASE @field
    WHEN NULL THEN ''
    ELSE @field
END
```

or:

```
SELECT ISNULL(@field,'')
```

or:

```
SELECT COALESCE(@field,'')
```

Advanced Data Access and Modification Techniques

Each of these has different merits:

- CASE – the use of CASE here is pretty self explanatory. It is a very powerful tool that goes far beyond simple NULL validations.

- ISNULL has two parameters. It checks to see if the first is NULL and then returns the second (in the case above, an empty string) if it is. If the second parameter is NULL, NULL is still returned.

- COALESCE allows us to supply multiple parameters and it chooses the first non NULL value. For example, COALESCE(@field, @variable, @variable2 + '*', '') would first check @field, then @variable, and so on. This is the equivalent to a CASE statement that does:

```
SELECT CASE WHEN @field IS NOT NULL THEN @field
       WHEN @variable IS NOT NULL THEN @variable
       WHEN @variable2 + '*' IS NOT NULL THEN @variable2 + '*'
       ELSE ''
END
```

Hopefully, this section has highlighted some of the problems to bear in mind when programming with NULLs. They can be troublesome to implement, but there's no way to avoid having to deal with them.

Views

As we discussed in Chapter 3, views can be thought of as virtual tables and have most of the characteristics of a normal database table. As far as our SQL statements are concerned, they *are* tables, although they generally do not support modification statements (apart from in very specific circumstances). Indeed, we would not really want to use views for modification purposes as they are meant to simplify our viewing of data.

> *Note that views are not pre-compiled objects like stored procedures but, rather, are simply implemented as text that can be inserted into a query where needed, just as you insert a derived query into a statement.*

There are a few general cases where views will be employed in our database:

- To encapsulate implementation details – they can be used to hide a large number of joins from the user

- As a real-time reporting tool – they can be used to implement reports that touch our live data and don't affect performance, by specifying a set of known queries that users frequently employ

- As security mechanisms – by giving access to a view and not the base table, we can implement row based or column based security

We will look at these situations now.

Views as an Encapsulation Device

Views are excellent encapsulation devices. We can take our highly normalized tables, join them back to the other tables in our database, and give our users data presented as they expect it to be, hiding from them the underlying database and the complexities of the actual mechanism by which the data was accessed. Views can also screen out all the unwanted data, enabling the user to focus on what is really important.

Suppose that we have the following two tables in a sales database. The `item` table represents items that are for sale, and a `sale` table indicates the number of items sold:

```
--items that we sell
CREATE TABLE item
(
    itemId int NOT NULL IDENTITY,
    name varchar(60) NOT NULL,
    price money
)

--records sales
CREATE TABLE sale
(
    saleId int NOT NULL IDENTITY,
    itemId int NOT NULL,        --foreign key to the item table
    date datetime NOT NULL,
    itemCount int NOT NULL      --number of items sold
)
```

We might wish to build a view to encapsulate the item and the sales information into a single table for the user to view.

```
CREATE VIEW v_sale
AS
SELECT sale.saleId, sale.itemId, sale.date, sale.itemCount,
       item.name, item.price
FROM dbo.sale AS sale
JOIN dbo.item AS item
    ON sale.itemId = item.itemId
```

Now, whenever the user needs to look at a sale, the view will save them from having to manually join in the `item` table. This is a pretty simple example, but when ten or more tables are included in a view, the time savings in coding can be pretty great. Plus, if the tables' columns change – or we do further normalization and, instead of storing the price in the `item` table, we store a reference to a separate `price` table where the value is stored – the user of the view never has to know about it.

Views in Real-Time Reporting

Real-time reporting is a term which indicates that a report can have no latency, that is, its data is continually updated. If we want immediate, up-to-the-second reports, one way to implement this is with a view. A view offers us a couple of benefits over writing a query directly against the tables, as you would with typical report-writing code:

- ❏ Views prevent *ad hoc* report queries – *ad hoc* querying against live tables can produce big performance hits. By building a view or views, we can attempt to channel any real-time querying needs into using a set of queries that have been optimized, tested, and have a smaller chance of affecting overall system performance.

- ❏ Views avoid locking – we can usually build reports in such a way that they will ignore locks in the database and, more importantly, do not *leave* locks in the database either. This is achieved by using the `readuncommitted` (or `nolock`) optimizer hint. This hint should only be used when estimated data is acceptable, as some of the records it reads may be in a transaction that could be rolled back. This way, no matter what the user tries to do with the view, it will not lock any resources.

Advanced Data Access and Modification Techniques

Going back to our tables, let's say the user needs to see up-to-the-minute sales figures on an hourly basis. We discover from the user that we can ignore those instances where a sale is recorded but might be removed later. So, we might create the following view for the user to build queries with:

```
CREATE VIEW v_saleHourlyReport
AS
SELECT item.itemId, dbo.date$removeTime(sale.date) AS saleDate,
       datePart(hour,sale.date) AS saleHour,
       sum(sale.itemCount) AS totalSold,
       sum(sale.itemCount * item.price) AS soldValue
FROM dbo.item as item (readuncommitted)
JOIN dbo.sale as sale(readuncommitted)
   ON sale.itemId = item.itemId
--group by item ID information, then the day and the hour of the day, to
--give what was asked
GROUP BY item.itemId, item.name, dbo.date$removeTime(sale.date),
         datePart(hour,sale.date)
```

Note that here we are using the `datePart` *system function for extracting the hour from the date, and Chapter 11's function to remove the time from the date.*

Now this query can be executed repeatedly with less effect on ongoing processes, since we have removed the chances of the data holding read locks as it is used (with the `readuncommitted` statements).

Of course, these measures are only as good as the tools that are built to use them. Even without locking, it is possible to use vast system resources if a view is joined to other views in an unfavorable manner.

Views as Security Mechanisms

There are two properties of views that we will make use of to build a more secure database. The first is assigning privileges to a user such that he can use a view, though not the underlying tables. For example, consider that we have a `person` table:

```
CREATE TABLE person
(
    personId int IDENTITY,
    firstName varchar(20) ,
    lastName varchar(40)
)
```

We could construct a view on this:

```
CREATE VIEW vPerson
AS
SELECT personId, firstName, lastName
FROM dbo.person
```

Selecting data from either of these returns the exact same data. However, they are two separate structures that we can separately assign access privileges to.

The second property of views which is useful as a security mechanism is the ability to partition a table structure, by limiting the rows or columns visible to the user. Suppose we have the following table structure:

441

Chapter 12

	Column1	Column2	...	ColumnN
Row1	Secretary1's salary	Secretary1's SSN		Secretary1's address
Row2	Manager1's salary	Manager1's SSN		Manager1's address
...				
RowN	CEO's salary	CEO's SSN		CEO's address

Views let us cut the table in sections that include all columns, but not all the rows, based on some criteria. This is **row-level security**, or **horizontally partitioning** our data. In our example, we might only allow Secretary1 to see Row1, while the rest of the rows do not even appear to exist:

	Column1	Column2	...	ColumnN
Row1	Secretary1's salary	Secretary1's SSN		Secretary1's address

Hence, by giving the view access to this row only, any user who has privileges for the view will only have rights to see this particular row.

Returning to our code example, we will take the previous view we created and use it as the basis for a very specific view – one that would only be of interest to the manager of the product with an `itemId` of 1. This will allow the manager to monitor the level of sales for this product over the course of a day:

```
CREATE VIEW v_saleHourlyReport_socksOnly
AS
SELECT itemId, saleDate, saleHour, totalSold, soldValue
FROM dbo.v_saleHourlyReport
WHERE itemId = 1
```

We would typically implement a far more comprehensive security plan than hard-coding an `itemId` in a view, but this is to give a quick example of row-level security. We will look at such a plan later in the chapter.

Alternatively, we could use **column-level security**. Unsurprisingly, this is also known as **vertically partitioning** the data, as we will be dividing the view's columns. In the `item` table we have three columns, `itemId`, `name`, and `price`. It would not be abnormal to allow every user of the database to see all of the items with their names, but price might be a different story altogether. Hence, we might put together a view like this:

```
CREATE VIEW v_itemNoPrice
AS
SELECT itemId, name
FROM dbo.item
```

Advanced Data Access and Modification Techniques

Of course, there is no reason why we cannot horizontally and vertically partition our tables at the same time, giving the user as small an about of data as need be:

	Column1
Row1	

Once we have built the necessary views, we would not allow access to the base table, but would give users who need to see the data access to the views instead. A more advanced discussion on security is included in the latter part of this chapter.

What's New in Views?

There are two very exciting new features for views in SQL Server 2000. These features are:

- View indexing
- Partitioning Views

Both of these features will be examined in some detail in the following sections.

Indexed Views

Indexing views is a very exciting feature, but one that is only available in the Enterprise version (and Developer and Evaluation versions) of SQL Server 2000.

By indexing a view, we now have the ability to build triggerless summary data, which is automatically maintained by SQL Server in a way that makes a usually tricky operation as simple as writing a query. Instead of the view definition being used as in ordinary views, the optimizer can choose to use the index, which has the current values for the index pre-materialized.

So, instead of building triggers that summarize our data in other tables, we could create a view. For example, going back to our `item` and `sale` tables, we could create the following view. Note that only schema bound views may be indexed. This makes certain that the tables and structures that the index is created upon will not change underneath the view.

```
CREATE VIEW v_itemSale
WITH SCHEMABINDING
AS
SELECT item.itemId, item.name, sum(sale.itemCount) AS soldCount,
sum(sale.itemCount * item.price) AS soldValue
FROM dbo.item
JOIN dbo.sale
ON item.itemId = sale.itemId
GROUP BY item.itemId, item.name
```

This would do the calculations at execution time. If this were not fast enough, or if it used too many resources to execute, we might add an index on the view like this:

```
CREATE INDEX XV_itemSale_materialize
ON v_itemSale (itemId, name, soldCount, soldValue)
```

SQL Server would then build the view and store it. Now our queries to the view will be *very* fast. However, while we have avoided all of the coding issues involved with storing summary data, we have to keep our data up to date. Every time data changes in the underlying tables, the index on the view will change its data, so there is a performance hit due to maintaining the index for the view. Hence, indexing views means that performance is great for reading but not necessarily for updating.

There are some other caveats too. The restrictions on what can be used in a view, prior to it being indexed, are fairly tight. The most important things that you may not do are:

- Use the SELECT * syntax – columns must be explicitly stated
- Use UNION in the view
- Use any subqueries
- Use any outer joins or recursively join back to the same table
- Specify the TOP keyword
- Use DISTINCT
- Include a Sum() function, if it references more than one column
- Use almost any aggregate function against a nullable expression
- Reference any other views
- Reference any non-deterministic functions

And this is not all! There are several pages of requirements that must be met, documented in SQL Server Books Online in the *Creating an Indexed View Section*, but these are the most significant ones that will need to be considered before using indexed views.

While this may all seem pretty restrictive, there are good reasons for all of these rules. For us to maintain the indexed view is analogous to us writing our own denormalized data maintenance functions. The more complex the query is to build the denormalized data, the greater the complexity in maintaining it. I'm speculating, but it's likely that these rules will get more and more lenient in newer versions of SQL Server.

Distributed Partitioned Views

A distributed partitioned view is basically like any other view, in that it represents data spread across several tables. However, these tables may exist on completely different SQL Servers. This process is known as **federation**. Here, we are referring to a group of servers which are independently administered, but which share the processing load of a system. This can bring incredible performance improvements by boosting the parallel I/O from the system.

As we are primarily interested in the design aspects of such view, we will look at the steps for building the schema:

- Take a table and create several replicas of it
- Partition the data along some value (month, type, etc.) into these tables, and apply a check constraint to enforce the partition
- Finally, define a view that uses UNION ALL (with no duplicate removal and no sort criterion) to combine the replica tables into a single result set

Advanced Data Access and Modification Techniques

For example, take our `sale` table. Say we have just two items – `ItemA` with `itemId = 1`, and `ItemB` with `itemId = 2`. We might then define the following tables:

```
CREATE TABLE sale_itemA
(
    saleId int NOT NULL,
    itemId int NOT NULL
    CONSTRAINT chk$sale_itemA$itemId$One CHECK (itemId = 1)
    itemCount int NOT NULL,
)
CREATE TABLE sale_itemB
(
    saleId int NOT NULL,
    itemId int NOT NULL
    CONSTRAINT chk$sale_itemA$itemId$One CHECK (itemId = 2)
    itemCount int NOT NULL
)
```

Next, we create a view that references these two new tables:

```
CREATE VIEW v_sale
AS
SELECT saleId, itemId, itemCount
FROM dbo.sale_itemA

UNION ALL -- no sort or duplicate removal

SELECT saleId, itemId, itemCount
FROM dbo.sale_itemB
```

SQL Server is smart enough to only use the table that is required and can automatically assign two processors, if available, to deal with this query.

There is some performance cost associated with going outside a server to process a query but, depending on how large the data set is, using federated partitioned views can create incredible performance gains. Obviously, we wouldn't use it to store a simple contact list but, when you are storing session information for half a million active Internet users at any time, it may very well pay to partition your data across multiple servers.

For more information, see *"Professional SQL Server 2000 Programming"* by Rob Vieira (*Wrox Press, ISBN 1-861004-48-6*).

Stored Procedures

Stored procedures are basically simple scripts that are stored in the database. The major difference between stored procedures and batches lies in performance, with stored procedures being precompiled.

In this section, we will not look specifically at how to build a stored procedure; rather, we will look at some of the features of stored procedures that are of interest when implementing a database system.

445

Stored procedures are very similar to user-defined functions, with a few important differences:

- Stored procedures return result sets in a very loose manner, in that we do not have to declare what we will be returning to the client, and we can return any number of result sets
- Stored procedures may have multiple output parameters, whereas scalar functions may only have a single return value of any type and may not have output parameters
- Scalar functions can be used in scalar expressions, while stored procedures cannot
- Stored procedures allow us to alter the database (in the form of updates, changing settings, etc.), whereas functions may not change anything during execution

Each of these distinctions will dictate when we use stored procedures as opposed to functions, especially the last two. In the rest of this section, we will look at:

- Returning values from stored procedures
- Error handling
- Using stored procedures for an encapsulation layer between our applications
- Using stored procedures as security mechanisms
- Using stored procedures to solve common problems

Regardless of your overall architecture, stored procedures are database features that every SQL programmer should use and use well. Writing efficient stored procedures takes a lot of skill and experience, so it is a good idea to experiment on dummy data and try out different construction methods.

Returning Values from Stored Procedures

There are three ways that stored procedures can communicate with the outside world:

- Return values – used to return a status value
- Output parameters – used to return single values through a parameter
- Result sets – used to return tables of information

Each of these has a very specific purpose that we will explore in the following sections.

Return Values

Unlike with user-defined functions, the RETURN statement of a stored procedure can only return an integer value, which is usually used to indicate status. The following is a common suggestion for a return value protocol, with the meanings for each value:

Value	Meaning
> 0	Procedure succeeded, with some meaning that can be inferred from the procedure definition.
0	Procedure succeeded, but no extended information can be learnt.
–1 to –99	Procedure failed with a system error. The meaning cannot be inferred, other than a system failure has occurred. –1 to –14 are the only values currently in use.

Advanced Data Access and Modification Techniques

Value	Meaning
–100	General user-defined error has occurred that cannot be handled in Transact-SQL.
< –100	Specific user-defined error message, based on whatever is built into the stored procedure.

> You should never use –1 to –14 to return information from a stored procedure. These values are used by SQL Server.

The reason for this protocol is fairly simple. If any error occurs in the stored procedure and you need to signal its caller, then a simple check for a negative return value shows there is a problem, and a non-negative return value indicates success.

For example, take the following simple procedure that returns an integer value passed to it:

```
CREATE PROCEDURE returnValue$test
(
    @returnThis int = 0
)
AS
RETURN @returnThis
```

If we execute this procedure, setting the values to a variable:

```
DECLARE @returnValue int
EXEC @returnValue = returnValue$test @returnThis = 0
SELECT @returnValue AS returnValue
```

we get the following return:

```
returnValue
---------------
0
```

The next stored procedure is set up to use the value from the first:

```
CREATE PROCEDURE caller$testreturnvalue
(
    @testValue int
)
AS

DECLARE @returnValue int
EXEC @returnValue = returnValue$test @testValue
SELECT @returnValue AS returnValue

IF @returnValue < 0 --negative is bad
    BEGIN
        SELECT 'An error has occurred: ' + CAST(@returnValue AS varchar(10))
```

```
                        AS status
    END
ELSE                -- positive or zero is good
    BEGIN
        SELECT 'Call succeeded: ' + CAST(@returnValue AS varchar(10))
                        AS status
    END
GO
```

Executing this with a negative value:

```
EXEC caller$testreturnvalue -10
```

tells us that an error has occurred:

```
returnValue
---------------
-10

status
----------------------------------
An error has occurred: -10
```

Obviously, if we change the parameter to a non-negative number, we get the message that no error occurred.

Output Parameters

Output parameters allow us to return a scalar value of any type to a calling procedure, and will allow the passing of the cursor data type if needed.

The output parameter is the best way to return a scalar from one procedure to another, since it is considered bad practice to use the return value for this purpose, even if the value we are returning happens to be an integer. We can have as many output parameters as necessary. Use the following syntax:

```
DECLARE @variable int
EXEC storedProcedure @variable = @variable OUTPUT
```

Note that you can increase performance in SQL Server applications by using output parameters to return a single row, which avoids the overhead of a result set.

Result Sets

Returning result sets to the client is as simple as including a SELECT statement in your code:

```
CREATE PROCEDURE test$statement
AS

SELECT 'Hi' AS hiThere
SELECT 'Bye' AS byeThere
GO
```

Advanced Data Access and Modification Techniques

Executing this stored procedure:

```
EXEC test$statement
```

will return two result sets:

```
hiThere
----------
Hi

byeThere
-----------
Bye
```

This seems very simple but bear in mind that, because stored procedures are precompiled batches of code, they must be self-contained. They should not contain code which requires interaction with the client, whether a human or another program. Stored procedures are not transactions by themselves and, if a connection cuts mid-way through a stored procedure, the rest of the procedure will not complete or roll back. This is why output parameters and return values are not available to the caller until *after* all result sets have been retrieved or canceled, and the stored procedure is finished.

Error Handling

Error handling in SQL Server code is one of its weakest points. There is no error trapping in SQL Server. However, we can always determine if a statement has caused an error, so we can take appropriate action.

Consider, for example, this call to a non-existent stored procedure:

```
EXEC dbo.doesntExist
```

This returns the following standard error message:

Server: Msg 2812, Level 16, State 62, Line 1
Could not find stored procedure 'dbo.doesntExist'.

If we look in the `master.dbo.sysmessages` table for error number 2812:

```
SELECT error, description
FROM master.dbo.sysmessages
WHERE error = 2812
```

we see the message, complete with all the static text needed to build the error message and a tag for holding the parameter values:

error	description
2812	Could not find stored procedure ' per cent.*ls'.

We can also create an error in code using the `RAISERROR` statement, which we have used before to send an error message to the client. `RAISERROR` is a very powerful and robust tool and we can do a lot more with it.

We can use the `RAISERROR` command to create our own messages and have them saved in the `sysmessages` table. It is important to mention how flexible `RAISERROR` is. It has built-in language support so, if you need to internationalize your database code, you can create versions of your messages in other languages. The appropriate message will be displayed according to the language setting of the user.

Using `RAISERROR` we can:

- Return an *ad hoc* message
- Return a message that we store in the `master.dbo.sysmessages` table with special formatting
- Return an error number (between 50000 and the maximum `bigint` value)
- Return a severity which tells us how bad the message is, from "informational" to "hardware corruption"
- Return a state value which indicates the source from which the error was issued

The simplest syntax for the `RAISERROR` command is:

```
RAISERROR <error number> <message>
```

This allows us to specify an error number and some text describing the error. The `message` value can be a `varchar` value or the contents of a `varchar` variable. For example:

```
RAISERROR 911911911 'This is a test message'
```

will return:

Server: Msg 911911911, Level 16, State 1, Line 1
This is a test message

So, in our stored procedures, we can build a statement that tests whether the output parameter value is less than zero and, if so, raises an error:

```
CREATE PROCEDURE test$validateParm
(
    @parmValue int
) AS

IF @parmValue < 0
   BEGIN
      DECLARE @msg varchar(100)
      SET @msg = 'Invalid @parmValue: ' + CAST(@parmValue AS varchar(10)) +
                 '. Value must be non-negative.'
      RAISERROR 50000 @msg
      RETURN -100
   END
SELECT 'Test successful.'
RETURN 0
GO
```

Advanced Data Access and Modification Techniques

Then, when we pass in a 0 to test it:

```
dbo.test$validateParm 0
```

We get:

```
---------------------
Test successful.
```

If we pass in a negative number, we get the error:

Server: Msg 50000, Level 16, State 1, Procedure test$validateParm, Line 11
Invalid @parmValue: -1. Value must be non-negative.

The other place where it is helpful to include an error message is after an INSERT, UPDATE, or DELETE statement. The reason is the same. If an error occurs, we can pinpoint exactly which statement caused the failure. Say we have the following table:

```
CREATE TABLE test
(
    testId int IDENTITY,
    name varchar(60) NOT NULL
    CONSTRAINT AKtest_name UNIQUE
)
```

We build the following stored procedure to create new values:

```
CREATE PROCEDURE test$ins
(
    @name varchar(60)
) AS

INSERT INTO dbo.test(name)
VALUES(@name)
IF @@error <> 0
    BEGIN
        -- raise an error that tells the user what has just occurred.
        RAISERROR 50000 'Error inserting into test table'
    END
GO
```

and then we execute a statement:

```
EXEC dbo.test$ins @name = NULL
```

The result is:

Server: Msg 515, Level 16, State 2, Procedure test$ins, Line 6
Cannot insert the value NULL into column 'name', table 'master.dbo.test'; column does not allow NULLs. INSERT fails.

Server: Msg 50000, Level 16, State 1, Procedure test$ins, Line 10
Error inserting into test table

The statement has been terminated.

This may seem to make the code messier, as we have error handlers everywhere, but it is crucial to check the return code and error status after every modification statement or stored procedure call. If we do this, we can see what error occurred and we know exactly where. This is very helpful as there will be occasions when, instead of inserting one row into a single table once, we might be inserting many rows into the table from our client application, or we might be calling this stored procedure from another server. This sort of error handling will save debugging time.

There are two things that we can do to improve SQL Server's error reporting:

- ❏ Build an error message mapping database, to map constraint messages to more meaningful custom messages
- ❏ Create an error message tag format to return extended messages to the client

Constraint Mapping

In this section, we will look at a technique to map the errors raised by our constraints to more comprehensible messages, which can be a largely automated process. The standard SQL Server constraint messages are not meant for end-user consumption. Consider the case where we have tried to enter a NULL value into a column – in this case a name column in the test table.

Server: Msg 515, Level 16, State 2, Procedure test$ins, Line 6
Cannot insert the value NULL into column 'name', table 'database.dbo.test'; column does not allow NULLs. INSERT fails.

By parsing some of the basic information from this message (the error number – which tells us that it is a NULL violation – and the column and table from the message):

Server: **Msg 515**, Level 16, State 2, Procedure test$ins, Line 6
Cannot insert the value NULL into **column 'name'**, **table 'database.dbo.test'**; column does not allow NULLs. INSERT fails.

we can produce the following error message, which is much better for the user:

You must enter a value for the name column in the test table.

Violations of non-NULL constraints are fairly simple to identify and report, but what about others? Consider check constraints. Imagine we add a check constraint to the test table to prevent Bob from accessing it:

```
ALTER TABLE dbo.test
ADD CONSTRAINT chkTest$name$string$notEqualToBob
CHECK (name <> 'Bob')
```

If a user now tries to enter Bob's name:

```
INSERT INTO dbo.test (name)
VALUES ('Bob')
```

the result is this standard SQL Server error message:

Advanced Data Access and Modification Techniques

```
Server: Msg 547, Level 16, State 1, Line 1
INSERT statement conflicted with COLUMN CHECK constraint
'chkTest$name$string$notEqualToBob'. The conflict occurred in database 'master', table 'test',
column 'name'.
The statement has been terminated.
```

We would prefer a custom message to be returned, should a user called Bob attempt to access the table. The standard error message is sketchy because we only get back the error definition, but we can use this as the basis of a custom message. To do this, we make use of the new extended properties that we discussed in Chapter 10.

In this case, we will create a property for the constraint that declares the message that we want violating users to see:

```
EXEC sp_addextendedproperty @name = 'ErrorMessage',
    @value =
        'You may not access the test table',
    @level0type = 'User', @level0name = 'dbo',
    @level1type = 'table', @level1name = 'test',
    @level2type = 'constraint', @level2name =
        'chkTest$name$string$notEqualToBob'
```

Once the extended property has been put into the database, SQL Server outputs the message as normal when the error arises. The client machine intercepts it, pulls out the constraint name, and queries the extended property to get the custom message, which is then sent to the client.

```
SELECT value AS message
FROM ::FN_LISTEXTENDEDPROPERTY('ErrorMessage', 'User', 'dbo', 'table', 'test',
    'constraint', 'chkTest$name$string$notEqualToBob')
```

So the user will see this new message:

```
message
------------------------------------------
You may not access the test table
```

This model can be extended to make it much more flexible, by automatically setting each of the possible constraints up with messages. Then we can map each message to a real message for the client. One thing, though. I generally prefer to have a method on the client to see the standard SQL Server error message, so that I can see what really happened (for example, an additional information button on the message dialog).

This method does cost another round trip to the server. A front end object could be coded such that, when we are developing our applications, we go to the server to process the error messages, but, when it comes to the release version of our software, we put the error messages into a DLL for faster reads.

Tagging Error Messages

Once we have mapped the messages that SQL Server sends to us, it is important to make sure that the messages which we send back to the client are as useful as possible.

When building *ad hoc* messages, we are very limited as to what we can return in a message. I add an encoded tag to the end of the message:

```
    'message text' +
            '<tagName1=tagValue1;tagName2=tagValue2;...; tagNameN=tagValueN>'
```

Here, each tag indicates a value that may be important to the client software, such as:

`obj`	The object that raised the error (P=procedure, TR=trigger, etc.).
`type`	The type of object that raised the error.
`call`	Previous call or action that caused the error.
`col`	Column values that required the error to be raised.
`key`	The key values of the row with the problem. This could be used if an entire batch of stored procedure calls were sent to SQL Server and we need to differentiate between them.
`action`	Specific action that the caller should take to repair the problem.
`severity`	Severity, like "warning", "severe", etc.
`occurrence`	Count of times that an execution of the same type might have taken place.

In our examples, we will be using the `obj`, `type`, and `action` tags for simplicity.

For example, in the block in each stored procedure where we declare our variables (such as variables to hold row counts, messages, etc.), we have the following:

```
--used to hold the first part of the message header
DECLARE @msgTag varchar(255)
--preset the message tag with the name of the object and its type
SET @msgTag = '<obj=' + object_name(@@procid) + ';type=P;'
```

Then, whenever we need to raise an error, we make a call like the following:

```
SET @msg = 'Ad hoc message' + @msgTag + ';action=(insert test)>'
RAISERROR 50000 @msg
```

and this returns a message like:

Server: Msg 50000, Level 16, State 1, Line 5
Ad hoc message<obj=test$ins;type=P;action=(insert test)>

This message makes it easier to find out exactly what was going on and where it occurred in the `test$ins` stored procedure. Stripping off the text between the < and > delimiters and parsing out each tag's value, to give a more readable message to the user, is simple as well. Now we can tell the client if our message is just a warning, or if it is more serious. This method has the advantage of not requiring any extra code.

Consider the following stored procedure. It simulates an error by setting the `@error` variable (that we typically would use to trap the `@@error` value) to a non-zero value:

```
CREATE PROCEDURE test$errorMessage
(
    @key_testId int
) AS

--declare variable used for error handling in blocks
DECLARE @error int,             --used to hold error value
        @msg varchar(255),      --used to preformat error messages
        @msgtag varchar(255)    --used to hold the tags for the error message

--set up the error message tag
SET @msgTag = '<' + object_name(@@procid) + ';type=P'
              + ';keyvalue=' + '@key_routineId:'
              + CONVERT(varchar(10),@key_testId)

--call to some stored procedure or modification statement on some table

--get the rowcount and error level for the error handling code
SELECT  @error = 100            --simulated error

IF @error != 0                  --an error occurred outside this procedure
   BEGIN
       SELECT @msg = 'A problem occurred calling the nonExistentProcedure. ' +
                     @msgTag + ';call=(procedure nonExistentProcedure)>'
       RAISERROR 50000 @msg
       RETURN -100
   END
```

This procedure is fairly long, yet all it does is raise an error! Unfortunately though, nearly all of this code (except the error tagging code) is generally required when we are calling other stored procedures or making changes to other tables. We have to check the return value and the value of `@@error` every step of the way. Executing this procedure:

```
test$errorMessage @key_testId = 10
```

returns the following message:

Server: Msg 50000, Level 16, State 1, Procedure test$errorMessage, Line 23
A problem occurred calling the nonExistentProcedure.
<test$errorMessage;type=P;keyvalue=@key_routineId:10;call=(procedure nonExistentProcedure)>

This tells the support person a few things. First of all, there would probably have been an error raised before this message that told us what the real problem was. Secondly, the `nonExistentProcedure` was the source of the problem, it came from the `test$errorMessage` procedure, and the value of the `@key_routineId` parameter was 10.

Encapsulation

The encapsulation of SQL code from the user is one of the most important reasons for using stored procedures, allowing us to execute many commands with a single call to a stored procedure. This is fantastic for two reasons:

- *How an action takes place can change, so long as the action itself does not.* In other words, if the code we have written works, the actual implementation does not matter. In this way, we can performance tune the inner workings of the stored procedure without having to change the interface that the external users see. We might even change all of the underlying table names and structures, yet the stored procedure will still have the same effect.
- *An interface can be built entirely by encapsulating SQL calls into stored procedures.* In this manner, the client programs would never embed any tricky calls in SQL to the database server, they would simply be able to use the stored procedures. This clarifies which operations can be performed as we can see the list of possible procedures.

I will try to demonstrate the first point with a quick example. Suppose you were asked to write a procedure that pulls the names of clients from the person table, and you've been given the following specifications:

- Name – person$get
- Parameters – @personId (int)
- Result sets – a single result set, containing a row from the person table comprising personId, firstName, and lastName, with personId filtered by the @personId parameter

You could produce the following code:

```
CREATE PROCEDURE person$get
(
    @personId int
) AS

SELECT personId, firstName, lastName
FROM person
WHERE personId = @personId
```

When just starting out in the SQL programming world, we might have produced the following, however:

```
CREATE PROCEDURE person$get
(
    @personId int
) AS

CREATE TABLE #person
(
    personId int
    firstName varchar(30),
    lastName varchar(30)
)

DECLARE @cursor cursor, @c_personId integer, @c_firstname varchar(30),
        @c_lastname varchar(30)

SET @cursor = cursor fast_forward for select personId, firstName, lastName
    FROM person

OPEN @cursor
```

```
        FETCH NEXT FROM @cursor INTO @c_personId, @c_firstName, @c_lastName

    WHILE @@fetch_status = 0
        BEGIN
            IF @personId = 1
                BEGIN
                    INSERT INTO #person
                    VALUES (@c_personId, @c_firstName, @c_lastName)
                END
            FETCH NEXT FROM @cursor INTO @c_personId, @c_firstName, @c_lastName
        END
    SELECT * FROM #person
```

While this code is riddled with bad SQL, it *does* work. It will return the proper values and, if the amounts of data are small, its performance won't be that much worse either. However, because we encapsulated the call, it is easy to rewrite this code in the proper fashion shown initially. What's more, the client software using this stored procedure need not change.

The last point I want to make is that, using stored procedures, we do not even need an actual table structure to start building applications. Using some form of code generation, we should be able to produce a set of methods (stored procedures) for our database that do nothing, but appear to the programmer as if they do enough to get started. Commonly called **dummy procedures**, they are often used to test the user interface before it is fully implemented.

In the previous example, we could have built the following dummy procedure to get the programmer started:

```
    CREATE PROCEDURE person$get
    (
        @personId int
    ) AS
    SELECT 1 AS personId, 'Joe' AS firstName, 'Jones' AS lastName
```

While this procedure doesn't do anything, and though it just ignores the parameter, it will return a row that an application programmer can use to see if a screen works while proper code is written. What is important is that the public interface is not violated.

Security

As with views, security in stored procedures is handled at the object level. Just because a user can use a stored procedure does not necessarily mean that he/she has to have rights to every object that the stored procedure refers to.

We can use stored procedures as our primary security mechanism by requiring that all access to the server be done through them. By building procedures that encapsulate all functionality, we then can apply permissions to the stored procedures to restrict what the user can do.

This allows us to have **situational control** on access to a table. This means that we might have two different procedures that do exactly the same operation, but giving a user rights to one procedure does not imply that he/she has rights to the other. So, if a screen is built using one procedure, the user may be able to use it, but not when the screen uses the other procedure.

Having two procedures that do exactly the same operation is far fetched, but it illustrates the fact that we can build objects that access the same tables, in different ways, and we can grant access independently of the underlying objects. We may have a summary procedure that gives a list of how many people there are whose name starts with the letter A, which a user may use, and a procedure that lists user names that he/she cannot use. A similar situation can be implemented with views but, of course, with procedures, we can not only look at data but we can create, modify, and delete it also. We will look in more detail at using SQL Security to lock down access to our objects later in the chapter.

Transaction Count

Aside from the obvious benefits of encapsulating SQL code from the user and establishing a security model, store procedures can be used to take care of the current transaction count – a very important factor when it comes to using transactions.

The transaction count (denoted by @@trancount) tells us how many active transactions are currently open. When we employ transactions in our batches of code, we must be very careful to open and close them before the end of the batch, so we don't leave any locks that might affect other users.

Whatever the transaction count was when you started the procedure, it must be the same value when you leave the procedure. This concept makes perfect sense, although it does make coding interesting. Take the following two procedures:

```
CREATE PROCEDURE tranTest$inner
AS
BEGIN TRANSACTION

--code finds an error, decides to rollback
ROLLBACK TRANSACTION
RETURN -100
```

and:

```
CREATE PROCEDURE tranTest$outer
AS
DECLARE @retValue int
BEGIN TRANSACTION

EXEC @retValue = tranTest$inner
IF @retValue < 0
   BEGIN
      ROLLBACK TRANSACTION
      RETURN @retValue
   END
COMMIT TRANSACTION
```

To see what is happening, we will consider the following call and slowly work through the execution. This can be a painful process, but in many cases it is the only way to completely understand the code:

```
EXEC tranTest$outer
```

1	tranTest$outer	DECLARE @retValue INT	Sets up the variable to hold the return value from the procedure	@retvalue = NULL
2	tranTest$outer	BEGIN TRANSACTION	Starts a new transaction	@@trancount = 1
3	tranTest$outer	EXEC @retValue = tranTest$inner	Calls the tranTest$inner procedure	
4	tranTest$inner	BEGIN TRANSACTION	Starts a second transaction	@@trancount = 2
5	tranTest$inner	ROLLBACK TRANSACTION	Rolls back all transactions	@@trancount = 0
6	tranTest$inner	RETURN -100	Returns a negative value to the calling procedure to tell it something happened	ERROR: Transaction count has changed
7	testTran$outer		Upon returning, the value of @retValue is populated	@retValue = -100
8	testTran$outer	IF @retValue < 0	Conditional to determine if an error has occurred	
9	testTran$outer	ROLLBACK TRANSACTION	Rolls back all transactions	ERROR: @@trancount already zero

Since the transaction count changed between step 3 when we started the procedure and step 6 when we ended it, we would have received the following error message:

Server: Msg 266, Level 16, State 2, Procedure tranTest$inner, Line 6
Transaction count after EXECUTE indicates that a COMMIT or ROLLBACK TRANSACTION statement is missing. Previous count = 1, current count = 0.

It is unreasonable to supply code into a stored procedure to check whether the transaction count has been changed by another process, so we have to rethink the problem. Instead of using straight transactions, we will begin a new transaction when we start the stored procedure, and then set a transaction save point. Note that we set a variable for the save point that is the procedure name plus the nest level, so it will be unique no matter how deep we have nested our procedure and trigger calls:

```
DECLARE @tranPoint sysname              --the data type of identifiers
SET @tranPoint = object_name(@@procId) + CAST(@@nestlevel AS varchar(10))

BEGIN TRANSACTION
SAVE TRANSACTION @tranPoint
```

So we recode our procedures in the following manner:

```
CREATE PROCEDURE tranTest$inner
AS
DECLARE @tranPoint sysname              --the data type of identifiers
SET @tranPoint = object_name(@@procId) + CAST(@@nestlevel AS varchar(10))

BEGIN TRANSACTION
SAVE TRANSACTION @tranPoint

--again doesn't do anything for simplicity
ROLLBACK TRANSACTION @tranPoint
COMMIT TRANSACTION
RETURN -100
GO


CREATE PROCEDURE tranTest$outer
AS
DECLARE @retValue int
DECLARE @tranPoint sysname              --the data type of identifiers
SET @tranPoint = object_name(@@procId) + CAST(@@nestlevel AS varchar(10))

BEGIN TRANSACTION
SAVE TRANSACTION @tranPoint

EXEC @retValue = tranTest$inner
IF @retValue < 0
   BEGIN
      ROLLBACK TRANSACTION @tranPoint
      COMMIT TRANSACTION
      RETURN @retvalue
   END
COMMIT TRANSACTION
GO
```

If we re-run our previous exercise:

```
EXEC tranTest$outer
```

1	tranTest$outer	DECLARE @retValue int	Sets up the variable to hold the return value from the procedure	@retvalue = NULL
2	tranTest$outer	DECLARE @tranPoint sysname SET @tranPoint = object_name(@@procId) + CAST(@@nestlevel AS varchar(10))	Sets up a name for the transaction save point	@tranPoint = 'tranTest$outer1'
3	tranTest$outer	BEGIN TRANSACTION	Starts a new transaction	@@trancount = 1

4	tranTest$outer	SAVE TRANSACTION 'tranTest$outer1'	Saves the transaction, but does not change @@trancount	@@trancount = 1
5	tranTest$outer	EXEC @retValue = tranTest$inner	Calls the tranTest$inner procedure	
6	tranTest$inner	DECLARE @tranPoint sysname SET @tranPoint = object_name(@@procId) + CAST(@@nestlevel AS varchar(10))	Sets up a name for the transaction save point	@tranPoint = 'tranTest$inner2'
7	tranTest$inner	BEGIN TRANSACTION	Starts a second transaction	@@trancount = 2
8	tranTest$inner	SAVE TRANSACTION 'tranTest$inner2'	Saves the transaction, but does not change @@trancount	@@trancount = 2
9	tranTest$inner	ROLLBACK TRANSACTION 'tranTest$inner2'	Rolls back to the tranTest$inner2 save point	@@trancount = 2
10	tranTest$inner	COMMIT TRANSACTION	Commits the transaction and returns @@trancount back to the value when we started the procedure in step 5	@@trancount = 1
11	tranTest$inner	RETURN –100	Returns a negative value to the calling procedure to tell it something happened	
12	testTran$outer		Upon returning, the value of @retValue is populated	@retValue = –100
13	testTran$outer	IF @retValue < 0	Conditional to determine if an error has occurred	

14	testTran$outer	ROLLBACK TRANSACTION 'tranTest$outer1'	Returns us back to our save point, no change to @@trancount	@@trancount = 1
15	testTran$outer	COMMIT TRANSACTION	Commits the final transaction	@@trancount = 0
16	testTran$outer	RETURN @retValue	Returns the return value of the inner call back to the caller	

This code helps prevent us from ever being out of the transaction protection – and, as a result, possibly having invalid data saved after the transaction is rolled back – since, as we saw, the code in the second stored procedure did not necessarily stop executing because of the transaction count error.

The code changes we have made really only apply to the inner stored procedure, in that failure of the inner transaction must not bring down the outer transaction. Failure of the outer transaction is not a problem since `@@trancount` would go to zero, which is where it started.

A positive side effect of all this is that we had the possibility to let the outer transaction occur. There are some cases were we might want to allow part of a transaction to complete when part of it failed, and this gives us that flexibility.

Common Practices with Stored Procedures

The real purpose of this section is to give the basic building blocks of common stored procedures – material that I have seldom seen in print or on the Internet. We will explore these procedures and discuss some of the pros and cons of each solution. Stored procedures are wonderful tools, though, as we will see, on occasion we are forced to hammer a square peg into a round hole.

We will build our objects to access the following table:

```
CREATE TABLE routine
(
    routineId int NOT NULL IDENTITY CONSTRAINT PKroutine PRIMARY KEY,
    name varchar(384) NOT NULL CONSTRAINT akroutine_name UNIQUE,
    description varchar(100) NOT NULL,
    timestamp ts_timestamp
)
```

To load some basic data into the table, we execute this script:

```
INSERT INTO routine (name, description)
SELECT specific_catalog + '.' + specific_schema + '.' + specific_name,
    routine_type + ' in the ' + specific_catalog + ' database created on ' +
    CAST(created AS varchar(20))
FROM <database>.information_schema.routines

SELECT count(*) FROM routine
```

Advanced Data Access and Modification Techniques

Here we will replace <database> with our database names. In my example I will use `Northwind`, `Master`, and `Pubs` for a total of around 1000 rows. I am executing these examples on a Pentium II 400 laptop with 256 MB of RAM – a pretty out of date computer. This will give us a baseline for some basic testing of stored procedure performance, as we look at possible ways to build stored procedures for our applications.

Retrieve

This code fills a list control in an application, and is a very common procedure in my applications. Each of the parameters is a filter to the list, so that the user can see the list in their own way. Here's the stored procedure:

```
CREATE PROCEDURE routine$list
(
    @routineId, int = NULL          --primary key to retrieve single row
    @name, varchar(60) = ' per cent'        --like match on routine.name
    @description varchar(100) = ' per cent' --like match on routine.description
)

-- Description : gets routine records for displaying in a list
--             :
-- Return Val  : nonnegative:  success
--             : -1 to -99:  system generated return value on error
--             : -100: generic procedure failure

AS

-- as the count messages have been known to be a problem for clients
SET NOCOUNT ON

-- default the @name parm to ' per cent' if the passed value is NULL
IF @name IS NULL SELECT @name = ' per cent'

-- default the @description parm to ' per cent' if the passed value is NULL
IF @description IS NULL SELECT @description = ' per cent'

--select all of the fields (less the timestamp) from the table for viewing.
SELECT routine.routineId AS routineId, routine.name AS name,
       routine.description AS description
FROM dbo.routine AS routine
WHERE (routine.routineId = @routineId
    OR @routineId IS NULL)
    AND (routine.name LIKE @name)
    AND (routine.description LIKE @description)
ORDER BY routine.name
RETURN
```

While the stored procedure itself is pretty rudimentary, we need to discuss the WHERE clause. I am checking all of the parameters against the set, regardless of which parameter the user is sending. SQL Server builds its plan based on the fact that some value is being passed in. So how does it perform? For average sized tables, extremely fast. It is not, however, the most optimal solution to the problem.

To show this, we will pull out the actual query from the stored procedure and execute it, wrapped with GETDATE() statements and turning SET STATISTICS IO on. This will allow us to check the performance of the code in a very straightforward way.

Note that this is just one of the performance tests to run on your code. Looking at the query plan in Query Analyzer is also a very good way to get an understanding of what is going on. I feel it makes it easier to follow an argument by looking at the amount of time, and how much I/O it takes to execute a statement.

Apart from timing the code, we will measure:

- **Scan count** – the number of scans through the table that were required
- **Logical reads** – the number of pages read from the data cache
- **Physical reads** – the number of pages that were read from the physical disk
- **Read-ahead reads** – the number of pages placed into the cache

Taking the logical reads and the physical reads together is a good indicator of how the query is performing. For larger queries and busier systems, logical reads will become physical reads as cache contention increases.

```
SET STATISTICS IO ON
DBCC freeproccache    --clear cache to allow it to choose best plan

SELECT GETDATE() AS before

--run the procedure version
EXEC routine$list @routineId = 848

SELECT GETDATE() AS middle

--then run it again as an ad-hoc query
SELECT routine.routineId AS routineId, routine.name AS name,
       routine.description AS description
FROM dbo.routine AS routine
WHERE (routine.routineId = 848 OR 848 IS NULL)
      AND (routine.name LIKE ' per cent')
      AND (routine.description LIKE ' per cent')
ORDER BY routine.name

SELECT GETDATE() AS after
```

This code gives us the following results (I haven't shown the actual results from the query to save space):

```
before
--------------------------------
2001-01-17 20:41:16.300
```

Table 'routine'. Scan count 1, logical reads 12, physical reads 0, read-ahead reads 0.

```
middle
--------------------------------
2001-01-17 20:41:16.330
```

Table 'routine'. Scan count 1, logical reads 2, physical reads 0, read-ahead reads 0.

```
after
--------------------------------
2001-01-17 20:41:16.330
```

This tells us that to execute the statement and retrieve the data took 0.03 seconds for the stored procedure, and less than 0.03 seconds for the ad-hoc version (the `datetime` data type's granularity is 0.03 seconds). Not an appreciable difference at all. Will this always be the case? No – as we will see when we execute this same test, filtering on the description column (which is not indexed):

```
SET STATISTICS IO ON
DBCC freeproccache       --clear cache to allow it to choose best plan

SELECT GETDATE() AS before

EXEC routine$list @description = 'procedure in the master named sp_helpsql per
cent'

SELECT GETDATE() AS middle

SELECT routine.routineId AS routineId, routine.name AS name,
       routine.description AS description
FROM dbo.routine AS routine
WHERE (routine.routineId = NULL OR NULL IS NULL)
  AND (routine.name LIKE ' per cent')
  AND (routine.description LIKE 'procedure in the master named sp_helpsql per
cent')
ORDER BY routine.name

SELECT GETDATE() AS after
```

After removing the actual rows returned from the results, this gives us the following:

```
before
---------------------------------
2001-01-17 21:13:49.550
```

Table 'routine'. Scan count 1, logical reads 2022, physical reads 0, read-ahead reads 0.

```
middle
---------------------------------
2001-01-17 21:13:49.620
```

Table 'routine'. Scan count 1, logical reads 19, physical reads 0, read-ahead reads 0.

```
after
---------------------------------
2001-01-17 21:13:49.640
```

Here we see that there is not much difference between the times taken to execute the tests, 0.07 against 0.02 seconds. But this time the stored procedure attempt requires ten times the number of logical reads. Since logical reads come directly from memory, this makes almost no difference even on my slow machine.

There are a couple of stored procedure alternatives. We could:

- Use the WITH RECOMPILE option in the stored procedure. This causes a new plan to be generated every time the query is executed. Building a plan takes time but, as a poor plan will lead to real performance problems, this is not a bad idea at all. Unless the procedure is called very frequently, the cost of compilation is usually quite small compared to the gain due to the better plan.

- Build an `IF THEN` nest, with every possible parameter combination that the user may send in, and custom build a query for each possibility. The main problem with this is that there are (n! + 1) possible combinations of parameters.

- Pick out individual cases and build additional stored procedures to handle the slow ones. In our case above with `description`, if this performance was not acceptable, a second stored procedure could be created that was faster. Then, before the `SELECT` statement, we break out into another stored procedure for the given case.

- Continue to implement using a stored procedure, but use a dynamic query. This solution will perform best, but when we execute code in a stored procedure, we lose the security benefits of stored procedures as the user then needs rights to run the dynamic query.

Let's demonstrate the dynamic query alternative. Here, we will build up the text into `varchar` variables and then run the query using `EXEC`:

```
CREATE PROCEDURE routine$list
(
    @routineId int = NULL,          -- primary key to retrieve single row
    @name varchar(60) = ' per cent',    -- like match on routine.name
    @description varchar(100) = ' per cent' -- like match on routine.description
) AS

--as the count messages have been known to be a problem for clients
SET NOCOUNT ON

-- create a variable to hold the main query
DECLARE @query varchar(8000)
-- select all of the fields from the table for viewing
SET @query = 'SELECT routine.routineId AS routineId, routine.name AS name,
                routine.description AS description
         FROM dbo.routine AS routine'

-- create a variable to hold the where clause, which we will conditionally
-- build
DECLARE @where varchar(8000) SET @where = ''  --since NULL + 'anything' = NULL

-- add the name search to the where clause
IF @name <> ' per cent' AND @name IS NOT NULL
   SELECT @where = @where + CASE WHEN LEN(RTRIM(@where)) > 0
   THEN ' AND ' ELSE '' END + ' name LIKE ''' + @name + ''''

-- add the name search to the where clause
IF @description <> ' per cent' AND @description IS NOT NULL
   SELECT @where = @where + CASE WHEN LEN(RTRIM(@where)) > 0
   THEN ' AND ' ELSE '' END + ' name LIKE ''' + @description + ''''

-- select all of the fields from the table for viewing
IF @routineId IS NOT NULL
   SELECT @where = @where + CASE WHEN LEN(RTRIM(@where)) > 0
   THEN ' AND ' ELSE '' END +
   ' routineId = ' + CAST(@routineId AS varchar(10))

-- create a variable for the where clause
DECLARE @orderBy varchar(8000)
```

```
    -- set the order by to return rows by name
    SET    @orderBy = ' ORDER BY routine.name'

    EXEC (@query + @where + @orderBy)
    GO
```

This procedure will run optimally for any set of parameters that are passed in but, for such a simple query, this is a lot of really hard-to-maintain code. Consider the fact that some basic stored procedures to retrieve a set of rows may have twenty lines or more of SQL, with quite a few different joins. Then you will begin to understand why dynamically building the query in a stored procedure (or even from the client) is such a hard thing to do.

In my experience, a procedure is optimized if it runs within specifications and does not interfere with other processes. I tend to generate database code that is as generic as the example list procedure, and optimize when needed. Seldom will I need to optimize this particular query but, in those cases where it runs too slowly or is causing other processes to wait, one of the listed alternatives will always fix the problem.

In the next three sections, we will look at stored procedures that create, modify, and destroy data. While retrieving data gave us difficulties, these types of data modification are pretty much plain sailing.

Although users will frequently demand to look at a thousand rows of data, rarely will they want to update a thousand rows at a time. It does happen, and we can code these statements when necessary, but data modification is generally done by primary key. Nearly every OLTP form I have been connected with over the years has followed the pattern of:

- Find a row from a list
- View the details of the row
- Modify the row, delete the row, or add a new row
- View the row after performing the action
- See the row in the list

In this section, we will look at building basic stored procedures which create, modify, and destroy single rows. From there, it should be easy to extend the examples to modify multiple rows, simply by repeating parts of the code.

Create

The CREATE stored procedure:

```
CREATE PROCEDURE routine$ins
(
    @name varchar(384),
    @description varchar(500),
    @new_routineId int = NULL OUTPUT
) AS

-- declare variable used for error handling in blocks
DECLARE @rowcount int,        -- holds the rowcount returned from dml calls
    @error int,               -- used to hold the error code after a dml
    @msg varchar(255),        -- used to preformat error messages
```

```
    @retval int,             -- general purpose variable for retrieving
                             -- return values from stored procedure calls
    @tranName sysname,       -- used to hold the name of the transaction
    @msgTag varchar(255)     -- used to hold the tags for the error message

-- set up the error message tag
SET @msgTag = '<' + object_name(@@procid) + ';type=P'

-- default error handling code used for most procedures
-- generic tran name generation guarantees unique transaction name,
-- even if the procedure is called twice in a chain, since if one is active
-- and another gets called it cannot be at the same nest level
SET @tranName = object_name(@@procid) + CAST(@@nestlevel AS varchar(2))


-- note that including this transaction is not actually necessary as we only
-- have a single statement. I like to include this just as a precaution for
-- when the need arises to change the code.

BEGIN TRANSACTION             -- start a transaction
SAVE TRANSACTION @tranName    -- save tran so we can rollback our action without
                              -- killing entire transaction

-- perform the insert
INSERT INTO routine(name,description)
VALUES (@name,@description)

-- check for an error
IF (@@ERROR!=0)
   BEGIN
   -- raise an additional error to help us see where the error occurred
   SELECT @msg = 'There was a problem inserting a new row into the ' +
       'routine table.' + @msgTag + ';call=(insert routine)>'
   RAISERROR 50000 @msg
   ROLLBACK TRAN @tranName
   COMMIT TRAN
   RETURN -100
   END

-- then retrieve the identity value from the row we created error
SET @new_routineId = scope_identity()

COMMIT TRANSACTION
GO
```

Now we test the code:

```
BEGIN TRANSACTION -- wrap test code in a transaction so we don't affect db
DECLARE @new_routineId int
EXEC routine$ins @name = 'Test',
   @description = 'Test', @new_routineId = @new_routineId OUTPUT
-- see what errors occur
SELECT NAME, DESCRIPTION FROM routine WHERE routineId = @new_routineId
-- to cause duplication error
```

```
    EXEC routine$ins @name = 'Test',
       @description = 'Test', @new_routineId = @new_routineId OUTPUT

    ROLLBACK TRANSACTION -- no changes to db
```

This returns two things. First, a resultset that has the new record in it:

```
name                   description
---------------------  ---------------------
Test                   Test
```

Then a set of three distinct messages:

Server: Msg 2627, Level 14, State 2, Procedure routine$ins, Line 29
Violation of UNIQUE KEY constraint 'AKroutine_name'. Cannot insert duplicate key in object 'routine'.

Server: Msg 50000, Level 16, State 1, Procedure routine$ins, Line 37
There was a problem inserting a new row into the routine table.<routine$ins;type=P;call=(insert routine)>

The statement has been terminated.

Our clients will need to translate the first message into something that the user can read. The second tells us what procedure was called and what it was trying to do, so we can debug.

However, note that, where the selecting procedure had trouble in building a decent WHERE clause for the optimizer, we are going to have to specify a fixed number of columns for the insert. This has a fairly annoying side effect of not allowing us to use the default values we have defined on our columns. This is not usually a problem as, when user interaction is required, any defaults that the user might choose will be shown on the UI, and any that they cannot change will not have to be a part of the INSERT statement.

Modify

Modifying or updating data in the table is again a fairly simple task:

```
CREATE PROCEDURE routine$upd
(
    @key_routineId int,  -- key column that we will use as the key to the
                         -- update. Note that we cannot update the primary key
    @name varchar(384) ,
    @description varchar(500),
    @ts_timeStamp timestamp   --optimistic lock
)
AS

-- declare variable used for error handling in blocks
DECLARE @rowcount int,        -- holds the rowcount returned from dml calls
        @error int,           -- used to hold the error code after a dml
        @msg varchar(255),    -- used to preformat error messages
        @retval int,          -- general purpose variable for retrieving
                              -- return values from stored procedure calls
```

```
            @tranname sysname, -- used to hold the name of the transaction
            @msgTag varchar(255) -- used to hold the tags for the error message

-- set up the error message tag

SET @msgTag = '<' + object_name(@@procid) + ';type=P'
                 + ';keyvalue=' + '@key_routineId:'
                 + CONVERT(varchar(10),@key_routineId)

SET @tranName = object_name(@@procid) + CAST(@@nestlevel AS varchar(2))

-- make sure that the user has passed in a timestamp value, as it will
-- be very wasteful if they have not
IF @ts_timeStamp IS NULL
   BEGIN
   SET @msg = 'The timestamp value must not be NULL' + @msgTag + '>'
   RAISERROR 50000 @msg
   RETURN -100
END

BEGIN TRANSACTION
SAVE TRANSACTION @tranName

UPDATE routine
SET NAME = @name, description = @description
WHERE routineId = @key_routineId AND timeStamp = @ts_timeStamp

-- get the rowcount and error level for the error handling code
SELECT @rowcount = @@rowcount, @error = @@error

IF @error != 0  --an error occurred outside of this procedure
   BEGIN
      SELECT @msg = 'A problem occurred modifying the routine record.' +
         @msgTag + ';call=(UPDATE routine)>'
      RAISERROR 50001 @msg
      ROLLBACK TRAN @tranName
      COMMIT TRAN
      RETURN -100
   END
ELSE IF @rowcount <> 1   -- this must not be the primary key
                         -- anymore or the record doesn't exist
   BEGIN
      IF (@rowcount = 0)
         BEGIN
            -- if the record exists without the timestamp,
            -- it has been modified by another user
            IF EXISTS ( SELECT *
               FROM routine
                  WHERE routineId = @key_routineId)
                  BEGIN
                     SELECT @msg = 'The routine record has been modified' +
                                ' by another user.'
                  END
            ELSE
               BEGIN
                  SELECT @msg = 'The routine record does not exist.'
```

Advanced Data Access and Modification Techniques

```
                    END
                END
        ELSE
            BEGIN
                SELECT @msg = 'Too many records were modified.'
            END

            SELECT  @msg = @msg + @msgTag + ';CALL=(UPDATE routine)>'
            RAISERROR 50000 @msg
            ROLLBACK TRAN @tranName
            COMMIT TRAN
            RETURN -100

    END

    COMMIT TRAN
    RETURN 0
```

I will not demonstrate this code; you will have to run it from the sample code on www.wrox.com. Note the use of the timestamp column as the optimistic lock, and how we deal with it:

❑   We try to do the update, using the primary key *and* the timestamp.

❑   Then, if there are no errors, we test to see how many rows are modified:

❑   If one row is modified, everything is great.

❑   If more than one row is modified, then too many rows are changed. It might be overkill to check for this, but it is a small cost to prevent a messy event from occurring. It is important to make sure that exactly what you expect to occur actually occurs. In this case, only one row should be updated, so we check to make sure that this happened.

❑   If no rows were updated, we check to see if the row with the primary key value exists in the table. If it does, then the row exists but it has been modified. Otherwise, it never existed in the first place.

We check each of these cases because it keeps stupid errors from occurring. Many times I have seen queries written to modify rows and, instead of passing in real values, they pass in zeroes. Five minutes using Profiler (the most important tool of the database code tester!) and the problems are found. Adding complete error handling to the procedure keeps every situation that may occur from biting us, with very little cost.

Note that, again, we have to update all of the columns at once. It would be deeply inefficient to write an update stored procedure that updated the columns based on which column was passed in.

One thing that can be done, however, is to take into consideration any columns that have extremely costly validations (or, in some cases, denormalization routines). We can take two paths:

❑   Break the statement into two updates. One to update the costly field(s) and another to update the others. This would only be proper if you have several fields and the costly fields are seldom updated.

❑   A more reasonable path (if there are only one or two fields to deal with) is to check to see if the values have changed, and then decide whether or not to update them. Build two (or more) possible update statements that update the fields in question.

Let's look at a part of the second path. We consider the case where changing the `description` field of our table causes all sorts of costly validations and denormalizations, taking well over a second to occur – but the value in the `description` column only changes 10 per cent of the time. We could replace:

```
UPDATE routine
SET name = @name, description = @description
WHERE routineId = @key_routineId AND timeStamp = @ts_timeStamp

-- get the rowcount and error level for the error handling code
SELECT @rowcount = @@rowcount, @error = @@error
```

with:

```
-- leave the timestamp out of this statement, as we do not want
-- to update the description field because the timestamp has changed
IF EXISTS (SELECT * FROM routine WHERE routineId = @key_routineId
           AND description = @description)
   BEGIN
      UPDATE routine
      SET name = @name WHERE routineId = @key_routineId
         AND timeStamp = @ts_timeStamp

      -- get the rowcount and error level for the error handling code
      SELECT @rowcount = @@rowcount, @error = @@error
   END
ELSE
   BEGIN
      UPDATE routine
      SET name = @name, description = @description WHERE routineId =
               @key_routineId
      AND timeStamp = @ts_timeStamp

      -- get the rowcount and error level for the error handling code
      SELECT @rowcount = @@rowcount, @error = @@error
   END
```

Notice that we do not change the meaning and we still check the same things out in the error handling code. It appears that the procedure will be slower to execute now as there is more code to deal with, and it will be slower when the description value is changed. However, over all, the total time executed for all calls will be significantly lower, since the `description` column will be checked far less and we will not incur those costs when it does not change.

Destroy

The destroy or DELETE stored procedure that we will demonstrate here is very similar to the update procedure, other than the fact that the row will no longer exist, of course.

```
ALTER PROCEDURE routine$del
(
   @key_routineId int,
   @ts_timeStamp timestamp = NULL   --optimistic lock
)
AS
```

```
-- declare variable used for error handling in blocks
DECLARE @rowcount int,         -- holds the rowcount returned from dml calls
        @error int,            -- used to hold the error code after a dml
        @msg varchar(255),     -- used to preformat error messages
        @retval int,           -- general purpose variable for retrieving
                               -- return values from stored procedure calls
        @tranname sysname,     -- used to hold the name of the transaction
        @msgTag varchar(255)   -- used to hold the tags for the error message

-- set up the error message tag
SET @msgTag = '<' + object_name(@@procid) + ';type=P'
                 + ';keyvalue=' + '@key_routineId:'
                 + CONVERT(varchar(10),@key_routineId)

SET @tranName = object_name(@@procid) + CAST(@@nestlevel AS varchar(2))

BEGIN TRANSACTION
SAVE TRANSACTION @tranName

DELETE routine WHERE routineId = @key_routineId AND @ts_timeStamp = timeStamp

-- get the rowcount and error level for the error handling code
SELECT @rowcount = @@rowcount, @error = @@error

IF @error != 0   -- an error occurred outside of this procedure
   BEGIN
      SELECT @msg = 'A problem occurred removing the routine record.' +
         @msgTag + 'call=(delete routine)>'
      RAISERROR 50000 @msg
      ROLLBACK TRAN @tranName
      COMMIT tran
      RETURN -100
   END
ELSE IF @rowcount > 1   -- this must not be the primary key anymore or the
                        -- record doesn't exist
   BEGIN
      SELECT  @msg = 'Too many routine records were deleted. ' +
         @msgTag + '; call=(DELETE routine)>'

      RAISERROR 50000 @msg
      ROLLBACK TRAN @tranName
      COMMIT tran
      RETURN -100

   END
ELSE IF @rowcount = 0
   BEGIN
      IF EXISTS (SELECT * FROM routine WHERE routineId = @key_routineId )
         BEGIN
            SELECT @msg = 'The routine record has been modified' +
                       ' by another user.' + ';call=(delete routine)>'
            RAISERROR 50000 @msg
            ROLLBACK TRAN @tranName
            COMMIT TRAN
            RETURN -100
```

```
            END
        ELSE
        BEGIN
            SELECT @msg = 'The routine record you tried to delete' +
                    ' does not exist.' + @msgTag + ';call=(delete routine)>'
                raiserror 50000 @msg
                -- the needs of the system should decide whether or
                -- not to actually implement this error, or even if
                -- if we should quit here and return a negative value.
                -- If you were trying to remove something
                -- and it doesn't exist, is that bad?
        END
    END

    COMMIT TRAN
    RETURN 0
```

The performance of the DELETE procedure is extremely good. We want to destroy one row by primary key, so we give it the primary key and the row is deleted. There is no chance of deleting only parts of the row, or of not passing in the correct number of values.

These are my four central stored procedures. We have now effectively built a set of access methods which will present a fairly easy-to-use interface for building an application. They will also provide hooks into the security system for our application, because we can clearly choose the operations that a user can perform at a finer grained level than INSERT, UPDATE, DELETE, or SELECT.

Obviously, I need more than these four stored procedures to build an application, but they cover 80 per cent of the requirements and allow the building of editing applications in a very generic manner. When the database interface always follows a very similar design, the code to access it can also follow a very generic path.

Batches of SQL Code

A batch of SQL code is one or more SQL statements executed by the server as a group. We will look at two different types of batches and the differences in how we must handle them. We will consider:

- **Single-statement batches** – these contain only a single statement to the server.
- **Multi-statement batches** – used to perform multiple operations in a way that a single statement, or even a single stored procedure, cannot easily do.

Note that the concept of single- or multi-statement batches has no meaning to SQL Server. It executes the whole batch, regardless of how many statements it contains, and returns whatever. We make the distinction because we must code differently for the two different cases.

> *One small point; in this section, we are not dealing with database creation scripts, which are one-time operations. In contrast, we are discussing building an application to touch and modify data.*

Single-Statement Batches

A single-statement batch is a single SQL statement – usually an INSERT, UPDATE, DELETE, or SELECT statement, but it can be a stored procedure or a system function like a DBCC.

Advanced Data Access and Modification Techniques

The only time when we do *not* have to consider adding extra code to execute a batch is when we execute a single statement. Note, however, that we are very limited as to what we can do with these statements. We can send a SQL statement of any type, but it is not possible to make more than one modification to the data. Hence, no pre-validation or manipulation of data is allowed, and error handling within the statement is effectively prohibited. For example, if we execute the following:

```
UPDATE customer
SET firstName = 'Andy'
WHERE customerId = 100
```

we cannot assume that this operation succeeded, as there may have been an error. It is incumbent on the actual calling program to check the error status and handle the errors itself. There is another concern, however. Does this row even exist? If not, your command will not update any rows. Many times I have seen statements (executed from VBScript in an ASP page) like this:

```
UPDATE customer
SET firstName = 'Andy'
WHERE customerId = 0
```

which was not executed because a user had misspelled a variable name, had forgotten to turn on `Option Explicit`, but *had* turned `On Error Resume Next` on. What is more, unless you remember to pass in the timestamp, or whatever optimistic locking value you have chosen for your database, *every time you modify a row*, the optimistic lock is valueless.

It is my suggestion that, if you are going to use batches of uncompiled code to do data modifications, then you should build a generic object to handle the modifications. Make sure as well that you get this object right, because experience has taught me that there are many ways to make a goofy mistake that is very hard to locate in your code.

Multi-Statement Batches

When discussing multi-statement batches, we will basically follow the same structure that we did in stored procedures. However, we must consider two topics that need a different treatment in this context:

- Transactions
- Handling errors

Transactions

As we noted in the *Transactions* section at the beginning of the chapter, it is very important that, when we converse with SQL Server, we make certain that we never start a transaction from our client software without closing it in the same batch. The only problem with this lies in the implementation because, every time we use the `GO` statement, Query Analyzer initiates a new batch.

Handling Errors

When we batch together multiple statements, we have to consider what to do in the case of failure. We have the `RETURN` statement when coding stored procedures, but `RETURN` does not work in a batch. When we decide that we are through with the batch and wish to quit, the way to deal with the situation is to set a variable and use it to conditionally execute blocks of code.

Suppose that we have statements that we want to execute, and we need to make sure that each of them runs prior to finishing. We put them in a transaction, but what if one fails?

```
BEGIN TRANSACTION
   <Statement1>
   <Statement2>
   <Statement3>
COMMIT TRANSACTION
```

We can code around it:

```
DECLARE @errornbr int,      -- holds error numbers after any statement
        @returnvalue int,   -- holds return values from stored procedures
        @errorout bit       -- flag to tell later statements to execute or not
SET     @errorOut = 1
BEGIN TRANSACTION

<Statement1>
SET @errorNbr = @@error
IF @error <> 0 or @returnValue < 0
   BEGIN
      RAISERROR 50000 'Error executing <statement1>'
      SET @errorOut = 0
   END

IF @errorOut = 1
   BEGIN
      <Statement2>
      SET @errorNbr = @@error
      IF @error <> 0 or @returnValue < 0
      BEGIN
         RAISERROR 50000 'Error executing <statement2>'
         SET @errorOut = 0
      END
   END

IF @errorOut = 1
   BEGIN
      <StatementN>
      SET @errorNbr = @@error
      IF @error <> 0 OR @returnValue < 0
         BEGIN
            RAISERROR 50000 'Error executing <statement2>'
            SET @errorOut = 0
         END
   END

IF @errorOut <> 0
   BEGIN
      RAISERROR 50000 'Error executing batch'
      ROLLBACK TRANSACTION
   END
ELSE
   COMMIT TRANSACTION
```

Once again don't forget that, if you hit an error in a trigger, the batch will come screeching to a halt and all of your exterior error handling will never be called. Coding all access in this manner is a good idea anyway because any constraint errors will not kill the batch.

Whenever you want to send multiple statements from the client and have them all execute or fail, you must use a scheme like this. Note that I have included lots of seemingly redundant error messages for debugging purposes. Obviously, a message about the first error that causes the batch to go wrong is the most important to get to the user, translated into a readable form for them.

Note the different shading of sections of this batch. If you are simply batching together a set of statements, probably with no resultsets, it should not be a problem to build a batching mechanism to add a set of statements to a queue and then build a script out of it. You might also add a bit of descriptive text to the error message, so that something like "Error executing <statement1>" becomes more along the lines of "Error deleting customer with customerId = 1234". When we go to execute this batch, the shaded parts are added to the ends, and we would add the error handlers after each statement.

Of course, this is not the only way to build an error handler. I frequently use another technique. Instead of using:

```
IF @errorOut = 1
```

to build up scripts, I code a GOTO in the error handler:

```
    <statement2>
    SET @errorNbr = @@error
    IF @error <> 0 OR @returnValue < 0
    BEGIN
        RAISERROR 50000 'Error executing <statement2>'
        GOTO errorOut
    END
```

and end the batch as:

```
    COMMIT TRANSACTION
    GOTO endOfBatch
errorOut:
    RAISERROR 50000 'Error executing batch'
    ROLLBACK TRANSACTION

endOfBatch:
```

This is an acceptable solution but it makes use of the dreaded GOTO statement. The primary value of this method is the ability to simply append the error code to the end of each statement, but basically this was a bit of laziness on my part. The most important thing is that we keep our batches safe and we make sure that the transaction is closed. If it does not close, two really freaky things will occur:

- ❏ Whatever data you have modified will be locked up tight, possibly causing other users to get blocked behind this transaction
- ❏ Since your application does not know that it is hanging a transaction, any other commands you send will also be running under this same transaction

As mentioned in *Error Handling* in the *Stored Procedures* section, make certain to complete any batches sent to the server, or completely cancel them. If an error occurs in the middle of the batch, the batch waits for someone to handle the error before moving on.

Chapter 12

Compiled SQL vs. Ad Hoc SQL for Building Apps

When building OLTP applications, we have to make a very big choice. Do we or don't we use stored procedures? And if we do, should we require that all database access go through them? In this section, we will examine the different arguments and give a recommendation for the best way to build applications.

Ad Hoc SQL

Ad hoc SQL is sometimes referred to as **straight SQL** as it is code that has nothing added to it. The "normal" way that most tools tend to want to converse with SQL Server is by using *ad hoc* batches of SQL code. As we have seen, code is very useful when batched together and, sometimes, this is the only way we can build scripts to do one-time changes to data. But what about when we are building a user interface to our OLTP system data?

Using uncompiled, *ad hoc* SQL has some advantages over building compiled stored procedures:

- More flexibility
- Faster development
- Better performance in some situations

More Flexibility

Because we build it at the very last minute, *ad hoc* SQL does not suffer from some of the stern requirements of stored procedures. For example, say we want to build a user interface to a list of customers. We have ten columns that can be added to the SELECT clause, based on the tables that are listed in the FROM clause. It is very simple to build into the user interface a list of columns that the user will be able to use to customize his/her own list. Then the program can issue the list request with only the columns in the SELECT list that are requested by the user. Since some columns might be very large and contain quite a bit of data, it is better to only send back a few columns instead of all ten.

For instance, consider that we have the view v_customer, with columns customerId, name, number, officeAddress (with each line of the address separated by slashes), phoneNumber, lastSaleDate, and yearToDateSales. We will certainly not want to show users the customerId, though we will always need it. If a user is in sales, he/she might set up a profile to return name, number, lastSaleDate, lastContactDate, and yearToDateSales. The user interface would send the following query to the server to get the requested rows:

```
SELECT   customerId, name, number, lastSaleDate, yearToDateSales
FROM     v_customer
```

Another user may simply want to see name and number, so we would execute the following:

```
SELECT   customerId, name, number
FROM     v_customer
```

This will save us bandwidth when transmitting the query back to the user. But we have still calculated yearToDateSales, lastContactDate, and lastSaleDate. As we've seen, in a well-designed database these values are likely to be calculated rather than stored, which will cause this query to incur a lot of unnecessary overhead.

In this case, we can split the query into two possibilities. If the user asks for a sales column, then the client will send the whole query:

```
SELECT  customer.customerId, customer.name, customer.number
      , sales.yearToDateSales, sales.lastSaleDate
FROM    customer
          LEFT OUTER JOIN
            (SELECT customerId,
              SUM(itemCount * pricePaid) AS yearToDateSales,
                MAX(date) AS lastSaleDate
            FROM    sales
            GROUP  by customerId) AS sales
            ON customer.customerId = sales.customerId
```

If the user does *not* ask for a sales column, the client will send:

```
SELECT customer.customerId, customer.name, customer.number
-- note the commas on the front of the row. This allows us to easily comment
-- out a row of columns easily, or programatically remove them in a real app
--       ,sales.yearToDateSales, sales.lastSaleDate
FROM    customer
--          LEFT OUTER JOIN
--              (SELECT  customerId,
--                  SUM(itemCount * pricePaid) AS yearToDateSales,
--                      MAX(date) as lastSaleDate
--                  FROM    sales
--                  GROUP  BY customerId) AS sales
              ON customer.customerId = sales.customerId
```

In this way we have the flexibility to only execute what is actually needed.

The same can be said for `INSERT` and `UPDATE` statements. One of the issues that we found when we built these two types of stored procedures was that it was very hard to vary the columns in the `INSERT` and `UPDATE` lists. It will be trivial (from a SQL standpoint) to build our applications to only include the columns that have changed in the column lists. For example, take the `customer` fields from above – `customerId`, `name`, and `number`. In our stored procedure, the `UPDATE` always had to send all the columns:

```
UPDATE customer
SET name = @name, number = @number
WHERE customerId = @customerId
```

But what if only the `name` column changed? And what if the `number` column is part of an index, and it has data validations that take three seconds to execute? Using straight SQL, we simply execute:

```
UPDATE customer
SET name = @name
    --   ,number = @number
WHERE customerId = @customerId
```

Faster Development

The speed of development is a sticky point in my opinion and depends solely on personnel. In shops where I have worked, it has been the case that one good SQL programmer could keep up with five or so UI programmers building applications and, by using code generators, we could push that up to ten or fifteen. However, there are two caveats to this. Firstly, good SQL programmers can be hard to find, and secondly, many managers don't feel the need to have programmers dedicated to SQL programming only.

So, if you do not have a dedicated query writer, developing user interface code by sending SQL query batches may be the way to go. However, it is worth mentioning that major holes will arise if the general rules (keep transactions in one batch and try to make one batch equal to one transaction) aren't followed.

Better Performance

Performance gains from using straight SQL calls are basically centered around the topics that we looked at in the previous section on flexibility. Because we can omit parts of queries that do not make sense in some cases, we do not end up in the situation where we are executing unnecessary code.

SQL Server 7.0 and 2000 do cache the plans of these calls, but bear in mind that the statements which are sent must be identical, except possibly for the scalar values in search arguments. Identical means identical; add a comment or even a space character and the plan is blown. SQL Server can build query plans that have parameters – which allow plan reuse by subsequent calls – but, over all, stored procedures are better when it comes to using cached plans for performance.

Compiled SQL

Compiled SQL is split into two types of objects. One type is stored procedures (and the functions compiled within them). The other type is triggers; we will not concern ourselves with triggers here as we have previously established that they are only useful in a very specific set of circumstances. In this section, we will look at the four particular properties of stored procedures that make them outstanding tools for building applications:

- They limit the access path to data
- Performance
- Encapsulation
- Security

Limited Access Path to Data

While a stored procedure can perform multiple operations, it appears to the user like a single call. As we discussed previously in the *Stored Procedure* section, we can build almost object-oriented methods for our database objects, such that the user never has to execute *ad hoc* query calls. This gives us a very large organizational gain. If we force users to only use stored procedures, we know the finite set of paths that users can take to access the data. Hence, if we have a performance problem, we can optimize the stored procedure in a rather simple manner (much as we did in the *Encapsulation* section above) instead of having to comb through lines and lines of code to find the problem.

Performance

Stored procedures can give us better performance by storing the optimized query plan the first time the procedure is executed. Subsequent calls use the exact same plan as the first. With all of the join types, possible tables, indexes, view text expansions, etc., optimizing a query is a non-trivial task which may take quite a few milliseconds. Now, admittedly, when you are building a single-user application, you will say who cares but, as your user numbers go up, this really begins to add up.

As we discussed in the *Ad Hoc SQL Better Performance* section a moment ago, SQL Server can cache plans of SQL calls and, even though there are a few stringent rules governing how this occurs, it can really make a difference.

However, when accessing stored procedures, the rules are far less stringent. Every time you call with any set of parameters, it uses the same plan (unless we force it not to using `WITH RECOMPILE`). This saves you milliseconds, which are important if you have lots of users on your system. While SQL Server does a pretty good job of caching *ad hoc* SQL calls, it is excellent when it comes to caching stored procedure calls.

One thing to understand is that stored procedures are optimized based on the initial parameters that are passed in. This very occasionally causes a problem if you run the exact same procedure with two different parameters. For example, we might have a table with a non-clustered index on a field, where 60 per cent of the items in the table have the exact same value while all other values in the table are unique. If your search argument is in the non-unique values, the index would not be the best way to retrieve the rows (since the overhead of fetching through the index to the data pages would likely be greater than just touching all of the data rows directly). If the search argument is against the unique values, using the index would be best. Whichever value is passed in first becomes the plan that is used by all subsequent queries.

There are two ways to deal with this, if it is a problem:

- Add the `WITH RECOMPILE` option to the stored procedure declaration, causing the plan to be dropped every time.
- Build a procedure that calls two other procedures, one for the unique cases and another for the non-unique. This is pretty cumbersome but, if it is a highly accessed stored procedure, then this would be the best way.

Encapsulation

One really great benefit of using stored procedures as an encapsulation layer between the user and the tables is that it simplifies calls to access data. Even a simple `SELECT` statement that accesses a single table can be difficult to formulate and send from the client, much less a multi-table query or even a multi-statement query. For example, consider this single table statement:

```
SELECT personId, firstName, lastName
FROM person
WHERE personId = 1
```

In pseudo-code, we might have to do the following:

```
query = "SELECT personId, firstName, lastName FROM person WHERE personId = 1"
```

We could then execute this using ADO, or some other set of objects that allow clients to consume data from SQL Server. If we were executing a stored procedure, we might simply do the following:

```
DIM query AS STRING
query = "EXECUTE person$get @personId = 1"
```

We can build this on the server as:

```
CREATE PROCEDURE person$get
(
    @personId  int
) AS

SELECT personId, firstName, lastName FROM person WHERE personId = @personId
```

The first thing you will probably notice is that the stored procedure took more effort to build. However, this is a very simple example. Considering that most `SELECT` statements in my code are at least five or six lines, and sometimes closer to fifteen or twenty, it is far easier for clients to use the code in a single line of text.

Consider also that, while our examples have been single statement queries, we looked earlier at multi-statement queries. When we need to execute more than one statement in a procedure, as when filling a temporary table or possibly even updating multiple tables, we have to use the far more complex batching syntax we looked at in the *Batches of SQL Code* section. Trying to build up the script programmatically and then execute it this way is pretty messy.

An encapsulation layer of stored procedures between the user and the tables also gives optimization benefits. As we discussed in the *Stored Procedures* section, because the details are encapsulated and therefore hidden from the user of the data, and because we have a finite set of queries to optimize, when a user says that a given procedure is slow, we can fix it easily. While perfect optimization can be more difficult to attain using a stored procedure, they lend themselves to code reuse.

Security

We can restrict users' access to specific stored procedures and, consequently, specific base tables. The result is that, by employing stored procedures, it is easy to build a proper set of rights that limits the user to seeing only what we want them to see.

Tips to Consider

Each of the two choices has pros and cons. On the one hand we have *ad hoc* SQL. This is very flexible – leading to faster development times but some associated mild performance hits. All that flexibility can also create chaos when trying to performance tune the application. On the other hand, by using stored procedures for access we save some compilation time on multiple uses, and gain encapsulation of the database structure from the actual user of the data – in essence putting a protective database access tier between the user and the data itself.

All things considered, the best choice for most OLTP databases is to build them using stored procedure access. You might guess that the primary reason for this is performance. Using stored procedures enhances performance, especially when you have extremely busy databases. However, once Microsoft added query plan caching for straight SQL calls, caching the kinds of queries that OLTP databases make is usually not such a big problem, so they have eliminated a great deal of this value.

Consequently, the greatest reward from stored procedure use is encapsulation. Maintaining a layer between applications and data structures is an invaluable tool for building solid applications and reducing maintenance costs.

The key to this is simple. Once users have worked with the application for a while, changes are inevitable. With stored procedures, we can encapsulate these changes to tables and never have to change our applications. Stored procedures also make our applications cleaner by taking much of the error handling of DML operations out of the presentation code. When we send batches of code to SQL Server, we are basically sending a stored procedure definition anyway, so why not build the SQL once and use it generically?

Security Considerations

Security is another database administrator job that we need to understand at a fairly high level, so that we can architect suitable applications that protect, not so much against improper data, but against improper data usage.

How data access applications will use the security is something that we will routinely have to specify. We will discuss how to design a security plan for our database, and we will look at how we can make use of the SQL Server security in our own code. We will shy away from any really technical security discussions – such as whether or not to use trusted connections (Windows Authentication) or standard SQL Server security – largely because, from a design standpoint, we don't really care. Inside the database the security will be set up exactly the same.

Using SQL Server security, we will want to build a security plan that will prevent any unwanted usage of our objects by any user, whether part of our organization or a hacker. As data architects, it is extremely important to carefully design our security needs in terms of who can do what with what (as we started to do with our use cases back in Chapter 5). Our goal is to allow the user to perform whatever tasks they need to, but to prohibit any other tasks, nor let them see any data that they should not. Creating roles and associating users to them is a fairly easy task using the Enterprise Manager, and one that we will not be looking at.

In SQL Server, we can control rights to almost every object type. The following table shows the kinds of operations that we will be interested in dealing with for each object type, with regard to security in our databases:

Object	Rights
Table	SELECT, INSERT, UPDATE, DELETE
View	SELECT, INSERT, UPDATE, DELETE
Column (View and Table)	SELECT, INSERT, UPDATE, DELETE
Function	EXECUTE
Stored Procedure	EXECUTE

There also exists a References *right on tables that is not pertinent to this discussion.*

We can then grant or deny usage of these objects to our users. We certainly don't want to have to grant access to each user individually, as we may have a multitude of users in our databases. So SQL Server provides us with the concept of a **role** (previously known as groups in SQL Server 6.X and earlier) which we can grant rights to and then associate with users.

Every user in a database is a member of at least the public role, but may be a member of multiple roles. In fact, roles may be members of other roles. Take, for example, any typical human resources system that has employee information like name, address, position, manager, pay grade, etc. We will likely need several roles, such as:

- HRManagers – can do any task in the system
- HRWorkers – can maintain any attribute in the system, but approval records are required to modify salary information
- Managers – all managers in the company would be in this role, but they can only see the information for their own workers
- Employees – can only see their own information, and can only modify their own personal address information.

Each of the roles would then be granted access to all of the resources that they need. A member of the Managers role would probably also be a member of the Employees role. Then, as stated, they could see the information for their employees, and also themselves.

There are three different commands that SQL Server uses to give or take away rights from each of our roles:

- GRANT – gives the privilege to use an object.
- DENY – denies access to an object, regardless of whether the user has been granted the privilege from any other role.
- REVOKE – used to remove any GRANT or DENY permissions statements that have been executed. Behaves like a delete of a permission.

Almost every permission statement that you will execute will be a GRANT statement. Typically, we will simply give permissions to a role to perform tasks that are very specific to the role. The DENY command should only be used as more of a punishment type command as, no matter how many other times you have granted privileges to an object, the user will not have access to it while there is one DENY. As an example, take the HR system we were discussing just. We would not deny access to the Employees role, since Managers are employees also and would need to have rights to it.

Once we have built all of our objects – including tables, stored procedures, views, etc. – we can grant rights to them. We have already mentioned in the object specific sections that – with stored procedures, functions, and views – we do not have to grant rights to the underlying objects that are used in these objects. This is true as long as the user that builds the object is also the user that owns the object. As we will build our objects as the database owner, this is not usually a problem.

One additional issue that we should note is that each database has a special set of built-in roles:

- db_accessadmin – users associated with this role can add or remove users from the database
- db_backupoperator – users associated with this role are allowed to back up the database
- db_datareader – users associated with this role are allowed to read any data in any table
- db_datawriter – users associated with this role are allowed to write any data in any table
- db_ddladmin – users associated with this role are allowed to add modify or drop any objects in the database (in other words, execute any DDL statements)
- db_denydatareader – users associated with this role are denied the ability to see any data in the database, though they may still see the data through stored procedures
- db_denydatawriter – much like the db_denydatareader role, users associated with this role are denied the ability to modify any data in the database, though they still may modify data through stored procedures
- db_owner – users associated with this role can perform any activity in the database
- db_securityadmin – users associated with this role can modify and change permissions and roles in the database

Deciding on whether to make your users members of any of these roles is totally up to the situation. I like to build a user administrator role – a user who can add users to the database and associate them with roles. Building an application that displays these values is a fairly easy task with SQLDMO (SQL Distributed Management Objects). Then, once a user has been created by the DBA, the user in the administrator role can associate them to their database roles.

Programmatically, we can determine some basic information about a user's security information in the database:

- `is_member(<role>)` – tells us if the current user is the member of a given role
- `user` – tells us the current user's name
- `permissions(object_id('<objectName>'))` – lets us see if a user has rights to perform some action

For example, we could build a query to determine all of the routine stored procedures that the user can execute:

```
SELECT specific_name ,
       CASE WHEN permissions(object_id(specific_name)) & 32 = 32
       THEN 1
       ELSE 0
       END AS CAN EXECUTE
FROM information_schema.routines
WHERE specific_name LIKE 'routine$ per cent'
```

When we execute it, we get the following list:

specific_name	canExecute
routine$del	1
routine$ins	1
routine$list	1
routine$upd	1

If you have limited access to the base tables, you have already built every bit of security into your system that the user or programmer will ever need to deal with. For example, take the four procedures we have listed above. By restricting access to the `routine$list` procedure, the user interface can look in this access list and determine if it should even try to execute the list. The same is true for the `insert`, `update`, and `delete` procedures. If the UI cannot use the `routine$del` procedure, it won't even show Delete in its menus.

`PERMISSIONS()` is a very versatile function that can be used to determine if a user can do most operations in SQL Server (consult SQL Server Books Online for more information) . When building applications, we will try our best to use the facilities of SQL Server for our security needs – this will help us to avoid building tables of users and their rights ever again.

In the rest of this section, we extend this concept of using SQL Server security to deal with few methods that we will occasionally have to employ. We will look at:

- Row-level security
- Column-level security

Row-Level Security

This generally refers to the situation where we want to give a user the rights to use a table, and use all of the columns of the table, but we don't want them to be able to see all of the rows, based on some criteria.

Chapter 12

Row-level security was very difficult to implement in previous versions of SQL Server. In SQL Server 2000, we can build a fairly simple solution to this problem with user-defined functions.

For our first example, let's use the `artist` and `album` tables from the previous chapter. We are going to deal with only letting the users see Beatles albums if they are a member of the `BeatlesFan` role. Assuming we have created the role, we will create the following user-defined function:

```
CREATE VIEW v_album
AS
    SELECT albumId, name, artistId FROM dbo.album
    WHERE artistId <> 1 --Beatles
        OR is_member('BeatlesFan') = 1
GO
```

Then we select from it:

```
SELECT *
FROM dbo.v_album
```

This returns:

albumId	name	artistId
3	quadraphenia	2
9	tommy	2

because I am not a member of the `BeatlesFan` role. This is certainly not very robust. What if we want to deny users from seeing other artists' work? We need to extend the example. We could build a table with `group` to `artist` relationships, here named `rlsAlbum` (`rls` meaning row-level security).

```
CREATE TABLE rlsAlbum
(
    rlsAlbumId int NOT NULL identity, artistId int, memberOfGroupName sysname
)
```

We then build a view that correlates the security to the `artist` table:

```
--we build a view that includes our row level security table.
ALTER VIEW v_album
AS
SELECT album.albumId, album.name, album.artistId
FROM   dbo.album AS album
        JOIN (SELECT   DISTINCT artistId
                FROM rlsAlbum
                    WHERE is_member(memberOfGroupName) = 1) AS security
                    ON album.artistId = security.artistId
GO
```

Then we select from the view before adding any groups:

```
--executed as member of no group
SELECT * FROM v_album
```

and we get no rows:

```
albumId   name                                       artistId
--------- ------------------------------------------ ---------
```

Next, we can add some groups to the `rlsAlbum` table to let the `db_owners` and other logical roles see the values in the table:

```
--db_owner, probably added in insert trigger on albumTable
INSERT INTO rlsAlbum(artistId, memberOfGroupName)
VALUES (1, 'db_owner')
INSERT INTO rlsAlbum(artistId, memberOfGroupName)
VALUES (2, 'db_owner')

INSERT INTO rlsAlbum(artistId, memberOfGroupName)
VALUES (1, 'BeatlesFan')
INSERT INTO rlsAlbum(artistId, memberOfGroupName)
VALUES (2, 'WhoFan')
GO
```

When we select from it, we get:

```
albumId   name                                       artistId
--------- ------------------------------------------ ---------
1         the white album                            1
2         revolver                                   1
4         abbey road                                 1
8         rubber soul                                1
10        yellow submarine                           1
11        please please me                           1
9         tommy                                      2
3         quadraphenia                               2
```

Now, if the users do not have rights to the base table, they will not be able to see any rows, unless you have specifically given rights to view to the role that they are a member of.

Column-Level Security

SQL Server security does have facilities to grant and revoke rights to a particular column, but they are painful to use. They also will not work when we use views and stored procedures to access our data, as objects use the security of their *owner*. If we want to use stored procedures to access all of our data (which is my preference), we need to look at different possibilities

In this section, we will give a possible alternative to building multiple views or procedures to vertically partition our data. A possible way to implement this is to use a technique very like the row-level example to blot out a column that the user does not have rights to see. Using SQL Server permissions, we can extend our previous view to only return values for columns that the users have access to:

```
ALTER VIEW v_album
AS
SELECT album.albumId, --assume the user can see the pk pointer
CASE WHEN PERMISSIONS(OBJECT_ID('album'),'name') & 1 = 1
THEN NAME
```

```
    ELSE NULL
    END AS NAME,
    CASE WHEN PERMISSIONS(object_id('album'),'artistId') & 1 = 1
    THEN album.artistId
    ELSE NULL
    END AS artistId
    FROM dbo.album AS album
    JOIN (SELECT DISTINCT artistId
    FROM rlsAlbum
    WHERE is_member(memberOfGroupName) = 1) AS security
    ON album.artistId = security.artistId
```

Note that we return NULL as the indicator here, because the column is a not-NULL value. In some cases, like when NULL is actually an allowable value for a column, we might need to add an additional column – perhaps something like canSeeNameFl (bit) – which tells the application if the user is allowed to see the column or not.

This may cause a bit of overhead, but then, almost any solution for column- and row-level security will. The important aspect of this solution is that we can now use this view in a stored procedure and, regardless of who owns the stored procedure, we are able to restrict column usage in a very generic manner that only uses SQL Server security.

Cross Database Considerations

So far, all of the code and issues we have discussed have been concerned with the local database. In general, apart from the fact that the data is not within the same logical unit of work, there is little difference in accessing data beyond the confines of the local database. This generally makes working with the data harder, especially since foreign key constraints cannot be used to handle referential integrity needs. Additionally, because the other database will be backed up and dealt with differently, we lose some of the protection we have in a single database world.

While accessing data in outside databases causes difficulties, sometimes it is unavoidable. A typical example might be trying to tie an off-the-shelf system into your home-grown system. It might be easier to access the tables from a different server rather than trying to include them in your database.

In this section, we will identify some of the issues that arise when working with other databases. We will break things into two sections:

- Same Server
- Different Server

Same Server

Accessing data in a different database but on the same server is pretty similar to the normal (same database, same server) situation. There are a few issues, however – regarding naming, security, and data modification – that we should examine.

Same Server Naming

This is pretty simple. To access data beyond our database, we simply include the database in the name of the object we are accessing. We use the following convention:

```
<databaseName>.<owner>.<objectName>
```

This is true for tables, stored procedures, functions, etc.

Same Server Security

Each database has a unique db_owner. Consequently, one db_owner cannot create a procedure that accesses data in another database without being given permission to do so by its db_owner.

If we have two databases on the server, there is currently no way to correlate the two owners and allow them to transfer rights to objects via a stored procedure. For example, consider this procedure:

```
CREATE PROCEDURE dbo.procedure$testCrossDatabase
AS
SELECT field1
FROM database2.dbo.table
GO
```

The user will not only need access privileges to the procedure$testCrossDatabase procedure but, in the database2 database, we will have to grant them explicit access to the database *and* the object.

Worse still, the same is true for triggers. Since the user will likely not even see the data that the trigger will validate against, it seems dangerous to have to give them full rights to the table on the other database just to validate a value.

Because of these problems, it might be advantageous to replicate a copy of the data that you need to do validations against into your other database, depending on the actual size of the data in question, of course. This will keep your data protected from viewings, but is certainly more costly than doing a cross database lookup.

Same Server Data Modification

In the first part of this chapter, we looked at how SQL Server uses transactions and locks to make certain that our operations either finish totally or not at all and, more importantly, without interruption from other processes. There is no difference in coding when we access data in a different database. We simply use the same syntax and touch the data in both databases. The same transaction mechanisms work seamlessly in either case.

For example, say we have an old in-house requisitioning system, and a new purchasing system that was created by a different company. When we built the former, we included a table which was a queue of items that the purchasing people needed to purchase, and which showed where the items were to be delivered to. Now that we have the new third-party purchasing system, we want to utilize its purchase order functionality. We would like to automatically create a purchase order when a requisition is accepted by the person with authority. So, in the requisition$finalize stored procedure, the call to INSERT INTO the aforementioned queue will be changed to INSERT INTO the purchase order table:

```
CREATE PROCEDURE requistion$finalize

...misc code removed for clarity...

BEGIN TRANSACTION
INSERT INTO dbo.requisitionStatus (requisitionNumber, statusId)
VALUES (@requisitionNumber, @statusId)
--error handling

INSERT INTO purchasing.dbo.purchaseOrder(number, date)
VALUES (@purchaseOrderNumber,getdate())
--error handling

--also insert items
COMMIT TRANSACTION
```

Because the two databases are on the same server, the operation appears seamless to the user. However, since there are now multiple transaction logs in the mix, SQL Server cannot do a simple transaction. It must use a very important concept called a two-phase commit.

Two-phase commit

The two-phase commit is basically a protocol that allows a server to communicate to a database that it wants to perform tasks in two different logical areas as a transaction. The same protocol is used when COM+ is using COM objects to perform non-database tasks within a transaction. Using COM+, we can mix transactions of database objects with file system objects, using the two-phase commit to pretty much ensure transactional integrity (there is some possibility of failing to finish a transaction on one source and not another, simply because of latency, but the possibility is very small).

Keep in mind that the controller starts transactions just as it normally does. A transaction is started on each individual database or resource exactly as it would be if it was the only transaction. Then, when we send the final commit to return the transaction count to zero, the two-phase commit begins.

- **Prepare phase** – Sends a prepare message to each of the resources and tells it to finish up the transaction. The resource then takes care of all logs and does everything necessary to make the transaction action permanent. When it finishes, it messages the transaction initiator, and tells it whether or not it was successful.

- **Commit phase** – Once it receives successful messages from the resources, a final message of commit is sent to each resource. If either of the resources claims failure, then all transactions are rolled back.

During the commit phase, if a command is received by one of the resources but not by another and the controller should fail, you may lose work. There is no way around this. However, this is *extremely* improbable as these commands go really fast and, during the commit phase, there should be no possibility of blocking occurring – we already have the items locked and all that is left is to send out the final commit command.

Different Server (Distributed Queries)

I just want to make brief mention of distributed queries, and introduce the functions that can be used to establish a relationship between two SQL Servers, or a SQL Server and an OLE DB or ODBC data source. There are two methods that can be used:

- **Linked servers** – we can build a connection between two servers by registering a "server" name that we then access via a four part name (`<server>.<database>.<owner>.<table>`), or through the `openquery` interface
- **Ad hoc connections** – Using the `openrowset` or `opendatasource` functions, we can get a table of data back from any OLE DB source

Just as our transactions could span multiple databases, we can also have transactions that span different servers using T-SQL. If needed, we can update data in our distributed data source by using the Distributed Transaction Controller (DTC) service that is a part of SQL Server and COM+. We use the following command:

```
BEGIN DISTRIBUTED TRANSACTION

UPDATE externalServer.database.owner.table
...

COMMIT TRANSACTION
```

We can write our code almost exactly as if it were on the same server. Note that, if we had written `BEGIN TRANSACTION` instead of `BEGIN DISTRIBUTED TRANSACTION`, the transaction would have been local to this server, and the action that touched the other server would not be part of the transaction.

We will not be going into the details of these commands, as they can be quite complex and have many different settings for many different situations. I have seldom used them in building OLTP systems and prefer, when possible, to import/replicate all data into the same SQL Server – mostly for speed purposes. Linked servers are used frequently when establishing replication relationships. For more information on distributed queries and replication, see SQL Server 2000 Books Online, or "*Professional SQL Server 2000 Programming*" by *Rob Vieira* (*Wrox Press, ISBN 1-861004-48-6*).

Case Study

We are now ready to begin building the access to the database structures that we created in the past two chapters. For this part of the case study, we have three specific tasks to deal with. These tasks will allow the other programmers who are working on our database to begin writing actual code to use the structures:

- Create the base modification stored procedures (insert, update, delete) – which are sometimes referred to as the CRUD procedures (create, read, update, delete) – as well as a list procedure and a domain fill for our domain tables.
- Build custom stored procedures that support the important tasks of our system, as noted in the use case diagram.
- Specify a set of security groups, and outline what objects they will probably have use of at a very high level.

Base Stored Procedures

Referring back to our diagram in Chapter 10, we will build the following four stored procedures, for four different tables:

- `transaction$ins`

Chapter 12

- bank$upd
- payee$del
- account$list

We will also build a `transactionType$domainFill` procedure. Note again that this code can be downloaded from www.wrox.com.

Transaction Insert Procedure

This is essentially the insert stored procedure that we developed earlier in this chapter, with a few more comments. In this procedure, we insert every field in the table, and include error handling to get back extra information if an error occurs. As usual, we must bracket the `transaction` table name, since it is a reserved word.

```
CREATE PROCEDURE transaction$ins
(
    @accountId int,
    @number varchar(20),
    @date smalldatetime,
    @description varchar(1000),
    @amount money,
    @signature  varchar(100),
    @payeeId int,
    @transactionTypeId int,
    @new_transactionId int = NULL OUTPUT   --contains the new key
                                           --value for the identity
                                           --primary key
) AS
  BEGIN


    --error handling parameters
    DECLARE  @msg AS varchar(255),       -- used to preformat error messages
             @msgTag AS varchar(255),    -- used to hold the first part
                                         -- of the message header
             @tranName AS sysname        -- to hold the name of the savepoint

    -- set up the error message tag and transaction tag
    -- (nestlevel keeps it unique amongst calls to the procedure if nested)
    SET  @msgTag = '<' + object_name(@@procid) + ';TYPE=P'
    SET  @tranName = object_name(@@procid) + CAST(@@nestlevel AS VARCHAR(2))

    BEGIN TRANSACTION
    SAVE TRANSACTION @tranName

    INSERT INTO [transaction](accountId, number, date, description, amount,
                     signature, payeeId, transactionTypeId )
       VALUES(@accountId, @number, @date, @description, @amount, @signature,
              @payeeId, @transactionTypeId )

    -- check for an error
    IF (@@error!=0)
       BEGIN
       -- finish transaction first to minimize chance of transaction
```

```
                -- being hung waiting on a message to complete
                ROLLBACK TRAN @tranName
                COMMIT TRAN
                SELECT @msg = 'There was a problem inserting a new row into ' +
                              ' the transaction table.' + @msgTag +
                              ';CALL=(INSERT transaction)>'
                RAISERROR 50000 @msg
                RETURN -100
            END

    -- scope_identity keeps us from getting any triggered identity values
    SET @new_transactionId=scope_identity()

    COMMIT TRAN

    END
```

Bank Update Procedure

In the update procedure, we will simply update the name of the bank to the value passed in. Note the timestamp parameter and how we use it to implement an optimistic lock for the users of this procedure.

```
CREATE PROCEDURE bank$upd
(
    @key_bankId int,  -- key column that we will use as the key to the
                      -- update. Note that we cannot update the primary key
    @name varchar(384),
    @ts_timestamp timestamp -- optimistic lock
)
AS
-- declare variable used for error handling in blocks
DECLARE @rowcount AS int,      -- holds the rowcount returned from dml calls
        @error AS int,         -- used to hold the error code after a dml
        @msg AS varchar(255),  -- used to preformat error messages
        @retval AS int,        -- general purpose variable for retrieving
                               -- return values from stored procedure calls
        @tranname AS sysname,  -- used to hold the name of the transaction
        @msgTag AS varchar(255) -- to hold the tags for the error message

-- set up the error message tag
SET @msgTag = '<' + object_name(@@procid) + ';TYPE=P'
            + ';keyvalue=' + '@key_bankId:'
            + CONVERT(varchar(10),@key_bankId)

SET @tranName = object_name(@@procid) + CAST(@@nestlevel AS VARCHAR(2))

-- make sure that the user has passed in a timestamp value, as it will
-- be very wasteful if they have not
IF @ts_timeStamp IS NULL
    BEGIN
        SET @msg = 'The timestamp value must not be NULL' +
            @msgTag + '>'
        RAISERROR 50000 @msg
        RETURN -100
    END
```

```
BEGIN TRANSACTION
SAVE TRANSACTION @tranName

UPDATE bank
SET name = @name
WHERE bankId = @key_bankId
   AND autoTimestamp = @ts_timeStamp

-- get the rowcount and error level for the error handling code
SELECT @rowcount = @@rowcount, @error = @@error

IF @error != 0   -- an error occurred outside of this procedure
   BEGIN
      ROLLBACK TRAN @tranName
      COMMIT TRAN
      SELECT @msg = 'A problem occurred modifying the bank record.' +
         @msgTag + ';CALL=(UPDATE bank)>'
      RAISERROR 50001 @msg
      RETURN -100
   END
   ELSE IF @rowcount <> 1   -- this must not be the primary key
                            -- anymore or the record doesn't exist
   BEGIN
      IF (@rowcount = 0)
         BEGIN
            -- if the record exists without the timestamp, it has been modified
            -- by another user
            IF EXISTS (SELECT * FROM bank WHERE bankId = @key_bankId)
               BEGIN
                  SELECT @msg = 'The bank record has been modified' +
                              ' by another user.'
               END
            ELSE    -- the primary key value did not exist
               BEGIN
                  SELECT @msg = 'The bank record does not exist.'
               END
         END
      ELSE       -- rowcount > 0, so too many records were modified
         BEGIN
            SELECT @msg = 'Too many records were modified.'
         END

   ROLLBACK TRAN @tranName
   COMMIT TRAN
   SELECT @msg = @msg + @msgTag + ';CALL=(update bank)>'
   RAISERROR 50000 @msg
   RETURN -100

   END

COMMIT TRAN
RETURN 0
```

Payee Delete Procedure

In terms of its code, the payee delete is very much like the update. This procedure allows the user to delete a payee record from the table.

```
CREATE PROCEDURE payee$del
(
    @key_payeeId int,
    @ts_timeStamp timestamp = NULL   --optimistic lock
)
AS
--declare variable used for error handling in blocks
DECLARE @rowcount AS int,        -- holds the rowcount returned from dml calls
        @error AS int,           -- used to hold the error code after a dml
        @msg AS varchar(255),    -- used to preformat error messages
        @retval AS int,          -- general purpose variable for retrieving
                              -- return values from stored procedure calls
        @tranName AS sysname,    -- used to hold the name of the transaction
        @msgTag AS varchar(255)  -- used to hold the tags for the error message

-- set up the error message tag
SET     @msgTag = '<' + object_name(@@procid) + ';TYPE=P'
                + ';keyvalue=' + '@key_payeeId:'
                + convert(VARCHAR(10),@key_payeeId)

SET     @tranName = object_name(@@procid) + CAST(@@nestlevel as varchar(2))

BEGIN TRANSACTION
SAVE TRANSACTION @tranName

DELETE payee
WHERE  payeeId = @key_payeeId
   AND @ts_timeStamp = autoTimestamp

-- get the rowcount and error level for the error handling code
SELECT @rowcount = @@rowcount, @error = @@error

IF @error != 0  -- an error occurred outside of this procedure
   BEGIN
       SELECT @msg = 'A problem occurred removing the payee record.' +
              @msgTag + 'call=(delete payee)>'
       ROLLBACK TRAN @tranName
       COMMIT TRAN
       RAISERROR 50000 @msg
       RETURN -100
   END
ELSE IF @rowcount > 1  -- this must not be the primary key anymore or the
                       -- record doesn't exist
   BEGIN
       SELECT @msg = 'Too many payee records were deleted. ' +
              @msgTag + ';call=(delete payee)>'

       ROLLBACK TRAN @tranName
       COMMIT TRAN
       RAISERROR 50000 @msg
```

```
                RETURN -100
        END
ELSE IF @rowcount = 0
    BEGIN
        IF EXISTS (SELECT * FROM payee WHERE payeeId = @key_payeeId)
            BEGIN
                SELECT @msg = 'The payee record has been modified' +
                              ' by another user.' + ';call=(delete payee)>'

                ROLLBACK TRAN @tranName
                COMMIT tran
                RAISERROR 50000 @msg
                RETURN -100

            END
        ELSE
            BEGIN
                SELECT @msg = 'The payee record you tried to delete'
                              ' does not exist.' + @msgTag +
                              ';call=(delete payee)>'
                    RAISERROR 50000 @msg
                        -- it depends on the needs of the system whether or not you
                        -- should actually implement this error or even if
                        -- if we should quit here, and return a negative value.
                        -- If you were trying to remove something
                        -- and it doesn't exist, is that bad?
            END
    END

COMMIT TRAN
RETURN 0
```

Account List Procedure

To build this procedure we need to include the account information and a few possible filters – in this case, `number`, `bankId`, and `bankName`. When we see a list of accounts, we will want to see the bank information too, so we will join this in.

```
CREATE PROCEDURE account$list
(
 @accountId int = NULL,         -- primary key to retrieve single row
 @number    varchar(20) = ' per cent', -- like match on account.name
 @bankId    int = NULL,
 @bankName  varchar(20) = ' per cent'
)
AS

-- as the count messages have been known to be a problem for clients
SET NOCOUNT ON

-- default the @number parm to ' per cent' if the passed value is NULL
IF @number IS NULL SELECT @number = ' per cent'

-- select all of the fields (less the timestamp) from the table for viewing.
```

```
SELECT account.accountId, account.bankId, account.number,
       bank.NAME AS bankName
FROM dbo.account AS account
JOIN dbo.bank AS bank
   ON account.bankId = bank.bankId
WHERE (account.accountId = @accountId OR @accountId IS NULL)
  AND (account.number Like @number)
  AND (account.bankId = @bankId OR @bankId IS NULL)
  AND (bank.NAME LIKE @bankName)
ORDER BY account.NAME

RETURN 0
```

Transaction Type Domain Fill Procedure

The domain fill procedure is used to fill a combo box of transaction types, like on a transaction form. Note that we turn the site name into a description field, even though there is a description field in the table. This is because, even if there was not a name or a description in the table, we would still return a description to make user coding simpler.

```
CREATE PROCEDURE transactionType$domainFill

AS

   BEGIN

   -- all domain fill procedures return the same field names, so that the
   -- user can code them the same way using a generic object
   SELECT transactionTypeId AS ID, transactionType.NAME AS description,
   FROM transactionType
   ORDER BY transactionType.NAME

   END
```

Custom Stored Procedures

We will focus on two of the use cases and consider how we might build stored procedures to support them. We will look at:

❑   Balance Account

❑   Get Account Information

Balance Account Use Case

Referring back to our use case diagram in Chapter 5, we identified a use case entitled Balance and described as, "Allows user to reconcile items that have been reported by the bank." We will not be writing any actual SQL code for this use case, but we will consider this fairly complex situation and how we will solve it in our database.

497

To perform the balancing operation, we will probably need to have the following stored procedures coded:

- `Statement$insert`, `statmentItem$insert`, and possibly `statement$insertItems`. Since we will possibly be downloading the `statementItem` records from an Internet site, we might use the last procedure to load the values into a temporary table and insert the lot at once. We could add an `INSTEAD OF` trigger to put all of the invalid rows into an exception handling table when they are retrieved from the download file.

- `transaction$listPossibleMatchesToStatementItems` – this procedure would do a join of unreconciled transactions to `statementItems` and give all of the exact matches, based on `transaction.number` to `statementItem.number` for checks, and `transactionType` if available. We would need to make certain that the join produces a one-to-one relationship for `transaction` to `statementItems`.

- `Transaction$reconcile` – this will allow us to associate a `transaction` with a `statementItem` for reconciliation.

- A batch of stored procedure calls would need to be coordinated from the screen that uses the `transaction$listPossibleMatchesToStatementItems` to execute the query.

- We would need a procedure much like our generic `transaction$list` filtered by account, to only show unreconciled items.

- `statementItem$list` – this would give us a list of items that have not been associated with a given `transaction`. This procedure and the previous one would give us the ability to have a side-by-side form (UI again) that we could use to associate items.

- `Statement$finalizeReconciliation` – this would place a record in the `accountReconciliation` table to tell the statement that it is finished. We would want to add a trigger to the statement table that checks to make sure that the total credits and total debits (positive and negative transactions) in the `transaction` table matched the totals in the statement. An enhancement to the requirements of the system might be to allow an offset transaction to be automatically added to the table, to balance the statement when a small error could not be tracked down.

Keep in mind that I have added to the requirements for the system in the last bullet. This functionality should be considered an enhancement and discussed with the project manager and the user. This may not be a feature that the client wanted or it may have slipped their mind. Throughout the process of implementing the system, you will think of new and cool features to add to the project. The architecture that you are creating should be clean enough to support new features, but never add new features to a product that are not in the specifications without getting client agreement (and an increase in your fee).

As you can see, this is quite a list of procedures to write. Depending on the coding staff, the next step would likely be to have stub versions of these procedures written so that UI coders can continue with their work. We have also discovered a few additional triggers that need to be written to cover the `statement` and `accountReconcile` tables. Discovering additional triggers and requirements will not be uncommon – no design process is perfect.

Get Account Information Use Case

We should be able to support this use case with a fairly simple stored procedure, so we will write it here. We will consider that the UI has been specified to give a list of accounts, with a way to drill down and see current information, including:

- Current balance (total debits, total credits)
- Total unreconciled amounts
- Total number of transactions
- Last statement date
- Last reconcile date

So we write the following procedure:

```
CREATE PROCEDURE account$getAccountInformation
(
   @accountId int
) AS

-- Note that because we built our transaction table using a reserved word,
-- we have to use bracketed names in our query.

SELECT account.accountNumber,
       statement.DATE,         -- if this value is NULL then no statements
                               -- ever received
       accountReconcile.DATE,  -- if this value is NULL, then the account
                               -- has never been reconciled
    SUM([transaction].AMOUNT) AS accountBalance,
    SUM(CASE WHEN [transaction].AMOUNT > 0
       THEN [transaction].AMOUNT
       ELSE 0
    END) AS totalCredits,
    SUM(CASE WHEN [transaction].AMOUNT < 0
    THEN [transaction].AMOUNT
    ELSE 0
    END) AS totalDebits,
    SUM(CASE
    WHEN transactionReconcile.transactionReconcileId IS NOT NULL
       THEN transactionAmount
       ELSE 0 END) AS unreconciledTotal
FROM  dbo.account AS account
--  accounts may have no transactions yet
    LEFT OUTER JOIN dbo.[transaction] AS [transaction]
       --  transaction may not have been reconciled yet
       LEFT OUTER JOIN dbo.transactionReconcile AS transactionReconcile
          ON [transaction].transactionId =
                                    transactionReconcile.transactionid
       ON account.accountId = [transaction].accountId
       --  account may never have recieved a statement
    LEFT OUTER JOIN dbo.statement AS statement
       LEFT OUTER JOIN dbo.accountReconcile AS accountReconcile
          ON statement.statementId = accountReconcile.statementId
       ON account.accountId = [transaction].accountId
WHERE accountId = @accountId
GROUP BY account.accountnumber, statement.DATE, accountReconcile.DATE
```

Security for the Case Study

Lastly, we need to specify our security. Our example does have two security roles specified, and we probably will want to add another role for administration purposes:

- ❑ `AccountUser` – based on the use case diagram, this role will simply be able to view account information. The custom stored procedure `account$getAccountInformation` would certainly be required, as well as any supporting stored procedures to build the form.

- ❑ `AccountingClerk` – as specified, this role will have rights to every defined procedure in the system.

- ❑ `UserAdministrator` – this role would be a member of the `db_securityadmin` and `db_accessadmin` fixed database roles.

There is some ambiguity in the specifications, but we have chosen to implement a user that can view all account information – `AccountUser`. We certainly need to ask the project manager and the client whether certain accounts should be off limits to certain users. If so, then we might want to add a row-level security system to implement this.

Summary

In this chapter, we have looked at many of the most important issues that we should be aware of when implementing data access and modification in our applications.

We have discussed the pros and cons of using stored procedures, *ad hoc* SQL, and views. We emphasized what can be done to tackle errors – error handling being one of SQL Server's weak points – and we looked at implementing security through stored procedures and user roles.

We have looked in detail at transactions and locking, temporary tables, `NULL`s, and cursors. Finally, we drew up some of the core stored procedures required to implement our case study database.

Hopefully, this chapter has answered many of your questions regarding data access and modification, and has raised your awareness of important issues. It should be interesting to see how these ideas affect your own designs.

In the next chapter, we will look at one of the most difficult tasks for the database designer – translating system requirements into actual hardware requirements.

Advanced Data Access and Modification Techniques

transaction

transactionId: int NOT NULL
accountId: int NOT NULL (FK) (AK1.1)
number: varchar(20) NOT NULL (AK1.2)
date: smalldatetime NOT NULL
description: varchar(1000) NOT NULL
amount: money NOT NULL
signature: varchar(20) NOT NULL
payeeId: int NULL (FK)
userId: int NULL (FK)
statementItemId: int NULL (FK)
transactionTypeId: int NOT NULL (FK)
autoTimestamp: timestamp NOT NULL

accountReconcile

accountReconcileId: int IDENTITY
statementId: int NOT NULL (FK) (AK1.1)
reconcileDate: smalldatetime NOT NULL (AK1.2)
autoTimestamp: timestamp NOT NULL

13
Determining Hardware Requirements

Introduction

This chapter is comprised of tasks that do not play a large role in database design, and are therefore not normally considered part of the data architect's remit. However, now that we have physically implemented our design, we have some idea of the volume of data the hardware will be required to handle. In considering these requirements the rest of this chapter exists not as a complete resource on hardware design but more as a primer for such matters, since we will not always have the luxury of database administration staff to handle them.

The hardware configuration that SQL Server runs on top of can make or break you. How do you know how much hardware is really needed by your applications? How do you know if your applications have grown to the point where they are now overloading your system? This chapter will give you the information you need when choosing the hardware on which your database will be hosted. More specifically, we will see how much space your database will need (a topic known as **volumetric analysis**), and look at the performance of your server.

Volumetric analysis is a process in which we examine the types of data stored and its expected rate of growth. An analysis of the types of databases you will encounter is necessary. Following this, we will engage in formulaic analysis of tables and attempt to simplify this analysis for the vast majority of cases. Archiving of old, unused data is an important and often overlooked area of performance improvement.

Server performance involves analyzing the various properties of a server and the database system.

Types of databases

Obviously there are innumerable applications with a plethora of databases that support them. While it is always difficult to draw clear distinct lines, databases are generally separated along two lines, On-Line Transactional Processing (OLTP) and On-Line Analytical Processing (OLAP). We are going to take a look at each of these in turn.

OLTP

OLTP databases generally have highly normalized tables that experience growth through numerous short transactions. Point-of-sales or bank account Automatic Telling Machine (ATM) databases are good representations of OLTP databases. Due to the normalized nature of the tables, row sizes and index usage are usually minimized. The main tables in these databases will generally grow at a constant rate of X (a calculable number of) rows per time period. This time period could be hours or days, or indeed, months or years. As you seek to gather the data storage requirements for the OLTP database, you will need to gauge this growth rate, forecasting it as accurately as possible.

Some OLTP databases may support more than one application, a good example being accounting applications, where you might have a separate database for each of the general ledger, accounts payable, and accounts receivable modules. On the other hand, due to the nature of SQL Server security and system table infrastructure, you will often see such applications written with a single database for all these modules. Thus, such an accounting database may have subsets of tables that support individual general ledger, accounts receivable, and accounts payable modules. Essentially, from a volumetric growth perspective, these subsets can be looked at as individual applications of tables and analyzed separately.

OLAP

OLAP databases are used for summarizing and reporting on the data generated from OLTP applications and non-relational sources. Take, for example, an insurance company that collects claims data in one of their OLTP databases. They might have separate OLAP databases that summarize this data for the purposes of regulatory requirements and business-decision analysis reports. Some will call these databases operational data stores and reserve the OLAP acronym for the specialized star-schema databases that are a further refinement of the operational data store. For our purposes, we will use the common acronym OLAP when talking about reporting databases running on top of the SQL Server engine.

Data is generally loaded into these databases through discrete batch loads during less busy periods. Usage is primarily limited to read-only selects, whilst tables are often denormalized and will frequently have large row sizes, in an effort to reduce the number of joins used in queries. To speed the execution of queries, each table in an OLAP database usually possesses many indexes. These databases grow, based on the anticipated growth of their source feeds. However, the indexes must always be accounted for as well. Also, as new reporting requirements occur, new tables and/or new indexes will be added.

Just as in life, everything is not black and white. While most databases generally will either be of the OLTP or OLAP type, a few will support applications that have both OLTP and OLAP components. A payroll database, for example, will provide the routine OLTP transactional entries related to ongoing pay cycles. At the same time, quarterly and annual report tables of an OLAP nature will often be generated from this data to supply governmental tax requirements. Again, in this instance, the OLTP and OLAP portions of the databases should be analyzed separately.

Growth of OLTP Tables

Not all of the tables in an OLTP database can be expected to grow at the same rate. Some of them will capture everyday data (a publishing house may expect to receive new orders daily), whilst others will expect less rapid growth (we would hope to get new customers, but not at the same rate as that which we receive orders). We will now go on to look at these scenarios in more detail.

Rapid Growth

Usually, most OLTP applications will have two to five tables that contain the vast majority of the data for the application. The size of the tables would usually be a factor of volume increasing constantly over time. A purchasing application, for example, will usually have a `PurchaseOrder` and a `POLineItem` table. For each purchase order, you would have one or more line items in the `POLineItem` table. In many applications, you might have a variety of sub-applications.

For example, an HR-Payroll application would have a set of tables that primarily support the HR side of the application and a set for the payroll side of the application. In the former, tables covering the history of the employees' human resource attributes of training, assignments, personal data, and company data would capture much of the data. In the latter, history tables covering payments to the entire sundry list of salary payments, taxes, and deductions from salary would contribute to most of the growth of the database.

Slow Growth

In addition to these tables are secondary tables that increase over time, but less rapidly. In the purchasing application, this would include the domain table that covers the list of vendors, purchasers, and allowable products. In the HR-Payroll application, this would cover the employee personal and corporate assignment tables. These tables increase over time, though at a much slower pace than the main transaction tables of the application. Often these tables are relatively small compared to the main tables and, if accounted for with a large estimate, can be assumed to be constant over the life of the application.

No Growth

Obviously, there are certain domain tables that will usually be populated initially and have very little change over the life of the application. For the purchasing application this would cover attributes of the purchase order such as unit-of-issue. For the HR-Payroll application, this would include such domain tables as job codes and their descriptions. These tables can generally be assumed to be constant over time after their initial load. Thus, while you are calculating table growth, you don't have to factor the time element into the size of these tables. In fact, if your time period for analysis is long enough, you can often totally ignore these tables for size calculation purposes, dramatically simplifying your task.

To summarize, a single OLTP application will often have twenty to forty tables. Two to five main tables would grow at a continuous rate and would take up the vast amount of the space requirements. Some supporting domain tables would grow at a slower rate. Other domain tables would receive an initial load and their growth (and often size itself) is negligible over time.

Growth of OLAP Tables

OLAP tables are also expected to grow. There may be many reasons for this – the amount of data from the OLTP database will have an effect, or the number of pre-calculated queries may change. We will now go on to look at these types of growth.

Batch Growth

OLAP databases, due to their often denormalized nature, will have fewer domain tables and more summary tables that experience routine batch growth. Typically, OLAP databases will take one of two forms. A large operational data store will have a number of large summary tables with some supporting domain tables. Where a specialized OLAP engine is not used, some OLAP databases will have a star schema, a single large summary table with rays emanating to a number of domain tables.

The volumetric growth of an OLAP database has a number of factors, such as the underlying data and its growth, the amount of denormalization necessary to speed queries, and the frequency with which data is introduced into the database from the source or sources. Almost all growth can be defined as discrete events. The most obvious growth of the database is due to the routine batch loads from one or more sources. Each source needs to be analyzed based on the periodicity of the batch feeds and the amount of growth this translates to in the summary tables of the OLAP database.

Not to be confused with this routine entry of data from various sources is the denormalization and summarization that often occurs in OLAP databases. While the data might be loaded in and this causes growth, data will also be summarized in "time batches". For example, tables with different levels of detail might be loaded for periods covering quarter-to-date, year-to-date, prior year, and older-than-prior-year time periods. Care must be taken to estimate the potential geometric growth factor this can have on OLAP database growth.

OLAP databases are well known for combining heterogeneous data sources to provide analysis. Along with these disparate sources, you will have to account for their disparate batch load frequencies. Batches may range from daily to quarterly depending on the source and allowable latency in your reporting requirements.

Growth Through Company Growth

Less obvious in the growth of an OLAP database is the growth of a company. Since OLAP databases are often used for executive reportage, the database needs to be sized to accommodate not only the growth of its original sources, but also the growth due to mergers and acquisitions of the parent company. For example, a medical insurance company might build an OLAP database providing profit and loss reportage on claims from a specific geographic area. When it acquires another insurance company covering a separate geographic area, suddenly the original database must now accommodate the data from this acquisition in order to give an accurate profit and loss statement for the new, expanded company.

Coincident with our thoughts about growth here due to mergers and acquisitions, you might do well to consider designing your OLAP table structures very generically with variable size columns. SQL 2000 introduces the `SQL_variant` datatype and this is a place where you may want to take advantage of it. Implicit with the use of variable size columns and SQL_variant columns is that they take more space than a simple integer or a big integer column for the same representation. Further, certain functions (`AVG`, `SUM`, etc.) cannot be used on `SQL_variant` columns.

"We Need More Reports!"

Remember also that OLAP databases play a vital role in getting timely and valuable analyses of information to the key decision-makers in the organization. As the data begins flowing in and business decisions are made, as often as not, a need for new reports and information is realized. Accommodating this need often means new summarization of the data or a new column and/or index on an existing table.

Don't Forget the Indexes

In OLAP databases, the volumetric impact of indexes cannot be overlooked. A single table with tens of Gigabytes of data may have an equal amount of data necessary for indexes. Thus, as the calculation of table volume is discussed, the equally important calculation of index sizes will also be discussed.

Calculating Complete Table Size

As you would expect, table size is roughly the product of the number of rows and the row size. However, a number of factors increase the complexity of the calculation. These include the number and type of indexes, the index key columns, the number and percent usage of variable length columns, and the size of text and image blobs.

The following steps can be used to estimate the amount of space required to store the data on a table.

1. Compute the space used by the data in the table.
2. If one exists, compute the space used by a clustered index.
3. If any exists, compute the space used by each non-clustered index.
4. Add these values together.

SQL Server Books Online does a nice job of explaining how tables and indexes are sized based on these parameters. What is not included there, however, is a programmatic method for performing the tedious job of gathering information on column size, column characteristics, and index key columns and then completing the calculations. We have included a set of three stored procedures with this book for just this job, and we will be working through them shortly.

The three procedures (explained in detail below) that need to be created in the `master` database are:

- `sp__table$calcDataSpace`
- `sp__index$getKeyData`
- `sp__table$indexSpace`

To use the procedures, you first need to actually create the empty tables and indexes in the `master` database. Additionally, you need to have thought through the expected row size and the percentage that variable length columns will be filled. These procedures were designed for SQL 7 and SQL 2000 and will not be valid for SQL 6.5.

Data Size Calculation

First we need to compute the space used by the data in the table. For our purposes, we are going to assume that you have already created the table with its appropriate columns and indexes. Alternatively, you can work through the Case Study at the end of the chapter. If you have variable length columns such as `varchar`, `nvarchar`, and `varbinary`, then, for our purposes, you will need to make an estimation of the percentage that these columns will be filled. For the `sp__table$calcDataSpace` procedure we will be outlining below, this is a single value for all columns. This is a single number for the whole table we will store as `@variFillPercent`.

> With the introduction of user-defined extended properties (discussed in Chapter 10) in SQL 2000, you can now create a **percentFillExpectation** property for each of your variable length columns that are programmatically accessible. This is just one of the many ideas that developers and DBAs are going to come to terms with for using these user-defined extended properties.

The size of a table is based on the number of columns, the length of those columns, and the number of rows. First we need some basic information. This section will walk you through the build-up of the procedure sp_table$calcDataSpace. The variable declarations are assumed. The default page size for SQL 2000 is 8192 bytes. You can get this programmatically using the following query:

```
SELECT @pagesize = low FROM master.dbo.spt_values WHERE number = 1 AND type = 'E'
```

For planning purposes, you will need to estimate the number of rows that you expect in the table. If you want to default to the number that are already in the table, you can get this programmatically through the following query:

```
SELECT @rowcount = rows FROM sysindexes WHERE object_name(id)= @tablename
                                        AND indid IN (0,1)
```

We then need the number of variable length columns, the size of those variable length columns (which is a function of their maximum size times the percent that you expect them to be filled, @variFillPercent), the total column count, and the size of fixed columns. The following two queries return these results, the key difference in the queries coming in the variable column value from the systypes table:

```
SELECT @varicolcount=count(c.name), @maxvaricolsize=ROUND((@variFillPercent *
ISNULL(sum(c.length),0)),0) FROM syscolumns c JOIN systypes t
    ON c.xusertype = t.xusertype
join sysobjects o on c.id = o.id WHERE t.variable = 1 AND o.name = @tablename
    GROUP BY o.name

SELECT @columncount=count(c.name)+@varicolcount,
    @fixcolsize=ISNULL(sum(case WHEN c.length IS NULL THEN t.length ELSE c.length
    end),0)
FROM syscolumns c JOIN systypes t ON c.xusertype = t.xusertype
JOIN sysobjects o ON c.id = o.id WHERE t.variable = 0 AND o.name = @tablename
```

A portion of each row is reserved for calculating the nullability of each column. This is a bitmapping for each column plus some overhead. The section of the row is called the null bitmap. We only need the integer portion of the calculation and the query to calculate is:

```
SELECT @nullBitmap=2+FLOOR((@columncount+7)/8)
```

If there are any variable length columns, we will adjust the maximum variable length column size for a row by adding two bytes for the table and two bytes for each variable length column:

```
SELECT @maxvaricolsize=@maxvaricolsize+2+@varicolcount*2
```

Determining Hardware Requirements

The full row size is the sum of the fixed column size, the null bitmap size, the max variable column size, and the data row header of four bytes:

```
SELECT @maxrowsize = @fixcolsize+@nullbitmap+@maxvaricolsize + 4
```

Next, we have to be concerned whether the table is a heap of rows or ordered by a clustered index. If the latter is true, then we need to calculate the amount of free space between rows due to a fill factor of less than 100. Each table always has a row in `sysindexes` with either an index ID of 0 for a heap table without a clustered index, or an index ID of 1 for a table physically sorted along the clustered index key. Obviously, if the table is a heap table with no fill factor, we don't need to find the fill factor and calculate free space. We extract the fill factor with the following query:

```
IF ((SELECT indid FROM sysindexes WHERE object_name(id) = @tablename
   AND indid IN (0,1)) = 1)
SELECT @fillfactor=OrigFillFactor FROM sysindexes
   WHERE object_name(id)=@tablename AND indid = 1
```

> **The default for fill factor is 0; legal values range from 0 through 100. A fill factor value of 0 does not mean that pages are 0 per cent full. It is treated similarly to a fill factor value of 100 in that SQL Server creates clustered indexes with full data pages and non-clustered indexes with full leaf pages. It is different from 100 in that SQL Server leaves some space within the upper level of the index tree. For the purposes of table data space calculation here, a fill factor of 0 will be identical to a fill factor of 100.**

If we have a heap table, we will continue the formula for calculating the number of free rows per page by setting the fill factor to 100. Once we have the fill factor for a table ordered by a clustered index, we calculate the amount of free space inserted in each page:

```
SELECT @freeRowsPerPage = (@pagesize*(100-@fillFactor)/100/(@maxrowsize+2))
```

Notice that if the fill factor is 100, the above query will always have a zero value for free rows per page. This is true whether the table is a heap table or ordered by a clustered index with a fill factor of 0 or 100.

Before we look at the next query for calculating the total data space in a table, a little explanation is necessary. Embedded in this query is a formula for the number of rows in a page. This is represented programmatically by `FLOOR((@pagesize-96)/(@maxrowsize+2))`. It is the space on the page not used by row points and page headers, `@pagesize-96`, divided by the `rowsize` plus two bytes between each row, `@maxrowsize+2`. We then use the `FLOOR` function to round the quotient down to the nearest integer since rows cannot span pages and a complete row must fit on each page. From this result we subtract the number of free rows per page. The resulting number of useful rows per page is then divided into the estimated or actual `rowcount` set forth earlier to yield the total number of pages our data would need. Round up using the `CEILING` function to get complete pages. You could stop at this point if you are only interested in the number of pages you need. Multiplying by the actual page size yields the number of bytes that the data would need.

```
SELECT @data_space_used = @pagesize *
   CEILING(@rowcount/((FLOOR((@pagesize-96)/(@maxrowsize+2)))-@freeRowsPerPage))
```

Chapter 13

Reviewing Index B-Tree Structures

Before we begin calculating index space, it is helpful to review how indexes are put together. Indexes are essentially shortcut pointers to rows in a database. All indexes contain at least one level, the Root Node level. This is a single page where queries of the index begin. Unless the table is so small that the root node page is also the bottom level leaf node page on a non-clustered index, the root node will point to the next level in the index. This may be a page from an index node level or it may be a page from the one and only leaf node level. Each index node level points to a lower index node level until the leaf node level is reached. As you can see from the figure below, this example index has three levels, the root node level, a single index node level, and the leaf node level.

The leaf node level is going to take one of three forms. If the index is a clustered index, the leaf node level is the actual data sorted along the clustered index key. The remaining two forms of leaf nodes are for non-clustered indexes and depend on whether the table has a clustered index or not. If the index is a non-clustered index on a table with a clustered index, each row of the leaf node level will contain pointers to the corresponding clustered index key for that row. Thus the size of each row in the leaf row level in this instance is essentially the size of the clustered index key.

Brief mention should be made here that this is the principal reason for keeping clustered index keys very short. When a query gets through traversing a non-clustered index in this form, it must then traverse the clustered index to find the actual row. Remember, the shorter your index key, the fewer levels your index will have.

The third form of leaf node is for a non-clustered index on a table without a clustered index (a.k.a. a heap table). Each row in the leaf row level is an eight-byte (four bytes for the page pointer and four bytes for the row offset on the page) row pointer to the actual row in the table.

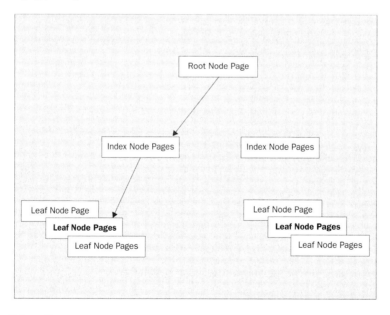

To summarize this section:

❏ For clustered indexes, leaf node pages are the data pages.

- For non-clustered indexes on a table with a clustered index, leaf node pages contain pointers to a clustered index key.
- For non-clustered indexes on a table without a clustered index, leaf node pages contain pointers to the actual rows on the table.

When an index has fewer node levels, it is said to be "flatter". You can see that flatter indexes means fewer page reads for a query since each node level is a page read. Fewer page reads means less of that expensive disk activity and fewer CPU cycles. Overall, flatter indexes are better when you need to go all the way to the table data to obtain your information. The concept of covered indexes is a trade-off mentioned elsewhere in this book.

Index Size Calculation

The space taken up by the data in a table is only half of the equation for the total space used by a table. The other half is the space taken up by indexes. With OLAP databases, it is not terribly unusual to see total index space used, equal or exceed that used by the actual data.

We will be looking at two more stored procedures, sp__table$indexSpace and sp__index$getKeyData. The first, sp__table$indexSpace is the main procedure while sp__index$getKeyData is an auxiliary procedure called from the first. As we outlined above for table size calculations, we are making a simplification by estimating the percentage that variable length columns will be filled. As above, variable declarations are assumed.

> When you run the **sp__table$indexSpace** procedure, in addition to the overall size of the table, you will get information on the size of the data alone in the table, the size of each index, and how many B-tree node levels are necessary for a given record count in the table.

We begin our analysis of sp__table$indexSpace by getting some housework out of the way. We need the pagesize for the server, the number of rows for the table if not supplied as an input parameter, and the overall space consumed by just the data. The pagesize and row count queries were outlined above in the *Data Size Calculation* section. To get the space used for the actual data, we will call the stored procedure sp__table$calcDataSpace whose analysis is outlined above.

Next we create a temporary table, #keyColumns with columns for index ID, column name, column length, whether the column is variable or not, and the fill factor from the index of the index ID. We pass this table name off to the stored procedure sp__index$getKeyData, whose sole task is to populate the #keyColumns table.

In sp__index$getKeyData, a cursor is set up on the index ID for each index, whether clustered or non-clustered, on the table. If there are no indexes, the @@fetchstatus for the cursor will be less than zero and we'll return to the main procedure, otherwise we cursor through the index IDs.

Every index will always have at least one column in it. To get the data for this column to put in #keyColumns (the name of which was passed into the procedure as the variable @tempTableName), we will generate a character string dynamically and execute it. Dynamic character string execution is a great skill to master so it is worth going through the query below in detail.

Loaded into the variable `@exct_stmt` is a USE statement for the database name. Then we generate an INSERT for the temporary table `#keyColumns` (passed as `@tempTableName`) and its columns, `indid`, `colname`, `variable`, `collength`, and `fill_factor`. The data loaded into these columns is the index ID from the cursor, `@indid`, the column name generated by the `INDEX_COL` function, the variable value for the column `datatype` from `systypes`, the length of the column from `syscolumns`, and the fill factor value, which is also part of the cursor key. After we load up the string into the `@exct_stmt` variable, we simply execute it inside a set of parentheses.

```
SELECT @exct_stmt = 'use ' + quotename(@dbName, '[')+ ' INSERT ' +
quotename(@tempTableName,']') + ' (indid,colname,variable,collength,fill_factor)
SELECT
'+convert(varchar(10),@indid) + ', INDEX_COL('+quotename(@tablename,'''')+',' +
convert(varchar(10),@indid) + ',1),
t.variable,
c.length,' +
convert(varchar(3),@fill_factor)+
' FROM '+@dbname+'.dbo.syscolumns c
JOIN '+ @dbname+'.dbo.systypes t
ON c.xusertype = t.xusertype
WHERE c.id = '+convert(varchar(16),@objid)+'
AND c.name=INDEX_COL('+quotename(@tablename,'''')+
    ','+ convert(varchar(10),@indid)+',1)'
EXEC (@exct_stmt)
```

If you do not understand how to execute character strings, it will prove helpful to consider this procedure in more detail. Open the code for the procedure in SQL 2000 Query Analyzer. The color-coding in Query Analyzer will be very helpful in understanding what we are doing. Notice that since we use the `INDEX_COL` function, we don't have to make a call on the `SYSINDEXES` table. Trust us, you don't want to have to call `SYSINDEXES` to get out column names. The `INDEX_COL` function is more than sufficient.

After we get the first column name, we use the increment key ID field for the `INDEX_COL` to get the next column name. If the column name is NULL, we know that we have exhausted the columns for a particular index and we go to the next index in the cursor if there is one. While the column name from the `INDEX_COL` function is not NULL, we loop through a WHILE loop, executing a character string similar to that above to insert the next row into `#keyColumns`.

When we have exhausted the last column for the last index, we return control to the `sp_table$indexSpace` procedure with a now populated `#keyColumns` table.

First we test `#keyColumns` to see if the table has a clustered index. If so, we set a flag variable in our procedure to indicate that there is a clustered index. This is important for two reasons. Remember that from the index structure review above, the leaf node level for a clustered index is the data. We already have this information from the `sp_table$calcDataSpace` procedure. Secondly, if we have a clustered index, each row in the leaf level of any non-clustered indexes will be the size of the clustered index key rather than an 8 byte row pointer. This is how we test for the existence of a clustered index, whose index ID is always 1:

```
IF EXISTS (select 1 from #keyColumns where indid = 1) select @clus_flag = 1
```

We then branch conditionally into calculating the non-leaf level sizes of the clustered index or immediately continue by calculating the size of any non-clustered indexes. Since we can have up to 253 non-clustered indexes, we set up a cursor to work through each non-clustered index based on their index ID from the data in `#keyColumns`. With the exception of the leaf level, the calculation of the sizes of the other levels for all indexes is similar.

We begin by calculating the key size for the index. In an index page, the key length is the row size. This is very similar to calculating the row size in `sp_table$calcDataSpace` above and we will not go through the specific details, except to say that the data in this case comes from the `#keyColumns` table that we generated rather than the actual system tables as in `sp_table$calcDataSpace`. Here are the three summations from the `sp_table$indexSpace` procedure for the respective cases of a clustered index row size, a non-clustered index row size on a table with a clustered index, and a non-clustered index row size on a heap table.

```
@CIndex_Row_Size = @Fixed_CKey_Size + @Variable_CKey_Size + @CIndex_Null_Bitmap + 1
+ 8

@Index_Row_Size= @Fixed_Key_Size+@Variable_Key_Size+@Index_Null_Bitmap+1+

@CIndex_Row_Size

@Index_Row_Size=@Fixed_Key_Size+@Variable_Key_Size+@Index_Null_Bitmap+1+8
```

Notice that, in the latter two instances for non-clustered index row size, the difference in the sums is the difference between the clustered index row size, `@CIndex_Row_Size`, and the set value for a heap table row pointer of 8 bytes. Furthermore in the first instance, note that the clustered index row size, `@CIndex_Row_Size` will always be at least 10 bytes and, more likely, at least 13 bytes in size. 13 bytes is the case where your clustered index is a single 4 byte integer column. Some would think that we are making the point that it might be better to not have a clustered index. Not at all! When intelligently done, a clustered index can give significant performance gains. The point we are making is to keep your clustered index key size and row size as small as is practical due to the feedback effect on non-clustered index row size.

> **Think of it this way. Reducing your clustered index key length by one byte will cause a reduction in one byte for every single row of every single page of every single level of every single index on your table outside the clustered index leaf node level. It adds up. It means flatter indexes and faster queries.**

After we have the key length for the index, we have to calculate the leaf level size first (or in the case of the clustered index, the index level immediately above the leaf level). If this level has only one page, we don't have to go any further. If it is more than one page in size, we have to calculate the next level up progressively until we get to the point where a level is only one page in size. This level is, by definition, the root node level. Here is the `WHILE` loop code for looping through index level page calculations while checking whether that particular level is only one page in size:

```
SELECT @this_Num_Pages_Level =
CEILING((@Num_Rows / @Index_Rows_Per_Page - @Free_Index_Rows_Per_Page))
SELECT @Num_Index_Pages = @this_Num_Pages_Level
WHILE @this_Num_Pages_Level > 1
  BEGIN
    SELECT @level_cnt = @level_cnt + 1
    SELECT @this_Num_Pages_Level =
CEILING(@this_Num_Pages_Level/@NL_Index_Rows_Per_Page)
    SELECT @Num_Index_Pages = @Num_Index_Pages + @this_Num_Pages_Level
  END
```

First we calculate the number of pages for the current level, `@this_Num_Pages_Level`. We have already initialised the `@level_cnt` variable with a value of 1. We add `@this_Num_Pages_Level` to the overall count we are keeping for the number of pages in the index, `@Num_Index_Pages`. While `@this_Num_Pages_Level` is greater than one, we loop through and calculate the number of pages for each successively higher index level until we get to the root level consisting of a single page. The calculations for the clustered index are similar.

At this point, we have calculated the pages necessary for each index and the number of b-tree levels for each index. We report this information out and add it to the overall page count we are keeping for the entire table. When we have finished with the indexes, we add the index page count to the data page count to get the overall table size.

Obviously, over time, data increases in tables and indexes. Is there any way to intelligently reduce the number of records in a table and the number of levels in your indexes? We will discuss this in the section on archiving data below.

Transaction Log Size

Once you have calculated estimates for all your table sizes, you also need to account for transaction log sizes. Generally, transaction logs are initially set as a percentage of database size. This percentage is based primarily on the expected transaction level and the rate that transaction logs are dumped to either disk or tape.

For OLTP databases where transactions are the bread and butter of the database, it is not unusual to see transaction log sizes exceeding 50 per cent of the database size. OLAP databases, on the other hand, routinely operate with 10 per cent or less dedicated to a transaction log.

This brings up the issue of recovering transaction logs since the ability to recover them will affect their size. For large batch loads, in SQL Server 7.0 a procedure was often developed where the transaction log was placed in `truncate log on checkpoint` mode while a batch load was taking place. The developers of SQL Server 2000 recognized this routine process and added a Bulk-Logged option to the transaction logging process.

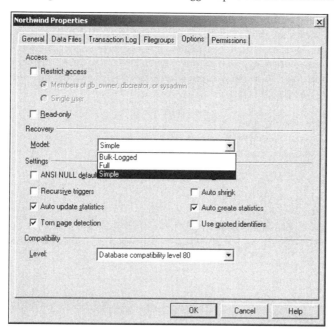

A Full recovery model is where the individual transaction, including bulk inserts and SELECT INTO's can be recovered transaction by transaction. It will make for large transaction logs, particularly for OLAP databases that have large batch transactions.

The Bulk-Logged model is a compromise, normally reserved for OLAP databases. Here, for bulk insert, SELECT INTO, and BCP, batches of inserts are recorded instead of individual transactions. It can mean that in the event of a failure, whole batch transactions may need to be manually repeated, but at the gain of smaller transaction logs.

The Simple recovery model is synonymous with setting a database to truncate log on checkpoint in SQL 6.5 and 7.0. Essentially, a database is recoverable to the last full backup and no further in this model. It is usually recommended for non-production environments.

So how much transaction log is enough? Generally start small and turn on and monitor auto growth for the transaction log files. We recommend starting with 20 per cent of expected data size for an OLTP database and 5 per cent for an OLAP database in Bulk-Logged recovery mode.

Archive Data When it Makes Sense

Given all these sources of data, it can quickly be seen that even in a moderately sized company, the volume of data can become huge. This is particularly relevant in the denormalized OLAP world. Very early in a volumetric sizing analysis, a decision needs to be made on if and when data will be archived off the main database to a long term "offline" storage container (tape, Write-Once, Read Many (WORM) drive, CD-ROM, DVD...). While data may no longer be needed for reportage or transactional processing, there may be a legal or regulatory reason that the data must be maintained. You need to remember that while these regulations very often specify a time requirement for maintaining the data, they seldom specify the media (paper hardcopy, read only storage, rotating disk, clay or stone tablet...) that the data is stored on. It can get very expensive to keep massive amounts of data spinning around for years and years when it may more appropriately be "shelved" on read-only media.

Even if the data is not huge and it can still stay in a SQL Server database, it may make sense to archive it away from your main tables. As we have pointed out earlier in the book, the single greatest expense that we always seek to minimize in database usage is reads from disk. The more data we need to read from disk, the slower an application will appear to an end user. If reads from disk are considered to be slow, reads from archived, offline storage can be an order of magnitude (or more) slower. A general rule of thumb is that no data should be archived from disk where there is a routine operational need to access that data.

On the other hand, once data is no longer routinely operationally necessary, it should aggressively be archived off either to another table, another database, another server, or a totally different medium. The gains from querying smaller indexes and, less desirably, tables can become enormous. What does "routine operational need" mean? The emphasis here should be on the word "routine". Where data is accessed monthly, quarterly, or even yearly, it might be best to keep it spinning on a hard disk.

Non-routine events would fall under the heading of IRS audits, legal suits, and company acquisitions. Such non-routine events happen rarely. When they do, the time expense of loading the data into either hard disk or RAM from an offline storage device and the customized querying that may be needed are usually acceptable expenses to the database operating system and the DBA.

Chapter 13

The Cost of Archiving

Like all performance improvements, every optimization needs to be analyzed from a cost-benefit standpoint. While the benefits include increased performance, the costs of archiving are primarily threefold. The first is the cost of the archive subsystem and its physical implementation. First off, there might be the up-front cost of a dedicated Write-Once, Read-Many drive, for instance. Additionally, the server engineers have to develop and maintain skills for its implementation and maintenance.

We shouldn't gloss over the word *maintain* too quickly in the previous sentence. We all know that the rapid pace of changes in software is matched by the pace of improvements in hardware. If you are an old hand like me, you can remember that little more than a decade ago we were running around with TRS-80 processors and 5¼ inch (or worse still 8 inch) floppies. Think of what it would take to load up and read an 8 inch floppy today. This doesn't even get into the software formatting of the disk implicit to the operating system it was saved under. Imagine that you have a requirement to save data for 25 years. You need to account for the "costs" of being able to either read data from an *ancient* format or for periodically re-formatting that data from old media onto more modern media.

Once the physical archive storage device exists, additional and significant costs can be generated in intelligently removing the data from the active online databases. As often as not, some detailed analysis is very necessary. Heaven forbid that you archive business data that is operationally necessary. The cost and time for this analysis needs to be factored into your design.

> **Archiving data doesn't mean we are throwing it away; you still have to be able to use it.**

Finally, there is the cost of designing the code necessary to access the data once it is archived. There may be a non-routine, exceptional need for the data. It is incumbent on the archive designer to account and prepare for this exceptional need.

Archiving Details

Now that you are totally convinced of the need for archiving, you need to know the details. Obviously, every database is going to have differing criteria depending on the parameters that I've previously set forth. But, you should generally start thinking about archiving by looking at the following areas.

- Archiving by time period
- Archiving by fact table date-partitioning
- Archiving by completed transaction
- Accessing archived data

Archiving by Time Period

Briefly, we need to begin by discussing the concept of fact tables. Fact tables are generally the largest tables in the database because they contain detailed data about the underlying transactions.

The most obvious method of archiving is to pull historically old data from fact tables and populate a parallel table structure with the archived data. While usually straightforward, as in "We will archive all data that is three years old", some things may not be obvious. Sometimes fact tables may have several dates associated with them. For example, a purchase order detail record may have the date the purchase order was initiated, multiple dates it was approved at various levels of approval authority, the date the purchase order was submitted to the vendor, the date the vendor acknowledged receiving the purchase order, the date or dates that the order was fulfilled, and the date that the purchase transaction was finally completed. It is not unusual to see six months or a year go by before some purchase orders are finally fulfilled, particularly on manufacturing contracts. Do you want to archive based on the date the purchase order number was assigned or based on the date that the purchase order was finally fulfilled? This is the work of a skilled data analyst who gets paid well. And it could be you.

What about domain tables that support fact tables? Take the vendor table that provides a `vendor_id` column to the purchase order detail record. Generally, you will have a foreign key on the purchase order record referencing the primary key on the vendor column. Take the instance where a vendor goes out of business. Now it is three years later and you have archived all rows that this vendor record key supported from your purchase order rows. All of the sudden, you no longer have programmatic enforcement of the primary keys persistence by a row with the foreign key. You need to think of such things as you prepare to archive. As we all know, good programmers make it work: great programmers make it break correctly.

Archiving by Fact Table Date-Partitioning

Much of the data that we insert into our databases is easily partitioned along date lines. For example, ATM transactions have a very definite date on which they were conducted. Further, once they have been recorded, the data is essentially read only. Rather than going back and undoing a disputed transaction, another correcting transaction is entered at a later date. Thus, it is easy to see how all the transactions for a particular month could be inserted throughout the month in a particular table. For example table `ATM_200104` (or actually a subset of dated tables with referential integrity that would really cover all the ATM transactions) could be all the ATM transactions for the month of April in the year 2001. Once April is over, no more transactions will go in this table. Once the bills for April of 2001 are issued and summary tables for OLAP analysis have been generated, this table is a great candidate for archival onto read only media. Such huge fact tables are routinely offloaded onto tape, CDROM, or DVD for infrequent reference. Now that you know this, you can understand why the bank charges you a hefty fee for a copy of a previous monthly statement. In some instances, companies will simply refuse to generate duplicate detail records from these fact tables (short of court action).

Archiving by Fact Table Characteristics

Similar to archiving by date-partitioned fact tables, individual rows can also be archived from online tables according to a particular set of circumstances for the row. In this case, we are not taking the whole table off line. Rather, we are culling individual rows and groups of rows from tables based on specified criteria. A good example might be a transaction completed more than two years ago. Obviously, while the transaction is open and has detail records inserted against it, you wouldn't want to archive it. Even after it is recently closed, you wouldn't want to archive it because it is still used for year-to-date and last-full-year reporting and analysis. Depending on your business rules, though, a transaction more than two years old might be a prime target for archiving.

Another example of a row that might be archived based on specified criteria would be a row representing a potential customer who never materialized. You might have a customer table listing all your current, previous, and prospective customers. You use this table not only to record customer activity but also as a sales generation tool for mailings and leads. Routinely, potential customers are put into the tables in lists that your company buys from a list broker. Many of these potential customers will be turned into customers. Many will not. Periodically you would want to prune this list to make your queries easier. You specify criteria for archiving off potential customer "dead wood". Such criteria might be "never was an active customer" and "we've carried him on the list for three years with no activity generated". Remember, though, you paid good money for this list. You don't just delete these potential customers. They go in the ever expanding *dead wood* archive table or tables on read only media. Who knows? You may be able to bring this wood back to life and move the row back to an active customer. You may be able to build up such a list that you could sell to another company and recoup part of the cost of the original list. If you threw the data away, you would have to go through the expensive process of a human operator regenerating the data. It may be much cheaper to do a relatively slow, but cheap, query of your archive table.

> **When designing a database, the moment you start thinking about putting large amounts of data into a table is the moment you should start thinking about archiving data out of the table.**

It is important to note: Archiving should not be an afterthought to designing a database and an application. Archiving can represent a significant area for performance gains. If, however, your table structure is not designed to support archiving, or applications were not designed to access archived data, you may be out of luck. It will be very hard to sell the customer the idea of removing data from their database, paying the cost of redesigning the application or database, and giving you more money to do this once the original application is online. Worse still, when your application starts choking on data that should otherwise be archived, the customer will blame you.

Accessing Archived Data

So now you have gone through and taken data out of your large fact tables or removed the fact tables from active usage entirely in the case of date-partitioned fact tables. Two questions come to mind: How do you get back to this data when you need it? And, if you offloaded data onto alternative media, what is the shelf life of these?

Regarding the first question, an application will often be made archive-aware by inserting a small row in the active table keyed to the archived row. When a user requests this archive row, a process is set in place to deal with the request. This may involve a simple query to another table, a juke box loading up a CD-ROM, a message sent to a computer room attendant to mount a tape, or a message sent back to the original user asking them if they really, really need this data.

Much of this process depends on how the data is archived. If the archived data is still in the database, but just moved to an alternate location (so that queries of the main fact table are faster and the indexes flatter), then getting to the data will be almost transparent to the users. At the other extreme, when the archived data is stored on reel-to-reel tapes that have to be mounted manually, the end user may decide that they don't really need the data.

The second question to keep in mind when archiving data, is the issue of the data being on alternative media, and its shelf life. More and more, when data is archived off, it is being placed on either CD-ROM or DVD-ROM. What about the case where it is placed on magnetic tape? We recently came across a story about the National Aeronautic and Space Administration (NASA) in the United States. NASA satellites routinely download information onto tape for later study and analysis by scientist in NASA-funded laboratories. The amount of data is staggering. It turns out that this tape has a shelf life of 10 years. It also turns out that if NASA took all the tape drives that are serviceable today to begin recopying this data onto more reliable and longer lasting media, it would take significantly longer than 10 years. In short, be careful where you store your archived data if you have a requirement to use it later.

Server Performance

We could present an intricate analysis of the memory breakdown of exactly what aspects of RAM are inhabited by each portion of SQL Server. This subject, though, has been exhausted by other tomes, most notably *"Inside Microsoft SQL Server 2000" (Microsoft Press, ISBN 0735609985)*. We will limit our analysis to a quick overview, emphasizing where you can obtain the greatest performance gains.

Memory Subsystems

In short, if there is any money left over in the budget for your hardware, the first rule of SQL Server performance tuning is to use this money for RAM. SQL Server thrives on RAM. While we will go into depth on disk sub-system performance gains, the performance gain you get from RAM is, dollar for dollar, greater than that of disk subsystems.

Within reason, you should seriously consider getting the maximum amount of RAM that your motherboard can hold. If you don't do so, make sure you buy RAM chips that maximize each RAM slot on the motherboard, by getting the largest possible memory module size possible for the slot, as this will make any future memory upgrades easier.

As an example, you are buying a server that has 8 RAM slots with a capacity of 512 MB in each slot for a total maximum of 4 GB. You have checked your budget and can justify only 2 GB in your boss's mind. There are two different ways that your server vendor can fill this requirement. The cheaper way is with 8 RAM chips of 256 MB each. The better way and the price that you want to present to your boss is 4 RAM chips of 512 MB each, leaving four empty slots. The slight premium you pay for this configuration will more than pay for itself, when your data requirements expand and you need to buy that extra 2 GB.

Memory Subsystems on Windows NT Server

Speaking of 4 GB of RAM, there are some limitations for the operating systems on which SQL Server runs. While SQL Server will run on Windows 9x/ME systems, we're only going to look at SQL Server on the Windows NT/2000 product line. An important point to note about the Windows 9x OS family is that since they have a different virtual memory design from Windows NT and Windows 2000, the algorithms used for SQL Server optimization are different.

Windows NT Server comes in two different flavors, the standard edition and the enterprise edition. While both of the Windows NT versions support a maximum of 4 GB of RAM, they divide this 4 GB differently. The standard edition will only support a maximum of 2 GB of memory dedicated to any one process. This dedicated memory includes both RAM and virtual memory, where a portion of the hard disk is set aside to act like RAM, albeit very, very slowly. Thus, even though you might have 4 GB of RAM in your server, the service process that starts at operating system boot-up and in which SQL Server runs would be able to only use 2 GB of this memory. The other 2 GB would be set aside for the operating system. The enterprise edition raises this level to 3 GB, allowing essentially a 50 per cent boost in performance. This is done through a `BOOT.INI` switch.

Memory Subsystems on Windows 2000 Server

Windows 2000 memory architecture is a little more complex. To begin with, there are now three flavors of the OS; Standard, Advanced, and Data Center. Standard is much like the standard version of Windows NT. It will support 4 GB of RAM, with a maximum of 2 GB for any single process.

The Windows 2000 Advanced server scales up to 8 GB of RAM. It does this in two different ways. The first is called Application Memory Tuning or 4-gigabyte-tuning (4GT). 4GT is very similar to the way the NT Enterprise version handles memory. It is for applications that run on servers with between 2 and 4 GB of RAM and has a maximum process limit of 3 GB.

To make full use of the 8 GB of RAM on Windows 2000 Advanced Server, you will need to implement Physical Address Extension (PAE) X86. The hardware requirements for PAE X86 are more stringent than those for 4GT. To determine if your hardware is supported, the Windows 2000 Hardware Compatibility List should be consulted (http://www.microsoft.com/windows2000/upgrade/compat/), searching for the keywords Large Memory.

Technology	Hardware requirements	
Physical Address Extension (PAE) X86	❑	Pentium Pro processor or later
	❑	4 gigabytes (GB) or more of RAM
	❑	450 NX or compatible chipset and support or later
Application memory tuning, also known as 4 gigabyte tuning (4GT)	❑	Intel-based processor
	❑	2 gigabytes (GB) or more of RAM

With PAE X86 implemented, both SQL Server 7 and SQL Server 2000 Enterprise Editions use Microsoft Windows 2000 Address Windowing Extensions (AWE) to address approximately 8GB of memory. In SQL 2000, this is on a per instance basis since it supports more than one instance of SQL Server. Each instance using this extended memory, however, must have its memory allocated manually instead of letting SQL Server manage it automatically using its dynamic memory management routines.

Windows 2000 Data Center is the most ambitious operating system Microsoft has ever marketed. In addition to supporting up to 32 processors, using PAE X86, it will support 64 GB of RAM. Only SQL 2000 Enterprise Edition is set up to run in this environment. Additionally, the Windows 2000 Data Center Server operating system will only load up on an approved hardware configuration. Approved hardware configurations are available under the Windows Data Center Program and are available from major vendors such as Compaq, Dell, Unisys, IBM, and Hewlett-Packard. Unisys, for example, markets the ES7000 with 32 CPUs and up to 64 GB of RAM. Its disk I/O subsystem supports up to 96 channels.

Memory Performance Monitoring

Now that you know the memory limitations in SQL Server imposed by the operating system, what can you do to optimize that memory and determine if you need more? This is where we get into what is popularly called *The Art of Performance Monitoring*.

Determining Hardware Requirements

We will generally focus our efforts on tuning SQL Server 7 and SQL Server 2000 engines. These engines made dramatic improvements over SQL Server 6.5 in their memory management algorithms. Unlike SQL Server 6.5, they dynamically acquire and free memory as needed. It is typically not necessary for an administrator to specify how much memory should be allocated to a SQL Server 7 or SQL Server 2000 Server, although the option still exists and is required in some environments.

Due to the dynamic nature of the memory in SQL Server 7 and SQL Server 2000, Microsoft removed support for one of the most useful tools available in SQL Server 6.5, DBCC MEMUSAGE. Now, to get this information, you have to monitor a variety of performance counters in the Buffer Manager object and the Cache Manager object since the information is no longer statically mapped in a table like sysconfigures. While this handy tool is listed as "Unsupported" now and no longer returns the breakdown of memory usage, try running it. You will see that this unsupported snap shot continues to return the top 20 list of buffered tables and indexes. This can be a very handy list. When analyzing performance of an individual application in a test environment, it can be invaluable.

The Art Of Performance Monitoring

Performance monitoring is an art, in that it is a combination of talent, experience, knowledge, and sometimes just plain luck. How do you know if you can do it? You have to try, try, and try again. Keep at it, read up on it. Keep a performance monitor continually open against your production server. Here are some good guidelines to get you started.

   1. Make sure that you are running your typical processes (SQL Server) and work loads (queries and stored procedures) during your monitoring.

   2. Don't just do real-time monitoring of your servers. Capture long running logs. In Windows NT, install the Datalog/Monitor service from the NT Resource Kit; this functionality is available out of the box in Windows 2000.

   3. Always have disk counters turned on by running from a command prompt the command DISKPERF -Y and then rebooting. Even in a production environment, the overhead is minimal; the last thing you want to do in the middle of a crisis where logical and physical disk counters are necessary is to have to reboot.

   4. For routine, daily, desktop monitoring, set up the chart window with an interval of 18 seconds. In both the Windows NT PerfMon and the Windows 2000 MMC SysMon, this will give your chart a Window of 30 minutes. For me, this has proven to be the ideal interval for both seeing the past and minimizing the impact on the server.

   5. Utilize SQL Profiler for individual queries and processes in coordination with PerfMon or SysMon to get a good picture of the impact of individual queries.

   6. Know the terminology of Performance Monitoring. Objects are lists of individual statistics available. An example is the Processor object. A counter is a single statistic that falls under the heading of an object. An example is the per centProcessor Time counter under the Processor object. An instance is further breakdown of a counter statistic into duplicate components. Not all counters will have separate instances. The per centProcessor Time counter has instances for each processor and a _Total instance as a summary of all processor activity.

7. Know your tools. While you may know how to set up a chart in PerfMon, learn how to set up a log with Datalog or Performance Log. Other tools to be familiar with are DBCC MEMUSAGE, Task Manager, and SQL Enterprise Manager Current Activity.

8. Don't be afraid to experiment. The BackOffice Resource Kit has tools in it for creating test data (DataSim), creating test databases (DBGen), and simulating loading from multiple clients (SqlLS).

SQL Performance Monitoring and Bottlenecks

Bottlenecks occur when the hardware resources cannot keep up with the demands of the software. For example, when a software process or combination of processes, wants more I/O from a disk than the disk can physically deliver, a bottleneck occurs at the disk. When the CPU subsystem becomes too saturated and processes are waiting, a bottleneck has occurred. Bottlenecks are usually fixed in one of two ways. The first is to identify the limiting hardware and increase its capabilities. In other words, get a faster hard drive or increase the speed of the CPU. The second way is to make the software processes utilize the hardware more efficiently. This could be done by putting an index on a table so that either the disk I/O necessary to service a query is reduced, or the CPU units necessary to process a join are lessened.

The following are five key areas to monitor when tracking server performance and identifying bottlenecks. Each bottleneck candidate will have varied performance monitoring objects and counters to consider.

- Memory usage – SQL Server needs, relative to itself and to the operating system memory. If SQL Server has enough memory but the operating system is starved of memory such that it has to frequently swap through the pagefile to disk, overall performance will suffer dramatically.

- CPU processor utilization – High CPU utilization rates indicate the CPU subsystem is underpowered. Solutions could be upgrading the CPU or increasing the number of processors.

- Disk I/O performance – Failure of the disk or disk controller to satisfy read or write requirements in a timely manner impacts performance.

- User connections – Improperly setting the number of user connections could rob memory otherwise available to SQL Server.

- Blocking Locks – One process keeps another process from accessing or updating data. This is particularly noticeable to users and is the cause of some of your most severe performance problems from a user perspective.

Memory Tuning: The Operating System and SQL Server

Start your intensive analysis of memory by looking at two counters,

- Memory: Available Bytes
- Memory: Pages Faults/sec

The Available Bytes counter tells how much memory is available for use by processes. The Pages Faults/sec counter tells us the number of hard page faults, pages which had to be retrieved from the hard disk since they were not in working memory. It also includes the number of pages written to the hard disk to free space in the working set to support a hard page fault.

A low number for `Available Bytes` indicates that there may not be enough memory available or processes, including SQL Server, may not be releasing memory. A high number of `Page Faults/sec` indicates excessive paging. Further looks at individual instances of `Process:Page Faults/sec` to see if the SQL Server process, for example, has excessive paging. A low rate of `Page Faults/sec` (commonly 5-10 per second) is normal, as the operating system will continue to do some house keeping on the working set.

As previously noted, starting with SQL Server 7, memory is auto-tuning by default. In general, though, you want to give SQL as much dedicated memory as possible. This is mostly dependent on what other applications may be running on the server. By using the `sp_configure` stored procedure, you can set the values to `MIN SERVER MEMORY` and `MAX SERVER MEMORY` to dedicated values.

If SQL Server is the only application on the server, set `MIN SERVER MEMORY` and `MAX SERVER MEMORY` to the same value. If SQL Server co-exists with one or more applications, lower the `MIN SERVER MEMORY` setting to account for the memory demands of the other application(s). If the other application fails to start in a timely manner, it may be because SQL Server has been operating at or near the `MAX SERVER MEMORY` setting and is slow in releasing memory to the new, and now starved, application. In this instance, lower the value of `MAX SERVER MEMORY`. Obviously, `MAX SERVER MEMORY` always needs to be greater than or equal to `MIN SERVER MEMORY`.

> If you have installed and are running the Full-Text Search support (Microsoft Search service, also known as MSSearch), then you must set the max server memory option manually to leave enough memory for the MSSearch service to run. Microsoft supplies a handy formula here: Total Virtual Memory – (SQL Server MAX + Virtual Memory for Other Processes) = 1.5 * Server Physical Memory.

Once we have tuned the SQL Server memory settings, it is a good idea to decide if you want SQL Server 7/2000 to tune the process memory automatically or have values set for the configuration. For better performance, you can lock the amount of working set memory that SQL Server reserves. The trade-off here is that you may receive "out of memory" messages from other applications on the same server. If you do decide to fix the amount of working set memory, two configuration settings are necessary. First, equalize the `MIN SERVER MEMORY` and `MAX SERVER MEMORY` settings. Then turn on the `SET WORKING SET SIZE` configuration flag using `sp_configure`. `MAX SERVER MEMORY` should generally not exceed the RAM available for the server.

SQL Server 2000 Dynamic Memory Tuning

Just how does dynamic tuning work? The screenshot below shows the memory property settings for an instance of SQL Server 2000. This instance is called `CD1\MS8D1`. This means that it is on server CD1 and is a second or later instance since the default first instance would simply have the name of the server. Deep down under the covers, the instance is running with a process identified by `MSSQL$InstanceName`, in this case `MSSQL$MS8D1`. The default instance, like in SQL Server 6.5 and SQL Server 7.0, has a process name of `MSSQLServer`. Instance `CD1\MS8D1` has a minimum setting of 60 and a maximum of 512, which is the total RAM installed on this particular server. With these settings, you would think that when you start up instance `CD1\MS8D1`, it would immediately take 60 MB of RAM and could potentially take all 512 MB. This isn't the way dynamic memory works.

When you first start an instance of SQL Server 2000, it initially takes 8-12 MB of RAM. It will only acquire more RAM for its process as users connect and workload increases. In the case of `CD1\MS8D1`, it will gradually increase its memory space allocated to the `MSSQL$MS8D1` process. Once it reaches the threshold of the configure value of 60 MB, it will not go below this setting. At the same time, as workload increases, the instance will gradually acquire memory. It will, however, not reach 512 MB, the value of installed RAM on the server. Instead, Microsoft designed a series of algorithms that kick into place. These algorithms have two specific goals.

❑ Maintain the operating system's free memory within 4-10 MB
❑ Distribute memory between instances of SQL Server based on their relative workloads

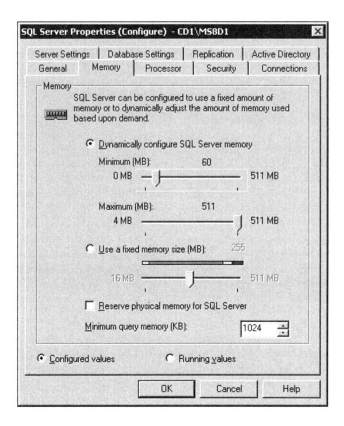

Free Memory Target

As previously noted, the maximum setting for instance CD1\MS8D1 in the above screenshot was 512 MB, the value of installed RAM on the server. Experiments by Microsoft have shown that maintaining 4 to 10 MB of memory on a Windows server will minimize page file swapping. The specific value that the SQL Server seeks to maintain in this 4-10 MB window is called the Free Memory Target. The algorithms were designed such that, as SQL Server consumes more and more memory for its data cache, the amount of free memory for the OS decreases. When the 4-10 MB threshold is reached, SQL Server will stop acquiring memory. The Free Memory Target is at 10 MB for a lightly loaded SQL Server system and gradually goes down to 4 MB for a heavily loaded SQL Server. This Free Memory Target is a reflection of the page life expectancy in the SQL server buffer pool. When a server is heavily loaded, pages are more frequently loaded into the buffer cache and old pages are removed, decreasing page life expectancy. As page life expectancy goes down, SQL Server will maintain OS free memory at the low end (4 MB) of the target 4-10 MB range. When less busy and page life expectancy goes up, it maintains a Free Memory Target closer to 10 MB.

Thus, going back to our instance of CD1\MS8D1, the maximum memory will never approach 512 MB of RAM. Rather, it would probably be somewhere around 460 to 470 MB since a relatively clean operating system takes 30-40 MB of RAM and the Free Memory Target of 4-10 MB of RAM is always maintained free for the OS, in order to avoid paging.

So what happens when you are running SQL Server and it is maintaining a Free Memory Target of 4-10 MB of RAM available for the operating system, and you suddenly start a large process that consumes 20-25 MB of RAM? It turns out that SQL Server will dynamically reduce its memory in data cache to maintain the 4-10 MB of free OS memory. It can do this very quickly, on the order of several MBs per second.

Multiple Instance Memory Tuning

When SQL Server has to share the operating system with another process, for example with the Microsoft Search service, SQL Server's maximum memory has to be manually configured. As you probably know by now, SQL 2000 allows multiple instances of SQL Server on the same operating system. This is true whether the operating system is Window NT or Windows 2000. What about this situation where two or more instances of SQL Server are installed on the same server?

In this case, SQL Server is smart enough to balance the loads between the two instances. Remember from the previous section our instance CD1\MS8D1. Obviously, the default instance is called CD1. We'll look at these two instances, but the theory would be the same for three or more.

> How many instances can you run on a single server? Microsoft recommends one, the default instance, for a production server. We've heard of separate tests running 10 and 16 successfully. We certainly don't recommend more than 10. Generally, you would want to run multiple instances on a single server to support, for example, a development environment in one or more instances and a quality assurance or testing environment in another instance. All of this is, of course, contingent on the overall capabilities of the hardware underneath the instances.

On system start-up, each of the instances, CD1 and CD1\MS8D1, will immediately acquire 8-12 MB of RAM. They will remain at this level until user connections and workloads start increasing on one or both. They will then acquire RAM independently of one another only until the operating system has 4 to 10 MB of free RAM available as outlined in the previous section. At this point, they start competing with one another for memory based on their Free Memory Target values.

As an example, if the default instance has heavy workload, its Free Memory Target will be around 4 MB. The CD1\MS8D1 instance is more lightly loaded and has a Free Memory Target of 10 MB. Assume that only 7 MB of free memory are available for the OS. As you would expect, the heavily loaded CD1 instance with a target of 4 MB will keep on acquiring memory. Since the lightly loaded CD1\MS8D1 does not see 10 MB free, it will release memory to the operating system to try and reach its target of 10 MB free. Don't think about how much memory is allocated to each process. Rather, think about the page life expectancy and the value of its corresponding Free Memory Target for that instance.

A negative feed back loop is thus set up to balance the amount of memory each instance acquires relative to its workload. As the CD1, the heavily loaded instance, gets more memory, it can keep pages in memory longer, increasing its page life expectancy. As page life expectancy goes up, the Free Target Memory value, which had been 4 MB, goes up. On the lightly loaded instance, CD1\MS8D1, memory is released so that the SQL Server attempts to raise the operating system's free memory to the 10 MB target. As memory is released, pages are kept in memory for a shorter period, decreasing their page life expectancy. As page life expectancy goes down, the Free Target Memory value goes down from 10 MB. At some point, the lightly loaded instance will have released enough memory (at least down to its minimum value) such that the Free Memory Target of the two instances are the same.

What is the final result? The Free Memory Target (and corresponding page life expectancy) of the two instances is the same. The heavily loaded instance is still heavily loaded. Except, now given the approximately 460 MB of RAM available to all SQL Server instances, the heavily loaded instance has, as an example, 430 MB of RAM allocated to it. The lightly loaded instance has around 100 MB of RAM. The equilibrium lasts only as long as the relative workloads of the instances remain steady. As soon as the workload on one or the other instance increases or decreases, the page life expectancy and corresponding Free Memory Target will respond and drive the instances to a new equilibrium.

SQL Server Process Memory Tuning

Once you have gotten the overall OS and SQL server memory tuned, look further at the SQL Server memory usage. Four counters are desirable here:

- ❑ `Process: Working Set:sqlservr`
- ❑ `SQL Server: Buffer Manager: Buffer Cache Hit Ratio`
- ❑ `SQL Server: Buffer Manager: Free Buffers`
- ❑ `SQL Server: Memory Manager: Total Server Memory (KB)`

The `Working Set:sqlservr` instance shows the amount of memory that SQL Server is using. If the number is consistently lower than the amount SQL Server is configured to use by the `MIN SERVER MEMORY` and `MAX SERVER MEMORY` options, then SQL Server is configured for too much memory. Otherwise, you may need to increase RAM and `MAX SERVER MEMORY`.

`Buffer Cache Hit Ratio` should be consistently greater than 90. This indicates that the data cache supplied 90 per cent of the requests for data. If this value is consistently low, it is a very good indicator that more memory is needed by SQL Server. If `Available Bytes` is low, this means that we need to add more RAM.

When `Free Buffers` is low, this means that there is not enough RAM to maintain a consistent amount of data cache. It too is indicative of a need for more memory.

If `Total Server Memory` for SQL Server is consistently higher than the overall server memory, it indicates that there is not enough RAM.

Adjusting Server Performance

If this server is dedicated to SQL Server or if SQL Server is considered to be the most important application on the machine, there is a configuration change that you can supposedly make to increase performance. You can control the relative amounts of processor time that will be given to foreground applications compared to background applications. The default value for Windows NT is to give foreground applications the highest priority and therefore, the best response time.

To configure this setting, open **Control Panel** from the **Settings** folder menu of the **Start** menu. Open the **System** applet in **Control Panel** and select the **Performance** tab, as in the screenshot below. Use the slider control on this tab to adjust the foreground and background priorities. In Windows NT Workstation, the OS scheduler will always give background threads 2 clock ticks. Clock ticks can be 7-15 ms depending on the Hardware Abstraction Layer (HAL). Depending on the position of the slider, the foreground applications will get either 2, 4 or 6 clock ticks for each thread, corresponding to **None** to **Maximum**.

Determining Hardware Requirements

A little known fact is that in Windows NT Server, this has absolutely no impact. The slide on the GUI works, but nothing changes underneath. All threads get 12 clock ticks. Period.

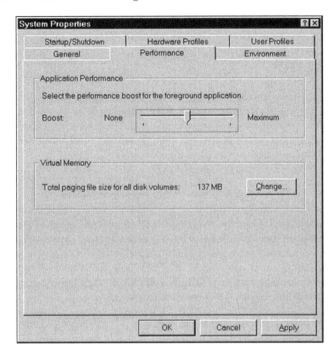

Unlike Windows NT Server, Windows 2000 Server actually works. But it is a little simpler. In both the server product and the workstation product, called Windows 2000 Professional, you get the dialog box shown in the following screenshot, by clicking the **Performance Options** button in the **Advanced** tab of the **Control Panel | System** applet.

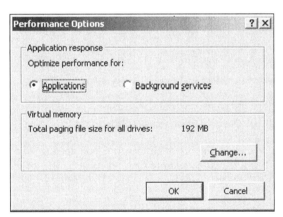

When you optimize performance for Applications in Windows 2000, you get the background thread to foreground thread ratio of 2 clock ticks to 6 clock ticks that Windows NT workstation uses when it is optimized for foreground applications. When you select the Background services choice for Windows 2000, you get the performance of Windows NT Server, 12 clock ticks for all threads.

527

It is recommended that you should keep this at the Background services selection on all Windows 2000 servers running SQL Server to provide equal processor time to both foreground and background applications. This will give the Microsoft SQL Server services a greater percentage of the processing power since it is almost always run as a background service.

CPU Subsystems

The CPU subsystem is the heart and soul of your server. As such, it is a primary candidate for performance tuning. In recent years, symmetric multi-processor (SMP) configurations have abounded. Windows NT server supports four processors out of the box with no special vendor hardware abstraction layers (HAL). Windows 2000 Server maintained support at four processors while Windows 2000 Advanced Server raises this bar to eight processors. The Windows 2000 Data Center Server further raises this up to 32 processors. You're talking some significant computation at this level.

Should you use Windows 2000 or Windows NT? Definitely Windows 2000. For a four-processor server, Windows 2000 shows a 68 per cent performance improvement over a similarly equipped Windows NT Server. Windows NT doesn't even support anything over four processors, short of specialized OEM builds. Windows 2000 also supports processor affinity. This is where a process such as the SQL Server process is assigned to one or more processors. This effectively replaces the SMP Concurrency that was written out of SQL Server as a configuration option after SQL 6.5. Please note, just as in SQL 6.5 with SMP Concurrency, you should use caution when using processor affinity since it will often have the impact of keeping a process such as SQL Server from being able to use a less used processor.

Currently there appears to be a price-performance "sweet spot" at the four-processor level. So how should you configure SQL Server to maximize CPU utilization? For SQL Server 7 and SQL Server 2000, one thought is necessary – hands off! While some arguments may have been made for tuning a CPU subsystem in SQL Server 6.5, SQL Server 7 and SQL Server 2000 are highly tuned to take maximum advantage of any CPU set-up that you throw at it.

CPU Performance Monitoring

In CPU performance monitoring, we are going to be using several counters:

- `Processor: per cent Processor Time`
- `Processor: per cent Privileged Time`
- `Processor: per cent User Time`
- `System: per cent Total Processor Time`

Generally, CPU performance monitoring is straightforward. You need to start by monitoring `Processor: per cent Processor Time`. If you have more than one processor, you should monitor each instance of this counter and also monitor `System: per cent Total Processor Time` to determine the average for all processors.

Utilization rates consistently above 80-90 per cent may indicate a poorly tuned or designed application. On the other hand, if you have put all the other recommendations of this book into use, they may indicate a need for a more powerful CPU subsystem. In general, I would spend a little bit of time analyzing the applications before immediately going out and buying three more processors. Spending this time experimenting to discover CPU performance problems and correcting them through software improvements will often keep you from just spending money on a more powerful CPU that only "covers up" poorly written software for little or no time.

Determining Hardware Requirements

If you do see high CPU utilization, you will then want to monitor `Processor: per cent Privileged Time`. This is the time spent performing kernel level operations, such as disk I/O. If this counter is consistently above 80-90 per cent and corresponds to high disk performance counters, you may have a disk bottleneck rather than a CPU bottleneck.

What about SQL Server? `Processor: per cent User Time` measures the amount of processor time consumed by non-kernel level applications. SQL is such an application. If this is high and you have multiple processes running on a server, you may want to delve further by looking at specific process instances through the instances of the counter `Process: per cent User Time`. This can be very useful for occasions such as when our operating system engineers installed new anti-virus software on all our servers. It temporarily brought them to their knees until we were able to determine the culprit through analyzing `Process: per cent User Time` for the anti-virus software instance.

Textile Management

In the parlance of CPU utilization, threads are a single process run by a CPU. Threads are managed by the operating system in kernel mode. SQL Server can maintain up to 255 open threads, with each thread utilized for batch processing. With the introduction of SQL Server 7, a new term was introduced, **fibers**. While threads are handled by the operating system in kernel mode, fibers are handled in user mode by the application itself.

In a high capacity OLTP environment, the number of batches and thus threads thrown at a CPU subsystem may be very high, typically approaching the configured default of 255 threads. Each time a thread context is switched for a CPU, the CPU has to come out of user mode, go through a context switch to kernel mode, take up the new thread, and then context switch back into user mode. For a CPU, a context switch is relatively expensive.

With fibers, SQL Server will spawn a few threads and then have multiple fibers in each thread. The management of fibers is relegated to the SQL Server application level code rather than the operating system kernel. Since fibers run in user mode, when the CPU switches between one fiber and another in the same thread, there are no context switches for the CPU. The difference in CPU cycles between a CPU taking up a new thread that has to go through a context switch down into kernel mode and back out, and a CPU taking up a new fiber that doesn't undergo this process is an order of magnitude.

Fibers are not for every situation. Fibers are confined to a single thread, which is always assigned to a single CPU. Thus, while a process thread could be serviced by one CPU and then another, a process fiber would be confined to a single CPU. OLTP applications are emphasized since they typically have very short, defined transactions running in a process, be it contained in thread or fiber. Use the following checklist in order to determine if fibers may be for you:

1. Your server should be entirely dedicated to SQL server usage and generally use it for an OLTP environment

2. You are experiencing a very high CPU utilization rate (> 90 per cent)

3. You see an abnormally high rate of context switches using the counter `System:Context Switches/sec`

If these parameters fit your system, you may want to experiment with fiber usage by switching the "lightweight pooling" configuration setting from 0 to 1.

Disk Subsystems

The second most important system characteristic for good performance of your SQL Server application is the disk subsystem. Remember, performance is mostly determined by maximizing the number of data reads from high-speed memory. Getting this data in and out of high-speed memory and storing it is the responsibility of the disk subsystem.

The Basic Disk Subsystem

The basic disk subsystem involves a hard disk and a hard disk controller interfacing with the motherboard. Hard disks have various performance characteristics. We can look at them from the standpoint of reading and writing, the standpoint of reading data off the disk sequentially or randomly, and the standpoint of how fast the disk is turning.

The reading characteristics are naturally different from the writing characteristics of a disk. As you would expect, writing is relatively slow compared to reading. Thus, we want to minimize the waiting time for disk writes. SQL Server naturally optimizes this by using a combination of individual worker threads and the lazy writer system. These two systems combine to scan through the buffer cache in active memory and decrement a counter indicating the relative busyness of a page in the buffer cache. Accessing the page causes an increment in its counter. In this way, frequently accessed pages are maintained in the buffer cache. If a buffer cache page's counter reaches zero and the page's dirty page indicator is set, either an individual worker thread or, less frequently, the lazy writer will schedule a flush to disk of the page. The key is that this is done asynchronously with the thread's read efforts so that waiting time for writing is minimized.

Reading data from the disk is where most performance gains are concentrated. It is much more efficient to read data sequentially (rather than randomly) off a disk. Thus, the use of clustered indexes for loading large amounts of data into the data cache for analysis is always optimal.

Finally, if you are given a choice between a disk that turns at 7200 RPM and 15,000 RPM, naturally choose the latter. Disks that turn faster get the data under the read head faster and into the data cache faster. Of course, they are more expensive.

You may have the fastest hard disk in the world, though, and have a poor performing system if you don't have a good controller interface between the hard disk and the motherboard. The controller's performance is measured in bit path throughput. 64 bits is obviously better than 32.

What is also important about controllers is their caching capability. Today's controllers have both read-ahead and write-ahead or write-back caching capability. When a controller reads ahead, it uses sophisticated algorithms to anticipate data needs and place this data in fast cache before the CPU is ready for it. Write-ahead or write-back caching involves the controller posting data to high-speed cache and returning a completion status to the operating system. The data is then actually written to the disk by the controller, independent of the operating system. Significantly, caching capability is marked by the amount of very high speed RAM dedicated to caching this information. Again, more is better but also more expensive.

Write-caching and SQL Server

Many controllers have a feature called Write Caching. This is where the controller will receive the data from the operating system and essentially tell the operating system that the data is written to disk, when in fact, it has been stored in high speed RAM for eventual writing to disk.

This can be highly problematic. SQL Server's whole scheme of ensuring data integrity in the event of a server failure is dependent on transaction logs being written to disk before the underlying tables are actually changed on disk. With a write caching controller, the SQL Server can be mistakenly told that a transaction log is sitting firmly on a hard disk, when in fact it is still residing in the high speed RAM of the caching controller. If during that moment the server fails, the integrity of SQL in recovering committed transactions and rolling back dirty transactions is potentially defeated.

Most medium to high-end servers today have write-caching controllers with on-card battery backups just for the controllers and their array of disks. In the instance of this battery backup, you should be safe in turning on write-caching controllers. However, what happens if the battery goes bad? The server engineers will tell you not to worry. They get alarms/paged. However, it is our personal experience that even with a very competent set of server engineers and a high-end server from one of the leading and best known server manufacturers, we only found out that the first of two redundant power supplies for a server had failed when the second one also failed and brought down the whole server. Even though paging was turned on, for some reason it didn't work.

In short, with very, very few exceptions, Microsoft almost always recommends that write caching be turned off on controllers through which SQL writes to disk. From our experience, we heartily agree. Except for a very few OLTP applications, this small performance hit is well offset by the extra hours sleep your DBA will get. Just think of it this way. Remember the first (and hopefully only time) you typed a ten page term paper into a word processor and, without frequently saving, the lights blinked? If you are going to turn write-caching on, you really need to have a very compelling performance reason and very high confidence in the hardware, engineers and systems maintaining and monitoring it.

The RAID Subsystem

Disks and controllers can be joined together in Redundant Array of Inexpensive Disk (RAID) combinations. The primary purpose of such combinations is to provide fault tolerance (in other words redundancy) such that the failure of any one component will not bring down the whole system. RAID combinations can be either software-based, where the NT or Windows 2000 operating system maintains the array, or hardware-based, where a specialized controller maintains the RAID configuration.

Generally there are three plus one ways of looking at a RAID configuration. The three ways are called RAID 0, RAID 1, and RAID 5. The extra one is called either RAID 10 or RAID 0+1. RAID 0, RAID 1, and RAID 5 are found in both software and hardware solutions. RAID 10 is only found in hardware solutions.

RAID 0

RAID 0 is where data is striped across disks in blocks, usually about 64 KB each. A single controller or the operating system would write a 64 KB block to one disk and then proceed to write a block to the next disk. Writing to and reading from such arrays can be extremely fast. Reads and writes are rapid, as you have multiple drive heads, which can read the blocks of data concurrently.

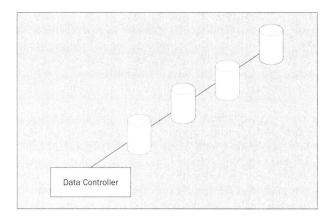

Many people will tell you that RAID 0 is not really RAID since it isn't redundant. We personally agree. If any one of the disks fails, then your system comes to a screeching halt and you may have (gasp!) lost data. There is an advantage in RAID 0 in terms of speed. Since no parity information is maintain on any other disks, data is written rapidly in stripes or blocks of data across each disk. Similarly, for reads (and particular sequential reads), the performance can be extraordinarily good. In addition to its speed, though, another advantage of the RAID 0 configuration is that it can support very large arrays. Even though it is not really a "redundant" array, it is important to detail it, since its performance means that it is one of two RAID configurations that will come into play later when we discuss RAID 10, the other being RAID 1.

RAID 1

RAID 1 is called **mirroring** when one controller mirrors two disks, or **duplexing** when two controllers each control a separate disk to maintain mirrored copies of data. Often, the term mirroring is used when duplexing would be more technically correct. It is usually enough to know that identical subsystems are being referenced. Essentially, two identical disk volumes, A and B, are set up. When data is written to A, it is simultaneously written to B. The volumes are kept in perpetual synchronization. When either A or B fails, the disk subsystem doesn't miss a beat. It just raises (hopefully) all sorts of alarms to tell you that it is no longer redundant. In order to recover, you have to "break the mirror", snap in a new drive and re-synchronize the mirror. Most subsystems that support mirroring will let you do this without ever taking down the server. What suffers? Remember the "I" in RAID? It stood for inexpensive. With RAID 1, you have to buy two bytes of storage for every one byte of data. In addition to costs, a disadvantage of the RAID 1 configuration is that it can only be as large as a single hard disk size.

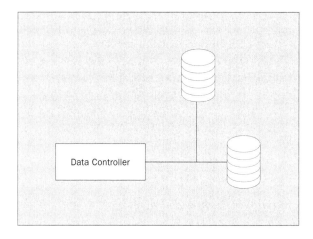

RAID 5

RAID 5 is the most common RAID configuration and like RAID 0, data is written across a set of disks in blocks. However whilst RAID 0 only requires two disks, RAID 5 requires at least three or more disks. Each stripe though, will now have a parity block written to alternating disks. For example, if you have four disks in a RAID 5 array, every stripe will write three blocks of data and one block of parity information. The parity information will be rotated from disk to disk such that no one disk has all the parity information.

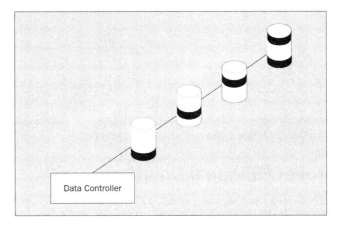

When a single disk fails in a RAID 5 array, the other disks will pick up the load. When the read should have come from the failed disk, the controller or operating system will read the parity information and compare it to the data from all the other intact disks, computing the data that would otherwise be present on the failed disk.

> **RAID 3 is very similar to RAID 5, except that rather than spreading the parity across all disks in the array, a single disk is used for the parity storage and all other disks are used for data storage.**

Quite obviously a disk failure in a RAID 5 configuration means that data reads become significantly slower than a failure of a RAID 1 system, where data reads are not really affected. Just as obviously, the overhead to maintain redundancy is only 1/n of your storage space, where n is the number of disks participating in the array. Another advantage of RAID 5 arrays is that the array can be sized very large. I've seen RAID 5 arrays with hundreds of GB. For the vast majority of mid-range servers and applications, hardware-based RAID 5 is the disk subsystem of choice.

RAID 10 – where 0+1 does not equal 1

As you can see, RAID 0 has the best throughput and extensibility of all arrays but no redundancy. RAID 1 has the best redundancy, but is very limited in its extensibility. Thus, the best RAID arrays on the market today are those that are characterized as RAID 0 + 1 or RAID 10. To build a RAID 10 array, you first make two separate but identical RAID 0 arrays where data is striped in blocks across two or more disks. These two identical RAID 0 arrays are then mirrored to each other. This solution is only implemented by high-end RAID controllers.

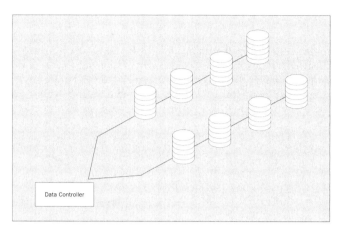

While RAID 10 is often considered one of the best RAID solutions, it should be pointed out that RAID 5 and RAID 1 are often used because of their lower cost and equal redundancy.

Multiple Controller/Channel Solutions

Up to now, we have only been addressing a single channel of data. Many controllers can have dual channels and certainly you can install extra controllers on a server. Remember, SQL Server is essentially a multi-level system. When a single record is written to disk, it is preceded by the transaction log write and, as often as not, accompanied by one or more index writes. Alongside the SQL writes, the NT or 2000 OS is continually pruning the operating system memory and paging inactive memory to disk. If these writes can be written by different controllers to different disk array subsystems, then the transaction throughput will be multiplied.

Data reads from disk to data cache can also greatly benefit from multiple channels. A well-optimized database will have complementary tables that are most frequently joined. By putting the data from one table on controller A, the indexes from that table on controller B, the data from another table on controller C, the indexes from that table on controller D, and TempDB on controller E, the data reads can be happening simultaneously. And fast.

Overall, while RAID 0+1 would probably be the fastest single disk subsystem, given the same amount of budget, a better buying decision would be made for most applications by buying three or four RAID 5 subsystems. Then the transaction logs would be dedicated to one subsystem, the data from some tables and indexes from others to another subsystem, and the remaining tables and indexes from the first tables on the third. The page file and other OS components may be on the fourth, if it is available.

Another viable solution that is frequently used is to put the write-intensive transaction log on a RAID 1 mirrored configuration. RAID 1 writes are faster since mirrored drives are doing simultaneous writes and don't have the overhead of calculating and writing the parity bit for a stripe. Since the data requires more extensibility, one or more RAID 5 subsystems are incorporated for the data and indexes.

Disk Tuning and Performance Monitoring

An earlier section about *The Art of Performance Monitoring* made mention of setting up disk performance counters. The overhead of the disk performance counters on processor CPU utilization is very small. In the early days of Windows NT, it was said that the overhead of disk performance counters was, at worst, one-half of one percent of processor utilization on a single CPU 486DX66 server. With Pentium 3's running at 10+ times that clock speed today in symmetric multi-processor environments, the concern about disk performance counters is negligible.

Determining Hardware Requirements

The greatest risk of bottleneck, after memory, is equally shared between the disk subsystem and the processor(s). A table scan on a large table can literally bring a server to its knees. Worse still, an ill-advised cartesian join of two large tables is a death sentence for disk performance. You will want to be monitoring disk performance when such events creep into your systems (and they will at the worst possible times). Imagine the head of Human Resources trying to run a summary query during payroll processing. It happens.

Begin disk performance monitoring by looking at the following counters:

- `PhysicalDisk: per cent Disk Time`
- `PhysicalDisk: Current Disk Queue Length`
- `PhysicalDisk: Avg. Disk Queue Length`

Applications and systems that are I/O-bound may keep the disk constantly active. This is called disk thrashing.

> **You should always know how many channels, what types of arrays, how many disks are in each array, and which array/channel your data and transaction logs are located on before you start thinking about disk performance tuning.**

The `PhysicalDisk: per cent Disk Time` counter monitors the percentage of time that the disk is conducting check the `Physical Disk: Current Disk Queue Length` counter to see the number of requests that are queued up waiting for disk access.

It is important at this point to be familiar with your disk subsystem. If the number of waiting I/O requests is a sustained value more than 1.5 to 2 times the number of spindles making up the physical disk, you have a disk bottleneck. For example, a RAID 5 configuration with seven spindles/disks would be a candidate for disk performance tuning should the `Current Disk Queue Length` continually rest above 12-14.

To improve performance in this situation, consider adding faster disk drives, moving some processes to an additional controller-disk subsystem, or adding additional disks to a RAID 5 array.

Most disks have one spindle, although RAID devices usually have more. A hardware RAID 5 device appears as one physical disk in Windows NT PerfMon or Windows 2000 SysMon. RAID devices created through software appear as multiple instances.

> *WARNING: The `per cent Disk Time` counter can indicate a value greater than 100 per cent if you are using a hardware based RAID configuration. If it does, use the `PhysicalDisk: Avg. Disk Queue Length` counter to determine the average number of system requests waiting for disk access. Again, this is indicative of a performance problem if a sustained value of 1.5 to 2 times the number of spindles in the array is observed.*

User Connections

In SQL Server 6.5, user connections were an important tuning option. SQL Server 7 and SQL Server 2000 have reduced this importance. User connections in these versions are a dynamic, self-configuring option. In most cases you shouldn't need to adjust the user connections settings because if 100 connections are necessary, 100 connections are allocated. Running the following commands will give the current settings of user connections and the maximum allowed number of user connections:

```
EXEC sp_configure "user connections"
SELECT @@MAX_CONNECTIONS
```

You may use `sp_configure` to tune the number of user connections, but we highly recommend avoiding doing this in SQL Server 7 and SQL Server 2000. Each user connection consumes about 40 KB of memory. When you start specifying the maximum number of user connections instead of letting SQL Server maintain the number, the allocation of memory is no longer dynamic. Instead, 40 KB of memory times the number of maximum users set will be consumed immediately. Generally you would only want to configure the number of user connections in an environment where spurious users could spawn a large number of user connections.

> Many administrators and managers confuse User Connections and Client Access Licenses (CALs). They are apples and oranges. In SQL 2000, a CAL is a license for a single device (usually a computer, but it could be your cell phone) to connect to SQL Server. The people who manage your licenses should explicitly assign it to the device. Once that device is licensed with a single CAL, it can connect and open as many User Connections as the server will allow. If your mode of licensing for your CALs is PER SEAT, it can open additional User Connections to other SQL Servers. It is not unusual to see a single computer with a single PER SEAT CAL open 20+ User Connections to one server and five to another server. In short, there is no correlation between Users Connections and CALs. Please don't think that this short explanation solves all your legal issues (which is what a CAL essentially is). Microsoft's licensing structure is more complex than this short explanation about the difference between User Connections and CALs. The professional thing to do is READ YOUR LICENSES.

It is important to monitor user connections in your performance tuning. The counter is `SQL Server:General:User Connections`. In a troubleshooting or testing environment, you may want to monitor `SQL Server:Databases:Active Transactions:database`.

The number of user connections is based on the requirements of your application and users. OLE DB applications need a connection for each open connection object. ODBC connections are spawned for each active connection handle in an application. DB-Library uses a connection for each occurrence of the `dbopen` function. n-tier applications that make use of connection pooling would tend to minimize the number of open connections.

Since SQL Server is a transaction logging system, what you may want to be aware of is the presence of long running transactions. It is commonplace to dump the transaction logs every hour or two. The transaction log is maintained open back to the longest open transaction. If a transaction remains open for an extended period of time, the transaction log will grow and grow, with each dump getting larger and larger. In a default situation, SQL Server will automatically grow the transaction log. It can get really huge and we've seen it reach the capacity of a disk. We've traced third party applications that begin a session with a DB-Library `dbopen` function call, immediately followed by a `BEGIN TRAN` statement. Monitor the sizes of your transaction log dumps. If they get progressively larger throughout the day for a particular database, you may have this condition. You can see long running open transactions by issuing the T-SQL command:

```
DBCC OPENTRAN <database>
```

You may even consider writing a T-SQL job that alerts you to the presence of long running open transactions.

Locking and Blocking

Locks in and of themselves are a very good thing. They guarantee that the data you read is the data actually in the database. Locks held too long are a problem. They lead to what we call blocking.

Blocking Demonstration

Start Query Analyzer. Open two connections to the same server. Then tile the windows vertically by using the menu option **Windows | Tile Vertically**.

In the first window type and execute the following code:

```
USE pubs
GO
SELECT au_fname FROM AUTHORS -- (NOLOCK)
   WHERE au_lname = 'Green'
```

You should return a value of **Marjorie**.

In the second window type and execute the following code:

```
USE pubs
GO
BEGIN TRAN
  UPDATE authors SET au_fname = 'Harry'
  WHERE au_lname = 'Green'
-- ROLLBACK TRAN
```

Ensure that there are two dashes in front of the `rollback tran` statement. You should get a message back.

(1 row(s) affected)

Now re-execute the first query. Open a third window (by typing *Ctrl – N*) and run the command:

```
sp_who2
```

Scroll through the list and notice the `blkby` column. This shows that your select transaction is blocked by your update transaction. Close the third window. If necessary, realign your windows using the **Windows | Tile Vertically** menu option again. In your update transaction window, highlight the phrase ROLLBACK TRAN and execute it. Notice what happens to the select query.

Try the experiment again, only this time, un-comment the (NOLOCK) clause by removing the two dashes from in front of it. Since you are now using NOLOCK you will not see your select statement blocked in SP_WHO2 this time. This is a good example of a dirty read.

Monitoring Blocking

Sometimes things just don't get better. In SQL Server 6.5, there was a very handy performance counter, SQLServer-Locks:Users Blocked, that we always used to show active blocking on our servers. This was such an important counter, that we would magnify the scale of the counter by 10 and increase the width of the counter line to a very thick line. Thus, when even a single lock popped up on our servers, a large thick line popped up in our performance monitor charts.

Unfortunately, this counter went away in SQL Server 7 and stayed away in SQL Server 2000. What to do?

Use the `User Definable Counters`. Most people never use these counters and don't know how they work. In SQL Server 6.5, when a counter was called, it automatically updated itself. In SQL Server 7 and SQL Server 2000, it doesn't. Each user defined counter has to be explicitly updated with an integer value by running the stored procedure `sp_user_counterX Y`, where X is the user defined counter number and Y is the integer value assigned to the counter.

In SQL Enterprise Manager, for the SQL Server, drill down in the management tree to **Management| SQL Server Agent| Jobs**. Right click **Jobs** and choose **New Job**. Then enter a name and description for User Defined Performance Counter 1.

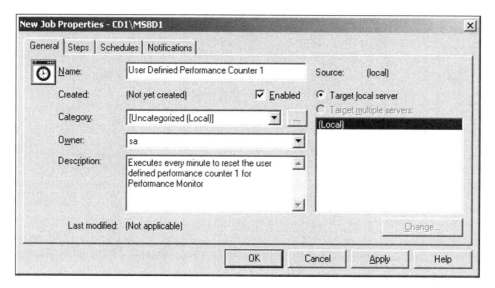

Click the **Steps** tab and then the **New** button to add a step. In the **New Job Step** dialog window, create a single step called **Reset Counter** in this job with the following T-SQL script executing in the `master` database:

```
SET NOCOUNT ON
DECLARE @blocks int
SELECT @blocks = count(blocked) FROM
        master.dbo.sysprocesses (nolock)
   WHERE blocked > 0
EXEC sp_user_counter1 @blocks
GO
```

Determining Hardware Requirements

The window should look like this:

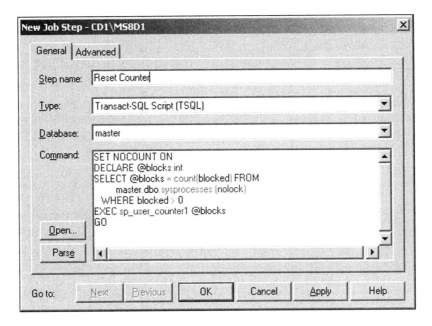

Click **OK** to close the **New Job Step** dialog box.

In the **Schedules** tab, click the **New Schedule** button. Radio the **Start whenever the CPU(s) become idle** option since we want this job to happen in the background and not interfere with more important ones.

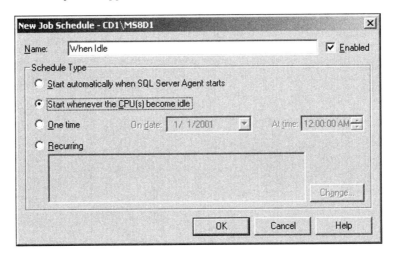

Click **OK** to save this schedule and **OK** in the **New Job Properties** to save the job.

Now in either Windows NT PerfMon or Windows 2000 SysMon, add the instance SQLServer:User Settable:Query:User counter1. Run the blocking tests outlined in the *Blocking Demonstration* section, to verify your work.

If you decide you want to add other user defined performance counters later, you would just add them to the T-SQL script in the Reset Counter step you defined above, and invoke the counter in Windows NT Performance Monitor or Windows 2000 SysMon.

Case Study

In this segment of our case study, we will look at taking the volumetric values we gathered in Chapter 8, and finally turning them into real numbers. In the following table we have taken the table from the end of Chapter 8 and will now extrapolate what the new values will be since we now have some new tables. Most notable of these are the following three rows:

Table Name	Initial Rows	Growth in Rows per Month	Max Rows
Deposit	0	5	4000
Check	0	245	10000
directWithdrawal	0	50	1000

In our tables we took the sub-typed tables of transaction and turned them into the table transaction. We will add them all together into a single row:

transaction	0	300	15000

We do the same for each of the tables and arrive at the following table of the conditions of initial row size, row growth, and maximum expected rows:

Table Name	Initial Rows	Growth in Rows per Month	Max Rows
account	1	0	20
accountReconcile	0	1	36
address	50	30	600
addressType	5	0	10
bank	1	0	5
city	450	20	25000
payee	100	30	300
payeeAddress	100	30	600
payeePhoneNumber	100	30	600
phoneNumber	50	30	600
phoneNumberType	5	0	10
state	50	0	70
statement	0	1	36

Determining Hardware Requirements

Table Name	Initial Rows	Growth in Rows per Month	Max Rows
statementItem	0	300	15000
statementType	3	0	5
transactionAllocation	75	400	12000
transaction	0	300	15000
transactionAllocationType	20	0	40
transactionType	3	0	5
user	10	2	50
zipCode	1000	10	99999
zipCodeCityReference	1100	10	99999

Next we need to calculate the sizes of the tables. Using the sp__table$indexSpace procedure, we will calculate values for initial rows, growth in rows per month, and maximum rows conditions. For each table, an assumption needs to be made regarding the percentage to which variable length columns are filled. For the purposes of this case study, we will assume 50 per cent. A sample query for maximum row condition in the transaction table is shown below. There are three variable length columns in the transaction table, number which is VARCHAR(20), signature which is VARCHAR(20), and description which is VARCHAR(1000). The 50 per cent assumption would need to be evaluated with these in mind.

```
EXEC SP__Table$IndexSpace
    @tablename = 'transaction',
    @variFillPercent = 50,
    @num_rows = 16000
```

The results for all tables and all conditions we have considered are presented in the table below. As you look at the results for each table, notice that the growth per month does not seem to be cumulative. This is because we were using the rows per month as the input parameter for rows for the stored procedure sp__table$indexSpace. Whether there is one row or several, the output of the procedure will always be in discrete 8 KB multiples. Thus, the size is particularly relevant for the initial row size and maximum row conditions. Also, remember, that as an index grows, the node levels gradually fill up. At a certain point, they will need to "grow" an additional leaf node level. Thus, index growth in general will be non-linear, particularly for larger tables.

The clustered index size is relatively flat (a single root node page of 8 KB) for virtually all conditions. This is because the clustered index that we are talking about here is the single root node page that points to the page of the actual data. All of our clustered indexes are single column keys of a 4-btye integer datatype, and 455 of these page pointers will fit on the root node page. This will almost always yield the flattest realistic clustered index you can have. Once the data pages exceed the 455 page count, the clustered index will increase in levels and include an additional index node level. This is only seen in the transaction table for the max row condition. Due to the relatively large row size of the transaction table (remember that the description column is VARCHAR(1000) and we assume it is 50 per cent filled), the number of pages exceeds the 455 page threshold.

Since all of our tables have clustered indexes, it might be more accurate to say the clustered index size is the sum of the "CInd Size" column and the "Data Size in KB" column, which is actually the leaf node of the clustered index. We break these out in the stored procedure and below for analysis purposes.

Table	Condition	Rows	Data Size In KB	CInd Size	CIndex Lvls	NCInd Size	NCInd Lvls
account	Initial Row Size	1	8	8	1	8	1
account	Growth Per Month	0	0	0	0	0	0
account	Max Rows	20	8	8	1	8	1
accountReconcile	Initial Row Size	0	0	0	0	0	0
accountReconcile	Growth Per Month	1	8	8	1	8	1
accountReconcile	Max Rows	36	16	8	1	24	2
address	Initial Row Size	50	24	8	1	32	2
address	Growth Per Month	30	16	8	1	24	2
address	Max Rows	600	272	8	1	296	3
addressType	Initial Row Size	5	8	8	1	8	1
addressType	Growth Per Month	0	0	0	0	0	0
addressType	Max Rows	10	8	8	1	8	1
bank	Initial Row Size	1	8	8	1	8	1
bank	Growth Per Month	0	0	0	0	0	0
bank	Max Rows	5	8	8	1	8	1
city	Initial Row Size	450	32	8	1	40	2
city	Growth Per Month	20	8	8	1	8	1
city	Max Rows	25000	1456	8	1	1496	3
payee	Initial Row Size	100	8	8	1	8	1
payee	Growth Per Month	30	8	8	1	8	1
payee	Max Rows	300	24	8	1	32	2
payeeAddress	Initial Row Size	100	8	8	1	8	1
payeeAddress	Growth Per Month	30	8	8	1	8	1
payeeAddress	Max Rows	600	24	8	1	32	2
payeePhoneNumber	Initial Row Size	100	8	8	1	8	1
payeePhoneNumber	Growth Per Month	30	8	8	1	8	1
payeePhoneNumber	Max Rows	600	24	8	1	32	2
phoneNumber	Initial Row Size	50	8	8	1	8	1
phoneNumber	Growth Per Month	30	8	8	1	8	1
phoneNumber	Max Rows	600	32	8	1	40	2

Determining Hardware Requirements

Table	Condition	Rows	Data Size In KB	CInd Size	CIndex Lvls	NCInd Size	NCInd Lvls
phoneNumberType	Initial Row Size	5	8	8	1	8	1
phoneNumberType	Growth Per Month	0	0	0	0	0	0
phoneNumberType	Max Rows	10	8	8	1	8	1
state	Initial Row Size	50	8	8	1	8	1
state	Growth Per Month	0	0	0	0	0	0
state	Max Rows	70	8	8	1	8	1
statement	Initial Row Size	0	0	0	0	0	0
statement	Growth Per Month	1	8	8	1	8	1
statement	Max Rows	36	8	8	1	8	1
statementItem	Initial Row Size	0	0	0	0	0	0
statementItem	Growth Per Month	300	32	8	1	24	2
statementItem	Max Rows	15000	1584	8	1	600	2
statementType	Initial Row Size	75	8	8	1	8	1
statementType	Growth Per Month	400	48	8	1	32	2
statementType	Max Rows	12000	1264	8	1	672	2
transaction	Initial Row Size	0	0	0	0	0	0
transaction	Growth Per Month	295	176	8	1	24	2
transaction	Max Rows	15000	9144	32	2	640	2
transactionAllocation	Initial Row Size	1	8	8	1	8	1
transactionAllocation	Growth Per Month	0	0	0	0	0	0
transactionAllocation	Max Rows	20	8	8	1	8	1
transactionType	Initial Row Size	3	8	8	1	8	1
transactionType	Growth Per Month	0	0	0	0	0	0
transactionType	Max Rows	5	8	8	1	8	1
user	Initial Row Size	10	8	8	1	8	1
user	Growth Per Month	2	8	8	1	8	1
user	Max Rows	50	16	8	1	8	1
zipCode	Initial Row Size	1000	32	8	1	40	2
zipCode	Growth Per Month	10	8	8	1	8	1

Table continued on following page

Table	Condition	Rows	Data Size In KB	CInd Size	CIndex Lvls	NCInd Size	NCInd Lvls
`zipCode`	Max Rows	99999	2544	8	1	2656	2
`zipCodeCityReference`	Initial Row Size	1000	32	8	1	40	2
`zipCodeCityReference`	Growth Per Month	10	8	8	1	8	1
`zipCodeCityReference`	Max Rows	99999	2936	8	1	2944	2

The total space for the table would thus be the data size plus the size of the clustered and non-clustered indexes. Our tables have only one non-clustered index on each of them for the alternative key. Obviously, as you add more non-clustered indexes for performance reasons, you would then need to review the results from `sp_table$indexSpace` for each additional non-clustered index that you add and the row total conditions listed above.

Summary

In this chapter we have taken a look at how you can estimate what requirements your database will have, not just at the time of deployment, but also in a year or so down the line. Data sizing, index sizing, and row estimations are intricately tied to future performance. Archiving is one of the most overlooked methods for obtaining significant performance improvements in a mature database. We have looked at the most important hardware requirements, those of storage space, processing power, and online memory. Consistent with this is a requirement on your part that you spend time familiarizing yourself with the performance analysis tools so that, when push comes to shove, you will have the skills to isolate causes of performance problems. More specifically, we saw what hard drive configurations are available and what they offer us in terms of performance and data redundancy. Obviously, the higher processor speed and the more memory you acquire, the better. But we also saw how important it is to configure SQL Server to take advantage of the processor and memory, especially where it might be fighting for resources with other applications. We are now in a position to finish our design project, which we will go on to do in the next chapter.

14

Completing the Project

Introduction

Throughout the past thirteen chapters we have taken our database system from conception to a working database. We have gathered data on what the user wanted, built models of this data, created tables, considered various safeguarding mechanisms and finally added code to act as a kind of tier between the user and the data. So our development work is at an end then? Well, though the OLTP part of the system is now complete, we still have a few things to tidy up.

- **Performance Tuning** – Though we have touched on performance tuning in previous chapters we have mostly been concerning ourselves with how transactions can affect the system.

- **Reports** – Now that our OLTP database has solidified and we are able to work with it, we can optimize it for the reporting needs that we determined in the logical design phase. For larger mission-critical projects (especially those involving vast amounts of data, or even mechanical clients tearing away at the data twenty-four hours a day) we may need to take the additional step of building a read-only copy (or partial copy) of the data for reporting. This will decrease the contention for data in our primary databases. We will look at designing a read-only database to meet such needs. We will also mention a few other uses of read-only extracts other than simple reporting, such as building an operational data store (ODS).

- **Enterprise Modeling** – As corporate data architects one of our jobs is to build a model that not only encompasses the work we have done on one project, but all projects that came before it, and even out-of-the-box packages that were built by different vendors. The goal of enterprise modeling is to keep a record of all of the data in our organization in order to enhance overall normalization on a corporate level.

❑ **Three-Phase Implementation** – This refers to the setting up of a design and implementation cycle involving Development, Quality Assurance (QA) and Production phases. We will discuss how to construct such an environment.

We will present a few guidelines for protecting yourself against system problems in the Production phase such as power outages and general hardware failures. Whilst the Production phase system set up is not strictly the responsibility of the data architect, in my experience, the data architect *is* often involved and can end up taking the blame if the proper backup and disaster recovery plan was not specified in the architecture for the system.

Performance Tuning

The performance tuning process is complex, and is completely separate from database design. We should also bear in mind that it is a never-ending process. Developers may need performance enhancements, and testers (especially those performing stress testing) will hopefully find almost every additional place to tune performance. Once the real system is up and running, we will again tune performance.

Performance tuning is the responsibility of the DBA and not the Data Architect. Nevertheless, when designing the database we must be aware of critical matters that will affect the DBA's task, and should consult them regularly. The following list represents reasons why we have skirted away from a deep discussion of performance tuning during our design:

Performance tuning should not be a matter of guessing – Performance must be considered over the entire system, and basing your performance considerations on previous experiences is not always optimal. SQL Server provides some extremely powerful tools for tracking down problem areas in our systems. By using the SQL Server Profiler, we can determine which queries take a long time to run, and look at how long processes take before and after a change. This, coupled with good stress testing, can determine if indexes, hardware improvements, or even denormalization is the best thing for the overall system package. It should be noted in passing that performance testing does not mean distorting the database model through de-normalizing, and indeed, denormalization for the sake of it may well lead to degraded performance when attempting to manipulate the database tables. While denormalization may be desirable in some cases, you begin to reintroduce the kinds of modification anomalies that we strove to remove in the normalization process. We either have to live with these anomalies or we have to write additional code to deal with them. An effective database administrator who can tune a database without having to carry out denormalization is worth their weight in gold.

Performance tuning changes in SQL Server versions – Whilst earlier versions required the designer to perform a large amount of manual optimisation, recent versions (7.0 and 2000) have added a rich layer of functionality to performance tuning. Generally I have now found it's often best to give back control of optimization to SQL Server. Further details on this can be found in *"Professional SQL Server 2000 Programming" (Wrox Press, ISBN 1861004486)*.

Superfluous indexes are very costly – In a system that is write-intensive, such as an OLTP database, too many indexes can cause performance problems. This is due to the fact that when changes are made to the underlying structure, we greatly increase the cost of doing inserts, updates, or deletes because both the table structures and indexes have to be manipulated. When building such a database, the use of indexes can be an appealing solution, but the overall performance of the system can be affected, especially if the data is continually being added to. On the other hand, in the case of a database or even a table that is not modified often, appropriate use of indexes may be a real boost to performance.

When performance problems arise we can use the SQL Server Profiler to see the exact calls that our clients are making. The Query Analyzer then allows us to consider the following:

- **Query Plan** – By looking at how SQL Server is planning on performing the query, we can see if it is making any illogical assumptions that we need to improve upon, either by rewriting our queries (like removing data from the query that we never make use of), using optimizer hints to tweak the query, or possibly adding indexes, but with suitable caution as mentioned above.
- **Statistics Time and Statistics IO** – We can set the Query Analyzer to return information about how long the query took, or how much and what types of disk activity the query required.
- **Index Tuning Wizard** – Using this tool will determine if you have optimal indexes being used in your database.
- **DBCC Commands** – DBCC stands for database consistency checker, and there are quite a few very useful DBCC commands that can be used for performance tuning. These include `SHOW_STATISTICS`, which shows statistics pages for indexes to help determine why they are used/unused, and `SHOWCONTIG`, which shows how fragmented a table or an index is.

These tools only scratch the surface. There are many other methods that we can use to tune our queries, databases, and servers to obtain maximum performance. Creating indexes is always a valid thing to do to boost performance, but too many can cause real problems. Limited denormalization may be undertaken, such as dropping back a level in particular tables where there is a problem (usually associated with dropping back from Fourth Normal Form or higher), but only after some level of testing has been performed.

For a good place to get started tuning SQL Server databases consider the following books:

- *"Inside SQL Server 2000"* (Microsoft Press, ISBN 0735609985)
- *"Professional SQL Server 2000 Programming"* (Wrox Press, ISBN 1861004486)
- *"Professional ASP Data Access"* (Wrox Press, ISBN 1861003927)

Read-Only Support Databases

If our reporting needs are not real time, that is, we can allow some latency between the current data and the data that users are dealing with, then we can build a read-only database that mirrors our active databases. Users who need to run expensive queries against the data could then utilize this read-only database. Depending on how the database is utilized (and after we have loaded the data into the database), it is possible to set the database as read-only by using the following:

```
EXEC sp_dboption '<databaseName>', 'read only', 'true'
```

We can then flip the switch back to writeable mode whenever we need to load more data into the database (though it isn't possible to set it to read-only when you wish to refresh the database). Setting the database to read-only has a very great benefit of telling SQL Server that it does not actually have to use locks on database resources, since no one can make changes to the data or structures of the database. Basically, we try to do all writes to the read-only database when no users want to read the data.

Chapter 14

The question to answer before we go any further is: "Why build a read-only database?

The answers to this question are one or all of the following:

1. To maximize concurrency in our user database systems
2. To maximize performance on a set of queries
3. To consolidate data from multiple sources

The bottom line is, that whilst all of our data ought to have had its original home in a proper normalized OLTP database, there are situations where this will definitely not be the case:

- **Legacy databases** – mainframes are classically referred to as legacy systems, but as the years begin to pass since the mini and even PC platform began developing server platforms, we can get legacy databases based on any platform.
- **User databases** – unfortunately, not all databases are built on a database server. Many exist as Access, Foxpro, or other database platforms.
- **Other** – categorized as other because there are too many to mention. Spreadsheets, text files, and many other ways of storing data may be in use in a particular organization, and required for entry into the read-only systems.

Once we have transformed the data from our databases into the read-only system, we get the following benefits:

- **Limited contention** – since all users of the database will be unable to modify the data, there is very little chance of concurrent users locking the same piece of data from one another. Whenever we can guarantee that no process will write to the database, we can set the database to read-only and no locks will be able to run. If we have a continuously updating system, we could run reports in the repeatable read isolation level which will mean we need never worry about an outside process changing the results of our reports as we run them. Note, of course, that we cannot eliminate contention within our hardware subsystem, or indeed loading methods, since whatever portion of the data is being copied from our OLTP system will be blocked to users whilst the transfer is taking place.
- **Fast performance** – depending on the situation, specific queries in our user database can be optimized, or if desired, we can move all querying out of the user databases. Bear in mind that greater performance benefits will be attained when the read-only databases do not reside on the same server as the user databases.

In the following section we will look at a few possibilities for structuring our read-only database, discuss the effect on performance, give a few tips on implementing the solution, and finally, a few examples of how to employ such databases in the real world. It should be noted that we are not going to the level of data warehouse or data mart (implemented in OLAP) in our discussions. Instead, we are looking at more generic solutions to immediate problems as we discussed in Chapter 9, such as heavy use clients, *ad hoc* reporting of current data, and ODSs. Read activity is a very important part of allowing our OLTP system to stay as normalized as possible, by taking load off our servers and especially by reducing contention between readers and writers.

Modeling the Transformation

In this section we will use the following set of four simple tables for illustrative purposes:

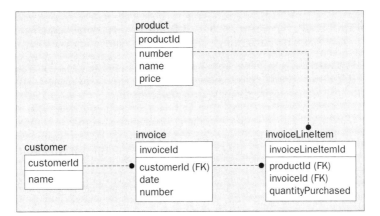

It should be obvious that it is a simplified model of an invoice system, and that we have, for example, ignored the fact that the price value will change over time. However, this set of tables will serve as an illustration of a common system from which reports need to be generated. In reality, we may have a much more complex situation like this:

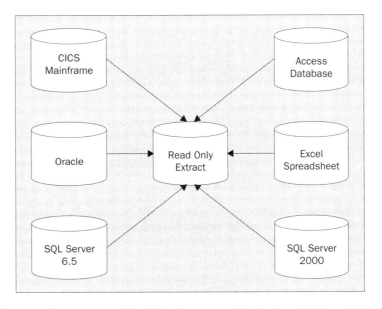

Which means that your data store could pull data from more that just one database. Note that I included an Excel spreadsheet on the diagram – this is not a mistake! It is not uncommon for a spreadsheet to become the "home" of a piece of data especially where there isn't the technical expertise to create and administer a database. Note of course that we aren't advocating the use of spreadsheets as data stores, simply admitting that it does happen frequently. Fortunately, we can import data from almost anywhere either by using Data Transformation Services, building ADO clients, or by utilizing some of the functions in SQL Server that we have discussed.

Modeling a read-only system is the same as the task of modeling the OLTP database, except that we can largely ignore normalization rules. There are two methods that I have found useful for performing this task. One is very pragmatic and the other is an open-ended solution that allows a more free form perusing of the data:

- **Table Oriented** – A very open method of building a reporting database, where every important table that does not simply contain domain data is represented.

- **Solution Oriented** – If we have a very specific problem to solve, there is generally no need to take as drastic an approach as the previous method. We will discuss why we might want to just include what is necessary to meet a particular need.

Bear in mind, that as always, I am not stating that these are the only methods for doing this sort of operation. The methods listed here are intended to be as much food-for-thought as they are precise solutions to a particular problem. Since we are looking at read-only databases, the only requirement is that the data in the database matches the source data in value at some recognized point in time. Beyond that, structure is of lesser concern, precisely because the data is not modified, except by system processes, isolated from the user.

Table Oriented

What we will endeavour to do is to take a copy of our OLTP database and expand each entity so that it includes as much data from parent tables as possible. In our example scenario, the invoice table has the customer table as a parent, and the invoiceLineItem table has invoice and customer on one path, and product on another. In this case, the essence and definition of the invoiceLineItem table includes both the definition of what was purchased and the invoice, customer and product.

There are benefits to this approach, as any time a user wants to see an invoiceLineItem they will usually want to know which customer purchased it. Hence we include a reference to the customer in the invoiceLineItem table. One concept in this scenario does not change, in that every attribute of an object must describe the object, even if only indirectly. Since we will include customer information in the invoice line item, we are clearly breaking normalization rules, though the values in the table do actually describe something about the invoice line item, namely the customer who purchased it.

We can also include additional columns for summary data that pertains to the object. If we want to store the sum total of all invoice items, then we store it in the invoice table, and not the invoiceLineItem table. The goal is not to totally eliminate joins, but to have as few as possible in order to maintain a reasonable logical structure whilst maximizing our overall performance.

> *One additional concern must be mentioned. Disk space. Our disk space needs for such a database, fully expanded into the final format, will be large and in some cases may actually be prohibitive depending on the size of the source data. Obviously the entire system would not have to be done this way if only small parts were required for queries.*

The first step is to walk down our relationship trees and move attributes down. From our example diagram, we work from top to bottom, starting with invoice, adding the parent fields like so:

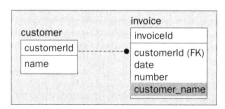

Completing the Project

`customer_name` is now a part of the `invoice` table, since the invoice is for a customer. The `customerId` column already exists in the `invoice` table, so no need to do anything there. The next step is to look at the `invoiceLineItemTable`. We include the attributes of the `invoice` and `product` tables and come to:

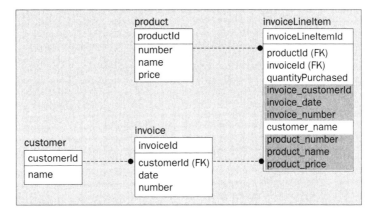

The next step is to take any values on which we might need to perform calculations or string concatenation operations, and add a field to contain the result. In the `invoiceLineItem` table, we have a `quantityPurchased` column as well as a `product_price` column, and we would want to multiply together the values of these fields to find the value of the line item, so we add a column to hold this value:

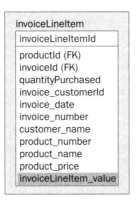

The last step is to go back up the chain and summarize all children. In this case, we can take the `invoice` to `invoiceLineItem` relationship and summarize all products on an invoice:

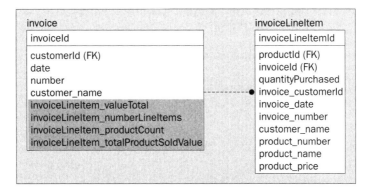

553

Take for example the `invoiceLineItem_valueTotal` column. This will be filled with the summation of all `invoiceLineItem_value` (`quantityPurchased * productPrice`) columns for a given invoice. The `invoiceLineItem_numberLineItems` would be the total count of line items.

We do the same for `product`, and then `customer`, to arrive at the following diagram:

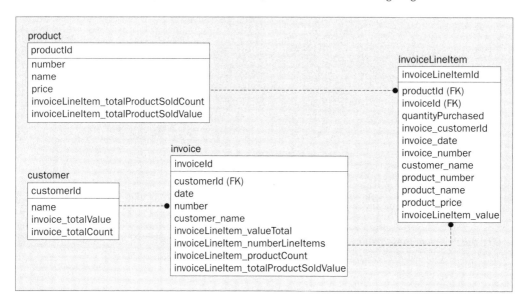

There are a few benefits of this approach.

- **Ease of use** – Since all related data is in the same table, having a user or programmer build a report using a tool such as Seagate Crystal Reports is relatively easy.

- **Recognizable data** – Users will know the names of the tables, and the fields within the tables, since we have gone to great lengths to make sure that we have named our objects in a way that is meaningful to them.

- **Useful summary data** – The goal is to simply try to push data down the tree to eliminate joins. What this does is to place all of the data that we will need at one level in the relational hierarchy of the database.

- **Relatively easy to implement** – In most cases we perform simple queries that include one or more children and one or more parents. This is not to oversimplify of course, as everything will depend heavily on how complex your database structures are.

For example, to load the `product` table, we could run the following code:

```
INSERT orderReport.dbo.product (productId, number, name, price,
                                invoiceLineItem_totalProductSoldCount,
                                invoiceLineItem_totalProductSoldValue)
    SELECT product.productId, product.number, product.name, product.price,
        SUM(invoiceLineItem.quantityPurchased)
            AS invoiceLineItem_totalProductSoldCount,
        SUM(product.price * invoiceLineItem.quantityPurchased)
            AS invoiceLineItem_totalProductSoldValue
```

Completing the Project

```
FROM order..product AS product
JOIN order..invoiceLineItem AS invoiceLineItem
    ON product.productId = invoiceLineItem.productId
GROUP BY product.productId, product.numnber, product.name, product.price
```

Not every answer will be readily available, but we are basically trying to allow *ad hoc* reporting by making the data output easier for the user to understand. This is possible because we have removed all hierarchy from the data model and have put the data right where the user needs it. For example, if we want to know the total value of product number 'XYY43233' that was invoiced in January 2001 to `customerId` 10, we might simply code a SELECT from a single table:

```
SELECT sum(invoiceLineItem_value)
FROM invoiceLineItem
WHERE invoice_customerId = 10
   AND invoice_date < 'Feb 1 2001'
   AND invoice_date >= 'Jan 1 2001'
   AND product_number = 'XYY43233'
```

Alternatively we could transform the data, pre-aggregating difficult values, and (once we have moved the data to the read-only database), consider using views to perform any reasonably simple calculations. This will certainly lower the coding needed to set up this read-only database system, as well as reducing the data space requirements. Using views in this way may prove more efficient than coding, whilst also allowing more flexibility if the reporting requirements change at some future date.

Solution Oriented

The solution-oriented method of creating a read-only database is easier to explain than the table-oriented method. In some cases we simply need a way to get certain data faster than we can retrieve it from our OLTP database, and we can build a solution oriented extract of our data to do so.

Instead of building the entire database model as we did previously, we could decide to provide answers to a very specific set of questions. Take, for example, a report of customers and the products purchased by them in the past week, month and year. Using the same database illustration from the previous example, we could build a query using nothing but the `invoiceLineItem` table, and if we do decide to build a full table-based database as before, we could create an additional table to handle this situation.

However, consider a situation where a query takes forty minutes to execute from the original OLTP database, and the sales staff need this data at their fingertips quickly and efficiently. In this case we may simply want to build a table like this:

customerProduct
customerId
productId
customer_name
product_name
product_price
product_number
week_quantityPurchased
week_valuePurchased
month_quanityPurchased
month_valuePurchased
year_quanityPurchased
year_valuePurchased
build_date

At the most basic level, the table will contain the answer to their query. Here, we have intersected the `customer` and `product` tables, and provided data for the product sales for the past week, month and year. This model is extendable in that if a requirement was made such that a user wanted to summarize on types of products, we could add a field for type, but unless we are dealing with tens of thousands of products, it is probably fine to allow summation by grouping on the type of product.

We include the ID columns as the primary key, in order that this table can be linked to the original OLTP. In addition to this summary table, the user might need more detailed customer information, in which case we can add a child table to supply this information.

The place that I use this kind of summary data the most often has nothing to do with sales but rather web content, like to serve up a set of pages personalized to a user type. The normalized internals of a web content database may be extremely ugly, yet we must maintain a very high level of concurrency when presenting pages, as well as letting the user do whatever he or she wants with the OLTP data they require. Once the content is prepared, say for a corporate front page of a site, a read-only version of the data might be built to support the web site.

What we end up with here is a very denormalized database, possibly containing one single table. So while it is similar to the table-based solution, in this case we have fewer tables (and so a smaller subset of data) and each of these tables are oriented around a specific query rather than around an identifiable object.

Performance

As with the OLTP system, we again have to consider performance when creating our read-only database, but this time we do want to make a pre-emptive strike, in that we not only performance guess, but we take it to the extreme and cover any and all scenarios for database use. Since the consistency of the read-only data is handled by the transformation subsystems, all we need to care about is making the reporting run fast. In this section we will look at two of the most important issues for the read-only system, hardware and indexes.

Hardware

As this topic was covered in the previous chapter, we will just remind you of the importance of not skimping on hardware when building the read-only system. It may even be advantageous to have a separate server to house the data, depending on the size of your operation. If we physically locate the read-only data on the same server as the one running the OLTP database, while we will reduce contention within the database, we can still end up with hardware contention. Even if you have built the best disk subsystem possible, you may still have to purchase an extra server due to processor limitations in simultaneously handling users running long reports and other users trying to update the OLTP master database.

Indexes

In building a read-only database, indexes are intrinsically part of the design, especially as we allow true *ad hoc* querying of the data. Since the read-only database will be updated infrequently, putting in too many indexes is unlikely to be a major problem. This of course depends on the actual size of the database, since if you have a terabyte in your read-only system, it may not be feasible to do what I am suggesting here.

In the *ad hoc* environment, one strategy that will give great benefits is to index every column individually in your table. Consider our example of the `invoiceLineItem` table we built for our table-oriented extract:

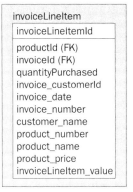

On this table we would build indexes on all of the columns individually. This will allow the optimizer to choose to use any or several of the indexes on the table to perform the query, using a covered query.

> *A covered query is one where SQL Server does not have to look into the actual tables to get the data it needs. Since the nodes of the index contain the data that is needed to build the index, if we only reference columns in an index or indexes, SQL Server will never have to read from the actual data.*

Note that we can even include indexes on columns that it might otherwise seem silly to index. Take the case of a column that contains gender ("M", "F"). This is generally considered a horrible index for finding values. However, if we want to see how many male or female values are in a table, we can perform a covered query on the gender index, and thereby only access the gender column. This will save large amounts of IO because it will be a very thin index, and is certainly more efficient than touching all data pages, especially in the read-only expansions of our tables.

Take for example, a query to access the `invoiceLineItem` table:

```
SELECT sum(invoiceLineItem_value)
FROM invoiceLineItem
WHERE invoice_customerId = 10
    AND invoice_date < 'Feb 1 2001'
    AND invoice_date >= 'Jan 1 2001'
    AND product_number = 'XYY43233'
```

From the `invoiceLineItem` table we have only accessed the `invoiceLineItem_value`, the `invoice_customerId`, the `invoice_date` and the `product_number` columns. By having an index on each column we have given SQL Server the chance to decide what the best first step is, by using the index statistics to ask a few simple questions:

- How many rows will I get back from `invoice_customerId = 10`?
- How many rows will I get back from `invoice_date < 'Feb 1 2001'` and `invoice_date >= 'Jan 1 2001'`?
- How many rows will I get back from `product_number = 'XYY43233'`?
- How expensive will it be to go get the `invoiceLineItem_value` value from the table rather than from the index?

557

The optimizer will not only choose the best plan, but also determine whether we have one invoice or a million between the specified dates, as well as the likelihood of a row even existing with the specified `product_number`. We don't do this in our OLTP database due to the large overhead in maintaining the indexes, but we presume that in most cases we will do our writes to the read-only database when no users want to read the data.

Latency

Latency in this case refers to the amount of time it takes for a piece of data to be created before it is available in our database. In this section we will look at the factors surrounding the latency of our read-only database.

Determining Build Frequency

Determining how often to update the read-only database depends on several factors, which are explained in the following list. We should make it clear that because financial and network resources are limited, in practice you'll never be able to reach the ideal of instant updates.

- **How often the user needs it** – if the data is needed immediately, then we may have to pull out all the stops to get it there as rapidly as possible.

- **How busy the OLTP server actually is** – if the server is used to store measurements from manufacturing robots, or to handle online orders, it may not be feasible to analyze the data immediately due to the load on the database servers.

- **Connection Properties** – depending on the connection speed, competing demands on our bandwidth, and the relative proximity of the OLTP system to the read-only version, it may not be reasonable to move massive amounts of data across the network during business hours.

- **Connection Status** – When it comes to some clients who receive the extracts, they may not even be able to connect to the server except on demand. This might include a Pocket PC or laptop user who gets a copy of the data from the server.

- **Data size** – the quantity of important data in a system varies from a few records to terabytes of data. If we consider an OLTP system with 200 gigabytes of data, we might not be able to extract the whole database, but it will certainly be possible to extract and aggregate a certain amount of data for faster use. Data size brings up the unfortunate truth that the more that we need to take the additional steps to build a read-only database, the harder it actually becomes to implement. In some cases we may be able to carry out incremental updates, as there is rarely a need to ship the entire database every time.

- **Availability of resources** – if you can only afford a base level server, it may actually hurt more to spend the time transforming the OLTP data into a read-only database, rather than carrying out some denormalization of the OLTP data in the same database and building stored procedures/views as necessary.

I would like to build you a matrix of the factors surrounding latency, but I can't. There is no single function or set of functions that we can use to decide what to do and when. The interplay between these factors is complex and each project must be treated individually in determining update frequency, though the individual user's needs come first wherever possible.

Implementation

Implementation of read-only databases is much easier to deal with than OLTP databases. We have three facilities readily available to us for transforming the data from the OLTP database.

- **DTS** – A powerful tool for transforming data from one form to another. It allows for graphical transformation of the data, as well as the use of scripting languages (VBScript, JavaScript) in the transformations.

- **Stored Procedures** – We can write queries that take data in one form and insert it as rows into the new database. For many jobs this is the cleanest and fastest way to build the transformations, especially when they operate between databases on the same server.

- **Replication** – Used as a tool to replicate data from database to database, a really neat manner of implementing the transformation is by using **stored procedure replication**. In this manner we can publish one database to another, overriding the typical SQL inserts, updates, and deletes for replication and using stored procedures instead. In the read-only database, we can build stored procedures to handle each situation where a record or table is modified and have the data in the summary tables change accordingly. A drawback to this plan is that we must still implement the initialization stored procedures which can be really tricky, since instead of doing clean transformations, we have to add to or subtract from summaries.

  As an example let's say that we have a running total on the `customer` table of all purchases that have been made. We would need to code an `INSERT` stored procedure that increments the value of the running total. For a `DELETE`, we would decrement the value, and for a modifying `UPDATE` command, we would have to subtract the previous value and add the new value.

  We can also use replication as our distribution agent to re-distribute the entire extracted database to all users.

  For more information on both DTS and Replication we refer the reader to "Professional SQL Server 2000 DTS" (Wrox Press, ISBN 1861004419) and "Professional SQL Server 2000 Programming" (Wrox Press, ISBN 1861004486).

With each of these tools, you can create extracts to suit a variety of needs. Let's consider a situation where we have an order processing establishment in Nashville, and a headquarters in New York. Whilst orders are both taken and invoiced in Nashville, the corporate headquarters, to which reports summarizing sales are sent, is located in New York. Since the headquarters in New York does not have enough space to house any of the primary corporate computers, the following design is devised:

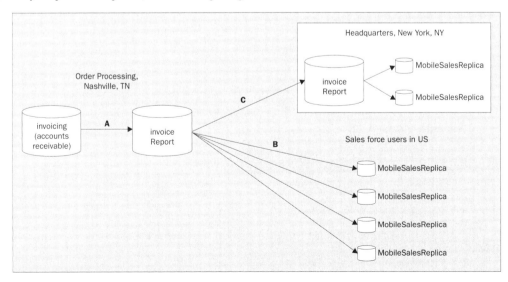

We have three separate problems to deal with in turn:

- **Transforming the data (A)** – We have to take the normalized data and turn it into the extract.

- **Loading the data onto lightweight clients (B)** – This is unlikely to entail loading all the data onto the client; but rather a very small, very specific data set that enables the user to do his job better.

- **Loading the data from one physical plant to another (C)** – With our business becoming more and more globalized, we need to be able to transport our data across a network.

We will now go on to look at each of these concerns individually.

Transforming the Data

To transform the data from the original normalized format, there are two possible courses of action:

- **Wipe and start again** – Anytime we build a read-only database, we always have to create a method of initially loading the database. If transformations are required, we will have to synchronize the database with the OLTP database's current state. If the size of the data is reasonably small and there is a period of time when usage of the database is low, we can simply delete the data and start over. This is the easiest method to use when you need to create a daily extract.

- **Transactionally using replication procedures** – If we must keep the data updated frequently, or the data is too large to handle by wiping and synchronizing, we can write replication procedures to maintain the data in the database.

As an example, let's code a procedure from our four-table example, and look at what we will have to do when a new `invoiceLineItem` record is inserted. We will not only have to insert a new `invoiceLineItem`, but also update the `product` table, as well as the other tables up the relationship chains:

```
CREATE PROCEDURE invoiceLineItem$replInsert
(
    @invoiceLineItemId int,
    @productId int,
    @invoiceId int,
    @quantityPurchased int,
) AS

--transaction and error handling not present for clarity

INSERT INTO invoiceLineItem (invoiceLineItemId, productId, invoiceId,
    quantityPurchased, Invoice_customerId,
    invoice_date, invoice_number,
    customer_name, product_number, product_name,
    product_price, invoiceLineItem_value)
SELECT @invoiceLineItemId, @productId, @invoiceId,
    @quantityPurchased, Invoice.customerId,
    invoice.date, invoice_number,
    customer.name, product.number, product.name,
    product.price, invoice.quantityPurchased * @quantityPurchased
FROM invoice
    JOIN customer
```

```
        ON customer.customerId = invoice.customerId
        ON @invoiceId = invoice.invoiceId
        --cross join is used because in a normal query we would join
        --these two sets to the invoiceLineItem table, which is represented
        --by the variable values, guaranteeing a cartesian product of two
        --single rows, which return a single row.
        CROSS JOIN product
        ON product.productId = @productId

    UPDATE product
        --add the quantity purchased to the products sold count
    SET invoiceLineItem_totalProductSoldCount =
        invoiceLineItem_totalProductSoldCount + @quantityPurchased,
        --add the quantity purchased * price to the products sold value
        invoiceLineItem_totalProductSoldValue =
        invoiceLineItem_totalProductSoldValue +
        price * @quantityPurchased,
    WHERE productId = @productId

    --same type of thing for invoice and product

    GO
```

Note that we won't do any summarizing, since we only insert a row at a time. However, we have to offset the amounts that are inserted. In general, this should run pretty fast. Unfortunately this may actually be more costly than deleting all the data and summarizing it again for data sets subject to constant change (these are generally smaller in nature). It may be best to try out simply truncating the data and adding it back to start with, since this requires much less effort on our behalf.

Loading the Data onto Lightweight Clients

Lightweight clients are those working with either laptops or PDAs. The best method for implementing an "on demand" client when working with disconnected clients is to implement **pull replication subscription** (since we do not have control over when and where they will connect from). This allows the client to connect whenever they want, and in much the same way as a mail program calls to the server to get our e-mail, SQL Server on the client calls the main server and requests any changes. This type of replication can also be used in cases when we need to update rows in other tables.

Loading the Data from One Physical Plant to Another

In this case **transactional replication** (where every transaction that is applied to one database will be used for replication) would be the way to go, with as much latency as the client can allow, or at the very least, tuned to happen primarily when loads are lowest on the servers.

> Note that any type of replication uses the transaction log to do the synchronization, so if you have made many changes to any of the databases and want to replicate them, the transaction log will continue to grow until the Distribution or Merge Agent has been able to apply all of the log entries to the target database.

Uses

We will take the opportunity here to briefly list a few possible uses of read-only databases:

- **Simple Reporting Needs** – simple here refers to single database type report extracts.

- ❑ **Operational Data Store** – The database where we consolidate data from all our external sources.
- ❑ **Web sites** – since most of the content from a web site is read only, any of the content that users need can be transformed from normalized structures into a format which is tailored to any particular site.
- ❑ **Laptop computers** – We might wish to factor in users of portable computers (who may be carrying around copies of sales figures or even actuarial tables), so that they have instant access to the latest figures.

Obviously the sky's the limit in this case. By separating the heavy readers of the data from the heavy writers, we give both sets of users a tremendous boost in performance. We will now take a deeper look at a couple of read-only database uses:

Simple Reporting Needs

Note that when I say simple I am referring neither to the queries that we can support, nor the complexity of reports, but rather to the work involved in setting up the reporting. In general, we will create our reporting databases from a single database. This is a fairly common use of read-only databases, since with only a small amount of work, we can give the user what they need in order to answer questions, without fear of their accidentally modifying something in the primary system.

Generally we can go down two paths in this case. We can support particular reports that the user needs, much like we did in the `customerProduct` table earlier:

We do this by removing all joins and giving them a report that they can customize the parameters on. Since most reports are based on a single result set of information, this works really well for less knowledgeable clients with very specific needs.

If we have more knowledgeable clients, however, then we could implement something closer to the table based solution we developed previously.

English Query

A tool for *ad hoc* reporting that I wanted to make sure you have heard of is **English Query**. It is a product that ships with SQL Server (since version 6.5) and is used to put a very natural language interface on a SQL Database, by translating a question such as:

What was the total value of EPROMs that was invoiced to Bob's electronics last year?

into a native SQL call to our extract table above:

```
SELECT sum(invoiceLineItem_value)
FROM invoiceLineItem
WHERE product_name = 'X'
    AND customer_name = 'Bob''s electronics'
    AND invoice_date >= 'jan 1, 2000'
    AND invoice_date < 'jan 1, 2001'
```

Of course it would also work against OLTP databases as well, and could create the following query:

```
SELECT sum(invoice.quantityPurchased * @quantityPurchased)
FROM invoiceLineItem
    JOIN invoice
    JOIN customer
    ON customer.customerId = invoice.customerId
    ON invoiceLineItem.invoiceId = invoice.invoiceId
    JOIN product
    ON product.productId = invoiceLineItem.productId
WHERE product.name = 'X'
    AND customer.name = 'Bob''s electronics'
    AND invoice.date >= 'jan 1, 2000'
    AND invoice.date < 'jan 1, 2001'
```

If this sounds like magic, it is not. There is a very detailed Semantic Modeling Format (which is an XML based language) that we must use to store a "model" of the database with descriptors for every table, attribute, and relationships, so that *total value* and *were invoiced* in our question can be turned into both of the above queries, in different databases. We would, of course, have to model the entire database that we wanted English Query to recognize in order for it to be able to perform these queries.

For more information on English Query we refer the reader to "Professional SQL Server 2000 Programming" (Wrox Press, ISBN 1861004486).

Operational Data Store

This is a database where we take all of the data from any (and possibly all) of our databases, as illustrated in the following diagram:

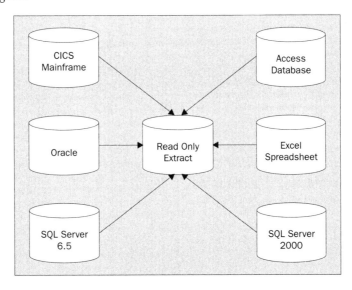

Chapter 14

It is the database where we consolidate data from all of our external data sources. In the ODS, we will employ many of the normalization (and for reporting, some denormalization) techniques that we have used to build our OLTP database, in order to create a reasonably up-to-date set of data. This will allow us to make decisions which will enable the overall business organization to run more efficiently.

The ODS will contain a model that is pretty much like our OLTP database, with some degree of denormalization. The goal is not to build one ODS per OLTP database, rather it is to merge organizational data from ALL corporate sources into a common storage, fully cleaned and with common data matched to common data. For example, say we have two databases, one out-of-box, and one in-house developed, with each database employed by different business units. Not surprisingly, each database has a vendor table filled with vendors that each unit does business with.

The first step to take is to model each of the source databases using common terms. For example, we may have two databases that each models the vendor tremendously differently:

Either:

Or:

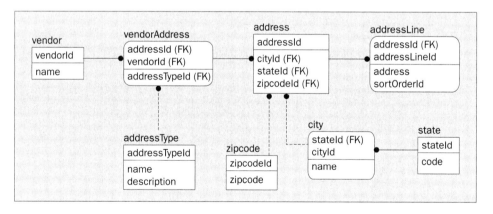

In the case of these tables, the path to take would likely be to build our ODS model using the normalized structures and transform the data from the first structure into the second. The distressingly difficult part of building the ODS is merging existing databases. Thinking back to the first chapter, we had this diagram:

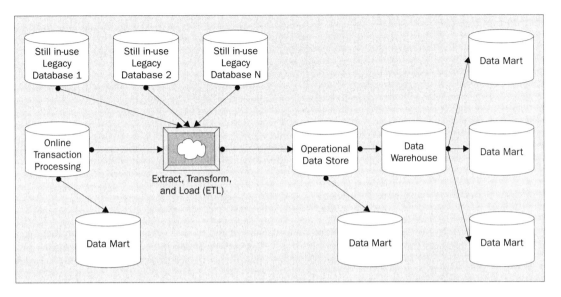

All data flows through this ETL cleaning cycle to get the data from each database matched up with the corresponding data from the other databases. In the final ODS, we will want to store the data in exactly the same manner for every instance of it, so if we have ten vendor tables in ten different databases (or spreadsheets, or whatever data storage is in use) and we have five different spellings of the name 'Joe's Fish Market' ('Joe''s Fish Market', 'joes phish markt', 'joe fish', and 'joe market') which all represent the same fish market, we consolidate the contents from all these rows into the same row in our ODS.

Obviously I have not given you enough information to build a complete ODS; rather I have tried to provide sufficient information for the reader to begin to ruminate on how to start the build process.

Enterprise Data Models

The concept is relatively straightforward. An **Enterprise Data Model** is a model that will show us every table and every relationship in every database that we deal with. In this way it allows the architect to have a complete overview of all the data that the corporation uses. Sounds like a good idea. Unfortunately achieving a perfect Enterprise Data Model would be amazing.

In our Case Study system that we have been building throughout the book, we have nearly twenty tables in order to perform a very small function. Now consider a corporation of almost any size and how much more complex its banking system would be, containing, for argument's sake, around two hundred tables. Then note that most corporations have more than one database that they have created, and several more management systems that they have purchased from vendors, that in many cases require interfaces from other systems. This can lead us to a system such as is shown schematically in the next diagram:

Chapter 14

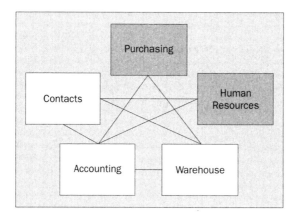

The darkened rectangles denote systems that have purchased, and the lines represent where an interface is built. Each of these systems will require hundreds of tables in their own right, and we have probably built several tables to support each communication between them. The goal of an enterprise model is to fuse all of the models into one "grand model", where we can see all of the interactions and get a clear picture of what we have and how they interact. This is no a simple task, whatsoever, for several reasons:

- **Sheer volume of the data** – Suppose that our example above contains one thousand tables.
- **Proprietary nature of third-party systems** – Even some of the best third-party tool developers feel the need to hide the implementation details of their systems from prying eyes. The business case for such schemes aside, it makes understanding/using the data next to impossible.
- **Multiple database server types** – SQL Server 4.2, 6.5, 7.0, 2000; Oracle 6, 7, 8; Informix; etc. leave us confused as to exactly what is going on in the server.
- **Fluctuations in the model** – Keeping a data model synchronized with a single database is a pretty steep task without very strict rules governing who can change it.
- **Cost** – considering the rest of the bulleted points, this operation can be quite expensive.

We can remove some of these issues by deciding to simply implement a logical enterprise model, quite possibly removing proprietary systems from our view, and including only the interface tables (either ones we create to interface with processes, or actual system tables that we care about). This leads us to a totally different problem, namely that of ensuring that the logical model for one database squares with its physical model. A further complication is that some of the systems that we will create may include multiple "modules" of a given system, such as an accounting system:

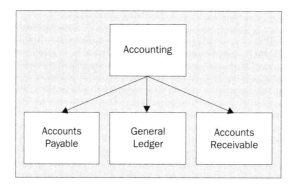

566

Completing the Project

The goal of any section in this book is to outline a situation, a description of the problem, and then suggest what to do about it. In this case, the answer is not easy. The only way to keep a logical model in sync with the physical model and more importantly, the physical implementation, is by being disciplined. The only way to take the smaller models and build an enterprise model is again through discipline. Fixed processes must be in place to take code from the on-paper stage to the built stage.

Changes to the database schema need to follow some process such as:

- Create or modify the logical model to contain all of the data that it currently needs to store.
- Update the physical model to reflect these changes in the manner decided.
- Make changes to physical structures.
- Update the enterprise model to reflect the current status of the system every time anything changes.

How to actually turn the goal of an enterprise model into reality will depend heavily on what tools you use to model your data and enterprise. It is critical to find the right modeling tool and repositories, which will allow you to build the model and maintain it over time as your situation changes.

Moving From a Test Environment

When developing software, we have to be realistic. Our design will never be perfect, and neither will the coding. If it were, we could just develop new software, then hand it over to users and move to the next project. The second reality is that once the users have had an opportunity to use the software, there will be changes required. Typically, there is an iterative process which we use to develop databases, involving three key stages:

- Development
- Quality Assurance
- Production

Each environment plays a fundamental part in the process of getting code created, tested, and utilized by users. The goal is to have a process where our code moves through a series of phases that appear like:

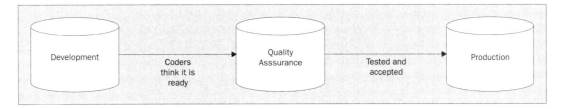

Code starts in the Development database, then moves into Quality Assurance (QA), and finally into Production. While this is the goal, it is certainly not reality. It is almost impossible to develop a system of any complexity and not find any errors. Usually, at a minimum, the process is more like:

Chapter 14

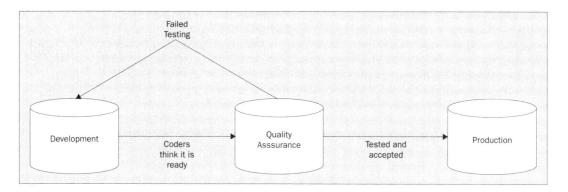

And realistically, we could draw lines from every database to every other database. However, when bugs are located in Production, in most cases we still have to go through this same cycle of developing code, testing the code for quality and finally into Production.

In addition to this three-phase model, it is common to have a Pre-Production phase in between QA and Production, depending on the importance of the system. We may also have two or more QA databases for different types of testing (load testing, user acceptance testing, validity testing to determine that all algorithms are proper) again based on the system and requirements. Some organizations will need to have multiple development areas to maintain different versions of the code to support the Production system that the users are currently using, and another for a new version.

However, we will be looking at this in more of a minimal fashion, as no matter how many actual systems you have to deal with, you will have the same areas to contend with.

Development

This is the environment in which we will build our databases to start with (and what we have assumed throughout the text so far). In this area, we should not have any users or testers, but rather we have the architects, DBAs, user interface programmers, database coders etc. testing out and creating new code.

Development Hardware

The hardware for Development should be minimal, but reasonable. If your test server is as powerful as your Production database servers, the developers will tend to try to use every bit of it to solve the problem, and it will be very hard to discover that you are going to have any kind of tuning issues with the data once it moves to Production. The same kind of thing is true when it comes to networking bandwidth. If you are building a WAN application with a 2 Mbit connection between client and server, and you are building your applications on a 100 Mbit network, it can be difficult to develop the proper solution.

Bear in mind, however, that the server should not be so slow as to impede process. Finding the proper balance for a Development environment is a difficult task, and it is probably better to err on the side of too much hardware. This decision must also be tempered with the knowledge that most test servers are not simply used for one database system and end up chock full of databases, both developing new software and testing out new versions of vendor built software.

Quality Assurance

Once software (or parts of the software) has been developed to a level where it is supposed to be ready to be given to users, it must be tested. The QA environment is used as a proving ground in several ways:

- **Quality testing** – Ensuring that the software (database and code that accesses the database, like the UI) performs as the programmers advertise, as well as checking that the system meets the users' needs. This will include testing the validity of the system (that all algorithms are correct) security audits, and basically that every thing works.
- **Load testing** – Used to put the software through a realistic (and in many cases beyond realistic) load to see if it can handle the loads it will be exposed to in Production.
- **Acceptance Testing** – Before the user can begin to utilize the new database or certain changes in it, the users will typically have to approve of the software that has been written, in order to agree that it does everything that was on the initial specification.

QA Hardware

The key to the right level of QA hardware is scale. Not every organization will be able to completely duplicate the hardware of their Production servers, as the server(s) may end up costing a large percentage of the entire budget for the system being developed. However, consider it this way. If the entire QA system is 10 per cent as powerful as the Production one, we should be able to handle 10 times as much activity on the Production system. Note of course, that rarely will we be able to scale every part of our system to exactly the same levels, but a great administrator should be able to approximate the process and get a reasonable scale factor for testing.

Minimal hardware is required for the other task of QA, which is to make sure that what has been developed meets specifications. During such testing the stress testing hardware will more than suffice for running test scripts that identify inputs to processes/procedures and corresponding proper values, as well as application testing.

Production

The Production environment is where the user actually uses the database. Once we have promoted code from Development, through the QA process, in theory, it should be bug-free (of course, in practice it generally takes a few cycles through the Development to QA path to get it close to bug-free). Whilst setting up the Production database is not the Data Architect's job, in my experience, the Data Architect *is* often involved with specifying how this system is used and maintained (especially in smaller organizations) and can take a good amount of blame if the proper database and hardware are not specified.

In Chapter 13, we gave a basic introduction to some of the hardware issues that you will face, as well as some formulas/stored procedures that we can use to help assist with the database sizing issues. We also calculated the sizes (and projections of future sizes) of the data that will be stored in our database. In most cases, this will be entirely the job of the DBA, but it is critical that you understand the basics, as not all DBAs understand hardware fully, and in many cases there may not even be a dedicated DBA, so you may have to participate in a request for hardware for a database system.

Chapter 14

Maintenance and Disaster Recovery Plans

While we will not be looking at how to back up databases, we do need to discuss a few of the important factors to consider when the system gets moved towards Production. Generally, this kind of information would likely be specified when the Data Architect has nearly finished the job. There are two areas of concern here; maintenance and disaster recovery, and there is a difference.

For both a maintenance plan and a disaster recovery plan, we are out to save ourselves from simple hardware and software problems like UPS failures (uninterruptible power supply, basically a battery backup), and hard disk crashes. These are relatively straightforward problems to deal with, as long as the DBA understands a few particulars:

- **Size of Data** – Using the formulas we discussed in the previous chapter, we can give projections of the size of the data based on its expected growth, as estimated at the end of the logical design phase.

- **Acceptable Loss of Data** – This one is easy! None. Of course, this is not a valid answer, as we have to accept that we will always have some window of time when there is a loss of data due to a massive system failure. However, as the acceptable risk time gets smaller, the cost of meeting this goal goes up exponentially. If we can lose a day's data, we simply have to back up every night onto some storage that is not located on the same machine. If an hour is acceptable loss, we can do the same thing with transaction logs while users are using the data, and we can eliminate almost any loss of data using clustering techniques (there is always some minimal latency that cannot be avoided). Of course clustering is far more expensive than a tape drive and with clustering you still need the tape drive. Cost, of course, is more of a matter for the client and the project manager to duke it out over.

- **Acceptable Level of Service** – This would generally be some indication of the expected load at different times during the day. It would also detail the expected/contracted uptimes that the database must be active. Of course, this sounds quite like the *Acceptable Loss of Data* bullet, as the expected level of service is full barrel, anytime the client wants it; but this is not a realistic expectation, and will not be contracted as such. To completely cover this requirement, we must also have an understanding of how long it will take to bring the servers back on line.

For a disaster recovery plan, we have to plan for "real" problems, such as hurricanes, fires, tornados, and even a blown transformer from neighboring building works. A full plan would simply be an extension of the maintenance plan, but will escalate from hardware failures to include:

- **Power failures** – Power failures are a very important concern. How many times have we heard stories about the online retailer that was down for a few hours? Not a great way to get recognition. Having a generator that will kick in well before the UPS gives way is the best way to make certain that that you will have no interruptions in service, regardless of the power supply.

- **Weather Disasters** – What if all of the power is out due to a hurricane? Or a tornado? Or even a flood? In a global economy, if your server is down for a week, you will likely be in the nightly news (or worse the financial news), and you may have sunk your company. You will probably need to have this covered with out of town servers.

- **Other Disasters** – Disasters come in all shapes and sizes, and we cannot even begin to make an exhaustive list. Building wiring faults, poorly set up systems, mice, insects, a volcano eruption, or (unfortunately) even the poorly planned software upgrade can all cause your system to be down for an unacceptable amount of time.

The last, and certainly most important, issue surrounding maintenance and disaster recovery plans is testing them. The best laid plans of mice and DBAs...or something like that. You can build the most impressive disaster recovery plan with the most impressive generator and UPSs, but if you only stock enough fuel to run the generators for a day; and subsequently an ice storm hits, taking the power out for two days, and you are not the only place that needs fuel, then your plan will be somewhat ineffectual. In the same manner, if you pull the plug on the main UPS only to discover that you cannot get the generator running in time before your UPS runs out of juice, then, in a word, ouch!

Case Study

In this final case study we find ourselves with one last remaining task to perform, that of building a reporting database. If we really were building this system, we probably would not actually build a reporting database, as our system is small with low concurrency requirements. However, for completeness we will build a table to support a specific report that we discovered in the Case Study segment in Chapter 8. It was described as:

> **User Activity** – A list of all transactions attributed to a given user, or simply grouped by user. Also needs to be able to show any transactions that have not been attributed to the user who actually spent the money.

Hence we need to get the tables related to the transaction, which are as follows:

- **transaction** – the transaction itself
- **account** – the account that the check came from
- **bank** – the bank where the account is held
- **payee** – for checks, and possibly others based on the `transactionType` table
- **user** – a list of users who are known to the system that write checks
- **transactionType** – classifies the type of transaction
- **transactionReconcile** – if a record exists in this table for the transaction, it has been reconciled

The relation between these is summarized in the figure below:

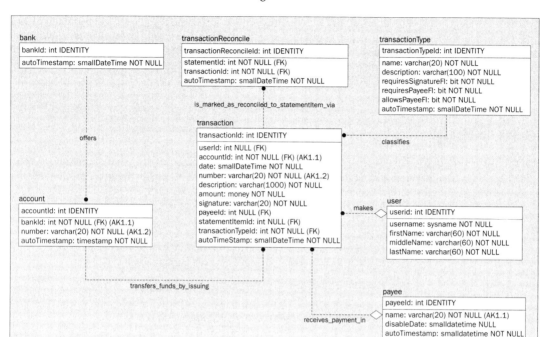

We will roll up many of the fields in these tables into a single table as follows:

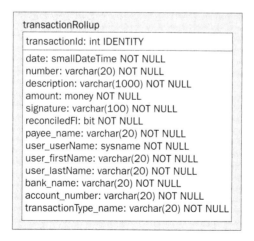

Since our system is not high access, we will simply build a stored procedure to truncate the data in the `transactionRollup` table, and replace it with the proper values. Instead of moving this table to a different database, we will choose to place it in the same database and never give users access to modify it. For smaller systems, this allows you to give users a read-only extract without needing to build an additional database.

In the following code, we build the transform procedure. While it is pretty long, it is also pretty straightforward. It simply resolves all of the joins to the parent tables of the `transaction` table:

```sql
CREATE PROCEDURE transactionRollup$transform
AS

--declare variable used for error handling in blocks
DECLARE @rowcount int, --holds the rowcount returned from dml calls
    @error int, --used to hold the error code after a dml
    @msg varchar(255), --used to preformat error messages
    @retval int, --general purpose variable for retrieving
    --return values from stored procedure calls
    @tranName sysname, --used to hold the name of the transaction
    @msgTag varchar(255) --used to hold the tags for the error message
--set up the error message tag
SET @msgTag = '<' + object_name(@@procid) + ';type=P'
    + ';keyvalue=' + '@key_bankId:'
    + convert(varchar(10),@key_bankId)

SET @tranName = object_name(@@procid) + cast(@@nestlevel as varchar(2))

BEGIN TRANSACTION
SAVE TRANSACTION @tranName

TRUNCATE TABLE transactionRollup
IF @error != 0 --an error occurred outside of this procedure
    BEGIN
    SELECT @msg = 'A problem occurred truncating the transactionRollup table'
    + @msgTag + 'call=(truncat transactionRollup)>'
    rollback TRAN @tranName
    COMMIT TRAN
    RAISERROR 50000 @msg
    RETURN -100
    END

INSERT INTO transactionRollup (transactionId, date, number, description,
    amount, signature, reconciledFl,
    payee_name, user_userName, user_firstName,
    user_middleName, user_lastName, bank_name,
    account_number, transactionType_name)
SELECT xaction.transactionId, xaction.date, xaction.number,
    xaction.description, xaction.amount, xaction.signature,

    --if the outer join to the transactionReconcile table leaves the
    --not nullable field null in the join. Hence if we check for null
    --in this field, we can tell if the record has been reconciled
    CASE WHEN transactionReconcile.transactionReconcileId IS NULL
    THEN 1
    ELSE 0
    END AS reconciledFl ,
    payee.name, user.userName, user.firstName, user.middleName,
    bank.name, account.number, transactionType.name

FROM dbo.xaction AS xaction

    --get the account and bank
    JOIN dbo.account AS account
    JOIN dbo.bank AS bank
    ON bank.bankId = account.bankId
```

```
            ON xaction.accountId = account.accountId

            --get the type of the transaction
            JOIN dbo.transactionType AS transactionType
            ON transactionType.transactionTypeId =
            xaction.transactionTypeId
            --not all transactions will have a payee
            LEFT OUTER JOIN dbo.payee AS payee
            ON payee.payeeId = xaction.payeeId

            --not all transactions have to be associated to user
            LEFT OUTER JOIN dbo.user AS user
            ON user.userId = xaction.userId

            --left outer join in case the value has not been reconciled yet
            LEFT OUTER JOIN dbo.transactionReconcile AS transactionReconcile
            ON transactionReconcile.transactionId = xaction.transactionId

        IF @error != 0 --an error occurred outside of this procedure
          BEGIN
            SELECT @msg = 'A problem occurred truncating the transactionRollup table'
            + @msgTag + 'call=(truncat transactionRollup)>'
            ROLLBACK TRAN @tranName
            COMMIT TRAN
            RAISERROR 50000 @msg
            RETURN -100
          END

        COMMIT TRANSACTION
```

Of course we have listed other tasks, such as setting up Production environments, performance tuning, etc. However, these tasks are beyond the scope of this case study, and were covered more to note their existence for times when we get called in to help specify hardware, such as when the DBA staff all land new jobs at the latest Internet start up. Having an understanding of how everything works, even if we never have to turn SQL Server's knobs and dials, is very important.

Summary

In this chapter we have considered some of the issues that we may well face at the end of our design projects, just as we are thinking about packing up and moving on to the next job.

We began by discussing the need for performance tuning, and recommended building queries and performance tuning after design. SQL Server is a great performer, so the practice of pro-actively tuning SQL Server queries, even before they have been executed once, can do more harm than good.

We then discussed all of the basics of building read-only extracts of our databases. The easy part of this task is to model what we want the data to look like, but the other tasks, such as setting up replication, using DTS, etc. are a lot more complex and involve other individuals such as the DBA. Included in this discussion was the idea of maintaining an Enterprise Model outlining all of our database resources. The most important reason to do this is to ensure that we store any one piece of data only once in a database.

Finally, we had a high level look at how to organize our development environment, utilizing a three-phase iterative process involving Development, Quality Assurance and Production. Such a cycle requires consideration of issues such as hardware, size of data and the nature of testing that we need to perform. We also looked at the need for devising both maintenance and disaster recovery plans.

Having looked at all these issues we should then be able to send the database off to the users and let them begin using our creation, whilst we proceed off into the sunset to face the next great database challenge.

Professional SQL Server 2000 Database Design

Codd's 12 Rules for an RDBMS

While most of us think that any database that supports SQL is automatically a relational database, this is not always the case, at least not completely. In Chapter 3, we discussed the basics and foundations of relational theory, but no discussion on this subject would be complete without looking at the rules that were formulated in 1985 in a two-part article published by *ComputerWorld* (Codd, E. F., *"Is Your DBMS Really Relational?"* and *"Does Your DBMS Run By the* Rules?" *ComputerWorld*, October 14 and October 21, 1985). They are also outlined at http://luna.pepperdine.edu/gsbm/class/ckettemborough/Codd12R.html and in '*Fundamentals of Database Systems' (The Benjamin Cummings Publishing Co., ISBN 0805317538)*. These rules go beyond relational theory and define a more specific set of criteria that need to be met in a RDBMS, if it is to be truly relational.

It may seem like old news, but the same criteria are still used today to measure how relational a database is. These rules are frequently brought up in conversations when discussing how well a particular database server is implemented.

We present the rules, along with brief comments as to how SQL Server 2000 meets each of them, or otherwise.

Rule 1: The Information Rule

All information in a relational database is represented explicitly at the logical level in exactly one way – by values in tables.

This rule is basically an informal definition of a relational database and indicates that every piece of data that we permanently store in a database is located in a table. In general, SQL Server 2000 fulfills this rule, as we cannot store any information in anything other than in a table. The variables used in this code cannot be used to persist any data and therefore they are scoped to a single batch.

Rule 2: Guaranteed Access Rule

Each and every datum (atomic value) in a relational database is guaranteed to be logically accessible by resorting to a table name, primary key value, and column name.

This rule basically stresses the importance of primary keys for locating data in the database. The table name locates the correct table, the column name finds the correct column, and the primary key value finds the row containing an individual data item of interest. In other words, each (atomic) piece of data is accessible by the combination of table name, primary key value, and column name. This rule exactly specifies how we access data in SQL Server. In a table, we can search for the primary key value (which is guaranteed to be unique, based on relational theory) and once we have the row, the data is accessed via the column name.

Rule 3: Systematic Treatment of NULL Values

NULL values (distinct from empty character string or a string of blank characters, and distinct from zero) are supported in the RDBMS for representing missing information in a systematic way, independent of data type.

This rule requires that the RDBMS support a distinct NULL placeholder, regardless of data type. NULLs are distinct from an empty character string or any other number, and are interpreted according to the ANSI_NULL setting. When the ANSI_NULL setting is set on, NULLs are treated properly, such that NULL + 'String Value' = NULL. If the ANSI_NULL setting is off, which is allowed for backward compatibility with SQL Server, NULLs are treated in a non-standard way such that NULL + 'String Value' = 'String Value'.

Rule 4: Dynamic Online Catalog Based on the Relational Model

The database description is represented at the logical level in the same way as ordinary data, so that authorized users can apply the same relational language to its interrogation as they apply to regular data.

This rule requires that a relational database be self-describing. In other words, the database must contain certain system tables whose columns describe the structure of the database itself, or alternatively, the database description is contained in user-accessible tables.

This rule is actually becoming more of a reality in each new version of SQL Server, with the implementation of the INFORMATION_SCHEMA system views. However, it is not exactly true because our view of the system catalog is not in a normalized form; if it was, then we could access the data in the same manner as user tables. Consequently we have to find information on the database schema by using the SQL Server system functions to mine out additional information from the catalog.

Rule 5: Comprehensive Data Sublanguage Rule

A relational system may support several languages and various modes of terminal use (for example, the fill-in-blanks mode). However, there must be at least one language whose statements are expressible, by some well-defined syntax, as character strings, and whose ability to support all of the following is comprehensible: data definition, view definition, data manipulation (interactive and by program), integrity constraints, and transaction boundaries (begin, commit, and rollback).

This rule mandates using a relational database language, such as SQL, although SQL is not specifically required. The language must be able to support all the central functions of a DBMS – creating a database, retrieving and entering data, implementing database security, and so on. Transact-SQL fulfils this function for SQL Server and carries out all the data definition and manipulation tasks required to access data.

Rule 6: View Updating Rule

All views that are theoretically updateable are also updateable by the system.

This rule deals with views, which are virtual tables used to give various users of a database different views of its structure. It is one of the most challenging rules to implement in practice, and no commercial product fully satisfies it today.

A view is theoretically updateable as long as it is made up of columns that directly correspond to real table fields. In SQL Server, views are updateable as long as you do not update more than a single table in the statement; nor can you update a derived or constant field. SQL Server 2000 also implements INSTEAD OF triggers that you can apply to a view (Chapter 11). Hence, this rule is technically fulfilled using instead-of triggers, but in a less than straightforward manner.

Rule 7: High-level Insert, Update and Delete

The capability of handling a base relation or a derived relation as a single operand applies not only to the retrieval of data but also to the insertion, update, and deletion of data.

This rule stresses the set-oriented nature of a relational database. It requires that rows be treated as sets in insert, delete, and update operations. The rule is designed to prohibit implementations that only support row-at-a-time, navigational modification of the database. This is covered in the SQL language via the INSERT, UPDATE and DELETE statements.

Rule 8: Physical Data Independence

Application programs and terminal activities remain logically unimpaired whenever any changes are made in either storage representation or access methods.

Applications must still work using the same syntax, even when changes are made to the way in which the database internally implements data storage and access methods. This rule is tougher to implement than other rules, and implies that the way the data is stored physically must be independent of the logical manner in which it is accessed. This is saying that users should not be concerned about how the data is stored or how it is accessed. For example:

- **Adding indexes** – indexes determine how the data is actually stored, yet the user, through SQL, will never know that indexes are being used.
- **Modifications to the storage engines** – from time to time Microsoft will obviously have to modify how SQL Server operates. However SQL statements must be able to access the data in exactly the same manner that they did in any previous version.

Microsoft has put a lot of work into this area, as they have a separate relational engine and storage engine and OLE DB is used to pass data between the two. Further reading on this topic is available in SQL Server 2000 Books Online in the *Database Engine Components* topic.

Rule 9: Logical Data Independence

Application programs and terminal activities remain logically unimpaired when information preserving changes of any kind that theoretically permit unimpairment are made to the base tables.

Along with Rule 8, this rule insulates the user or application program from the low-level implementation of the database. Together they specify that specific access or storage techniques used by the RDBMS, and even changes to the structure of the tables in the database, should not affect the user's ability to work with the data. This rule is quite difficult to implement, since the goal is to be able to shield the table structures from the actual users of the table. In this way, if I add a column to a table, and if tables are split in a manner that does not add or subtract columns, then the application programs that call the database should be unimpaired.

For example, say, we have the following table:

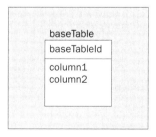

And we vertically break it up into two tables:

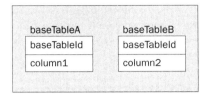

And if we then create this view:

```
CREATE VIEW baseTable
AS
SELECT baseTableId, column1, column2
FROM baseTableA
JOIN baseTableB
   ON baseTableA.baseTableId = baseTableB.baseTableId
```

The user should be unaffected. If we were to implement INSTEAD OF triggers on the view that had the same number of columns with the same names, we could meet this need. Note that the handling of identity columns can be tricky in views, as they require data to be entered, even when the data will not be used. See Chapter 11 for more details.

In Chapter 12, we discussed using distributed partitioned views to break up tables horizontally into identically structured tables. These new tables are then accessed using a view that joins the tables back together thereby allowing them to be treated as a single table. This actually fulfills the criteria for Rule 9.

One thing of note: we can fulfill the requirements of this rule by implementing a layer of abstraction between the user and the data using stored procedures; the stored procedures would then become the "users" of the data.

Rule 10: Integrity Independence

Integrity constraints specific to a particular relational database must be definable in the relational data sublanguage and storable in the catalog, not in the application programs.

A minimum of the following two integrity constraints must be supported:

- **Entity integrity:** No component of a primary key is allowed to have a NULL value.
- **Referential integrity:** For each distinct non-NULL foreign key value in a relational database, there must exist a matching primary key value from the same domain.

This rule says that the database language should support integrity constraints that restrict the data that can be entered into the database, and the database modifications that can be made. In other words, the RDBMS must support the definition and enforcement of entity integrity (primary keys) and referential integrity (foreign keys).

This rule requires that the database must be able to implement constraints to protect the data from invalid values and that careful database design is needed to ensure that referential integrity is achieved. SQL Server 2000 does a great job of providing the tools to make this rule a reality. We can protect our data from invalid values for most any possible case using constraints and triggers. Most of Chapter 11 is spent covering the methods that we can use in SQL Server to implement integrity independence.

Rule 11: Distribution Independence

An RDBMS has distribution independence. Distribution independence implies that users should not have to be aware of whether a database is distributed.

This rule says that the database language must be able to manipulate data located on other computer systems. In essence, we should be able to split the data on the RDBMS out onto multiple physical systems without the user realizing it. This is beginning to become a reality with SQL Server 2000. With SQL Server 2000, the notion of federated database servers seamlessly sharing the load becoming a reality. More reading on this subject can be found in the SQL Server 2000 Books Online in the *Federated SQL Server 2000 Servers* topic.

Rule 12: Non-Subversion Rule

If an RDBMS has a low-level (single-record-at-a-time) language, that low-level language cannot be used to subvert or bypass the integrity rules or constraints expressed in the higher-level (multiple-records-at-a-time) relational language.

This rule basically requires that alternate methods of accessing the data are not able to bypass integrity constraints, which means that users will not be able to violate the rules of the database in any way. For most SQL Server 2000 applications, this rule is followed, as there are no methods of getting to the raw data and changing values other than by the methods prescribed by the database. However, there are two places where the rule is violated in SQL Server 2000:

- **Bulk Copy** – by default, the bulk copy routines can be used to insert data into the table directly and around the database server validations.
- **Disabling constraints and triggers** – there is syntax to disable constraints and triggers, thereby subverting this rule.

It is always good practice to make sure you use these two features carefully. They leave gaping holes in the integrity of your data, since they allow any values to be inserted in any field. Since you are expecting the data to be protected by the constraint you have applied, data value errors may occur in the programs that use the data without revalidating it first.

Conclusions

Codd's 12 rules for relational databases can be used to explain much about how SQL Server operates today. These rules were a major step forwards in determining whether a database vendor could call his system "relational", and presented stiff implementation challenges for database developers. Fifteen years on, even the implementation of the most complex of these rules is becoming achievable, though SQL Server (and others RDBMS) still falls short of achieving all their objectives.

Index

A Guide to the Index

This index covers all numbered chapters and the Appendix. It is arranged alphabetically, word-by-word, with Symbols and numerals preceding the letter A.

Where a main heading has both page references and subheadings, the unmodified page references include any major treatments of the topic, while the sub headings indicate pages where specific aspects only are mentioned.

Acronyms, rather than their expansions, have been selected as main entries on the grounds that unfamiliar acronyms are easier to construct than to expand

Symbols

 # prefix, local temporary tables, 256, 421
prefix, global temporary tables, 421
$ (dollar sign) delimiter, 301
@@error variable
    accessing error numbers from SQL, 357
@@rowcount variable
    interrogating after SET statements, 358
@@trancount variable, 407
    stored procedures must leave unchanged, 458
@name
    and other extended property sproc parameters, 309
@parmname= syntax
    user defined functions, 339
[] (square brackets)
    enclosing SQL Server object names, 256
    enclosing table name which is a reserved word, 315
"" (double quotes)
    enclosing SQL Server object names, 256
<searchConditions> value
    check constraints, 351
4GT (4 Gigabyte Tuning), 520

A

abbreviations
    naming of attributes should avoid, 115
    naming of entities should avoid, 111
    naming rule exceptions, 259
abstract entities, 73
acceptance testing, 569
access contention
    see also **concurrency.**
    avoiding in widely distributed systems, 245
    ad hoc user queries as a source of, 229
    read-only support databases minimize, 550, 556

access privileges see **data access.**
accessing archived data, 518
ACID (Atomicity, Consistency, Isolation and Durability) properties, 406
    locking keeps transactions compliant with, 411
actors, use case models, 105
    checking register case study, 133
    including security information, 203
ad hoc queries
    table-oriented read-only databases, 555
ad hoc SQL, 478, 480
addresses
    case study normalization demands, 167, 169, 190, 316
    multiple entities determine uniqueness, 170
    examples of First Normal Form violations, 149, 150
    examples of locator attributes, 77
ADO (ActiveX Data Objects)
    API cursors, 425
    may send transactions in multiple batches, 419
AFTER triggers, 371
    AFTER update triggers, 292
    enforcing mandatory relationships with, 375
    introduced, 360
    matching zipcodes with cities, 400
    multiple AFTER triggers, 372
    range checking, 376
    transaction allocation check, 401
age of data
    archiving by time period, 516
aliases
    user-defined data types allow, 277
alphabetization
    see also **sort order.**
    collation types and, 286
    collation in checking register case study, 330
    languages other than English, 287
ALTER TABLE statement
    adding constraints with, 300
    introduced, 299

alternate keys
  Boyce-Codd normal form, 164
  implementing to enforce uniqueness, 297
  introduced, 52
  representation in IDEF1X standard, 112
  role in maintaining uniqueness, 50
  uniqueness enforced by constraints not indexes, 294
analysis paralysis, 215
ANSI_NULLS option, 436
ANSI_PADDING option, 270
API cursors, 425
Application Memory Tuning, 520
application types
  determine number of user connections, 536
approximate numeric data, 265
architecture limitations
  demands placed on the database and, 204
archiving, 515
  accessing archived data, 518
  costs of archiving data, 516
  fact table date partitioning, 517
  flagging archived data, 518
  hardware and software obsolescence, 516
  should not be an afterthought, 518
arrays
  using temp tables as, 423
artificial keys
  row identification using, 52
atomicity
  access to external tables, 388
  attributes, requirement of First Normal Form, 148
  checking register case study, 166
  OLTP transactions and, 15, 406
  optionally cascading deletes, 390
  transaction property, 406
  updating telephone area codes and, 151
attributes
  adding descriptive information, 132
  attributes of attributes, 46
  BCNF, must fully depend on a key, 162
  building standard, using IDEF1X domains, 114
  checking for third normal form violations, 159
  checking register case study, 90
  columns identified with, 45
  definitions, checking register case study, 141
  deriving from sample documents, 90, 92
  difference from columns, 77, 111
  domains and, discovering in data from customers, 70
  Enterprise Manager diagramming tool, 130
  finalizing definitions, 326
  First Normal Form, must be atomic, 148
  history, fourth normal form violations and, 185
  identifying additional data, 87
  identifying those that describe an entity, 75
  moving, when building read-only databases, 552
  multi-valued, fourth normal form and, 176, 182
  naming conventions, 115
  order is not inherent in, 46
  relationship with keys and normalization, 153
  representation in IDEF1X standard, 111
  Second Normal Form, must describe the entire key, 154
  tabulated examples, with entities and domains, 78

audit
  defer audit trails to physical design stage, 73
  requirements, 33
auto dealership example
  use of summary data, 161
Available Bytes counter, 522
AWE (Address Windowing Extensions), 520

B

Back Office Resource Kit
  source of performance tuning tools, 522
balance account use case
  custom stored procedure, 497
balanced trees see **B-trees.**
bandwidth
  reducing, using a thick client, 239
bank register
  deriving attributes from electronic format, 93
bank statement
  sample, as source of attribute information, 92
banking example see **case study.**
batching
  batch growth of OLAP databases, 506, 515
  database calls over moderate connections, 231
  SQL statements executed as a group, 474
  transactions should not span boundaries, 418
  transactions with the GO statement, 410
BCNF see **Boyce-Codd Normal Form.**
before triggers see **INSTEAD OF triggers.**
BEGIN DISTRIBUTED TRANSACTION, 491
BEGIN TRANSACTION statement, 406
BETWEEN operator, WHERE clause, 267
bias, floating-point values, 265
bigint data type, 261
binary collation example, 288
binary data types, 269
binary relationships, 61
binary tree example, 423
bit column
  GROUP BY clause, using tinyint data type, 262
bit data type, 261
bitmasks
  columns_updated() returns, 363
bitwise operations
  binary data types don't support, 269
blanks
  checking for, using UDFs, 352, 393
BLOB (Binary Large Objects)
  storage by SQL Server, 269
  table of domains, case study, 140
blocking
  access, caused by lock escalation, 229
  access, caused by locks held too long, 537
  connections, repeatable reads and 414
  key cause of bottlenecks, 522
  testing with user definable counters, 539
book publishing example
  Second Normal Form violation, 154, 156
  Third Normal Form violation, 158
  use case models, 107, 203

Books Online, 48, 256
    Create Index topic, 290
    Creating an Indexed View, 444
    Database Engine Components, 580
    definition of null values, 434
    deterministic and non-deterministic functions, 346
    distributed queries and replication, 491
    extended properties, 313
    Federated SQL Server 2000 Servers, 582
    locks, 412
    Performing Transactions in ADO, 419
    permissions function, 485
    replication from other databases, 235
    sizing tables and indexes, 507
    SQL-DMO, 237
    System Stored Procedures, 308
Boolean data type
    bit, as SQL Server's closest approximation, 261
    use of smallint as, not justified, 262
bottlenecks
    disk and CPU, 529
    disk performance and, 535
    possible causes, 522
bought-in systems
    inaccessiblity of implementation details, 566
Boyce-Codd Normal Form
    checking register case study, 168, 172
    clues to violations as for 2NF and 3NF, 165
    replacement for second and third normal forms, 162
bracketed notation, 256, 315
B-trees
    indexes implemented using, 290
    using to calculate index space, 510
budget
    effect on performance optimization options, 233
Buffer Manager: counters, 526
bugs
    see also **error handling; programming.**
    associated with use of NULLs, 437
built-in functions
    UDFs cannot include, 345
bulk copying
    intermediate tables to cut overheads, 418
    violates Codd's twelfth RDBMS rule, 582
bulk logged transactions, 514
bulk update locks, 412
Business Analyst role, 26
business decisions see **decision support.**
business layer
    connection pooling by object broker in, 243
    enforcing business rules, 243
business rules
    best implemented on the server, 245
    care required in formulating, 84
    coding in functional language, not in SQL, 243
    defined, 83
    defining in data structures, 187
    discovering in data from customers, 70, 83, 98
    enforcing with INSTEAD OF triggers, limits on, 382
    enforcing with triggers, 359
    implementation by middle-tier services, 387
    importance of complete discovery, 83
    optional rules in case study, 402
    sharing between middle tier and database, 388
    table of new processes in banking example, 99
    usage, and relation to predicates, explained, 50

C

caching
    by disk controllers, 530
    database calls over moderate connections, 231
    pages to speed data accesss, 530
    query plans, 480
    validation data, can compromise data integrity, 388
    write caching, 530
CAL (Client Access Licences)
    distinction from user connections, 536
calculated columns, 258, 282
    see also **computed columns.**
    building read-only databases, 553
camel notation, 110
candidate keys
    avoiding duplicate information, 50
    Boyce-Codd normal form, 164, 170
capitalizing words in strings, 345
    see also **case sensitivity.**
    INSTEAD OF trigger to capitalize names, 382
    user defined function for, 339
cardinalities
    enforcing, as use for after triggers, 376
    of relationships, discussed, 61
    table showing six possible cardinalities, 120
    use of, to mean rowcounts is ambiguous, 53
cascading modifications
    cascading deletes using an AFTER delete trigger, 378
    cascading inserts using AFTER triggers, 375
    cascading updates and deletes, 302
    error handling from within triggers, 370
    foreign keys and cascading deletes, 300
    INSTEAD OF triggers ignore cascading updates, 382
    optionally cascading deletes, 389
    setting child key references to NULL, 303
CASE keyword
    use to allow for possible null values, 438
case sensitivity
    see also **capitalizing words in strings.**
    changing collation to introduce, 287
case study (checking register).
    applying business rules, 391
    Boyce-Codd Normal Form, 168
    building a reporting database, 571
    building the database access structures, 491
    building the physical implementation, 313
    check constraints and UDFs, 392
    data model after Boyce-Codd normalization, 172
    data model after full normalization, 194
    data modeling, 135
    data types, 323
    data usage and reporting, 210
    default constraints, 392
    delete stored procedure, 495
    domain fill procedure, 497
    entity discovery, 88
    external systems, 214
    First Normal Form violations, 165
    Fourth Normal Form violations, 188
    information gathering stage, 33
    insert stored procedure, 492
    introduced, 19
    listing stored procedure, 496
    marking document attributes, 90
    object listing, 94
    optional business rules, 402

case study (checking register) Cont'd
  physical model, 330
  physical-only columns, 319
  range checking, 397
  reporting, 212
  security issues, 500
  simple client-server topology, 245
  table of domains, 140
  table of entities, attributes and domains, 94
  transaction subtype, 313
  update stored procedure, 493
  use case modelling, 133
  volumetric analysis, 215, 540
casting
  can cause problems with variant data, 273
  datetime data to a string, 396
  scalars to a binary collation, 288
catalog, dynamic on-line
  Codd's fourth rule for an RDBMS, 578
categorization relationships, 124
  complete and incomplete categories, 125
CEILING function, 509
character data
  char data type, 270
  drawbacks of using to store other data, 270
  dynamic character string execution techniques, 511
  specifying Unicode in strings, 271
check constraints, 350
  checking register case study, 392
  deriving from domain lists, 393
  function-based, 354
  inter-column dependencies solved by, 55
  introduced, 49
  one of five constraint types, 347
  rules using should be enforced at database level, 388
  <searchConditions> value, 351
  triggers may perform better in validation, 357
  validating ranges using, 397
  violations, custom error messages, 453
CHECK option
  check constraint, 350
CHECK_CONSTRAINTS listing
  Information Schema, 307
checking register case study see **case study.**
checks (banking)
  sample, as source of attribute information, 90
Chen ERD methodology, 129
child tables
  problems from deleting parent records, 233
  setting foreign key references to NULL, 378
client executable code
  securing data integrity with, 336
client software
  encapsulation protects from SQL changes, 457
clients (community) see **customers.**
client-server systems
  checking register case study, 245
  connection speed effects, 231
  ideal system, between think and thin client, 241
  large systems depart form simple architecture, 232
  simplest configuration for SQL Server use, 242
  thick and thin clients, 239
clustered indexes, 291
  calculating testing for presence of, 512
  checking register case study, 541
  factors favoring the choice of, 291
  free space from fill factor, 509
  normalization and use of, 146
  primary keys specification defaults to, 297
  reasons to keep index keys short, 510, 513
  reasons to keep row size short, 513
clustered servers, 234, 570
clustered tables
  non-clustered indexes on, 293
COALESCE function
  check constraints, 351
  use to allow for possible null values, 438
Codd, Edgar F
  database rules, 52, 54, 577
  relational database pioneer, 12, 148
  relational operators formulated by, 56
coding see **programming.**
COLLATE clause, 287
collation types, 286
  see also **sort order.**
  checking register case study, 330
colleagues
  getting designs validated by, 198
column constraints
  type of check constraint, 350
column domains see **domains.**
COLUMN_DOMAIN_USAGE listing
  Information Schema, 308
COLUMN_PRIVILEGES listing
  Information Schema, 307
column-level security, 442, 487
columns
  attributes of, 46
  defining using CREATE TABLE, 258
  distinction from attributes, 77, 111
  headings and bodies, 54
  indexing all, in read-only support databases, 556
  limiting visibility with views, 441
  maximum permitted number, 258
  normalization reduces number, 147
  physical and computed, 258
  SQL Server definition, 45
  whether order is inherent in, 46
  which are costly to update, 471
COLUMNS listing
  Information Schema, 306
  INSERT statement, 362
columns_updated() function, 363
COM (Component Object Model)
  COM object instantiation, 237
  COM+ use of two-phase commit, 490
COMMIT TRANSACTION statement
  introduced, 407
communicates relationship
  use case models, 106
communication
  across design team members, 27
compiled SQL, 480, 482
  see also **stored procedures; triggers.**
  compared with ad hoc, 478, 480
composite keys
  non-foreign keys suggest 2NF violation, 157
  Second Normal Form applies to, 153
compound keys, 138
computed columns, 258
  see also **calculated columns.**

588

concurrency
see also **access contention; locking**.
conflict with consistency, 415
control of, 284, 411
maximizing, with read-only databases, 550
conditional inserts
using INSTEAD OF triggers, 383
conference planning example
resolving ternary relationships, 177
conflict resolution see **access contention**.
connection loss
minimizing effects by batching transactions, 419
Connection Objects, ADO
may cause locking problems, 420
connection pooling
performed in business layer of n-tier system, 243
technique for multi-user systems, 234
connection speed
WANs and web applications, 231
connections to other systems
pre-existing data may require, 32
consistency
see also **data integrity**.
conflict with concurrency, 415
transaction property, 406
constant expressions
default constraints, 348
constraint errors
from triggers cause rollbacks, 369
mapping to user-friendly messages, 452
CONSTRAINT_COLUMN_USAGE listing
Information Schema, 307
CONSTRAINT_TABLE_USAGE listing
Information Schema, 307
constraints, 346
adding with ALTER TABLE, 300
disabling violates Codd's twelfth rule, 582
end-of-transaction, not avialable in SQL Server 2000, 193
errors from triggers cause rollbacks, 369
errors, mapping to user-friendly messages, 452
five types introduced, 346
introduced and classified, 49
securing data integrity with, 336
triggers compared with, 359, 371
contact design model
multi-valued attribute example, 183
contention see **access contention**.
context-switching
use of fibers avoids, 529
contracts and work orders
source of data rules, 32
copy databases
see **read-only copy databases**.
corporate data structure
four functional modules, 14
costs of archiving data, 516
coupling
interfacing with external systems, 207
covered queries, 557
CPU subsystem
monitoring, not tuning performance of, 528
CREATE FUNCTION statement, 337
CREATE TABLE statement, 255
defining columns using, 258

CREATE TRIGGER statement, 360
CREATE VIEW statement, 437, 440, 441
creating single rows, 467
cross joins
example of the product operator, 58
cross-database data access, 488
databases on different servers, 490
databases on the same server, 488
cross-database relationships, 304
crow's foot symbols, 128
CRUD (Create, Read, Update, Delete) procedures, 491
CURRENT OF keyword, 427
cursor types, 426
downgrading, 428
effect on sort order example, 432
importance of specifying, 433
cursors, 425
circumstances in which to use, 429
direction, 426
not permitted as a column data type, 276
updatability, 427
use by volume-estimating stored procedure, 511
custom data types, 48
custom error messages, 452
check constraint violations, 453
tagging values to include in, 453
custom stored procedures
calculating complete table size, 507
calculating index size, 511
customer consultation
establishing reporting requirements, 200
identifying further sources from, 35
interview process guidelines, 28
marking up interview notes, 88, 90, 98
must precede data modelling, 25
reviewing first draft document, 88
suggested questions for interviews, 30
customer perceptions
prototyping can distort, 28

D

data access
see also **security issues**.
access to partitioned data, 442
allocating privileges to security roles, 484
from a different database, 488
limiting paths, using stored procedures, 480
performance of systems with high data volumes, 228
protecting against unauthorized, 483
restricting access to views instead of tables, 441
through table, column and primary key, 578
Data Architect role, 26
data conversion plans, 208
data cubes
as data mart querying technology, 22
introduced, 17
data dependencies
three types identified, 55
data domains see **domains**.
data duplication
normalization helps minimize, 146

data integrity
  see also **consistency**.
  bulk copying and disabling constraints and triggers, 582
  concurrency control by locking and, 284, 411
  locking isolation levels and, 415
  middle tier and database involvement, 388
  OLTP primary goal, 14
  problems from importing data, 388
  problems from using spreadsheets, 31
  problems with pre-aggregated data, 229
  schema binding and data protection, 342
  securing, four methods compared, 335
  value of triggers in ensuring, 388
  validation data caching could compromise, 388
  write caching could compromise, 531
data loss
  acceptable levels for maintenance plans, 570
data marts
  accessible via tools not involving coding, 18
  data warehouse segments, 17
  distinguished from OLAP and cubes, 22
data modeling, 103
  see also **logical modeling; modeling methodologies**.
  alternative to unwieldy lists, 97
  case study physical model, 330
  checking register case study, 135, 172
  data models introduced, 103
  identifying processes relevant to, 85
  invoice system for transforming to read-only, 551
  logical and physical models distinguished, 108
data modification, 405
  allowed with stored procedures but not UDFs, 446
  Codd's seventh rule for an RDBMS, 579
  cross-database data access, 489
  INSTEAD OF triggers suit generic extensions, 383
  INSTEAD OF triggers, examples of use, 382
  problems caused by 2NF violations, 155
  problems caused by 3NF violations, 158
  problems caused by ternary relationships, 178
  SQL statements obey Codd's seventh rule, 579
data ownership, 202
  see also **database owner role**.
data protection see **data integrity**.
data scrubbing, 236
data size calculation
  using a stored procedure, 507
data sources
  consolidating into read-only databases, 550
data sub-language
  Codd's fifth rule for an RDBMS, 579
data transformation
  example corporate solution, 560
data types
  chosing to match logical domains, 260
  cursor, declating a variable as a, 426
  cursor, passing using output parameters, 448
  example of a SQL Server domain, 47
  general classes suffice for logical design, 48
  <genericDatatype> placeholder, 348
  inheritance of in IDEF1X, using domains, 113
  securing data integrity with, 336
  table of 'primitive' data types, 47
  transformation of logical domains into, 323
  user-defined, 48
data usage, 198, 202
  checking register case study, 210

data validation
  exception-handling tables, 384
  check constraints, finding invalid data, 356
  handling errors from within triggers, 370
  involving inter-table comparisons, 388
  multi row validation with triggers, 364
  range checks using AFTER triggers, 376
  record catalog numbers example, 353
  rules, 32
  rules, unsuitable for client enforcement, 241
  single row validation code, 356
  using thick and thin clients, 239
data volumes
  see also **volumetrics**.
  consequences of deleting parent table records, 233
  estimating, for hardware needs, 503
  estimating, for variable length columns, 508
  factors in calculating for tables, 507
  source of reporting problems, 227
data warehousing
  as decision support tool, 16
  contrasted with OLTP, 13
  diagram of a typical architecture, 19
  read-only support database alternative, 550
  storage optimized for reporting, 13, 16
Database Administrator see **DBA role**.
database design
  adherence to standards and normalization, 145
  as art and science, 11
  compared to building construction, 219
  diagram of typical large system, 18
  history, 12
  importance of approaching in stages, 70
  information gathering stage, 25
  logical and physical design distinguished, 22
  process stages enumerated, 21
  separate roles distinguished, 26
  should incorporate archiving plans, 518
  development slowed by technology, 12, 157
  tools provided by SQL Server, 235
database development
  an iterative process, 567
database engine
  relational and storage engines distinct, 580
database level locking, 411
database objects
  as entities in a database, 72
  controlling access rights, 483
  heirarchy used by extended properties, 309
  SQL Server 2000 reporting tools for, 304
database owner role, 255, 257
  db_owner and other built-in roles, 484
  user defined functions, 339
database structure
  described within the database itself, 578
  divorcing yourself from, at discovery stage, 70
database tables see **tables**.
databases
  see also **read-only copy databases**.
  access and modification techniques, 405
  database generation tools, 250
  defined, 42
  end-user, as pre-existing data source, 31, 550
  growth of, through company growth, 506
  merging into an ODS, 564
  OLTP and OLAP, 504

590

distributed queries

databases (cont'd)
  programming, has parallels with object orientation, 45
  recursive triggers set at database level, 367
  relational model, 42
  reorganization, to cope with high data volumes, 228
  rules to assess whether truly relational, 577
  theory, 41
databases other than SQL Server
  access as linked servers, 236
  replication from, 235
Datalog/Monitor, 521, 522
date information
  archiving by time period, 516
  checking whether a date is in the future, 395
  datepart system function, 441
  storage and manipulation of dates, 267
  use of dates in keys not recommended, 323
datetime data type, 266
  cases where user-defined data types are preferable, 267
  removing hour from, using datepart system function, 441
  removing time from, with a UDF, 396, 441
  removing time from, with an INSTEAD OF trigger, 398
  technically violates First Normal Form, 152
db_owner see database owner role.
DBA (Database Administrator) role
  distinct from database designer, 11, 26
  hardware specification, 503, 569
  performance tuning part of, 548
DBCC (Database Consistency Checker), 429, 549
DBCC MEMUSAGE, 521, 522
DBCC OPENTRAN
  detecting long running transactions, 536
DDL (Data Definition Language)
  needed by relational language to build DML objects, 61
DEADLOCK_PRIORITY property, 417
deadlocks, 417
debugging
  bugs associated with the use of NULLs, 437
decimal data type, 262
decision support
  day-to-day, based on ODS, 16
  OLAP reporting demands and, 506
  primary use of data warehouses, 16
declarative key constraints, 289
decomposition
  ternary relationships, 182
default constraints, 347
  checking register case study, 392
default isolation level
  read committed as, 413, 415
defaults
  ensuring singularity of, with AFTER triggers, 376
degrees of relations, 46
DELETE statements
  INSTEAD OF triggers may need to repeat, 380
  stored procedure alternative, 472
DELETED table
  temporary table used by triggers, 361
delimiters
  bracketed notation, 256, 315
  clue that existing data is not in 1NF, 153
  naming constraints, 301
  SQL Server naming convention, 256

denormalization, 188
  coding round denormalized data, 157
  complex reporting situations may justify, 229
  introduction of summary data, 255
  last resort of performance tuning, 548, 549
  problems from denormalized external systems, 206
  read only copies of data, 244
  some required in an ODS, 564
  treatment of subtypes may involve, 253
  update stored procedures and, 471
deny command, 484
dependent entities, 109
  foreign keys present in primary key, 109
derived tables, T-SQL
  alternative to temporary tables, 422
descriptive information
  adding to graphical data models, 131
descriptive properties
  communicating with developers, 308
desktop databases
  possible location of pre-existing data, 31
destroy stored procedure, 472
determinants
  must all be keys in Boyce-Codd normal form, 163
developers
  communicating with, 304
  speed of, using ad hoc SQL, 480
development databases
  contain data with no business value, 250
development phase
  hardware requirements, 568
dial-up access see mobile clients
difference operator
  NOT IN SQL operator and, 60
dimension tables
  fact tables and, 17
dimensions
  limits for a database table, 258
dirty reads, 537
disabling constraints and triggers
  violates Codd's twelfth RDBMS rule, 582
disaster recovery, 570
discovery and logical design
  discovery process introduced, 70
  report discovery strategy, 200
discriminators
  categorization relationships, 124
  checking register case study, 314
disk reads
  can determine perceived performance, 515
disk striping (RAID), 531, 533
disk subsystem
  disk performance counters, 534
  importance of familiarity with, 535
  multiple disk controllers, 534
  performance tuning, 530
disk thrashing, 535
DISKPERF -Y command, 521
DISTINCT keyword
  project operator example, 57
distributed computing
  clustered servers and, 234
  database applications typically involve, 21
  widely distributed systems, 245
distributed partitioned views, 444
distributed queries, 490

Distribution Independence
Codd's eleventh rule for an RDBMS, 582
divide operator, 60
DML (Data Manipulation Language)
commands derived from basic relational operators, 61
DMO (Data Management Objects), 237
code to instantiate and connect to, 237
displaying database security roles, 484
documentation
checking register case study, 34
completing the data documentation tasks, 86
crucial importance in database projects, 26, 201, 210
data modeling as alternative to unwieldy lists, 97
disguising sensitive information on samples, 36
final review, 209, 219
future requirements, 210
identifying information elements in, 70
need for constant updating, 70
documents
as entities in a database, 73
domain entities see domain tables.
Domain Key Normal Form, 187, 241
domain predicates, 142
domain tables, 119
changes to, supporting fact tables, 517
characterised by slow or no growth, 505
checking regster case study, 316, 492
external system interface problem caused by, 205
DOMAIN_CONSTRAINTS listing
Information Schema, 308
domains
attributes and, discovering in data from customers, 70
building does not imply implementation, 115
column domains introduced, 46
creating during normalization process, 167, 184, 189, 191
deriving check constraints from domain lists, 393
discovered at the same time as attributes, 75
discovering an attribute's possible domain, 77
implementing with triggers and stored procedures, 49
inheritance depends on modeling tools, 114
logical, checking register case study, 140
logical, transformation into data types, 323
matching data types to, 260
names, table with equivalent data types, 323
representation in IDEF1X, 113-114
tabulated examples, with entities and attributes, 78
usage explained with examples, 49
using as a column template, 260
DOMAINS listing
Information Schema, 308
double quote delimiters, 256
downgrading cursor types, 428
downloading data
large transfers may be broken down, 232
DROP commands
schema binding and, 343
DTC (Distributed Transaction Controller), 236
code example also using linked servers, 236
transactions spanning different servers, 491
DTS (Data Transformation Services), 236
data integrity problems from data imports, 388
read-only databases and, 559
scheduling tasks with SQL Server Agent, 239

dummy procedures, 457
duplexing (RAID 1), 532
durability
transaction property, 406
dynamic memory allocation
upset by specifying user connections, 536
SQL Server 2000 tuning, 523
dynamic queries
stored procedures and, 466

E

email
addresses violate First Normal Form, 148
SQL Mail facility, 238
empty strings
checking for, using UDFs, 352, 393
encapsulation
code within stored procedures, 455, 481
code within UDFs, 352
joins etc, to hide them from users, 439
user-defined data types as a tool for, 278
end-user databases
source of denormalized data, 550
English Query, 562
Enterprise Data Models, 565
logical enterprise model, 566
Enterprise Manager
creating security roles using, 483
diagramming tool, 130-131
query window as example of a thin client, 240
setting user definable counters, 538
entities
adding descriptive information, 132
attributes as identifiers for, 75
attributes must all describe, in 2NF and 3NF, 163
checking register case study, 88, 135
child and parent, defined, 116
conceptual versions of tables, 44
database tables should each represent single, 147
discovering in data from customers, 70
enforcing entity integrity, 581
Enterprise Manager diagramming tool, 130-131
expanding for reporting databases, 552
First Normal Form rows must have same number of values, 150
ideas as abstract entities, 73
identifying from customer documentation, 71
must be relations and single-themed, 195
naming, 110
relationships and, 70, 116
removing unnecessary, before implementation, 317
representation in IDEF1X standard, 109, 111
tabulated examples, with attributes and domains, 78, 94
tabulated, for office supplier example, 74, 82, 94
entity integrity, 581
error handling
see also data validation.
client and server side, 241
implementing with triggers, 369
multi-statement batches, 475, 477
statements which violate constraints, 357
stored procedure for testing messages, 454
stored procedure to examine output parameters, 451
stored procedure to examine return values, 447
stored procedures, 449

error messages, 357
    customizing using a mapping table, 452
    deadlock, error number 1205 signifies, 417
    error numbers, significance of, 357
    including after modification statements, 451
    stored procedure return values and, 446

error reporting
    user-defined data types using rules, 278

error variable
    accessing error numbers from SQL, 357

ERwin modeling tool
    representation of alternate keys, 112

ETL (Extract, Transform and Load) operation, 19, 565

events
    as entities in a database, 73

exception-handling tables, 384

exclusive locks, 412

EXEC statement
    user defined functions, 338

execution order of triggers, 374

exponent, floating-point values, 265

extended properties
    defining and adding programmatically, 309

extends relationship
    use case models, 106, 135

extent locking, 411

external systems
    checking register case study, 214
    import layers to reduce coupling with, 207
    interfacing needs, 204

F

fact tables
    archiving by row characteristics, 517
    archiving by time period and, 516
    dimension tables and, 17

facts
    modifying records with variable numbers of, 151

fault tolerance
    provided by RAID combinations, 531

federated partitioned views, 534

federation
    Codd's eleventh RDBMS rule, 582

fibers
    non-kernel applications use instead of threads, 529
    when to use, 529

field format
    generic checks with UDFs, 353

field values
    supplying initial, with default constraints, 350

fieldnames with number suffixes
    clue that existing data is not in 1NF, 153

fieldnames with repeating key prefixes
    clues that existing data is not in 2NF, 156

fieldnames with shared prefixes
    checking register case study, 169
    clue that existing data is not in 3NF, 161

Fifth Normal Form, 187

fill factors, 509

First Normal Form, 148
    checking register case study, 165
    clues that existing data is not in 1NF, 152
    datetime data type technically violates, 152
    examples of violations, 148

    requirement for record type occurrences to be different, 150
    same number of values in all entity instances, 150

flagging
    archived data, 518
    records which it is impracticable to delete, 233

flat indexes, 511, 513

floating point values, 265
    comparing with = problematic, 266
    float data type, 265
    inability to represent some values exactly, 265

FLOOR function, 509

fn_listextendedproperty system function, 309, 313

foreign characters *see* **languages other than English.**

foreign key constraints
    one of five constraint types, 347
    rules using, should be enforced at database level, 388

foreign keys
    absent from primary keys of independent entities, 109
    cascading deletes and multi-database relationships, 300
    error-proneness in unnormalized databases, 146
    introduced, 53
    primary keys migrated as, in one-to-n relationships, 61
    present in primary key of dependent entities, 109
    referential integrity and, 581
    representation in IDEF1X standard, 113, 116
    role names for attributes used as, 121
    setting to NULL in child tables, 378

forms
    scattered data sources, 33

4 Gigabyte Tuning, 520

Fourth Normal Form, 176
    addresses ternary relationships, 176
    checking register case study, 188

Free Memory Target, 524-525

Full Text Search, 238

functional dependencies, 64
    higher normalization forms and, 153, 155
    non-key attributes in third normal form, 158
    second normal form, 154

functions
    using in default constraints, 349

fundamental processes, 85

future dates
    checking for, with a UDF, 395

future requirements
    documenting, 210

G

generic data types
    string as, in check constraints, 351

generic entities
    categorization relationships, 124

get account information use case
    custom stored procedure, 498

global temporary tables
    viewable by any connection or user, 421

GO statement
    batching transactions, 410

GOTO statements, 477

grant command, 484
granularity
  lock types and, 411
graphical representations see data modeling; use case models.
GROUP BY clause
  bit column using tinyint data type, 262
  using clustered indexes, 291
grouping data on the second, 282
Guaranteed Access Rule
  Codd's second rule for an RDBMS, 578
GUID (Globally Unique Identifiers)
  example of domain specification in IDEF1X, 114
  uniqueidentifier data type, 275

H

handheld devices see mobile clients.
hardware
  see also disk subsystem; memory.
  CPU subsystem performance, 528
  determining requirements, 503
  development phase requirements, 568
  memory needed by server connections, 234
  need for adequate provision, 233
  performance of read-only databases and, 556
  quality assurance phase requirements, 569
  systems with high data volumes, 228
'has a' relationships
  example of one-to-X relationship, 80
heaps
  tables without clustered indexes, 292, 509
heavy use webservers, 243
heterogeneous data sources, 236
hexadecimal integers
  representing a bitmask, 363
hierarchical relationships, 63, 122
  diagrammatic representation, 116
high-level data modification
  Codd's seventh rule for an RDBMS, 579
historical information
  data warehouse storage, 16
history of database design, 12
horizontally partitioning data, 442
Hungarian notation, 259

I

IDEF1X (Integration Definition for Information Modeling)
  methodology, 105
  domains and inheritance of data types, 113
  introduced, 104
  naming relationships, 126
  representation of entities in, 109
  treatment of relationships, 116
identification numbers
  use for char data type, 270
identifier-dependent entities, 109
identifiers
  attributes suggested as suitable, 76
identifying relationships, 117
  diagrammatic representation, 116
  Information Engineering, 128
  second normal form violations and, 155

dentity columns
  CREATE TABLE statement, 264
IEEE
  standard for floating point values, 265
IGNORE_DUP_KEY option, 295
images
  image data type, 269
  performance issues with storage, 269
implementation
  differences from logical design, 226
  tasks to be finished before starting, 198
implicit conversions, 263
import layers
  interfacing with external systems, 207
importing data
  data integrity problems, 388
increment, identity columns, 264
independent entities, 109
  foreign keys absent from primary key, 109
indexed views, 443
  restrictions on prior content, 444
  use to allow complex searches, 229
indexes
  calculating data volumes for tables, 507
  calculating size using custom stored procedures, 511
  DBCC commands, 549
  enforcing unique values, 294
  flattening and query performance, 511
  growth tends to be non-linear, 541
  Index Tuning Wizard, 549
  leaving to performance tuning stage, 299
  literal defaults need care, 348
  maximum number of bytes per entry, 258
  maximum number of clustered and non-clustered, 258
  naming is optional, 298
  normalization reduces need for, 147
  OLAP database volumes should include, 504, 507
  read-only support database may have many, 556
  software approach to treating bottlenecks, 522
  too many bring performance problems, 548
  use to implement unique constraints, 289
Information Engineering methodology
  non-required relationships, 128
  representation of relationships, 128
Information Rule
  Codd's first rule for an RDBMS, 577
Information Schema
  introduced, 55
  parameters view, 428
  prefered to system stored procedures, 305
  reporting on table structures, 305
informative error messages, 452-453
inheritance
  data types, using IDEF1X domains, 113
  using domains depends on modeling tools, 114
in-line table-valued functions
  executing with table commands, 342
  UDF type, 341
INSERT statements
  columns list interrogated by triggers, 362
  INSTEAD OF triggers may need to repeat, 380
  should never be coded without insert lists, 283
  stored procedure alternative, 467
INSERTED table
  INSTEAD OF trigger example using, 378
  temporary table used by triggers, 361

INSTEAD OF triggers, 378
  creating an exception handling table, 383
  ignore cascading modifications, 382
  introduced, 359
  multi-row range checking difficult, 381
  problems with the operation of, 379
  removing time from datetime values, 398
  using to modify views, 386, 579
integers
  incrementing with a scalar UDF, 338
  int data type, 261
integrated database design
  four functional modules, 14
integrity constraints
  entity and referential integrity, 581
Integrity Independence rule, 52, 54
  Codd's tenth rule for an RDBMS, 581
intelligent keys, 138
intent locks
  intent shared, intent exclusive and shared with intent exclusive, 412
interfaces
  external systems, 204
  flexibility of, using ad hoc SQL, 478
intermittent connections
  see also **mobile clients.**
  read-only database replication, 561
  read-only database update frequency, 558
internationalization
  complicates storage of telephone numbers and addresses, 149
intersecting tables
  intersect operator, 59
  solution oriented models, 556
inter-table and inter-row constraints
  enforcing with triggers, 359
inter-table validations
  rules using, should be enforced at database level, 388
interview technique, 29
intrinsic data types, 260
invalid data see **data validation.**
invoice system
  model of, for transforming to read-only, 551
IP (Internet Protocol) addresses
  First Normal Form and unsigned integers, 149
  storage in SQL Server requires bigint, 261
'is a' relationships
  example of one-to-n relationship, 81
IS NULL operator, 436
is_member function, 485
ISNULL function
  use to allow for possible null values, 438
isolation
  transaction property, 406
isolation levels
  locking duration and, 412, 415
  specifying using optimizer hints, 416

J

job scheduler
  SQL Server Agent as, 239
join operator, 58

joins
  chaining together, 58
  encapsulation of, using views, 439, 440
  including subqueries in, 422
  illustrating SQL difference from procedural programming, 20
  minimizing in read-only databases, 552
  multiple data channels can speed data reads, 534
  using clustered indexes, 291

K

key or key-range locking, 411
KEY_COLUMN_USAGE listing
  Information Schema, 307
keys
  attributes and, relationship and normalization, 153
  determinants as, in Boyce-Codd normal form, 163
  implementing, 289
  naming convention for primary and alternate, 298
  "nothing but the key", 159
  "the key, the whole key and nothing but the key", 153
  use of dates in, is inadvisable, 323

L

LAN (Local Area Networks) breakdowns
  minimizing effects by batching transactions, 419
languages other than English
  changing collation to alphabetize correctly, 287
  supported in RAISERROR, 450
laptop users see **mobile clients.**
latency
  real-time reporting, 440
  decision support systems, 230
  read-only support databases, 549, 558
lazy writer system, 530
leaf nodes, 290
  clustered and non-clustered indexes, 510
legacy data
  see also **pre-existing data.**
  data warehouse incorporating, 17
legacy systems
  see also **pre-existing systems.**
  possible location of pre-existing data, 31
  problems interfacing with denormalized, 206
  source of denormalized data, 550
legal values
  methods of restricting listed, 46
levels of service
  maintenance planning and, 570
  Service Level Agreements, 33
licences, importance of reading, 536
lightweight clients see **mobile clients.**
LIKE mask
  function-based check constraint, 354
linked servers, 236, 491
  code example, also using DTC, 236
list controls
  filling, example stored procedures, 463
listing relationships, 82
literal defaults, 348
live data
  development databases shouldn't contain, 250
  reporting from, using views, 439

load balancing

load balancing
  offered by server clustering, 234
  switch, for heavy use web servers, 243
load testing, 569
local temporary tables
  scoped to SQL Server connections, 421
locators
  addresses as examples of attributes, 77
locking, 411
  avoiding using views, 440
  blocked access caused by lock escalation, 229
  lock modes, 411
  lock types in order of increasing granularity, 411
  optimistic and pessimistic locks, 284
  query optimizer choses types, 411
  risk of, from use of T-SQL cursors, 425
LOCK-TIMEOUT property, 418
logging
  defer providing, to physical design stage, 73
logic
  separation in three-tier and n-tier systems, 242
  three-value logic involving NULLS, 434
logical data independence
  Codd's ninth rule for an RDBMS, 580
  providing using views, 54
logical design
  final stages of, 197
  general datatype classes suffice for, 48
  reasons to stray from, during implementation, 251, 255
logical domains see **domains**.
logical modeling
  checking register case study, 172, 194
  correcting errors, 318
  denormalization inappropriate during, 188
  entities as conceptual version of tables in, 44
  implementation independence, 108
  logical enterprise model, 566
  models should be living documents, 110
  normal forms should be considered during, 148
  primary keys. choice of during, 163
  summary data absolutely prohibited, 161
logical reads
  performance mesures, 464
long transactions
  minimizing effects of, 418
looping
  SELECT on joined tables is equivalent to, 20
lossy decompositions, 179
lurking multi-valued attributes, 182, 189

M

maintenance
  maintenance plans, 570
  problems of archiving systems, 516
mandatory relationships
  enforcing with AFTER triggers, 375
  mandatory non-identifying relationships, 119
mantissa, floating-point values, 265
many-to-many relationships, 63, 125
  diagrammatic representation, 117
  resolution entities, 126
masks
  see also **bitmasks**.
  use for data validation, 354

Maybe (NULL comparisons)
  logical equivalent of Unknown, 435
MDS (MetaData Services), 305
MDX (Multidimensional Exressions)
  data mart access need not depend on, 18
media
  archiving policy and storage media, 516, 519
memory
  dynamic memory tuning, 523
  importance of maximizing RAM, 519
  management by SQL Server 7 and 2000, 521
  management under AWE, 520
  operating system free memory, 524
  process memory tuning, 526
  requirements of other applications, 523
  requirements of server connections, 234
  tuning, counters available, 522
  tuning, multiple server instances, 525
  Windows 2000 Server optimization, 520
  Windows NT Server optimization, 519
merge replication, 235
  widely distributed systems, 245
metadata
  elements of a relation (column), 54
  procedures, Information Schema views and system sprocs, 305
Microsoft Corporation see individual product names.
middle-tier services
  business rule implementation moved to, 387
migrated attributes, migrated keys see **foreign keys**.
migration of primary keys
  as foreign keys in one-to-n relationships, 61
  identifying and non-identifying relationships, 117
  naming primary keys to facilitate, 115
mirroring (RAID), 532, 533
mobile clients
  see also **intermittent connections**.
  merge replication especially suits, 235
  ODS suitability for peripatetic staff, 16
  read-only databases, 561-562
  remote staff may depend on dial-up access, 231
modeling methodologies
  see also **data modeling; Enterprise Manager; IDEF1X; Information Engineering; use case models**.
  introduced, 104
  key to Enterprise Data Modeling, 567
  representation of relationships, 128
modifying data
  accessing changes with triggers, 361
  drawbacks to modifying views, 386
  flexibility of, using ad hoc SQL, 479
  including error messages, 451
  makes clustered indexes less attractive, 292
  modifying views with INSTEAD OF-triggers, 386
  single rows, with stored procedures, 467
  typical pattern of operation, 467
modifying lists
  problems caused by First Normal Form violations, 150
money data type, 263
movie rental example see **video library example**.
MS_Description table, 310
multi-database relationships
  foreign keys, 300
multi-part fields
  modifying, 151
multiple data channels, 534

multiple disk controllers, 534
multiple joins, 58
multiple keys
    Boyce-Codd Normal Form recognizes, 162
multi-statement batches, 475
    introduced, 474
    row update errors, 475
multi-statement table-valued functions, 345
multi-tier design see n-tier configurations.
multi-valued dependencies see MVD.
mutable rules
    candidates for stored procedure enforcement, 389
    examples that appear fixed, 391
MVD (multi-valued dependencies), 65
    contact design model, 184
    fourth normal form allows only one, 176

N

@name
    and other extended property parameters, 309
named relations, 43
naming conventions
    see also **terminology**.
    alternative table naming styles illustrated, 256
    attributes, 115
    cross-database data access, 489
    database objects,110, 115, 256
    default constraints, 347
    entities, 110
    extended properties, 309
    keys and indexes, 298
    problems from uninformative column names, 206
    relationships, 126, 300
    SQL Server four-part scheme, 257
    table columns, 259
    table-oriented read-only databases, 554
    user defined functions, 338
natural keys
    checking register case study, 137
    should be unique identifiers, 76
natural language interface
    English Query, 562
nchar, nvarchar and ntext data types, 271
nested subqueries
    example of use instead of cursors, 429
nested triggers, 366
network access
    SQL implementation required for efficiency, 21
network topologies, 239
    see also **n-tier configuarations; client-server systems**.
    client to data configurations, 242
    connection speed for client server access, 231
    designed to minimize performance problems, 230
    three-tier and n-tier systems, 242
newId() function, 275
NO ACTION option
    cascading deletes, 303
NOCHECK option
    check constraint, 350, 352, 356
NOCOUNT option, 279
non-alphabetic characters
    clue that existing data is not in 1NF, 153

non-binary relationships, 63
non-clustered indexes, 292
    checking register case study, 544
non-deterministic functions, 345
non-identifying relationships, 118
    diagrammatic representation, 116
    mandatory and optional, 119
    third normal form violations and, 158
non-key attributes
    interdependency violates third normal form, 157
non-required relationships
    Information Engineering, 128
non-specific relationships see **many-to-many relationships**.
Non-Subversion Rule
    Codd's twelfth rule for an RDBMS, 582
normal forms see **Boyce-Codd Normal Form; Domain-key Normal Form; Fifth Normal Form; First Normal Form; Fourth Normal Form; Second Normal Form; Third Normal Form**.
normalization, 145
    see also **denormalization**.
    adjusting performance while preserving, 227
    advanced, 175
    checking register case study model after, 194
    ignoring rules with read-only databases, 552
    introduced, 12
    reasons for normalizing data structures, 146
    seven types of normal form accepted, 147
    table summarizing normal form requirements, 195
    treatment of subtypes may compromise, 253
Northwind example database
    Enterprise Manager diagramming tool, 130
NOT IN operator
    difference operator and, 60
ntext, nchar and nvarchar data types, 271
n-tier configurations, 242
    connection pooling, 234, 243
    problems for data protection, 387
null bitmaps, 508
NULL constraints
    introduced, 49
    not technically constraints, 347
    rules using, should be enforced at database level, 388
null values, 433
    Books Online definition, 434
    bugs associated with using, 437
    can cause problems with variant data, 273
    CASE keyword, use to allow for, 438
    child table foreign key references, 378
    Codd's third rule for an RDBMS, 578
    comparisons, 434
    need for and desirability discussed, 52
    normalizing reduces, 146
    NULL specifications for logical domains, 323
    specifying columns as nullable, 280
    transformation query illustrating problems caused by, 437
    user-defined data types handle inconsistently, 279
numeric data
    numeric data type, 262
    precise and approximate data types, 260
NUMERIC_ROUNDABORT option, 263
nvarchar, nchar and ntext data types, 271

O

object listing
  checking register case study, 94
object orientation
  'is a' relationships parallel subclasses, 81
  analogy with table rows and columns, 45
objects see **COM; database objects.**
ODBC (Open Database Connectivity)
  API cursors, 425
  data sources and distributed queries, 490
ODS (Operational Data Stores), 563
  consolidated data for day-to-day reporting, 15
  format, key to data warehousing transformations, 19
  merging data involves finding common terms, 564
  OLAP definition and, 504
  suitability for peripatetic staff, 16
OLAP (Online Analytical Programming)
  as data mart querying technology, 22
  characteristics of databases, 504
  data volumes should include indexes, 504, 507
  table growth and factor affecting, 505-506
old code see **legacy systems; pre-existing systems.**
OLE DB
  API cursors, 425
  data sources and distributed queries, 490
  DTS and DTC require compliant sources, 236
OLTP (Online Transaction Processing)
  banking illustration, 15
  characteristics of databases, 504
  contrasted with data warehousing, 13
  growth rates of tables, 505
  normalized structure of, 14
  optimized for transaction speed, not reading, 13, 15
  problems with, addressed by ODS, 15
on-demand connections
  read-only database replication, 561
  read-only database update frequency, 558
one-to-many relationships, 62, 117
  Enterprise Manager diagramming tool, 130
one-to-n relationships, 61
  one-to-one or one-to-many, 80
one-to-one or more relationships, 120
one-to-one relationships, 62
one-to-X relationships
  table showing possible cardinalities, 120
operating system free memory, 524
Operational Data Stores see **ODS.**
operators
  Codd's eight relational operators, 56
  distinct from SQL keywords, 57
  elements of relational algebra, 56
  modification and retrieval types, 60
optimistic locking, 284
  checking register case study, 319
  use by update stored procedure, 471
optimizer hints
  adjusting lock types, 411
  avoiding locking using views, 440
  listed, 416
  specifying isolation level using, 416
optional business rules
  checking register case study, 402
optional relationships, 119
  diagrammatic representation, 116
  Information Engineering, 128
  must be non-identifying, 120

optional values see **null values.**
optionally cascading deletes, 389
organization chart
  example of recursive relationships, 123
outer joins
  as source of null values, 433, 437
output parameters
  stored procedures, 448
ownership
  see also **data ownership; database owner role.**
  specifying for UDFs, 339

P

PAE (Physical Address Extension) X86, 520
page life expectancy, 524, 525
page locking, 411
page size
  accessing programmatically, 508
page splits
  using clustered indexes, 292
page transfers
  number depends on indexes, 147
Pages Faults/sec counter, 522
paper files
  possible location of pre-existing data, 31
PARAMETERS listing
  Information Schema, 306
parent deletes
  setting foreign key child references to NULL, 378
parentheses
  always required in UDFs, 338
parity information (RAID 5), 533
peer review process, 198
people
  as entities in a database, 72
PerfMon (Windows NT), 521
  testing blocking with user definable counters, 539
performance issues
  ad hoc queries, discouraging by providing views, 440
  ad hoc queries, using SQL, 480
  add indexes at tuning stage, 299
  adjusting without sacrificing normalization, 227
  architecture limitations and, 204
  cursors, 428
  deletions and record disablers, 286
  disk reads and off-line storage, 515
  distributed partitioned views, 444
  flattening indexes, 511, 513
  image storage, 269
  indexed views, 443
  major coding issues, 420
  maximizing on queries with read-only databases, 550
  numbers of users as a factor, 234
  read-only databases, 556
  reporting, 227
  servers, 519
  text field storage, 271
  triggers and check constraints, 357
performance monitoring, 520
  as an art, guidelines to, 521
performance problems
  avoiding by using views, 439
  denormalization and, 188
  networking configurations to combat, 230
  page splits and, 292

performance problems (cont'd)
  unnormalized systems, due to extra
    programming, 146
  use of summary data, 161
performance tuning, 548
  CPU subsytem, 528
  disk subsystem, 530
  disk subsystem, counters, 535
  five key areas which can cause bottlenecks, 522
  Query Analyzer role in, 549
  Windows 2000 Performance Options, 527
permissions function, 485
person entity
  Boyce-Codd normal form example, 162
personal names
  examples of First Normal Form violations, 149
pessimistic locking, 284
phantom rows, 413, 414
physical data independence
  Codd's eighth rule for an RDBMS, 580
physical implementation
  illustrative scenarios, 225
physical model
  checking register case study, 330
physical reads
  performance mesures, 464
PhysicalDisk: counters, 535
physical-only columns, 283
  checking register case study, 319, 320
pictorial representations see **data modeling; use case models.**
places
  as entities in a database, 72
pointers, page and row, 510
portables see **mobile clients.**
power supply failures, 570
pre-aggregated data
  data integrity problems with, 229
precise numerica data, 260
precision
  decimal data type, 262
  storage requirement for numeric data types and, 263
predicates, 50
  data input rules for tables, 56
pre-existing data, 31
  see also **legacy data.**
  finding errors in with check constraints, 356
  merging into an ODS, 564
  must meet constraints before triggers are
    applied, 375
pre-existing systems
  see also **legacy systems.**
  dangers of emulating, 33
  data conversion may invalidate, 208
  infering business rules from old code, 84
  problems arising from need to interface with, 204
preliminary documentation
  checking register case study, 36
  identifying entities by analyzing, 71
  supplementary questions after analyzing, 75
primary key constraints, 347
primary keys
  checking register case study, 139
  choice of, in logical modeling, 163
  entity integrity and, 581
  entity name repeated in attribute name, 115

First Normal Form entities require, 150
foreign keys in one-to-n relationships, 61
IDEF1X entities must have, 111
implementing tables with meaningless keys, 296
locating data within a database, 578
logical changes effect on implemented keys, 320
may not have optional attributes, 120
migrating pointer unsuitable for implementation, 296
migration distinguishes identifying and non-identifying
  relationships, 117
migration, naming to facilitate, 115
physical-only columns, 320
role in maintaining uniqueness, 50
specification defaults to a clustered index, 297
use by update stored procedure, 471
process memory tuning
  counters available, 526
process models see **use case models.**
processes
  discovering in customer interview notes, 98
  identifying from customer documentation, 86
  table of new processes in banking example, 99
processor affinity, 528
processor time
  adjusting allocation to foreground and background
    applications, 526
Processor:% counters
  CPU performance monitoring, 528
product operator
  cross joins as example of, 58
programming
  additional, load of in unnormalized systems, 146
  coding applications, distinct from object
    creation, 406
  coding triggers, CREATE TRIGGER statement, 360
  logical errors due to NULLs, 437
  problems avoided by third normal form, 159
  problems caused by BCNF violations, 165
  problems caused by First Normal Form violations, 150
  problems rectified by Second Normal Form, 155
  relational and procedural, contrasted, 20
  round normalization problems, 157
Project Manager role, 26
project operator
  DISTINCT keyword as example of, 57
project planning, 209
  checking register case study, 217
  information gathering stage, 25
  importance of documenting scope, 27
proprietary systems
  inaccessiblity of implementation details, 566
prototyping a database
  risk of distorting customer expectations, 28
prototyping reports
  checking register case study, 213
  choice of data to present in, 201
publications
  replication definition of, 235
pull replication subscription, 561

Q

quality assurance
  see also **performance tuning; testing.**
  second phase in database development, 567

queries
  customizing client queries, 479
  embedding user-defined functions, 337
  factors contributing to efficiency, 406
  flattening indexes and performance, 511, 513
  maximizing performance with a read-only
    database, 550
  performing covered queries, 557
  writing to allow for null values, 438

Query Analyzer
  dynamic character strings execution, 512
  error messages seen by, 357
  role in performance tuning, 549

query optimizer
  can make use of constraints, 346
  read-only database with all columns indexed, 558
  row-level lock escalation, 229
  stored procedures easier to optimize, 482
  unique indexes assist working of, 295

query plans
  reuse, 480, 482
  role in performance tuning, 549
  stored procedures reuse, 480

questions
  suggested for initial customer interviews, 30

QUOTED_IDENTIFIER option, 256

R

RAID (Redundant Array of Inexpensive Disks), 531
  advantages of a multiple RAID 5 system, 534
  RAID 0, 531
  RAID 1, 532
  RAID 5, as subsystem of choice, 533
  RAID 10, 533

RAISERROR statements
  interrogating after SET statements, 358
  stored procedures, 449

RAM see **memory**.

range checking
  checking register case study, 397
  generic field format checks with UDFs, 353
  INSTEAD OF triggers difficult to use for, 381
  using AFTER triggers, 376

RDBMS (Relational Database Management Systems) see
  databases.

read committed isolation level, 413
read uncommitted isolation level, 412
read-only copy databases, 234, 549
  checking register case study, 571
  choice of model depends on users, 562
  example corporate solution, 560
  heavy use web server configuration, 243
  implementation, 558
  justifications for, 550
  possible uses tabulated, 561
  returning to writeable mode, 549
  update frequency, 558
  using to protect the primary database, 549
  web applications using solution oriented
    methods, 556

read-only operations
  user-defined functions restricted to, 337

real data type, 265

real-time reporting, 440

RECOMPILE option
  stored procedures, 465, 481

reconfiguring servers
  testing nested and recursive triggers, 368

record disablers, 286

recording artists example database, 336
  accessing using a UDF, 340
  column-level security, 487
  row-level security, 486

records of activities
  as entities in a database, 74

recursive relationships, 63, 122
  diagrammatic representation, 116

recursive tree example, 423

recursive triggers, 367

redundant data
  normalization helps minimize, 146

referential integrity
  cross-database RI with triggers, 359
  foreign keys and, 581
  OLTP transactions and, 15

REFERENTIAL_CONSTRAINTS listing
  Information Schema, 307

relational databases see **databases**.

relational operators
  retrieval operators formulated since Codd's, 61

relations, 44
  all entities must be relations and single-themed, 195
  origins of relational database, 43

relationship trees
  building read-only databases, 552

relationship types
  between database tables, 80
  less common types described, 122

relationships
  adding descriptive information, 131
  binary and non-binary, 61
  checking register case study, 90, 137
  Chen ERD methodology, 130
  cross-database, need triggers, 304
  discovering in data from customers, 70
  enforcing mandatory, with AFTER triggers, 375
  Enterprise Manager diagramming tool, 130
  Enterprise Manager tool won't cover triggers, 131
  entities and, 116
  identifying and non-identifying, 117, 118
  implementing, 299
  naming, 300
  representation by methodologies other than
    IDEF1X, 128
  table of symbols used in Information
    Engineering, 128
  table of types in IDEF1X, 116
  table showing possible cardinalities, 120
  tabulated for office supplier example, 82
  treatment by data modeling methodologies, 116
  verb phrases make into readable sentences, 126

reorganization of databases
  coping with high data volumes by, 228

repeatable read isolation level, 413, 414, 550

repeating groups of data
  clue to 3NF violations, 161
  clues to 2NF violations, 156

repeating key prefixes
  to fieldnames, clues to 2NF violations, 156

replication, 235
    alternative to cross-database data access, 489
    distributed partitioned views, 444
    implementing read-only databases, 559, 560
    may be needed for dial-up access, 231
reporting, 199, 227
    checking register case study, 212
    complexity of reports and performance, 228
    data required should be identified early, 30
    data volumes and performance, 227
    data warehouses optimized for, 13
    day-to-day, based on ODS data, 15
    demand for decision support, 506
    frequency, 230
    key issue in physical design, 227
    performance of read-only databases, 556
    problems from complex searches, 229
    real-time reporting using views, 439, 440
    simple needs, read-only databases for, 562
    standard and specialized reports, 200
    timeliness of data required, 229
    using a copy database to boost performance, 228
reporting databases see read-only copy databases.
reporting tools
    database objects, 304
    table oriented approach leads to ease of use, 554
reserved keywords, 256, 315
resolution entities, 126
restaurant database example, 43
restrict operator
    WHERE clause as example of, 57
result sets
    classed as unnamed relations (tables), 43, 56
    stored procedure SELECT statements return, 448
    table data type exists to store, 276
retrieving records
    from lists, example stored procedures, 463
    large transfers may be broken down, 232
return values
    stored procedures, suggested protocol for, 446
RETURNS clause
    mandatory for UDFs, 338
review
    design stage, frequently neglected, 22
    first draft document, 88
revoke command, 484
RFP (Request For Proposal)
    source of data rules, 32
RFQ (Request For Quote)
    source of data rules, 32
rights see data access.
role names
    attributes used as foreign keys, 121
roles (security), 483
ROLLBACK TRANSACTION statement, 407
rolling up subtypes, 253
root node level
    detecting, in index size calculation, 513
rounding, 263
ROUTINE_COLUMNS listing
    Information Schema, 306
ROUTINES listing
    Information Schema, 306

row identifiers
    artificial keys, 52
    avoiding duplicate rows, 50
row locators, 292
    heaps, include page and offset, 293
row locking, 411
row update errors, 475
row-based operations
    archiving selected fact table rows, 517
    using cursors, 425, 426
rowcount
    @@rowcount variable after SET statements, 358
    use of term cardinality for, is ambiguous, 53
rowguidcol property, 275, 297
row-level security, 442, 485
rows
    accessing individual rows with a cursor, 429
    limiting visibility with views, 441
    maximum permitted number of bytes, 258
    SQL Server definition, 45
rowversion data type see timestamp columns.
rules
    user-defined data types using, 278

S

safeguarding data see data integrity.
SAVE TRANSACTION statement, 409
savepoints, 409
    set by stored procedures, 459
scalability
    see also users, numbers.
    needs to be known before implementation, 204
scalars
    output parameters to return, 448
    scalar expressions can use UDFs but not sprocs, 446
    scalar functions, UDF version, 338
scale
    decimal data type, 262
scenarios
    illustrating possible physical implementations, 225
schema binding, 342
    introduced, 309
    use advisable on production systems, 343
    needed for views to be indexed, 443
schema locks, 412
SCHEMATA listing
    Information Schema, 306
scope creep
    role of documentation in avoiding, 27
scope, transactions
    batching transactions, 410
scripting
    SQL Profiler as aid to, 310
<searchConditions> value
    check constraints, 351
search requirements
    reporting problems from complex searches, 229
searching
    case sensitive data can cause problems, 287

601

Second Normal Form

Second Normal Form, 153
   applies to composite keys, 153
   clues that existing data is not in 2NF, 156
   identifying relationships and violations of, 155
security issues
   see also **data access.**
   checking register case study, 500
   cross-database data access, 489
   preventing unwanted access or modification, 202
   roles, creating with Enterprise Manager, 483
   situational control of table access, 457
   stored procedures, handled at object level, 457
   stored procedures, hiding base table details, 482
   views, hiding base table details, 439, 441
seed, identity columns, 264
SELECT statements
   stored procedure alternative, 463
   user defined functions, 338
selective rollback, 409
self-referencing relationships, 63, 122
   diagrammatic representation, 116
Semantic Modeling Format
   English Query, 563
sensitive information
   disguising on sample documents, 36
serializable isolation level, 413, 415
servers
   adjusting server performance, 526
   clustering, load balancing and breakdowns, 234
   distributed partitioned views over several, 445
   importance of shifting processing load onto, 20
   multiple server instances, memory tuning, 525
   nested triggers set at server level, 366
   performance issues, 519
   reorganizing to cope with high data volumes, 228
   two or more needed for development, 233
   web applications, with read-only database copies, 243
SET (OPTION) see option name.
SET command, cursors, 426
set-based operations
   alternatives to cursors, 425, 429
severity levels, error messages, 357
shared locks, 411
shared with intent exclusive (locks), 412
sign offs
   advisability of regular, 88
   final documentation review, 219
   problems which can be avoided with, 210
single-statement batches, 474
single-statement table-valued functions, 341- 342
size limits
   components of database tables, 258
size of databases see **data volumes; volumetrics.**
smalldatetime data type, 266
smallint data type, 261
smallmoney data type, 263
smart keys, 76, 138
SMP (Symmetric Multi-Processor) confgurations, 528
snapshot replication, 235
snowflake schemas, 17
software licenses, 233
solution oriented models
   reporting databases, 552
"somewhere in between"
   ideal client-server system, 241

sort order
   see also **collation types.**
   cursor use to implement artificial sort order, 430
sp__index$getKeyData stored procedure
   auxiliary role, 511
   introduced, 507
sp__table$calcDataSpace stored procedure, 507, 508
sp__table$indexSpace stored procedure, 511
   checking register case study, 541
   introduced, 507
sp_addextendedproperty stored procedure, 309
sp_adduser stored procedure, 430
sp_column_privileges stored procedure, 307
sp_columns stored procedure, 306
sp_configure stored procedure, 366
   adjusting server memory allocation, 523
   limiting numbers of user connections, 536
sp_databases stored procedure, 306
sp_datatypes_info stored procedure, 308
sp_dboption stored procedure, 281, 367
   setting database as read-only, 549
sp_dropextendedproperty stored procedure, 309
sp_fkeys stored procedure, 307
sp_help stored procedure, 281
sp_helpconstraint stored procedure, 298, 307
sp_helptext stored procedure, 306
sp_pkeys stored procedure, 307
sp_server_info stored procedure, 305
sp_special_columns stored procedure, 307
sp_sproc_columns stored procedure, 306
sp_statistics stored procedure, 307
sp_stored_procedures stored procedure, 306
sp_table_privileges stored procedure, 307
sp_tableoption stored procedure, 271
sp_tables stored procedure, 306
sp_updateextendedproperty stored procedure, 309
sp_usercounterX Y stored procedure, 538
sparse tables, 272
specialized reports, 200
specific entities
   categorization relationships, 124
spreadsheets
   commonly used as data stores, 551
   data integrity problems from using, 31
SQL (Structured Query Language)
   see also **T-SQL.**
   compiled and ad hoc compared, 478
   data architect needs to maintain coding skills, 405
   data modification statements obey Codd's seventh rule, 579
   entire interfaces can be built of sprocs, 456
   operators as relational algebra of, 56
   requires atomic fields, 150
   triggers, SQL statements in, 360
   T-SQL as Microsoft version, 20
SQL Mail, 238
SQL Profiler see **SQL Server Profiler.**
SQL Server
   database diagramming tool from version 7.0, 130
   evaluation of NULLs, 435
   relational database models and, 42
SQL Server 2000
   compliance with Codd's RDBMS rules, 577
   dynamic memory tuning, 523
   source of information on features of, 250

SQL Server 2000 new features
  bulk logged transactions, 514
  calculated columns fully supported, 282
  cascading updates and deletes with declarative RI, 303
  collation setting is flexible, 287
  extended descriptive object properties, 308
  indexed and partitioned views, 443
  indexed views, 229
  schema binding, 309
  user defined functions, 336
  variant data storage, 272
SQL Server Agent
  scheduling jobs using, 239
SQL Server Books Online see **Books Online.**
SQL Server optimizer see **query optimizer.**
SQL Server Profiler, 521
  as aid to scripting, 310
  role in performance tuning, 549
  use to check applications being redesigned, 160
SQL Server Security, 483
  row-level and column-level security, 485
sql_variant data type, 272
  discovering the data type of a stored value, 273
  storage of extended descriptive information, 308
SQL-DMO see **DMO.**
SSN (Social Security Number)
  user-defined data type example, 278
staff expertise
  specialists required in large projects, 233
standard attributes
  building using IDEF1X domains, 114
standard reports, 200
star schemas, 17, 504, 506
state diagrams
  fourth normal form violations and, 185
Statistics IO, 549
  performance testing using, 463
Statistics Time, 549
status information
  fourth normal form violations and, 185
storage media
  archiving policy and, 519
stored procedure replication
  implementing read-only databases, 559
stored procedures, 445
  see also **compiled SQL.**
  batches compared to, 445
  calculating complete table size, 507
  calculating index size, 511
  can be rewritten yet still work, 456
  checking register case study, 491
  common uses, 462
  creating single rows, 467
  custom, for checking register case study, 498
  deleting single rows, 472
  encapsulation the greatest benefit from, 482
  enforcing business rules, 389
  error handling, 449
  error handling by calling from triggers, 370
  executing for each row in a set, 429
  implementing a column domain with, 49
  implementing read-only databases, 559
  limiting access paths to data, 480
  modifying data, 467
  optionally cascading deletes, 390
  overriding business rules, 391

  performance mesures, 464
  query plans reused by, 480
  RECOMPILE option, 465, 481
  result sets returned by SELECT, 448
  returning values from, 446
  securing data integrity with, 336
  security handled at object level, 457
  should avoid client interaction, 449
  transaction count must not be changed by, 410, 458
  truncating rolled up tables, 572
  UDFs compared to, 446
  updating single rows, 469
  user-defined functions compared to, 337
  views compared to, 439
string data type
  generic data type in check constraints, 351
strings
  see **capitalizing words in strings; character data.**
subqueries
  example using nested subqueries instead of cursors, 429
  including in joins, 422
subscriptions
  replication definition of, 235
substring() function, 151
sub-type relationships, 124
  checking register case study, 136
  diagrammatic representation, 117
sub-types
  checking register case study, 313
  reasons to stray from logical design, 251
summary data
  building with indexed views, not triggers, 443
  checking register case study, 168
  clue to 3NF violations, 161
  incorporating into read-only databases, 552, 554, 556
  reasons to stray from logical design, 255
  summarizing transaction data into ODS, 16
support databases see read-only copy databases.
symbols
  use case models, 106
sysmessages table, 450
SysMon (Windows 2000), 521
  testing blocking with user definable counters, 539
sysname data type, 313
System Architect role, 26
system architecture
  demands placed on the database and, 204
  often complex, with varying connection speeds, 232
system catalog
  Codd's fourth RDBMS rule, 578
system stored procedures
  see also **sp_; stored procedures.**
  appropriate to use cursors when executing, 429
  Information Schema alternative, 305
System:% Total Processor Time
  CPU performance monitoring, 528

T

table constraints
  type of check constraint, 350
table data type
  not permitted as a column data type, 276

603

table joins

table joins *see* joins.
table locking, 411
table oriented models
   benefits of the approach, 554
   reporting databases, 552
TABLE_CONSTRAINTS listing
   Information Schema, 307
TABLE_PRIVILEGES listing
   Information Schema, 307
tables
   accessing from within a UDF, 340
   building database tables, 249
   combining with various operator types, 57
   conceptual versions are entities, 44
   CREATE TABLE statement, 255
   exception handling, 384
   factors in calculating table volumes, 507
   growth of case study tables, 540
   growth of OLAP tables, 505
   growth of OLTP tables, 505, 506
   mathematically described as relations, 43
   naming conventions, 256
   partitioning by time, archiving and, 517
   partitioning structure with views, 441
   permanent data must reside within, 577
   queries may access up to 250, 422
   relational database theory and, 43
   relationships between tables, types of, 80
   terminology illustrated by sample, 43
TABLES listing
   Information Schema, 306
tag format
   extending error messages, 452, 453
telephone numbers
   checking register case study, 169, 392
   examples of First Normal Form violations, 149
   problems posed by varying formats, 80
   updating area codes, atomicity and, 151
templates
   using domains as, for columns, 260
temporary tables
   DELETED and INSERTED tables, 361
   derived tables as alternative, 422
   hash as identifier for, 256
   local and global, distinguished by prefixes, 421
   multi-statement table-valued functions instead of, 345
   needed less often under SQL Server 2000, 421
   recursive tree displays using, 422
   UNION [ALL] operator alternative to, 422
terminology
   see also naming conventions.
   database tables and relational theory, 43
   Performance Monitoring, 521
   SQL's preferred to that of relational theory, 64
   table converting SQL Server and relational theory, 65
ternary relationships, 63, 177
   addressed by fourth normal form, 176
   Fifth Normal Form, 187
   resolving, 179
testing
   see also performance tuning; quality assurance.
   performance of stored procedures, 463-464
   protecting data while testing triggers, 365
   stored procedure performance, 463-464
   types of testing, 568, 569

text data type, 271
"textile management", 529
thick and thin clients, 239-240
thin tables, 147
Third Normal Form, 157
   clues that existing data is not in 3NF, 161
   need for normalization beyond, 175
threads
   non-kernel applications use fibers, 529
three-phase model
   database development, quality assurance and production, 567
three-tier configurations, 242
three-value logic, 434
time information
   see also date information.
   storage and manipulation of, 267
timeliness
   decision support systems, 229
timestamp columns
   timestamp data type, 273
   use by update stored procedure, 471
   use for optimistic locking, 284
   use of datetime data type, 267
tinyint data type, 262
tools *see also* modeling methodologies.
   provided by SQL Server, 235
topologies *see* network topologies.
trancount variable, 407
   stored procedures must leave unchanged, 458
transaction logs
   sizes in OLTP and OLAP databases, 514
transaction support
   involving more than one server, with DTC, 236
   OLTP data integrity and, 14
transactional replication, 235
   appropriate to remote databases, 561
transactions, 406
   best kept short and in a single batch, 416, 418
   best kept short to minimize deadlock risk, 418
   completing partially, 462
   consequences of failing to close in batches, 477
   detecting long running, 536
   end-of-transaction constraints not avialable in SS2K, 193
   introduced, 15
   locking as control mechanism for, 411
   modifying statements should be inside, 358
   multi-statement batches, 475
   rollbacks affect all triggers, 369
   rolling back after testing code, 365
   stored procedure transaction count errors, 458
   using two-phase commit, 490
transform procedure
   checking register case study, 572
transformation queries
   example illustrating problems caused by NULLs, 437
triggers, 359
   see also compiled SQL.
   basic format, 375
   solving inter-row dependencies with, 55
   solving inter-table dependencies with, 56
   care over including statements returning resultsets, 359
   cascading modifications that need triggers, 303
   checking zipcodes match with cities, 400

uses relationship

triggers (cont'd)
  constraints compared with, 346, 371
  cross-database data access, 489
  cross-database relationships and, 304
  disabling violates Codd's twelfth rule, 582
  discovering need late in the design process, 498
  error handling using, 369
  execution order, 374
  implementing a column domain using, 49
  indexed views as alternatives to, 443
  looping stored procedures as alternative, 430
  may perform better than check constraints, 357
  multi row validation, 364
  multiple triggers for the same action, 366
  multiple triggers should be used with care, 374
  need to test, embedded in transactions, 365
  optimistic locking using, 284
  pre-existing data must pass constraints, 375
  relationships implemented in, 131
  removing time from datetime values, 398
  securing data integrity with, 336
  testing nested and recursive, 368
  value in ensuring data integrity, 388
truncate log on checkpoint, 514
TRUNCATE TABLE statement, 373
truth tables
  comparisons involving NULLS, 434
T-SQL (Transact-SQL)
  see also **SQL**.
  comprehensive data sub-language, 579
  cursor solutions often slower than set-based, 425
  derived tables, 422
  introduced, 13
  list of commands excluded from triggers, 359
tuples, 44
  table rows as, 45
two-phase commit, 236
  cross-database data modification, 490

U

UDF (User Defined Functions), 337
  accessing variable length column data, 508
  cannot include built-in functions, 345
  checking for empty strings, 352
  checking register case study, 393
  cursors and non-local objects, 346
  in-line table valued functions, 341
  multi-statement table-valued functions, 345
  range checking example, 397
  schema binding and, 342
  specifying the owner, 339
  stored procedures compared to, 446
  versions described, 338
  will not accept user-named parameters, 339
UDT (User defined Data Types), 48, 277
  cannot apply changes once set, 280
  handle variables inconsistently, 279
  manipulating dates and times, 267
UML (Unified Modeling Language)
  object oriented parent of use case models, 104
Unicode charater set
  allowed in non-delimited names, 256
  changing collation to sort, 287
  nchar, nvarchar and ntext data types, 271
UNION operator, 59
  alternative to using temp tables, 422

distributed partitioned views, 444
  multi-row tests with triggers, 365
unique constraints, 347
  use with alternate keys, 294, 297
unique identifiers
  see also **GUID**.
  keys as, in Boyce-Codd normal form, 162
  timestamps as unique values, 274
unique indexes
  enforcing unique values, 289, 294
  use with alternate keys, 297
uniqueidentifier data type, 297
  setting as auto-generating with rowguidcol, 275
Unknown
  "Maybe" as logical equivalent, 435
unnamed relations, 43, 56
updatability of views
  Codd's sixth rule for an RDBMS, 579
update function, triggers, 362
update locks, 412
UPDATE statement
  SET clause interrogated by triggers, 362
  stored procedure alternative, 469
  updating cursors, 427
update stored procedure
  columns costly to update, 471
updates
  criteria for updating a row, 292
  frequency, read-only support databases, 558
  updating single rows, 469
  updating support databases, 549
upper case see **capitalizing words in strings; case sensitivity**.
usability
  reduced with thin clients, 240
use case models, 105
  checking register case study, 133, 218
  classes of relationship, 106
  custom stored procedures from, 497, 498
  descriptive tables for use cases, 107
  including security information, 203
  introduced, 103
user defined counters, 538
user defined data types see **UDT**.
user defined error numbers, 358
user defined functions see **UDF**.
user function, 485
user interfaces
  unaffected by stored procedure changes, 457
user named parameters
  user defined functions will not accept, 339
user privileges see **data access**.
users
  see also **customers consultation**.
  controling access to data with stored procedures, 480
  effects of multi-tier design on different types, 387
  importance of early identification, 30
  monitoring important user connections, 536
  numbers and concurrency, 202, 204
  numbers and performance optimization, 234
  numbers a problem with classic client-server configurations, 242
  representation in use case models, 105
  self-configuring connections from SQL Server 7, 535
  transactions scoped to entire user connections, 410
uses relationship
  use case models, 106, 135

605

V

validation *see* **data validation.**
value of data
    establishing for database projects, 31
value types
    incapable of being represented by float data type, 265
varbinary data type, 269
varchar data type, 270
variable length data, 269
    accessing fill factors with UDFs, 508
variables
    declaring as a cursor data type, 426
    user-defined data types handle inconsistently, 279
variant data *see* **sql_variant data type.**
verb phrases
    can be read in either direction, 127
    naming relationships, 126
vertically partitioning data, 442
    column-level security alternative, 487
video library example
    categorization relationships, 124
    mandatory relationships, 119
    treatment of subtypes, 251
views, 439
    Codd's sixth rule for an RDBMS, 579
    compared to stored procedures, 439
    drawbacks to modification statements on, 386
    Information Schema as set of, 305
    INSTEAD OF-triggers overcome single-table restrictions, 387
    introduced and their uses discussed, 54
    modifying using INSTEAD OF-triggers, 386
    partitioning table data, 441
    providing abstraction layers using, 207
    restricting access to, rather than tables, 441
    table-oriented read-only databases, 555
    use as an encapsulation device, 439
VIEWS listing
    Information Schema, 306
virtual columns *see* **calculated columns.**
Visio modeling methodology, 105, 130
Visual Basic
    Booleans and use of smallint data type, 262
volumetrics
    see also **data volumes.**
    archiving policy should be decided early, 515
    checking register case study, 215, 540
    introduced, 503
    planning for, 208

W

WAN (Wide Area Networks)
    connection speed over, and data access, 231
    practicability of edits and reports over, 244
Waterfall Method, 100
weather, 570
web applications
    connection speed over, and data access, 231
    read-only copies of data, 234, 244
    read-only databases, 562
    solution oriented read-only databases, 556
WHERE clauses
    BETWEEN operator, 267
    including all columns in, for optimistic locking, 284
    restrict operator example, 57
Windows 2000 Data Center OS, 520
Windows 2000 Server
    CPU performance improvement over NT, 528
    memory optimization, 520
Windows Authentication, 483
Windows NT Server
    CPU performance less than 2000, 528
    memory optimization, 519
wipe and start again
    implementing read-only databases, 560
WITH option *see* **option name.**
Working Set:sqlserver, 526
write caching, 530
    could compromise data integrity, 531
wrting to disk
    optimized by lazy writer system, 530

Z

Zip codes, 191
    validating match with cities, 399

p2p.wrox.com
The programmer's resource centre

A unique free service from Wrox Press
with the aim of helping programmers to help each other

Wrox Press aims to provide timely and practical information to today's programmer. P2P is a list server offering a host of targeted mailing lists where you can share knowledge with your fellow programmers and find solutions to your problems. Whatever the level of your programming knowledge, and whatever technology you use, P2P can provide you with the information you need.

ASP — Support for beginners and professionals, including a resource page with hundreds of links, and a popular ASP+ mailing list.

DATABASES — For database programmers, offering support on SQL Server, mySQL, and Oracle.

MOBILE — Software development for the mobile market is growing rapidly. We provide lists for the several current standards, including WAP, WindowsCE, and Symbian.

JAVA — A complete set of Java lists, covering beginners, professionals, and server-side programmers (including JSP, servlets and EJBs)

.NET — Microsoft's new OS platform, covering topics such as ASP+, C#, and general .Net discussion.

VISUAL BASIC — Covers all aspects of VB programming, from programming Office macros to creating components for the .Net platform.

WEB DESIGN — As web page requirements become more complex, programmer sare taking a more important role in creating web sites. For these programmers, we offer lists covering technologies such as Flash, Coldfusion, and JavaScript.

XML — Covering all aspects of XML, including XSLT and schemas.

OPEN SOURCE — Many Open Source topics covered including PHP, Apache, Perl, Linux, Python and more.

FOREIGN LANGUAGE — Several lists dedicated to Spanish and German speaking programmers, categories include .Net, Java, XML, PHP and XML.

How To Subscribe

Simply visit the P2P site, at **http://p2p.wrox.com/**

Select the 'FAQ' option on the side menu bar for more information about the subscription process and our service.

Programmer to Programmer™

Wrox writes books for you. Any suggestions, or ideas about how you want information given in your ideal book will be studied by our team. Your comments are always valued at Wrox.

Free phone in USA 800-USE-WROX
Fax (312) 893 8001

UK Tel. (0121) 687 4100   Fax (0121) 687 4101

Professional SQL Server 2000 Database Design - Registration Card

Name	
Address	

What influenced you in the purchase of this book?	How did you rate the overall contents of this book?
☐ Cover Design	☐ Excellent ☐ Good
☐ Contents	☐ Average ☐ Poor
☐ Other (please specify)	

City _____ State/Region _____
Country _____ Postcode/Zip _____
E-mail _____
Occupation _____
How did you hear about this book? _____
☐ Book review (name) _____
☐ Advertisement (name) _____
☐ Recommendation _____
☐ Catalog _____
☐ Other _____

Where did you buy this book? _____
☐ Bookstore (name) _____ City _____
☐ Computer Store (name) _____
☐ Mail Order _____
☐ Other _____

What did you find most useful about this book? _____

What did you find least useful about this book? _____

Please add any additional comments. _____

What other subjects will you buy a computer book on soon? _____

What is the best computer book you have used this year? _____

Note: This information will only be used to keep you updated about new Wrox Press titles and will not be used for any other purpose or passed to any other third party.

Check here if you DO NOT want to receive support for this book ☐

NB. If you post the bounce back card below in the UK, please send it to:

Wrox Press Ltd., Arden House, 1102 Warwick Road,
Acocks Green, Birmingham B27 6BH. UK.

Computer Book Publishers

NO POSTAGE
NECESSARY
IF MAILED
IN THE
UNITED STATES

BUSINESS REPLY MAIL
FIRST CLASS MAIL   PERMIT#64   CHICAGO, IL

POSTAGE WILL BE PAID BY ADDRESSEE

**WROX PRESS INC.,
29 S. LA SALLE ST.,
SUITE 520
CHICAGO IL 60603-USA**